Amateur Gemstone Faceting

Volume 2

Expanding Your Horizons

TOM HERBST

FACE
TABLE
BOOKS

Scan this code to visit
www.facetingbook.com

Book design and formatting: Tom Herbst
tom@facetingbook.com

Copyright © Tom Herbst, 2014
All rights reserved

ISBN-13: 978-3-00-047475-0

"True glory consists in doing what deserves to be written; in writing what deserves to be read; and in so living as to make the world happier and better for our living in it..."

- Pliny the Elder

Table of Contents

NOTE: Volume 1 contains Chapters 1 to 9 and the Glossary. Chapters 10 to 20 appear in Volume 2 (this book). You can search by topic in the merged index appended to each volume.

Volume 1

Volume 2

for Matthew and Timothy

10

Gemstone Mathematics and Geometry

The foreword to the first volume of this book noted that gemstones occupy a unique space in Man's consciousness. On the one hand, they are objects of great mystery and beauty, seemingly half of this world and half of some transcendent place. On the other hand, the visual impact of gemstones is a direct, comprehensible consequence of the interaction of light with matter, and these interactions are ultimately governed by mathematics and geometry.

This chapter presents the essentials of gemstone mathematics and geometry. It begins with an introduction to trigonometry and the fundamental relations that govern the paths that light rays take through a gem via refraction. It then explains the procedures necessary to adjust the pavilion or crown angles of a gemstone using tangent ratio scaling. Hints on using pocket calculators, gem design software, and spreadsheet programs to determine this scaling are accompanied by good reasons for making the adjustment, as well as some very good reasons not to.

Section 10.7 clarifies the concept of gemstone symmetry and the transposition of cutting designs to a different index wheel. The chapter ends with a discussion of matching gem designs to a particular piece of rough and mathematical strategies for assessing and maximizing yield.

10.1 Introduction

Sorry.

Sorry in advance.

Here you are, with a brand new book on faceting in your hands, and the first thing that hits you is a whole bunch of math. To make it up to you, here is a nice picture of a faceted tourmaline:

Feeling better? Good.

Actually, I'll try to make this as painless as possible, sticking to just those "need to know" topics and focusing the main text on how the math can help you cut. Nevertheless, I hope you will gain some appreciation of the beauty of mathematics. Our hobby, after all, wouldn't be possible without it. For those interested in learning more, there are several mathematical diversions set apart in gray "highlight" boxes like the one on the opposite page.

Figure 10-1 A nice picture of a faceted tourmaline. No math here…

10.2 Sines of the Times – A Trigonometric Primer

Mathematics and physics are the tools which allow us to describe and predict the interaction of light with matter – in other words, they explain the thing that puts the sparkle in our gemstones. The next chapter focuses on the optical aspects of this interaction. This chapter will equip you with the mathematical methods necessary to understand these interactions and turn them to your advantage. It begins with a primer on trigonometry.

Trigonometry is the mathematics of triangles. Logically enough, the name itself comes from the Greek *trigonon*, or triangle, and *metron*, a measure. And again, logically enough, we use the Greek name for this branch of mathematics, since it was the ancient Greeks who pioneered the study of relationships between the lengths of the sides of a triangle and its angles (see "Don't know much trigonometry…don't know much about history…" on the opposite page).

Trigonometry is the beating mathematical heart of a number of disciplines, including navigation, chemistry, biology, architecture, astronomy, economics, and a whole lot more. As you shall soon see, trigonometry is pretty useful in faceting, as well. Ray tracing (Section 10.3) and tangent ratio scaling (Section 10.5) are two prominent applications.

So Trigonometry: Trigonon Metron…measuring triangles. How should a primer on the measurement of triangles begin? How about with a triangle…

Figure 10-3 shows a simple triangle with sides of length *a*, *b*, and *c* and angles *A*, *B*, and *C*. Note that this book adopts the usual convention of using capital letters to label the an-

Don't know much trigonometry…don't know much about history…

(with apologies to Sam Cooke)

Trigonometry quite rightly has a Greek name, given the pioneering work of Euclid, Archimedes, and others. Nevertheless, the history of trigonometry is basically a history of the world's great civilizations.

The ancient Egyptians and Babylonians did not possess the concept of angles, but they used the relationships between the sides of triangles extensively in their construction and scientific work. For example, the pyramid builders employed surveyors, known as *harpedonaptai* or "rope stretchers," who used knotted ropes and a knowledge of the ratios of sides of triangles to produce right angles (see Figure 10-2). By our definition of trigonometry – the measurement of triangles – this is the real deal.

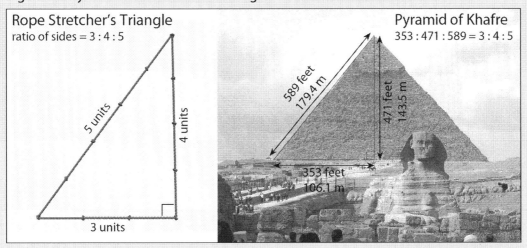

Figure 10-2 The Egyptians used a loop of knotted rope (left) to reproduce known angles, such as the 90° angle in a triangle with lengths 3, 4, and 5. This required twelve equally spaced knots around the loop. Such a triangle figures prominently in the dimensions of the great pyramid of Khafre outside Cairo (right – photo by Hamish2k at wikipedia.org).

The Greeks took things to a new level, developing and using angle measures, as well as demonstrating a number of geometric rules that are the equivalent of modern trigonometric theorems. The great Indian mathematicians of the 5th century made significant contributions, including the first recorded tabulation and use of the sine and cosine functions (see page 5). Given their discoveries in related areas such as optics and physics (see Chapter 11), it will come as no surprise that Islamic scholars were pushing the state of the trigonometric art around the turn of the first millennium, introducing several new functions and using their skills to understand the motion of heavenly bodies. At about the same time, Chinese mathematicians independently developed essentially the same understanding and skill with trigonometry.

Notice anyone missing in this parade of great civilizations? It is a curious fact of history that European mathematicians and scientists were basically ignorant of trigonometry until a rather embarrassingly late date. In fact, knowledge of trigonometric relations and methods only reached Europe via Latin translations of earlier Persian and Arabic works.

You've probably heard of Nicolaus Copernicus, the great 16th century Polish astronomer who finally placed the sun in its rightful place at the center of the solar system. Previous orthodoxy held that everything revolved around the earth. In his ground-breaking treatise on the subject, Copernicus devoted two full chapters to an explanation of the basics of trigonometry. Without this primer, his European contemporaries would have been woefully unprepared to understand his revolutionary work (sorry for the pun).

You should therefore consider yourself lucky. Not only can you benefit from more than two thousand years of intellectual investment in trigonometry in your gem cutting, but also you only have to plow through one chapter of the stuff. Onward!

gles, while lowercase letters denote the length of the opposite sides. The small box in the lower right corner indicates that the angle *C* is 90°, a "right" angle. This is therefore a "right-angled triangle" and the longest side is called the *hypotenuse*. The following text will focus on angle *A*, hence the labeling of its particular *opposite* and *adjacent* sides.

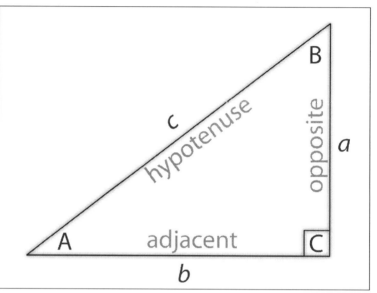

Figure 10-3 A right-angle triangle to illustrate the fundamentals of trigonometry (see text).

What do you remember about triangles? Probably a couple of things, at least. You probably recall that the sum of the angles of a triangle is always 180°. This means that the angles *A* and *B* in Figure 10-3 must add up to 90°, since the third angle is a right, or 90°, angle. Note that this summing to 180° business is true for all triangles, not just right-angled ones. This information will be useful later on.

You probably also remember Pythagoras' Theorem. This theorem states that, in a right-angled triangle, the square of the length of the hypotenuse is equal to the sum of the squares of the other two sides. In other words, for the triangle pictured in Figure 10-3, $c^2=a^2+b^2$. You won't need this theorem at all. Why did I bring it up? Well, Pythagoras was a pretty interesting guy and he appears to have discovered the "sum of angles equals 180°" rule as well. Not only that, his father was apparently in the gem trade and probably trained young Pythagoras in the lapidary arts. In other words, good old Pythagoras was very likely a kindred spirit.

Figure 10-4 Pythagoras as rendered by Raphael in The School of Athens, a fresco painted ca. 1511 in the Apostolic Palace at the Vatican.

Back to trigonometry, or the measurement of triangles. Imagine yourself as an ancient Greek colleague of Pythagoras. How can you actually measure a triangle?

Clearly, you will need to quantify the lengths of the sides of the triangle and measure the angles somehow. The sides are easy: just grab a measuring stick, now called a ruler, and have at it. The angles are a bit trickier, however. Recall that you are in ancient Greece and cannot toddle over to the stationery store for a protractor.

Since ancient times, important angles have been measured as ratios of lengths. For example, a road which rises 528 feet in a mile has a 10% grade, since a mile contains 5280 feet. Using the ratio to represent the angle has the great advantage of being independent of the actual distances or units of measure. That 10% grade remains the same, even if you only measured 264 feet of rise over half a mile of road. It is also the same if you used a meter stick instead of a ruler marked off in feet.

It seems natural, then, to characterize the angles in a triangle using the ratios of the lengths of the sides. After all, it was good enough for the pyramid builders, and their handiwork has been making a significant impression for nigh on 5000 years (see page 3). Measuring angles via the ratio of lengths is exactly what trigonometry does.

The three basic ratios are the *sine*, the *cosine*, and the *tangent*, conventionally abbreviated to *sin*, *cos*, and *tan*, respectively. For angle *A* in Figure 10-3, the definitions of these ratios are:

$$\sin(A) = \frac{\text{opposite}}{\text{hypotenuse}} = \frac{a}{c}$$

$$\cos(A) = \frac{\text{adjacent}}{\text{hypotenuse}} = \frac{b}{c}$$

$$\tan(A) = \frac{\text{opposite}}{\text{adjacent}} = \frac{a}{b}$$

The sine, cosine, and tangent have inverse functions as well. Again, for angle *A* in Figure 10-3:

$$A = \sin^{-1}\left(\frac{a}{c}\right) = \cos^{-1}\left(\frac{b}{c}\right) = \tan^{-1}\left(\frac{a}{b}\right)$$

Here's how to interpret the inverse trigonometric functions: the inverse sine function, $\sin^{-1}(x)$, returns the angle whose sine value is *x*. Put another way, it tells you which angle has the given opposite / hypotenuse ratio. The inverse cosine and tangent functions have similar definitions. You may occasionally see the inverse trigonometric functions under a different name, such as invsin, invcos, invtan, or arcsin, arccos, arctan. Such nomenclature is particularly prevalent in computer programming languages, since it is not easy to enter superscripted characters (such as "-1") in software code. Don't be fooled. These are all simply the inverse functions of the classic trigonometric ratios.

Incidentally, you will usually find your trigonometric functions helpfully clustered together on your calculator. More often than not, you access the inverse function using the Shift or 2nd Function key (Figure 10-5).

That's it. Class dismissed. See? Trigonometry was easy.

Actually, before you leave class, take another quick look at Figure 10-3. Notice that the "road grade" measurement of angle is actually the tangent function. In other words, the road with a 10% grade has an angle whose tangent is 10% or 0.1. Tap, tap, tap on the calculator…this is a shade under 6°.

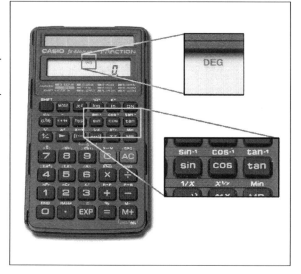

Figure 10-5 Pocket calculators make trigonometric calculations a breeze. Use the Shift or 2nd Function key to access the inverse trigonometric functions, and make sure the calculator is set to use degrees (note the small "DEG" symbol).

Optional Fun for the Trigonometrically Inclined

Note: This material is truly optional: you don't need to understand it to grasp the mathematics and geometry of gemstones. Nevertheless, the following should help you develop an intuition for how angles and their trigonometric relations work, and this undoubtedly will help you cut better gems.

If you play around a bit, you might notice another neat thing about the definition of the trigonometric ratios. If you add up the square of the sine and cosine of an angle, you get:

$$\sin^2(A) + \cos^2(A) = \left(\frac{a}{c}\right)^2 + \left(\frac{b}{c}\right)^2 = \left(\frac{a^2 + b^2}{c^2}\right)$$

Notice anything about the last part of this equation? (hint: I was lying about your not needing Pythagoras' theorem again…). Yes. The top part of the equation, $a^2 + b^2$, is actually equal to c^2, since the square of the hypotenuse of a right-angled triangle is equal to the sum of the squares of the opposite sides. This means that:

$$\sin^2(A) + \cos^2(A) = 1$$

Note that this makes no assumption about the size of angle *A*, and hence it is true for all angles. This type of rule has a special name, a trigonometric *identity*, and in fact, this particular identity is a special one indeed. It is known (fanfare, please) as the *Pythagorean Trigonometric Identity*.

Actually, the Pythagorean Trigonometric Identity leads to an insightful way of looking at the definition of sines, cosines, and tangents. Imagine a circle of radius one (inch, meter, light-year…it doesn't matter). To jog your memory, this is known as a *unit circle*. Consider the angle *A* between the horizontal line going through the center of the circle and any point on its circumference (Figure 10-6).

Because the radius has length = 1 and will always be the hypotenuse, you know that the sine of angle A is just the y value of the point and the cosine is just the x value. The tangent is y/x. Now imagine that A can vary. With the help of Figure 10-6, you can immediately write down a whole bunch of things you didn't know before.

1. The sine (y value) of 0° is zero and the cosine (x value) is one. The tangent (y/x) of 0° is also zero.

2. As the angle increases, the sine and tangent increase while the cosine decreases. At 45° the sine and cosine are equal and the tangent is therefore 1. For angles above 45°, the sine is greater than the cosine and the tangent is greater than one.

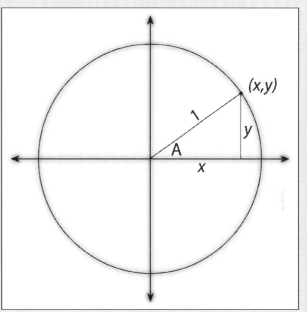

3. At 90°, the sine is one and the cosine is zero. The tangent of 90° is infinity, since 1 divided by 0 is an infinitely large number. Don't try this on your calculator.

4. Beyond 90°, the sine starts going down again, and the cosine is actually negative (as is the tangent)! Don't try this on your faceting machine.

Figure 10-6 A circle of radius 1 can help you understand the relationships between the sine, cosine, and tangent.

5. Similarly odd things happen as you pass 180° – both the sine and cosine are negative, but the tangent is positive. Between 270° and 360° (or 0°), the sine and tangent are negative and the cosine is positive.

At this point, you should be able to look at an angle and make a rough guess of the values of the sine, cosine, and tangent, or at least know which is bigger than which, whether they are positive or negative, or whether the tangent is bigger or smaller than one.

This trigonometric intuition can be really helpful to your faceting, for example in evaluating how a certain change of facet angle will affect the light rays via Snell's Law (Section 10.3) or in reckoning new cutting angles via tangent ratio scaling (Section 10.6).

At the very least, you should have a sense of the size of the numbers you expect in your faceting-related calculations. Believe it or not, you may occasionally hit the wrong key on your calculator or computer.

10.3 Using Trigonometry: Refraction, Snell's Law, and the Critical Angle

You can now test your newly acquired trigonometric skills in a real world situation relevant to faceting. The most obvious application of trigonometry is in the calculation of the path that light takes as it passes through a gemstone, a process that is governed, as we all learned on our mother's knee (or at least in Chapter 11.4), by *Snell's law of refraction*.

Note that this material is a bit out of place: Chapter 11 goes into great detail on how Snell's law works, gives proper credit for its discovery, and even provides an amusing derivation based on the problem of saving a drowning man. This section and the next one will just the use the darn thing.

Stated simply, Snell's law says that when light enters a medium of differing refractive index, the ray is bent by an angle whose relationship to the incident angle and the refractive indices of the two media is:

$$n_1 \cdot \sin(\theta_1) = n_2 \cdot \sin(\theta_2)$$

See Figure 10-7 for the exact meaning of these angles and indices.

Time to start playing with light. Figure 10-8 shows a side view of a standard round brilliant gem, with canonical proportions for quartz: pavilion mains and breaks at 43° and 45°, respectively, and the canonical 47° - 42° - 27° sequence for the crown. And by "canonical," I mean part of the canon of gem cutting as set down by Vargas. Compare Figure 10-8 with Figure 6 of *Faceting for Amateurs*.

An incoming light ray has just struck the table facet at an angle $\theta_1 = 25°$ from the vertical. Because the gem has a higher refractive index than air (n_2=1.54 for quartz versus n_1=1.0 for air), the ray will be bent, entering the stone at an angle θ_2 closer to the vertical. Specifically, Snell's law says:

$$\theta_2 = \sin^{-1}\left(\frac{n_1 \cdot \sin(\theta_1)}{n_2}\right)$$

which, for an incident angle of 25° into quartz gives a refracted angle a shade under 16° (Figure 10-8).

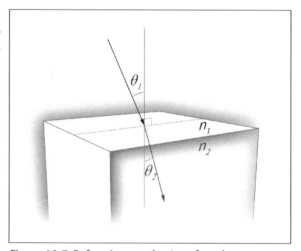

Figure 10-7 Refraction at the interface between two media of differing refractive index. Note that the incident angle θ_1 and the refracted angle θ_2 are measured with respect to the perpendicular to the surface. Since angle θ_2 is smaller than θ_1, Snell's Law, coupled with your understanding of the behavior of the sine function, tells you that n_2 is greater than n_1. See "Optional Fun" on page 6 if this unclear.

What happens next? Well, that all depends on which way the light ray is headed, and more specifically, on what the ray hits next. Let's assume the situation in Figure 10-8, in which the ray continues downward and strikes one of the pavilion mains. Figure 10-9 follows the action.

If the light ray strikes the pavilion at an angle greater than the critical angle, total internal reflection, or TIR, will occur and the ray will continue onward to the right (if this is un-

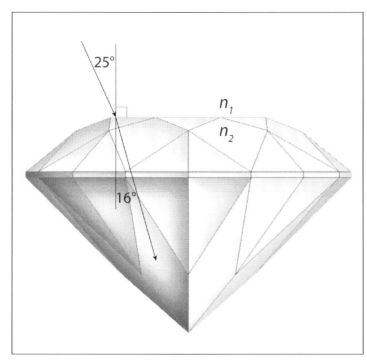

Figure 10-8 A light ray striking the table facet of a quartz gem. The incident angle is 25° and the refracted angle is 16°.

clear to you, review the material in Chapter 11.7). If, on the other hand, this angle is less than 40.5°, the critical angle for quartz, the ray will leak out of the bottom of the gem. Happily, your hard-won knowledge and understanding of trigonometry will tell you that the angle is in fact 59°, well above the danger zone. Read on to learn why.

Time to gird your loins…here comes the trigonometry. The angle in question is *TPQ* in Figure 10-9, since *PQ* is the perpendicular to the pavilion main facet. Note the nomenclature: the angle where the ray strikes the pavilion is labeled *TPQ*, since it is the angle between points *T*, *P*, and *Q*.

Here's how you know that *TPQ* is 59°. The angle *ACB* is 43°, the cutting angle of the pavilion mains. Angle *ABC* is 90°, and hence you can immediately write down that angle *BAC* is 47°, since you know that the angles of a triangle must add up to 180° (see! this is useful stuff).

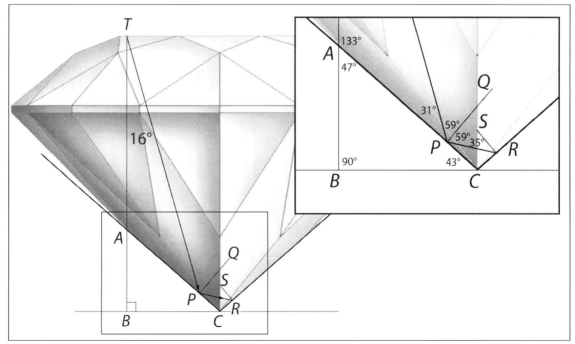

Figure 10-9 The light ray has struck the pavilion main facet at point P. The inset drawing illustrates the details explained in the text.

Angle *BAT* is really just a straight line, in other words 180°. Boom! You automatically know that *PAT* is 180° – 47° or 133°, and angle *APT* is 31°, since *ATP* is 16°, the original refracted angle, and the sum over the triangle must again be 180°. Recall that line *PQ* is the perpendicular to the pavilion main. Hence, *APQ* = 90°. This means that *TPQ*, the incident angle where the ray strikes the pavilion main, is 90° - 31° or 59°, which, you are now relieved to discover, is well above the critical angle.

Whew! That was a little harder than it originally looked! And the light ray's work has just begun, since it will, in fact, reflect off the pavilion main at 59° and head across the culet to the pavilion main on the other side (a reflected ray always has the same angle as the incident ray). What happens next again depends on the angle of incidence – *PRS* this time – and, of course, the refractive index.

Want to flex your trigonometric muscles? Prove to yourself that angle *PRS* is in fact 35°, which for this gemstone, means that the ray escapes. The only trigonometric information you need is the fact that the sum of the angles of a triangle is 180° and that a "straight-line" angle like *BAT* is also 180°. By the way, if you want to take a break from the math, Chapter 11.9 follows a very similar set of rays through a gemstone using neat 3D pictures, and without an equation in sight.

10.4 Applied Mathematics: Capture the Light

The simple mathematical principles explained in the foregoing sections allow you to make some pretty powerful general statements about how gemstones perform. Let's take an important example: common sense says that gems work best when they capture incoming light from a variety of directions, bounce it around a couple of times, and then send it back upward to the viewer. The more light that they capture this way, the more they sparkle and shine. What can trigonometry tell you about this?

Broken down to its simplest form, this common-sense statement really means that if a particular gemstone produces total internal reflection at both bounces within the pavilion (points *P* and *R* in Figure 10-9), there is a very good chance that the light will come out of the crown and produce pleasing results. This, in turn, means that the angles *TPQ* and *PRS* must both be above critical. If not, light will escape out of the bottom of the gem. Short version: two bounces, good…zero or one bounce, bad.

Yes, of course rays can enter the crown through other facets besides the table. The example shown here is perhaps the simplest case, and you are welcome (and now equipped with the tools) to try more complicated geometries. However, your intuition probably tells you that if a gemstone does a great job with table rays, it will probably perform pretty well with light entering the crown breaks, mains, and stars.

So, how can you determine which gemstones do well and which do not?

Let's begin by casting the mathematics from the previous section into a more general form. Figure 10-10 shows the various angles from Figure 10-9 in terms of the incident and refracted angles *i* and *r*, as well as *p*, the facet angle of the pavilion mains. From the figure, the incident angles for the first and second bounces are *TPQ* = *p* + *r* and *PRS* = 180° – *3p* – *r*. Again, you may want to use the mathematical tools in this chapter to convince yourself of this.

You know from Snell's Law that sin(*i*) = *n* sin(*r*). Note that from here on, the text presumes that n_1=1 for air and n_2=n, the refractive index of the gem material. You should therefore be able to make a plot of the angles *TPQ* and *PRS* for different incident angles *i*, assuming,

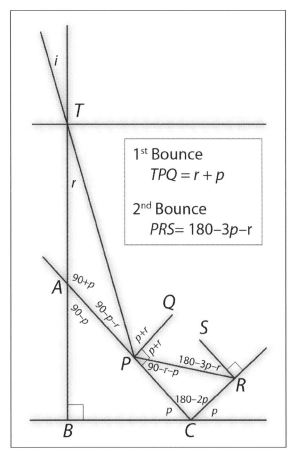

1st Bounce
$$TPQ = r + p$$

2nd Bounce
$$PRS = 180 - 3p - r$$

Figure 10-10 The ray angles from Figure 10-9 expressed in terms of the incident and refracted angles i and r and the facet angle of the pavilion mains, p.

of course, that you know both the refractive index n and the facet angle of the pavilion mains, p. Such a plot will show which range of incident angles produce zero, one, or two pavilion bounces. In other words, the plot will illustrate how well a particular gem captures light.

To determine n and p, you can pick your favourite gem material and design. The following calculations examine three gemstone materials, quartz, corundum, and zircon, and assume a pavilion main angle $p=40°$. Why 40°? As "A Critical Look at Culets" on page 64 demonstrates, the range of culet angles in real-world gem designs is surprisingly small. In fact, a single value, say 40°, represents a reasonable choice for essentially all gemstone materials. If you don't believe me, go look at Chapter 11.7 or chew on the following fact: centuries of optimizing the production of diamonds ($n=2.42$) has lead to a consensus choice of culet angle: about 40°.

Ok. Let's set $p = 40°$ and get on with it. Figure 10-11 plots the first and second pavilion incident angles (TPQ and PRS) for quartz ($n=1.54$), corundum ($n=1.76$), and zircon ($n=2.00$).

What's going on in these plots? Take a look at the topmost one, for quartz. The horizontal axis shows the input angle of the ray entering the table of the gemstone (angle i in Figure 10-10). The two curves, labeled "First Bounce" and "Second Bounce" are angles TPQ and PRS in Figure 10-9 and 10-10. The horizontal dashed line indicates the critical angle, which is 40.5° for quartz.

Note that essentially the entire "First Bounce" curve is above the critical angle, and hence total internal reflection will take place, even with quartz. Yes, the extreme left end of the curve may be problematic. This area corresponds to rays striking the table at 0° incidence, *i.e.* vertically. These rays pass directly into the gem without bending (obvious, now that you know that the sine of 0° is zero). They then strike the pavilion at an angle equal to the culet angle, p, which is 40°. This is slightly less than the critical angle, and hence light rays coming from straight up can go straight through. This is all a very roundabout way of saying that 40°, although a pretty good choice overall, may not be the ideal culet angle for quartz. And yes, this is why the "canonical" standard round brilliant proportions for quartz on page 8 call for a culet angle greater than 40°.

The situation is quite different for the "Second Bounce" in quartz, however. Note that the curve plunges below the critical angle for incident angles above 30° or so. These rays will happily bounce off the pavilion mains once, but not twice: the ray's second encounter with

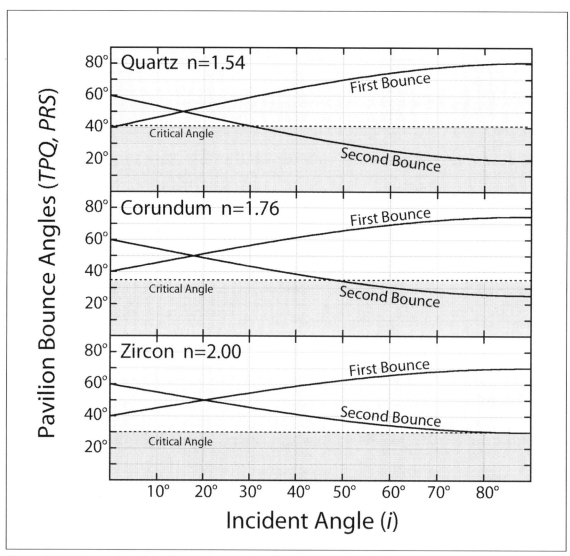

Figure 10-11 The angles of the first and second pavilion bounces for a light ray entering the table for quartz (top), corundum (middle), and zircon (bottom). The horizontal dashed line indicates the critical angle for each material. Note that quartz runs into trouble – the second incident angle is below critical – for light entering the table at angles greater than approximately 30°, while zircon is fine for essentially all input angles.

the culet facets will not produce total internal reflection, and the light will leak out. This means that a quartz SRB gemstone has a "capture cone" of about 30°. In other words, light rays entering the table within 30° of vertical will experience two bounces and have a good chance of contributing to the brightness and sparkle of the gem.[1]

Now look at the other two plots. For corundum, (middle plot), leakage occurs for table incident angles above 50°, while for zircon (bottom), essentially all input angles produce double TIR goodness.

Figure 10-12 shows schematically the SRB capture cone for various gemstone materials. As expected, the higher refractive index gems do a better job of collecting light from a broad range of input angles. This is one reason why high-index stones appear brighter and flashier.

---

[1] Note that an incident angle of only 25° causes leakage on the second bounce in Section 10.3, but there, the culet angle is 43°, not 40°. Perhaps 40° is a good angle after all!

There is one last chapter to this mathematical tale. Figure 10-12 significantly underemphasizes the value of a wide "capture cone." It turns out that a 60° cone captures *much* more light than a 30° cone. This is because the amount of light depends on the "area of sky" from which the gem can gather photons (Figure 10-13). How big is the area of sky for a given angle? The derivation is well beyond the scope of this chapter, but here's the answer for a cone whose opening angle is θ from the vertical :

$$\text{Area} = \pi \cdot \big(1 - \cos(\theta)\big)$$

where π is 3.14159..., the ratio of the circumference of a circle to its diameter. Incidentally, our old friend Archimedes (see page 3 and Chapter 20.2.1) worked this area relation out more than two thousand years ago. Now that you are no longer frightened (if you ever were) by trigonometric calculations, you can figure out on your pocket calculator that, for example, a YAG gem (n=1.84) with a 60° capture cone gathers 3.7 times as much light as a quartz gem (n=1.54) with a 30° cone.

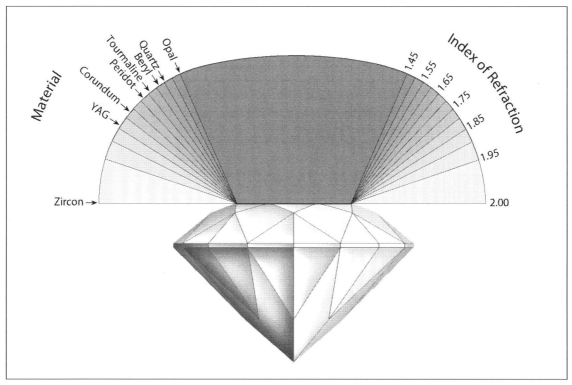

Figure 10-12 The range of incident angles for light entering the table of a gemstone which produces two total internal reflections in the pavilion. A little trigonometry shows that for lower refractive indices (darker areas), only light striking the table relatively close to perpendicular will bounce twice and re-emerge out of the crown. For higher index materials, a much broader range of incidence angles will contribute to the brightness of the gem, and materials with an index of 2 or above will capture essentially all rays.

The pocket-protector crowd will point out at this stage that all of these calculations are a simplification, since not every point on the table can gather light from the entire capture cone – we have, after all, been considering the somewhat optimistic case of light striking the culet facet on the same side of the gem as the incident ray. Fair enough. In fact, this example makes several assumptions that reasonable people could question, despite their overprotectiveness of their shirt pockets. Nevertheless, the overall message remains the same: higher index gems will capture more light from more angles and channel it more magically up to your eyes.

A second more indirect message, which you have hopefully absorbed without pain, is that trigonometry can be very useful in gaining insight into how real-world gemstones perform. Interested in learning more about tracing light rays through gems? Chapter 15 explains the process in detail, and will even help you produce your own photo-realistic computer images using exactly the principles explained here.

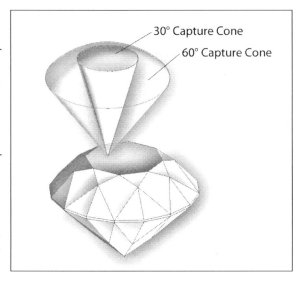

Figure 10-13 Wider capture cones gather much more light into the gem. For example, the 60° cone shown here accepts almost four times as much light as the 30° cone.

10.5 Stretching / Shrinking and the Tangent Ratio

Unless you really get into the game of tracing light rays through gems, by far the most common trigonometric calculation you will undertake will be scaling the pavilion or crown using the *tangent ratio* method.

Figure 10-14 explains how tangent ratio scaling works. By applying a mathematical operation to the gemstone design angles (see Section 10.6 below), you can raise or lower the crown, pavilion or both. The result is a shallower or deeper gemstone with the same basic design. In other words, the facet arrangement would appear unchanged when viewed from above or below (the plan views), whereas a side view would show the scaling. Figure 10-15 tries to capture this process using a 3-dimensional drawing.

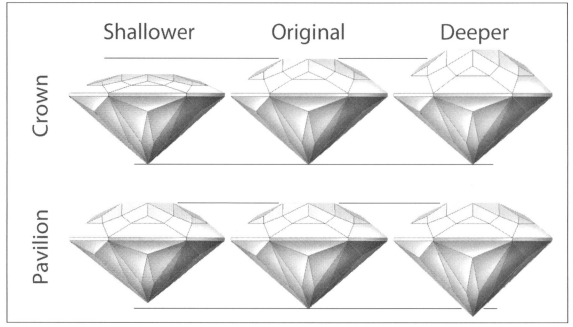

Figure 10-14 The tangent ratio scaling method allows you to raise or lower the crown and/or the pavilion of a gemstone without changing the basic design.

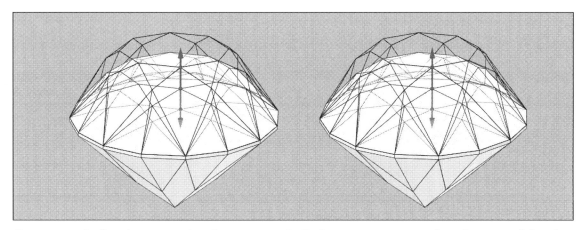

Figure 10-15 Scaling the crown using the tangent ratio. Each vertex moves up or down (see arrows), but does not shift along the other two dimensions. This is a 3D pair of images. Cross your eyes to see the effect and refer to page 74 for more information on seeing these images in 3D.

Why shrink or stretch a gemstone? It turns out there are several reasons to scale pavilions and crowns, and at least as many reasons not to…

10.5.1 Going Thinner…

There are multiple situations which may call for a shallower crown. For example, the usual and highly recommended faceting order calls for the pavilion to be cut first (see "The Great Debate: Pavilion-First or Crown-First?" on page 304 of Volume 1). When you get to the crown, you may find that you have insufficient remaining material to complete the gem. Flattening the top half of the stone somewhat may save your bacon. Similarly, you may discover a previously unseen flaw or inclusion. Adjusting the dimensions might allow you to transfer the problem from the stone to your splash pan. Other circumstances that may call for a flatter crown include recovering from a cutting error – which none of us makes, of course – or re-cutting a worn or damaged gem.

I am a strong advocate of optimized gemstone cuts, and hence feel compelled to note that reducing the height of the crown will almost certainly have a negative effect on the performance of a well-designed gem. As with selecting the initial set of angles, it is always a good idea to check the consequences of scaling the crown with one of the software tools out there (see Chapter 15.3). If you are running out of gem material or are compensating for an internal flaw, cutting error, or wear and tear, it may be a better idea to go with a thinner girdle rather than scaling the crown.

While the arguments listed above for thinning the crown apply in principle to the pavilion as well, the risk of windowing (Section 10.4) and even worse performance argues strongly against doing so. In almost all cases, it is better to accept an inclusion, cutting error, or a somewhat thinner girdle than to monkey around with reducing the pavilion angles.

10.5.2 Going Thicker…

Well, if slimming down isn't such a great idea, how about scaling things up? A number of authors have recommended deepening the crown or, if necessary, the pavilion, in order to increase yield. Others argue that a scaled up stone produces longer light paths and hence can enrich the colour of pale gemstone material.

I'm not buying. For one thing, there are better ways of increasing yield than willy-nilly stretching of the design to fill the volume of gem rough. Taking greater time and care in matching the cut to the raw material is a good place to start (see Chapter 6.7 and Section 10.8.2 below). More importantly, thickening the crown, or especially the pavilion, will change the gem design and optical performance, perhaps catastrophically. Finally, stretching the crown or pavilion may not increase the yield as much as you think – a thicker girdle is probably a much more sensible approach (see "Weight Gain and Girdles…" on page 44).

As to the longer light paths, I am again skeptical. Increasing the depth of a typical gem may add a millimeter to the total path length of a light ray passing through it. Because of the way light interacts with matter and colour absorption occurs (Chapters 11 and 12), this will produce only a slight deepening of colour in most instances. Besides, changing the design may very well cause substantially *shorter* light paths, due to sub-optimal reflections, light leakage, etc.

To summarize, deeper gems do in fact weigh more and may have longer light paths, but optimization issues make it difficult to recommend this course. To quote the Good Book: "What is a man profited, if he shall gain the whole world, and lose his own soul?" Yes, you can add a few milligrams of weight or a millimeter of light path by deepening a design, but you may very well lose the character and visual impact – the soul – of the gem. In other words, proceed with caution and use one of the software tools described in Chapter 15.3 to verify that your adjustments make sense.

10.6 Tan Ratio Mathematics

So much for the reasons to scale (or not to scale) a gemstone. How do you actually go about doing it? How does tangent ratio scaling work?

Let's take a simple example to illustrate the process. Unless you are cutting freestyle, and hence are a braver and more skilled person than I, you are almost certainly working from a faceting diagram. Although they have historically come in many forms, most modern faceting diagrams adhere to a basic convention of listing index wheel settings and cutting angles, usually in the correct sequence for producing the gem. Chapter 5.1.1 explains faceting diagrams in detail, and you should review that material if the concept of sequenced index and angle settings is not clear.

Figure 10-16 shows the cutting prescription for a standard round brilliant gem in quartz. You want to cut the design in fluorite, which will be problematic, since the pavilion main angles are 41°, considerably below the critical angle for fluorite (44.4°). You decide to deepen the pavilion mains by about 4° via tangent ratio scaling. In other words, you want to end up with pm=45°.

The process of tangent ratio scaling involves four distinct steps:

1. **Select a reference cutting angle from the original prescription.** In principle, you can pick any angle (except the girdle) from the list, but I usually choose either the mains (pavilion or crown) or the tier with the most facets. Why? The tan ratio calculation will

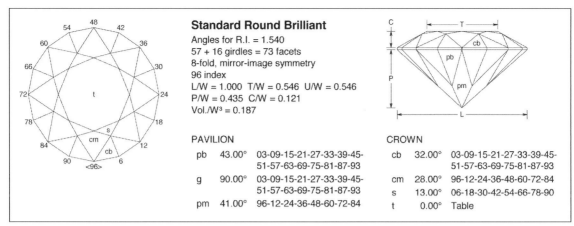

Figure 10-16 A standard round brilliant designed for quartz. Yes, this is not a canonical SRB (see page 8).

transform this reference angle into the desired target angle. Controlling the mains is clearly "critical" for gem performance, and choosing a nice round target number (like 45°) for the most important and/or frequently cut facet just makes life easier. Let's select the 41° pavilion mains as the reference:

$$\text{reference angle} = \text{original pm} = 41°$$

2. **Determine the target angle for the transformation.** This is the final value that the previously selected reference angle will have. Note that a lot of experience and judgment should go into this step. For example, I typically select a target angle based on a combination of computer optimization (Chapter 15.3.2) and the size and type of gem rough. Here, for the sake of simplicity, we have assumed a target value of 45° for the pavilion mains, since this puts things safely above the critical angle for fluorite:

$$\text{target angle} = \text{new pm} = 45°$$

3. **Calculate the tangent ratio for the transformation.** This is just a fancy way of saying (surprise!) the ratio of the tangents of the two angles. In other words:

$$\text{Tan Ratio} = TR = \frac{\tan(\text{target angle})}{\tan(\text{reference angle})} = \frac{\tan(45°)}{\tan(41°)} = 1.150$$

Yes, this calculation is simplified somewhat by the (now) well-known fact that the tangent of 45° is exactly one (see "Optional Fun for the Trigonometrically Inclined" on page 6).

4. **Transform all of the pavilion angles using the formula:**

$$\text{new angle} = \tan^{-1}\left(TR \cdot \tan(\text{original angle})\right)$$

Table 10-1 shows the transformed angles for the fluorite standard round brilliant.

(Note also that there is yet more fun for the trigonometrically inclined! "Raising the Roof" on page 29 provides a derivation of these formulae, based on the trigonometry discussed at the beginning of this chapter.)

Table 10-1 The transformed angles for the fluorite SRB.

Facet	Original Angle	New Angle
pb	43.00	47.01
g	90.00	90.00
pm	41.00	45.00

Yes, you should calculate all of the angles, including the reference, which in this case is the pavilion mains. And yes, you better end up with the reference angle (41°) transformed to the target angle (45°) or something has gone wrong. It is also reassuring that the girdle angle stayed at 90°, although your knowledge of trigonometry should tell you that this would obviously happen. If it is not obvious, turn back to page 6.

Caveat time (again!). Although the math worked out well, and all the pavilion angles are well above critical, transforming the design in this way and immediately putting stone to lap is a terrible idea. Check the new angles with a suitable software tool and read "The Terrible Transform" on page 20 to learn more.

Eagle-eyed readers should have spotted something about this transformation: for all the fancy trigonometric gymnastics, we ended up with angles that are almost exactly 4° higher than the originals (with the obvious exception of the girdle).

Why not do as the old masters did and just add 4° to each angle?

Great question. In fact, in most cases you can safely transform a gem by adding an offset to each setting, *as long as all of the angles are fairly close to the reference angle*. See "A Classical Case of Error" below for a more complete discussion of whether and when to use the traditional approach.

A Classical Case of Error

The classical "seat of the pants" method for scaling the pavilion or crown of a gem design is to add or subtract an offset angle for all of the facet tiers. How well does this work, and how can you ensure that the seat of your pants is not where you get bit?

Let's take a look…and now that we are all happy trigonometrists, we can make this a very exact and logical look.

In the fluorite SRB case discussed here, the "seat of the pants" approach transforms the original angles to the new angles by adding an offset of 4°. In other words, the classical transformation is:

$$A_{\text{new}} = A + 4°,$$

where *A* and *Anew* are the original and transformed pavilion angles, respectively. The tangent ratio transformation is:

$$A_{\text{new}} = \tan^{-1}\left(TR \cdot \tan(A)\right).$$

Recall that the value of *TR* is 1.150, based on the reference (41°) and target (45°) angles, which were different by 4°.

The basic question boils down to this: How good an approximation to the correct tangent ratio transformation is the classical method? Stated mathematically for the case under consideration, how close is $A + 4°$ to $\tan^{-1}(TR\tan(A))$? Figure 10-17 shows the error in degrees for a range of original design angles. This is basically a plot of the difference between the two methods for different input angles.

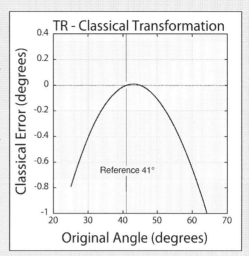

Figure 10-17 demonstrates a couple of things. First, the classical and tangent ratio methods are essentially indistinguishable when the angles are close to the reference. For example, with the reference at 41°, the error in the classical approach exceeds 0.2° only for angles below 34° and above 52°. Cutters may argue whether 0.2° is a big error or not – it depends a great

Figure 10-17 The difference between the classical technique of adding an offset angle and the proper tangent ratio calculation. The horizontal line indicates zero error.

deal on how well your machine is aligned and how much care you take – but the point remains that the classical approach is a reasonable approximation over a reasonable range of angles. The danger lies out in the wings of the curve, below 29° and above 57°, say. Out there, the error in adopting the classical approach exceeds half a degree, which is a serious problem for just about any gemstone cut on any machine.

The bottom line is that you can safely use the classical method, as long as all of the angles in the design are relatively close. Nevertheless, the tangent ratio method always produces the correct answer, and given the availability of inexpensive calculators, computer software, and online tools (see Section 10.6.1), there is really no reason not to do things right.

One final note before moving on: a review of the material at the beginning of this chapter, as well as "Raising the Roof" on page 29, should make it clear to you that the tangent ratio, or *TR*, is a very special number. It is not just an abstract factor for multiplication in the formula. *TR* is, in fact, the ratio of the height of the pavilion or crown after transformation to the height before. That last sentence was important. You may want to read it again.

For example, if you scale a pavilion that was 6 mm deep using $TR = 1.2$, the new pavilion will be 7.2 mm deep. This can be extremely valuable information. For example, you may discover an inclusion in the future crown after completing the pavilion and girdle of a gem. You can physically measure the location of this flaw, in millimeters above the girdle, for example. Knowing the original dimensions of the completed stone (see Section 10.8.3), and the required flattening of the crown in millimeters to avoid the problem, you can immediately determine *TR* and hence all of the transformed angles. Turning the previous example around illustrates the procedure. Imagine you have a crown that is nominally 7.2 mm deep, but you discover an inclusion which forces you to shave off 1.2 mm. Here, the TR factor to shrink the crown will be 6.0 / 7.2 or about 0.83.

The Terrible Transform

At this point, you will not be surprised to see me roll out my usual caveat that it is an excellent idea to check the impact on optical performance of any pavilion or crown transformation before doing anything rash.

Don't believe me?

Take a look at Figure 10-18. This is a GemRay rendering of the SRB discussed in this section, cut in quartz (n=1.54) and in fluorite (n=1.43). See Chapter 15.3.1 to learn how this image was created.

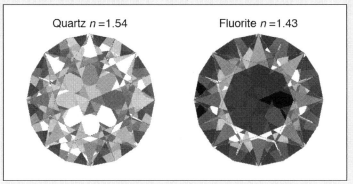

Your lack of surprise should continue: an unmodified quartz SRB does not do too well in fluorite. In particular, the pavilion mains allow light to leak out of the bottom of the stone. The GemRay analysis shows that the fluorite SRB returns only about 50% of the light that hits it, compared to about 88% for the quartz gem.

Figure 10-18 GemRay rendering of a standard round brilliant cut in quartz (left) and fluorite (right). Without modification, the design windows horribly in the lower index material.

This section has focused on scaling the pavilion using the tangent ratio method to ensure that the pavilion mains lie above the critical angle. This should solve all your problems, right?

Wrong.

Figure 10-19 shows the outcome of scaling the gem as described in the adjacent text, resulting in 45° pavilion main facets.

Is total internal reflection at the pavilion mains now working?

Yes. Apparently not very well, but yes.

Is the gem itself now working?

No. Definitely not. Not very well at all.

In fact, the same GemRay analysis of the scaled design shows a light return only slightly above 30%, considerably lower than the unaltered version. It seems that in this case, tangent ratio scaling is worse than doing nothing at all!

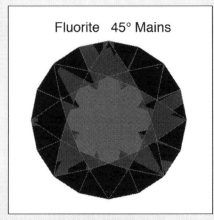

Figure 10-19 Scaling the pavilion to produce 45° mains eliminates the windowing in the center of the gem, but the overall light return is much worse.

Yikes! Are you surprised now?

Don't despair, dear reader. All is not lost. For example, the fluorite gem rough is not lost, since you took some very sage advice and checked the performance before lowering the stone to the cutting lap. Also, at this point, a little experience can be brought to bear. Put the calculator away for a moment…

The problem with fluorite is its narrow tolerance of angles, basically its narrow "capture cone" (see Section 10.4 earlier in this chapter). Experienced cutters have a number of tricks for helping low-index material perform, and one of the best of these is the *apex crown*. An apex crown is basically a domed crown without a table facet. It has the optical effect of gathering more rays into useful directions, hence increasing the capture cone. Exactly what you need.

Figure 10-20 shows the standard round brilliant minus its table facet and with a slight optimization performed to the pavilion and crown angles using the tools described in Chapter 15.3.

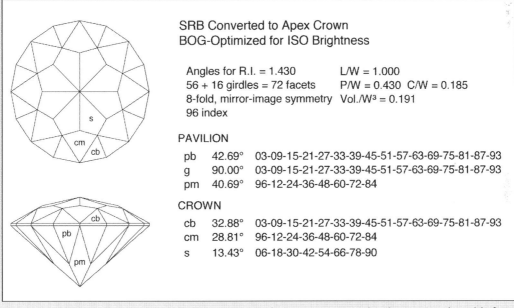

SRB Converted to Apex Crown
BOG-Optimized for ISO Brightness

Angles for R.I. = 1.430   L/W = 1.000
56 + 16 girdles = 72 facets   P/W = 0.430 C/W = 0.185
8-fold, mirror-image symmetry   Vol./W³ = 0.191
96 index

PAVILION

pb	42.69°	03-09-15-21-27-33-39-45-51-57-63-69-75-81-87-93
g	90.00°	03-09-15-21-27-33-39-45-51-57-63-69-75-81-87-93
pm	40.69°	96-12-24-36-48-60-72-84

CROWN

cb	32.88°	03-09-15-21-27-33-39-45-51-57-63-69-75-81-87-93
cm	28.81°	96-12-24-36-48-60-72-84
s	13.43°	06-18-30-42-54-66-78-90

Figure 10-20 The standard round brilliant converted to an apex crown by eliminating the table facet and optimizing the pavilion and crown angles.

"Wait a minute!" you declare…"both the pavilion main and break facets are now below the critical angle for fluorite!"

Very true and very well spotted, but since there is no longer a large table facet, few if any rays will hit the pavilion exactly vertically. This is part of the genius of the apex crown.

How well does this slightly modified SRB perform? Figure 10-21 shows the GemRay results. The domed crown has spread uniform facet goodness across the entire gem, and the light return has increased to over 80%, essentially the same value as for the original design in quartz.

Yes, things are less than perfect at the very center of the stone, but considering that this is fluorite and you were staring at almost three times lower light return, this is an excellent outcome. I would happily and confidently cut such a gem at this point.

Fluorite Apex Crown

Figure 10-21 All is not lost. Converting the design to an apex crown, coupled with a slight optimization of angles, returns excellent performance to the fluorite gem.

10.6.1 Doing the Calculation

The previous section discussed the mathematics and motivation for performing the tangent ratio calculation. This section explains how to actually *do* it – that is what tools to use and how to get them to work. Note that the following instructions continue the example of tangent ratio scaling the pavilion of a quartz SRB for fluorite, despite the fact that you now know that this might not be such a great idea (see "The Terrible Transform" on page 20). Recall that the goal is to end up with 45° pavilion mains, above the critical angle for fluorite.

Going Retro – The Pocket Calculator

I am unashamed to admit that, when I was learning mathematics, going retro meant a slide rule and log tables (anyone else remember those?). For a 21st century faceter, using a pocket calculator should be plenty passé.

Performing tangent ratio scaling on a calculator is straightforward, although it can be tedious and, for this reason, prone to error. The example below assumes a garden-variety calculator with built-in trigonometric functions (Figure 10-5). And, despite the fact that it will evoke nostalgic memories of heated debates at college, I refuse to be tempted into a discussion of the relative merits of Reverse Polish Notation. If you are one of the many who do not know what the heck I am talking about – or worse, believe that I have just made some sort of crude ethnic slur – spend a minute on wikipedia and have pity on the rest of us.

Here are the steps:

1. Make sure that the calculator is set to do trigonometry in degrees, not radians or (horrors) gradians. This usually means pressing a special key or setting a certain mode (see Figure 10-22). You can do a quick check that you have the correct setting by evaluating the tangent of 45 (enter 45 and then press the tan key). The answer, as you know, should be one.

2. You should have the value of the tangent ratio (*TR* in the previous section) at hand and ready to use. As emphasized repeatedly, settling on a good value for *TR* may involve

optimization calculations such as those described in Chapter 15.3.2. In this example, *TR*= 1.150 (see page 17). Incidentally, you will be using this *TR* value multiple times, so write it down somewhere or, even better, store it in a memory register of the calculator.

Figure 10-22 A calculator properly set up for degrees will return the value one for the tangent of 45°. Note the small DEG symbol indicating the correct mode (Figure 10-5 shows it more clearly).

3. For each angle in the pavilion or crown to be scaled, evaluate the new angle using the formula from page 17:

$$\text{new angle} = \tan^{-1}\left(TR \cdot \tan(\text{original angle})\right)$$

This involves using the inverse tangent function, which probably doesn't have its own key. Instead, you will likely have to hit the Shift, 2nd Function, or Inverse button then the tangent key (see Figure 10-5).

For example, in order to transform the 43° pavilion breaks of the fluorite SRB, I had to execute the steps illustrated in Figure 10-23 on my cheapo Casio calculator (which for all its cheapo-ness works wonderfully, and for which I would have traded almost anything in college).

Figure 10-23 The calculator keystrokes to transform an angle via the tangent ratio. Note that the MR ("Memory Recall") button retrieves the value of TR from storage.

The answer is 47.01°, which I dutifully noted down in my log book and which was eventually transcribed into Table 10-1 in the previous section.

That's all there is to it. Go through the angles one by one, take care in making entries on the calculator, note the answers down, and abracadabra! You have your transformed prescription. As mentioned before, it is always a good sanity check to verify that your reference angle does indeed transform into the target angle.

Software Tools – GemCAD

Both versions of GemCAD, the original DOS program and the much-improved GemCAD-Win, make tangent ratio conversion a breeze, and they are only a download away at www.gemcad.com (see Chapter 15.3.1). Explaining how these programs work is well beyond the scope of this chapter (and indeed this book). Nevertheless, the following paragraphs should help you get the results you need. Note that these instructions assume that you have an input GemCAD file of the standard round brilliant, called SRB.GEM. You can download a copy of this file at www.facetingbook.com.

Tangent Ratio Scaling with DOS GemCAD

Double-click the GemCAD icon to start the program. If this is the first time that you have run GemCAD, you may have to answer some questions for the initial configuration (see the program documentation). Note that in the following, GemCAD commands and program output are **boldfaced**. Also note that GemCAD distinguishes between upper and lower case. For example, the **T** and **t** commands do very different things.

Use the **O** command or navigate the menus (**F1-File : F1-Open**) to open the SRB.GEM file. You should see something like Figure 10-24. Press **F10** to return to the main menu.

This is the original gem. You can see the cutting instructions using the **l** (lowercase L) command (or **F6-Diagram Menu : F1-List to scrn**). Note that the pavilion facet pm at 41° is the reference angle. Press **any key** to return to the drawing.

To tangent ratio the pavilion, place the cursor on a pm facet (see the cross-hair in the lower left panel of Figure 10-24), and press **T**. Alternatively, select **F3-Edit Menu: F6-Tan Ratio** and then click on facet pm. GemCAD should prompt you with: **Angle was 41.00. New Angle?**

If you can't find the Edit Menu, you are probably still in the File sub-menu or the Diagram sub-menu. Press **F10** and try again. If you see a different angle in the prompt, make sure that you have the cursor in the correct location (see figure), and double check the cutting instructions with the **l** key.

Enter the target pavilion angle (**45**) and hit **return**. GemCAD will redraw the gem with the appropriately scaled pavilion. The drawing may look very similar, but you can confirm the change by again listing the cutting instructions on the screen. You can save the gem under a new name (**S** or **F1-File Menu: F3-Save as**).

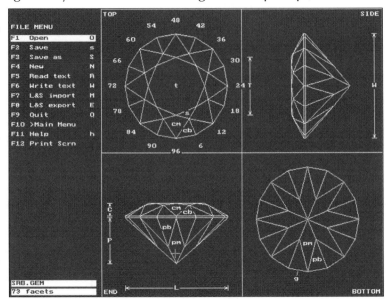

Figure 10-24 The original SRB.GEM file loaded into DOS GemCAD.

To get a hardcopy of your results, select **F6-Diagram Menu: F2-List to file** or press **L**. Enter a file name, such as **SRB_TR.txt**. GemCAD will produce a plain text listing that you can use to cut the stone. Alternatively, you can print out the modified GemCAD file using the GemPrint program. To quit GemCAD, use the **Q** command or **F1-File Menu: F9-Quit**.

Tangent Ratio Scaling with Windows GemCAD

The Windows version of GemCAD represents a significant improvement over the original DOS version. I use GemCadWin regularly and recommend it highly. To get started, double-click the GemCAD icon. Use the **Open** command in the File menu to load SRB.GEM. Figure 10-25 shows what you should see.

To perform the tangent ratio, place the crosshair cursor on a pm facet and **left-click**. Alternatively, you can **click** on the appropriate line in the cutting prescription at the bottom of the screen. In either case, a dialog box should appear (Figure 10-26).

Enter the desired target angle (**45**) in the New angle box at the bottom. Click the **Apply** button to scale the pavilion. Note that if you clicked in the prescription listing rather than on the diagram, a somewhat different dialog box appears, but the procedure is identical.

As with the DOS version, you should save the gem under a new name (**File Menu: Save as**). You can now print out the modified design using **File Menu: Print**.

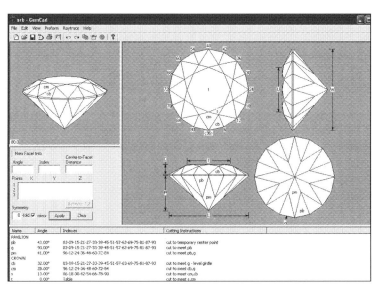

Figure 10-25 (left) GemCADWin has loaded the SRB prescription.

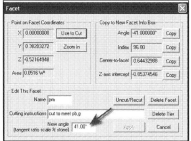

Figure 10-26 (below) Clicking on facet pm brings up a dialog box. The arrow indicates the New angle box to perform the tangent ratio.

Software Tools – Excel

In many ways, spreadsheets like Microsoft Excel and its freeware equivalents are the perfect type of software for tangent ratio calculations. Gem cutting instructions are inherently tabular, and the formula capabilities of these programs allow you to perform the same calculation on a whole column of numbers at once. Excel, also produces easy to read printed output that you can use right at the faceting machine.

Figure 10-27 shows the SRB prescription entered into a simple Excel spreadsheet. Refer to the many user guides to learn how to do this. Note that this is how I organized the prescription. Other layouts are possible, as long as you keep the group of pavilion and crown angles together. Note also that your initial display may look somewhat different. For example, I have used some settings in the format menu to set the angle output to two decimal places.

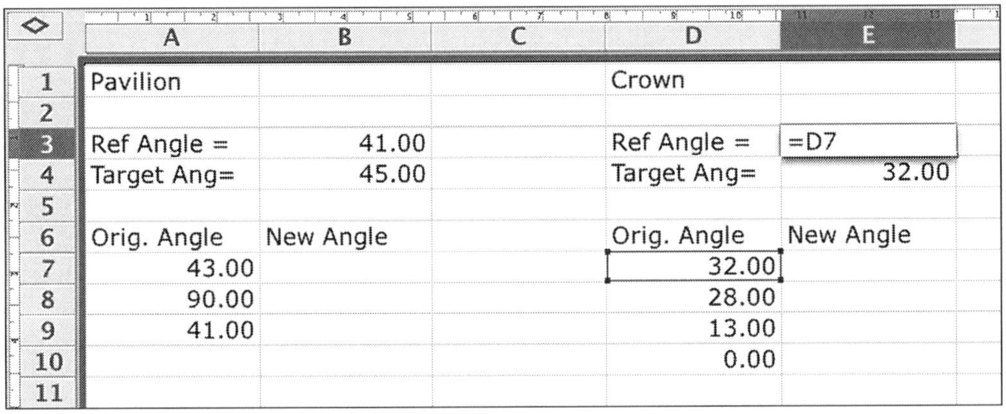

	A	B	C	D	E
1	Pavilion			Crown	
2					
3	Ref Angle =	41.00		Ref Angle =	=D7
4	Target Ang=	45.00		Target Ang=	32.00
5					
6	Orig. Angle	New Angle		Orig. Angle	New Angle
7	43.00			32.00	
8	90.00			28.00	
9	41.00			13.00	
10				0.00	
11					

Figure 10-27 The standard round brilliant entered into Excel. The Crown Reference Angle has been set to cell D7, which is the crown break facet at 32°.

You should notice a couple of additional aspects of this spreadsheet. First, there are title headers for the new pavilion and crown angles, but no values yet. Excel is going to fill those entries. Second, the Reference Angles are linked to the appropriate cells in the table below. The figure shows the entry for the Crown Reference Angle. **Double clicking** and then entering the command **=D7** sets the contents of this cell equal to the contents of cell D7, the crown break facets. A similar operation set the Pavilion Reference Angle to A9, the pavilion mains at 41°.

Now on to the calculation. The desired target angles are already in place: 45° for the pavilion and 32° for the crown. The crown reference and target angles are identical, since this exercise scales the pavilion angles only. Getting the tangent ratio calculation to work involves entering an appropriate formula in cells B7-B9, (and E7-E9 if you want to scale the crown as well). The procedure is identical to the =D7 formula described in the previous paragraph, although this command will be a little more complicated.

Recall that the tangent ratio formula is:

$$\text{new angle} = \tan^{-1}\left(\frac{\tan(\text{target angle})}{\tan(\text{reference angle})} \cdot \tan(\text{original angle})\right)$$

See Section 10.6 for a refresher if this is not absolutely clear.

Referring to the cells in Figure 10-27, you can write this formula for the first angle of the pavilion as:

$$B7 = \tan^{-1}\left(\frac{\tan(B4)}{\tan(B3)} \cdot \tan(A7)\right)$$

This equation should somehow go into cell B7. Here's how you do it. **Double click** cell B7 and then enter the following:

$$= \text{DEGREES(ATAN(TAN(RADIANS(\$B\$4))/TAN(RADIANS(\$B\$3))} * \text{TAN(RADIANS(A7))))}$$

Hit **Enter**. Boom! The correct value, 47.01° appears! Actually, I got 47.0097835° until I set the formatting to two decimal places – see Figure 10-28.

Take a closer look at this Excel formula. You should be able to recognize it as the New Angle formula from above. Three things deserve clarification. First, Excel operates in radian angle units, not degrees. You therefore have to use the DEGREES and RADIANS conversion commands at the appropriate places to get what you want. Second, mathematics in Excel usually operates in terms of a *relative* offset from the current cell. For example, the last part of the formula calculates the tangent of cell A7. Because the formula itself sits in cell B7, Excel takes the value from the cell one over to the left. Copying this formula into cell G12 would make Excel replace A7 with F12 in the calculation, again one cell to the left. A bit confusing, admittedly, but it works.

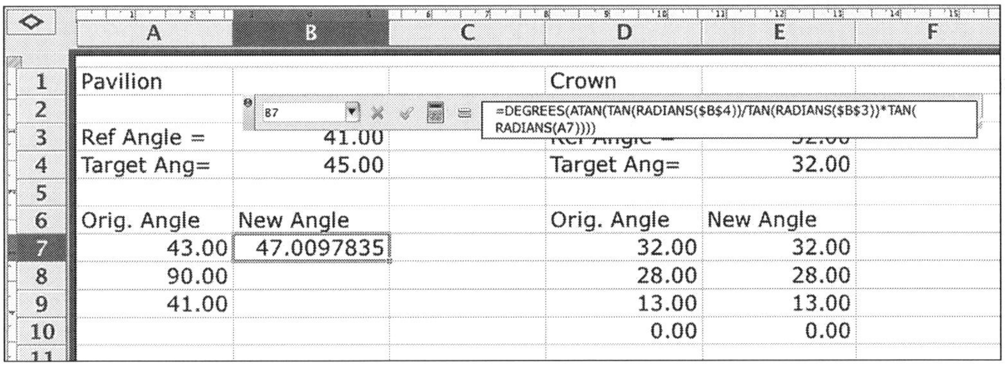

◇	A	B	C	D	E	F
1	Pavilion			Crown		
2		B7 ▼ ✕ ✓ 📷 ≡		=DEGREES(ATAN(TAN(RADIANS(B4))/TAN(RADIANS(B3))*TAN(RADIANS(A7))))		
3	Ref Angle =	41.00		Ref Angle =	32.00	
4	Target Ang=	45.00		Target Ang=	32.00	
5						
6	Orig. Angle	New Angle		Orig. Angle	New Angle	
7	43.00	47.0097835		32.00	32.00	
8	90.00			28.00	28.00	
9	41.00			13.00	13.00	
10				0.00	0.00	
11						

Figure 10-28 Entering the formula into cell B7 using the pop-up formula box.

The third curious aspect of this formula relates to the dollar symbols. To convert the remainder of the pavilion angles, you will want to copy this formula to their respective cells, but there is a problem with relative offsets: the locations of the reference and target angles are *fixed*. Wherever you go in the table, you will need a fixed, not relative, address. Excel uses fixed addresses when you place a '$' character in the cell reference. Referring to the formula, then, Excel interprets B4 as the contents of the cell at position B4, independent of where the formula actually resides.

The final step involves copying this formula to the appropriate cells for the remaining pavilion angles. This is actually fairly easy, provided that you know the trick. **Click** on the cell (B7) containing the formula. It should become outlined with an additional small box on the lower right. **Click** on this small box and **drag** the region downward to cover cells B8-B9. When you release the mouse, Excel will calculate the remaining pavilion angles (Figure 10-29).

The exact same procedure holds for the crown angles, should you choose to transform them. In this instance, the formula in cell E7 would be:

$$= \text{DEGREES(ATAN(TAN(RADIANS(\$E\$4))/TAN(RADIANS(\$E\$3))} * \text{TAN(RADIANS(D7))))}$$

After checking the answer, you can apply this formula to cells E8-E10 as explained above.

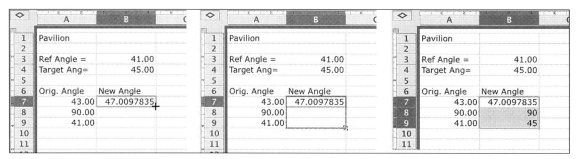

Figure 10-29 Select B7 and then click in the lower right of the cell, where the cursor becomes a cross-hair (left panel). Drag the selection area downward and release (center panel). This causes the formula to be applied to the remaining cells (right panel). Note that the girdle and pavilion mains end up at the correct values.

This may strike you as a great deal of work, but you now have a working Excel spreadsheet. For example, try entering a different target angle in cell B4. As soon as you hit Enter, Excel recalculates the entire pavilion for you. You can also try using a different reference angle by linking B3 to the pavilion breaks in cell B7.

You will probably want to save the Excel file twice, once under a name like SRB_TR, and again as a generic tangent ratio template. At any time and for any gem, you can simply open the template, enter the new angles, and stretch the gem to your heart's content.

Online Tools

Guess what?

There is a lot of stuff on the Internet. A lot. Some of it is even interesting and useful. For example, there are online resources that let you easily calculate tangent ratio transformations for gemstones. The first (as far as I know) and the best (as far as I am concerned) of these is at rockhounds.com.

Figure 10-30 shows the online tangent ratio calculator. It operates essentially identically to the Excel spreadsheet described in the previous section: type the Reference and Target Angles into the boxes at the top, and then enter the individual facet angles in the table below. Clicking Submit for Processing initiates the calculation. As always, it is a good idea to include the Reference Angle in the calculation as a sanity check. It should, of course, end up being the Target Angle.

Bob Keller created this tool, and his site includes a great deal of additional information, including an excellent description of the tangent ratio method. You can find the online calculator at:

http://www.rockhounds.com/rockshop/gem_designs/tangent_ratio_form.html

and the description at:

http://www.rockhounds.com/rockshop/gem_designs/tangent_ratio

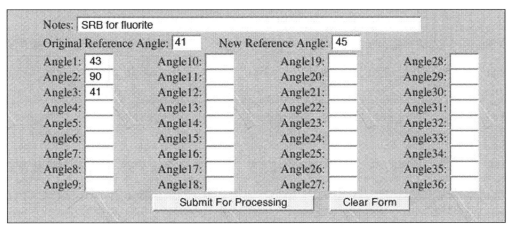

Figure 10-30 Bob Keller's online tangent ratio calculator.

10.6.2 Tangent Ratio – The Summary

Uniqueness and cut quality distinguish amateur faceting from department store gems, and one important way of ensuring consistent high quality is to always cut your stones at the best angles. There are multiple ways of determining these angles, ranging from heeding received wisdom to using sophisticated optimization tools. The tangent ratio method provides a simple and easy way of scaling the pavilion or crown of a gemstone to achieve your desired outcome.

Although there may be very good reasons for scaling a gemstone, there can also be serious pitfalls. For example, it is not always wise to simply scale the shallowest pavilion angle to a degree or two above the critical angle for a particular gemstone material (see page 20 and page 64). Readily available software tools exist to help you assess the impact of any change to a gem design, and it is an excellent idea to check things before cutting the stone.

Whether you use a simple pocket calculator, a gem design program, a spreadsheet, or an online widget, executing the tangent ratio calculation has never been easier. Such tools are not a replacement for your brain or careful practice, however. Keep thorough notes of which angles you used and what worked well.

Raising the Roof…(A Nuts and Bolts Derivation of the Tan Ratio Method)

Note: This is not required reading – you should be able to understand and use the tangent ratio method without it. Nevertheless, it offers an opportunity to use the trigonometric skills you have acquired in previous sections, and it will hopefully give you a deeper insight into how gems and gem design work. It might even help you with your teenagers…

Imagine for a moment that you are the proud parent of a teenager who, much to your surprise, ended up considerably taller than you. Given the trend in average human height over the last couple of centuries, this should have been no surprise at all, but there you are. Of course, being a teenager, he (or she) insisted on moving into that small room above your barn-style garage, not that living with the rest of the family is uncool or anything (Figure 10-31). The problem is that the roof is too low, and there

is a very real prospect of your teenager suddenly sitting up in bed, causing skull damage, roof damage, or both.

You have to find more room, but there is another problem. Your local neighbourhood planning authority will not permit you to change the architectural style, raise the outside walls, or expand the floor plan of the building. Clearly, you have to raise the roof. But how can you do this while ensuring that all the walls, roof segments, and joists line up?

Figure 10-31 The barn-style garage, future home of your very cool teenager.

Here's an idea: draw the building plan of the second floor on a rubber sheet, and then stretch the sheet vertically and measure the results (see Figure 10-32). This gives the required headroom, allows you to measure the required angles, and guarantees that the thing can actually be nailed together. It also leaves the top view of the building completely unchanged.

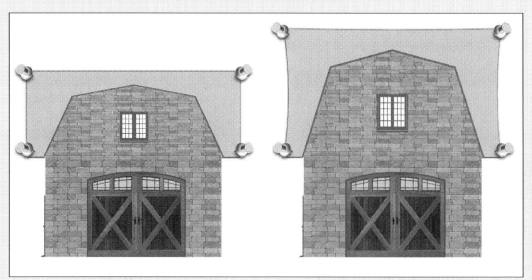

Figure 10-32 Drawing the second floor on a rubber sheet lets you raise the roof to increase headroom.

While this is a nice little domestic story about architectural problem solving, you can quite legitimately ask at this point what the heck it has to do with gem cutting.

The answer should be fairly obvious by comparing Figure 10-32 and Figure 10-14. While most of us don't have the wherewithal or the taste to have a gem-like geodesic dome for a garage, the two situations are essentially identical. The mathematical operations required for scaling the pavilion or crown of a gemstone without changing its plan view are the same as for raising the roof of your barn-style garage.

Figure 10-33 shows the geometry of the situation in more formalized terms. The stretching trick means increasing the heights *BD* and *AE* without changing the distances *CD* and *DE*. The rubber sheet in this mental experiment stretches uniformly. This means that all the vertical distances change by the same fractional amount. Thus, for example, if you stretch the rubber vertically so that it is twice as tall, all points on the sheet move a factor two apart up-down but keep the same separation left-right. In other words, both *BD* and *AE* will double in length.

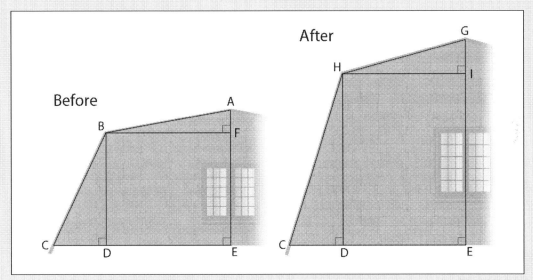

Figure 10-33 Schematic diagram for raising the roof. Points A, B, and F move upward to G, H, and I, respectively, while points C, D, and E remain fixed.

What has this exercise in elasticity revealed?

In order to scale the garage roof (or pavilion or crown), you must adjust the vertical height of the roof vertices (or facet intersections) by a constant ratio. What does this mean for the roof (cutting) angles? In other words, how do you transform angle *BCD* into *HCD*, and angle *ABF* into *GHI*? (refer to page 9 if you don't understand this convention for labeling angles).

You know that you have to change the vertical sides of the triangles by a constant ratio while keeping the horizontal sides fixed. We are talking ratios here. More specifically, measuring the ratios of the sides of triangles. Where have you heard that before? Hint: How do you say triangle in Greek? How do you say measure in Greek?

Look at the first roof angle, labeled *BCD* in Figure 10-33. Referring back to the definition of the trigonometric functions (Section 10.2), you recognize that angle *BCD* is given by:

$$\tan(BCD) = \frac{BD}{CD}$$

Similarly, after stretching the roof, angle *HCD* is:

$$HCD = \tan^{-1}\left(\frac{HD}{CD}\right)$$

where I have sneakily deployed the inverse tangent function to isolate angle *HCD*. Take the value of *CD* from the first equation:

$$CD = \frac{BD}{\tan(BCD)}$$

and plug it into the second:

$$HCD = \tan^{-1}\left(\frac{HD \cdot \tan(BCD)}{BD}\right)$$

What next? Well, you already know something about the heights *BD* and *HD*. They are related by your constant ratio. Let's call this ratio *TR* (play Tangent Ratio foreshadowing music here). Say, for example, that you wanted to increase the height of your teenager's room by 50%. This would mean that *TR* = 1.5.

$$TR = \frac{HD}{BD} \quad \text{or} \quad HD = TR \cdot BD,$$

which causes a lot of nice cancellation in the equation for *HCD*:

$$HCD = \tan^{-1}\left(TR \cdot \tan(BCD)\right)$$

Bingo! This is the familiar equation for tangent ratio scaling. Re-organizing this a bit, you get:

$$TR = \frac{\tan(HCD)}{\tan(BCD)}$$

What does this tell you? This equation says that in order to raise the roof or stretch a gemstone, you have to scale things by the ratio of the tangents – the Tangent Ratio.

For the second part of the roof line, the exact same type of manipulation yields:

$$GHI = \tan^{-1}\left(TR \cdot \tan(ABF)\right)$$

since you also have to scale the vertical side *AF* by the factor *TR* to get *GI*. This may take one extra step to convince skeptics, since the original problem talked about the full height *AE*, not *AF*, at the beginning. The proof is simple – try it yourself.

Punctilious readers and geometrical purists will point out at this stage that this uniform stretching is not strictly necessary. For example, you could have raised beam *BD* without raising *AE*, giving a flat rooftop (Figure 10-34).

There are at least a couple of problems with this suggestion, beyond the obvious fact that it comes from an overly punctilious and pure source. First of all, scaling only one of the beams clearly changes the architectural style of the roof, an option not permitted by the local punctilious purists at the housing authority. Of course, it also changes the visual character of the gem. The second reason is less obvious, particularly looking at a two-dimensional representation of the situation. It turns out that scaling the height of the different beams (or vertices) by different ratios can cause *rotation* of the roof planes (or facets) joining them. This is particularly true for complex roof lines and all but the simplest of gemstones.

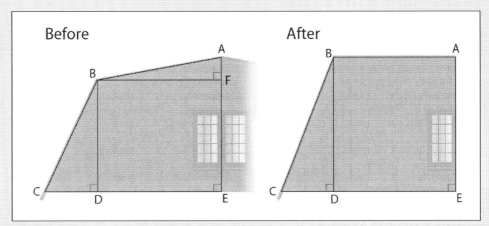

Figure 10-34 Another way of raising the roof.

This rotation of the facets means that the index wheel settings will change, as well as the cutting angles. While this might work out, it probably won't. You will in all likelihood be left with a mess: fractional index settings, missed meet points, confusion, and a semi-infinite amount of cheater use. Short version: adjusting the vertex heights by the same ratio, the tangent ratio, lets you scale the pavilion or crown with ease.

10.7 Gemstone Symmetry and Transposing to Another Index Wheel

Gemstone symmetry is a concept that is often mentioned but is poorly understood. If you have examined a modern gemstone design, such as that produced by GemCAD (Chapter 15.3.1), you have almost certainly seen declarations such as "8-fold, mirror image symmetry," "6-fold, radial symmetry," or "1-fold, mirror image symmetry." What do these terms mean?

Gemstone symmetry comes in two flavours: mirror-image and radial. The easiest way to think of mirror-image symmetry is to ask whether a design changes if it is flipped across a line. If it doesn't change, then the design is mirror-image symmetric. The name comes from the fact that this flipping procedure is equivalent to placing a mirror along the line of symmetry perpendicular to the page (Figure 10-35). Do the real and reflected parts of the diagram combine to recreate the original? If they do, then the design has mirror-image symmetry.

As its name suggests, radial symmetry relates to rotation. Here, the test for symmetry is to *rotate* the design rather than to flip it. For example, the gem design in Figure 10-36 would be identical if rotated by 90°, 180°, or 270° about its center. This gem design has radial symmetry.

For both mirror-image and radial symmetry, there is a measure of how many directions of symmetry exist. This is where the 8-fold and 6-fold come in. The "fold" value measures the number of symmetry lines around the gem for mirror symmetry, or the number of steps to a full rotation for radial symmetry. For example, a sixteen-sided standard round brilliant design would look the same if you placed the mirror across any of the eight pairs of equally spaced opposite vertices. You can try it yourself with Figure 10-16 on page 17. The SRB thus has "8-fold, mirror image symmetry."

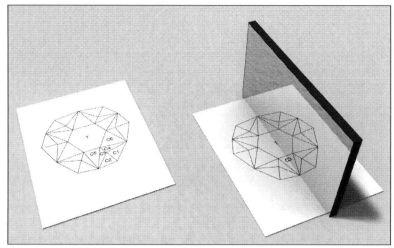

Figure 10-35 Mirror-image symmetry. This is the crown of the Briar Rose design (see Chapter 18).

A couple of notes for the sharp-eyed reader. First, the SRB has 8-fold symmetry, not 16-fold symmetry. This is because each placement of the mirror corresponds to a line connecting a *pair* of vertices, and there are only eight such pairs. Effectively, placing the mirror between vertex 1 and vertex 9, say, is the same as placing the mirror between vertex 9 and vertex 1. It is also equivalent to flipping the mirror around 180°.

I know. You're confused (heck – I'm confused). Here's another way to think about it. Imagine the mirror placed up-down, dividing the SRB design into left and right halves. Whether the shiny side of the mirror faces left (vertex 1 – vertex 9) or faces right (vertex 9 – vertex 1), the test answers the same question: does the left side look exactly like the right side flipped over? This measurement produces one symmetry axis, not two.

The second note is more semantic than conceptual. The standard round brilliant actually has radial symmetry as well. Rotating the gem by an eighth of a revolution leaves you with an identical gem. Why is it assigned mirror-image symmetry? The unsatisfying answer is that it just is. At some level, you can consider the symmetries as a hierarchy, with mirror-image above radial. A gemstone exhibiting both types

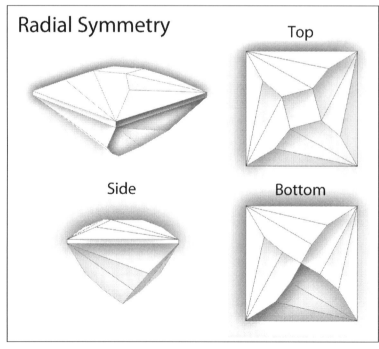

Figure 10-36 A gemstone has radial symmetry if rotating it by a fraction of a turn leaves the design unchanged.

is labeled with the highest order of symmetry, in other words, mirror-image. Incidentally, not all gemstones with mirror-image symmetry have radial symmetry. The heart cut is a straightforward example.

Purists could argue that a heart, does, in fact, have one-fold radial symmetry. If you split a full rotation into N equal steps for N-fold radial symmetry, then one-fold corresponds to a complete rotation of 360°, bringing you back exactly to where you started. Of course, by this definition, every gemstone (and indeed every object in the Universe) has one-fold radial symmetry.

What's My Symmetry?

Here's a fun exercise. Reproduced below are the top views of several gem designs from Chapter 19. Try to figure out each type of symmetry. You can find the answers in the cutting diagrams starting on page 334.

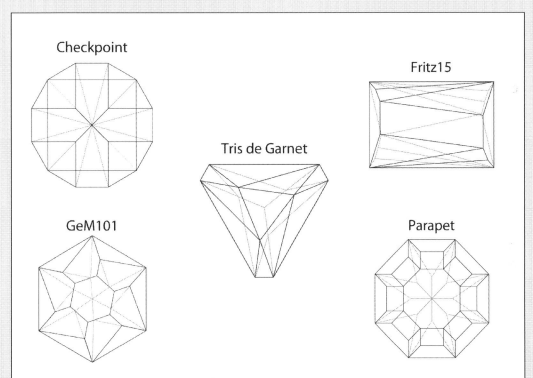

Checkpoint

Fritz15

Tris de Garnet

GeM101

Parapet

Figure 10-37 Try to determine the type of symmetry for each gem. These are top views, with the crown outlined in black and the pavilion in gray. Refer to Chapter 19 for the correct answers.

All this talk of symmetry has some serious real-world consequences. The reason is that the symmetry of your gem design may be different from the symmetry of your index wheel.

For example, a gemstone design with five-fold radial symmetry will have facet tiers distributed every 72° around the gem, since 360 / 5 = 72. More than likely, your faceting machine has a 96-tooth index wheel, and thus you can measure angles in units of 360 / 96 = 3.75°. How do you make steps of 72° out of units of 3.75°? Do the math. You cannot. You would need 19.2 gear teeth on your machine to produce a rotation of 72°.

Oops.

In fact, your 96-tooth wheel is not capable of producing five-fold symmetry. This problem has lead most manufacturers of modern faceting machines to offer exchangeable index wheels. Table 10-2 lists the most common types and their symmetries.

Table 10-2 Common index wheels and their symmetries.

Number of Teeth	Symmetries
32	2, 4, 8
48	2, 3, 4, 8
64	2, 4, 8, 16
72	2, 3, 4, 6, 8, 9, 12, 24
77	7, 11
80	2, 4, 5, 8, 10, 16, 20
96	2, 3, 4, 6, 8, 12, 16, 24
120	2, 3, 4, 5, 6, 8, 10, 12, 15, 20, 24

There are a couple of messages, both of them inaccurate, that a brief perusal of Table 10-2 can convey. The first is that more is better. While it seems obvious (and mathematically, it is obvious) that a wheel with a larger number of teeth generally has more symmetries, there is a point at which practicalities take over. I own a 120-tooth index wheel, but I almost never use it. Why? Because there are too many darn teeth! As the number of teeth on the gear grows, it becomes easier and easier to mis-index, in other words to screw up. This, coupled with the fact that the lion's share of modern gemstone designs use the 96-tooth gear, means that I very rarely need to exchange wheels.

The second message is that you can always cut a gem with a certain degree of symmetry using a wheel that supports that symmetry.

Also wrong.

How can this be? Well, it turns out that gemstone prescriptions consist of more than just a statement of symmetry. The distribution of index settings *between* the major lines of symmetry is also important.

Here's a concrete example: a couple of pages back, I asserted that a standard round brilliant has 8-fold mirror-image (and radial!) symmetry. A 72-index wheel supports 8-fold symmetry (see Table 10-2), but it cannot cut an SRB. The problem arises when you chop up the circle into eight pie-shaped slices: the 72-tooth index wheel provides *nine* teeth per slice. Unfortunately, the additional facets (breaks, stars, etc.) of a standard round brilliant don't fall at these locations.

Let's take a closer look. Referring to Figure 10-16, the standard round brilliant on a 96-tooth wheel has facets at settings 3-6-9-12-18-...96, in other words, every third tooth or every 11.25°. The 72-tooth wheel has teeth every 360° / 72 = 5°.

When do these line up? Table 10-3 shows the answer. A 72-index wheel is capable of producing only the pavilion and crown main facets! Setting out to cut an SRB on such a wheel would produce nothing but headaches and frustration. Similar problems would occur if you tried the gem on an 8-fold symmetric 80-tooth gear.

Table 10-3 The index wheel settings for a standard round brilliant on a 96 and 72-tooth wheel. The first two columns in each table show the index wheel settings and the corresponding facets cut on a 96-tooth wheel. The SRB facets are labeled as pavilion main (pm), crown main (cm), pavilion break (pb), girdle (g), crown break (cb), and crown star (s). Column 3 is the quill rotation angle, which is 3.75° times the index setting. The final column lists the corresponding number of 72-index teeth to set the same angle. With the exception of the pavilion and crown mains, all of the facets would require fractional index settings on a 72-tooth wheel.

96-Tooth Index	SRB Facet Name	Quill Rotation Angle (°)	Number of 72-Index Teeth	96-Tooth Index	SRB Facet Name	Quill Rotation Angle (°)	Number of 72-Index Teeth
96	pm, cm	0.00	0	48	pm, cm	180.00	36
3	pb, g, cb	11.25	2.25	51	pb, g, cb	191.25	38.25
6	s	22.50	4.5	54	s	202.50	40.5
9	pb, g, cb.	33.75	6.75	57	pb, g, cb.	213.75	42.75
12	pm, cm	45.00	9	60	pm, cm	225.00	45
15	pb, g, cb	56.25	11.25	63	pb, g, cb	236.25	47.25
18	s	67.50	13.5	66	s	247.50	49.5
21	pb, g, cb.	78.75	15.75	69	pb, g, cb.	258.75	51.75
24	pm, cm	90.00	18	72	pm, cm	270.00	54
27	pb, g, cb	101.25	20.25	75	pb, g, cb	281.25	56.25
30	s	112.50	22.5	78	s	292.50	58.5
33	pb, g, cb.	123.75	24.75	81	pb, g, cb.	303.75	60.75
36	pm, cm	135.00	27	84	pm, cm	315.00	63
39	pb, g, cb	146.25	29.25	87	pb, g, cb	326.25	65.25
42	s	157.50	31.5	90	s	337.50	67.5
45	pb, g, cb.	168.75	33.75	93	pb, g, cb.	348.75	69.75

How do you avoid this problem?

The easiest and cheapest strategy is to stick to designs for which you already own the proper index wheel. The next easiest but more expensive strategy is to buy more wheels. Although prices seem high, you are likely to spend as much on a good piece of gem rough as you would on a new index wheel.

The most difficult route, although again cheap, is to attempt to *transpose* the gem design to your index wheel. This essentially means lining up the teeth on the drawing with the teeth on your machine. There are a number of ways of doing this.

10.7.1 Transposing with Paper

The classic reference books on gem cutting are filled with charts, diagrams, and nomograms to help with faceting-related calculations. Most of these functions, including transposition, have been taken over by computerized tools. Nevertheless, the Index Transposition Wheel is a visually beautiful and still useful device.

Figure 10-38 shows an Index Transposition Wheel for the popular index gears in Table 10-2. Using it is straightforward and fun. Locate the rings corresponding to the index wheel in the design and the one on your machine. Then, using a transparent straightedge, line up each index setting in the design ring with the cross-hair at the center of the wheel. The index wheel setting that you want is at the intersection of the straightedge and the ring corresponding to the gear installed on your machine. Hopefully.

For example, placing the straightedge between index 12 on the 96-tooth ring and the central target shows that this setting corresponds to 8 on a 64-tooth wheel and 15 on a 120-tooth wheel (among other possibilities). If the straightedge intersection falls between the marks on the machine's ring, you have a fractional index. This could be a problem – see Section 10.7.3 below.

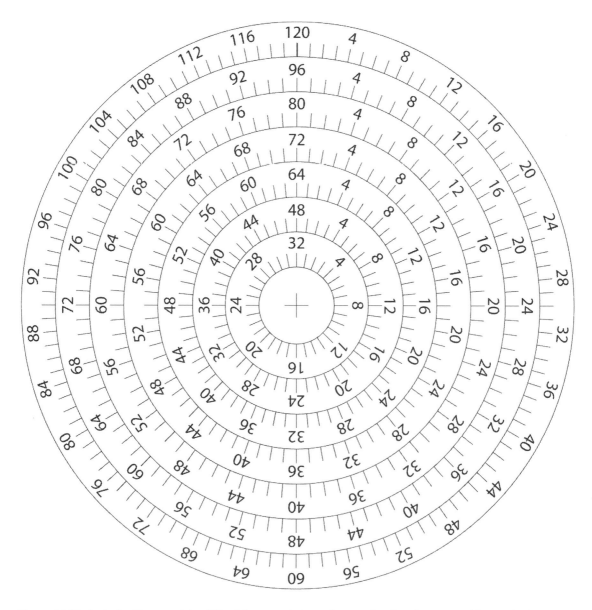

Figure 10-38 An Index Transposition Wheel for gem designs. See text for details. As an additional educational exercise, you might want to try demonstrating to yourself the problem with cutting the SRB from Figure 10-16 on a 72 or 80-tooth index wheel.

10.7.2 Transposing with Silicon

The mathematics behind the elegant Index Transposition Wheel is surprisingly prosaic. In order to transpose a design index setting D to a machine index setting M, the calculation is:

$$M = D \cdot \frac{NM}{ND}$$

where, ND and NM are the number of gear teeth for the design and machine, respectively. Following the example of the previous section, transposing index 12 on a 96-tooth wheel to a 64-tooth wheel gives:

$$M = 12 \cdot \frac{64}{96} = 8$$

At this stage of this chapter, I don't need to explain how to actually do the calculation. You can use a pocket calculator (don't forget to be careful and take notes), an Excel spreadsheet, or even an online tool if you can find it.

GemCAD also offers index transposition. In the original DOS version, press **g** or select **Index Gear** from the **Parameter** menu. In Windows GemCAD, select the **Index Gear...** command under the **Edit** menu.

10.7.3 Checking the Results

In all cases, check whether any of the resulting indices are fractional – that is, not a whole number. If you manage to transpose your design without any fractional indices, congratulations! You are lucky, and you should probably double-check your work. If you have a few fractional indices which are close to whole numbers (10.1, 35.9, etc.), then you might want to risk cutting the gem by rounding off to the nearest whole index. If you end up with a lot of fractional indices, or a few instances where the number came down right in the middle between integers, watch out.

Heroic and / or foolhardy cutters can in fact cut accurate gemstones with fractional or split indices. This is what the index splitter, or cheater, does, after all. You should be able to measure directly, or consult the user manual, to find out how many turns of the cheater correspond to a single index tooth. You should then be able to accurately dial in fractional indices and have at it. Of course, on a typical gem, this might involve accurately adjusting and keeping track of literally hundreds of cheater settings without error. Like I said, heroic and / or foolhardy.

10.8 Estimating and Calculating Gemstone Size and Yield

If you are anything like me, you want to know the moment you purchase a rough stone how big the resulting gem will be. And if you are anything like me, your early hopes are often dashed against the rocks of faceting reality. Nevertheless, there are ways to assess both the physical size and carat weight of your gemstones long before you pop them off the dop.

Specifically, measurements of the physical size of the gem rough, coupled with some numbers from the information block of the faceting diagram, can produce surprisingly accurate estimates fairly early on in the process. Such estimates can be essential for planning the remaining steps required to complete the gem. For example, if you have a requirement for a certain final weight, minor adjustments to the geometry of the design can get you where you need to go.

Chapter 5.5.5 already covered some of this material in the context of cutting your first gemstone. This section takes a more complete look at the mathematical information contained in a modern gem cutting diagram and how you can put that information to use.

10.8.1 Gemstone Geometry and the Information Block

Figure 10-39 shows the various directional views and the information block found in the header of a modern gem-cutting diagram. In this instance, the gem is Sakhir from Chapter 19.3.4, and the output is from the excellent GemCAD program (see Chapter 15.3.1).

In terms of determining size and yield, the critical area of the information block is at the bottom. Based on the shape of the stone, GemCAD has calculated various important geometrical factors, such as L/W, C/W, Vol./W³, etc. Other programs should provide similar information.

The first thing to note is that all of these factors are ratios, that is, one value divided by another. The directional views of the gemstone illustrate the meaning of the various symbols.

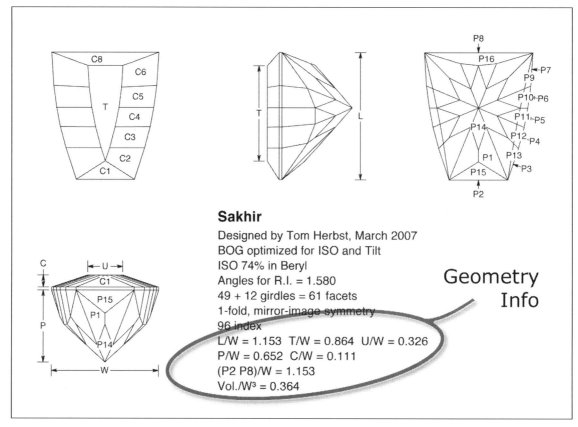

Sakhir

Designed by Tom Herbst, March 2007
BOG optimized for ISO and Tilt
ISO 74% in Beryl
Angles for R.I. = 1.580
49 + 12 girdles = 61 facets
1-fold, mirror-image symmetry
96 index
L/W = 1.153 T/W = 0.864 U/W = 0.326
P/W = 0.652 C/W = 0.111
(P2 P8)/W = 1.153
Vol./W³ = 0.364

Geometry Info

Figure 10-39 The top, side, end, and bottom views, as well as the information block, of the Sakhir gem design. The last four lines of the information block contain important mathematical information about the geometry of the gem.

Specifically, they are:

L – Long dimension of the stone

W – Short dimension of the stone

T – Long dimension of the Table

U – Short dimension of the Table

C – Height of the Crown

P – Depth of the Pavilion

The reason for the ratios should be obvious. The program does not know how big your gemstone actually is, but the relative lengths will be independent of the size. In other words, a one carat Sakhir and a one hundred carat Sakhir will both have L/W=1.153.

A few other things are worthy of note. First, the length and width directions of the gem are always perpendicular to each other and aligned with the screen. The L direction is always the longer of the two. Similarly, T and U are always perpendicular to each other and T is always larger. Note also that these ratios correspond to the maximum dimension in the appropriate direction. This means, for example, that a symmetrical six-sided stone will have L/W=1.155, not 1.0. This may seem odd, but you can prove it to yourself using the hexagonal GeM101 design in Chapter 5.1.1. The various ratios can be measured from flat to flat (as with L for Sakhir), from point to point (as with W), or even from point to flat.

The volume factor Vol./W^3 is the ratio of the volume of the gem to the cube of the width W. You can think of this factor as the volume relative to a cube whose edge length is the width of the stone. It turns out that the volume factor is also a measure of the overall geometry of the design. Longer, thinner gems will have a larger L/W ratio and, in general, a larger Vol./W^3.

The height C of the crown and the depth P of the pavilion are always measured from their respective girdle lines (examine the lower left gem drawing in Figure 10-39). Hence, there is no explicit information about girdle thickness. Nevertheless, GemCAD uses the actual girdle thickness created by the designer to determine the volume factor Vol./W^3. In other words, if I had generated the GemCAD design of Sakhir with a thicker girdle, the volume factor would be larger, but none of the other geometrical ratios would change. You can take advantage of this fact to increase yield – see "Weight Gain and Girdles..." on page 44.

Note that there is one unusual ratio in Sakhir's information block. GemCAD has calculated the value (P2 P8)/W. It does this whenever there are two labeled girdle facets on exactly opposite sides of the stone, *i.e.* index 0 and 48. This ratio can be used to give additional information about the dimensions of the gem, since it corresponds to the distance that one would measure with calipers placed between the labeled girdle facets. In the case of Sakhir, P2 and P8 also correspond to the long dimension of the gem. Hence, the (P2 P8)/W ratio is identical to L/W.

While the preceding paragraphs may have demystified faceting diagrams somewhat, you can legitimately ask what purpose is served in providing the so many geometrical ratios. As you will see, they can be extremely useful in determining whether a given design is well matched to your piece of gem rough, and also how large a gem can be cut from it. In addition, you can use the volume ratio to predict the final carat weight of your masterwork in progress.

10.8.2 Using the Ratios 1 – Fitting Design to Rough

Let's say you want to cut your own Sakhir out of a nice piece of morganite you picked up. The design is already optimized for beryl, so happily no transformations or scaling will be required. Your morganite is mostly clean, and careful examination has shown that there is a promising flawless region that is about 12 x 9 mm and 8 mm thick.

Your understanding of the geometrical ratios will let you answer at least two critical questions: 1. Is Sakhir a good match to your piece of rough? 2. Assuming no screw-ups or hidden flaws, how big a gem will you get?

The two questions are closely related, and they both require an additional simple calculation of the *depth* of the gem design. Recall from the previous section that GemCAD reports the L/W, C/W, and P/W ratios, but not the *total* depth, which we will call D. In fact, for consistency and comparison, you should focus on D/W, that is, the ratio of D to the width of the stone. You can readily estimate D/W by adding up the crown, pavilion, and girdle using the formula:

$$D/W = C/W + P/W + 0.02$$

which assumes the "classic" girdle height equal to 2% of the width W of the gem. For Sakhir, D/W=0.783.

You now know Sakhir's ultimate external "envelope." Independent of the actual final size in millimeters, you will need a volume of material whose dimensions are a multiple of:

$$L/W \times 1 \times D/W$$

You should recognize this as length x width x depth, where I have cleverly simplified W/W to the number one – all those years of college seem to have paid off. The actual values for Sakhir are 1.153 x 1 x 0.783.

How well do these dimensions match the rough and how big a gem can you get? The clean area of morganite is 12 x 9 x 8 mm. Given these proportions, you clearly want to try fitting L along the 12 mm direction, W along the 9 mm direction, and D along the 8 mm direction.

The maximum possible gemstone size would then have L = 12 mm. You can divide Sakhir's dimensions by L/W and then multiply by 12 to get the physical size of such a gem:

$$\frac{L/W \times 1 \times D/W}{L/W} \cdot 12 = 12 \times 10.4 \times 8.1 \text{ mm, scaled to maximum } L$$

Therefore, cutting a Sakhir with L=12 mm would require a piece of gem rough at least 12 x 10.4 x 8.1 mm. Unfortunately, the piece of morganite is somewhat smaller.

This exercise illustrates that W is the problem. When you matched the long dimensions of design and rough, the required depth (8.1 mm) is only slightly more than the available depth (8 mm), whereas the required width (10.4 mm) is considerably greater than what you have (9 mm).

At this point, you should recognize that the largest possible stone has W=9 mm. Nevertheless, it is a worthwhile exercise to scale Sakhir's dimensions and prove it:

$$\frac{L/W \times 1 \times D/W}{D/W} \cdot 8 = 11.8 \times 10.2 \times 8 \text{ mm, scaled to maximum } D$$

$$\frac{L/W \times 1 \times D/W}{W/W} \cdot 9 = 10.4 \times 9 \times 7.0 \text{ mm, scaled to maximum } W$$

As expected, scaling Sakhir to the 8 mm depth produces a stone that is too wide: 10.2 mm with only 9 mm available. The maximum gem size is therefore 10.4 x 9.0 x 7.0 mm.

So. How good a fit is this?

This is inevitably a subjective question. There will always be a better fit out there somewhere, but is it worth searching for a design you like that has a length to width to depth ratio corresponding exactly to 12 x 9 x 8? I don't think so.

You can make a very crude estimate of "goodness of fit" of a design to a particular piece of rough by asking how much of the original volume of gem material the scaled design fills. The maximum Sakhir has dimensions 10.4 x 9.0 x 7.0 mm and therefore needs a rectangular volume of 655 cubic millimeters (the volume of a rectangular solid is length x width x height). The clean volume of gem rough is 12 x 9 x 8 mm, or 864 cubic millimeters. The scaled Sakhir therefore exploits about 75% of the available material. This is fairly decent as these things go, so overall, I would say that Sakhir is a good design for the morganite. Note that you could also play a bit with the girdle thickness (see next page), and don't forget the lessons you learned starting on page 228 of Volume 1.

Both experienced gem cutters and mathematicians are probably pulling their hair out about this calculation, so here come the caveats. First and foremost, gemstones aren't rectangular solids. Stated simply, they are wide in the middle at the girdle, tapering to a culet or keel on one side and tapering to a flat table on the other. Therefore, making judgments about the available rough or the "goodness of fit" on the basis of rectangular volume is a gross simplification. For example, there may be an ugly inclusion somewhere deep in the rectangular volume that has absolutely no effect since it will be cut away. Also, slavishly following this procedure for comparing designs to gem rough may lead to the ludicrous conclusion that a pre-form is a bad match to its intended final shape.

Clearly, as with many aspects of our hobby, the path to success combines common sense and mathematical calculations, doled out in appropriate proportions. Oh…and I have tried it: pulling your hair out doesn't help.

10.8.3 Using the Ratios 2 – Estimating Yield

The ratios in the information block can also help you estimate *yield*, in other words, to make a decent guess at the final carat weight of your gemstone. And as an extra bonus, if you have done all the work in the previous section and / or understood the material in Chapter 5.5.5, this one will be easy.

The critical ratio for estimating weight is of course the volume factor Vol./W³. If you know the width W of the gem – for example, by going through the exercise in the previous section –

then Vol./W³ tells you its volume. And, given the volume and the density of the gem material, you can readily calculate the weight, since density is simply the weight per unit volume. It sounds a lot more complicated than it is.

Let's estimate the carat weight of the maximum Sakhir that will fit in the morganite rough from the previous section. The biggest possible gem is 10.4 x 9.0 x 7.0 mm. This means that W=9.0. The volume factor Vol./W³ is 0.364. Therefore, Vol.=0.364 W³, which for W=9.0 gives a volume of 265.4 cubic millimeters.

There is a range of published densities for beryl (see Chapter 14.1), and individual samples of any gemstone material can vary somewhat. Adopting a value in the middle of the range gives about 2.78 grams per cubic centimeter.

Note that the gem volume calculation is in cubic millimeters, while published density values are in units of cubic centimeters. Wouldn't it be nice if our gems were so big that we measured their volume in cubic centimeters as well? One can always dream, but in the meantime, you will need to perform a simple conversion. With 1000 cubic millimeters in a cubic centimeter, the choice is yours: convert the gemstone volume to cubic centimeters (answer: 0.2654) or convert beryl's density to grams per cubic millimeter (answer: 0.00278).

Whichever you choose, simply multiply the density by the volume to get the weight. The answer is 0.738 grams or 3.69 carats. For future reference, the formula for the complete calculation is:

$$\text{Carat Weight} = 5 \cdot \text{density} \cdot \text{volume factor} \cdot W^3$$

A few concluding notes deserve mention. First, your gemstone will almost certainly not end up exactly this weight. In addition to variations in the density of real-world materials, you will likely make small errors in assessing the clean volume of rough. Also, these calculations leave no margin for cutting, pre-polishing, and polishing. Finally, very few gemstones end up exactly as you expect them to. Hidden flaws, cutting errors, and good old Murphy's Law can always exert their insidious influence. The lesson? Don't count your carats before they're cut (see page 164 of Volume 1), and if you have to meet a certain requirement (gem size, carat weight), leave yourself some wiggle room.

Weight Gain and Girdles...

I know. Bad title. Not only is it vaguely sexist, but also it is vaguely fifty years out of date.

The following paragraphs unify the material covered in this chapter, in the sense that they invoke trigonometry, tangent ratio scaling, and estimating the yield of a gemstone. Yes, I could have forced an index wheel switch in as well, but that would have been just a little too cute...

The question at hand focuses on the yield from a piece of gem rough and the contention held by many authorities, including some textbooks, that deepening a gemstone via tangent ratio scaling is a good away to maximize it.

Horsepucky.

Tangent ratio scaling fundamentally changes the optical performance of a gemstone, and in my view, should be used only for improving that performance. A well-designed gem should already have the optimal angles, and if it doesn't, tools exist to find them and change them.

Yes, I have been banging away on this particular drum for half of this chapter, but the issue of optimal angles is unquestionably vital to the visual impact of your gems, and consequently, to your personal satisfaction with faceting. Here come more bangs…

Let's take a concrete example, or better yet, a tourmaline example. Good tourmaline gem rough runs upward of $15 per carat at current (2014) prices. Let's also adopt the rule of thumb that for smallish (1-5 carat) gems, the finished, per-carat value is roughly ten times higher than the rough price (see Chapter 6.5). Thus, your $15 per carat tourmaline should sell for $150 per carat when you are done. Increasing the yield on a 4-carat finished stone by 15% corresponds to a cool one hundred bucks. How can you earn that Benjamin while maintaining high quality and self respect?

(Parenthetical Remark: Lord knows that I, of all people, should not view faceting as a money-making proposition…correction…Wife knows that I, of all people, should not view faceting as a money-making proposition. For most of us, cutting gems is just an enormously rewarding hobby. Nevertheless, it can be very satisfying, dare I say rewarding, to increase the yield of expensive gem rough, even by a small amount. For example, modest increases in yield can push certain finished stones over a psychological barrier, such as 1.0 carats, 2.0 carats, etc. – see "Excluding Inclusions – The 1 carat boundary" on page 144.)

So. Back to the example. You have a nice piece of tourmaline rough that should yield a 4-carat standard round brilliant, according to the calculations explained in this section. Let's see how you can make it close to a five-carat stone – specifically a 4.7-carat stone that is worth $100 more. The example presumes the classic, not canonical, proportions for the SRB used throughout this chapter (see Figure 10-16), since they are not too far from optimal for tourmaline:

| pavilion mains: 41° | crown mains: 28° |
| pavilion breaks: 43° | crown breaks: 32° |

Incidentally, this discussion also assumes that the geometry of the rough does not allow simple scaling of the whole gem, since I hope that you will always try to cut the biggest, good quality gem out of a particular piece of raw stone. Put another way, the real goal here is to increase the volume factor Vol./W^3 by about 15%.

Given these geometrical constraints, the conventional options are rather limited: scale the pavilion or scale the crown. Experience and the other sections of this chapter tell you that this road is paved with peril. In particular, changes to the pavilion angles of a well-designed gem usually end badly, for example in a fish-eye.

A few minutes of play with the software tools described in Chapter 15.3 illustrate the dilemma. Pavilion main angles below about 38° and above 42.5° cause the optical performance of the SRB to tank badly. There is considerably more freedom with the crown: the break facets can range between about 20° and 35° before things seriously go south. There is an additional problem, however. It is a general characteristic of gemstones that shallow crowns perform well with deep pavilions and deep crowns perform well with shallow pavilions (see, for example, Figure 18-47). The other combinations, shallow crowns and shallow pavilions or deep crowns and deep pavilions, simply don't work out. Unfortunately, it is exactly this last combination – a deep crown coupled with a deep pavilion – that would increase your yield.

Let's give it a try anyway. Deepening the pavilion using the tangent ratio to transform the mains from 41° to 42.5° produces a 3% increase in yield. Stretching the crown so that the breaks are 35° pushes the yield up about 4%. Doing both increases the yield by 7%, although for the reasons laid out in the previous paragraph, this is not a particularly good idea. In fact, it produces a gem with about 30% lower light return and a very unattractive reflection pattern (Figure 10-40).

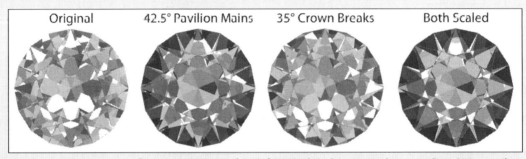

Figure 10-40 GemRay reflectance patterns for (left to right) the original tourmaline SRB, pavilion mains scaled to 42.5°, crown breaks scaled to 35°, and both pavilion and crown scaled. The calculated light return values are 94, 89, 75, and 67 percent, respectively. The tilt performance of the modified gem suffers as well.

The moral of this story is that scaling the pavilion or crown to increase yield will probably not help much, and if you push it too far, it could seriously damage your goods.

All is not lost, however. Four paragraphs back, I mentioned that the *conventional* options were limited to scaling the pavilion and scaling the crown. Who wants to be conventional? There is, after all, a third, oft-ignored component in the anatomy of a gemstone: the girdle.

Scaling the girdle represents a very interesting option for increasing yield. First and foremost, a modest increase in the thickness of the girdle has little effect on the gem's optical performance. Also, the girdle is, by definition, the thickest part of the stone, and hence increasing the height at that location has the maximum effect. Convention (there's that word again) holds that the girdle should be cut to 2% of the width of the gem, yet in the real world, this is quite narrow and potentially makes the stone susceptible to breakage during mounting. A thicker girdle reduces the chances of chipping and breakage while setting in jewelry, and the added bulk preserves more gem material if you ever have to re-cut the crown or pavilion. Finally, increasing the girdle thickness is *easy*: just cut it thicker. No fancy scaling or tangent calculations involved.

Figure 10-41 shows the "classic" standard round brilliant cut with 2, 4, 6, 8, and 10% girdles. Even if money were not involved, I would have no qualms about cutting a gem with a 6% girdle. I would consider going even higher if the stone was small. In fact, in my household, smaller rough usually means more valuable rough – top tourmaline, sapphire, etc. – for which improvements in yield are proportionately more important.

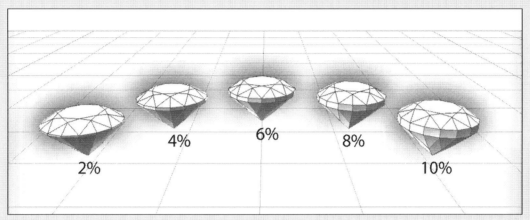

Figure 10-41 Standard Round Brilliant gems with a girdle thickness of 2, 4, 6, 8, and 10 percent of the total width of the stone.

How much yield will thickening the girdle buy? Figure 10-42 plots the increase in yield as a function of the girdle width. For a classic SRB, a gem with a 6% girdle has a volume factor 16% higher than one with a 2% girdle. There's your hundred bucks.

Of course, and as always, several caveats are in order. First, the gem rough must be of a size and shape to allow the thicker girdle. Due to the form of many tourmaline crystals and the fact that the C-axis often presents the best colour, this will frequently be the case. Second, a thicker girdle may be incompatible with your planned setting. Check before you cut. Finally, even with sustained optical performance and increasing yield, there is a limit to how far you want to push this. The 10% girdle in Figure 10-42 does not look overtly silly, but it is getting there.

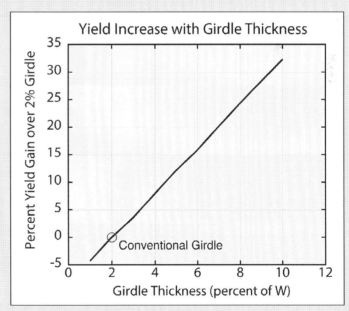

Figure 10-42 The increase in yield for various girdle thicknesses relative to the conventional 2% girdle. The gem is a classically proportioned SRB.

The conclusion? A thicker girdle may be the key to higher yield. Give it a try.

11

Gemstone Optics

Of all the properties of gemstones, it is their optical characteristics – that is, the way in which the gem material interacts with light – that determine their quality and emotional impact. This chapter explains how a number of optical phenomena, including refraction, reflection, and dispersion, produce the brilliance, sparkle, and fire that give life to our gemstones.

After an explanation of the wave nature of light, the chapter explores the origin and consequences of colour in gems. The polarization property of light waves leads to the well-known effects of birefringence and pleochroism. The chapter then provides both an intuitive and mathematical introduction to Snell's Law, Total Internal Reflection, and Fresnel Losses, all of which are at the core of how gems perform. The concluding section follows the 3-dimensional journey of a light ray from the sun to your gemstone to your eye.

11.1 Introduction

First of all, don't panic.

You don't really need a profound grasp of optics nor an advanced degree in mathematics to understand how gemstones work. After all, the cutters who developed and refined the most successful designs, such as the standard round brilliant and emerald cuts, were artisans and artists, not physicists. Nevertheless, a basic understanding of how light interacts with matter to produce the effects we so much desire – brilliance, sparkle, fire, etc. – will help you make better design and cutting decisions, as well as enhance your appreciation of the results.

11.2 Catch a Wave

Here's a fundamental question that you have probably asked yourself more than once: what is light?

It's not a simple question. In fact, the nature of light and how it behaves in the world around us has been at the center of the physical sciences for at least 2000 years. Intellectual giants such as Euclid, Ptolemy, Newton, and Einstein have all struggled with this question, and it is only in the last couple of centuries or so that a coherent, consistent picture has emerged (see opposite page).

We now understand that light is an *electromagnetic wave*. No, this is not just an incomprehensible name for an incomprehensible phenomenon. We are all familiar with the effects of electric and magnetic fields in everyday life. They are the phenomena that attract small pieces of paper to an electrically charged comb, or iron filings to a magnet. What physicists in the mid 19th century realized is that light is actually an *oscillating* disturbance of electric and magnetic fields, in other words, a wave (Figure 11-1). These oscillating fields interact with the atoms in matter, such as those in a crystal of gem material.

Note that the oscillation of the electric and magnetic fields in Figure 11-1 are perpendicular to each other and to the direction the wave is travelling. Note also that the height of the wave in the figure represents the strength of the corresponding electric or magnetic field at that point (P for example). Unlike with ocean waves, nothing actually moves up and down or back and forth.

How can you characterize these light waves?

An examination of Figure 11-1, coupled with a bit of inspired head scratching, should lead you to the answer. There are four properties that completely describe an electromagnetic wave passing a certain reference point in space:

- the intensity or *amplitude* of the oscillation.

- the distance from one peak to the next, known as the *wavelength*.

- the orientation of the wave, called the *plane of polarization*.

- the *phase*, which describes where in a particular wave the reference point finds itself, for example rising up to a crest or at the bottom of a trough.

An Electromagnetic Wave

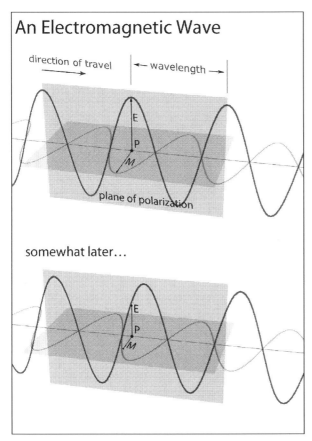

Of these four, only the wavelength and polarization are of particular interest to the hobby faceter, because they have a direct effect on light's interaction with the gem material. The wavelength of light corresponds to its *colour*: blue light has a shorter wavelength than green light, which in turn has a shorter wavelength than red light (see Section 11.2.1). Polarization (Section 11.2.2) is responsible for *birefringence* and *pleochroism*. Birefringence, among other effects, produces the facet doubling you see in zircon, while pleochroism results in orientation-dependent colour in gemstones, such as sapphire, tourmaline, and most spectacularly, iolite.

Figure 11-1 Light is an electromagnetic wave. Here, the wave is traveling from left to right past a point P. In the top frame, the electric (E) and magnetic (M) fields at P are at a maximum. Slightly later (bottom frame), the wave has moved onward, and the fields are reduced. The plane of polarization of the light is by definition the same as that of the electric field.

Look! Up in the Sky. It's a Wave! It's a Particle! No! It's a Wavicle!

The wave nature of light, now universally accepted, has by no means been the conventional wisdom during the last millennium. One of the first investigators to examine this issue was Ibn al-Haytham, born in Basra Iraq in 965 AD. al-Haytham was an astronomer, engineer, mathematician, and philosopher – essentially the Isaac Newton of the Muslim world, and he is credited with advancing the first theory of light as a stream of energetic particles that travel at finite speed.

Some 700 years later, Isaac Newton proposed a similar particle theory of light, arguing in his famous work *Opticks* that light must be a particle – a corpuscle in 17th century scientific lingo – since it was known that waves can bend around solid objects whereas light always travels in straight lines.

In the meantime, Newton's colleague and nemesis, Robert Hooke, was advancing a wave theory of light. This would not be the only time that these two found themselves on different sides of a discussion. See page 54 and Chapter 8.11.1 for more fireworks.

The Dutch physicist Christiaan Huygens advanced his own wave theory for light a couple of decades after Hooke, but such was the reputation of Isaac Newton that the particle theory was held to be gospel for the better part of a century.

Things began to go pear-shaped (or perhaps, wave-shaped) for the particle theory in the 19th century with the observation that light does indeed bend around objects. The theoretical work of James Clerk Maxwell in the 1870's, coupled with experimental verification by Heinrich Hertz and others (see Figure 11-5), seemed to put the final nail in the coffin of Newton's corpuscular theory.

Somehow, however, you can't keep a good theory down, and the idea of light as particles experienced a renaissance at the beginning of the twentieth century, thanks to Albert Einstein and others. In 1905, Einstein was able to explain an enduring mystery of experimental physics, namely the *photoelectric effect*, by postulating that light is indeed a stream of energetic particles.

Nevertheless, the wave-like behaviour of light was undeniable, and it took a twenty-year debate in the scientific community, along with the development of the theory of relativity and quantum mechanics, to come to a final understanding.

Physicists now speak about the *wave-particle duality*, that is, light (and in fact all matter and energy) displays properties of both waves and particles. Can't decide between calling light a wave or a particle? Come up with a new name! How about *wavicle*? I kid you not.

Although this solution may be unsatisfying to those who always want a clear winner in a debate, the notion of the wave-particle duality is by no means a cop out. Both sides were right, and the real error was in trying to force a poorly understood phenomenon into a strict categorization.

Light really does have both a particle nature and a wave nature. It turns out that in order to explain the phenomena associated with gemstone optics, the wave nature usually suffices, and the balance of this chapter will speak of light as waves, not particles.

11.2.1 Wavelength

Colour describes our visual perception of the wavelength of light. The human eye is sensitive to electromagnetic radiation with wavelengths ranging from about 3/8 to 3/4 of a micron. A micron is a thousandth of a millimeter, but you may be more familiar with Angstroms, which are one ten-millionth of a millimeter. In these units, the visible spectrum ranges from 3,800 Angstroms in the violet to 7,500 Angstroms in the red. Shorter wavelengths correspond to *ultraviolet* light (remember that ultraviolet "black light" at the disco that made your eyeballs and teeth look weird? Good. Me neither), while longer wavelengths are known as *infrared* light (Figure 11-2).

The colour of light can also be described by its frequency, that is, the number of wave crests that pass a certain point per second. Identifying "colour" with frequency is more common at radio wavelengths, which are longward of the infrared in Figure 11-2. For example, your local "Classic Rock 104.6" bathes you in electromagnetic waves at a rate of 104.6 million crests per second. No wonder you can't stop tapping your feet...

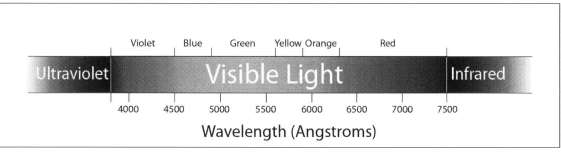

Figure 11-2 Visible light corresponds to wavelengths between 3,800 and 7,500 Angstroms.

11.2.2 Polarization

One individual light wave has a single plane of polarization. In other words, the direction of oscillation of its electric field stays constant as it travels along (see Figure 11-1). A whole bunch of light waves, however, will typically have wildly differing planes of polarization. Polarization refers to the overall amount of alignment of these planes.

Most of the light around us is unpolarized, that is, the individual electric fields are randomly oriented. However, some interactions of light with matter can vary strongly for different orientations. For example, the scattering of sunlight off the asphalt of a highway can preferentially reflect one plane of polarization versus another. How can you cut down the glare on a late afternoon freeway cruise? Wear Polaroid sunglasses, which cancel one orientation (the preferentially reflected one), while allowing the perpendicular polarization to pass through.

Polarization also plays a critical role in modern flatscreen display technology. Try tipping your head from side to side while wearing polarized sunglasses in front of a computer monitor or television. Pretty cool, eh? Try the same while looking at different parts of the sky on a cloudless late afternoon. More coolness. Polarization is behind all of these phenomena.

With your shades still on, hold up and rotate a piece of tourmaline in front of the flatscreen display or sky (also see Figure 12-13). Cool upon cool. Polarization is important to gemstone optics because, like the asphalt highway, many gem materials treat different planes of polarization differently. For example, birefringent gemstones have a different index of refraction for light waves with one polarization compared to waves with the perpendicular polarization. Section 11.4 below explains why this can be important, while Chapter 12.4 deals with birefringence and its effects in detail.

11.3 How Light Rays Interact with Matter

We all know that light rays, whether in the beam of a laser pointer or from the headlights of a car, travel in straight lines (more or less...see the discussion of waves versus particles starting on page 51). What is less obvious in our day-to-day experience is that light travels at a finite speed, is reversible, and can, in fact, change direction when it encounters an object. The remainder of this chapter provides an overview of how the effects of finite speed, reversibility, and changing direction put the sparkle into faceted gemstones.

11.3.1 It's Not Only a Good Idea – It's the Law

In the early 1900's, Albert Einstein demonstrated that there is an absolute speed limit in the universe: the speed of light. More specifically, the limit is the speed of light *in vacuum*, about 186,282 miles per second or 299,792 kilometers per second. Nothing can go faster. Light travels more slowly when traveling through matter, whether it be air, water, or the transparent body of a gemstone, and this reduction in speed is a basic property of that matter. All of the optical effects relevant to faceting follow from this simple fact.

Figure 11-3 Albert Einstein established the universal speed limit.

Scientists usually use the symbol *c* when referring to the speed of light. Yes, this is the *c* in Einstein's famous formula $E=mc^2$, which tells you how much oomph you can extract by converting a mass *m* into energy. Given that *c* is a couple of hundred thousand miles per second, such conversion is very powerful indeed: one gram of matter, say that nice five-carat garnet, could power a typical home for almost 3,000 years, if converted entirely to energy!

As emphasized above, light travels more slowly than *c*=186,282 miles per second when it passes through matter, and each type of matter has a specific speed reduction factor. This factor is known as the *refractive index* or *index of refraction*. The common symbol for the refractive index is *n*. Thus, the speed of light in a material with refractive index *n* is *c* ÷ *n*.

You are almost certainly familiar with the refractive index. It is the number which determines the critical angle for a gem material (see Section 11.7 below). Want to impress your friends at the lapidary club? Mention casually that the speed of light in uvarovite is just a shade under 100,000 miles per second. At that speed, a light ray can enter a gemstone, bounce around a couple of times, and exit again in less than a tenth of a nanosecond (one ten-billionth of a second). That's not much time for your well-planned facets to do their magic, so you better get them right.

Measuring The Speed of Light

More than two centuries before Einstein, scientists throughout Europe knew that the speed of light was finite – in other words, light rays require a nonzero interval of time to travel from one point to another. Einstein merely (merely!) proved that this speed was an absolute limit in the universe.

Measuring the speed of light experimentally proved to be enormously difficult, however. Many of the great luminaries of the physics world, including Galileo, Newton, and Robert Hooke, took part in this great challenge (a little closer to our lapidary hearts, it turns out that some of these individuals also locked horns in trying to explain how polishing works – see Chapter 8.11.1). After many attempts and mixed success, the French physicists Hippolyte Fizeau and Léon Foucault, who coincidentally were born in the same week in Paris in 1819, succeeded in accurately measuring the speed of light using a clever rotating apparatus and a distant mirror (see Figure 11-4).

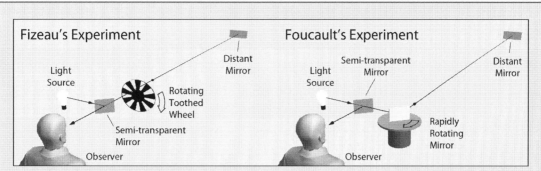

Figure 11-4 The Fizeau (left) and Foucault (right) experiments for measuring the speed of light.

Hippolyte Fizeau used a rotating toothed wheel and a semi-transparent flat mirror to make his measurement. Light bounces off this mirror and passes through a gap in the wheel on its way to a second, distant mirror several miles away. After reflection, the light returns to the rotating wheel, which has moved by a small amount during the journey. At certain rotation rates, everything works beautifully, and the returning ray passes through a subsequent gap in the wheel and eventually into the observer's eye. At lower or higher rates, however, the wheel has not rotated by a full gap and the light is blocked. Knowing the number of teeth in the wheel, as well as its rotation rate and the distance to the far mirror, lets you calculate the speed of light directly. Fizeau's estimate was 194,000 miles per second (313,000 km/sec), about 4% high.

In Foucault's arrangement, light bounces off a rotating mirror and travels a long distance – over 20 miles (35 km) in his experiment – to a second, flat mirror. The returning light bounces off the rotating mirror once again and makes a measurable spot. The trick to the experiment is that the mirror can rotate by a small angle during the time that the light is traveling out to the flat mirror and back. By varying the rotation rate of the mirror, Foucault was able to measure the displacement of the reflected spot and hence the speed of light. His value, published in 1862, was 185,000 miles per second (298,000 km/sec), very close to the correct answer.

Incidentally, many modern optical alignment procedures adopt an approach reminiscent of Fizeau and Foucault's experiments. The optical alignment scheme for dop transfer described in Chapter 7.6.4 is one such example.

11.3.2 What's Really Going On?

The interaction of light with matter is actually a fairly complicated business, but if you understand a little about radios, you are well on your way. The simplest radio transmitter is a wire connected to some circuitry that produces an oscillating electric voltage (Figure 11-5). When you switch it on, the electrons in the wire move back and forth in response to the voltage. Moving charge means a moving electric field, and this in turn means a moving magnetic field (think of the charge moving around the coil of an electromagnet). These choreographed oscillating electric and magnetic fields are in fact an electromagnetic wave. In this case, it is a radio wave, which heads outward from the wire in all directions.

On the receiving end, exactly the opposite happens. The incoming electromagnetic wave causes the electrons in the receiver wire to oscillate, which produces a voltage that is detected and converted into sound. How we got from this simple elegance to Top 40 radio is beyond me...

What does any of this have to do with gemstone optics?

Well, the classical picture of any material, including your favourite lump of rock, is of a three dimensional lattice of small oscillators based on electrons and atomic nuclei. Each of these oscillators acts like a tiny radio receiver and transmitter. When light – that is, an electromagnetic wave – falls on the material, the oscillators act like radio receivers, and the electrons jiggle in response to the incoming wave. These jiggling electrons, in turn, act as a transmitter, re-creating the electromagnetic fields, which allow the wave – the light – to propagate onward (Figure 11-6).

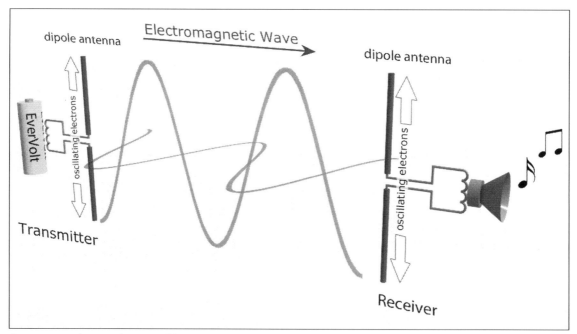

Figure 11-5 The simplest possible radio transmitter and receiver. Heinrich Hertz used a similar device in the 1880's to demonstrate the wave nature of light (see page 52). Oscillating electrons in the transmitter create an electromagnetic wave. On the receiving end, exactly the opposite happens. The incoming electromagnetic wave causes the electrons in the receiver wire to oscillate, which produces a voltage that is detected and converted into sound.

Ok. One more time. What does this have to do with gemstone optics?

Ah. Great question. You should have asked earlier. The key to gemstone optics is *refraction*, and this depends on slowing down the light (see next section). It turns out that the oscillators within your crystal of gem material are not perfect, and in fact, the speed of the re-radiated wave depends on how imperfect they are. For all real-world materials, the oscillating electrons produce a slower electromagnetic wave than one traveling in vacuum. Specifically, there are *natural frequencies* associated with optical materials. These natural frequencies are determined by the chemical makeup and structure of the crystal – effectively the stiffness of the springs in Figure 11-6. The speed of the re-radiated wave depends on the difference in frequency between the incoming light and these natural frequencies. Different materials have different natural frequencies, and hence light travels at different speeds within them. As

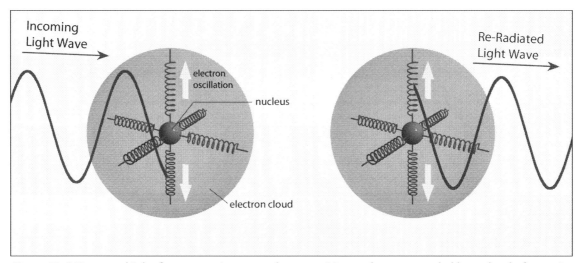

Figure 11-6 You can think of one atom in a crystal as a positive nucleus surrounded by a cloud of negative electrons and connected to its neighbours by springs. The incoming light (left) causes the electrons to oscillate and, in turn, re-radiate the light (right). Note that the electrons, not the nuclei, oscillate in response to the wave. The strength of the "springs" determines the natural frequency of oscillation and hence the speed of the re-radiated wave (see text).

you will see below, it is this difference in speed that produces refraction, which ultimately makes our gemstones sparkle. In addition to refraction, these internal forces and frequencies are responsible for the full range of optical phenomena we associate with gemstones, including colour, birefringence, pleochroism, etc. Chapter 12 provides additional detail (see in particular, Chapters 12.3 and 12.4).

I hope that you have enjoyed this little excursion into electromagnetism, but as a gem cutter, you really only need to understand *how*, not *why*, it happens. In other words, you need to understand refraction and Snell's Law.

11.4 Refraction

When a ray of light leaves one type of material (i.e. air) and enters another (i.e. uvarovite), it will, in general, have to change speed, unless the two materials have identical refractive indices (which air and uvarovite do not – see page 54). The previous section explains why this happens.

The natural effect of this change in speed is a bending or *refraction* of the light ray. This phenomenon can be understood in a number of different ways, but perhaps the most straightforward approach is to examine the consequences of *Fermat's principle of least time*.

Pierre de Fermat was a 17th century mathematician who realized that a ray of light traveling between two points will take the quickest path – hence the name *principle of least time*. In a single medium, such as air, this path is clearly a straight line. If the ray encounters differing media, however, its speed will change and a straight path is no longer the quickest.

Figure 11-7 Pierre de Fermat, seventeenth century lawyer and amateur mathematician. He is perhaps best known for his "Last Theorem," which was discovered by his son in the margin of a notebook. Despite intense effort by mathematicians, the theorem was not proven until 1995, almost four hundred years later.,

A simple analogy is to imagine yourself walking along the seashore, when you spot a struggling swimmer a certain distance along the beach (see Figure 11-8).

What is the quickest way to rescue the drowning man? You can run faster on land, so it makes sense to plan more of your path there. A straight line in the example shown would be half on land and half in water (right panel of Figure 11-8), so clearly it is not optimal. Running all the way along the beach and then diving in is also less than ideal. The fastest path lies somewhere in between. Exactly where depends on how fast you – or the light ray – can travel in each of the two environments.

Figure 11-8 Saving a drowning man at the beach. The fastest route to the struggling swimmer is not the shortest distance.

Interested in learning more? Section 11.5 uses the swimmer analogy to derive exactly how light behaves as it passes from one material into another, a process governed by *Snell's Law.*

11.4.1 Refraction and Snell's Law

Snell's law gives the direction of light rays as they pass from one medium to another. In Figure 11-9, light strikes the interface between the two materials at an incident angle θ_1, and it travels onward at transmitted angle θ_2.

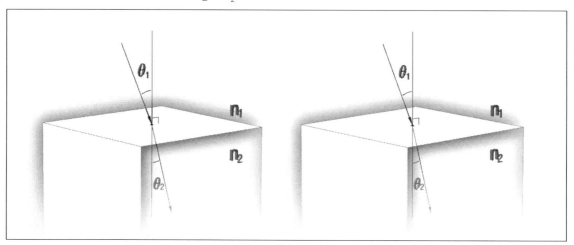

Figure 11-9 The angle of incidence and refraction for two media of refractive index n_1 and n_2. Note that the angles are measured with respect to the perpendicular to the surface. Yes, this is the same drawing as Figure 10-7. To make it up to you, this one is in 3D! Cross your eyes to see the effect. Section 11.9 explains 3D imagery and can help if you have difficulty.

The relation between incident and transmitted angles is:

$$n_1 \cdot \sin \theta_1 = n_2 \cdot \sin \theta_2$$

where n_1 and n_2 are the refractive indices of the respective materials. Not sure what $\sin \theta$ means? See Chapter 10.2.

Let's take the simple example of a ray of light passing from air (n_1=1) into a diamond (n_2=2.42) and an amethyst (n_2=1.54). Figure 11-10 shows some rays, while Figure 11-11 plots the transmitted angle as a function of the incident angle.

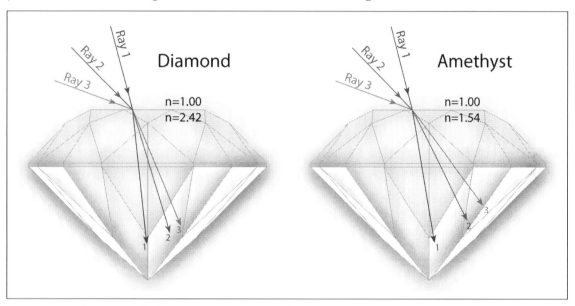

Figure 11-10 Three rays of light entering a diamond (left) and an amethyst (right). For the same incident angle, a diamond refracts the ray closer to the perpendicular (smaller θ2) than does an amethyst.

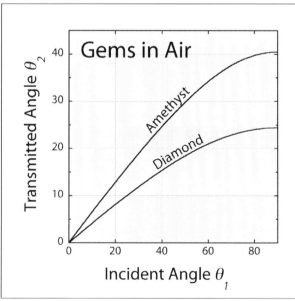

Figure 11-11 The transmitted angle θ2 as a function of the incident angle θ1 for diamond and amethyst in air.

As pointed out in Chapter 10.3, the ray transmitted into the gem is always closer to perpendicular – in other words, θ_2 is always smaller than θ_1. This explains the ability of gemstones to "collect" light from a large range of incident angles and redirect them into directions useful for the performance of the gem. Note also that this redirection is more effective for higher refractive index: for a given input ray, the value of θ_2 is always smaller for diamond than for amethyst. This greater refractive ability also means that, in general, the rays entering your eye from a diamond came from a wider spread of input angles. This translates to better subjective gem performance, since this wider range captures more photons and likely includes a greater variety of light sources, less head shadow, etc. See Section 11.9 below for more on light paths within a gem and Chapter 10.4 for additional detail on how refractive index influences the "capture cone" of light. Figure 15-9 illustrates the head shadow effect.

Credit where Credit is Due...

Interestingly, it appears that Snell was not the first to discover the law of refraction that now bears his name. Several other scientists had previously identified the principles governing the behaviour of light at the interface of two media.

Ptolemy worked on refraction in second-century Egypt, and six hundred years before Snell came on the scene, an Arab optician, Ibn Sahl, presented a geometric version of the law of refraction in a monograph of which only portions survive. An English astronomer, Thomas Harriot, worked out the angle relationships two decades before Snell, but never published the results. Curiously, neither did Snell. In fact, the French philosopher and mathematician René Descartes was the first to present the law in written form ten years after Snell's death, and the French still refer to the refraction law as "la loi de Descartes" (Descartes' law).

11.5 Deriving Snell's Law – A Mathematical Diversion

Danger! Mathematics ahead!

Actually the mathematics involved in deriving Snell's law is not that complicated and should be within the reach of any high school graduate. Nevertheless, if you feel unprepared – or more likely, uninterested – feel free to skip ahead. This section is definitely not required reading. Section 11.4 and Chapter 10 give you all you need to know.

You can derive Snell's law by following the analogy of a struggling swimmer at the beach (see Section 11.4). You must decide which path is quickest – that is, which path obeys Fermat's principle of least time. Stated another way: What are the exact angles which minimize the travel time to the swimmer?

This is a classic minimization problem, and high school calculus provides the answer: set up the equation describing the travel time in terms of something which you can vary, and then set the derivative of the equation with respect to this variable to zero. This sounds complicated, but it's not...just push on.

Look at Figure 11-12. Imagine that you are at point A on the beach and the swimmer is at point B in the water. The total distance between you is L along the land and W perpendicular to the waterline. The simplest way of thinking of the fastest route is to ask: "how far along the beach should I enter the water, in order to reach the swimmer as quickly as possible?" In other words, what is the distance x in Figure 11-12?

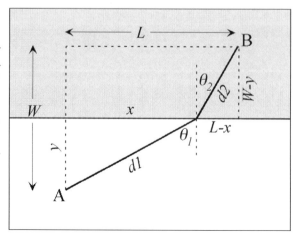

Figure 11-12 Mapping the fastest route to the swimmer. You are at point A on the beach, and the struggling swimmer is in the water at point B.

Recall that the time to reach a certain destination is the total distance divided by the speed. For example, it takes two hours to drive 120 miles at 60 miles per hour. The travel time T from point A to point B is then:

$$T = \frac{d_1}{S_1} + \frac{d_2}{S_2}$$

where S_1 and S_2 are your speeds on land and in water, respectively.

From the Pythagoras theorem (see page 4), you know that:

$$d_1 = \sqrt{x^2 + y^2} \quad \text{and} \quad d_2 = \sqrt{(L - x)^2 + (W - y)^2}$$

Finally, noting that the speed S is some constant maximum speed c divided by a factor called the index of refraction n (see Section 11.3.1 above), you get:

$$T = \frac{n_1\sqrt{x^2 + y^2}}{c} + \frac{n_2\sqrt{(L - x)^2 + (W - y)^2}}{c}$$

Pretty easy so far. Pause now and have a quick look at this equation. It expresses the total travel time to the struggling swimmer as a function of where you enter the water (x) and your running and swimming speeds (n_1, n_2). Note that y is fixed – it is your starting distance from the edge of the water. You can see how T depends on these quantities by assuming some reasonable values for L, W, y, etc. and plugging the numbers into a calculator.

For simplicity, let's assume that the swimmer is 200 meters along the beach and both you and your struggling friend are each 50 meters from the edge of the water. This gives L=200, W=100, and y=50. How fast can you run? When Roger Bannister broke the four-minute mile in 1954, he averaged (you guessed it) about 15 miles per hour. You may not be an Olympic athlete, but let's say you can sustain this pace for the couple of hundred meters necessary to rescue your friend. This is about 24 km/hr or 6 meters per second. The current world record for the 50-meter freestyle swim is about 21 seconds, an almost Herculean feat. Let's assume an adrenalin-fueled 20 seconds, or 2.5 meters per second in the water. For any faceter still listening, this difference in speed corresponds to a highly prized refractive index of 2.4.

Figure 11-13 plots the total travel time T for different entry points, x. It also shows the time required if your running speed and swimming speed were identical. Note that for the realistic case in which your can run 2.4 times faster than you can swim, the minimum is not at the midpoint. As expected, the best route is mostly on land. Also unsurprisingly, if you are just as fast on land as on water, the straight line route (*i.e.* x=100) is the best.

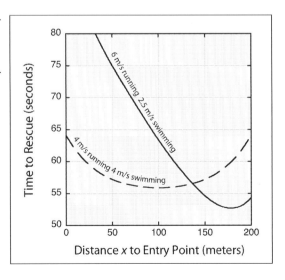

Figure 11-13 The time required to rescue the struggling swimmer. When you can run much faster than you can swim, the best strategy is to cover most of the distance on the beach.

Now the tricky part. You can find the minimum T for varying x by setting the derivative to zero. In other words:

$$\frac{dT}{dx} = 0$$

You may recall that this is effectively asking where the slope of the curve in Figure 11-13 is zero – in other words, where does the curve flatten out at its minimal value?

Don't worry if you don't remember how to take derivatives – here is the result (it is a fun exercise, if you are interested).

$$\frac{dT}{dx} = \frac{n_1 x}{c\sqrt{x^2 + y^2}} + \frac{n_2(L - x)}{c\sqrt{(L - x)^2 + (W - y)^2}} = 0$$

Notice something? The quantity:

$$\frac{x}{\sqrt{x^2 + y^2}}$$

is equal to x/d_1, and similarly, the quantity:

$$\frac{(L - x)}{\sqrt{(L - x)^2 + (W - y)^2}}$$

is equal to $(L - x)/d_2$

Chapter 10.2 informs us that the ratio of sides of a right-angled triangle can easily be expressed in terms of sines, cosines, and tangents. Applying this information to Figure 11-12 gives:

$$\frac{x}{d_1} = \sin(\theta_1)$$

$$\frac{(L - x)}{d_2} = \sin(\theta_2)$$

Plugging all of this into the derivative five equations up gives for the minimum travel time:

$$n_1 \sin(\theta_1) = n_2 \sin(\theta_2)$$

which is Snell's Law. Pretty neat, eh?

11.6 The Reversibility of Light

Figure 11-10 shows what happens to a ray of light when it enters a gemstone – in other words, when it travels from a medium with lower refractive index (higher speed) to one with higher refractive index (lower speed).

Of course, once the ray is inside the gem and encounters another facet, the opposite situation occurs. This raises the obvious question of what happens to light when it *leaves* a higher index medium and enters one with lower n.

The swimmer analogy and the principle of least time provide the common-sense answer. In this case, you are in the water and want to find the fastest route to rescue someone on the beach – perhaps your friend is choking on a corn dog. Common sense dictates that your fastest route out of the water is the same as your fastest route in. Another way of saying this is that Snell's Law applies, independent of whether n_1 or n_2 is larger.

A quick scan of the derivation of Snell's Law from Fermat's principle of least time (Section 11.5) shows that this intuition is obviously correct. In trying to find the fastest route, you have to minimize the total amount of time on the beach and in the water. The derivation makes no assumption about which part of the journey comes first, however.

This mental experiment illustrates a fundamental physical law: the *principle of reversibility* of light. Basically, this principle states that light paths are reversible, and it underlies a surprising amount of how the world around us works. For example, even a five year old playing hide-and-seek knows that if you can see the seeker, then the seeker can see you (or at least your eyes!). The next section explains how the reversibility principle plays an important role in gemstone optics.

11.7 Total Internal Reflection

If Snell's Law applies equally well to rays of light inside a gemstone, then the principle of reversibility says that you should be able to plot the equivalent angles for light emerging from a diamond or amethyst, simply by exchanging the axes of Figure 11-11. Figure 11-14 shows the result.

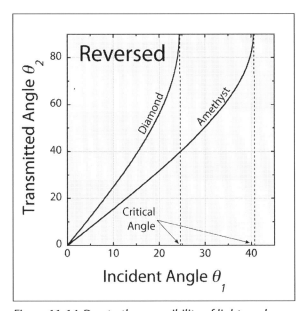

Figure 11-14 Due to the reversibility of light, exchanging the x and y axes in Figure 11-11 gives the angle of emergence of a light ray from a gemstone.

But wait. Something funny is going on here! For an incident angle of about 25°, the light emerges from the diamond essentially parallel to the facet (θ_2=90°). But what happens if θ_1 is larger than this value, if the emerging ray strikes the surface at an angle greater than 25°?

The answer to this question is the key to the beauty and performance of gemstones: *total internal reflection* or TIR. If the incident light strikes a low-index to high-index interface at an angle greater than a certain value, the rays are no longer transmitted. Instead they are reflected, exactly as though the facet was a mirror, not a window. Given proper angles, a gemstone produces many such total internal reflections, acting like a hall of mirrors, scattering and breaking up the incoming light.

The angle at which TIR begins is called the *critical angle*, θ_c

$$\theta_c = \sin^{-1}\left(\frac{n_{\mathrm{air}}}{n_{\mathrm{gem}}}\right) = \sin^{-1}\left(\frac{1}{n_{\mathrm{gem}}}\right)$$

where n_{air} and n_{gem} are the refractive indices of air and the gemstone material, respectively. Refer to Chapter 10.2 if you don't understand the sin⁻¹ function.

Yes, this is the critical angle you have heard about so often in connection with gem materials. It corresponds to the minimum pavilion angle to avoid a fish-eye, in other words, the minimum pavilion angle to ensure total internal reflection. Figure 11-15 plots the critical angle for common gemstone materials.

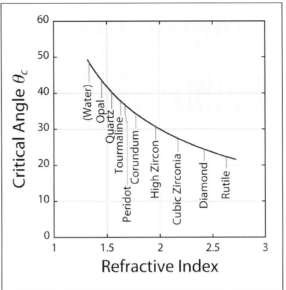

Figure 11-15 The critical angle for common gemstone materials.

A Critical Look at Culets

Every experienced faceter knows that the refractive index of the gem material determines the lowest acceptable pavilion angle. In fact, the "First Law of Faceting" states that the pavilion mains, or more generally, the shallowest culet facets, must be cut a couple of degrees above the critical angle. Failure to do so results in the dreaded "fish-eye" – light leaking out of the bottom of the pavilion.

What is less obvious and less well known is that very few modern gemstone designs are cut anywhere near the critical angle, particularly for high index material. For example, diamond has a refractive index of 2.42 and hence a critical angle just under 25°, yet most cut diamonds have a culet angle of about 40°, more than 15° above the critical value!

Don't believe me? "The Science of Art" on page 264 describes a simple analysis I performed on about 100 random gem designs optimized for a variety of materials. Among the many pieces of information included in this data set are the pavilion angles and the refractive index of the target gem material. Figure 11-16 plots the shallowest pavilion angle in the design as a function of refractive index for each gem. The solid line shows the critical angle for the same target materials.

Even the most casual glance at Figure 11-16 shows that the critical angle has very little to do with the actual pavilion angles of modern gemstone designs. Read that last sentence again: it sounds pretty radical, but it is completely true.

There are several morals to this story. The first has to do with selecting pavilion angles. Stated simply, you shouldn't just cut the pavilion to the critical angle, or two degrees above it, as dictated by the First Law. Nor should you target the critical angle when scaling the stone via the tangent ratio (see Chapter 10.5).

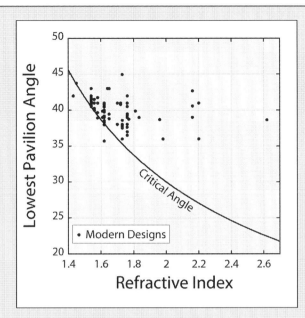

The second moral is that, while higher index materials generally lead to shallower gemstone designs, the difference can be surprisingly less than you assume. The final message is that a culet angle of roughly 40° represents a reasonable choice for essentially all gemstone materials with index higher than that of quartz, a fact that is exploited in some neat ray-tracing in Chapter 10.4.

Figure 11-16 The points indicate the lowest culet (or keel) facet angle as a function of refractive index for approximately 100 optimized gemstone designs. The solid line indicates the critical angle for windowing.

Real-World TIR: A Summertime Experiment

Here is a fun demonstration of total internal reflection that you can try the next time you are at a swimming pool. The only equipment you will need are a bathing suit (unless your name is Archimedes – see page 373), and if you feel more comfortable, swim glasses or diving goggles. You should also be able to hold your breath for at least 10-20 seconds, and it is a great help if the water is relatively calm.

Take a deep breath and slip gently under the surface of the pool. The goal is to look upward at the sky from inside the water, so try to sink to the bottom (blowing out some air can help here) and support yourself crab-like using your arms and legs.

Wait for the surface of the water to calm down, and then look carefully at your surroundings. Straight up, you should see the sun, sky, and clouds as normal, but further and further from the zenith, things will begin to appear strange. The view will be more and more compressed as you look toward the horizon, and eventually – a little more than halfway down – the sky will disappear entirely. Instead, you will likely see a solid colour, perhaps blue or white.

What you are seeing outside the circle of sky is, in fact, the bottom and sides of the swimming pool, due to total internal reflection. You can calculate the angle at which TIR sets in from the refractive index of water n=1.33. The critical angle is about 50° (Figure 11-15). If you were swimming in honey (ick), with a refractive index of 1.50 and critical angle $\theta c = 42°$, your cone of vision to the sky would be noticeably reduced. For higher index fluids, the view would be smaller still. Note also that such fluids can be extremely toxic as well as inarguably disgusting to swim in, so you should just take my word on this (and see "High Index Immersion Fluids" on page 101 of Volume 1).

Incidentally, total internal reflection is a serious safety issue for ice divers, those hardy souls who cut a hole in the frozen surface of a lake and go scuba diving. It is distressingly easy to get outside the cone of visibility of the access hole – you can only see it when you are directly below – and get lost. For this reason, ice divers always attach themselves to a rope leading out of the hole.

Figure 11-17 The view from the pool.

Imagine now that you are a ray of light inside a gemstone. Looking around, you would see the various facets, but in some directions, you would not be able to see out, just like in Figure 11-17. This means that light cannot reach you from the outside world along those paths. Due to the reversibility principle (Section 11.6), this also means that in those directions, you would not be able to escape. These are directions that exceed the critical angle, and total internal reflection will mirror you back into the gem. After that first bounce, you might be on a path which leads out of the gem, but your neighbouring ray, travelling at a slightly different angle, could get reflected once more. After this second bounce, that ray and its neighbours would have a third chance of escape. Some will and some will not.

This selective splitting of neighbouring light rays contributes greatly to the visual interest or scintillation of a gem. Turn to Section 11.9 for a more detailed, three-dimensional luminous journey through a gemstone.

11.8 Surface Reflections

Previous sections have examined two important effects governing the interaction of light rays with a gemstone: refraction and total internal reflection. The story is not complete, however, since there is a third important effect: *surface reflection*.

When light rays strike the interface between materials of different refractive index, the transmitted rays are bent, but a fraction of the light is reflected from the surface, exactly as though it was a mirror. In the case of total internal reflection, described in the previous section, all of the light is mirrored – hence the term "total." Here, we are talking about *partial* surface reflections.

You are certainly familiar with the effects of partial surface reflection. It is the physical phenomenon which causes even a clean window to act as a partially reflecting mirror. Partial surface reflection produces faint double images in most regular mirrors as well (see page 278 of Volume 1). It also causes reflections off well-polished facets when you examine your stones for scratches under a powerful lamp (see Figure 5-51).

Self Reflection

Remember Narcissus, the beautiful but self-absorbed young boy of Greek mythology? Wandering through the forest one day, he comes across a deep pool of liquid with refractive index 1.33 (normal people would call this a pond). Narcissus bends over to drink and sees his reflection for the first time. The child he beholds is beautiful, and Narcissus falls in love. Of course, the boy soon realizes that he is seeing himself, and that he will never be able to act on his infatuation. He tears at his clothes and body and collapses and dies on the shore of the pond. The legend concludes with the Narcissus flower, commonly known as the daffodil, springing up from the point where he expired.

Had young Narcissus spent more time at the faceting machine, rather than hunting stags and prancing about with nymphs, he would have immediately realized that the dim figure visible in the pool was the result of partial surface reflection, and not a viable object of affection.

Interestingly, Narcissus and his problems of self-reflection live on in the modern optics industry. Ghosts and double images caused by the partial surface reflection of bright objects off the film (or nowadays the CCD) in a camera are known as "Narcissus ghosts."

Figure 11-18 Narcissus struggling with surface reflections (painting by Caravaggio, ca. 1595).

As with refraction and TIR, the refractive index is the key. The amount of light reflected from a surface depends on the index of refraction on each side of the interface. Specifically, the fraction R of light reflected is:

$$R = \left(\frac{n_1 - n_2}{n_1 + n_2} \right)^2$$

where n_1 and n_2 are the two indices of refraction. This is known as the *Fresnel reflection law*, after the French physicist Augustin-Jean Fresnel, who correctly derived the equations governing the effect. Figure 11-19 plots the amount of surface reflection for light entering a gemstone from air ($n_1=1$).

Technically speaking, this formula only holds for light that strikes the surface of the gem nearly perpendicularly – that is, the incident angle in Snell's law is near zero degrees. It turns out that with real-world materials and non-perpendicular incidence, one polarization of the light experiences a greater surface reflection while the other experiences less. This explains the situation with the afternoon sunlight and asphalt described in Section 11.2.2. Nevertheless, over reasonable ranges of angles, the net effect is small, and the Fresnel reflection law represents a good approximation.

As you can see from Figure 11-19, surface reflections can be significant for higher index materials. For example, almost twenty percent of the light striking a diamond never makes it into the gem.

Incidentally, optical designers call this phenomenon "Fresnel loss." Optical designers are a pretty grim lot, however, and it is unnecessarily pessimistic for faceters to refer to surface reflections as *losses*. Why? Because this light gives the gemstone its characteristic and often beautiful *luster* (see Chapter 12.7.2). Also, note that the light rays must not only *enter*, but also *leave* the body of the gemstone before you see them. Fresnel "losses" affect the departing ray in the exact same way: some fraction of the light – about 17% in diamond – bounces back into the stone to produce a more interesting and beautiful gem. See the next section for more on the often surprising trajectories that light can take on its way from the surface of a gemstone to your eye.

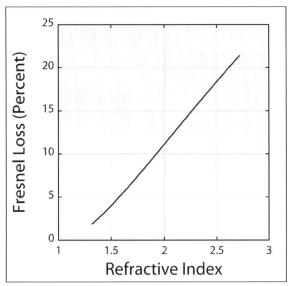

Figure 11-19 The "Fresnel Loss," or fraction of light reflected at the surface when light enters a gemstone material from air.

Fresnel Gains

The name Fresnel (pronounced "fray-nell") is probably familiar to you. In addition to working on the wave theory of light, Augustin-Jean Fresnel is credited with the invention of the Fresnel lens, those floppy plastic sheets that seem to pack an absurd amount of magnifying power.

The principle of the Fresnel lens is very simple. A strong lens requires strong curvature. Normally, this would mean a very thick, heavy, and expensive piece of glass. Fresnel's insight was that you could break up such a lens into a series of concentric zones, each of which has the correct curvature for that location (Figure 11-20).

Fresnel came upon this idea in connection with his day job as commissioner of lighthouses for the French government in the early 1800's. His innovation allowed an enormous concentration of light and was widely copied. Fresnel lenses also play a vital role on aircraft carriers. The infamous "meatball" approach slope indicator on a carrier deck uses a simple arrangement of Fresnel lenses to supply a reliable visual guide to approaching pilots.

Perhaps the most common use of Fresnel lenses is in the head and tail lights of automobiles, where an embossed pattern on the lamp assembly provides proper aiming and shaping of the light beam. Finally, Fresnel lenses will hopefully soon play a major role in supplying renewable energy: the efficiency and output of expensive solar cells can be multiplied significantly with inexpensive plastic Fresnel concentrators. Thanks Augustin-Jean. Dare I say that your loss is our gain?

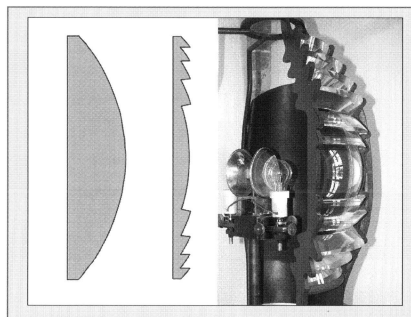

Figure 11-20 A u g u s t i n - Jean Fresnel invented the Fresnel lens, which uses a concentric series of curved zones to replace a conventional, thick lens (left). Fresnel first used these lenses in lighthouses, and the lamp assemblies from these life-saving beacons remain a marvel of opto-mechanical engineering (right – image courtesy of Hannes Grobe).

11.9 Different Paths: A 3D Journey of Light

So much for theory. What does all of this refraction and reflection mean for gemstones?

Great question. And perhaps the best way to answer it is by following the light. Here is where it all comes together. Let's take a light ray's three-dimensional journey through a gemstone, applying what you have learned.

11.9.1 A Walk in the Garden

Light is everywhere around us – we literally soak in a bath of photons every day. These photons can take long and indirect paths between their source and our eyes. For example, that lovely daffodil in your garden is visible only because some photons made the 93 million mile journey from the sun to strike that single spring flower. The daffodil absorbed some of this light, particularly blues and greens, (see "Why is Grass Green?" on page 86 for more on this). The remainder, much of it yellow, bounced off the flower, and some of this ended up entering your eye.

But what exactly does "entering your eye" mean?

Clearly, the light rays have to be in the right place at the right time. During a stroll on a bright afternoon, your pupils may be only 2-3 millimeters in diameter and they move with your body at perhaps three miles an hour. The rays of light scattered from the flower have to hit that tiny, moving target.

But there's more. In addition to being at the correct location at the right time, the light rays have to be moving in the proper *direction*, in order for your brain to sort out where they came from. Many trillions of photons enter your eyeballs every second, and without some notion of their direction of origin, you would not be able to make visual sense of the world around you. That notion of direction comes from the lens at the front of your eye: it maps different incoming ray directions onto different locations on the light sensitive retina, located at the back of your eye (see also Chapter 15.6.2).

Thus, at a given moment in time, a particular ray has to be at the correct location and travelling in the appropriate direction to be identified with the flower. But not every ray of light that satisfies these conditions travelled the same path. For example, some rays traveled from the sun and were scattered off clouds before hitting the daffodil. If they arrive at your eye at the same time and with the same direction, their light will contribute to your perception of the colour and brightness of the flower.

Enough with the daffodils. We are gem fanatics, not flower people, after all (see page 213 of Volume 1). Back to gemstones...

11.9.2 Light Rays and Gemstones

Back from the garden? Good.

This section applies what you have learned in earlier sections of this chapter, including your walk in the garden, to the question of what happens when light rays interact with gemstones. As an added bonus, it will do so using cool three-dimensional figures. Wheee! For math mavens, Chapters 10.3 and 10.4 put this action on a firm trigonometric footing.

Figure 11-21 shows a light ray striking the table of a standard round brilliant gemstone cut in sapphire. There are two versions of the image, one for the left eye and one for the right. Hold the page about a foot away from your face and cross your eyes to make the images merge. You should now see three images total, and the central one should appear three-dimensional. How cool is that?

If you have difficulty seeing the effect, look at "Depth of Perception and Perception of Depth..." on page 73, as well as "Seeing in 3D" on page 74. Don't worry if it doesn't work – you will not miss any important information – and above all, do not persist if you feel discomfort in crossing your eyes. We all have enough headaches as it is.

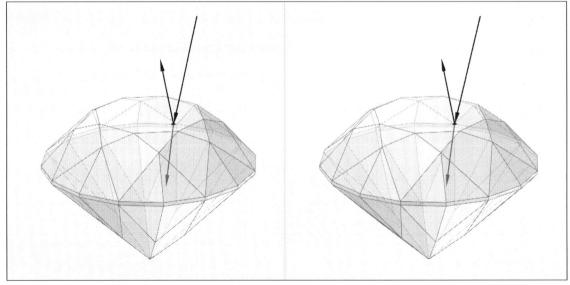

Figure 11-21 Light strikes the table of an SRB. Fresnel loss causes a fraction of the rays to reflect off the surface, while the remainder enters the gem. Some reflected rays will have the appropriate direction to be seen.

What happens when the rays hit the surface? Section 11.8 explains that, due to the difference in refractive index between the air and the gem, some fraction of the light will reflect off the surface in a process known as Fresnel loss. For sapphire with an index of refraction of 1.76, this will be about 7% (see Figure 11-19). Those reflected rays with the correct geometry to enter the viewer's eye will present a faint reflection of the gem's surroundings.

The remaining 93% of the incoming rays pass through the table, where they are bent by an amount appropriate to their incident angle and the index of refraction of sapphire (Section 11.4). It appears that Snell, Descartes, and the others were actually on to something...

The surviving bundle of rays continues onward into the gem, striking one of the pavilion facets, in this instance at an angle of 46° (Figure 11-22). This is well above the critical angle of sapphire (34.5°), and hence Total Internal Reflection (Section 11.7) takes place. The rays head across the culet to the other side of the stone.

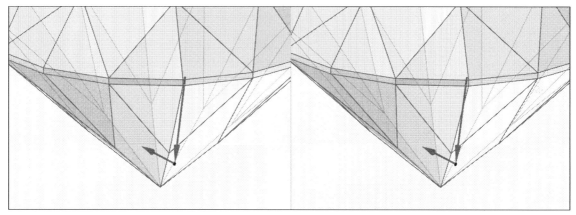

Figure 11-22 The rays continue into the stone and strike a pavilion facet, where total internal reflection sends them back into the gem.

A few fractions of a nanosecond later, the light rays encounter a different pavilion facet on the opposite side of the gem (Figure 11-23). Here, too, Fortune has smiled on these gentle photons, and once again the incident angle is above critical. TIR sends the rays upward toward the crown.

The rays' journey is almost done. When they again strike the table – this time very close to the crown stars – they exit the gemstone bent somewhat outward by refraction (Figure 11-24). As before, those rays which have the appropriate trajectory will enter the viewer's eye.

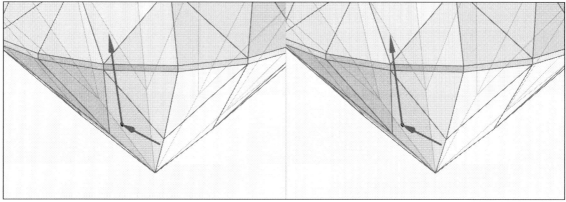

Figure 11-23 The rays cross the pavilion and strike another main facet, again above the critical angle. The totally reflected rays then head upward.

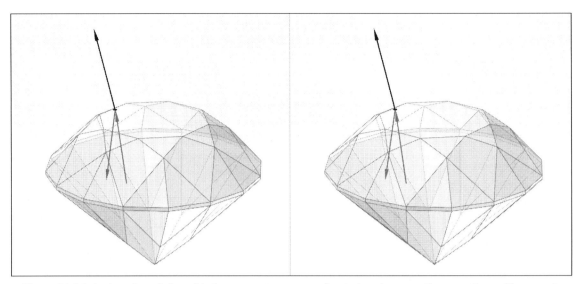

Figure 11-24 At the edge of the table facet, most rays are refracted and escape the gem. Fresnel loss again causes a 7% reflection, and those rays head back into the stone.

Actually, not all of them escape. In fact, Augustin-Jean Fresnel has been sitting quietly for the last two reflections and now insists on being heard. Section 11.8 explains that partial surface reflection will occur, independent of whether the light is entering or leaving the gem. In fact, 7% of the rays which have made it back up to the table facet still have some work to do. They continue on back into the gemstone to find their own particular destiny…

The story is not complete, however. Recall from your garden jaunt that light can take many paths on its way from the sun to the daffodil to your eye. The same situation applies to gemstones. In fact, well designed gems scramble and mix the light so wonderfully well that rays coming from completely different directions can eventually leave the stone at almost the exact same place and in almost the exact same direction. Figure 11-25 shows an example.

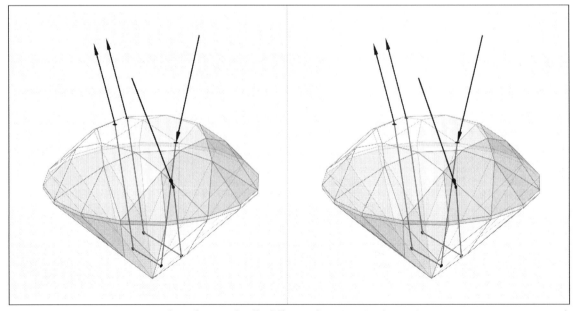

Figure 11-25 Two rays approaching from radically different directions in the environment emerge next to each other and parallel. To the observer, the stone slices up the scene and scrambles it, producing rich scintillation.

This mixing of rays from a complex, interesting lighting environment produces enchanting colours and scintillation, the true magic of gemstones. Turn to Chapter 15.6 for more on light paths through gems.

Depth of Perception and Perception of Depth…

The figures in the adjacent text attempt to recreate a three dimensional image on a two dimensional page. They do this by exploiting the fact that humans, with the possible exception of cinematic pirates, have two eyeballs that are well separated on the fronts of their heads. These two eyeballs look at the world from slightly different angles and hence see slightly different scenes, a phenomenon known as *parallax* (Figure 11-26). Our brains automatically reconstruct the three dimensional distribution of objects we see based on these two viewpoints.

You can mimic the parallax effect with the double images in this book by crossing your eyes until the diagrams merge to a 3D version in the middle. Note that for this to work, the left-eye view must be on the right, and the right-eye view on the left. The arrangement in Figure 11-26 is deliberately incorrect. Try to see the 3D effect and compare with Figure 11-27.

Look again at Figure 11-27 without crossing your eyes. You should notice that the two drawings are slightly different. One has been created from the left-eye's point of view, while the other portrays the scene as viewed by the right eye. Crossing your eyes causes the left-hand image seen with your right eye to merge with the right-hand image seen with your left eye. The result is a scene with all the appropriate depth cue differences that you experience in real life – a true 3D image.

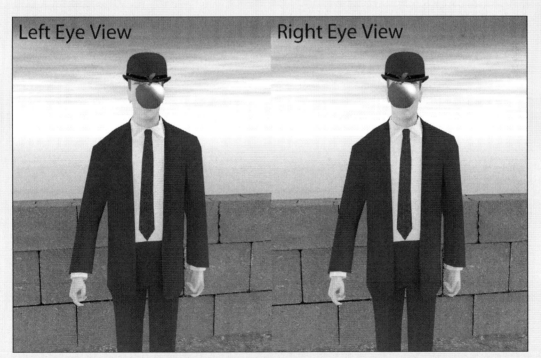

Figure 11-26 Our eyes see slightly different versions of the world around us, allowing our brains to perceive the scene in 3D.

Figure 11-27 The previous frames arranged properly for 3D viewing.

Seeing in 3D

A substantial number of people will have difficulty seeing the 3D effect in these images. For some, the act of crossing their eyes can be difficult or impossible. Others may have one eye that is considerably stronger or *dominant*, complicating the merging process necessary to see the effect.

Don't worry if you have difficulty. It definitely takes practice. Also, these diagrams are an attempt to illustrate in a fun way the path of a light ray through a gemstone. It is by no means necessary to see the 3D image in order to follow the path.

Here is a tip that may help. We naturally cross our eyes to focus on an object very near to us. You can try holding your finger or a pen about halfway between you and the page. When looking at the drawing, you should see two images of the closer object. Move your fingertip or pen back and forth and left and right until these two images lie just below the culet of the stone (Figure 11-28). When you are happy with the arrangement, try to focus on your finger or pen. To do so, you will naturally cross your eyes the correct amount (Figure 11-29).

Maintain focus on the nearer object. In the background, you should see three gems. The central one is the merged 3D image. Do you see it?

Finally, if you experience headache or other discomfort while looking at these images, please stop. As mentioned above, the 3D effect, while fun, is not necessary to understand what's going on. You can also try viewing the "wigglegrams" of these figures at this book's website: www.facetingbook.com

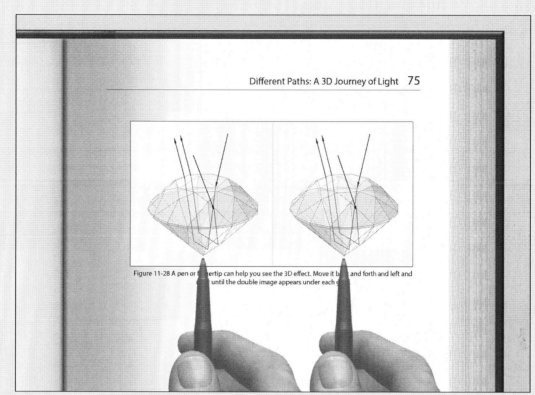

Figure 11-28 A pen or fingertip can help you see the 3D effect. Move it back and forth and left and right until the double image appears under each gem.

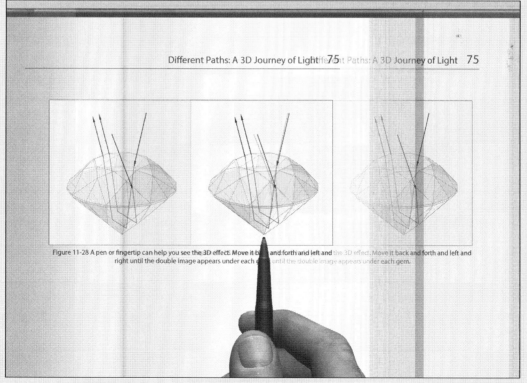

Figure 11-29 When you focus on your pen or fingertip, the gem images in the background should merge to a 3D view

12

Gem Material Properties

Gem materials are distinguished and identified by their *properties*, that is, their observable and measurable characteristics. Because of their overwhelming importance to gem performance, faceters typically consider the *optical* properties of a material separately, and lump everything else under the moniker *physical* properties. Of course, this division is somewhat artificial, since both the optical and physical properties of a gem material arise from its underlying composition and structure.

This chapter examines gem material properties from both a scientific and practical viewpoint. It begins with a discussion of the chemical composition of gemstones at the atomic and molecular level. The heart of the chapter follows, with a detailed look at the essential optical properties of gemstones. This includes an extensive examination of the phenomenon of colour in gemstones in all its diverse forms. Subsequent sections explain refractive index, dispersion, and a few less commonly discussed optical properties, such as transparency and luster.

The latter part of the chapter looks at physical gemstone properties, including density and hardness. It then draws the connection between crystal systems and crystal habit and the related properties of cleavage, fracture, and streak.

These optical and physical material properties have a direct influence on identifying, orienting, cutting, and polishing gemstones. Understanding them will make you a better faceter.

12.1 Why Properties Count

As a beginning faceter, you soon learn that there are two kinds of cutters out there. The first understands the chemical composition, crystal system, optical axes, and other assorted bits of information about the gem material at hand. The other cutter just knows a pretty stone when he or she sees one and leaves it at that.

While fascination and emotional response are admirable and highly understandable reactions to the magic of gemstones, let me try to convince you to be a little more like the first person than the second.

By my count, there are about half a dozen good reasons to familiarize yourself with the optical and physical properties of gemstone materials. First, an understanding of these properties will help you make intelligent buying decisions. Different types of gem rough have characteristic colours, crystal shapes and densities, for example, allowing you to distinguish at a glance – or a heft – between garnet and tourmaline, or topaz and quartz. You will also be able to identify the optical axes and how they relate to the overall shape of the stone. Pleochroic material can exhibit dramatically different colours along different crystal directions. For such gemstones, an ideal match of the design to the rough can produce a unique, bewitching gem, while getting this wrong may result in a muddy mess. Understanding the optical properties will thus help ensure that a particular piece of rough will result in both high yield and pleasing colour.

Back in your workshop, knowledge of the gemstone properties will help you to prepare and orient the rough for cutting. For example, a keen awareness of heat and mechanical shock sensitivity, as well as being able to identify the orientation of cleavage planes, can help you avoid a highly educational yet emotionally traumatizing disaster.

Information about the physical properties of the material is important even after you are done and are ready to mount your gem. Softer stones – those with Mohs hardness under 7 – do not do well in the rough-and-tumble world our fingers encounter. Rather than a ring mounting, such gems would fare better in a pendant or earring. Also, cleavage planes and careless crimping of mount pins are a deadly combination.

In addition, if you are a commercial cutter, or even just trying to impress your brother in law, being able to speak intelligently about gemstones can lead to more sales or higher prices or even just an ounce of respect, thank you very much.

Finally, knowing more about your craft is *fun*. The interaction of light with matter is a fascinating topic with a rich history (see Chapter 11.3 for an all too brief overview). The physical chemistry of gemstone materials is equally interesting, and it is very satisfying to know not only *how* a certain material looks, but also *why* it looks that way. In sum, learning about the optical and physical properties of gemstones inevitably brings a deeper involvement in the faceting process, and a deeper involvement leads to better results.

12.2 Gemstone Chemistry

The first chapter of the first volume of this book begins with the essential question "What is a gem?"

The simple answer, respectfully extracted from the *Oxford English Dictionary*, is that a gem is "a precious stone of any kind, especially when cut and polished for ornament." This answer unavoidably prompts further questions (what is a stone? what is precious?) and ultimately points to the need for an understanding of the underlying chemical composition of gemstones. That's where this section comes in.

What is the chemistry of gemstones?

A simple answer to this question is that gems are *chemical compounds*, strongly bonded pairings of two or more *elements* forming a distinct chemical entity with unique properties. Elements, you will recall from high school chemistry, are the ultimate atomic building blocks of our universe. All the objects around us – the ground we walk on, the water we drink, the atmosphere we breathe, and the night sky we wonder at – are composed of various mixtures of a hundred or so of these chemical elements.

One man's soufflé is another man's scrambled eggs….

You probably remember a chart of the elements from your high school chemistry class. This elegant representation, known as the *Periodic Table*, organizes the 120 or so known elements according to their properties.

You may also recall another elegant representation, this one in song. Tom Lehrer's *The Elements* listed the 102 distinct chemical elements known at the time (1959), set to the music of Gilbert and Sullivan.

I am not sure which representation of the elements I liked more in high school, but I do remember being surprised at their diversity. Most of the elements, about 100, are solids while the bulk of the remainder are gases. Only two, mercury and bromine, exist in liquid form, at least under the conditions I would find comfortable (an additional four, rubidium, cesium, gallium, and francium, would liquefy in a sauna). Many elements are literally as common as dirt, while others can only be produced artificially in tiny, short-lived amounts in jaw-droppingly expensive particle accelerators. Even the names are interesting. Going through the choices and controversies associated with naming the elements is like reading a history of human science and culture. Both the Periodic Table and Lehrer's song are excellent jumping-off points for your wiki explorations. I recommend them highly.

Despite this huge variety, it turns out that most of the chemical elements are exceedingly rare, and the overwhelming majority of the objects we encounter each day, including gemstones, are composed of only a handful of them. Oxygen, silicon, aluminum, iron, calcium, sodium, potassium and magnesium are on average hundreds to thousands of times more common in the earth's crust than the remaining ninety naturally occurring elements. Thus, the diversity of the world around us, and in fact, the diversity of gemstone materials, is not so much a matter of *composition* as *structure*.

There are many arresting examples of how the same basic composition, coupled with a seemingly insignificant difference in structure, can make a huge change in chemistry. Take, for example, nitrogen and oxygen, by far the most abundant elements in our atmosphere (over 99% by volume). Sandwiching a single nitrogen atom between a pair of oxygen atoms produces NO_2, commonly known as nitrogen dioxide, a reddish brown, highly toxic gas and major atmospheric pollutant. Taking a pair of nitrogen atoms and gluing an oxygen on the side gives you N_2O, nitrous oxide, an invisible, mostly harmless substance commonly known as laughing gas.

Structure is critical to the properties and performance of gemstones as well. Not convinced? Have you been breathing laughing gas? Think pure carbon, as in the graphite in your pencil lead. Think pure carbon, as in colourless D-type diamonds. See "Diamonds are Forever...?" on the opposite page to learn how structure, not composition, produces remarkable differences between the two naturally occurring forms of pure carbon.

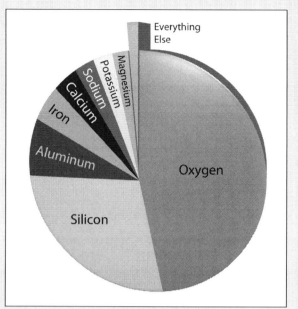

Figure 12-1 *The elemental constituents of Earth's crust by weight. Although almost 100 elements occur naturally, only a few account for the vast majority of the world around us.*

As with most simple answers – even those from the eggheads at Oxford – this one gets a bit more complicated. In fact, there are gem materials that are not chemical compounds. You may have heard of one of these: diamond. Diamond is pure elemental carbon, albeit put together in a very special way (see opposite page). There is at least one more element that can be made into faceted gemstones in its pure form: sulfur. Like diamond, elemental sulfur has some unique properties that make it a challenging substance to facet (see "Faceting Fire and Brimstone..." on page 146).

All right then. Apart from the glaring exception of diamond and the amusing exception of sulfur, all gemstones are in fact compounds.

Actually, it gets a bit more complicated than that as well.

Oh boy can it get complicated. Gemstone compounds can represent the simple pairing of two elements into a large, ordered mass, as with the sodium and chlorine crystal known as halite to you and me, and as salt to normal people. Alternatively, the basic chemical unit of some gem materials can be an extraordinarily large and complex molecule. Common elbaite tourmaline is an excellent example. Its basic molecule is $Na(Li,Al)_3Al_6(BO_3)_3Si_6O_{18}(OH)_4$, consisting of an eye-watering 54 separate elemental atoms. The complexity can also occur on larger scales. Opal is a mixture of tiny cristobalite spheres made of SiO_2 (essentially glass, and a seemingly simple molecule) suspended in a gel of silica and water (more SiO_2 and good old H_2O). The chemical formula of opal seems absurdly simple – $SiO_2 \cdot nH_2O$ – but try crushing some glass in water. I suspect that you will not end up with gem-grade, iridescent, black opal. See Section 12.7.4 to learn what puts the magic in opals.

Entire textbooks have been written on the subject of the chemistry of minerals. Turn to Chapter 9 to learn how to continue your explorations.

12.3 Colour

Needless to say, it is the optical property known as *colour* that is the most important to hobby faceters. Colour is what sets apart Paraiba tourmaline, which may be worth considerably more gram-for-gram than diamond, from its essentially chemically identical, but much more common and affordable cousins.

Curiously, given its overarching importance to our craft, there is no objective measure of gemstone colour outside of the diamond industry. You will undoubtedly run across comparison charts, either in paper form or, even worse, on your uncalibrated computer monitor, but subjective factors, such as lighting and the personal taste of the observer, have overwhelmed efforts to create a standard. In gem colour, beauty is truly in the eye of the beholder.

It is also interesting that this most predominant characteristic is a notoriously poor diagnostic when trying to identify gemstones. For example, it can be virtually impossible to distinguish a topaz from an aquamarine based on colour alone, and there is a rich and seemingly shady history of famous rubies which turned out to be garnets or spinels.

Despite these difficulties, understanding the origin and use of colour in gemstones will enhance your faceting experience and lead to more satisfying results.

Diamonds are Forever…?

Did Ian Fleming get it right?

Are diamonds truly forever?

Diamonds are certainly extraordinary gemstones. They have the highest hardness and highest thermal conductivity of any natural material, and with a melting temperature of 6400°F (3550 C), they can certainly put up with a great deal of abuse. In fact, gem quality diamonds were used as optical windows for cameras on the NASA Pioneer and Soviet Venera probes to Venus. With surface temperatures in excess of 850°F (450 C) and a sulfuric-acid atmosphere at a pressure almost one hundred times greater than Earth's, Venus can be a pretty rough place. Indeed, for all their diamonds and high tech engineering, none of the dozen or so American and Soviet Venus probes survived for more than a couple of hours on the surface.

Still, diamonds are pretty stable. Right?

Not necessarily. Diamonds are a pure crystalline form of the element carbon. It turns out that there are other forms of pure carbon, including graphite, which you can find at the heart of any good old number 2 pencil. And, as it turns out, graphite is a chemically more stable form of carbon than diamond, at least under normal temperature and pressure conditions.

This means that every diamond on the surface of the earth is slowly, inexorably turning into graphite.

You read that right. Your $5000 engagement ring is relentlessly metamorphosing into pencil lead. Luckily, the process is imperceptibly slow, and for all human intents and purposes, diamonds are forever. Perhaps Malcolm Forbes said it best: "diamonds are nothing more than chunks of coal that stuck to their jobs."

Scientists call such different forms of the same chemical element *allotropes*. You may also see the term *polymorph*, which refers to the same property for any crystalline material, including chemical compounds, not just elements (see page 79). The two common allotropes of diamond are quite different (see Table 12-1), underlining the importance of structure versus composition in the optical and physical properties of materials.

Table 12-1 The two common allotropes of carbon, diamond and graphite, are quite different sides of the same coin.

Diamond	Graphite
Diamond is hard (Mohs 10)	Graphite is soft (Mohs 1-2)
Diamond is an excellent electrical insulator	Graphite is a good conductor
Diamond is the ultimate abrasive	Graphite is a very good lubricant
Diamond crystallizes in the isometric system*	Graphite crystallizes in the hexagonal system*
Diamond is transparent	Graphite is opaque
A gram of diamond costs about $20,000	A gram of graphite costs about 7 cents

* see Section 12.10

Carbon actually has some other interesting allotropes, in addition to diamond and graphite. *Graphene* consists of a single, sheet-like layer of carbon atoms bonded together much like graphite. This material is poised to have a huge impact on several green technologies, including solar energy, electric vehicles, and bio-fuel production. *Fullerenes* are large carbon molecules in the form of spheres, ellipsoids, or tubes. Named after Buckminster Fuller, the American architect who invented the geodesic dome, these carbon allotropes hold great promise for developments in material science, electronics, health, and nanotechnology. Just type "graphene," "buckyballs" or "carbon nanotubes" into your favourite search engine to get a sense of the potential of these materials.

The short version? Diamonds aren't truly forever, but they are forever to you or me, and their allotropes may hold the key to everyone's future.

12.3.1 An Absorbing Hobby

Colour in gemstones is *subtractive*. Rather than emitting light of a certain colour, gemstones receive a broad spectrum of photons from the environment, absorb specific wavelengths, and then return the remainder to the viewer. The relative amounts of these remaining wavelengths produce the colour we perceive. For example, if green, yellow, and red are absorbed relatively strongly, the gemstone will appear blue (see "Why is Grass Green?" on page 86).

In almost all instances, it is absorption due to individual atoms that produces the colour in gemstones. For example, trace amounts of the element chromium or vanadium within the crystal lattice of beryl are responsible for the vivid green hue that makes an emerald an emerald. The same crystal with iron impurities will produce the entrancing blue of aquamarine. Pure beryl, known as goshenite, is colourless (see Table 12-2).

Note that I was careful to use the phrase "in almost all instances" in the foregoing paragraph. At this point in this book, it should be clear to you that very little is cut-and-dried in this business. Yes, selective absorption by atoms within gem crystals is usually the source of colour, but there are prominent exceptions. Among these are good old common smoky quartz, whose gray to brownish hues arise from flaws in the internal crystal lattice, usually induced by radiation damage. The two famous diamonds mentioned in "The Cost of Colour" on the next page provide an additional instructive example of how assumptions about the origin of colour can be wrong. The brilliant blue of the Hope diamond arises from absorption by boron, an elemental impurity within the diamond crystal. The Dresden Green is another case entirely, however. Here, the colour is due to missing carbon atoms within the regular structured lattice of the gem. This affects how light interacts with the crystal and produces absorption at the red end of the spectrum. The result? A green diamond!

Who's Hue?

As if things weren't confusing enough.

In your faceting ramblings, you will almost certainly hear the colour of gemstones described using terms like hue, saturation, and tone.

What's wrong with good old red and blue?

Actually, the terms hue, saturation, and tone have very specific meanings when it comes to gemstone colour.

Hue refers to the actual colour of the gem. The technical definition, according to the *Commission Internationale de l'Eclairage* (the CIE, or International Commission on Illumination) is "the degree to which a stimulus can be described as similar to or different from stimuli that are described as red, green, blue, and yellow…" These four colours are, in fact, the four unique hues in human perception. In other words, good old red and blue are hues.

Saturation, sometimes referred to as colourfulness or chroma, is the perceived intensity or richness of colour. More specifically, saturation measures how close the sample is to the pure colour and how far away it is from grey. A bandana faded with use, while more comfortable, is less saturated than a new one.

Tone refers to how light or dark a particular colour appears. Sometimes referred to as value or lightness, the tone relates directly to how much bulk absorption occurs in a gemstone.

The hue, saturation, and tone completely describe a particular colour, and in fact, these values form the basis of a very important colour model known as HSL (hue-saturation-lightness). Other well-known colour models include RGB (red-green-blue), an additive colour scheme which you may know from playing with your computer, and CMYK (cyan-magenta-yellow-black), a subtractive model used in the print industry. See "Why is Grass Green?" on page 86 for more on additive and subtractive colour.

Precious opal is an even more spectacular example of how non-absorptive colour can appear in a gemstone. Section 12.2 explains that, in this mineral, stacked microscopic spheres of a silicate mineral called *cristobalite* are embedded in a gel of silica and water. The quasi-regular stacking of the spheres acts like a diffraction grating, similar to the hologram imprinted on a credit card. The resulting multi-colour play of light, though absorbing, has nothing to do with absorption (turn to Section 12.7.4 for more on colour in opal).

The Cost of Colour

Interestingly, achroite, the colourless form of tourmaline, is quite rare, yet it is considerably less valuable than the much more common coloured varieties, particularly the intense blues and greens. This trend is generally true in coloured gemstones: the value increases with colour saturation, sometimes dramatically, up to a certain level, at which point the material is deemed too saturated to produce an appealing gem. The per-carat price then falls rapidly. In this sense, a plot of value versus saturation resembles an inverted "U".

As often seems to happen, diamonds break all the rules, and in fact, among the most valuable gems of this type are the colourless "very fine white" D grade diamonds. Faint hints of any colour, particularly brown or yellow, make a big difference at the cash register. Of course, in its own ornery way, diamond breaks its own broken rule: the actual kings of the diamond hill are the intensely coloured stones, most famously exemplified by the blue Hope diamond (see page 4 of Volume 1) and the Dresden Green (see page 160 in this volume). The value versus saturation plot for diamonds is thus an upright "U", exactly the inverse of coloured gemstones.

Wykoff has a great deal to say about the curious behavior of the cost of colour in the first chapter of his excellent *Techniques of Master Faceting*. Chapter 9 of this book can help you hunt down this and other reference works.

12.3.2 Colouring Agents

Which impurity produces which colour?

Simple question. Not so simple answer. Take, for example, one of the most important colouring agents in gemstones: chromium. Chromium interlopers in the crystal lattice are what make an emerald green (see page 82), but they are also what make a ruby red. To close this absorbing circle, chromium is also responsible for the spectacular green-red colour-change seen in alexandrite (Section 12.3.5).

Beryl exemplifies beautifully how minute amounts of chemical impurities can produce dramatically different colour. Even atoms of a single impurity species can have a different effect depending on the overall charge of the atom, its so-called *oxidation state*. For example, Fe^{++} is iron that has lost two of its electrons. This is called the *ferrous* state of iron and it produces the blue of aquamarine. Fe^{+++}, on the other hand, has lost three electrons and is called *ferric*. Ferric impurities are responsible for the greenish gold of heliodor. Table 12-2 lists the colouring agents and oxidation states responsible for the diversity of beryl. Clearly, both the atom type and oxidation state influence gem colour.

Who You Calling Idiochromatic?

Mineralogists have a special name for the atoms that create colour in gemstones: *chromophores*, a very suitable name, from the Greek *chroma* or "colour" and *phoros* or "bearer." The most common gemstone chromophores are titanium, vanadium, chromium, manganese, iron, cobalt, nickel copper, uranium, nitrogen and boron.

These chromophores act in two fundamentally different ways. In *idiochromatic* materials, they form part of the basic chemistry of the gemstone. Such materials always occur in various shades of the base colour produced by the chromophore. In other words, they all have the same hue (see "Who's Hue?" on page 83). For example, peridot, the most common idiochromatic gem, has chemical formula $(Mg,Fe)_2SiO_4$ and derives its distinctive green colour from its iron (Fe) content.

Allochromatic materials, on the other hand, do not produce selective absorption in their pure form, which is therefore colourless. In such gems, trace impurities are responsible for the colour we perceive. Common allochromatic gemstones include beryl, corundum, quartz, tourmaline, topaz, and spinel.

Pure, and hence colourless, allochromatic gem materials can be quite rare, although this scarcity does not always drive up the cost (see "The Cost of Colour," opposite). In fact, some types, such as spinel, have such an affinity for allochromatic chromophores that the pure, white form simply does not exist in Nature (see "Real Synthetics" on page 221 of Volume 1).

It turns out that most of the common colouring agents, such as vanadium, chromium, manganese, iron, etc., lie in a certain area of the periodic table of elements (see page 79 and Table 12-3). There are very good reasons for this, involving electron orbitals, charge transfer and so forth, but they are *way* beyond the scope of this book. Interested students of chemistry are encouraged to consult some of the references in Chapter 9.

Table 12-2 The origin of colour in various types of beryl.

Impurity	Beryl Type (colour)
none	Goshenite (colourless)
Chromium: Cr^{+++}	Emerald (intense green)
Vanadium	Emerald* (intense green)
Iron: Fe^{++}	Aquamarine (blue)
Iron: Fe^{+++}	Heliodor (greenish-yellow)
Iron: Fe^{++} & Fe^{+++}	Green Beryl (green)
Manganese: Mn^{++}	Morganite (pink)
Manganese: Mn^{+++}	Red Beryl (red)
Uranium	Golden Beryl (yellow)

*classification of vanadium beryl as emerald has been controversial

The interaction between a host gem crystal and foreign atoms is a complex business, and it is difficult to predict how the presence and chemical state of impurities will affect the overall colour of a stone. This uncertainty is a well known fact of life for those who try various means to improve the colour of gemstones (see Chapter 13.1).

Table 12-3 The dominant elemental impurities responsible for colour in well-known gem species.

Colourant	Gem Type (colour)
Chromium	Alexandrite (red/green), Demantoid Garnet (green), Emerald (green), Red Spinel (red), Ruby (red), Tourmaline (green)
Cobalt	Spinel (blue)
Copper	Malachite (green), Sunstone (red, schiller), Tourmaline (blue, paraiba)
Iron	Amethyst (purple), Aquamarine (blue), Chryso-beryl (yellow-green), Citrine (pale yellow), Green Beryl (pale green), Heliodor (green-yellow), Indicolite Tourmaline (blue), Peridot (green), Pyrope Garnet (red), Sapphire (yellow), Topaz (yellow)
Iron and Titanium	Sapphire (blue)
Iron, Titanium and Chromium	Sapphire (purple, violet)
Magnesium and Chromium	Sapphire (orange)
Manganese	Andalusite (green), Morganite (pink), Red Beryl (red), Tourmaline (pink)
Uranium	Golden Beryl (yellow), Zircon (blue)
Vanadium	Emerald (green), Grossular Garnet (green), Tanzanite (blue-purple)

Why is Grass Green?

Every book on parenting should include a section on this stuff, because sooner or later, your kid will ask. The origin of colour in the wider world around us, including in grass and gemstones, is interesting and not at all simple.

Scientists and colour specialists, such as those in the electronics and print industries, speak of two types of colour: additive and subtractive. As their names suggest, the process of building a certain hue depends on adding up individual wavelengths of light in the first instance, and subtracting away colours in the second. For example, in order to create the colour purple additively, one must combine equal amounts of red and blue light. All colours combined additively in equal proportion will produce "white" light, which may, depending on the overall brightness, appear pure white, gray or, when the proportions are zero, black.

Most objects around us don't actually produce light, however – try to admire that beautiful sapphire in a darkened room sometime. In order to exhibit colour, these materials must *subtract* away certain wavelengths of the light falling on them, leaving their characteristic colours behind. They do this via the process of *absorption*, and the *absorption spectrum* of a material is a characteristic optical property that can be used for identification. Gemologists use a well-named device known as a *spectrometer* to measure the absorption spectrum of gemstones. These instruments can range from a simple hand-held unit costing a few tens of dollars up to laboratory-grade bench spectrometers, which will set you back several thousand (Figure 12-2).

So, back to the kid's question. Grass is green because it contains an important molecule known as chlorophyll. Chlorophyll is the stuff that makes photosynthesis possible, and photosynthesis is what puts the oxygen in the air, feeds us, and generally makes Earth a nice place to live. Plants, algae, and plankton use photosynthesis to convert carbon dioxide into usable energy, largely in the form of sugars. The energy to drive this reaction comes from sunlight, in particular, the red and blue-violet colours of the solar spectrum. The chlorophyll molecule absorbs strongly at these wavelength and barely at all in the green part of the spectrum. The result? Incoming yellowish-white light is turned into green (see Figure 12-3).

Figure 12-2 An inexpensive handheld spectrometer. This model from Krüss offers variable focus and spectral resolving power. Expect to pay between $200 and $300 for this type of instrument.

It is a curious paradox that we think of the vegetation around us as green, when the plants actually prefer everything but green. A nice meal of red or blue light is fine…hold the greens.

Incidentally, this preference for the extreme ends of the visual spectrum is the reason why high efficiency grow lights are bluish or orange-red in colour. No need to waste energy on undesirable green. And, in a curious echo of colour-change in gemstones (Section 12.3.5 below), plants seem to react differently to blue versus red light. Horticulturists insist that the initial growth phase of a plant is encouraged by blue light, whereas the later, flowering stage requires reddish light.

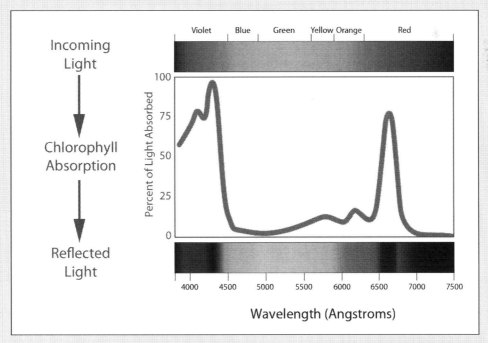

Figure 12-3 Chlorophyll absorbs the blue-violet and red parts of the incoming light, leaving a luxuriant green colour behind. Review the material in Chapter 11.2 if you have difficulty understanding this figure.

> Gemstones operate on the exact same principle (minus all that metabolism of sugar and flowering). The hue of a gem is determined not by the colour it adds, but rather by that which it subtracts.

12.3.3 Colour Variety

Gemstones come in all colours of the rainbow, and many more besides. From the entrancing dark purple-blue of tanzanite, through the intense green of emerald, to the yellows and oranges of zircon, to the rich magenta and red of garnet, there is a gemstone out there for every taste.

It is a close call between sapphire and tourmaline as king of the chromatic hill. Both of these gemstones come in an almost unbelievable variety of colours. Diamond, which few amateur faceters actually cut, arguably shares the crown. Garnet is a close second to these three, with beryl, topaz, spinel, quartz and zircon a more distant third. Table 12-4 organizes the more common gem types by colour. Other books, such as Schumann's *Gemstones of the World* (see Chapter 9), contain a much richer compendium.

Table 12-4 Common gemstones ordered by colour. This list is far from exhaustive, and in fact includes only the materials from Chapter 14.

Colour	Common Gem Species
black	Diamond, Fluorite, Garnet, Opal, Quartz, Spinel, Tourmaline
blue	Apatite, Beryl, Corundum, Diamond, Fluorite, Garnet, Iolite, Opal, Quartz (synthetic), Spinel, Sunstone, Tanzanite, Topaz, Tourmaline, Zircon
brown	Amber, Andalusite, Apatite, Chrysoberyl, Corundum, Danburite, Diamond, Fluorite, Garnet, Opal, Peridot, Quartz, Sphene, Spinel, Topaz, Tourmaline, Zircon
colourless	Amber, Apatite, Beryl, Corundum, Danburite, Diamond, Fluorite, Garnet, Iolite, Opal, Quartz, Scapolite, Spinel (synthetic) Sunstone, Topaz, Tourmaline, Zircon
green	Andalusite, Apatite, Beryl, Chrysoberyl, Corundum, Diamond, Fluorite, Garnet, Opal, Peridot, Quartz, Sphene, Spinel (synthetic), Sunstone, Topaz, Tourmaline, Zircon
orange	Amber, Corundum, Diamond, Fluorite, Garnet, Opal, Quartz, Sunstone, Topaz, Tourmaline
pink	Andalusite, Apatite, Beryl, Corundum, Danburite, Diamond, Fluorite, Garnet, Quartz, Scapolite, Spinel, Topaz, Tourmaline
purple	Apatite, Corundum, Diamond, Fluorite, Garnet, Iolite, Quartz, Scapolite, Spinel, Tanzanite, Tourmaline
red	Andalusite, Chrysoberyl (alexandrite) , Corundum (ruby), Diamond, Fluorite, Garnet, Opal, Quartz, Sphene, Sunstone, Spinel, Topaz, Tourmaline
white	Opal
yellow	Amber, Andalusite, Apatite, Beryl Chrysoberyl, Corundum, Danburite, Diamond, Fluorite, Garnet, Iolite, Opal, Peridot, Quartz, Scapolite, Sphene, Sunstone, Topaz, Tourmaline, Zircon

Table 12-4 underscores a point made in Section 12.3: it can sometimes be difficult to distinguish gemstone materials based on colour alone. Even within an individual gem species and hue, the variation can be dramatic. You should use the colour, as well as all the other diagnostic tools at your disposal, to help you identify a particular gemstone type.

12.3.4 Depth of Colour

Have you ever seen a "Siberian" amethyst next to its paler Rose de France cousin? The contrast is almost as remarkable as the difference in cost: top Siberian amethyst points can fetch more than ten times as much per gram as Rose de France, even though the two are physically and chemically almost identical. The difference, of course, is *depth of colour.*

Two factors determine the depth of colour of a gemstone. The first is the intrinsic amount of absorption in the material, that is, how much light gets absorbed per unit length. A one centimeter slab of Siberian amethyst will absorb a lot more green, yellow, and orange light – thus leaving blue and red, which combine to purple – than would a similar sample of Rose de France (see Figure 12-4).

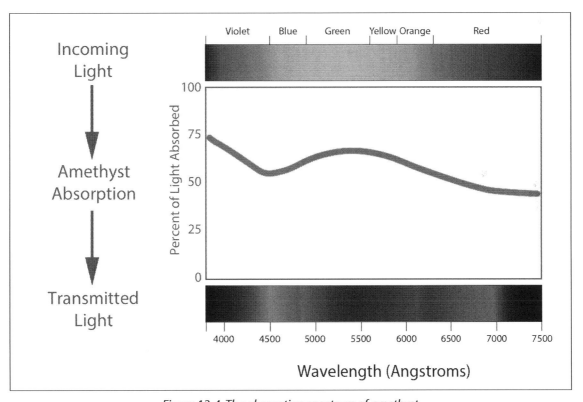

Figure 12-4 The absorption spectrum of amethyst.

The second factor determining depth of colour is the distance that a light ray must travel through the stone. Longer light paths mean more selective absorption and deeper, richer, saturation. The pathlength is a function of both the size and the design of a particular gem. Chapter 11.9 follows a light ray's path through a gemstone. A review of that material should make it clear that larger, deeper gems will display more saturated colours than smaller, shallower stones.

You can and should use this information to your advantage. For example, there are gem designs that are explicitly tailored to paler gem rough. One of these is the *barion* (see page 246), whose deeper belly produces longer light paths and hence enriches the colour. A modified emerald cut with deeper pavilion angles can achieve the same effect (but see Chapter 10.5.2 for a somewhat contrarian view of these design strategies).

Typically, deeper, more intense colour means greater value and a more vivid gemstone, but as often happens, you can have too much of a good thing. It is very easy to cut a gem that has *too much* colour. Figure 12-4 shows that amethyst absorbs most strongly in the green-yellow-orange range of the spectrum, but its absorption is by no means zero elsewhere. Without proper care, the combination of intrinsic absorption, rough size, and cut design could result in an amethyst with too much absorption – a dark and unattractive gemstone.

As with pale material, there are some strategies for improving the appearance of saturated gem rough. For example, shallower designs lead to shorter light paths and hence less absorption. For the same reason, smaller stones work better in saturated rough than do larger ones. Cutting for brilliance and sparkle is not necessarily a good idea. These characteristics depend on multiple reflections and long light paths. Instead, you should concentrate on getting photons through the stone. Simple reflector or emerald-style pavilions work best.

In extreme cases, you can try cutting below the critical angle, since in any case, you are only going to get a couple of bounces before all the light is absorbed. Some commercially cut garnets have the back of the stone hollowed out to lighten the colour. Of course, these strategies only work in open-type mountings, such as pendants and earrings, which allow light to enter the back of the gem. Chapter 16.5.2 provides more tips on dealing with colour and saturation, and Chapter 19.2.3 contains a gem design that takes this approach to the limit.

When is Too Much Too Much?

How can you tell if a stone is too intensely coloured and may produce a dark gem?

That's an easy one. Just cut it and see. Although less than completely satisfying, this answer is at least honest. One of the most fascinating and frustrating aspects of our hobby is that surprises are the norm, not the exception. A particular gem will turn out lighter or darker than expected, or perhaps even a different hue altogether. However, as you gain experience as a faceter, you will be able to control this unpredictability somewhat, and tip the balance more toward the fascinating than the frustrating.

What to do?

Well, first, here is something not to do. It can be very tempting to look at gem rough by holding it up against a light source, such as the sky, an incandescent bulb, or a flashlight. While this is an excellent means to examine the stone for internal flaws (see Chapter 5.3.1 and page 201 of Volume 1), it is not a good way to gauge how dark a gem will ultimately be.

Figure 12-5 The white paper test will show whether gem rough is too dark to cut. The Mali garnet and blue-green tourmaline to the top and right are fine. The pyrope garnet to the bottom left is not.

To judge colour saturation, experienced cutters usually use the "white paper test." Place the gem rough to be examined on a clean piece of white paper in good lighting conditions. Yes, you should bring your own paper on buying expeditions (see Chapter 6.2.2). If you are sorting through rough at a gem show, ask the dealer for a white plastic tray. Examine the stones carefully. The colour you see will be a rough approximation of the final colour of the gem. Any material that is too dark to show appealing colour under these circumstances will simply not produce an attractive gem. Period. Put it back.

Cut for Brilliance? Cut for Colour?

All this talk of absorption and the strategies for deepening or lightening colour prompts an obvious question:

Can't I have it all? Rich colour, brilliance, scintillation, a nice house in the country with a white picket fence?

Sadly, no.

Almost every piece of gem rough that you will encounter will have its strengths and weaknesses, and these characteristics will more than likely dictate how best to cut the stone. You may pick up a piece of pale, perfectly clean aquamarine that promises lovely colour when you look down the long c-axis (see Figure 12-33). Don't be fooled. The white paper test (see above) will give you a good idea of the eventual saturation of the gem. It will probably also tell you that cutting for colour will be hopeless. On the other hand, its internal clarity could yield a brilliant brilliant.

The same goes for that rich red almandine garnet that is amazingly inexpensive. Rich colour often means a dark gem; believe your eyes and the white paper test. Brilliance and scintillation require the interplay of multiple reflections within the body of the stone, and it just ain't gonna happen if the white paper makes the rough look like a piece of coal. Cutting for colour may be possible, but beware.

The unfortunate truth is that precious little gem rough has the ideal amount of saturation to produce *both* rich colour *and* brilliance. Did you notice the use of the words "precious" and "rich" in the previous sentence? Yes, this material is expensive. Chapter 16.5.5 has a great deal more to say on the tradeoff between colour and brilliance.

12.3.5 Changing Colours

"It is the eye of ignorance that assigns a fixed and unchangeable colour to every object"

- Paul Gauguin

Gauguin sure got that one right, and you do have to admit that he was an expert on the subject. In fact, it is largely the ever-changing play of light and colour in gemstones that fuels their unique appeal. Beyond the dynamic effects due to lighting and motion, however, it turns out that the intrinsic colour of a gem can itself be subject to change. This section examines three types of mutability of colour in gemstones: colour-change due to the spectral makeup of the lighting environment, artificial treatment of gemstones to improve colour, and fading and modification of colour due to external influences. Note that this categorization distinguishes these effects from stable, multiple, colours in a *single* gemstone, a topic discussed in Section 12.3.8.

Colour-Change Gemstones

A number of coloured gemstones, most notably garnet, spinel, chrysoberyl, and sapphire, exhibit the unique property of showing different body colour under different lighting conditions. For example, colour-change garnets will appear green in sunlight and red under incandescent light. If you have not seen the effect, beg, borrow or steal one of these gems. They are remarkable.

How can a stone change colour in this way? The answer is straightforward once you are armed with the knowledge of how subtractive colour works in a gemstone. Let's take the example of alexandrite, the most famous and sought-after type of natural, colour-change gemstone. Alexandrite is a variety of chrysoberyl, known to the Pocket Protector types as beryllium aluminum oxide or $BeAl_2O_4$. In alexandrite, chromium atoms have replaced some of the aluminum in the crystal lattice.

Recall from Section 12.3.2 that chromium is a notorious colouring agent in gems (in fact, the name chromium comes from *chroma*, the Greek word for colour). The effect of these chromium atoms is to produce two broad bands of absorption in the violet and in the yellow-orange range (see Figure 12-6). If absorption is low, transmission is high. This means that alexandrite transmits well in two windows centered on greenish-blue and red.

The two absorption bands, coupled with the spectral makeup of the incoming light, produce the magical colour-change in alexandrite. Under incandescent lighting, which contains plenty of red light but very little blue, the gem appears reddish. It would do a fine job of transmitting blue, but there just isn't any around. The opposite situation occurs under bluish-white lighting, such as that produced by fluorescent tubes. Here, the alexandrite transmits the abundant shorter wavelength photons, and therefore appears greenish-blue.

Note that the detailed chemical makeup of alexandrite varies from specimen to specimen. This has the effect of modifying the absorption spectrum, and hence the range of colour change. The most valuable alexandrites produce an intense red to green shift. These stones are exceedingly rare, and a one-carat gem can cost tens of thousands of dollars. Synthetic alexandrite has been around since the mid-1970's and offers a considerably more affordable alternative (see Table 12-5 and Chapter 6.6).

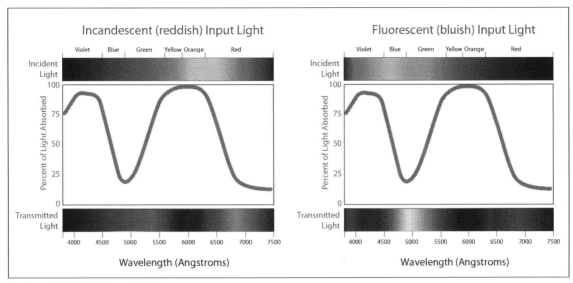

Figure 12-6 The absorption spectrum of alexandrite. Note the two broad bands of absorption. Depending on the mix of incident colours, alexandrite gems can appear either red (left) or greenish-blue (right).

The other natural colour-change gemstones operate on the identical principle: chemical impurities (usually chromium or vanadium) in the crystal cause a double-humped transmission spectrum. Altering the colour balance of the incident light then produces the dramatic colour shift. As with alexandrite, stones exhibiting a significant colour change are rare in nature and command premium prices. Synthetics are available for several of the popular colour-change species (Table 12-5).

Table 12-5 Natural and synthetic colour-change gemstones. See also Table 6-1.

Gem Material	Colour-Change (incandescent –> fluorescent)*	Synthetic Available?
Alexandrite (Chrysoberyl)	pink/red –> greenish blue	Yes
Diaspore (also called zultanite)	brown/pink –> green	No
Fluorite	pink/purple –> blue/green	No
Garnet	red/purple –> green green/blue –> purple ("reverse alexandrite effect")	No
Sapphire	purple –> blue pink –> greenish	Yes
Spinel	purple/pink –> purple/blue, purple/violet –> blue	Yes
Tourmaline	orange –> purple green/blue –> purple ("reverse alexandrite effect")	No
Cubic Zirconia	Various	Yes (only)

The colour-change tabulated refers to the shift going from reddish to bluish input light. For example, alexandrite shifts from pink/red to greenish blue when changing from incandescent to fluorescent lighting or from incandescent to daylight.

Simple Colour-change?

So. Colour-change in gemstones is straightforward and the result of selective bands of absorption in the material. If you know the absorption features and the spectrum of the illumination, you can figure out the colour-change…

Not so fast. In fact, the perception of colour in general, and of colour-change in particular, is a complex mix of multiple factors. These include the adaptation of the eye to certain colours and the spectral sensitivity of the eye's cone photoreceptors, in addition to the factors mentioned above. It is for this reason that it can be particularly difficult to capture on film – or these days on CCD – the perceived colour shift of a gemstone under different conditions. We are living in a world of premium asking prices for natural colour-change gem rough. Hence, it is important that you examine potential purchases in person, or at least have an ironclad return guarantee.

12.3.6 Artificial Treatment for Colour

Given that a difference in hue can increase the value of a gem a hundredfold or more, it will come as no surprise to you that people try to alter the intrinsic colour of gemstones. Also, given that purely "natural" gemstones command a considerably higher price than those that are perceived as synthetic or artificially modified, it will come as no surprise to you that such modifications are not always openly declared.

There are three types of gemstone treatment for colour: heat, radiation, and diffusion. In addition, there are other techniques, such as oiling and laser drilling, which can improve the chromatic appearance of a gem – for example, by masking inclusions. The history, practice, and ethics of gemstone treatment is a vast and interesting topic. Turn to Chapter 13 to learn more.

12.3.7 Slow Colour Changes and Fading

The ancient Greek philosopher Heraclitus captured an essential truth in saying that "everything changes but change itself." Indeed, the notion of eternal change has enlivened not only philosophy, but also such seemingly diverse pursuits as subatomic physics and political campaigns.

Change is central to gemstones as well, and as it turns out, change is not always a good thing. Yes, using treatments to enhance the colour or clarity of a gem is generally beneficial, but there are a number of gemstone types that don't take well to change. Specifically, exposure to moderate heat, direct sunlight, or even air can cause their beauty to fade.

Perhaps the most striking example of this sensitivity is deep blue or *maxixe* beryl. Exposure to light or heat can cause the rich blue colour to fade within days. Maxixe is definitely an evening gemstone. In addition, some types of amethyst, as well as rose quartz and kunzite, can lose colour saturation in direct sunlight. Exposure to ultraviolet light can cause colour shifts in zircon.

One type of light-induced colour-change seems to be reversible. If kept in darkness, *tenebrescent* zircon is a vivid orange or orange-red. When exposed to daylight, the colour fades to a beige-brown within minutes. Returning the gemstone to darkness restores the vibrant orange within a day or two, at which point the whole process can be repeated.

Opals exhibit their own type of change due to interaction with the air around us. This type of gem is actually a mineraloid gel of silica and water (see page 80). It is the water in this mixture – up to 30 percent in some types of opal – that causes the sensitivity to air.

Opals can, in fact, dry out with time, a phenomenon that leads to colour fading due to milkiness, internal "crazing" and other uglies. Reputable rough dealers will store their opals under dry conditions for months or years before selling, in order to identify susceptible stones. Nevertheless, like me, you may end up with a favourite gemstone that simply doesn't like being out in the open air. Luckily, soaking the opal in water can restore its original appearance. Yes, my wife's custom jewelry box does, in fact, feature a jar of good old H_2O. And yes, you mineralogy experts out there, I know that this is not supposed to work, due to the nature of the chemical bonding of water in opal. I can only say that, in ignorance, I tried it, and in ignorance, I found that it worked. Maybe it's something in our water...(see also Section 12.13.1).

12.3.8 Multi-Colour Gemstones

Which famous physicist first published the idea of the space-time continuum, that is, the concept that the three dimensions of space and the one dimension of time are parts of a single, four-dimensional way of looking at the universe? If you answered Albert Einstein, good for you. You would be wrong, but good for you. It was a fine guess.

Actually, the honour goes to Edgar Allan Poe – yes, the creepy raven guy. The first known published work connecting space with time was his essay *Eureka* (1848), which included the statement that "space and duration are one." It also included a description of the Big Bang and an expanding universe almost a century before it became scientific orthodoxy.

Well, good for Edgar Allan Poe. But what does this have to do with gemstone colour?

I am glad you asked. The previous section dealt with gemstones that change colour with *time*, either due to illumination effects, artificial treatment, or exposure to the environment. This section examines gemstones that change colour in *space*, that is at different locations on the stone, while the next section discusses gem types whose colour changes when the crystal is viewed from different directions. Sort of a gemological space-time continuum.

Yes, that is a pretty lame analogy. I promise not to do it again. Quoth the author, "Nevermore."

Colour Bands and Zones

Section 12.3.1 explains that colour in gemstones arises due to absorption, either from chemical impurities or the structure of the crystal lattice. These effects can, of course, vary from place to place within a single gemstone. The result is colour banding or zones – regions in which the hue, saturation or tone differs from the bulk of the material (see "Who's Hue?" on page 83 for an explanation of hue, saturation, and tone).

Tourmaline is perhaps the best-known example of a gem material exhibiting bands or zones of colour. The separation can either be along the axis of crystal growth, as in classic bi-colour and tri-colour tourmalines, or radial within the crystal, as in so-called "watermelon" tourmaline (see Figure 12-7). For this species, the different colours reflect changes in the chemistry of the surrounding liquid during crystallization.

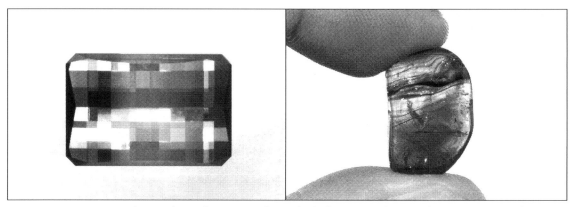

Figure 12-7 A green-clear-red tri-colour tourmaline, which this grayscale reproduction miserably fails to portray (left). Viva Italia! A tumbled multi-colour "watermelon" tourmaline (right).

Note that you should exercise some care in cutting bi-colour and tri-colour tourmaline, since the transition zone between colours can be susceptible to parting and fracture.

Quartz can also present two or more colours in a single stone. Ametrine, which is half amethyst and half citrine, is the most striking example. In this instance, it is the oxidation state of the iron impurity that determines the colour (see Section 12.3.2). Heat can alter this oxidation state, and in fact, almost all citrine on the market is heat-treated amethyst (see Chapter 13.3). In naturally occurring ametrine, temperature gradients during formation lead to the spatial variations in the oxidation state, and hence the colour. As with citrine, most commercial ametrine has been treated.

Figure 12-8 Ametrine is bi-colour amethyst-citrine. The rightmost gemstone is tri-colour: amethyst, clear, and citrine quartz.

Other gemstone materials exhibit banding and colour zones to various degrees. For example, most sapphire rough will have some spatially varying colour, in addition to its native pleochroism (see below). Bi-colour zircon also exists (Figure 12-9).

As with dichroism and pleochroism (see next section), colour banding and zones may require careful orientation of the rough prior to cutting. Chapter 6.7 addresses this issue.

Figure 12-9 A bi-colour brownish-gold and clear zircon. Anyone else a fan of Haribo Happy Cola?

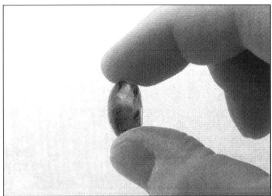

12.4 Birefringence and Pleochroism

Want to impress a kid? Show him or her a piece of iolite, that amazing gemstone material that changes colour from deep blue to straw-yellow to clear, depending on which way you hold it. Want to impress a highly trained physicist? Do the exact same thing.

In the case of the child, it is the eye-popping wonderment of seeing something that is seemingly magical. For the PhD physicist, it is the dizzying, side-slipping knock to his (or sadly all too rarely, her) world view…"I thought I understood everything. Magic doesn't exist. How can this possibly happen?"

Actually, the physics of materials such as iolite has been fairly well understood since the middle of the nineteenth century. Mineralogists use the term *dichroic* to describe materials which show two distinct colours in different directions and *trichroic* to identify those which show three (like iolite). The more general term, *pleochroic* encompasses both dichroic and trichroic materials. As you shall see, all of these colour effects arise due to *birefringence*, which is a fancy way of describing a material that exhibits different refractive indices along different crystal directions.

Note: Chapter 11.3 describes how light interacts with matter, and specifically, how the properties of the crystal lattice can influence the propagation of electromagnetic waves. It is worthwhile to review that material before proceeding.

Refer to Figure 12-10, Figure 12-11 and Chapter 11.3.2. Recall that the incoming electromagnetic wave "shakes" the electrons, and that the speed of the re-emitted light depends on the strength of the "springs" of the crystal lattice.

Now imagine that the material is *anisotropic* – that is, it has different properties in different directions along the crystal. Specifically, you can imagine that the springs in the "x" direction in Figure 12-10 have a different stiffness than those lying along the "y" and "z" axes.

You learned in Chapter 11.3.2 and 11.4 that "spring strength" relates directly to the speed of light, and that the speed of light in the material determines the angle of refraction. Thus, if unpolarized light enters such an anisotropic material, it encounters two different refractive indices along different directions of the crystal lattice. The light splits into two polarized rays, which follow different paths through the crystal. Materials which display this property are termed *birefringent*.

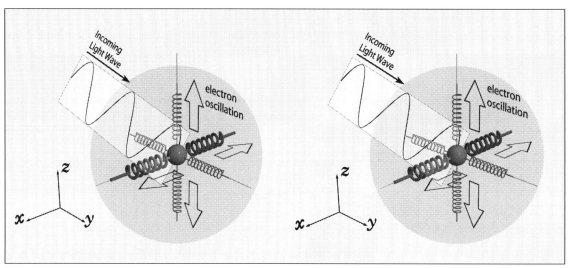

Figure 12-10 A light ray interacting with an atom in a birefringent gemstone. This phenomenon arises in aniso-tropic materials when the "spring strength" is different along different crystal directions. Compare this drawing with Figure 11-6. Note that this is a 3-D image. Cross your eyes to see the effect, and refer to page 74 if you have difficulty.

This birefringence is a familiar effect to rockhounds: it is responsible for the splitting of light rays by a crystal of calcite (Figure 12-12). Physicists and gemologists quantify the amount of birefringence or *double refraction* in a sample as the difference in refractive index for the two directions:

$$\Delta n = n_e - n_o$$

where n_e and n_o are the refractive indices for the two polarization directions.

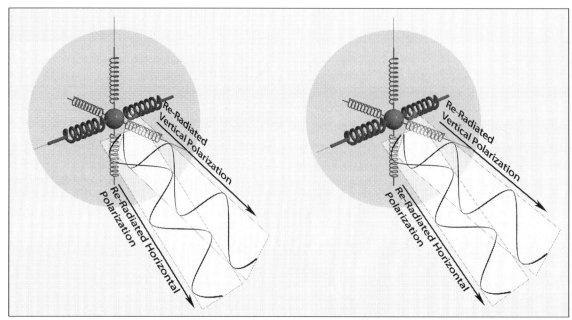

Figure 12-11 After interacting with the electrons, the emerging light wave splits into two distinct polarized waves that take two different paths through the crystal. Differences in the absorption properties for the two polarizations can lead to colour differences in different directions, the phenomenon known as pleochroism. Note: this is a 3-dimensional figure.

The splitting of light rays in birefringent materials can have a significant influence on the appearance of gemstones. Depending on the direction of the optical axis with respect to the table, pleochroic gems such as zircon can exhibit "facet doubling," the faceter's equivalent of what is happening in Figure 12-12. Rutile, sphene, and to a lesser extent, peridot can also display noticeable facet doubling. While I do not find this effect unattractive (it is pretty cool

physics, after all), facet doubling can lend a fuzzy appearance to the gem. Here again, careful orientation of the rough can reduce the effect. Happily for those trying to minimize double refraction, there will always be a direction for which the incident rays do not split. This direction corresponds to the optical axis of the stone, and placing the table perpendicular to it will minimize facet doubling. As a bonus, this will often produce the most intense and pure colour as well.

Figure 12-12 Birefringence is the splitting of light rays due to anisotropic effects, here in a crystal of Icelandic spar or calcite.

In addition to different light speeds, anisotropic materials can also exhibit different absorption properties in different crystallographic directions. You know from earlier in this chapter that colour in gemstones is fundamentally an absorption effect. Since the incoming rays have split, each of the daughter rays may experience different absorption and hence emerge with a different colour. As a consequence, such a material will appear to have a different body colour when viewed from different angles. The result is the magic of iolite.

Due to the symmetry of their "springs," minerals of the tetragonal, trigonal, and hexagonal crystal system can only produce two distinct colours and are hence dichroic (see Section 12.10 for an explanation of crystal systems). Members of the orthorhombic, monoclinic, and triclinic group can show three colours and are called trichroic.

Of course, if a material has no direction-dependent properties, there can be no splitting and no pleochroism. Such materials are termed *isotropic* and include members of the cubic crystal system, as well as amorphous materials such as glass and opal. Table 12-6 lists the properties of common pleochroic gemstones..

Because pleochroism is fundamentally a polarization effect, examining a stone using polarized light can help you identify it, locate the optical axes, and isolate the two or three fundamental colours. Yes, you can use that old pair of fisherman's sunglasses (Figure 12-13), but beware: the darkening and colour shift due to the intrinsic colour of the lenses may make this option worse than using nothing at all.

Instead, you should own and use a simple gemological instrument known as a *polariscope*. These devices come in a number of different configurations, but perhaps the simplest and most effective is the birefringent *dichroscope*. Recall from page 97 that randomly polar-

Table 12-6 Pleochroism of some common gemstone materials (adapted from Schumann, 1997 and online sources).

Gem Material	Strength	Colours
Andalusite	strong	light green, pinkish-orange, yellow
Beryl		
Aquamarine	distinct	blue, greenish blue, different tones
Emerald	distinct	green, blue-green, yellow-green
Golden beryl	weak	lemon-yellow, yellow
Heliodor	weak	golden-yellow, green-yellow
Morganite	distinct	pale pink, blue-pink
Chrysoberyl	very weak	red, yellow, green
Alexandrite	distinct	red-violet, yellow-red, dark green
Corundum		
ruby	strong	yellow-red, deep red
sapphire		
blue	distinct	dark blue, greenish-blue
green	weak	green, greenish-yellow
orange	strong	yellow-brown, orange, colourless
purple	distinct	purple, light red
yellow	weak	yellow, light-yellow
Iolite	strong	deep blue, yellow, colourless
Peridot	very weak	colourless, pale green
Quartz		
amethyst	very weak	purple, gray-purple
citrine	weak	yellow, light-yellow
rose quartz	weak	pink, pale pink
smoky quartz	distinct	brown, red-brown
Tanzanite	very strong	purple, blue, brown-yellow
Topaz		
blue	weak	light blue, pink, colourless
brown	distinct	yellow-brown
green	distinct	pale green, blue-green
pink	distinct	pink, pale pink, colourless
Tourmaline		
blue	strong	light blue, dark blue
green	strong	dark green, yellow green
pink	distinct	light red, yellow-red
red	distinct	dark red, light red
yellow	distinct	dark yellow, light yellow
Zircon		
blue	distinct	blue, yellow-gray, colourless
brown	very weak	red-brown, yellow-brown
green	very weak	green, brown-green
red	weak	red, light-yellow
yellow	very weak	honey-yellow, yellow-brown

ized light entering a birefringent crystal will split, with the two polarizations taking different directions through the material. A properly sized and oriented entrance window at the input side of such a crystal will thus produce two side-by-side images at the output side, each with its own polarization (Figure 12-14). Looking at a sample of gem rough with such a device will then show you two adjacent views through the material in perpendicular polarizations. Any difference in brightness or colour indicates a pleochroic material, and the orientation of zero difference shows you the optical axis of the crystal. By rotating the sample, you should also be able to discern the two or three intrinsic colours. Simple, elegant, beautiful.

Chapter 20.3 contains a more complete explanation of dichroscopes, including instructions on how to build your own for under two dollars.

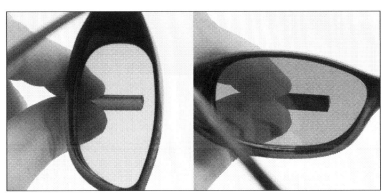

Figure 12-13 Pleochroism is a polarization phenomenon, here seen with fisherman's sunglasses and a tourmaline crystal with a closed c-axis. To see the effect, you need to hold the stone in front of an intrinsically polarized light source, such as a flat screen display or the blue sky 90° from the sun.

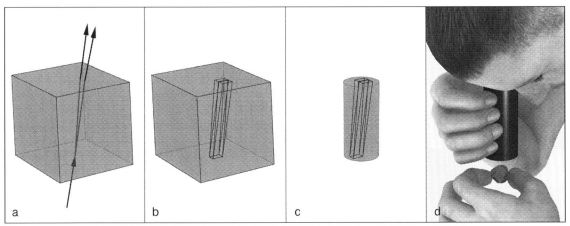

Figure 12-14 Operating principle of a simple calcite birefringent polariscope, or dichroscope. Light rays from below enter the crystal and split according to polarization, taking different paths (a). If oriented properly, an input window on one side of the crystal will produce two output windows, one for each polarization (b). Trimmed to a convenient size (c) and mounted in a sturdy holder (d), the calcite crystal becomes a dichroscope, which can be held against a sample of gem rough to identify the optical axis and dominant body colours.

12.4.1 Gem Design and Orientation for Pleochroism

In addition to providing a fun little example of seemingly magical physics, dichroism and trichroism have a direct impact on the appearance of a gemstone. For example, some tourmalines display complete absorption along one axis of the crystal – a phenomenon often referred to as a "closed c-axis." Viewed along their length, such stones are opaque black, hardly an appealing colour for a gem. Other samples may show a pleasing green or turquoise colour in one direction, and a considerably less aesthetic brownish-green along another (see Figure 6-26).

There are design and orientation choices which can help you get the most out of pleochroic gemstones. Turn to Chapter 6.7.1 for practical advice.

Figure 12-15 A pleochroic tourmaline showing yellow-green colours along the up-down direction and pale blue-green left and right.

12.5 Refractive Index

The second most important gemstone optical property after colour is the *refractive index*, also frequently called the "index of refraction" or simply the "index." The refractive index measures the amount of refraction that a medium can produce and it is a unique property of the material. As Chapter 11 and the previous sections have attempted to explain, refraction in gemstones arises due to the interaction of electromagnetic waves with the electrons and nuclei of the crystal lattice.

Actually, you don't really need to understand the detailed physics of the interaction of light with matter in order to understand refraction, but you should at least take on board the notion that refraction is *everything* in terms of gemstone performance. No refraction means no total internal reflection, and no total internal reflection means no sparklies. End of story.

Those other chapters and sections explained *how*, and to some extent, *why* refraction works. This section will concentrate on refraction as a gemstone material property – that is, as a characteristic that can be used in gemstone design, material identification, and so forth.

12.5.1 Refractive Index and Gemstone Design

The refractive index of a particular piece of rough has an important influence on the selection of gemstone design.

First, and most importantly, the refractive index determines the critical angle – that angle at which total internal reflection can occur (review the material in Chapter 11.7 if you don't understand this statement). This, in turn, determines the minimum depth of the gemstone design. A higher refractive index means a smaller critical angle and hence, shallower gem designs can, in principle, work (Figure 12-16). For more on this "critical" issue see Chapter 10.4 and "A Critical Look at Culets" on page 64.

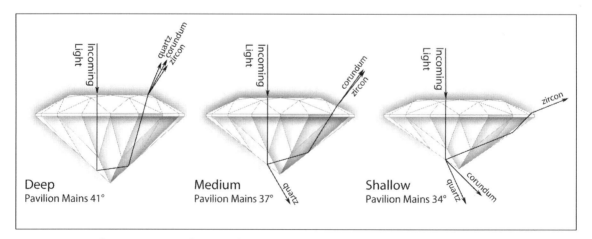

Figure 12-16 Light rays entering deep, medium, and shallow gemstones. Each figure follows three rays, corresponding to gems made of quartz (n = 1.54), corundum (n = 1.76), and zircon (n = 2.00). Note that zircon produces total internal reflection for deep, medium, and shallow gemstone designs, while quartz works only in deeper cuts. Chapter 10.4 examines this process in much greater detail.

This ability to produce sparkle in shallower gemstone designs has multiple benefits:

- Shallower gems will have a larger top-view outline for a given carat weight, and hence appear bigger and more valuable. They will also work well in just about any setting – deep bellies are particularly troublesome in rings, for example.

- It is not only the first bounce in a gemstone (as in Figure 12-16) that counts. Higher index materials will produce a second internal reflection for a larger range of incident angles, reducing windowing and light loss. They will therefore be brighter and livelier in realistic, mixed lighting environments. See Chapter 10.4 for more.

- Elongated, culet (i.e. non-keel) gem designs require a range of pavilion angles: relatively shallow in the long dimension and steep in the short. For example, a brilliant oval will have shallower culet facets along the length of the stone and steeper ones across the width. The ability of higher index materials to work over a larger range of incident angles allows such designs to work. The classic (and unappealing) "bowtie" effect in low-index oval gems is an example of this (Figure 12-17).

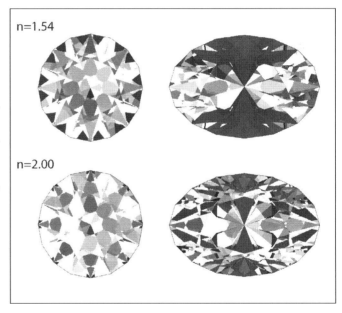

Figure 12-17 Computer renderings of a standard round brilliant (left) and a 1.5:1 ratio oval brilliant (right). The upper two images are rendered in quartz (n=1.54), while the lower two are for zircon (n=2.00). All gems keep the minimum pavilion angle at 41°, safely above the critical angle for quartz. The elongated design has a range of pavilion angles, and the lower index material simply cannot cope. The result is the dreaded "bowtie" effect. Thanks to Bob Keller for the original idea – Google "Bow Tie Blues" to see his clear explanation of this phenomenon.

n=1.54

n=2.00

Of course, all of this wonderfulness comes at a price. Literally. Whether you are talking chrysoberyl, corundum, spinel, or (shudder) diamond, you will almost always pay more per carat than for beryl, tourmaline, quartz, or (shudder) fluorite. There are notable exceptions to this rule, however. For example, top colour tourmaline can command sapphire-like prices, and some higher index materials, such as garnet and zircon, can be surprisingly affordable.

Tailoring Gem Designs to the Refractive Index

By now, it should be clear that you ignore refractive index at your peril when you select a gem design for a given piece of rough. Luckily, there are some general guidelines for choosing (and modifying) gem designs that will help you avoid unattractive windowing, bowties, and other nasties.

The best strategy is to pick a gemstone design from a reputable source that is already optimized for your selected material. All modern published designs will specify a target refractive index (Figure 12-18).

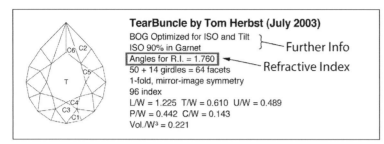

TearBuncle by Tom Herbst (July 2003)
BOG Optimized for ISO and Tilt
ISO 90% in Garnet } Further Info
Angles for R.I. = 1.760 Refractive Index
50 + 14 girdles = 64 facets
1-fold, mirror-image symmetry
96 index
L/W = 1.225 T/W = 0.610 U/W = 0.489
P/W = 0.442 C/W = 0.143
Vol./W³ = 0.221

Figure 12-18 Published gemstone designs should specify the design refractive index. Further information about materials with suitable index of refraction may appear elsewhere in the header or in the cutting notes. This design is available at www.boghome.com.

As a general rule, you can cut most designs in (somewhat) higher index materials without modification. However, it is risky to execute a certain design in lower index or significantly higher index material. For example, a cut designed for tourmaline ($n = 1.62$) will almost certainly be fine in rhodolite garnet ($n = 1.76$), but don't expect it to work in quartz ($n = 1.54$) or cubic zirconia ($n = 2.17$).

In those instances where your chosen rough has lower or significantly higher index than the design target, you can try to raise or lower the pavilion angles using the tangent ratio method (see Chapter 10.5). Of course, a well-designed gemstone cut requires more than just having the pavilion facets above the critical angle. The designer has very likely tried different combinations of angles and facet placement to achieve a certain effect. Departing radically from these may not produce a pleasing gem. Chapter 10.5 rants about this issue at great length.

There are a number of software tools to help you evaluate and modify gemstone designs in different index materials. Among these are GemCAD and BOG, both described in Chapter 15.3. There are also some tricks which can help with lower refractive index materials, for example apex crown facets (see page 21). Finally – and yes, I have said this many times before – there is no substitute for experience and experimentation.

12.5.2 Refractive Index of Common Gemstone Materials

Table 12-7 lists the refractive index for common gemstone materials. The table also shows the amount of birefringence (see page 98) and the dispersion, an optical property discussed in the next section. Note that these data also appear in the relevant tables of material properties in Chapter 14. Schumann and Vargas (see Chapter 9.3), as well as the online web resources listed in Chapter 15.8.6, contain much more complete information on the optical constants of gemstone materials.

12.5.3 Measuring Refractive Index

The refractive index is an excellent diagnostic tool for identifying gem materials. If you can measure the refractive index of a sample, you have a very good idea of what it is, and can avoid misidentification and fraud. Gemologists use a *refractometer* to do this. These devices take advantage of the fixed relationship between the critical angle and the refractive index. Figure 12-19 and the following paragraphs explain the principle.

Light enters the refractometer with a range of input angles and strikes a hemisphere of high index glass. The gem to be measured is placed against the flat face of this hemisphere, usually with a liquid to ensure good optical contact. Assuming that the gem has lower refractive

Table 12-7 The refractive index, birefringence and dispersion for common gemstone materials. The birefringence is the difference between the maximum and minimum refractive indices, while the dispersion numbers represent the change in refractive index going from blue to red light. See Section 12.6 for details and page 210 for info on the Cauchy B Value. Data assembled from the references in Chapter 9.3 and online sources.

Gem Material	Refractive Index	Birefringence	Dispersion (BG)	Cauchy B Value
Amber	1.539-1.545	none	–	–
Andalusite	1.627-1.649	0.007-0.013	0.016	0.0049
Apatite	1.628-1.649	0.002-0.006	0.013	0.0040
Beryl	1.562-1.602	0.004-0.01	0.014	0.0043
Chrysoberyl	1.746-1.763	0.007-0.011	0.015	0.0046
Corundum	1.762-1.788	0.008	0.018	0.0055
Cubic Zirconia	2.150-2.200	none	0.06	0.018
Danburite	1.630-1.636	0.006-0.008	0.017	0.0052
Diamond	2.417-2.419	none	0.044	0.013
Feldspar/Sunstone	1.525-1.548	0.01	0.012	0.0037
Fluorite	1.433-1.448	none	0.007	0.0021
Garnet	1.734-1.940	none	0.014-0.057	0.012
Glass (Obsidian)	1.400-1.600	none	0.01	0.0031
Iolite	1.542-1.578	0.008-0.012	0.017	0.0052
Opal	1.370-1.520	none	–	–
Peridot	1.650-1.703	0.036-0.038	0.02	0.0061
Quartz	1.540-1.553	0.009	0.013	0.0040
Scapolite	1.540-1.579	0.006-0.037	0.017	0.0052
Sphene	1.843-2.110	0.1-0.192	0.051	0.016
Spinel	1.712-1.762	none	0.02	0.0061
Tanzanite	1.691-1.700	0.009	0.03	0.0092
Topaz	1.609-1.643	0.008-0.016	0.014	0.0043
Tourmaline	1.614-1.666	0.014-0.032	0.017	0.0052
Zircon	1.810-2.024	0.002-0.059	0.039	0.012

index than the glass, total internal reflection will occur at the glass-gem interface when the incident angle is greater than the critical angle:

$$\theta_c = \sin^{-1}\left(\frac{n_{\mathrm{gem}}}{n_{\mathrm{glass}}}\right)$$

See Chapter 11.7 if the previous sentences don't make sense to you. For angles smaller than θ_c, the light will refract into the gemstone and be scattered away.

The effect of all this is that a light-dark shadow line will appear on a marked scale placed on the output side of the glass hemisphere. When properly calibrated, this scale gives the refractive index of the gem directly. (Note that a light ray emerging from the center of a sphere always strikes the surface at a 0° angle, and hence will experience no refraction at the glass-air interface. This is why a hemisphere is used.)

Testing a gem is simplicity itself. Place a facet, typically the table, on the center of the hemisphere, hold the device up to the light, and read off the answer. Compared to other gem

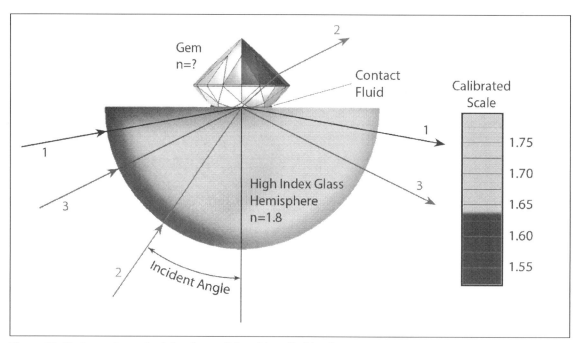

Figure 12-19 Operating principle of a traditional handheld refractometer. Rays incident on a hemisphere of high index glass at angles greater than the critical angle for the glass-gem interface experience total internal reflection (Ray 1). Rays below this critical angle (Ray 2) enter the gem and are scattered away. A calibrated scale on the output side of the hemisphere will then show a light-dark shadow transition at angles corresponding exactly to the critical ray (Ray 3). See text for further details.

identification techniques, this method has considerable advantages. First, unlike physical probes, such as the scratch and streak tests (Sections 12.9.2 and 12.11.3), the refractometer is essentially non-contact and completely non-destructive. The technique also works well with mounted stones, unlike diagnostics such as specific gravity. On the other hand, because it depends on good optical contact with the stone, a standard refractometer does not work well with gem rough.

Unsurprisingly, real-world refractometers are somewhat more complex than the one shown in Figure 12-19; they frequently contain additional lenses, mirrors, polarizers, and other doo-dads to make operation easier, more accurate, and comfortable. You can expect to pay one hundred dollars or less for a cheap handheld device, and up to a thousand for a top-quality laboratory grade instrument.

Do you really need a refractometer?

No. Definitely not. Purchasing gem rough from a reputable dealer is the best defense against fraud (Chapter 6 provides further tips). Nevertheless, if you deal with a lot of gemstones, particularly if they are already faceted, a refractometer can be an invaluable aid.

Figure 12-20 A commercial gemological refractometer. Note the polarizing filter, which allows separate measurement of the refractive indices of pleochroic materials. Image courtesy of Krüss Optronic, at www. kruess.de.

Mind Bending Refraction

Have you ever explained to a child that nothing can go faster than the speed of light? Inevitably, you will get the question "Ok, but if you *could* go faster than the speed of light, what would happen?"

Good for the kids. Asking such questions means that they are thinking outside of the box, and thinking outside of the box is usually necessary to arrive at creative, elegant solutions to the world's problems. So what if Einstein established the ultimate universal speed limit? See Chapter 11.3.1 for more on this.

Of course, as faceters, we recognize that this ultimate speed limit means that the refractive index of all materials must be greater than or equal to one.

Actually, it is not always so.

In fact, most materials exhibit a refractive index slightly less than one for very short wavelengths of light, for example high energy X-rays, which lie to the left of the ultraviolet in Figure 11-2. This has some pretty interesting consequences, not the least of which is a phenomenon known as total *external* reflection (read that again…yes, *external*). Total external reflection is used to produce high efficiency X-ray mirrors in space telescopes and other applications.

At this point, that pesky kid (bless his or her heart for reading Chapter 11) has already spotted the problem. If the refractive index is less than one, doesn't this mean that Einstein's rule has been broken? Doesn't this mean that something is going faster than the speed of light?

Well spotted. In fact, old Albert has an out. When speaking of electromagnetic waves, there are actually two types of speed, the *phase* velocity and the *group* velocity. The group velocity is the one that has to obey the speed limit, whereas the phase velocity is the one that is determined by the index of refraction. Normally, the distinction is not important, but watch out at X-ray wavelengths.

If thinking about refractive indices between zero and one bends your mind uncomfortably, fasten your safety belt and put on a helmet.

In the mid-1960's, a Russian theoretical physicist named Victor Veselago hypothesized that a substance with a *negative* refractive index could exist without violating the fundamental laws of physics. Such substances are known as *meta-materials*, and in fact, they have been produced in the laboratory in the last decade. So far, they work mostly at radio wavelengths (longward of the infrared in Figure 11-2), but optical materials are on the way.

A negative refractive index has some *really* interesting consequences. Snell's law still applies, but with one index being negative, the refracted light stays on the same side of the line perpendicular to the surface (see Figure 12-21). It turns out that this property can lead to essentially perfect optical lenses. Lord only knows what kind of gem performance this would produce (actually, probably not very good, since total internal reflection cannot occur). Finally, the Doppler effect is reversed – in other words, light from a source approaching you shifts to lower frequencies. If they actually produce this stuff in paint form, I'm tossing out my radar detector…

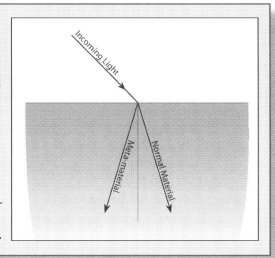

Figure 12-21 Metamaterials have a negative refractive index and bend the incoming light on the same side of the surface perpendicular.

12.6 Dispersion

Mother Nature has thrown us a bit of a curveball with birefringent and pleochroic materials: their refractive index and absorption properties change as a function of direction in the crystal, complicating our lives in terms of rough selection, orientation, and gem design (see Section 12.4). Yes, carefully navigating these waters can produce a jewel of profound beauty and mystery, but these effects can also wreck you on the rocky shores of muddy colours, over-dark gems, and fuzzy looking facets (to say nothing of overwrought metaphors).

If birefringence and pleochroism are a curveball, then *dispersion* is a nice slow pitch right over the middle of the plate (This is the last metaphor in this section. I promise). All real-world materials exhibit dispersion – a variation in refractive index with wavelength. Some particularly prized gem species are strongly dispersive, that is, the refractive index changes a lot.

If you've made it this far into this book, you almost certainly know that dispersion causes the "fire" in gemstones, the lovely flashes and interplay of colour that makes a diamond, well, a diamond. This fire arises due to our old friend, Snell's law (Chapter 11.4), and the wavelength dependence of the refractive index.

Here's how it works. When white light strikes a facet obliquely, the variation in refractive index with wavelength causes the transmitted rays to bend over a range of angles, spreading out into a little spectrum, just as with a prism. All gem materials have a higher refractive index for blue light than for red. Hence, the blue rays are bent more strongly (Figure 12-22).

From that point onward, the gem goes to work. Total internal reflection bounces the light around, and in a well-designed gemstone, sends most of it back out through the crown to our wondering eyes (see Section 10.4). The initial spread of angles means that different colours take different paths through the gem, however, and when the light emerges, it is full of sparkle, fire, and magic.

Of course, it is an oversimplification to credit the fire in a gemstone entirely to that initial dispersing of light on entry. First, and most obviously, the colours will be dispersed again

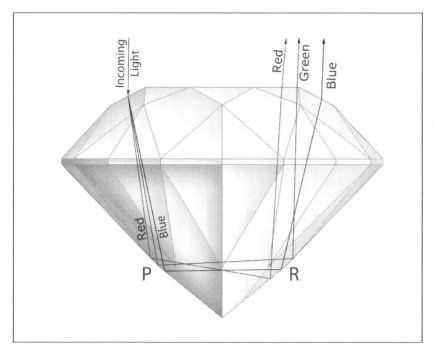

Figure 12-22 Dispersion in gemstones spreads the incident light by wavelength, creating flashes of colour known as fire. Note that there may be facet junctions at the points labeled P and R. The resulting discontinuity in refection angle will further split the colours.

when the light leaves the gem. Note that the bounce angle of total internal reflection does not depend on wavelength – it is a pure mirror-like or "specular" effect – but *whether* reflection occurs *will* vary with colour. For example, one can imagine ray directions within the gemstone that allow the red light (lower refractive index) to escape while causing total internal reflection of the blue. Finally, the initial dispersion of the light into a small rainbow can produce additional fire when that rainbow is split at facet edges (Figure 12-22).

Conversational Dispersion

I distinctly remember my first transatlantic trip in the early 1980's. Flying from Montreal to Brussels was like stepping into another world: the language was (more or less) the same, but literally everything else seemed different. This sense of remoteness was enhanced by my first attempt to call my family at home. In those days, you had to enter a shop-front telephone agency, pay your fee, and wait to be assigned to a telephone box.

However, the real surprise was the *delay*. At that time, most transatlantic communication relied on geosynchronous satellites, which are really far away: about 26,000 miles (42,000 km). Expressed in more relevant units, the round trip for the radio waves is about a third of a second, which can really screw up the natural rhythm of a two-way conversation.

Of course, all of this has changed, thanks to optical telecommunication fibers. Yes, the first transatlantic cable was laid more than a century and a half ago, but the capacity of copper wire limits the number of simultaneous conversations to a few tens, hundreds, or in the best case, thousands of calls. Nowadays, everything, including telephony, is digital, and engineers talk in terms of several terabytes of data per second for transatlantic fiber. To put that in perspective, such a cable can support about one and a half billion simultaneous conversations, more than enough to allow everyone in North America and Europe to chat on the phone at the same time.

Guess what limits the communication capacity of optical fiber...

Surprisingly, it is not absorption. The high-purity glass of modern optical fiber permits error free communication, even over hundreds of miles of transatlantic cable. Repeaters installed along the link re-boost the signal.

The real problem is *dispersion*, the same phenomenon that puts fire in our gemstones. Even the best fibers have a slight variation in refractive index with wavelength, and this means a slight difference in speed. The resulting dispersion causes a clean pulse at the input end of the fiber to be spread and eventually mixed with its neighbours, destroying the signal (Figure 12-23). Narrow wavelength-range laser light can help, but for really long cables, engineers install "dispersion compensators," specially prepared lengths of optical fiber with the opposite dispersion. These tighten up the pulses and preserve their precious information.

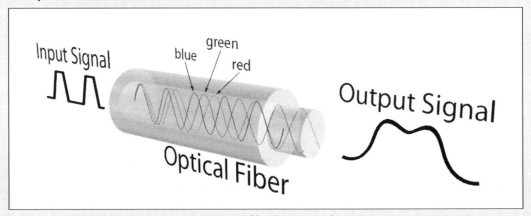

Figure 12-23 Dispersion in an optical fiber limits its information carrying capacity.

Some optical fibers display birefringence as well. This can cause problems because pulses with one polarization arrive earlier than those with the perpendicular polarization. (Careful readers will have spotted a problem: how can an amorphous material like glass be birefringent? It turns out that manufacturing flaws, external stress, and imperfections in the glass are the culprit. Although tiny, this birefringence can build up a significant effect over several thousand miles.)

There is a clever engineering solution to birefringence as well. Polarization maintaining fibers are the equivalent of fishermen's sunglasses (Figure 12-13), allowing only a single polarization to travel along the fiber.

I really don't think about it anymore, but every transatlantic telephone call is a tiny miracle of optical engineering, overcoming the effects of dispersion to place that family member only a tiny fraction of a second away.

12.6.1 Measuring Dispersion

Rainbows are visions, but only illusions, And rainbows have nothing to hide...

- Kermit the Frog, The Rainbow Connection
(music and lyrics by Paul Williams)

No indeed. Nothing to hide. In fact, the rainbow, and its gemological cousin, the spectrum, can tell a great deal about the nature and chemistry of the underlying gem material. Section 12.3 explains how absorption – essentially characteristic dark bands in the rainbow – leads to colour in a gemstone and can help in identification. This section focuses on how the change in refractive index across the spectrum, the *dispersion*, can be used as a characterization and identification tool.

How do you measure a rainbow? Or, more specifically, how do you characterize the amount of dispersion, the change in refractive index with wavelength?

There are a number of standardized metrics for quantifying dispersion. Some, such as the *Abbe number*, are best suited to optical design (see "A Gem-Cutter's Abbe Number?" on page 113). Dispersion relates to the change in refractive index with wavelength. Logically, then, any measure of dispersion should quantify this change. The most commonly used measurement in the mineralogical world is:

$$Dispersion = n_G - n_B$$

where the G and B subscripts refer to two very specific wavelengths, 4308 Å and 6867 Å, respectively. These are the wavelengths of the so-called B and G Fraunhofer lines, narrow dark absorption features seen in the Sun's spectrum (Figure 12-24). They are named after the early nineteenth century German optician Joseph von Fraunhofer, who in addition to discovering his eponymous absorption lines, invented the spectrometer (page 86) and developed a number of precision polishing machines. I think he would have liked faceting…

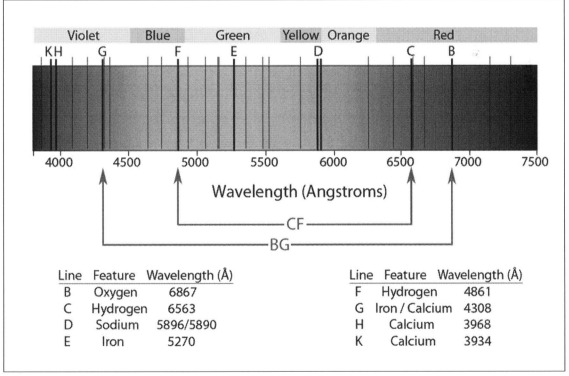

Line	Feature	Wavelength (Å)
B	Oxygen	6867
C	Hydrogen	6563
D	Sodium	5896/5890
E	Iron	5270

Line	Feature	Wavelength (Å)
F	Hydrogen	4861
G	Iron / Calcium	4308
H	Calcium	3968
K	Calcium	3934

Figure 12-24 A spectrum of the sun showing the Fraunhofer lines (top) and the wavelengths and chemical species represented by the prominent features (bottom). The arrows indicate the BG and CF line pairs commonly used to quantify dispersion. Turn to Section 12.3 and Chapter 11.2.1 to learn more about spectra.

The choice of the B and G Fraunhofer lines seems very reasonable, since the dispersion effectively measures the difference in refraction between red and violet light, the two ends of the visible spectrum. Note, however, that some references use the "CF" dispersion, that is, between 4861 Å and 6563 Å. The argument for this pair of lines is that they cover the "heart" of the spectrum visible to human eyes, not the extremes, and hence better represent the mix of lighting that your gemstone is likely to encounter.

Table 12-7 on page 105 lists the BG dispersion of some common gemstone materials. As noted earlier, Schumann and other sources listed in Chapter 9.3 provide a much more extensive compendium.

Ok. Enough history and tables. How do you actually *measure* dispersion?

Since dispersion is the variation of refractive index with wavelength, it seems obvious to use your trusty refractometer (see Section 12.5.3) and some coloured filters to measure the index at several wavelengths, for example, at the B and G Fraunhofer lines. Easy, right?

Wrong. Unfortunately this straightforward approach runs into a number of difficulties. The first and perhaps most challenging of these is the fact that commercial refractometers are calibrated at the factory to operate well at a single wavelength, usually yellow light around the sodium D line at 5890 Å (yes, this is another of Joseph von Fraunhofer's famous lines – see Figure 12-24). If you move far from the D line, the accuracy of the refractometer disperses, so to speak. For example, you are likely to derive a negative dispersion in many gem materials for which the dispersion is actually positive. There are published papers outlining schemes for correcting the measurements, but these rely on your knowing the optical constants of the glass hemisphere within the refractometer, and there is no guarantee of reliable results.

A more fundamental issue is that BG dispersion uses red and violet wavelengths that are close to the limit of normal human vision – yes, as mentioned above, this is a good argument for abandoning this standard in the gemological world. It is hard enough finding suitable filters. Locating light sources bright enough to work at these extreme wavelengths will just compound your headaches (literally).

Of course, using a refractometer to measure dispersion brings with it all the challenges and requirements of making a straight-up refractive index measurement. For instance, the sample must be reasonably well polished and have a large, flat facet.

Oh. One more thing. Many gemological refractometers come equipped with a fixed, yellow filter, precisely to isolate the wavelengths around the D line. As anyone who has watched late-night infomercials knows, yellow lenses block blue and violet light.

Actually, the best way to measure dispersion is with a lab bench spectrometer, a serious piece of hardware whose cost could easily dwarf that of your faceting machine. It is also a bit clumsy to haul around to gem shows.

The summary? If you are a serious gem purchaser or a hard-core amateur mineralogist, you should invest in a bench spectrometer. A reasonably experienced eyeball can distinguish between high and low dispersion gem materials, based on the amount of colour flashes or fire. Beyond that, you will probably want to rely on other material properties to help you in identification.

A Gem-Cutter's Abbe Number?

Optical designers select custom mixtures of glass from a catalog containing literally hundreds of different varieties. To help manage this diversity, the manufacturers organize their offerings by both refractive index and dispersion, the latter expressed as the so-called *Abbe Number*.

The Abbe Number honours Ernst Karl Abbe, who among many other achievements, helped lay the foundation of modern optics. He also invented the first refractometer (Section 12.5.3), married a woman named Else Snell (Chapter 11.4.1), and introduced the eight-hour workday to Europe. What's not to like about that?

The Abbe Number is a hybrid of both refractive index and dispersion. Specifically, the definition of Abbe Number V is:

$$V = \frac{n_d - 1}{n_F - n_C} \, ,$$

where n_d, n_F, and n_C are the refractive indices of the material at the wavelength of the associated Fraunhofer lines (see Figure 12-24 – note that the "d" line arises due to helium and is very close to the pair of sodium "D" lines).

Take a close look at this equation. From a lens designer's point of view, it makes a great deal of sense. These happy folk are in the business of producing powerful optics with a minimum of colour distortion – something they call *chromatic aberration*. Yes, for some reason, they don't actually like dispersion and fire.

More power means more light bending capability and hence a higher refractive index. Less colour problems means lower dispersion. Looking back at the equation, higher refractive index means a larger numerator and lower dispersion means a smaller denominator. The bottom line? Larger Abbe number means good glass.

My optical designer friends are now assembling large chunks of flint glass to hurl at my skull, because of course, the story is a great deal more complicated than this. Nevertheless, the Abbe number is a very useful way of comparing the optical performance of different glasses.

Why not an Abbe number for gems?

In our case, of course, we want both the refractive index and dispersion to be high. That's what puts the sparkle and fire in a diamond, after all.

If we reformulate the equation thus:

$$G = (n - 1) \cdot (n_F - n_C)$$

then higher index, higher dispersion material will have a higher Gem-Cutter's Abbe Number. Note that both this equation and the original Abbe Number formula use the more sensible CF range of wavelengths. Sharp-eyed readers will also recognize that I have replaced one of the subscripts: rather than being restricted to yellow, helium "d" light, the Gem-Cutter's Abbe number uses the average refractive index n of the material across different samples, wavelengths, polarization states, crystallographic axes, and so forth.

Figure 12-25 shows the Gem-Cutter's Abbe Number for common gemstone materials presented in a format that will be warmly familiar to all optical designers (so you can put the glass chunks back down, please).

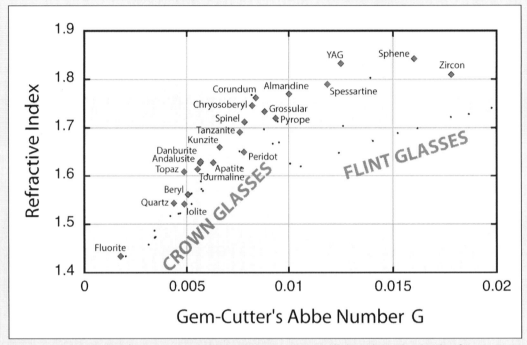

Figure 12-25 A chart of Gem-Cutter's Abbe Number, G. The small dots show the G value for common commercial glasses. Data for gem materials are from Schumann (see Chapter 9).

A couple of conclusions almost jump out of this plot. First, there are a few gem types that perform significantly better than others. That is, they have a higher G value than the bulk of materials with the same refractive index. Peridot and zircon are obvious examples.

The second conclusion is that my optical designer friends were right: the situation is indeed more complicated, and there are in fact, many optical glasses that outperform gemstones based on this criterion, sometimes spectacularly so. In fact, to achieve top performance, glassmakers deliberately formulate mixtures with strong dispersion that can be used to correct the chromatic aberration of other lens elements in the system. The figure also clearly shows why they were preparing to hurl flint-type glass at my skull…

12.7 Other Optical Properties

12.7.1 Transparency

Transparency measures the amount of light that can pass through a gemstone. For example, a material with intensely saturated absorption will not be transparent (see Section 12.3.4). Inclusions (Section 12.12) can also affect transparency. Foreign matter, air bubbles, and fractures will all scatter and absorb photons, reducing the fraction of light transmitted through the stone.

Gems that are partially transparent due to inclusions are termed *sleepy* or *milky* if the amount of internal scattering is low to moderate. Increased scattering to the point where light can pass through, but images cannot, leads to a stone being labeled *translucent* (think waxed paper). When inclusions, grains, and internal fibers block all light transmission, the material is deemed *opaque*.

Needless to say, faceters deal almost exclusively with transparent gemstones.

12.7.2 Luster

Luster describes the appearance of a gem in light reflected off its surface, and it depends on both the refractive index and surface properties of the stone (but not its colour). Recall from Chapter 11.8 that the refractive index determines how much light reflects from the gem due to "Fresnel loss," with higher indices leading to more reflection and greater luster. Some textbooks group other optical effects, such as cat's eye and schiller, under the rubric of luster, but these are strictly internal phenomena (see below).

Scientists classify the subjective appearance of a mineral's luster using a number of terms, such as *adamantine*, *vitreous*, or *resinous*. As indicated in Table 12-8, both reflection effects and the smoothness and microstructure of the surface determine the type of luster.

Table 12-8 Luster categorization. Additional terms, such as metallic, earthy, and waxy, exist for minerals but are not relevant to transparent, facetable gemstones.

Luster Type	Origin
Adamantine	Surface reflections, high polish, high refractive index (greater than 1.9); examples: diamond
Sub-adamantine	Surface reflections, high polish, medium high refractive index; examples: corundum, garnet
Vitreous (glassy)	Surface reflections, high polish, low to moderate refractive index; examples: many, including quartz, topaz, beryl, tourmaline, etc.
Resinous	Resin-like surface texture; example: amber
Greasy	Surface alteration and microscopic inclusions; examples: opal, iolite, halite
Pearly	Surface cleavages; examples: pearls, moonstone, talc
Silky	Fibrous grain; example: selenite

12.7.3 Cat's Eyes and Star-Stones

One of the very first and most prized stones in my mineral collection is a polished tiger-eye, purchased from a tourist gift shop on one of many family camping trips. I remember rocking the stone back and forth in wonder, marveling at how something so solid could look so liquid.

Cat's eyes and star-stones are the popular names for gems exhibiting the optical properties known more formally as *chatoyancy* and *asterism*. These phenomena occur when thread-like inclusions in a gemstone scatter the incoming light, sometimes in spectacular and un-expected ways.

If the inclusions are randomly aligned, or if the stone is not cut to enhance the effect, normal cha-toyancy occurs. This is what put the liquid magic in my piece of tiger-eye. When the threads are aligned along one direction, the scattered light forms a sin-gle band across the gem, producing the vertical slit effect known as "cat's-eye." Chrysoberyl, tourma-line, corundum, quartz, spinel and moonstone can display cat's eye. Formally, you should refer to only chatoyant chrysoberyl as cat's-eye; the others are denoted "cat's-eye quartz," "cat's-eye tourmaline," etc. Synthetics do exist (Figure 12-26).

Figure 12-26 A marble formed from synthetic cat's-eye glass.

The rarest and most highly prized form of this phenomenon occurs when the fibrous inclu-sions align along more than one crystal axis, producing the four or six-rayed magic of star-stones. Known formally as *asteria*, the star-stone effect appears most commonly in corundum. The Star of Bombay, a 182 carat blue star sapphire, is perhaps the best known of these gems. Two interesting facts about the Star of Bombay: it once belonged to Mary Pickford, and its entrancing colour was the inspiration for Bombay Sapphire gin.

Note that chatoyancy and asterism rarely go together with faceting. In order to enhance the visual effect, craftsmen almost always cut such gems *en cabochon*.

12.7.4 Wave Effects

The wave nature of light leads to all kinds of wonderful effects in gemstones. These include the fancifully named phenomena of iridescence, adularescence and labradorescence.

All of these effects result from the overlap of different light waves, whose direction and phase have been modified by structures on the surface or within the body of the gemstone (review the material in Chapter 11.2 if you don't understand the concept of light waves and phase).

For example, *iridescence* results from the interaction of light waves with uniformly spaced irregularities in a gem. These irregularities can be small fibrous inclusions or even variations in refractive index. This produces *diffraction*, the bending of light waves by obstacles whose size is comparable to the wavelength. Diffraction is what puts the rainbow of colours in the hologram on your credit card. Closer to our hearts, iridescence creates the bewitching play of colour in precious opal and the ethereal shades of "orient" on the surface of pearls. It also leads to the rainbow hues of twinning planes and internal fractures (see Section 12.12).

Adularescence is a special type of iridescence in which diffraction produced by alternating layers of two mineral types creates a milky glow that seems to arise from the heart of the gem. In moonstone, the best-known mineral displaying adularescence, the layers are sodium feldspar (albite) and potassium feldspar (orthoclase). Most moonstones display a whitish glow, but blue and orange specimens do occur. Other gem types, such as opal, quartz, and agate, can display adularescence, although the phenomenon is commonly termed "opalescence" for opals and "girasol" for quartz.

Labradorescence appears in (unsurprisingly) labradorite, as well as spectrolite, both feldspar minerals which contain thin layers of inter-grown twinning crystals. These layers produce highly directional colour. Hence, labradorite and spectrolite require careful orientation.

As with chatoyancy and asterism, most cutters opt for a cabochon form to highlight these wave phenomena. A prominent exception is contra-luz opal, which can produce spectacular faceted gemstones (Figure 12-27).

Figure 12-27 A faceted contra-luz opal displaying iridescence. This gem was cut well below the critical angle and mounted in front of a piece of black tourmaline to highlight the internal play of colour. The symbol appears due to unpolished facets. Normal lighting conditions (left) and side lit (right). This black and white image really doesn't do justice to the gem. See the original picture at http://www.boghome.com/ TomsPages/MyDesigns/OPace.html.

12.7.5 Aventurescence and Schiller

Aventurescence is an optical effect produced by tiny plate-like inclusions in a mineral. Unlike the wave effects described in the previous section, aventurescence does not rely on the wave nature of light. Instead, the platelets act like small mirrors, creating a glittering effect referred to as *schiller*. Aventurine feldspar, known more familiarly as sunstone, is the most prominent gem of this type and it is a favourite among faceters. Quartz can also display aventurescence, and there are synthetics. Note that mineralogists occasionally refer to adularescent and labradorescent displays as "schiller." With the prominent exception of sunstone, most aventurescent gems are cut en cabochon.

12.7.6 Fluorescence

Some materials, including some well-known gemstone types, have the ability to absorb photons of one wavelength and then re-emit that light energy at a completely different wavelength. The catch-all term for this physical process is *photoluminescence*. When the incoming photons are ultraviolet and the re-radiated light is visible, mineralogists speak of *fluorescence* (see Section 11.2.1 for more on ultraviolet light). The term is a natural, since the phenomenon was first observed in fluorite.

Fluorescence arises due to the gemstone's chemical makeup or as a result of flaws in its crystal structure. Typically, scientists characterize ultraviolet (UV) photons as either short wave (SW – those with wavelengths below 2540 Å), or long wave (LW – with wavelengths between 2540 and 3660 Å). Most of the "cardinal" gemstones (see Chapter 1.1.2) fluoresce under UV light. The exact type of response to SW and LW can be a powerful diagnostic tool for identifying the source region of a gem, and in particular if that source region is inside a high-tech factory.

About a third of natural white diamonds fluoresce blue, which occasionally surprises their owners at the discotheque (see page 52). Natural Mogok rubies also fluoresce, while specimens from other localities contain trace impurities of iron oxide and do not. Iron, it turns out, can completely suppress fluorescence. In emeralds, fluorescence can point to foul play: natural emeralds generally do not respond to UV light, while common synthetics glow red. Also, many of the crack-filling and other cosmetic materials applied to emerald will fluoresce. See Chapter 13.2 for more on emerald treatments.

Despite these high profile exceptions, fluorescence should only be used as supporting evidence in gem identification, since many species exhibit fluorescence that can vary wildly in strength from sample to sample.

12.8 Density

Have you ever hefted a piece of silver (colourless) topaz? It's worth trying if you haven't already done so. To the untrained eye or casual expert observer, a chunk of clear topaz may resemble quartz, but there is no way to confuse the two once they are in your hands. The difference, of course, is in their *density*.

Density, usually denoted by the Greek letter ρ (rho), is a physical property of all materials given by the ratio of mass m to volume V:

$$\rho = \frac{m}{V}$$

Silver topaz, for example, has a density of about 3.5 grams per cubic centimeter, whereas quartz is about a third less dense at 2.6 g/cc. Common gemstone materials range over a factor of approximately five in their bulk density, from amber (ρ = 1.1 g/cc) to cubic zirconia (ρ = 5.7 g/cc), but most lie in the range 2.5-3.5.

Differences in density can provide more than tactile surprise. If you have tried faceting a variety of materials, you have no doubt been pleasantly surprised at the carat weight of that modest-sized garnet, or equivalently been disappointed at the trifling weight of a pretty big amethyst.

Figure 12-28 puts this into direct visual perspective. It illustrates the relative size of a 1-carat gemstone cut from various materials. Of course, the corollary is also true: various gemstone types of identical physical size will have dramatically different carat weight.

While Figure 12-28 shows that a one carat amber gem is physically much more imposing than a one-carat sapphire, this is, needless to say, not the entire story. Anyone who has seen faceted amber next to a sapphire knows that other factors beyond pure size come into play when it comes down to visual impact.

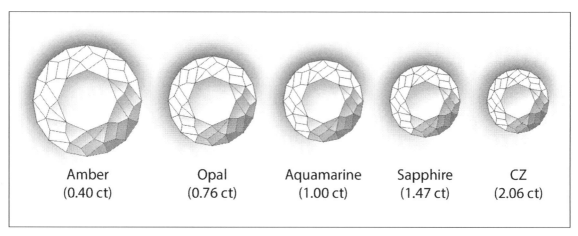

Amber   Opal   Aquamarine   Sapphire   CZ
(0.40 ct)   (0.76 ct)   (1.00 ct)   (1.47 ct)   (2.06 ct)

Figure 12-28 The relative size of identically cut, 1-carat gemstones of various materials. The label also includes a number in brackets indicating the carat weight of a gem of that material cut to the identical size as the aquamarine in the middle. This is the fabulous Viviant design, a creation of David Thompson, who introduced me to faceting (also see "Reinventing the Split" on page 229).

Note also that the figure assumes an identical gem design, with no account made for differing index of refraction. It is a pleasant side effect of how the Universe is put together that higher density materials tend to have higher refractive index as well (see "What You See is What You Get…" below). This means that you can generally cut a shallower stone from denser material, without having light leak out of the bottom of the gem. A shallower stone will have a larger top-view outline for the same total weight, and hence Figure 12-28 somewhat overstates the situation (if you didn't understand the last two sentences, it's time to review the material in the first half of this chapter).

What You See is What You Get…

Are the optical and physical properties of gemstones related?

Specifically, is there a relationship between the optical property of refraction and the physical property of density?

The adjacent text mentions that topaz looks like quartz, but is substantially more dense. If you have picked up and examined a few hundred pieces of gem rough in your life, you almost certainly have the subconscious notion that higher index materials, such as garnet and zircon, also tend to be heavier. This is why topaz is so surprising.

Figure 12-29 plots the refractive index of common gemstone types versus their bulk density and confirms this subconscious notion: with a few exceptions (including topaz), most gem materials follow a linear relation between these two quantities.

You will not be surprised to learn that others have thought of this and generated similar plots in the past. In fact, the empirical relation between density and refractive index has been recognized for a century and a half.

The Gladstone-Dale law, named after the British chemist John Hall Gladstone and the Reverend T. P. Dale, expresses this linear relationship:

$$n = \text{const} \cdot \rho + 1$$

Of course, as with any empirical law, the Gladstone-Dale relation shows *how* one thing correlates with another, but not *why*. Somewhat mysteriously, minerals with a mean molecular weight of about 20 show the tightest correlation (the mean molecular weight is the total number of protons and neutrons in a molecule divided by the number of atoms). This group of minerals includes many familiar gemstones, such as quartz, peridot, garnet, spinel, and corundum.

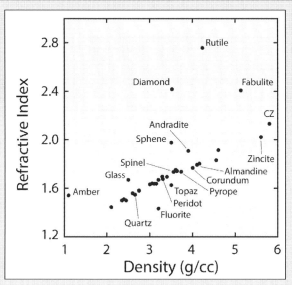

Figure 12-29 *A comparison of the refractive index and density of common gemstone materials. With the exception of a few outliers, there is a strong correlation between the two properties.*

The reasons for this are complex and not completely understood. It is nice to know that there is still plenty to learn about even the simplest properties of gemstones...

12.8.1 Density of Common Gemstone Materials

However you feel about the relative value and aesthetics of gemstone size versus sparkle (Section 12.8), it is clear that density can be used to distinguish one material from another. Table 12-9 lists the density of common gemstones. As always, references in Chapter 9.3, especially Schumann's *Gemstones of the World*, provide a much more complete compilation.

Table 12-9 *The density of common gemstone materials.*

Gem Material	Density (g/cc)	Gem Material	Density (g/cc)
Amber	1.05 - 1.09	Glass (Obsidian)	2.35 - 2.60
Andalusite	3.05 - 3.20	Iolite	2.58 - 2.66
Apatite	3.16 - 3.23	Opal	1.98 - 2.50
Beryl	2.66 - 2.87	Peridot	3.28 - 3.48
Chrysoberyl	3.70 - 3.78	Quartz	2.65
Corundum	3.95 - 4.05	Scapolite	2.57 - 2.74
Cubic Zirconia	5.6 - 6.0	Sphene	3.52 - 3.54
Danburite	2.97 - 3.03	Spinel	3.54 - 3.63
Diamond	3.50 - 3.53	Tanzanite	3.35
Feldspar/Sunstone	2.62 - 2.65	Topaz	3.49 - 3.57
Fluorite	3.00 - 3.25	Tourmaline	2.82 - 3.32
Garnet	3.41 - 4.30	Zircon	3.93 - 4.73

12.8.2 Measuring Density

If all we had to deal with was topaz and quartz, the technique of identifying gemstones by density would be easy and literally at our fingertips. Unfortunately, as Table 12-9 makes clear, a number of materials of similar visual appearance can also have similar density. For example, red spinel (ρ = 3.6 g/cc), rhodolite garnet (ρ = 3.8 g/cc), and ruby (ρ = 4.0 g/cc) can have a very similar look and heft. There can be no mistaking the differences at the cash register, however.

Given that it is such an accessible physical property, it should be easy to measure and compare the density of gemstone materials. Right?

Well, half right, anyway.

While the techniques for identifying gems by density are straightforward in principle, they can be somewhat trickier in practice. For example, they all presume that the stone is not mounted in jewelry. The classic gemological method is to see whether the sample floats in a liquid of known density. If it floats, the gem is less dense, and if it sinks, more dense. For a more accurate measure, the intrepid investigator can dilute a solution in which the stone sinks until the gem becomes exactly neutrally buoyant. The amount of added water allows a straightforward calculation of the density. Note that this method is not necessarily very wasteful of expensive testing fluid, since the solution can be restored to its original, reference density by evaporation in a steam bath.

Density versus Specific Gravity

You like potato and I like potahto, You like tomato and I like tomahto Potato, potahto, Tomato, tomahto, Let's call the whole thing off..."
— George and Ira Gershwin

As with the Gershwin brothers' famous vegetables, density and specific gravity are essentially two different ways of saying the exact same thing (and if you argue that tomatoes are fruit, the US Supreme Court disagrees – look it up).

Technically speaking, density is always expressed in units of mass per unit volume, such as grams per cubic centimeter or slugs per cubic foot (for non-American readers: this is not a joke). The specific gravity of a sample, on the other hand, is actually its density relative to a reference material, and hence has no units. However, since the reference material is water, and since water has a density of 1 g/cc, the answer comes out the same, at least for gemcutters and others who use the metric system.

For example, beryl has a density of 2.7 grams per cubic centimeter and a specific gravity of 2.7. For example, you like potato, and I like potahto...

By the way, for my American readers: beryl has a density of 5.24 slugs per cubic foot, but its specific gravity is still 2.7. In an amazing coincidence, my tomato/tomahto patch also has a density of 5.24 slugs per cubic foot, at least during harvest season (yes, this time it was a joke).

Ok. Just a few more words for the propeller-heads....

All water is not the same, and specific gravity is usually measured against a particular type of water, namely pure H_2O at 4°C (39.2° F). It turns out that water actually contracts between its freezing point at 0° C and plus four degrees, and then expands as it continues to warm. Therefore, pure water is most dense at 4 degrees, and scientists use this as a reference.

Is there a real difference after all? Well, the density of pure H_2O at 4°C is not exactly one gram per cubic centimeter – it's actually closer to 0.999972 g/cc. Therefore, technically speaking, the density and specific gravity of a substance according to these conditions differ by about one part in thirty-five thousand. Happy now? I didn't think so. Let's call the whole thing off…

The problem is that suitable liquids for the range of gemstone densities are few, far between, and generally very toxic. They include the charming fluid known as Clerici's solution, a witches-brew with the formal chemical name of thallium-formate-thallium-malonate. Its Material Safety Data Sheet (MSDS) reads like a script for a bad horror movie. As with many of the immersion fluids (see Chapter 4.5), you probably want to keep your distance.

Ok. Scrap the nasty fluids. Why not just measure the mass and volume directly? The mass is easy, since you probably already have accurate carat scales at hand, (Chapter 4.14).

So far so good, but the difficulty arises with measuring the volume. If we faceted cubes, the solution would be straightforward, since accurate calipers are standard equipment (Chapter 4.17), and the formula to calculate the volume of a cube from its edge length is pretty simple. Of course, a cube is a notoriously bad shape in terms of optical performance, and the gems we actually cut are of considerably more complex form.

A Sense of Scale, A Scale of Sense

Nerdy physics purists will point out at this stage that our scales measure weight, not mass, and that they should read out in Newtons, not grams or (yikes!) pound-force, not slugs. Of course, nerdy physics purists never get invited to the right kind of parties, so why should we listen to them?

Cool physics purists will point out to the people clustering around them that our fancy scales are calibrated to read out grams directly, provided that we operate them under standard conditions, that is, with normal gravity acting on them. And normal gravity is an absolute prerequisite for the right kind of party…

One option is to evaluate the volume of a gemstone using a tool such as GemCAD, which provides the volume-to-width ratio of a particular cut. Extracting the volume from the measured width is a snap (see Chapter 10.8.3).

Of course, this strategy assumes that you have the correct GemCAD file for the stone in question and that the cutter followed the instructions exactly. You also need to factor in the thickness of the girdle, which GemCAD output does not provide (see page 44). Finally, in many instances, you want to identify a gem material in rough form, long before it has reached its final, geometrically perfect and measurable shape.

Aha! you exclaim. Measuring the volume of irregular objects is easy – just drop the gem rough into a test tube filled with water and measure how much the water rises.

Again, this is simple in principle but difficult in practice. The so-called displacement technique works fine for boulders and engine blocks, but can get very tricky for small objects. A one gram sample of typical gemstone material is actually fairly tiny – seven or so millimeters on a side. Most of us don't have access to graduated cylinders of sufficient accuracy to measure the displacement of such small objects properly.

All is not lost, however. With a little patience, wire, and solder, you can fabricate a device for measuring the density of mineral samples with sufficient accuracy to distinguish rhodolite from ruby. We owe this invention to an ancient Greek mathematician and physicist named Archimedes. His famous Principle states that an object in a fluid experiences an upward, buoyant force equivalent to the weight of water it displaces. To calculate the density, all you have to do is measure the sample in air and in water. Still confused? Turn to Chapter 20.2 for a complete description of how Archimedes' Principle yields the density, and how you can build your own gizmo for identifying gemstones.

12.9 Hardness

When I was a kid, my grandfather would occasionally impart the following words of wisdom to me: "All men are created equal. It's just that some are more equal than others..." This would inevitably elicit a knowing nod and chuckle from me. A somewhat tentative knowing nod and chuckle, mind you, since I didn't have the slightest idea what he was talking about.

Now that I find myself in a similar position with respect to my own progeny, I tend to keep my mouth shut on the issue. This is for at least three good reasons. First, I believe that all men are created *different*, thank God. Second, knowing nods and chuckles from my children make me nervous, and third, I still don't have the slightest idea what my grandfather was talking about.

Difference is good, and in fact, if it weren't for differences, we wouldn't be able to enjoy the hobby we love. In particular, we are totally dependent on the difference in hardness of various materials when we cut gemstones. Our laps are impregnated with diamond, the hardest known natural substance, in order to remove gem material efficiently and consistently. If not diamond, we use aluminum oxide, which is corundum, the second hardest known natural substance.

Rubbing hard things against less hard things is the best way to make those less hard things look the way we want. Imagine trying to cut an amethyst with a quartz lap. Even worse, imagine cutting a chrysoberyl with it. Of course, only diamonds can cut other diamonds, and this has lead to all sorts of black magic to get the job done (see page 125).

In addition to serving your abrasive needs, differences in hardness can be a useful diagnostic for identifying gem materials. Also, hardness can and should influence your choice of cutting and polishing laps, and once the stone is complete, your mounting strategy. For example, household dust contains significant amounts of quartz, which has a Mohs hardness of 7 (see next section). It also contains a great deal of dead human skin cells, pollen, hair, and other things, which, though disgusting, are unlikely to damage your gemstones. Nevertheless, daily wear and tear can dull the polish of softer gems, particularly if they are mounted in rings. Anyone, like me, with a high school signet ring containing a cheapo glass "gem" can attest to that. The bottom line? Choose a pendant or earring setting for softer materials.

Origins: Pliny the Elder on Faceting

Given the central importance to human culture of manufacturing and shaping things, it should come as no surprise that knowledge of the relative hardness of natural materials goes back a long way. In fact, almost two millennia ago, Pliny the Elder mentioned embedding diamond in iron, in order to work on hard stones:

When, by good fortune, this stone (adamas or diamond) does happen to be broken, it divides into fragments so minute as to be almost imperceptible. These particles are held in great request by engravers, who enclose them in iron, and are enabled thereby, with the greatest facility, to cut the very hardest substances known...
- Pliny the Elder, *Historia Naturalis*, 37, 15

Figure 12-30 A portrait of Pliny the Elder from the 19th century. This portrait is the artist's impression. Unfortunately, we don't really know what the great man looked like, since no contemporary image has survived. See the frontispiece to this book and multiple references in the index, especially page 154, for more on Pliny.

Incidentally, for the geographical and technological circumstances in which Pliny found himself, it now appears unlikely that he was referring to tools impregnated with diamond. Emery, a naturally occurring abrasive consisting mostly of corundum, seems a much more likely candidate for Pliny's *adamas*.

Our amazement at Pliny's ancient description of modern faceting technique should be tempered somewhat by context. The same section which describes the embedding of abrasive particles in iron also points out that adamas "neutralizes poisons, dispels delirium, and banishes groundless perturbations of the mind..." Pliny also notes that the only way to cut a diamond is by repeated blows from the finest tempered iron, but this only works after steeping the gem thoroughly in the warm, fresh blood of a he-goat. Perhaps this is worth trying next time on that stubborn, scratch-prone facet?

12.9.1 Hardness of Common Gemstone Materials

It is clear from the discussion of the previous section that the hardness of a particular gemstone material has a direct impact on the cutting process. For example, with a given lap, it will take more work to produce a certain gem design in sapphire than in amber, since corundum is hard and amber is less hard. This difference can also help in material identification.

Of course, vague descriptions such as "hard" and "less hard" are of limited value in establishing cutting strategy or identification – you need an objective measure or physical unit that characterizes hardness.

This isn't so easy. Unlike density, which is the natural ratio of physically measurable properties (mass and volume), hardness is a more abstract concept. You can't go down to the corner hardware store and buy a hardness measuring device.

Directional Differential Hardness

While hardness is a useful property for identifying gem materials, it can get a bit tricky.

This is due to the fact that hardness relates directly to the strength of the chemical bonds holding the crystal lattice together, and these bonds can be different along different directions. This produces *directional differential hardness*, a fancy way of saying that a gem exhibits different hardness when tested in different orientations.

The result can occasionally be dramatic. Kyanite, a lovely blue polymorph (see page 82) of andalusite, has Mohs hardness 4-5 parallel to the c-axis and 7-7.5 perpendicular to the c-axis. Needless to say, cutting Kyanite without attention to this property leads to problems. Corundum also exhibits this type of behaviour.

In some crystals, the edges can be harder than the faces. For example, the edge or vertex of a topaz crystal can scratch the face of another otherwise identical stone.

Diamonds are perhaps the best example of the importance of directional differential hardness, In fact, were it not for the property that its crystals exhibit different hardness along different directions, it would be all but impossible to cut and polish diamond. Orientation is everything in the diamond-cutting world, since you have to arrange to bring the hard grain of the diamond in your tool into contact with the soft grain in the gem being cut. In practical terms, this means identifying the "on grain" direction of the gem and forcing it against the randomly oriented crystals of bort embedded in the cutting wheel. Happily, diamond forms in the cubic or isometric crystal system (Section 12.10), and hence exhibits no birefringence or pleochroism (Section 12.4). This means that concerns about direction-dependent colour and facet splitting are not an issue, and gem orientation is purely a matter of optimizing the shape of the rough with respect to the best cutting directions. Want to learn more? Wykoff's *The Techniques of Master Faceting* contains an entire chapter on diamond cutting. Chapter 9 will help you track down this and other reference works.

What to do?

Go with what you know. If object A can do some serious damage to object B without suffering much damage itself, then object A is harder than object B. This is the basis of the so-called scratch test, which has been credited to the 19th century German geologist Friedrich Mohs. In fact, this most common method for assessing the hardness of minerals dates back to Pliny, who not only recognized that diamond was really "hard", but also pointed out that counterfeit gems could be identified by what they can scratch and what can scratch them (see "Origins: Pliny the Elder on Faceting" opposite and page 141).

Although he may not have been first, Mohs was certainly more systematic than his forebears, and his eponymous test of hardness forms the basis for the most common measure, the Mohs hardness scale. Table 12-10 lists the reference materials that define the Mohs hardness scale. It also includes values for a couple of additional types of hardness measurement described in Section 12.9.3.

Table 12-11 shows the Mohs hardness for the most common gemstone materials. As always, better and more complete listings appear in the reference books listed in Chapter 9.3.

Table 12-10 Hardness and cutting resistance scales. Each of the reference minerals can scratch those of lower hardness and, in turn, be scratched by those of higher hardness. See text for details.

Reference Material	Mohs Scratch Hardness	Knoop Hardness	Cutting Resistance (Rosiwal)
Talc	1	1	0.03
Gypsum	2	32	1.25
Calcite	3	135	4.5
Fluorite	4	163	5
Apatite	5	430	6.5
Orthoclase	6	560	37
Quartz	7	820	120
Topaz	8	1340	175
Corundum	9	2100	1,000
Diamond	10	7000	140,000

Table 12-11 The Mohs hardness of common gemstone materials.

Gem Material	Mohs Hardness	Gem Material	Mohs Hardness
Amber	2 - 2.5	Glass (Obsidian)	5 - 5.5
Andalusite	6.5 - 7.5	Iolite	7 - 7.5
Apatite	5	Opal	5.5 - 6.5
Beryl	7.5 - 8	Peridot	6.5 - 7
Chrysoberyl	8.5	Quartz	7
Corundum	9	Scapolite	5.5 - 6
Cubic Zirconia	8.25 - 8.5	Sphene	5 - 5.5
Danburite	7 - 7.5	Spinel	8
Diamond	10	Tanzanite	6.5 - 7
Feldspar/Sunstone	6 - 6.5	Topaz	8
Fluorite	4	Tourmaline	7 - 7.5
Garnet	6.5 - 7.5	Zircon	6.5 - 7.5

12.9.2 Measuring Mohs Scratch Hardness

Measuring the Mohs scratch hardness of a valuable gemstone couldn't be easier. Just take a bunch of other valuable gemstones of known type and have at it. Nothing could be easier, particularly in comparison to explaining the aftermath to the owner of said valuable gemstones.

Yes, measuring hardness in this manner is far from the ideal of a "non-destructive test." In fact, it is largely for this reason that the Mohs scratch hardness test has been abandoned for all practical purposes in the gem trade. Other diagnostics, including observation of the optical properties, crystal habit, and density, are not only effective in identifying gem materials but also have the salubrious property of not inciting violence in the owner.

If you absolutely must try a scratch test, take a few sensible precautions. First, begin the test with the softest reference materials. If you try to identify an amethyst starting with diamond and working your way down through corundum and topaz, you will end up with three hideous scratches on your stone, rather than one. Second, pick a location on the sample where any damage you cause will be less noticeable. For a cut gem, this will be on the girdle. Finally, avoid cracked or otherwise imperfect surfaces. A crumbly zone can easily mimic a softer material.

12.9.3 Other Hardness Measures

There are many ways to skin a cat, and as you will see, there are many ways to destroy your valuable gemstone while trying to measure its hardness.

Sclerometer

The sclerometer is a device for performing the Mohs scratch test using a diamond pyramid under somewhat controlled conditions, hence yielding a more objective measure of hardness. There are two basic types of sclerometer. The first presses the diamond against the sample with a known, fixed force. The width of the resulting scratch then gives the hardness. The second type has a calibrated variable load. The operator steadily increases the force until a scratch appears, at which point the force is noted and translated to hardness.

Knoop, Vickers, and Brinnel Hardness Tests

These three types of test measure the effect of a known force driving an indenter into a sample. The extent of plastic deformation relates directly to the hardness. The Knoop hardness test is the most appropriate to gemology, since it involves a very small, elongated diamond pyramid and a correspondingly small amount of damage. The dimensions of the dent give the hardness value. The Vickers method is very similar, although the diamond indenter is usually a square, not elongated, pyramid, and the test is usually on a larger scale – larger forces, larger damage, and less precise measuring equipment. The Brinnel technique uses a spherical indenter, but is in most other respects comparable to Vickers. All three of these hardness tests find wide application in the field of metallurgy, but they are rarely used on gemstones.

Rosiwal Cutting Resistance

The Rosiwal test takes a completely different approach. Rather than assigning a hardness value based on a sample's resistance to scratching or indentation, the Rosiwal scale relates to how well a material can stand up to *abrasion*. Developed in the 1890's by the Austrian geologist August Rosiwal, this test involves grinding the sample against a fixed amount of calibrated abrasive until the abrasive is worn out and the cutting action ceases. The difference in weight of the sample before and after grinding provides a measure of its hardness. (Parenthetical remark: Details of the Rosiwal test are quite difficult to dig up. I found the foregoing information in a scholarly research article on the effect of studded snow tires on various types of road surface – the reference appears in Chapter 9.4.)

Table 12-10 lists the Mohs hardness, Knoop indentation, and Rosiwal cutting resistance values for the standard set of reference materials. A quick scan of the table makes it clear that an objective, simple, measure of hardness for gemstones remains an elusive goal. For example,

Mohs, Knoop, and Rosiwal seem to have quite different opinions on the relative hardness of corundum and diamond. Coupled with the fact that all of the methods described above are in one way or another fairly destructive (see page 126), this variability means that hardness has fallen out of favour since the time of Pliny as a way of identifying gemstones.

Despite these difficulties, Table 12-10 makes one point crystal clear: the standard Mohs scale is far from linear. Numerical differences aside, the more "objective" measures of hardness (Knoop and Rosiwal) can provide real guidance to faceters. For example, the increase in hardness from quartz to topaz (Mohs 7 to 8) is less than that from topaz to corundum (Mohs 8 to 9). Of course, if you have ever cut a sapphire, you knew this already.

You Think You're Tough? You're Not So Tough...

Have you ever watched a Formula 1 car race? Despite all the over-the-top commercialism and extravagant burning of fossil fuels, the Formula 1 circus is a showcase for some pretty impressive technologies. Nowhere is this more evident than in the field of materials science, exemplified by high tech composites like carbon fiber, which has largely replaced the steel and aluminum of the traditional automobile chassis.

Carbon fiber is amazing. Lighter than steel, yet considerably stronger, it has enabled manufacturers to develop racing cars that can reach 220 miles per hour (350 kph) with relatively modest-displacement 100 cubic inch (1.6 liter) engines. Carbon fiber has also enabled most drivers to walk away from some pretty horrific looking accidents.

Carbon fiber has a weakness, however, and it is the same weakness shared by its chemical cousin, the diamond. Both materials, while hard, are not *tough*. This comes as a bit of a surprise to racing fans, when they see shards of carbon fiber flying about at the slightest contact between cars, and to gem aficionados, who view diamond as the ultimate, resilient gemstone.

Materials scientists, including that breed known as mineralogists, distinguish between the *hardness* of a material and its *toughness*. Hardness measures how difficult it is to scratch a particular sample, while toughness relates to its resistance to breaking and chipping.

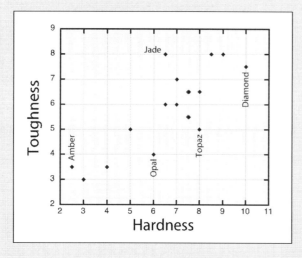

For most materials, the two go more or less hand-in-hand (Figure 12-31), but there are prominent exceptions and diamond is one of them. It is the king of gemstones (page 5 of Volume 1). A diamond is forever (page 81). And it is the hardest known natural substance (Table 12-10). It just ain't that tough. This turns out to be a

Figure 12-31 The toughness of common gemstone materials as a function of their hardness. Adapted from table 15 of Vargas' Faceting for Amateurs (see Chapter 9.1).

good thing, actually, since it is diamond's susceptibility to impact that permits the initial cleaving of the crystal in the cutting process. You don't even have to soak it in goat's blood (see page 124).

Topaz is another clear outlier. Although quite hard (Mohs 8), its perfect cleavage means greater sensitivity to a well-directed blow and hence reduced toughness.

Jade is a fascinating counterexample. With a hardness of 6.5, you would be forgiven for thinking that it is somewhat delicate and not suitable for really rough-and-tumble circumstances. Jade, however, is one of the toughest gemstones that we know, due to its fibrous microcrystalline structure. In fact, in addition to producing lovely faceted and carved gems, jade has been used over the centuries for some pretty extreme purposes, including as anvils and axe blades (see Figure 8-19). No word yet on its applicability to Formula 1 racing…

12.10 Crystal Systems

Who knew?

Who knew that the geometry of gem crystals involves a mathematics and formalism that is at the core of such diverse modern disciplines as semiconductor manufacturing, virology, and the biosynthesis of proteins?

Like I said, who knew?

I guess that it should come as no surprise that the forces which govern the assembly of something as magical as a gemstone may also influence other structures, both microscopic and large. Unfortunately, the casual faceter and amateur mineralogist will encounter a maelstrom of fairly complex terminology and math the moment he or she steps through the door into the wonderful world of crystal systems research.

Here is what wikipedia.org, that ubiquitous source of all information, has to say in its attempt to summarize the topic of crystal systems:

A lattice system is a class of lattices with the same point group… The lattice system of a crystal or space group is determined by its lattice but not always by its point group…A crystal system is a class of point groups. Two point groups are placed in the same crystal system if the sets of possible lattice systems of their space groups are the same. For many point groups there is only one possible lattice system, and in these cases the crystal system corresponds to a lattice system and is given the same name… The crystal system of a crystal or space group is determined by its point group but not always by its lattice. A crystal family also consists of point groups and is formed by combining crystal systems whenever two crystal systems have space groups with the same lattice.

It then goes on to conclude that *"in dimensions less than three, there is no essential difference between crystal systems, crystal families, and lattice systems."* Doesn't that make everything absolutely clear?

The good news is that you don't have to be an expert crystallographer (or linguist) in order to understand and appreciate the essence and beauty of crystal structure and systems. Here is the main point: all natural crystals come in one of seven forms – eight if you include "amorphous" materials such as glass and amber in the mix.

Recognizing these crystal systems in faceting rough can be a lifesaver when trying to identify gem materials and thereby avoid a scam. For example, if you have ever held a fluted, triangular, cushion-shaped crystal of natural tourmaline, you will always be able to recognize it (Figure 12-32).

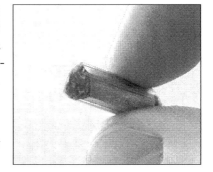

Figure 12-32 A crystal of natural tourmaline. Note the characteristic cushion triangle cross-section and the fluted outer walls of the crystal.

12.10.1 Crystal Systems and Habits

To prevent confusion later on, you should understand an important distinction made by mineralogists, namely the difference between crystal *systems* and crystal *habits*.

The crystal *system* is the underlying structure of the material, in other words, how it is put together at the microscopic level. The forces between separate atoms and molecules allow only a certain number of arrangements of angles between them. The result is a crystal lattice (uh oh…terminology alert) in one of seven possible forms: cubic, tetragonal, hexagonal, trigonal, orthorhombic, monoclinic, and triclinic. Oh yes, and amorphous, if you allow it…

The crystal *habit* is how a macroscopic crystal appears – what it looks like. In many instances, the crystal system expresses itself on these large scales, leading, for example, to the familiar hexagonal prism habit of aquamarine (Figure 12-33). Different conditions during crystal growth can lead to a wide variety of different outcomes (or habits), however. For instance, most sapphire crystals display the classic, tapering, hexagonal crystal habit, but those from Montana frequently appear flatter and tablet-shaped.

Figure 12-33 Aquamarine, a form of beryl, has characteristic crystals whose habit reflects its underlying hexagonal crystal system.

Mineralogists have come up with a large number of descriptive and occasionally fanciful names to describe crystal habits. These include acicular (needle-like), coxcomb (closely-spaced flaky crystals), drusy (minute crystals coating a surface), enantiomorphic (mirror-image), fibrous (displaying thread-like fibers), micaceous (sheet-like, as in mica), mamillary (rounded partial spheres…think malachite - I know, I know), plumose (feathery), sphenoid (wedge-like), tabular (flattened, tablet-shaped), and a couple of dozen more.

Once again, you don't need to memorize any terminology to understand and appreciate that the inter-atomic forces which create a particular mineral's crystal system can also produce an enchanting variety of crystal habits.

12.10.2 The Seven (or Eight, or Six) Crystal Systems

Right. Enough with the preliminaries. Let's get to the crystal systems themselves. As mentioned above, these systems reflect the underlying form of the crystal structure or lattice. Mineralogists classify these lattices, and hence the systems, in terms of so-called crystallographic axes. You can think of these as axes of symmetry and growth, or more practically, as the lines joining opposite faces or points of a perfect crystal.

For example, Figure 12-34 shows three perfect forms of the **isometric** or **cubic** crystal system. The lines joining opposite faces or points are all of equal length and meet each other at 90°. Examples of isometric gem crystals include fluorite, diamond, and garnet.

If the three crystallographic axes intersect at 90°, but one axis is shorter or longer than the other two, you end up with the **tetragonal** crystal system. This leads to crystal shapes such as elongated rectangular solids and dipyramids (Figure 12-35). Zircon is an example of a gem in the tetragonal crystal system.

In the **orthorhombic** crystal system, the three axes are again at right angles to each other, but each axis is of a different length (Figure 12-36). This leads to shapes such as rhombic prisms and dipyramids. Peridot, topaz, and chrysoberyl form in the orthorhombic crystal system.

The **monoclinic** crystal system also exhibits three crystallographic axes of different length. Two of the axes meet at right angles, while the third is inclined (Figure 12-37). This results in prisms with inclined end faces. Few common gem materials form in this crystal system. Perhaps the best known is kunzite or spodumene. If you have cut this material, you are probably terribly familiar with the effect of large-scale weak interatomic bonds.

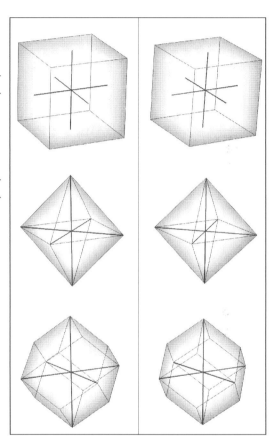

Figure 12-34 Three forms of the isometric or cubic crystal system: the cubic form, as in fluorite (top); the octahedral form of diamond and spinel (middle); and the 12-faced dodecahedron form of garnet (bottom). Note that these are three-dimensional renderings. Cross your eyes to see the effect and refer to Chapter 11.9 for more help on seeing these images in 3D.

The **triclinic** crystal system breaks all the rules. Not only are the three axes of different length, but also none of them meet at right angles (Figure 12-38). This leads to inclined, asymmetric prisms and dipyramids. There are no common gem materials in the triclinic system (apologies to the one kyanite cutter out there...).

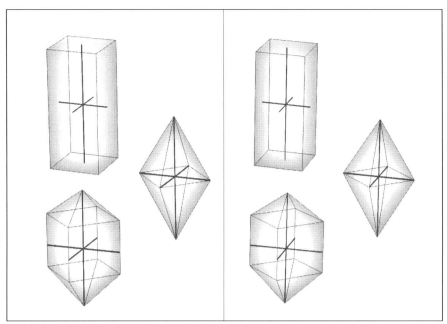

Figure 12-35 Three-dimensional representation of the tetragonal crystal system, which produces elongated rectangular prisms, dipyramids, and combinations of the two (top to bottom).

Actually, if you think triclinic broke the rules, consider the **hexagonal** and **trigonal** crystal systems. Not content with three, both of these systems have *four* crystallographic axes: three coplanar axes of equal length that meet at 120° and a fourth perpendicular to the plane (Figure 12-39).

The hexagonal and trigonal crystal systems are essentially the same – in fact, one school of mineralogical thought counts them as a single system. As their names imply, the major difference is that hexagonal crystals exhibit six-fold symmetry while trigonal crystals have

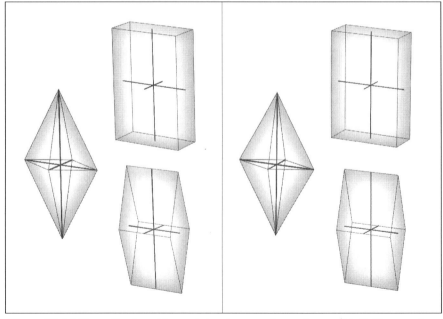

Figure 12-36 The orthorhombic crystal system produces dipyramids (left), as well as orthorhombic prisms (right).

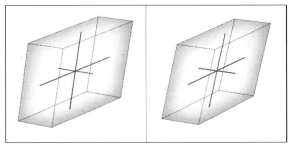

Figure 12-37 Three-dimensional image of the mono-clinic crystal system.

three-fold symmetry. This may be a distinction without a difference, since you can think of the hexagonal crystal as a cut-off version of the trigonal.

You can guess based on Figure 12-33 that beryl forms in the hexagonal crystal system. The trigonal system includes many other common gemstone materials, such as tourmaline, corundum, and quartz (but see "You take the high quartz" on page 135).

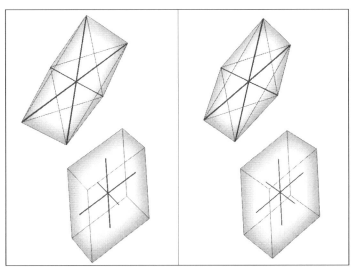

Figure 12-38 The triclinic crystal system produces inclined asymmetric prisms and dipyramids.

Whew! That makes seven crystal systems. Or six, if you are one of those who view hexagonal and trigonal crystals as two sides of the same coin.

Actually, there is an eighth system. Or a seventh. Materials which exhibit no long-range microscopic order or symmetry are termed **amorphous**. You could call this a non-crystalline crystal system. Examples of common amorphous gemstones include amber, obsidian, glass, and opal. Opal is particularly interesting because it is simultaneously amorphous and well ordered, consisting as it does of stacked spheres of silica (see page 80 and 84).

This ends the disquisition on crystal systems. There are two important things to remember. First, most rough gems will not look like their perfect crystal forms, so beware of identification based on the large-scale shape or habit. Nevertheless, *the angles between crystal faces will be preserved, independent of habit.* Spotting clean crystal faces at the appropriate relative angles can therefore aid enormously in your mineralogical sleuthing. The second thing

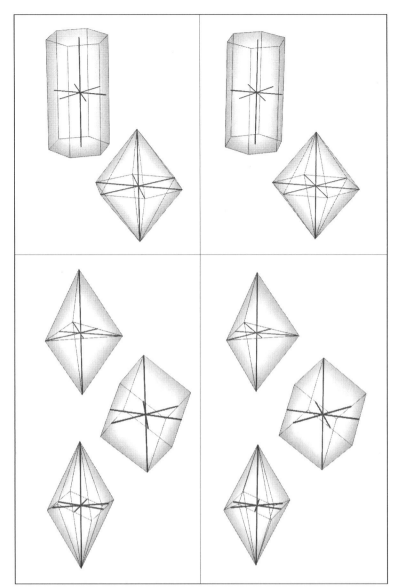

Figure 12-39 The hexagonal and trigonal crystal systems have four axes. The hexagonal prism and dipyramid (top) are typical shapes observed in the hexagonal crystal system, while the three-sided dipyramid, rhombohedron, and scalenohedron (bottom) are associated with the trigonal crystal system.

to remember is that the microscopic forces holding a crystal together lead to both strong and weak bonds. Because the atoms in a gem retain their relative positions over long distances within the crystal lattice, the strong and weak bonds are also spatially extended. This leads to directions along which the crystal is weak and can split rather easily. Yes, this is how cleavage planes arise (see next section).

Table 12-12 categorizes common gemstone materials by crystal system and gives an indication of habit and the importance of cleavage planes. It also lists fracture and streak properties (see below). And for those of you out there who are straining mightily to formulate a sophomoric joke for the next lapidary club meeting…yes, there are minerals with mamillary habit and perfect cleavage. My apologies to the non-troglodytes in the readership.

You take the high quartz, I'll take the low quartz…

…and you'll be in hospital afore me…
  (and apologies to my Scottish friends and forebears…)

And apologies to you, dear reader, for what may the most strained and obscure reference in this book, almost as strained and obscure as my attempts to sing these mangled lyrics. You see, I was digging up information on crystal systems, and I learned to my surprise that good old quartz, the material we all know and love, is actually a bit more complicated than I thought.

It turns out that the normal crystal system for quartz is trigonal. Normal in the sense that it is the one stable form at temperatures and pressures that you and I would find comfortable. This type of quartz is called "low" or α-quartz. Heat it up to a thousand degrees or so, and the situation changes, however. At these temperatures, and at high pressures, the quartz crystal transforms into so-called "high" or β quartz in the hexagonal system. Let it cool again, and it switches back to low quartz. These transformations involve a slight re-jiggering of the bonds between the silicon and oxygen atoms in the crystal. High quartz has a slightly lower density than low quartz, due to these modified bonds.

Incidentally, you may come across quartz crystals being marketed, no doubt at premium prices, as "high" or β quartz. Don't be fooled. Unless the salesperson is engulfed in roaring flames, it is very unlikely that his or her wares represent *true* high quartz. To be fair, some crystals retain the larger morphological characteristics, in other words the habit, of high quartz after cooling, but they are undoubtedly the run-of-the-mill low variety. To properly appreciate high quartz, you really have to get uncomfortable…

Whew! I hope that explains the strained obscurity in the first paragraph. I agree…there is no explanation for my singing.

12.11 Cleavage, Fracture, and Streak

No, Cleavage, Fracture, and Streak is not a firm of solicitors in a Dickens novel. They are, in fact, three diagnostic properties that distinguish gemstone materials on the basis of how they get damaged or destroyed. And yes, cleavage, fracture, and streak are not a good way of identifying potentially valuable faceted gemstones. They can be very helpful in distinguishing gems in rough form, however.

12.11.1 Cleavage

The previous section on crystal systems introduced the concept of cleavage as a natural consequence of weaker and stronger inter-atomic bonds in the crystal lattice. Basically, the large scale ordering of the atoms produces directions along which the crystal can part relatively easily, either by mechanical force, such as a blow, or by rapid temperature change. This property can serve as a useful diagnostic tool, since certain materials exhibit strong cleavage and can be identified by this in rough form (see Table 12-12 and "Finding the Cleavage Planes in Topaz" on page 137).

Table 12-12 The crystal system, habit, cleavage, fracture and streak of common gemstone materials. The bracketed values for cleavage refer to the number of distinct directions.

Gem Material	Crystal System	Common Habit	Cleavage?	Fracture	Streak
Amber	amorphous	nodular	none	conchoidal, brittle	white
Andalusite	orthorhombic	blocky, prismatic, euhedral	good	uneven, brittle	white
Apatite	hexagonal	euhedral, prismatic	indistinct	conchoidal, brittle	white
Beryl	hexagonal	columnar, prismatic	indistinct	conchoidal, brittle	white
Chrysoberyl	orthorhombic	columnar, tabular, prismatic, twinning	good	conchoidal, weak	white
Corundum	hexagonal	euhedral, prismatic, tabular	none	conchoidal, splintery	white
Cubic Zirconia	isometric	(manmade)	none	conchoidal, brittle	white
Danburite	orthorhombic	euhedral, prismatic	imperfect	uneven, conchoidal	white
Diamond	isometric	euhedral	perfect	conchoidal	white
Feldspar / Sunstone	triclinic	euhedral	perfect	grainy, splintery, brittle	white
Fluorite	isometric	coarse crystalline	perfect	conchoidal, brittle	white
Garnet	isometric	fine crystalline	indistinct	conchoidal, brittle	white
Glass (Obsidian)	amorphous	nodular	none	conch. very brittle	white
Iolite	orthorhombic	prismatic	good	conchoidal, uneven	white
Opal	amorphous	amorphous, nodular, reniform	none	conchoidal, brittle	white
Peridot	orthorhombic	crystalline, tabular	indistinct	conchoidal, brittle	white
Quartz	trigonal (α) hexagonal (β)	coarse crystalline, prismatic	none	conchoidal, very brittle	white
Scapolite	tetragonal	prismatic	good	conchoidal, brittle	white
Sphene	monoclinic	crystalline, tabular, wedges	good	conchoidal, brittle	reddish-white
Spinel	isometric	euhedral	indistinct	conchoidal	grayish-white
Tanzanite	orthorhombic	columnar, prismatic, striated	perfect	uneven, brittle	white
Topaz	orthorhombic	prismatic, columnar	perfect	conchoidal	white
Tourmaline	trigonal	prismatic, striated	indistinct	uneven, brittle	white
Zircon	tetragonal	crystalline, tabular, prismatic	indistinct	conchoidal, very brittle	white

Cleavage can be both a help and a hindrance. In relatively rare instances, for example in traditional diamond cutting, the craftsman can exploit natural cleavage planes to divide a large crystal in a (hopefully) controlled way. I am old enough to remember the classic 1970's automobile commercial which demonstrated the smoothness of the suspension by having a jeweler cleave a valuable diamond in the back seat of a moving car. I will also never forget the Saturday Night Live parody of this advertisement involving a mohel. Such amusing recollections will likely be your only exposure to cleavage as an aid to faceting, however. Most of our encounters with this phenomenon are of the negative type.

If you have spent any time in front of a faceting machine, you have almost certainly experienced cleavage. In my own cutting adventures, about 2% of the stones have parted suddenly and catastrophically along cleavage planes. I should say at this point that I almost never facet quartz, and rarely beryl, both of which are popular materials with little or no cleavage tendencies. In most instances, my problems arise with tourmaline splitting along a plane perpendicular to the long, c-axis. The experts will admonish me at this point that this phenomenon is not technically cleavage. Rather, it is the gem parting at weakened locations along the growth axis of the crystal due to changes in chemistry or other external factors. Different cause, same effect.

Finding the Cleavage Planes in Topaz

Topaz is a lovely material boasting the all-too-rare combination of pleasing colour, reasonably high refractive index, good dispersion, and low cost. But you have been warned. Cleavage kills, and topaz has cleavage in spades.

Should you be afraid of topaz?

Absolutely not. The first clue that topaz's notorious cleavage is less of a problem than you fear is the fact that this material represents a substantial fraction of the commercially cut coloured stone market. If topaz was completely intractable, mass producers of faceted gemstones would not go anywhere near it.

In fact, topaz presents few problems, provided that you take appropriate precautions. This boils down to avoiding the strongest cleavage planes for large facets, such as the table. The conventional wisdom is that any such facet should be oriented at least 7° away from the cleavage plane (see Figure 12-42). But how do you know where these dangerous planes are?

It is relatively easy to identify the cleavage plane if your topaz gem rough is in crystal form. Figure 12-40 shows the typical shape of natural topaz and identifies the primary

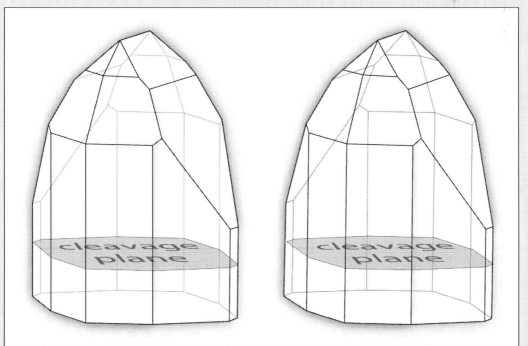

Figure 12-40 Typical crystal form of topaz and the dominant basal cleavage plane. This is another 3D diagram; see Chapter 11.9 for instructions on viewing these images in three dimensions.

cleavage. This is an instance of *basal cleavage*, since the cleavage plane lies parallel to the base of the crystal. In cutting such a stone, make sure that you orient the rough appropriately.

But what if your topaz doesn't show an obvious crystal form? This can happen with alluvial (river smoothed) samples, as well as commonly available pre-forms. Neither shape provides obvious clues to the orientation of the underlying crystal lattice.

Sunlight to the Rescue!

Luckily, there is a simple way to locate the primary cleavage plane of topaz. Take your gem rough outside on a sunlit day, or examine the stone under intense artificial light. With the sun or lamp over your shoulder, rotate the stone back and forth until you see a multitude of tiny sparkles (Figure 12-41). You are now looking down on the primary cleavage plane. Mark the location with a permanent ink pen and orient the rough accordingly.

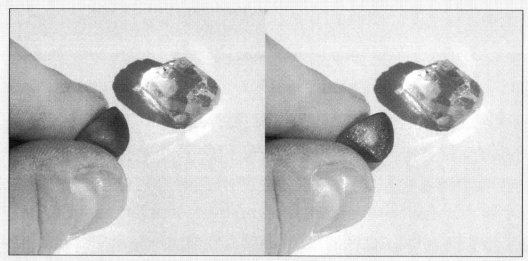

Figure 12-41 The topaz crystal structure is obvious in some pieces of gem rough, such as the clear sample pictured above. This makes avoiding the cleavage planes relatively straightforward. Alluvial material or pre-forms may not have a clear structure, however. Intense lighting can help. When properly oriented (right image), many tiny facets appear, revealing the primary cleavage plane.

What happened out there in the sunshine? Even when tumbled or ground smooth, topaz's natural crystal structure leads to tiny fractures revealing the orientation of the cleavage plane. Essentially, the action of tumbling the stone across a riverbed or pre-forming it on a grindstone pays little heed to the danger of cleavage. Therefore, cleavage occurs, albeit on a small scale. Each of these inadvertent fractures creates a tiny facet, which in turn creates the flash you see.

I have also experienced disaster with fluorite, which has perfect cleavage along four directions. Yes, I was asking for it. Somewhat surprisingly, I have had zero difficulty with topaz, which is notorious for its cleavage problems. The conventional wisdom, which I follow in all cases, is to identify the cleavage planes in a susceptible material and orient any large facets (particularly the table) at least 7-10° away from them (see Figure 12-42).

The reasons underpinning this strategy are not obvious until you try to cut a gem close to a cleavage plane. In fact, you could suggest that the table be placed perfectly parallel to the cleavage plane. In such a configuration, this most difficult of facets could be produced in final, perfect form by a well-placed blow.

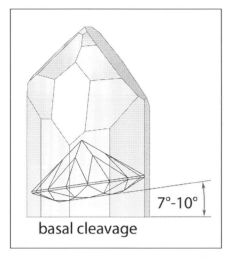

Figure 12-42 You should orient large facets, such as the table, at least 7-10° away from prominent cleavage planes.

Well, yes and no. In principle, such a strategy could work, but it turns out that few of us are equipped, in terms of both the proper tools and the emotional fortitude, to cleave a valuable gem. The emotional aspect is particularly true at the final stage of generating the table, at the conclusion of perhaps hours of investment at the machine. Cutting facets parallel or nearly parallel to a cleavage plane in the conventional manner can also be a nightmare. First, the grinding and cutting process inevitably results in impacts along the weaker crystal planes. This can cause large pieces of the gem to split off. Not good. Second, polishing near to a cleavage plane can produce unattractive "streaky" effects as individually well-polished crystal layers shear off. By far the safest strategy is to keep big, important facets well away from the cleavage planes, allowing these undesirable effects to occur elsewhere or, hopefully, not at all.

12.11.2 Fracture

Fracture describes the physical appearance of the surface of a mineral when it is broken under stress. It is obviously related to cleavage, since material with directional weakness in the crystal lattice will fracture selectively along planes. Nevertheless, mineralogists restrict the term "fracture" to characterize samples which have not experienced planar cleavage.

Fracture is also similar to cleavage in the sense that it can be a useful diagnostic in identifying gem materials in rough form. For example, the surface of quartz fractures in a distinctive way, producing the concentric pattern of arcs known as *conchoidal* fracture (see Figure 12-43). The name derives from the Greek word *konchoeides* (mussel-like) and is based on the resemblance of the fracture pattern to the ridged curves of a marine bivalve mollusk. Nicomedes studied the conchoidal form mathematically more than two millennia ago.

Figure 12-43 Conchoidal fracture patterns are characteristic of quartz crystals.

Other common types of fracture are splintery, hackly, fibrous, and uneven. Table 12-12 lists the fracture properties of common gemstone materials.

12.11.3 Streak

The streak property of a mineral refers to the colour of ground-up residue left on a hard surface when the sample is scratched across it. This colour represents the true underlying appearance of the material, since the scratching process generates microscopic crystals for which impurities play a very small optical role. I suppose that, technically speaking, streak belongs with the other optical properties in this chapter, but I place it here with the physical properties for two reasons: First, you have to get physical – that is, scratch the stone – in order to do the test; and second, like several other physical diagnostics, streak is almost never used anymore.

The streak can sometimes be surprisingly different from the bulk colour of the mineral. For example, hematite, which ranges in colour from silver-gray to black, produces a bright red streak (hence the name hematite, which comes from the Greek word for blood – think hemoglobin). Iron pyrite is another spectacular example. This yellowish-gold mineral – Fool's Gold to you and me – produces a black or greenish-black streak with the additional endearing property of smelling of sulfur. This makes for a pretty cool party trick…

Identifying minerals by streak has a long and rich history. As far back as Theophrastus (see opposite page), merchants used a "touchstone," a piece of hard black stone, such as slate, jasper, or basalt, to compare the streak left by suspect gold alloys with known, high-quality, standard samples. Modern mineralogists use a "streak plate," a flat, unglazed porcelain plate whose fine microstructure can readily reduce a mineral to a fine powder. Ceramic is quite hard and thus works well with most minerals, but for the hardest samples, the assayer can grind away a small amount of the mineral with a file and rub the resulting powder on the streak plate.

Despite its obvious coolness and long tradition, the streak property is rarely used in modern gemological identification. There are a couple of good reasons for this. First of all, the streak test is fundamentally destructive – you have to remove part of the stone in a moderately violent way. Few rough dealers will allow this, and it is completely out of the question for faceted gems, despite the published advice to scratch away at the girdle or some other less obvious location (I am guilty of this as well – see Section 12.9.2).

The second reason for the reduced popularity of this test is perhaps the more important one: the streak test is not particularly informative. Table 12-12 lists the streak colour of common gemstone materials. Notice anything? Yes, essentially all gems of interest produce white streaks. While the test could certainly distinguish a garnet from iron pyrite, if you have to scratch the darn things across a chunk of slate to tell them apart, you have more serious issues.

12.12 Inclusions

I could write a whole separate book on inclusions. I could, but I won't because I don't like inclusions. Yes, in some instances, such as emerald and demantoid garnet, inclusions can be a signature of natural origin and hence of enormous value. I would like such inclusions if I could afford to cut emerald and demantoid garnet, but I can't so I don't.

To be fair, not everyone takes such a negative view, and in fact, one of the online discussion groups features a popular forum called the "inclusion of the day." The visual appearance and

The Touchstone Touchstone…

In the oldest known published work on the subject of mineralogy, *On Stones*, the Greek philosopher and scientist Theophrastus of Eresus (371-287 BCE) describes the use of "Lydian stone," a touchstone, which has the "power…to test gold and silver." Writing some four hundred years later, Pliny the Elder (see page 124) referred to Theophrastus in describing the touchstone, and added that it can be a useful diagnostic for gems as well:

Nothing is more difficult than to distinguish the several varieties of this stone (carbunculus, or ruby)… They are counterfeited, too, with great exactness in glass; but the difference may be detected with the touchstone; the same being the case also with other artificial stones, as the material is always of a softer nature and comparatively brittle…
- Pliny the Elder, Historia Naturalis, 37, 26

Clearly, the touchstone's seemingly magical power to reveal fraud impressed the ancients, and the modern version of Theophrastus' test is still in use for quick evaluations of quality among jewelers and dealers in scrap gold. But the psychological influence of this magical power has extended further still. Whether it is famous Shakespearean clowns or Rossini operas, the concept of a touchstone has entered the culture as much more than a mineralogist's diagnostic tool.

We speak of a certain event or accomplishment as being the fundamental or quintessential feature, the *touchstone*, of a career or era. The opening up of the West was a touchstone of 19th century America. Touchstones also set the standard – one is tempted to say, the gold standard – of their times. *Easy Rider* was the touchstone movie of the 1960's. Wait…I have a great idea for the name of a film production company…

chemical makeup of inclusions can also be an invaluable clue to the geographical origin of a gem. For example, tiny crystals of rutile, spinel, zircon, and garnet are common inclusions in corundum from some regions, while other localities tend to produce calcite, mica, and graphite interlopers. Other site-specific flaws include "lily pads" in San Carlos peridot from Arizona and "horsetail" inclusions of chrysotile (asbestos) in Russian demantoid garnet.

The term *inclusion* has come to mean any internal flaw or foreign matter that disrupts or scatters light as it passes through a gemstone. Strictly speaking, fractures and other lattice phenomena in a pure crystal are not inclusions, but their effect is the same: they reduce clarity and, in almost all cases, have a negative influence on the optical performance of a gem. In severe instances, they can even increase the likelihood of breakage. Thus, as with the streak characteristics discussed in the previous section, inclusions are both an optical and physical property.

To clarify things, gemologists speak of two types of inclusions. *Intrinsic* inclusions occur in a "pure" crystal and include the phenomena of lattice dislocations, irregular growth boundaries, crystallization phase transitions, colour striations, and stress fractures.

Perhaps the best-known intrinsic inclusion is the twinning plane, in which two or more bulk crystals have grown together and produced a distinct boundary. This boundary often exhibits rainbow bursts of colour due to diffraction at the crystal interface. This is the same optical phenomenon that creates the lovely colours in opal (Section 12.7.4), but twinning can have a very dark side. Because it represents the boundary between two separate, stable crystals, the twinning plane can be weak and prone to fracture. Quartz and spinel are particularly vulnerable. If you want to chance it, most experts recommend orienting the twinning plane parallel to the girdle, exactly as with colour zones (see page 234 of Volume 1). This not only provides protection from mechanical shock, but also it spreads any visual funnies across the entire gem.

Extrinsic inclusions are everything else. If it doesn't belong there, it is an extrinsic inclusion. This category can include crystals of other gem species, fluid, gas, and even organic matter.

Extrinsic inclusions can form before, after, or at the same time as the surrounding gem. In the first case, an existing crystal or other foreign matter becomes enclosed in the growing parent gem. Simultaneous formation occurs when an inclusion develops from the same melt as the parent, but gets surrounded due to its slower crystal growth rate. Younger inclusions result from liquids entering fissures in the surrounding gem after formation.

12.12.1 An Inclusion Potpourri

Rather than a whole book, which I suspect neither of us would enjoy, the following paragraphs present a potpourri of interesting inclusion facts and phenomena. I note, however, in connection with my distaste for inclusions, that the word *potpourri* literally means "rotten pot" in the original French...

Ephemeral Inclusions

Inclusions can come and go. Literally. In the case of one mineral dissolved within another, the exact formation conditions of a gemstone will determine whether that foreign mineral stays in solution or crystallizes out to form a visible inclusion. Mineralogists call the latter process *exsolution*, and it is responsible for a number of important and interesting phenomena. For example, rutile (TiO_2) can be dissolved in quartz or corundum. If it exsolves, rutile needles may form. This leads to reduced clarity and in general, a less desirable gem. However, in certain instances, such as isolated needles in quartz (page 208 of Volume 1) or asteria in corundum (Section 12.7.3), the inclusions can substantially increase the value of the stone. The phenomenon of exsolution has been recognized for centuries and is routinely exploited for gem enhancement. For example, by varying temperature and pressure, experts can dissolve or exsolve rutile in sapphire more or less at will. This can help clarify a sleepy gem or intensify the star effect, respectively. Chapter 13.2 provides more information on such treatment.

Amber

Perhaps the most spectacular example of extrinsic inclusion occurs in amber, which is the fossilized resin of ancient trees. Amber deposits across the globe date from a few tens of millions to well over a third of a billion years go. All kinds of organic matter, including splinters of wood, flowers, fruit, insects, and even whole frogs, have been found encased in a golden time capsule of amber. These windows into our planet's biological past can be of enormous paleontological value, and they can even make for some pretty cool dinosaur movies. To tie all of this in a nice, neat bow, our old friend, Pliny the Elder (see page 124), noted the existence of insect inclusions in amber in his encyclopedic *Historia Naturalis*. Turn to page 154 to learn more about this remarkable document.

Multi-Phase Inclusions

Internal cavities, whether filled by liquid or gas, are also classified as inclusions. The liquid can be plain water or a chemical solution, while the gases are frequently air or carbon dioxide. When a pocket contains both gas and liquid, it is termed a *two-phase* inclusion. Occasionally, solid matter, such as recrystallized mineral, is also present. This produces a *three-phase* inclusion. Quartz, calcite, and amber are the most common hosts of such interlopers. As with organic material in amber, two and three-phase inclusions can provide valuable clues to the atmospheric and geological conditions prevailing at the time the gem formed. And, as with amber, collectors prize fine examples of such inclusions.

Euphemisms

The gem world has a rich tradition of sales-oriented language, and nowhere is this more true than in the often-shady world of marketing included stones. Cracks and internal fractures are given the harmless sounding name "feathers." When such lovely feathers occur in a still-forming gem, pressure, influx of fluid, or heat can cause partial healing, resulting in a "fingerprint," a dainty name for a very distracting patch of arcs and tiny cavities. Perhaps the most egregious example of gemological euphemism occurs in the high-stakes world of emerald marketing. This variety of beryl, while greatly valued for its rich green colour, is particularly prone to severe internal fracturing and inclusions. Dealers have adopted a variety of techniques to repair, or more often conceal, such flaws (see Chapter 13.2), and they have been equally creative in their verbal blandishments. The term *jardin*, literally "garden" in French, has become common usage to describe inclusions in emerald. Doesn't that sound nice?

12.12.2   Dealing with Inclusions

Whether you love inclusions or hate them, you are going to have to deal with them. The most obvious strategy for managing a bad inclusion in a piece of gem rough is to put the stone back down on the dealer's table. If that is not possible, either because you missed the opportunity to do so or the gem is otherwise too appealing, you will have to manage the situation at the orientation and cutting phases.

Chapter 6.7 explains strategies for orienting gem rough. In the case of inclusions, the basic idea is to place them in a location that will be cut away. Again, this may not be possible, in which case you should try to locate any uglies somewhere discreet, such as near the girdle. Another option is to hide them in the overall scintillation of the gem, for example, under the crown star facets. Whatever you do, you should avoid an orientation which places inclusions near the culet, since your one small flaw could be optically multiplied four, or eight, or sixteen times (see page 209 of Volume 1).

Inclusions present a further challenge to the finicky faceter. If a flaw breaks through the surface during fine cutting or polish, havoc will almost certainly ensue (see page 339 of Volume 1). There is nothing quite like the feeling of seeing an almost complete, almost perfect facet that has just been ravaged by the breakout of a nasty inclusion. Such breakouts inevitably force you to polish further, which can open up the flaw even more. This cycle of destruction sometimes continues to the point where it is easier and less stressful to recut the entire pavilion or crown. Short version: don't let inclusions anywhere near the surface of your gemstone.

Let me end this too long yet too short discussion of inclusions with a quote from Gerolamo Cardano, the great sixteenth century Italian mathematician, doctor, astrologer, and gambler.

(Given this range of pursuits, you will be unsurprised to learn that Cardano was a real character. Famously arrogant, he supported himself by gambling, since the local universities refused to hire him. In doing so, he helped lay down the foundations of the modern disciplines of probability and statistics. He also landed in hot water by casting the horoscope of Jesus Christ, an apparent publicity stunt viewed dimly by the religious authorities of the day).

Here is what Cardano had to say about inclusions:

"In precious stones, imperfections are in reality less common than in animals and vegetables; but they are more conspicuous in jewels, simply because their nature is more brilliant and more rare. For the same reason, great men appear to have more vices than common mortals; but this is a delusion and an error. The lustre of their fame and the splendour of their names render their faults only the more apparent; while the ignorant vulgar, under favour of their obscurity, escape having their vices noticed."

Figure 12-44 Gerolamo Cardano, one of the founders of the field of probability and statistics, thanks to some unhealthy habits.

Cardano's quote sums up the world of inclusions pretty well for me. His opinion? Sure, inclusions are bad, just like the character flaws of the great and presumably good, but they only look bad because their hosts are so fine. Sales talk. I suggest that we refer to the next embarrassing public peccadillo of a distinguished national leader as "jardin."

Excluding Inclusions – The 1 carat boundary

Deciding whether and how to exclude an inclusion is always tough. It is tough because this choice often involves reducing the ultimate size of the final gemstone. Of course, if careful orientation can send the flaw down the drain of your splash pan, fine. It's the rest of the time – the time governed by Murphy's Law – that you have to make a difficult decision.

Let me try to convince you that you should face this choice objectively, and in particular, with no direct concern about the final, exact carat weight of the gem. This is a somewhat forlorn hope on my part, because like everyone else, I have a psychological barrier to overcome: somehow, a 1.0 carat gem seems much more valuable than a 0.95 carat gem. This desire to get above a certain target weight might encourage you to make some non-optimal design and cutting choices.

A strong focus on the exact final yield will result in less than ideal outcomes. Perhaps Vargas said it best: "There can be little argument against a smaller perfect gem versus a large incorrectly cut one," (*Faceting for Amateurs*, 3rd edition, page 157) In fact, jewelry experts advise buyers to avoid 1.0-carat diamonds. A 0.9-carat gem will be virtually indistinguishable and will come at a substantially better per-carat price. As a direct corollary, a 1.1-carat stone will very likely be better cut.

12.13 Other Physical Properties

12.13.1 Heat Sensitivity

Some gemstones simply can't take the heat.

Whether it is exposure to warm, dry air, contact with molten dop wax, the heat of the polishing moment, or for some materials, even the warmth of a friendly hand, some gemstones just like to keep cool.

The dangers of overheating take two basic forms: dehydration and thermally induced breakage. Opals contain significant amounts of water in their chemical structure, and the presence of this water is essential to the optical performance of the stone. When exposed to hot, dry air, these gems can lose this water, resulting in changes of colour and transparency. In severe instances, small networks of cracks can appear, producing ugly regions of opaque "crazing" that ruin the appearance of the stone (see page 95). The only proper strategy for dealing with this phenomenon is to patronize reputable rough dealers.

The second insidious effect of heating arises from the phenomenon of *thermal expansion*. Most materials expand when heated, although there are some prominent exceptions. You are no doubt familiar with the phenomenon. Changing size with temperature is the reason

---

Bake and Shake...

Thermal shock can literally strain things to the limit, and even low sensitivity materials like quartz can blow up if they experience an extreme temperature change. Here's the war story: At a certain point in my faceting career, I was paranoid about stones breaking off the dop during polishing. As a result, I turned to some pretty extreme epoxy, which simply didn't release that well, even after an extended acetone soak (see "The Nightmare Stone from Hell™" on page 259 of Volume 1 for more on this difficult period of my life). My strategy was to place the stone and dop in the oven at a decent temperature for baking chicken (400° F or 200 C). After a quarter of an hour – not enough for chicken, incidentally – I would (carefully) try to pull the thing apart. It usually worked.

On one occasion, however, I was trying to release a very pretty synthetic blue quartz. Unfortunately, the rag I was using to grab the gem was a bit wet. The cold water touched the hot stone, I heard a distinct "click," and when things cooled down, I discovered to my horror that the gem had cracked (Figure 12-45).

The lesson? Don't do this. You don't need to use muscular epoxy to hold your gems in place, you shouldn't annoy the spouse by using kitchen appliances in your lapidary work, and you needn't expose any stone to a sudden temperature difference. Particularly one of a few hundred degrees...

Figure 12-45 A lovely blue synthetic quartz done in by thermal expansion.

why railroads and bridges have expansion joints, and it is why electrical wires sag lower in summer than in winter. However, when thermal expansion goes too far or too fast, disaster can result. Think about that glass fresh from the dishwasher that cracked when filled with cold liquid.

In the case of gemstones, excessive or too-rapid expansion can exceed the structural strength of the crystal, causing it to literally come apart at the seams. Opal, apatite, amber, calcite, and especially sulfur (see below) are extremely sensitive, while obsidian, glass, and tourmaline present a moderate risk. Essentially all other common gemstones have either low, very low, or no heat sensitivity. Chapter 12 of Vargas' *Faceting for Amateurs* contains a complete listing.

If you choose to facet a heat sensitive material, take appropriate precautions. In particular, use a cold dopping technique (see Chapter 7.2) and monitor the polishing process to prevent heat buildup. Additional bonus warning: acetone is a wonderful solvent for cold dopping adhesives such as epoxy and cyanoacrylate glue. Unfortunately, it is also a wonderful solvent for amber, a gem which usually requires cold dopping.

Heat treatment can, in fact, help in terms of improving colour, dissolving inclusions, and so forth. Chapter 13 contains more on its benefits. Perhaps the most interesting example of using heat to improve the appearance of a gem is the deliberate fracturing of amber by sudden cooling. When done properly, the thermal shock produces disk-like internal stress fractures known as "sun spangles." Yes, I know this sounds a bit like "jardin" (see page 143), but the effect is quite pretty.

A final, quick warning about heat: some gem materials, such as corundum, have little or no heat sensitivity, but beware! Dop wax is unquestionably heat sensitive, and unexpected warming of the stone during polishing can cause it to shift.

Faceting Fire and Brimstone…

With a few successful stones under your belt, you will inevitably start dreaming of more challenging gem materials. Peridot and corundum are obvious early choices due to their difficulty in polishing and hardness, respectively. But once those are conquered, where can the adventurous faceter turn?

There are a number of beautiful gem materials whose cleavage properties present a significant challenge to even experienced cutters. Spodumene, which comes in various colours and forms, including kunzite and hiddenite, can be hellishly difficult to facet due to its strong cleavage.

Other materials present a unique challenge. My favourite among these is sulfur. With a Mohs hardness of 1.5-2.5, it can hardly stand up to the wear and tear of traditional faceting, let alone be mounted in jewelry. But sulfur's most endearing property is its extravagant sensitivity to heat. As Schumann points out in *Gemstones of the World*, faceted sulfur crystals have a distressing tendency to explode when warmed by a human hand. More than enough challenge for anyone there…and no, I am not enough of an adventurer / masochist to have tried it.

12.13.2 Thermal and Electrical Conductivity

The thermal and electrical conductivity of a material refer to its ability to transmit heat and electricity, respectively. Both of these properties are used in gem identification, particularly with diamonds.

You can assess the thermal conductivity of a stone by picking it up. Some types, such as quartz, conduct heat fairly well and will feel cool to the touch. Its thermal conductivity is roughly three times higher than that of common glass, with which it can otherwise easily be confused. Other gemstones, such as amber, are poor thermal conductors and will feel warm to the touch.

Diamond is the king of thermal conductors: as with hardness, it is on the top of the heap of natural materials in terms of its ability to transmit heat. This fact formed the basis of most diamond testing equipment in the twentieth century, until a simulant with similar properties (silicon carbide, or Moissanite) came along in the late 1990's.

Very few gemstones conduct electricity. Prominent exceptions include minerals with a metallic luster, such as pyrite. Transparent gems generally do not, a fact exploited by "second generation" diamond testers. These devices contain two separate diagnostic mechanisms. The first, a traditional thermal conductivity tester, separates diamond and Moissanite from other gems, and a second probe of electrical conductivity isolates the true diamond from Moissanite. Note that neither test will succeed with synthetic diamonds, which are chemically identical to the real thing. CVD synthetics (see page 226 of Volume 1) are an exception. Fresh from the oven, they are decent electrical conductors, but this property can be modified by annealing (heat treatment). Note also that natural blue diamond is a modest electrical conductor, due to the presence of boron.

A final conductivity factoid: diamond's excellent thermal conductivity, coupled with it's low electrical conductivity, has led to a lot of research on how to incorporate diamonds in computer chips. Overheating is a major barrier to increasing the horsepower of microcircuits, and monocrystalline synthetic diamond, with the highest thermal conductivity of any known substance (five times that of pure copper), offers some enticing opportunities. Don't be surprised if your future smartphone is literally a jewel of modern engineering.

12.13.3 Pyroelectricity, Piezoelectricity, and Triboelectricity

Wow. Talk about a mouthful of technical terms. Pyroelectricity, piezoelectricity, and triboelectricity all refer to different ways that a gemstone material produces electric charge.

In the **pyroelectric** effect, a crystal develops an electric charge from one face to another, due to a heat-induced distortion of the lattice. This charge can be measured as a voltage difference, and indeed, pyroelectric materials are used as infrared heat sensors. Tourmaline is the best-known pyroelectric gemstone. The phenomenon has been recognized for quite some time. Our colleague Theophrastus (see page 141) noted that tourmaline will attract small bits of ash and straw when heated.

Piezoelectricity refers to the accumulation of charge when a material is physically compressed or stretched, and it is closely related to pyroelectricity. In fact, all pyroelectric materials are also piezoelectric. The converse is not always true, however, due to crystal symmetry effects. Piezoelectric materials have enabled a huge and diverse range of technologies, ranging from the press-to-spark mechanisms in gas appliances and cigarette lighters to the accelerometer in your smart phone. Again, tourmaline is the most prominent common gemstone exhibiting this phenomenon. You have probably experienced tourmaline's frustrating ability to pick up dust and debris, whether mounted on the dop or set in earrings. Pyro and piezoelectricity are responsible. Quartz is also piezoelectric.

Triboelectricity is an entirely different effect, in which a material acquires an electric charge by rubbing against another material. Triboelectricity is the secret behind the trick of attracting small balls of paper with a recently-used comb. Common quartz is triboelectric, but the granddaddy of such materials is amber. We've known about triboelectricity for a while as well: Thales of Miletus described the effect in amber more than two and a half thousand years ago. In fact, we owe essentially all of the modern vocabulary of electricity to this effect in humble amber: the Greek name for amber is *elektron*.

Tribo what?

Incidentally, you should not confuse triboelectricity with *triboluminescence*, which describes the ability of some materials to emit light when mechanically rubbed or stressed. Although not fully understood, triboluminescence appears to be related to the generation of electrical charge due to the breaking of chemical bonds. Diamonds can display this phenomenon, emitting flashes of light during cutting and polishing. Wint-O-Green Lifesavers are also triboluminescent – try crunching one between your teeth in front of a mirror in a darkened room. My favourite example, however, is a glowing ceremonial rattle developed by a Native American tribe living in central Colorado. This enterprising group, known as the Uncompahgre Ute, constructed the rattles from thin sections of buffalo hide stretched over a frame. They then placed transparent quartz crystals inside, which, when shaken, would rub and impact each other, emitting an eerie glow visible through the translucent skin. How cool is that? I want one.

12.13.4 Radioactivity

Thankfully, very few gemstones are radioactive, as this would more or less put a damper on their attractiveness as jewelry. In the majority of instances, radioactivity in minerals results from the decay of potassium, uranium, or thorium. The actual process is quite interesting. For uranium and thorium, *alpha decay* takes place. This involves the ejection of a helium nucleus – two protons and two neutrons – leaving a parent nucleus with a correspondingly lower atomic number (proton count) and mass. For example, when a uranium nucleus (92 protons and 146 neutrons) spontaneously emits an alpha particle, the result is a nucleus of thorium (90 protons and 144 neutrons) and a high-energy photon or *gamma ray*. In the case of potassium (19 protons and 21 neutrons), the radioactive process is known as *beta decay* and involves the conversion of one neutron into a proton and the ejection of an electron (beta particle) and a gamma ray. The aftermath is a nucleus that has one proton more and one neutron less, in other words a calcium nucleus with 20 protons and 20 neutrons.

It can get a bit complicated. For example, that thorium nucleus created by alpha decay will in turn break down by beta decay in a few weeks, producing a nucleus of an exotic-sounding element known as protactinium, as well as the usual electron and another photon. That protactinium nucleus does not have a long and happy life ahead of it, however. After only a few hours, it will, in turn, beta decay to a different type of uranium containing 92 protons but only 142 neutrons. Talk about déjà vu. At least this sort of uranium can hang around for awhile – a quarter million years on average – before jumping back on the radioactive merry-go-round and alpha-decaying to thorium again…this time it's thorium with 90 protons and only 140 neutrons. Guess what…that thorium nucleus ain't exactly stable either…

And now a brief intermission featuring a bit of faceting trivia. One of the giants of physics who managed to figure out all this subatomic complexity was Frederick Soddy. In addition to winning the 1921 Nobel Prize for his research on radioactive decay and isotopes, Soddy had the distinction of marrying Winifred Beilby, the daughter of good old Sir George, who promulgated the theory of aggregation and flow in polishing (see Chapter 8.11.1). End of intermission.

A few natural gemstones exhibit measurable radioactivity. For example, some zircon crystals contain trace amounts of uranium and thorium. In addition to causing mildly alarming "ticks" on a Geiger counter (see Figure 13-2), the breakdown of these elements leads to crystal damage known as metamictization, the process which produces low zircon. Turn to page 160 to learn more. Besides zircon, the table of common radioactive gemstones is mercifully short. Sphene is mildly radioactive, while orthoclase (feldspar) produces barely detectable radiation.

Want to live on the edge? Ekanite, a somewhat eclectic collector's gemstone, is a transparent calcium thorium silicate that will really bend the needles on your Geiger counter. If deadly opaque gemstones are more your style, the charmingly named mineral coffinite really fits the bill. This silicate mineral is a fashionable dead black in colour and contains about 75% uranium by weight.

So much for gemstones that are *naturally* radioactive. In its tireless attempts to improve the visual appearance of gems, the jewelry industry has come up with all sorts of imaginative treatments, including plonking the darn things into a nuclear reactor. Irradiation of gemstones is a surprisingly common practice, and it does produce more desirable colour. When executed improperly, however, it can also result in radioactive gems. Chapter 13.1 contains a much more complete description of gemstone irradiation and its possible consequences.

A final brief note on radioactive gems. Hobbyist faceters will occasionally encounter uranium glass, sometimes known as Vaseline glass. This greenish yellow material is a formulation of normal glass and a small amount of uranium – typically a couple of percent by weight, although it can go considerably higher. Uranium glass was quite popular for vases and tableware late in the late 19th century, but essentially disappeared after uranium became a strategic element during World War II. Faceting uranium glass remains controversial, as any reading of the online discussion forums will attest. Most samples are negligibly radioactive, but you may be unlucky enough to find an exception. Also, the impact of alpha-emitting material on the human body is quite different when admired as a flower vase versus inhaled into the lungs during fine cutting. I personally would never cut a gem out of uranium glass, not only due to the potential risk, but also because there are so many more beautiful, natural, and inarguably safe minerals out there.

12.13.5 Magnetism

Magnetism refers to the property of a material to be attracted by a magnet. As with radioactivity, very few gemstones exhibit significant magnetism. Hematite, which some hobbyists facet, is slightly magnetic in its natural form, but there are synthetic hematites which are strongly magnetic. Some types of synthetic diamond will also be attracted by a strong magnet, due to the presence of iron-nickel inclusions generated during manufacture. This effect can be used to detect forgeries.

In what must by now seem to be an inevitable refrain, it gets a bit more complicated. You see, there is magnetism and there is magnetism. More specifically, there is *ferromagnetism*, *paramagnetism*, and *diamagnetism*. **Ferromagnetism** is the one you are used to. The forces produced by ferromagnetism are strong enough to do practical things in the real world. For example, that attractive plastic sculpture of Homer Simpson holding the shopping list to the fridge uses a ferromagnet. Very few materials exhibit ferromagnetism, among them iron, nickel, cobalt, and some rare earth metals.

Paramagnetism occurs in materials which react to the presence of an external magnetic field by producing one of their own. The interaction between external and internal fields produces a weak attraction, one that is usually so small that specialized equipment is needed to sense it. **Diamagnetism** is similarly weak, but in this phenomenon, the material produces a magnetic field opposite to the applied one. The result is repulsion.

So. Back to gemstones, which according to the first paragraph of this section, do not exhibit significant magnetism. That is true of the gemstone itself, but it is not necessarily true of its chromophores (Remember chromophores? If not, flip back to page 85). It turns out that many of the prominent elements responsible for colour in gemstones are paramagnetic, and hence will be attracted to a strong magnet. Other gem materials and chromophores are diamagnetic and will be repelled. (Physics geeks will point out at this stage that everything in the Universe is diamagnetic...it's just that the weak repulsion is cancelled or overwhelmed in many materials by paramagnetic or ferromagnetic attraction.)

In any case, some gemstones will be attracted to a magnet while others will be repelled, for the most part depending on what type of chromophores are present. The effect is quite weak and to date, few gemological laboratories have the correct equipment for testing. Nevertheless, the field of magnetic gemstone identification appears quite promising – it can, for example, distinguish garnet from much more expensive red spinel and ruby (see page 121). You can actually demonstrate the effect yourself. I have managed to pick up a small Anthill garnet with a "supermagnet" extracted from a broken hard disk drive. Magnetic diagnostics may also help reveal the geographical origin of suspect gems. Google "magnetism in gemstones" to learn more.

13

Gemstone Treatments

Since antiquity, gemstones have been modified to improve their appearance, and this trend shows no sign of slowing down. New treatment techniques seem to appear every year, raising questions about authenticity, disclosure, and commercial ethics.

There are two basic types of gemstone treatment: those that seek to improve the colour and those that can conceal or even repair internal flaws. There are treatment types that can do both: for example, heat treatment is used for both colour improvement and dissolving inclusions.

This chapter examines the various types of gemstone treatment, including heating, irradiation, diffusion, injection of optical agents, and laser repair. The final section addresses the ethics of all of this technological trickery.

13.1 Colour Treatment

The most important determining factor in the value of a coloured gemstone is (surprise!) the colour. Aficionados can and will accept less than perfect clarity – and for some gemstone types, will insist on it (see Chapter 12.12). Colour, on the other hand, is nonnegotiable. You have likely noticed this in your own gem rough buying experience: differences in hue, saturation, and tone can drive the price up or down by a factor of ten or more.

For this reason, gem dealers have developed a variety of treatments for improving colour, and the potential for substantial economic gain has prompted them to subject their treasured rough to some fairly stressful situations. Modern gemstone colour treatment comes in three essential flavours: heating, irradiation, and diffusion.

Heating or "firing" involves raising the gemstone to high temperature, usually in an oxygen-rich or oxygen-poor atmosphere. Treatment temperatures range from a few hundred to a couple of thousand degrees Celsius, applied over a period of minutes to hours to days. This can involve a non-trivial investment in special equipment, and the process is not without its risks (see Section 13.1.2 below).

Radiation treatment subjects the gemstone to energetic photons (gamma rays) or subatomic particles, such as neutrons and beta particles (the historical name for high speed electrons). Some natural radiation treatment involves alpha particles, again a historical name, this time for energetic nuclei of helium atoms (see page 160).

The third type of common treatment aimed at improving colour is **diffusion**, in which the gemstone is heated to near-melting temperature in an environment rich in chromophore elements such as titanium or iron (see page 85). Shallow *surface diffusion* has been around for decades, but recently, much deeper and more difficult to detect bulk or *lattice diffusion* techniques have appeared.

Foiled Again

Actually, there is one more colour treatment beyond heating, radiation, and diffusion: foiling or surface coating. This involves the application of a thin film to the outside surface of the finished gem, often by vacuum deposition techniques. I hesitate to include surface coating among gemstone colour treatments, since it emphatically does not alter the body colour of the stone. I also hesitate because the resulting gems look, in my opinion, emphatically kitschy.

You have probably encountered surface treated gemstones in the form of *Mystic Topaz*, a trade name for colourless topaz with a thin, metallic surface layer applied. When done properly, such a layer will display iridescent interference effects, much like a soap bubble (see also Section 12.7.4). Unfortunately, the coatings are thin, mechanically delicate, and subject to chemical attack from common liquids such as household cleaners. Oh, and did I mention that they look kitschy?

Mystic topaz may be the best-known type of surface-treated gemstone, but it is by no means the first to come down the pike. Some two thousand years ago, Pliny the Elder referred to the application of foil to the back of gems to enhance their appearance, and the practice predates Pliny by almost as much time as he predates us (see "Ancient Treatments, Ancient Fraud" on page 154).

More recently, the foiling of gemstones to improve reflectivity and colour was a common and accepted practice in the 18th and 19th centuries. A basic understanding of optics, which you can glean from Chapter 11, and a glance at the gem designs of the time, particularly the rose cut (page 241), should make it obvious why help was needed. The revolution in gemstone design at the beginning of the twentieth century essentially doomed the art, and true "foil backs" are now a collectors item…emphatically kitschy, but still very collectible.

13.1.1 How Do Colour Treatments Work?

Heat treatment for colour relies on the fact that many gemstones derive their body colour from external trace contaminants, and it is the exact oxidation state of these interlopers that determines the resulting hue, saturation, and tone. Altering the oxidation state of a gemstone's chromophores will alter its colour. Chapter 12, and in particular Section 12.3.2, has a great deal more to say on this issue.

The gases used in heat treatment are either *oxidizing*, in other words oxygen-rich, or *reducing*, which is oxygen-poor. Typically, an oxidizing atmosphere will remove electrons from the chromophore, changing Mn^{++} to Mn^{+++}, for example. A reducing atmosphere has the opposite effect. Thus, much aquamarine has been heated in a reducing atmosphere to convert ferric chromophores (Fe^{+++}) to ferrous (Fe^{++}). This drives off undesirable yellow-green tones (see also Table 12-2).

Heating can alter the colour in other ways, for example by dissolving impurities such as rutile needles in sapphire. Of course, dispersing inclusions via heating will enhance clarity as well (see Section 13.2 below). Heating can also improve colour by allowing the chromophores to move about and become distributed more evenly, hence reducing the effects of banding and zones.

Irradiation operates in a completely different way. Chapter 11.3 describes how light interacts with matter, specifically how the incoming electromagnetic wave "shakes" the crystal lattice and produces the optical effects we observe. Furthermore, Chapter 12.3.1 explains how subtractive colour arises due to absorption of specific wavelengths of incoming light.

Radiation treatment of gemstones combines these two principles. Bombarding a crystal with energetic gamma rays or high-speed subatomic particles produces damage in the structure of the crystal lattice. For example, an atom can be knocked out of its usual location and an electron be trapped in the resulting "hole." As with the simple radio antenna described in Chapter 11.3.2, the electron reacts to the incoming electromagnetic wave and jiggles back and forth. This jiggling dissipates the energy of the wave, and the light is absorbed. The interaction of the electron with the wave and its surrounding atoms allows absorption over only a narrow range of wavelengths, however. The result is a "colour center," a small zone in the crystal which absorbs a certain colour of light.

Given enough colour centers, the overall absorption spectrum, and hence the colour of the gemstone, can be altered. Note that different types of damage sites absorb different wavelengths, and in fact a single radiation treatment may produce multiple absorption bands in the spectrum. Some of these bands are undesirable and may require further treatment (see "Singing the Heat and Radiation Blues..." on page 157).

Diffusion is in many ways a specialized type of heat treatment. Recall from above that heating in the presence of an oxidizing or reducing atmosphere can have a beneficial effect on colour by changing the oxidation state of impurities, dissolving inclusions, or dispersing natural or radiation induced colour centers. Diffusion takes this process one step further – by heating the gem in the presence of desirable chromophores, such as chromium or iron, the impurity atoms can be coaxed to enter the gemstone itself, diffusing inward from the surface and altering the overall colour.

Diffusion treatment first appeared in the late 1970's and to date, it has been applied almost exclusively to corundum. For example, heating off-colour red corundum in the presence of Cr_2O_3 powder allows the chromium atoms to diffuse into the stone, producing a richer and far more valuable red gem. Similarly, iron and titanium oxide powders can enhance the saturation of blue sapphire. Most recently, beryllium diffusion has been used to alter pink sapphire to the considerably more prized orange-pink padparadscha colour.

Ancient Treatments, Ancient Fraud

You don't actually need a modern oxidizing furnace or nuclear reactor to improve the appearance of a gemstone, and the potentially enormous gain in value means that the practice of gemstone enhancement is almost as old as jewelry-making itself.

In fact, there are references to gem manipulation as far back as Pliny the Elder's *Historia Naturalis* (Natural History), which was published in 77 AD. Pliny, an author, natural philosopher, and military commander, has the unique distinction among important historical figures of having died in a volcanic explosion, namely the 79 AD eruption of Vesuvius, which wiped Pompeii and Herculaneum off the map. Pliny is also responsible for what may be the most awesome quote of all time, at least for those poor, self-deluded wretches who see themselves as the next Hemingway:

> *"True glory consists in doing what deserves to be written;*
> *in writing what deserves to be read; and in so living as to*
> *make the world happier and better for our living in it..."*

The *Historia Naturalis* certainly deserves to be read. It is a remarkable, 37-volume encyclopedic overview of our understanding of the world in the first century. It includes books on mathematics, physics, geography, anthropology, medicine, zoology, botany, pharmacology, mining, and yes, precious stones and gems.

In the very last volume, Pliny describes the variety of gemstone types and their use for medicinal purposes and cures. The entire text has survived, and all 77 chapters of *The Natural History of Precious Stones* are available in modern translation on the web (Chap-

Figure 13-1 An 11th century illuminated manuscript of Pliny the Elder's masterwork, Historia Naturalis. This book is the source of much of our knowledge of the ancient world. As a fully connected citizen of the modern world, you can download and read the entire 37-volume edition in translation on the Internet (see Chapter 15.8.13).

ter 15.8.13 of this book will help you track it down). Among my favourites is Pliny's Chapter 11, intriguingly titled "Amber: The Many Falsehoods that have been told about it…," which includes the startling information that fiery red amber is, in fact, the hardened remains of male lynx urine. Amber of a paler, less pronounced, colour comes (of course) from the female.

Despite such quaint and arguably sexist content, Pliny provides considerable practical information on identifying gemstones, and in particular, determining whether they are fake or real. He describes dye processes intended to make quartz look like emerald, the use of metallic foil backings to brighten gems, and the counterfeiting of precious stones by cementing together less valuables materials, including glass.

As a good example to all of us, Pliny the Elder held the practitioners of gemstone fraud in healthy disdain. In describing the faking of *smaragdus* (emerald), he intones:

> "Nay, even more than this, there are books in existence, the authors of which I forbear to name, which give instructions how to stain crystal in such a way as to imitate smaragdus and other transparent stones…indeed, there is no kind of fraud practiced, by which larger profits are made."

The more things change, the more they remain the same. Turn to page 124 to learn more about Pliny the Elder and faceting.

Diffusion Confusion

Are diffusion-modified gems "real"? Is this treatment ethical? Section 13.5 tries to capture the current state of affairs concerning guidelines for disclosure of gem treatment, but here is a summary and an opinion: on the one hand, sapphire has been heat treated since antiquity, and it hardly seems a huge leap from baking a stone in normal sand to baking it in iron oxide (rust). On the other hand, there is no excuse not to disclose such treatment. Ask yourself a simple question: do you view a naturally occurring padparadscha sapphire as more "special" and hence valuable than one that has been created in a modern laboratory from common pink sapphire? Case Closed (or End of Story – see page 165)

If you gave the same answer as I did to that question, you will be happy to know that most diffusion treatment is relatively easy to detect. First, it is fundamentally a heat technique, and the usual diagnostics, such as modified inclusions and stress fractures, should give a strong hint that something unusual has happened to the stone (see Section 13.4). In fact, diffusion requires much higher temperatures than traditional heat treatment, and in the case of the shallower surface diffusion technique, must take place after the gem is cut (see below). Partially melted and dissolved internal flaws, and perhaps even modified facet edges, can point to funny business.

An even more obvious indication of trouble comes from the fact that diffusion acts from the outside in, and in the case of surface diffusion, the colour shift is often confined to a thin layer near the periphery of the stone. Because of this, gems are almost always surface diffusion treated after cutting. This leaves colour zoning and gradients that follow the shape of the gemstone, hardly to be expected in "natural" material. Dropping the gem into a suitable immersion fluid (unfortunately something nasty like methylene iodide for corundum – see Chapter 4.5) should reveal the anomalous colour distribution, which usually appears as increased saturation zones near facet edges. A much more aggressive (and destructive) test is to abrade away some of the gem material, perhaps on the girdle. Careful inspection with a loupe should reveal anything unusual in the distribution of colour.

Despite these relatively straightforward indicators of diffusion treatment, it is a depressing fact of life in the gem world that the counterfeiters are getting better and better at their craft, and even now, the deeper lattice diffusion treatments can be very difficult to detect. For the moment, we faceters can take comfort in the fact that the diffusion labs treat finished gemstones, not rough, but such deep lattice techniques are bound to make an appearance in uncut stones. Bulk gem dealers will be able to afford the necessary diagnostic tests, such as mass spectroscopy, but the rest of us may have to get used to the fact some of our "real" gemstones aren't. Section 13.4 provides more information on detecting gemstone treatment.

13.1.2 Home Colour Treatment?

These treatments are not risk free and should not be undertaken by the beginner or uninformed. They also require some fairly serious equipment. Please play safely or not at all.

What could go wrong? First of all, heating can cause internal stresses, fissures, or inclusions to express themselves in disastrously spectacular ways when a stone is heated. If you have never inadvertently placed a gem in the oven at several hundred degrees and then tried to handle it, then trust me, the experience can be bad for both gemstone and human (What? You haven't tried this? See "Bake and Shake…" on page 145). Nor does heating always produce reliable, predictable results. A milky-white, opaque amethyst is arguably not better than its purple progenitor, and messing up the heat treatment of a diamond can leave you with a rather less valuable noseful of carbon dioxide gas.

Radiation carries its own risks, particularly if you choose to build a nuclear reactor to treat stones in your basement. Linear accelerators and gamma ray sources are marginally safer, yet still insanely dangerous alternatives. There is also the distinct and nasty possibility of residual radioactivity, if the stones come from an unreliable source like your basement. See the next section for more on radiation safety in treated gemstones.

If you are serious about attempting heat treatment of gemstones, there are reference materials available in print form and on the Web to help you get started on your baking career. The same applies to diffusion. I will not even begin to point you in the right direction – as if there is a right direction – to get started with home radiation treatment.

Singing the Heat and Radiation Blues…

Section 13.1.1 explains how heating and irradiation can improve the colour of gemstones. One particular type of material, blue topaz, takes advantage of both techniques and provides the perfect case study of gem colour modification.

Blue topaz begins as colourless, gray, or pale yellow rough. In fact, this material is so common that the cost of production of blue topaz is dominated by the treatment, not the raw material. Drop a few pieces of colourless topaz into your neighbourhood linear accelerator or nuclear reactor, and you can create some pretty useful crystal lattice damage, specifically trapped electrons that absorb light at the blue and red ends of the spectrum.

The result is not pretty – usually brown or green or, if you are really lucky, brownish-green. The result is also radioactive. Wasn't that worth it?

Actually, it was. First, the induced radioactivity in topaz is relatively short-lived, and letting the stones "cool off" for a few weeks or months makes them perfectly safe (see Section 13.1.3). Second, not all topaz colour centers are created equal, and in fact, the blue-absorbing ones are less stable than the red-absorbing ones.

Time for the second weapon in the treatment arsenal: heat. The relative instability of the blue absorbing colour centers means that shaking the crystal lattice via heat can knock the trapped electrons out of these damaged areas, effectively healing the regions responsible for the brownish colour.

This time, the result is very pretty indeed: the vivid blue topaz that has become an enormously popular gemstone all over the world. Without irradiation and heating, gems of this colour would be so rare as to be unobtainable. Instead, lovely, flawless, blue topaz abounds and is sold at Wal-Mart, not Tiffany's.

What happens if something goes wrong?

> Well, unlike with other treatments, you get a do-over with topaz. For example, if the irradiated stones are overheated, all of the colour centers can heal, yielding the original colourless or gray material. No problem! Just head back to the neighbourhood reactor and try again…

13.1.3 Radiation Treatment and Safety

All this talk about nuclear reactors and linear accelerators is probably making you nervous.

Are irradiated gemstones safe?

The short answer is yes. In fact, the long answer is yes as well, provided that you get your gemstone rough from a reliable source. It is true that irradiated stones can be "activated" – that is, made radioactive – by such treatment (particularly by neutrons, as it turns out). Nevertheless, strict controls, both at the reactor facilities and by importers, ensure that any residual radioactivity has decayed to harmless levels before the material is released for sale. Geiger counters are cheap, and a company's reputation would be utterly destroyed by cutting corners in this area. If you feel concerned, you can let that lovely chunk of blue topaz roll around in your rough drawer for a few months before cutting it (I know…we never do that. We immediately cut everything that we buy.)

Of course, radiation never really goes away: the "half life" refers to the period of time in which half of the remaining radioactivity decays. After one period, you have one half; after two periods, one quarter; then one eighth, and so on. You never have zero, but you do get close enough.

We live in a partially radioactive world, and we just have to deal with it. For example, granite rock, airplane flights, and medical X-rays all expose us to radiation (see Table 13-1). Living safely means managing and controlling our exposure, and on the larger scale of things, gemstones are not a concern.

A number of years back, the Nuclear Regulatory Commission in the United States studied the level of exposure due to irradiated gemstones. The fact sheet on their web site (search for *Fact Sheet on Irradiated Gemstones* at www.nrc.gov) describes the results of that study, saying that "the NRC estimated that a person wearing a blue topaz stone at the highest level of radioactivity allowed for distribution under NRC regulations would receive an annual dose of 0.03 millirem. By contrast, a chest X-ray is about 60 millirem." Oh…and the NRC's annual whole-body safety limit is 5000 millirem.

Table 13-1 Some of the background sources of radiation in our daily lives. The maximum safe dose according to the Nuclear Regulatory Commission is 5000 millirem per year.

Radiation Source	Annual Dose (millirem)
Natural Background*	240
Radon (in affected areas)	1000
Medical X-rays	50
Nuclear test residue	0.5
Irradiated blue topaz worn daily	0.03

*depends strongly on location

Figure 13-2 shows me testing some of the zircons from my rough collection. For what it's worth, none of the zircons, nor any of the couple of hundred other stones I measured, moved the needles noticeably beyond the normal background. The display shows about 100 nano-Sieverts per hour, which is 10 micro-rem per hour. During the half-hour of my testing, the natural background ranged between 50 and 150 nano-Sieverts. Over a year, that gives a dose of a little under 100 millirem. The worldwide average per year is between 200 and 400 millirem from natural background and other sources (Table 13-1). It looks like there is not a lot of radon-bearing granite near my house. In any case, that 0.03 millirem you would get from an irradiated blue topaz is small indeed.

A final caveat: the preceding paragraphs have discussed the radiation safety of gemstones worn around your neck or measured on a table in my workshop. Clearly, grinding away at a material and potentially breathing the dust is a different matter. If you are concerned about the radiation safety of faceting, you can avoid materials such as topaz. And as always, the Web contains a great deal more information on this topic.

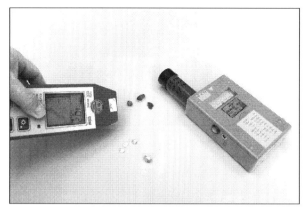

Figure 13-2 Testing gem rough for radiation with a modern dosimeter. Older models such as the one on the right will work fine. They can be purchased for modest cost in electronics surplus stores.

All Natural Colour Treatment

Have you ever been to a natural hot spring? At these seemingly miraculous locations, hot water – occasionally extremely hot water – bubbles up naturally from the earth, filling pools and allowing year-round comfortable bathing and balneotherapy (look it up). Perhaps the most famous of these springs is Iceland's Blue Lagoon, which attracts almost half a million visitors per year. Ironically, the Blue Lagoon is not fed directly from deep in the earth but rather from the outlet of an electric power plant, albeit a geothermal one.

Figure 13-3 Steam rises from the geothermal Blue Lagoon in Iceland.

It will not take many hours of pensive soaking in your favourite hot spring to realize that the inside of the earth is hot, and that gemstones receive natural heat treatment long before they are dug out of the ground. In fact, it is the existence of this natural geological furnace that justifies the claim that heat-treated stones are in fact "natural."

What is less obvious is that minerals within the earth receive natural radiation treatment as well. Thankfully, there are no inviting, warm pools of plutonium lying around on the surface of our planet, but it turns out that the interior of the earth contains a great deal of natural radioactivity – so much, in fact, that this radioactivity is the ultimate source of most geological heat, from volcanoes to that (perhaps now disturbingly blue) lagoon in Iceland.

The most common example of natural gemstone radiation treatment is smoky quartz. This type of rock crystal is good old SiO_2 which contains trace amounts of aluminum. Ambient radioactivity knocks electrons free, and they are subsequently trapped with the help of the aluminum, yielding the colour centers that give smoky quartz its characteristic gray-brown colour. With enough aluminum impurity and irradiation, smoky quartz can turn completely black, forming a mineral known as *morion*. The colour centers are stable, but heating can heal the crystal, restoring its clarity.

Some types of pink tourmaline owe their enchanting colour to natural radiation treatment. Initially pale, the crystal's manganese Mn^{++} chromophores gradually change to Mn^{+++}, thanks to gamma ray bombardment from radioactive potassium decay in the surrounding granite (see Chapter 12.3.2 for more on chromophores). The result is the lovely pink tourmaline that we all know and love.

The most spectacular naturally irradiated gemstones are the fancy green diamonds, and the most spectacular exemplar is no doubt the Dresden Green, a 41-carat natural green diamond that is the centerpiece of the treasury of the New Green Vault in Dresden, Germany (Figure 13-4). With the Hope Diamond at the Smithsonian in Washington (Chapter 1.1.2), the Dresden Green is an essential stop on any gem fancier's pilgrimage.

Figure 13-4 The Grünes Gewölbe or Green Vault in Dresden Germany, home to the most spectacular naturally irradiated gemstone in the world.

No overview of naturally irradiated gemstones would be complete without an homage to zircon. This often-overlooked gem not only exhibits lovely colour and breathtakingly high refractive index and dispersion, it also has the unique ability to radiation-treat *itself*. Naturally occurring trace atoms of uranium and thorium in zircon spontaneously decay, emitting alpha particles which cause radiation damage in the surrounding crystal lattice.

As with smoky quartz and diamond, this radiation damage produces colour centers, yielding an overall greenish or brownish cast in the stone. This process has been honoured with the fancy moniker *metamictization*, and given enough time and radioactivity, this natural treatment can even affect the refractive index and specific gravity of the material. Eventually, the radiation can completely compromise the crystal structure.

Yes, this natural radiation treatment is what distinguishes *high* zircon from *low* zircon. The crystal lattice of high zircon has suffered minimal radiation damage and has a refractive index of 1.95 and a specific gravity of 4.7. Add a bit of uranium and thorium, wait a while, and you end up with low or *metamict* zircon, whose refractive index and specific gravity are about 10% lower. As with other radiation induced changes, heating can restore the original properties. In fact, most blue zircons have had an artificial heat treatment after their lengthy, natural radiation bath (see Table 13-2).

13.2 Inclusion Treatment

Inclusions are the bane of any amateur faceter's existence. Despite our most heroic investigative efforts at the dealer's table, that lovely piece of gem rough inevitably ends up having an internal crack, bubble, or feather at the worst possible place. Inclusions have a strong influence on the value of rough and cut gemstones. As a result, and as with colour, the industry has developed a variety of techniques for reducing their visual impact. These techniques include heating, the application of optical agents, and laser drilling.

Heating improves the clarity of gemstones by dissolving internal flaws and in some instances, partially repairing fractures. Perhaps the best-known and most practiced instance of this is with corundum – ruby and sapphire. Needle-like crystals of rutile are a common inclusion in corundum. Heating such gems can cause the needles to dissolve into the crystal lattice and disappear. Interestingly, a different sequence of temperatures can encourage the rutile to re-crystallize or *exsolve*, forming the fibrous inclusions responsible for star sapphire (see Chapter 12.12.1).

There are a number of materials that can be applied to the surface of, or injected into, a gemstone to help disguise cracks and flaws. These **optical agents** work by minimizing changes in refractive index and hence distracting reflections. This is the exact same principle as an immersion fluid, which not only fills in surface imperfections but also reduces Fresnel reflection (see Chapters 4.5 and 11.8).

There are two types of optical agent used for this purpose: liquids, either oil or unhardened resin; and solids, either hardened resin or glass. The practice of oiling emeralds is the best known example of applied optical agents, and in fact, about 90% of commercial emeralds have been treated with cedar oil, Canada balsam, Opticon, or other natural and synthetic oils or resins. Solid fillings have been used for diamonds for some time, and indications are that glass-filled corundum is coming soon.

When openly declared (see Section 13.5 below), oiling with transparent optical agents is an accepted treatment for emeralds, although dishonest traders have been known to use green-coloured oil. This is essentially a dye treatment, which is not accepted. Careful examination under a microscope will usually reveal the presence of solid or liquid optical agents, due to the slight difference in colour and refractive index (see Section 13.4). Note that you should take extra care in cutting such stones. Not only are gems with significant structural flaws more susceptible to fracture, but also the cracks can take up unsightly cutting residue. Needless to say, you should never subject such gemstones to an ultrasonic cleaner.

Laser drilling has so far only been seen in diamonds. The goal here is to produce a tiny pipe between the surface of the gem and an internal inclusion. This pipe provides access for filling agents or bleach, which can reduce the visibility of the flaw.

13.3 Common Gemstone Treatments

So much for the theory. How likely is it that a particular piece of gem rough in your collection has been treated?

The answer depends entirely on the type of gem material. For some, such as blue topaz, the probability that it has been modified is essentially 100%. Other species, such as spinel and garnet, have no known or economically viable treatment. Table 13-2 attempts to capture the current (2013) situation regarding treatment of common gemstones. Given the economic forces at play, however, the status quo is certain to change. The best strategy is to review on a regular basis the information materials produced by the gem trade associations. Both the World Jewellery Confederation (CIBJO) and the American Gem Trade Association (AGTA) maintain listings of common treatments (see Chapter 15.8.3 for links). The online discussion groups are again a useful resource. A number of gemologists and other experts contribute frequently, and their insight into the current treatment landscape can be invaluable.

Table 13-2 Treatment of common gemstone materials. Information assembled from the CIBJO Gemstone Blue Book and the AGTA Gemstone Information Manual, as well as various online sources. Consult the links in Chapter 15.8.3 to learn more.

Material	Treatment
Amber	Heated to darken (surface layer) and clarify. Heated and quenched to produce "sun spangles" (see page 146). Occasionally dyed to add colour.
Andalusite	No common treatment.
Apatite	No common treatment.
Beryl	Aquamarine usually heat treated to change green-blue to blue. Morganite is heated to drive off yellow tones. Some beryl is also radiation treated (colourless to yellow, blue to green, pale to deep blue or *maxixe*, which can fade in sunlight). Most emerald is treated with optical agents. Some emerald dyed. Red beryl frequently oiled.
Chrysoberyl	No common treatment for transparent varieties. Some alexandrite oiled.
Corundum	Virtually all corundum is heat treated to improve clarity and colour. Some stones heated to enhance asteria (stars). Diffusion (see page 156). Some irradiation, which can turn colourless corundum yellow and pink corundum to padparadscha. Some glass or plastic filling. Some oiling. Some dyeing.
Cubic Zirconia	Not applicable – synthetic material.
Danburite	No common treatment.
Diamond	Radiation is used to produce fancy colours, especially green or blue. Adding heat treatment leads to yellow, orange, brown, pink, or occasionally red. High pressure, high temperature treatment can produce white, pink, or blue from off-colour material. Acid bleaching combined with laser drilling to treat inclusions. Glass filling. Some surface coating reported.
Feldspar / Sunstone	No common treatment.
Fluorite	Blue material heated.
Garnet	No common treatment, with the possible exception of demantoid.
Glass / Obsidian	No common treatment.
Iolite	No common treatment.
Opal	Depends on variety. Opaque opal frequently impregnated. Black opal substrate artificially darkened. Fire opal no common treatment.
Peridot	No common treatment. Occasionally filled with optical agent.
Quartz	Modest heating of amethyst can lighten it. Higher temperatures yield yellow, orange or yellow-green (almost all citrine and prasiolite on the market is "burnt" amethyst). Naturally occurring yellow quartz is quite rare. Oro verde or greened quartz is irradiated, as is some rose and smoky quartz.

Material	Treatment
Scapolite	Yellow material can be irradiated to deeper lavender.
Sphene	No common treatment
Spinel	No common treatment
Tanzanite	Essentially all rough tanzanite is reddish-brown. Heat treatment brings out the prized purple-blue colour and very occasionally green to green-blue. Some surface coating reported.
Topaz	Irradiation and heat (see page 157). Pink topaz routinely heated to drive off yellow and orange tones. Irradiated to produce green and occasionally yellow and orange. Surface diffusion and coating to improve / modify colour (see "Foiled Again" on page 152).
Tourmaline	Most green and blue stones are heat treated. Red occasionally. Some irradiated to intensify colour (i.e. to darken pink or turn blue to purple) and to drive off brownish tones. Some injection of filling agents. Some dyeing.
Zircon	Brown zircon heat treated to blue, light brown to clear (diamond simulant). Yellow-brown and red heated to golden colour. Irradiation of clear zircon produces brown or red.

13.4 Detecting Gemstone Treatments

Although detecting some of the more advanced gemstone treatments would require the services of a serious gemological laboratory, there are a number of tests you can make to double check the veracity of your gem dealer. Armed with a bit of knowledge and a half-decent loupe or microscope, you should be able to identify the signatures of laboratory modification.

The first bit of knowledge is an understanding of the current state of gemstone treatments (see previous section). It hardly makes sense to examine blue tourmaline for signs of heating, since much if not all of this material is treated with heat before sale. The obvious exception is the situation where a dealer claims that a sample has not been modified in any way, and is planning to charge you a correspondingly higher price as a result.

Evidence of heat treatment comes primarily in the form of modified inclusions. This can be the partial dissolution of silk and mineral inclusions or even stress fractures. In some instances, gas or fluid inclusions may show signs of rupture. Irradiation is very difficult to detect. The one exception is diamonds which have been treated to create fancy colours. Not only are these stones much more vividly coloured than their natural counterparts, but also careful examination may reveal colour zoning characteristic of radiation treatment. Surface diffusion can be easy to spot, but the deeper lattice type may require proper lab equipment (see "Diffusion Confusion" on page 156).

Life gets a bit easier for the treatment sleuth in the case of optical agents and fillers. Although techniques and materials have improved enormously over the centuries, there will always be at least a subtle change in refractive index, colour, or luster in the regions that have been filled. This can be seen with careful microscopic examination under good lighting. Some optical agents fluoresce under ultraviolet light, making your detective work a snap.

Laser drilling is also usually easy to identify. Once you have seen an example (and there are plenty of microphotographs on the Web), it will be hard to mistake a perfectly clean, perfectly straight, tube-like structure as the work of Nature.

Identifying gemstone treatment is one of the basic skills every gemologist needs to possess. This means that there are multiple resources out there for you to explore, ranging from asking a professional to examine your stone to taking a class or even a graduate gemologist's degree in the field.

13.5 The Ethics of Gemstone Treatment

As emphasized several times in this chapter, the potential gain in value that gemstone treatment brings has led to the establishment of a modern, efficient, and technologically adept industry. It has also led to a lot of fraud. At the level of your local gem rough dealer, this situation raises a number of additional ethical questions. Here's the important one:

Must all gemstone treatments be declared?

There are actually two answers to this: yes and no. From my viewpoint, a dealer who wishes my sustained business and respect must declare any and all treatments of which he or she is aware. So the answer is Yes. End of Story.

Why is gem treatment controversial?

As a gem lover, you may view this as a stupid question with an obvious answer. However, there are several consequences that may not be immediately clear, beyond the obvious fact that artificially modified gems are further from their natural origins than the untreated type.

First, the ready availability of souped-up stones could swamp the market, reducing the worth of "natural" gems. This has knock-on effects, ranging from lowering the value of your existing rough collection to worsening the already difficult economic situation for gem miners worldwide. Undeclared and undetectable treatment will also impact the overall reputation of the gem and jewelry world, affecting international conglomerates like DeBeers and hobby faceters alike. Finally, some treatments are not stable. Whether it is the slow reversal and fading of a colour treatment or the gradual yellowing, crazing or decay of an inclusion fill, a negative consumer experience with a poorly treated gem is bad for all of us.

The legal situation is (surprise! surprise!) a little more complicated.

The actual requirements on formal declaration of gemstone treatment vary from jurisdiction to jurisdiction. In the United States, the Federal Trade Commission is the ultimate arbiter on issues of business ethics, and they have a specific set of rules regarding the gemstone trade (see also page 218 of Volume 1).

You can and should read their entire online rule book, available at www.ftc.gov/bcp/guides/jewel-gd.shtm. The core of the matter appears in Article 23-22 of the Code of Federal Regulations:

FTC § 23.22 Disclosure of treatments to gemstones.

It is unfair or deceptive to fail to disclose that a gemstone has been treated if:

(a) the treatment is not permanent. The seller should disclose that the gemstone has been treated and that the treatment is or may not be permanent;

(b) the treatment creates special care requirements for the gemstone. The seller should disclose that the gemstone has been treated and has special care requirements. It is also recommended that the seller disclose the special care requirements to the purchaser;

(c) the treatment has a significant effect on the stone's value. The seller should disclose that the gemstone has been treated.

The last clause is the kicker, and is used regularly as an "out" to not declare a treatment. What does "significant" actually mean? Also, if a particular practice is essentially universal, the comparison with untreated material clearly breaks down.

I disagree with these views. In my opinion, clause (c) makes the answer to the question of declaration an emphatic yes. Both my common sense and my experience tell me that in all instances, a completely natural gem is far more valuable than one whose appearance is the result of human intervention. As I said, Yes. End of Story.

There are actually a few other influential regulatory bodies out there. The World Jewellery Confederation, known by its French acronym CIBJO (Confédération Internationale de la Bijouterie, Joaillerie, Orfèverie, des diamant, perles, et pierres) was originally founded in the 1920's with a mission, among other things, to safeguard public trust in the gem industry. The CIBJO Code of Ethics dedicates its membership to ensuring consumer confidence in its fair dealings, specifically stating, "the non-disclosure of treatments, and the passing off of partly or wholly synthetic stones and simulants as natural stones, is contrary to the interests of consumers."

The American Gem Trade Association (AGTA) came into being around a hotel swimming pool in Tucson on a rainy gem show evening in 1981. Now boasting more than a thousand members in the USA and Canada, the AGTA has formalized the declaration of gemstone enhancement using a system of codes that are becoming accepted worldwide (Table 13-3). The association also binds its membership to a higher standard of disclosure than required by the FTC. Quoting from the AGTA Code of Ethics and Principles of Fair Business Practice: "Merchandise must not be misrepresented as to its nature, authenticity, treatment and/or origin. Disclosure of treatment is mandatory…"

Table 13-3 American Gem Trade Association symbols for specific forms of gemstone enhancement. Adapted from the AGTA Gemstone Information Manual.

Symbol	Definition
N	Natural: No modification (or currently has no known modification process).
B	Bleaching: The use of heat, light and/or other agents to lighten or remove a gemstone's color.
C	Coating: The use of such surface enhancements as lacquering, enameling, inking, foiling or sputtering of films to improve appearance, provide color or add other special effects.
D	Dyeing: The introduction of coloring matter into a gemstone to give it new color, intensify present color or improve color uniformity.
F	Filling: The filling of surface-breaking cavities or fissures with colorless glass, plastic, solidified borax or similar substances. This process may improve durability, appearance and/or add weight.
H	Heating: The use of heat to effect desired alteration of color, clarity and/or phenomena. If residue of foreign substances in open fissures is visible under properly illuminated 10X magnification, H F should be used.
HP	Heating and Pressure: The use of heat and pressure combined to effect desired alterations of color, clarity and/or phenomena.
I	Impregnation: The impregnation of a porous gemstone with a colorless agent (usually plastic) to improve durability and appearance.
L	Lasering: The use of a laser and chemicals to reach and alter inclusions in gemstones, usually diamonds.

Symbol	Definition
O	Oiling/Resin Infusion: The filling of surface-breaking fissures with colorless oil, wax, resin or other colorless substances, except glass or plastic, to improve the gemstone's appearance.
R	Irradiation: The use of neutrons, gamma rays or beta particles (high energy electrons) to alter a gemstone's color. The irradiation may be followed by a heating process.
U	Diffusion: The use of chemicals in conjunction with high temperatures to produce ARTIFICIAL color change and/or asterism-producing inclusions.
W	Waxing/Oiling: The impregnation of a colorless wax, paraffin or oil in porous opaque or translucent gemstones to improve appearance.

It's unanimous then. Gemstone treatments are ethical, provided that they are completely disclosed. Incidentally, "completely disclosed" includes the use of clear language. As with synthetic material (Chapter 6.6), there is a strong motivation to employ euphemistic terms such as "enhanced" to describe gemstone treatment. The unambiguous AGTA codes in Table 13-3 go a long way toward solving this issue.

The field of gemstone treatment is vast, interesting, and rapidly evolving. No book on amateur faceting can do it proper justice. Point your web browser to the relevant links in Chapter 15.8.3 to learn more about the practice, ethics, and legality of gemstone treatments.

14

Common Gem Materials

Every book on faceting must contain a chapter listing the properties of gemstone materials. Having said that, I will forgive you for never actually consulting this chapter. Whenever I need to know the refractive index of spodumene, for example, I look it up on the Web. Also, there are entire excellent textbooks dedicated to exactly this topic (see Chapter 9.3).

Again, having said that, there is actually useful information buried in the tables on the following pages. In particular, the faceting tips and info listed for each gem species represent the gathered wisdom of many years of cutting, most of it from sources far more experienced than I am.

14.1 Common Gemstone Materials

The following pages list the optical, physical, and faceting properties of the most popular gem materials, while Section 14.2 contains more abbreviated information on less common gems. The division between the two groups is admittedly somewhat biased, in the sense that the first group contains the gemstones that I cut most. Nevertheless, the thirteen materials presented in this section surely represent well over 95% of current amateur faceting output, at least by the number of stones produced.

Each gemstone material appears on its own page, headed by its common name, chemical name, and chemical formula. A short description provides general information, followed by tables of the optical, physical, and faceting properties.

The optical properties include the body colour of the gem material, listed approximately in order of "prominence" to the amateur faceter. This is an admittedly arbitrary combination of how common, how popular, and how valuable a particular colour is. The refractive index entry often includes a single value in boldface, followed by two numbers in round brackets. The former is the commonly adopted value, while the latter represents the range of published indices. The variation occurs from sample to sample, and in the case of mineral groups, from species to species. The "low-medium-high" assessment of the dispersion and birefringence follows the conventions of Vargas' *Faceting for Amateurs* (see Chapter 9.1), while the description of pleochroic colours represents an amalgam of sources.

The physical properties should be self-explanatory. Refer to the relevant sections of Chapter 12 if you have difficulty understanding their meaning.

The final group of properties is arguably the most valuable to an amateur faceter. I have tried to assemble a reasonably complete list of source regions for each gem type. As with the colour property, the order of the Localities usually reflects the importance of each region. The Faceting Tips entry gathers together experience and wisdom on actually cutting and polishing the gems, while the Treatments field lists common laboratory modifications that you should watch out for. The final entry in the Faceting Properties table gives an estimate of Rough Cost and the availability of synthetics.

As hinted at on the previous page, this chapter is by no means the only or even the best source of information on the properties of gemstone materials. For example, Chapter 12 focuses exclusively on the optical and physical characteristics of gems, albeit on a property-by-property and not a material-by-material basis. Chapter 8 presents cutting and polishing tips, Chapter 13 discusses treatments, and you can learn more about rough cost and synthetics from Chapter 6.

Finally, turn to the printed resources listed in Chapter 9.3 and the websites catalogued in Chapter 15.8.6 for more complete, up to date information on gemstone material properties.

Beryllium Aluminum Silicate
$Al_2Be_3(Si_6O_{18})$

Beryl

Facetable beryl appears in many colours: *aquamarine* (blue to green), *emerald* (green), *golden beryl* (lemon-gold yellow), *goshenite* (colorless), *heliodor* (yellow-green), *morganite* (pink), and *bixbite* (red). Some references classify all non-emerald and non-aquamarine samples as *precious beryl*.

Optical Properties

colour	blue, blue-green, green, lemon-yellow, golden-yellow, yellow-green, colourless, pink, red
refractive index	**1.58** (1.562 - 1.602)
dispersion	0.014 - medium
birefringence	0.004 - 0.01 - low
pleochroism	dichroic – aquamarine: distinct - (colourless/light blue to blue, greenish bue); emerald: distinct (yellow-green to blue-green); golden beryl: weak (yellow to light-yellow); goshenite: no dichroism (colourless); heliodor: weak (gold-yellow to greenish-yellow); morganite: distinct (pale-pink to lavender-pink)

Physical Properties

hardness	7.5 - 8
density	2.66 - 2.87
crystal system	hexagonal
cleavage	indistinct
fracture	conchoidal, brittle

Faceting Properties

Localities	Many. Brazil, Colombia, Afghanistan, Pakistan, Zambia, Russia, Nigeria, Mozambique, Zimbabwe, USA, Australia, Madagascar, China, Tajikistan…
Faceting Tips	Emerald and bixbite almost always contain inclusions, which can weaken the crystal and lead to fractures. Otherwise, beryl presents no problems. Polish with alumina, cerium oxide, or diamond on all common laps.
Treatments	Natural aquamarine usually has a greenish hue. Blue material on the market is almost always heat treated. Emerald treatments include the injection of oils or synthetic fillers to stabilize the stone and improve colour. This type of treatment is not always reported. Other types of beryl may be heat treated or irradiated to improve colour.
Rough Cost	Strongly dependent on type. Pale aquamarine is available in perfect crystals at modest cost, making it an excellent choice for a first stone (see Chapter 5.2). Well-saturated aqua commands premium prices, comparable to excellent quality tourmaline, for example. The less popular types of beryl – goshenite, morganite, heliodor, and golden beryl – can be difficult to find, but are not expensive. Due to its popularity and mystique, emerald is among the most costly of the coloured gemstones. The profit motive encourages cutting at the source, and you may have difficulty locating decent emerald rough. Natural red beryl, or bixbite, is exceedingly rare in large, facetable sizes, and hence can be expensive. Synthetic emerald and bixbite exist.

Chrysoberyl

Beryllium Aluminum Oxide
$BeAl_2O_4$

Chrysoberyl appears in two common forms. Ordinary **chrysoberyl** produces excellent yellow to golden-green gemstones with plenty of sparkle. **Alexandrite** is a highly prized gem material which exhibits a distinct colour change (green in daylight to purple-red in incandescent light). Chrysoberyl is also the only true Cat's Eye (Chapter 12.7.3).

Optical Properties

colour	yellow, greenish-yellow, green, brownish-green, purple, red, colour-change (alexandrite)
refractive index	**1.75** (1.746 - 1.763)
dispersion	0.015 - medium
birefringence	0.007 - 0.011 - medium
pleochroism	dichroic – very weak (reddish to yellowish or yellow to pale green) Alexandrite displays distinct trichroism (red, orange-yellow, green)

Physical Properties

hardness	8.5
density	3.70 - 3.78
crystal system	orthorhombic
cleavage	good
fracture	weak, conchoidal

Faceting Properties

Localities	Brazil, Sri Lanka, Myanmar, Madagascar, Russia, Tanzania, Zimbabwe
Faceting Tips	Chrysoberyl is an excellent material for the amateur faceter. It cuts and polishes easily, albeit somewhat slowly due to its hardness. Polish with diamond or alumina on metal or composite laps.
Treatments	May be irradiated to improve colour. Some alexandrite may be oiled.
Rough Cost	Ordinary chrysoberyl commands a modest price in the rough market. Natural alexandrite rough is almost impossible to obtain and very expensive. Synthetic alexandrite is available.

Aluminum Oxide
Al_2O_3

Corundum

Corundum is available in a bewildering array of colours. Red corundum is called **ruby**. All other colours are **sapphire**. Pink-orange sapphires, known as **padparadscha**, are particularly prized, as are the more widely-known blue variety.

Optical Properties		Physical Properties	
colour	ruby: red sapphire: many. blue, orange, yellow, pink, green, purple, colourless, colour-change	hardness	9
		density	3.95 - 4.05
refractive index	**1.76** (1.762 - 1.788)	crystal system	hexagonal / trigonal
dispersion	0.018 - medium	cleavage	none
birefringence	0.008 - low	fracture	conchoidal, splintery
pleochroism	dichroic – varying, darker colours show stronger dichroism. ruby: strong (deep red to yellowish-red); blue: distinct (dark blue to greenish-blue); orange: strong (orange to yellow-brown or colorless); yellow: weak (yellow to light-yellow); green: weak (more or less yellow); purple: distinct (purple to pinkish)		

Faceting Properties

Localities	Australia, Myanmar, Sri Lanka, Thailand, USA (Montana), Brazil, China, Cambodia, Tanzania, Kenya, Malawi, Nigeria, Zimbabwe
Faceting Tips	Challenges: directional differential hardness, orange peel with bonded laps, colour banding, crystal shape vs pleochroism to maximize yield, frictional heating during polish, slow cutting due to hardness. Polish with diamond on ceramic or metal.
Treatments	Almost all corundum is heat-treated to dissolve silk and improve colour. Heat can also enhance asteria (star-stones). Other occasional treatments include diffusion, radiation, oiling, dyeing, and filling.
Rough Cost	Generally expensive, although smaller stones in less desirable or banded colours are affordable. Top colour rough, especially padparadscha, may be difficult to find at any price. Corundum is an important material in the opto-electronics industry, and synthetics are available in a multitude of colours at very low cost.

Cubic Zirconia

Zirconium Dioxide
ZrO_2

Cubic zirconia, also know as just zirconia or more familiarly as CZ, is a synthetic gemstone that first appeared in large quantities as a diamond simulant in the mid-1970's. With the addition of various doping materials, CZ can be synthesized in almost any colour, and it offers the faceter spectacular performance at a modest price.

Optical Properties

colour	many, including colour-change
refractive index	**2.18** (2.15 - 2.20)
dispersion	0.060 strong
birefringence	none
pleochroism	none

Physical Properties

hardness	8.25 - 8.5
density	5.6 - 6.0
crystal system	isometric / cubic
cleavage	none
fracture	conchoidal brittle

Faceting Properties

Localities	Many factories produce cubic zirconia, although some claim that those in Russia, the USA, and Britain produce the highest quality product.
Faceting Tips	Due to its hardness, you should polish cubic zirconia with diamond on metal or ceramic. A pre-polish with 8000 grit diamond can speed the final polishing phase. The material is brittle, so take extra care to prevent small fragments from producing scratches.
Treatments	Not relevant.
Rough Cost	Low. Expect to pay pennies per carat.

Various Metal Silicates
$X_3Y_2(SiO_4)_3$

Garnet

Garnet is not a single material but rather a group of related silicate minerals with similar chemistry and crystal structure. The main varieties are pyrope, almandine, spessartine, uvarovite, grossular, and andradite. Mixtures are common. For example, the very popular rhodolite species is a mixture of pyrope and almandine. Garnet is a close second to sapphire and tourmaline in terms of the variety of colours available.

Optical Properties

colour	red, purple, brown, orange, green, pink, yellow, black, colourless, colour-change
refractive index	1.73 (grossular) - 1.94 (andradite)
dispersion	0.014 (uvarovite) - 0.057 (andradite)
birefringence	none
pleochroism	none

Physical Properties

hardness	6.5 - 7.5
density	3.41 (uvarovite) - 4.30 (almandine)
crystal system	isometric / cubic
cleavage	indistinct
fracture	conchoidal, brittle

Faceting Properties

Localities	Many (alphabetical): Brazil, Canada, China, Germany, India, Italy, Kenya, Korea, Madagascar, Mali, Mexico, Myanmar, Namibia, Pakistan, Poland, Russia, South Africa, Sri Lanka, Switzerland, Tanzania, USA, Zaire...
Faceting Tips	Keep red garnets small to avoid over-dark gems. Some users report "orange peel" problems with Nubond laps (see page 341 of Volume 1). Polish with alumina or diamond on all common laps, or with diamond on ceramic.
Treatments	No commercially viable treatments, except heat treatment of demantoid.
Rough Cost	Varies widely. Common red garnets are very affordable, while the green varieties can rival sapphire in per-carat cost. Tsavorite, demantoid, and colour change garnets can be extraordinarily costly. Synthetics exist, including types such as YAG (yttrium aluminum garnet) and GGG (gadolinium gallium garnet), which do not exist in nature (see Chapter 6.6).

Glass

Amorphous Silicon Dioxide
SiO_2

Glass has been used as a simulant gemstone for thousands of years. Although at its heart a simple amorphous oxide of silicon, glass is available in an extraordinary variety of mixtures with correspondingly diverse properties. Faceters will prefer the higher index flint glasses (see page 113) as a practice material.

Optical Properties

colour	virtually all, including colour-change
refractive index	1.44 - 1.68 (specialty glasses can be much higher)
dispersion	variable. strong in lead glass
birefringence	none
pleochroism	none

Physical Properties

hardness	**5** (4 - 7)
density	**2.5** (2.2 - 5)
crystal system	amorphous
cleavage	none
fracture	conchoidal, very brittle

Faceting Properties

Localities	Very many. There are geographically-specific novelty glasses, such as those made by melting volcanic ash, i.e. Mt. St. Helen's glass.
Faceting Tips	Polish with cerium oxide or alumina. Some glass can be very brittle or heat sensitive.
Treatments	Not applicable
Rough Cost	Low

Hydrous Silicon Dioxide
$SiO_2 \cdot nH_2O$

Opal

Opal is an amorphous mineraloid consisting of cristobalite spheres in a water solution. In the most highly prized samples, diffraction due to the regular stacking of these spheres produces dramatic rainbow effects. The colour, transparency, and play of colour varies widely from species to species and sample to sample. Most opal is cut en cabochon, and the transparent jelly, fire, cherry, and hyalite varieties will be of greatest interest to the faceter.

Optical Properties		Physical Properties	
colour	jelly opal is clear, yellow, or bluish-gray; fire and cherry opal is orange to red; hyalite is colourless to gray	hardness	5.5 - 6.5
		density	1.98 - 2.5
refractive index	**1.45** (1.37 - 1.52)	crystal system	amorphous
dispersion	none tabulated	cleavage	none
birefringence	none	fracture	conchoidal, very brittle
pleochroism	none		

Faceting Properties

Localities	Australia, Mexico, Brazil, Central America, Indonesia, Japan, Russia, USA
Faceting Tips	Polish with cerium oxide. Soft and hence susceptible to scratching from contamination, including household dust. Can be very brittle and sensitive to mechanical shock. Heat sensitive. Interestingly, Vargas (see Chapter 9.1) reports several instances of opals cracking during the faceting process and subsequently showing no evidence of damage.
Treatments	There is no common accepted treatment for transparent opals, although there are reports of shady dealers using water, oil, or other transparent liquids to conceal flaws. Transparent opal should be "seasoned" by leaving it in open air for up to two years to ensure that the material will not become milky or crazed (see page 95). The opaque varieties are frequently impregnated to repair fractures. The rare and valuable black opals may have the substrate matrix artificially darkened.
Rough Cost	Modest for the transparent varieties. Samples with particularly fine play of colour can be costly. Synthetics exist, but are not an issue for the transparent, facetable types.

Peridot

Magnesium Iron Silicate
$(Mg,Fe)_2SiO_4$

Peridot has been a popular gemstone for centuries. It is unique among the common gem materials in having only a single body colour, green, although its intensity and hue can vary significantly. Peridot is also the only common idiochromatic gem (see page 85), with the distinct green colour arising from the presence of iron. Also known as chrysolite forsterite, or olivine, the mineral peridot is very common – anyone who has visited a green sand beach has literally been rolling in the stuff. Nevertheless, large clean crystals are relatively rare.

Optical Properties

colour	green, yellow-green, apple-green, olive-green, greenish-brown
refractive index	**1.67** (1.650 - 1.703)
dispersion	0.020 medium
birefringence	0.036 - 0.038 medium
pleochroism	dichroic – very weak (colourless or pale green to deeper yellow or olive-green)

Physical Properties

hardness	6.5 - 7.0
density	**3.3** (3.28 - 3.48)
crystal system	orthorhombic
cleavage	indistinct
fracture	conchoidal, brittle

Faceting Properties

Localities (alphabetical) Australia, Brazil, China, Egypt (Zabargad Island), Kenya, Mexico, Myanmar, Norway, Pakistan, Sri Lanka, South Africa, Tanzania, USA

Faceting Tips Polish with alumina or diamond on all common laps, or with diamond on ceramic. While cutting is generally problem-free, polishing can be unpredictable. Try switching laps or compounds. Some faceters recommend adding vinegar to the drip tank (but see page 298 of Volume 1). Flat "lily pad" inclusions are fairly common and can cause trouble if they come to the surface. Black carbon-spot inclusions are also commonplace. Some people find the facet-doubling due to birefringence distracting and orient the gem accordingly.

Treatments No common treatment, although bulk rough is often surface oiled. Occasional filling with optical agent.

Rough Cost Modest. Unlike most other types of gem rough, you can often find decent pieces of peridot that have been tumble polished. These can be a great value and offer the additional benefit of presenting a clean internal view and an unambiguous body colour. There are no economically viable synthetics.

Crystalline Silicon Dioxide
SiO$_2$

Quartz

Quartz is the second most abundant mineral in the Earth's crust (after feldspar), and it is very likely the most abundant mineral in every faceter's rough drawer. Facetable quartz species include rock crystal, amethyst, citrine, rose quartz, prasiolite, oro-verde, smoky quartz, and synthetics. Amethyst is the most valued variety. Although touted as the ideal beginner's gemstone material, polishing quartz can be problematic.

Optical Properties		Physical Properties	
colour	colourless (rock crystal), purple, purple-red (amethyst), yellow, orange, gold-brown (citrine), pink (rose), leek-green (prasiolite), yellow-green (oro-verde), brown, black (smoky), blue. Mixed amethyst-citrine is called ametrine.	hardness	7.0
		density	2.65
refractive index	**1.55** (1.540 - 1.553)	crystal system	hexagonal / trigonal
dispersion	0.013 medium	cleavage	none
birefringence	0.009 weak	fracture	conchoidal, very brittle
pleochroism	rock crystal: none; amethyst: weak (purple to grayish purple); citrine: weak (yellow to light-yellow); rose: weak (pink to pale pink); prasiolite: very weak (light green to paler green); smoky: definite (brown to reddish-brown)		

Faceting Properties

Localities	Brazil, Madagascar, Uruguay, Zambia, Myanmar, USA, Russia, Canada, Mexico, Sri Lanka, Switzerland, Argentina, Namibia, UK, Spain
Faceting Tips	Polish with cerium on a composite lap or with alumina on metal. Can be susceptible to "horse-hair" scratching and ripples. See Chapter 8.17.3 for polishing tips.
Treatments	Modest heating of amethyst can lighten its body colour. Conventional heat treatment of amethyst produces yellow, red-brown, green, or colourless stones. Natural citrines usually have no red tint. They are quite rare and most citrine material on the market is "burnt" amethyst. Prasiolite is also heat-treated amethyst as is most ametrine. Oro-verde is irradiated. Some smoky and rose quartz is also radiation treated.
Rough Cost	Generally low. Top "Siberian" amethyst can be moderately expensive, as can very transparent rose quartz. Synthetics exist, including colours, such as blue, which are not found in nature.

Spinel

Magnesium Aluminum Oxide
$MgAl_2O_4$

Spinel is actually a group of related minerals with similar properties. Its relatively high refractive index and dispersion make for a fine gemstone, and spinels have been popular for centuries, albeit occasionally masquerading as rubies and other more valuable stones. Synthetic spinel has been around since the 1800's.

Optical Properties

colour	red, yellow, brown, orange, blue, green, pink, violet, colourless, black. Also colour-change
refractive index	**1.72** (1.712 - 1.762)
dispersion	0.020 medium
birefringence	none
pleochroism	none

Physical Properties

hardness	8.0
density	3.54 - 3.63
crystal system	isometric / cubic
cleavage	indistinct
fracture	conchoidal

Faceting Properties

Localities	Tanzania, Myanmar, Sri Lanka, Afghanistan, Australia, Brazil, Tajikistan, Vietnam, Madagascar, Nigeria, Thailand, USA, Nepal
Faceting Tips	Polish with alumina or diamond on most common laps, or with diamond on ceramic. Cutting is problem-free, but polishing occasionally produces challenges. A fine pre-polish or changing lap direction can help.
Treatments	No common treatment, although reports of heat-treatment are increasing.
Rough Cost	Moderate to high. Large, flawless stones are very rare and expensive. Flame fusion and flux-process synthetics are available in a wide variety of colours, including colour-change.

Aluminum Fluoro-Hydroxyl-Silicate
$Al_2[(F,OH)_2/SiO_4]$

Topaz

Topaz is an extremely popular gemstone, due to its vivid colour, low cost, and relatively high refractive index. The name derives from Topazos, an island in the Red Sea now called Zabargad and the historical source of peridot. In fact, in his *Historia Naturalis*, our friend Pliny the Elder (see page 154) refers to topaz, but he was almost certainly discussing peridot. Although it has a bad reputation among faceters, topaz cuts and polishes relatively easily, provided that you take some care.

Optical Properties

colour	blue, greenish, yellow, pink-red, red, purple, brown, colourless
refractive index	**1.62** (1.609 - 1.643)
dispersion	0.014 medium
birefringence	0.008 - 0.016 weak
pleochroism	dichroic – blue: weak (light blue to pink or colourless); green: definite (pale green to paler or colourless); yellow: definite (honey to straw yellow); pink: definite (pink to pale pink or colourless); red: strong (deep red to pinkish red); brown: definite (brown to brownish yellow)

Physical Properties

hardness	8.0
density	**3.5** (3.49 - 3.57)
crystal system	orthorhombic
cleavage	perfect (1 direction)
fracture	conchoidal, uneven

Faceting Properties

Localities	Brazil, Afghanistan, Australia, Myanmar, China, Madagascar, Mexico, Namibia, Nigeria, Pakistan, Russia, Sri Lanka, USA, Zimbabwe
Faceting Tips	Polish with alumina or diamond on metal or composite, or with diamond on ceramic. Keep all large facets at least 7° away from the basal cleavage plane (see Chapter 12.11.1). If you notice shredding and abrasion at facet edges, try changing lap direction, hand pressure, etc. Note that some yellowish-brown varieties can fade in sunlight.
Treatments	Radiation and heat treatment is very common, particularly in the production of the popular blue colours (see page 157). Some surface diffusion. Vacuum-deposited thin films produce "Mystic Topaz" (page 152).
Rough Cost	Low to modest. The pink to reddish-orange variety known as imperial topaz can be very costly. Commercially-cut blue topaz gems are very common and inexpensive and can be an excellent source of "rough." Blue topaz is also readily available as pre-forms. See page 210 of Volume 1 for more. Synthetics exist but have difficulty competing with the low cost of natural material.

Tourmaline

Chemical name depends on type
$(Na,Ca)(Mg,Li,Al,Fe^{2+})_3Al_6(BO_3)_3Si_6O_{18}(OH)_4$

The tourmaline group of gemstones encompasses a variety of chemically complex silicate minerals. Tourmaline is very popular among faceters due to its entrancing range of colour. Indeed, single-coloured tourmalines are quite rare. Unlike most other common gemstones, tourmaline was unknown in western Europe until relatively recent times: the Dutch East India Company began importing the stones in the early 1700's. Tourmaline exhibits remarkable piezo- and pyro-electricity (Chapter 12.13.3). In fact, the Dutch named the mineral "aschentrekker," or ash-puller, and the name stuck for many years.

Optical Properties

colour	very many, including pink, red, yellow, brown, green, blue, purple, colourless, black, multi-coloured, colour-change…
refractive index	**1.63** (1.614 - 1.666)
dispersion	0.017 medium
birefringence	0.014 - 0.032 medium
pleochroism	dichroic, many colour combinations – red: definite (dark to light red); brown: definite (dark to light brown); green: strong (dark to yellow-green); blue: strong (dark to light blue)

Physical Properties

hardness	7.0 - 7.5
density	2.82 - 3.32
crystal system	trigonal
cleavage	indistinct
fracture	uneven, brittle

Faceting Properties

Localities	Brazil, Afghanistan, Australia, Myanmar, India, Madagascar, Mexico Nigeria, Pakistan, Sri Lanka, Tanzania, USA…
Faceting Tips	Relatively easy to cut and polish. Strong pleochroism, including "closed" crystal axes, may dictate rough orientation (see Chapter 6.7.1). Polish with alumina or diamond. Some stones are heat sensitive. Splitting can occur at colour junctions. Some faceters report "orange peel" problems with Nubond laps (Chapter 8.17.3).
Treatments	Green and blue crystals are usually heat-treated. Red tourmaline is occasionally heat-treated. Radiation can darken pink stones or turn blue to purple. There are reports of surface treatments, filling agents, and dyeing.
Rough Cost	Modest to high. Generally the yellow and off-green varieties are affordable, while the more desirable green, pink, red, and purple stones can be quite expensive. The blue indicolite material can be extraordinarily costly, while the neon green-blue paraiba species, if you can get it at all, requires a new adjective for expensive (see page 213 of Volume 1). Synthetics exist but are not currently economically viable.

Zircon

Zirconium Silicate
$ZrSiO_4$

Although zircon has been popular as a gemstone since ancient times, it is in many ways the dark horse of faceting materials. In addition to the benefits of high refractive index and dispersion, you can usually find clean, nicely-coloured samples at low to modest cost. Zircon is also relatively easy to cut and polish. Zircon is unique among common gemstone species in that it radiation treats itself: trace amounts of uranium and thorium break down over time, creating colour centers in the gem through a process known as metamictization. See page 160 for more.

Optical Properties

colour	yellow, golden-yellow, brown, orange, red, purple, blue, green, colourless
refractive index	**1.94** (normal or "high" zircon) **1.79** (metamict or "low")
dispersion	0.039 strong
birefringence	0.002 - 0.059 strong
pleochroism	dichroic – yellow: very weak (yellow to brownish-yellow); brown: very weak (yellowish to reddish brown); red: weak (red to orange-red); blue: distinct (blue to yellow-gray or colourless); green: very weak (green to brownish-green)

Physical Properties

hardness	6.5 - 7.5
density	3.93 - 4.73
crystal system	tetragonal
cleavage	indistinct
fracture	conchoidal, very brittle

Faceting Properties

Localities	Myanmar, Australia, Cambodia, Sri Lanka, Thailand, Brazil, Korea, Madagascar, Nigeria, Tanzania, Mozambique...
Faceting Tips	Polish with alumina on metal or composite, or with diamond on metal, composite, or ceramic. Zircon is somewhat brittle – avoid excess pressure during cutting and polishing. Facet-doubling due to strong birefringence may drive rough orientation.
Treatments	Most blue zircon has been heat-treated from brown material. This process also produces light brown and clear stones. Yellow-brown and red zircon are heat treated to gold-yellow. Irradiation of clear zircon produces brown or red stones.
Rough Cost	Modest. Synthetics exist, but do not appear to be economically viable.

14.2 Less Common Gemstone Materials

This section lists the basic properties of a dozen less common gemstone materials. As with Section 14.1, more complete information can be found in the reference books described in Chapter 9.3 and on the websites listed in Chapter 15.8.6.

Amber   Oxygenated Hydrocarbon $C_{10}H_{16}O$

Amber is an amorphous organic mineraloid (see Chapter 1.1.1). It is the fossilized resin of ancient pine trees, and in fact, particularly prized specimens can contain organic inclusions such as insects or even small amphibians (see Chapter 12.12.1). Transparent amber can be faceted, although its very low hardness makes it unsuitable for much jewelry.

colour	yellow, red, orange, and brown		
refractive index	**1.54** (1.539 - 1.545)	hardness	2.0 - 2.5
dispersion	none tabulated	density	1.05 - 1.09
faceting info	Amber is very soft. Cut with a fine lap to prevent clogging. Polish with alumina on a soft lap or with a tin oxide Ultra-lap. Amber will soften at about 300° F (150 C), not much higher than dop wax. Sensitive to thermal shock.		

Andalusite   Aluminum Silicate Al_2SiO_5

Named after the lovely Andalusia region of southern Spain where it was first discovered in transparent form, andalusite can make a striking gemstone. Andalusite displays strong, trichroic pleochroism, requiring careful orientation.

colour	yellow-green, green, brownish-red, red, pink, violet		
refractive index	**1.64** (1.627 - 1.649)	hardness	6.5 - 7.5
dispersion	0.016 medium	density	3.05 - 3.20
faceting info	Orient for best colour. Gem design should emphasize colour over sparkle (Chapter 16.5). Polish with alumina on composite or metal. Andalusite is brittle. Beware of the cleavage plane.		

Apatite   Fluoro or Chloro Calcium Phosphate $Ca_5(F,Cl,OH)(PO_4)_3$

Apatite produces a lovely gemstone, although its heat sensitivity and brittleness demand care in dopping, cutting, and polishing. Large, perfect, nicely coloured crystals are available at modest cost. Low hardness argues for an earring or pendant setting.

colour	pink, blue, yellow, green, violet, colourless		
refractive index	**1.64** (1.628 - 1.649)	hardness	5.0
dispersion	0.013 medium	density	3.16 - 3.23
faceting info	Very heat sensitive – use a cold dopping technique. The blue material can display strong blue to clear dichroism. Orient accordingly. Apatite is brittle; cut with a fine lap. Polishing can be problematic. Use alumina or cerium oxide on metal or a chrome or tin oxide Ultralap.		

Calcium Borosilicate Ca(B$_2$Si$_2$O$_8$)   Danburite

Although not well known as a gemstone, danburite is in many ways the ideal faceting material. Relatively large, clean rough is modestly priced, and danburite has decent refractive index and dispersion. As a final bonus, it presents few difficulties on the cutting or polishing lap.

colour	colourless, yellow, brown, pink		
refractive index	**1.63** (1.630 - 1.636)	hardness	7.0 - 7.5
dispersion	0.017 medium	density	2.97 - 3.03
faceting info	Danburite is relatively easy to cut and polish. Use alumina or diamond on composite or metal.		

Elemental Carbon C   Diamond

Diamond is currently the king of gemstones (see page 5 of Volume 1). Not unsurprisingly, many amateur faceters undertake to cut and polish a diamond at some point. Few follow through, due to multiple factors, including the difficulty in obtaining rough material and, of course, the stone's intrinsic hardness. As a true hobbyist, you should not be deterred. Just do your research and prepare...

colour	many. colourless, yellow, brown, blue, green, reddish, black		
refractive index	**2.41** (2.417 - 2.419)	hardness	10.0
dispersion	0.044 strong	density	3.50 - 3.53
faceting info	Only diamond can cut and polish diamond. Professionals use a cast iron lap spinning at high speed. Strong directional dependent hardness requires careful orientation. Beware of perfect cleavage. Wykoff's book (see Chapter 9.1) has an entire chapter on cutting and polishing diamond. There are a couple of commercial faceting machines designed to cut and polish diamond (see Chapter 2.5). Rough can be very difficult to obtain.		

Feldspar Group (including Sunstone)   Various Alkali Aluminum Silicates

Although feldspars as a group constitute up to 60% of the Earth's crust, facetable varieties are few and far between. The best known of these is sunstone, a so-called plagioclase feldspar. Tiny, oriented mineral platelets within sunstone create schiller, a spangling effect that can produce a dramatic gem (see Chapter 12.7.5). The most valuable samples show a distinct reddish body colour, occasionally surrounded by green.

colour	yellow, brown, gray, red, green, colourless		
refractive index	1.52 - 1.58	hardness	6.0 - 6.5
dispersion	0.012 medium-weak	density	2.62 - 2.65
faceting info	Although feldspar has perfect cleavage in two directions, this does not usually present a problem to the faceter. Nevertheless, beware of sharp corners. Polish with cerium oxide. Place colour spots near the culet (see Chapter 6.7).		

Fluorite   Calcium Fluoride CaF_2

Fluorite's poor optical properties – low refractive index and dispersion – are more than made up for by its variety and brilliance of colour. As a bonus, large, clear pieces of rough are available at a modest price. The perfect cleavage can cause difficulty at all stages of faceting, including dopping.

colour	many: yellow, green, blue, pink, purple, multi-colour, etc.		
refractive index	1.434	hardness	4.0
dispersion	0.007 weak	density	3.00 - 3.25
faceting info	Beware of perfect cleavage! Fluorite is soft and susceptible to parting. Cut slowly on a fine lap and polish with alumina or a chrome oxide Ultralap. Select designs for colour, not sparkle. Shock sensitive.		

Iolite (Cordierite)   Magnesium Aluminum Silicate $Mg_2Al_3(AlSi_5O_{18})$

Iolite's very strong trichroism requires careful cut selection and rough orientation, but it can produce lovely blue gemstones. Try cutting a perfect cube oriented on the optical axes to produce a striking demonstration of pleochroism.

colour	blue, pale yellow, colourless, brownish		
refractive index	**1.55** (1.542 - 1.578)	hardness	7.0 - 7.5
dispersion	0.017 medium	density	2.58 - 2.66
faceting info	Orient for best colour but be careful as larger stones can be dark. Cleavage planes occasionally present difficulty. Polish with cerium oxide or alumina. Inclusions common.		

Sodium Calcium Aluminum Silicate   Scapolite

Scapolite makes a fine gem, although it is a bit soft for the rough and tumble world of ring settings. Cutting and polishing are relatively straightforward, and large clean pieces are easy and inexpensive to obtain.

colour	yellow, pink, purple, greenish, colourless		
refractive index	**1.56** (1.540 - 1.579)	hardness	5.5 - 6.0
dispersion	0.017 medium	density	2.57 - 2.74
faceting info	Although it has perfect cleavage in two directions, scapolite rarely presents problems. Polish with cerium oxide or alumina on composite or metal laps.		

Calcium Titanium Silicate $CaTi(O|SiO_4)$ Sphene (Titanite)

Sphene's very high refractive index and dispersion make for a stunning gemstone, although large, clean rough can be difficult to find. Stick to earring or pendant mountings due to low hardness.

colour	yellow, brown, green, reddish		
refractive index	1.843 - 2.110	hardness	5.0 - 5.5
dispersion	0.051 strong	density	3.52 - 3.54
faceting info	Despite its cleavage planes, sphene is mostly problem free. Polish with alumina on metal or composite laps. Crystals are frequently twinned. Orient the twinning plane parallel to the table. Birefringence can cause facet doubling.		

Lithium Aluminum Silicate $LiAl(Si_2O_6)$ Spodumene (Hiddenite and Kunzite)

There are many faceter's war stories told about spodumene. Its perfect cleavage in two directions can ambush you at all phases of faceting. Nevertheless, spodumene produces a lovely pale gemstone.

colour	yellow, yellow-green, green, pink, colourless		
refractive index	**1.67** (1.660 - 1.681)	hardness	6.5 - 7.5
dispersion	0.017 medium	density	3.15 - 3.21
faceting info	Cut and polish very carefully - nothing coarser than 600 grit! Strong trichroism may dictate orientation, but keep large facets away from the cleavage planes. Nubond laps work well. Polish with alumina or cerium oxide at low speed.		

Tanzanite (Zoisite)   Calcium Aluminum Silicate $Ca_2Al_3(O|OH|SiO_4|Si_2O_7)$

Tanzanite is the ultimate gemstone marketing success. Although colourless to pink zoisite, often heavily included, had been known beforehand, the discovery of a bluish purple variety in the Merelani district of Tanzania in 1967 set the gem world on fire. Tiffany & Co. of New York renamed the material "tanzanite" and marketed it aggressively, stating that the gem could be found in only two places on Earth, Tanzania and Tiffany's. In its native form, tanzanite is strongly trichroic, showing purple, blue, and brownish-orange along the three crystal axes. Essentially all tanzanite is heat-treated, however, a process which drives off the orange-brown colour and leaves the crystal apparently (but not actually) dichroic purple-blue. Its strong commercial success as a cut gemstone means that little high-quality rough material appears on the market.

colour	blue, violet, purple, orange, brown, pink, colourless		
refractive index	**1.7** (1.691 - 1.700)	hardness	6.0 - 7.0
dispersion	0.030 medium-high	density	3.35
faceting info	Orient for best colour if the rough shape allows it. Despite the perfect cleavage in one direction, tanzanite does not usually cause problems. Polish with cerium oxide or alumina on metal or composite laps.		

15

Faceting on Your Computer

The advent of affordable, powerful home computers late in the twentieth century has changed the world in ways that were almost unimaginable only a generation before. For example, computers have injected into society a powerful, democratizing influence through the instant availability of information, and on a more mundane level, they have also freed many of us from the mechanical drudgery of calculations and record keeping.

As the 21st century dawns, these modern miracles have become an essential tool in almost all aspects of our lives. Whether on a desktop, in a schoolbag, or inside the guts of what looks like a mobile telephone, the computer has become an appendage to our active lives. And, as you shall see, computers can also be a valuable assistant in the art and craft of faceting.

This chapter begins with an overview of how to exploit your computing horsepower to enhance your hobby through learning, connecting with others, and engaging in that miracle and hazard of the modern age: online commerce. It then introduces and explains a number of software tools for gem design and optimization. This is followed by an introduction to three-dimensional rendering programs, including a detailed tutorial that should help you cut your first virtual gemstone using free, downloadable software. The penultimate section lists general-purpose auxiliary software to help you organize, finance, and communicate your lapidary achievements, and the chapter concludes on an overly ambitious note by attempting to gather together useful faceting-related web links.

15.1 Gemma Ex Machina

Computers…Humbug. Who needs `em?

You do. You really do.

Faceters tend to be a curmudgeonly lot, and sadly, any visit to a lapidary club will tell you that very few of us are spring chickens, to say nothing of being of the Internet Generation. Nevertheless, gem cutters are a do-it-yourself kind of crowd, always willing to try something new and not particularly interested in hearing how difficult or impossible a particular project will be. Why should it be different with learning to use a computer?

Ok, you say, it may well be true that you booked your last vacation online and did your Christmas shopping in a web browser rather than a shopping mall, but how can computers possibly help you facet?

Well, at the very least, they can help you book your trip to the Tucson show next February, and there is no end to the amount of gem rough, both good and bad, that you can order through eBay. Put another way, computers are a part of your life and faceting is a part of your life, so naturally, computers are very likely already a part of your faceting.

But there is more, much much more, that computers can do to enhance your gem cutting experience. The Foreword to this book and Chapter 16 emphasize that faceting occupies a special place at the junction of mathematics, physics, and art, and computers are particularly adept in all of these areas. This chapter provides an introduction to a variety of tools that will help you get the most out of both your computer and your faceting machine.

Breaking down Barriers

The barrier to entry into the world of computing has never been lower. Software and operating systems are far easier to understand than they were twenty years ago, and user accessibility and "friendliness" improve with each new release and upgrade. The short version? If you managed to facet that piece of spodumene, you shouldn't be scared of Windows.

Price ceased to be an issue toward the end of the first decade of the 21st century: usable portable computers now cost about as much as a couple of laps or twenty carats of good tourmaline. The short version this time? If you can afford a faceting machine and rough, you can afford a computer.

Here's a life lesson for all of us: A few years ago, I returned to the region where I grew up, bringing my then very young family with me. With the one exception of my grandmother, who was in her nineties at the time, every single family member, from my teenage nephews to my elderly aunts, had an opinion on the state of the Web and an attitude about social networking. The lesson? Computers: they're not just for neck-bearded geeks anymore…

15.1.1 Network Resources

We now take access to information for granted. For example, it is not unusual to see people settling an argument at lunch by looking up the answer on wikipedia with their mobile phones. Before the coming of the Web, tracking down a particular piece of information usually meant a trip to the bookshelf, if not the local library.

The same transformation has taken place in our hobby. If you need the refractive index of zircon, for example, you probably look it up on the Web. And, while I encourage you to peruse Chapter 14 for an interesting overview of the optical properties of various gem materials, such information is instantly accessible, given a network connection and an inexpensive piece of hardware.

The potential impact of the web goes way beyond tables of numbers, however. The following sections examine some ways in which you can use network resources to enhance your faceting experience.

A Day in the Life...

I remember the exact moment when I realized that the World Wide Web had changed everything. It was the early 1990's, and as an active scientific researcher, I had been using computer networks and e-mail for the better part of a decade. However, it took a cultural experience, specifically listening to a popular song on the radio, to bring home to me how transformative the Web had become.

The song, Run, Baby, Run by Sheryl Crow, contains the lyrics "She was born in November, 1963, the day Aldous Huxley died…" The line intrigued me, and I decided to try using the (then new) World Wide Web to find out exactly when Aldous Huxley died.

It took about ten seconds.

I was stunned. I merely typed "Aldous Huxley death" into the Alta Vista search engine (does anyone else remember Alta Vista?), and the answer came up. As Steve Jobs would say, "Boom." Try it with your current favourite search tool…I think that you will agree with Sheryl that that particular day was one heck of a day.

15.1.2 Learning

A common complaint about our hobby, in addition to the related issue of startup cost, is the lack of "critical mass" of faceters. There just aren't enough of us around.

This presents a serious challenge to anyone interested in taking up faceting. How does one learn? Without access to a lapidary club (see next section) and an experienced teacher, the barrier to entry can be daunting.

Computers can help. There are an increasing number of online resources to help you learn to polish gems. None of these is a substitute for a patient teacher (or a good book!), but you can, in fact, learn a great deal on the Web.

Surf Hunting

No, surf hunting is not some bizarre information-age sport like chess-boxing (not a joke...look it up on wikipedia). It is what I call the process of hunting for information while surfing the web.

You are probably more than familiar with online search engines, such as Google and Bing, and by now, you are probably reasonably proficient at formulating search terms to get what you want.

Here's a little challenge from Chapter 16.4: Use your favourite web search tool to track down an important document to faceting history, Marcel Tolkowsky's 1919 monograph on diamond design (see page 243).

Could you find it? Instant access to such documents, which are maintained on the Internet by passionate amateurs and professionals alike, is just one way in which the Web has rocked our world. Those of us who proudly post photographs of our cut gemstones will also note that the Web has worlded our rocks. You may now groan.

Section 15.8.13 at the end of this chapter contains the link to Tolkowsky's monograph. Don't peek!

15.1.3 Connecting

Do you belong to a lapidary club? I do.

It's not a bricks and mortar lapidary club. In fact, I don't know anyone who lives within 500 miles (800 km) of my home who is also an amateur gem cutter. My lapidary club exists on the Web, in the Cloud. My fellow club members come from North America, South America, Europe, Asia, and Australia. We meet once a day via an online user group, and less regularly via direct e-mail between ourselves. Real-world get-togethers, for example at large gem shows, are not uncommon.

I have had extended e-mail dialogs with my fellow cutters on both lapidary and other topics. In fact, I developed the BOG gemstone optimization program (see Section 15.3.2 below) in collaboration with enthusiasts on the other side of the planet. You, too, should be using the World Wide Web to connect with fellow faceters. The best way to get started is to join an online faceter's group, of which there several. See the online resources in Section 15.8.1.

15.1.4 Buying and Selling

Perhaps the biggest societal impact of the computer revolution has been in the area of commerce, the buying and selling of products. Web sites such as eBay and amazon.com are much more than the 21st century equivalents of the Sears catalog. By enabling instant communication around the world, the Internet has brought buyers and sellers together in ways that were never before possible.

Of course, such e-commerce brings risks along with the benefits. Cynics point out with some legitimacy that the web has enabled fraud and theft to take place at the speed of light. The online user group postings are filled with tales of horror about the differing interpretations of "loupe clean," "overnight delivery," and "money back guarantee." With many sellers located in other countries and other jurisdictions, going after the bad guy can be infinitely more complex than raising a stink at the shop counter.

Having recognized these difficulties early on, most e-commerce websites offer an additional degree of security via escrow-type exchange of funds: the money travels to a third party such as PayPal, and is not released until the customer is satisfied. Reputable websites also maintain a record of comments and user satisfaction reports. You should pay attention to and use this information. In addition, online user groups and mailing lists (see Section 15.8.1) are an excellent source of information on businesses, both reputable and otherwise.

For those of us who cannot get to the large gem shows (see Chapter 6.2.2), the Web lets us shop the world from our desktops for equipment and gem rough. Nevertheless, the ancient adage "caveat emptor" – buyer (and seller) beware – should definitely be the operative principle in the world of faceting e-commerce.

YouTube – It's Not Just for Piano-Playing Cats Anymore.

With an upload volume of about half a million videos each day, at a mind-bending rate of more than *100 hours* of new content every *minute*, YouTube has something for everyone. Some may argue that YouTube does indeed have a whole lot of something, most of it for almost nobody, but the presence of a powerful and easy to use search engine means that locating that one video on flugelhorn felines is just a couple of keystrokes away.

Type the word "faceting" into the YouTube search box and hit return. You should be rewarded with thousands of videos on the subject. At least this is how many I got in early 2014 – I am sure that you will find more. They range from instructional videos on meet point faceting to documentaries on large scale cutting enterprises in East Asia. In terms of hardware, you should find explanations of everything from jamb peg machines to computer controlled CNC robots. The range of gemstones and rough portrayed is equally staggering.

While no substitute for a good book on the subject – not that I am in any way biased in the matter – YouTube can be an excellent resource for learning and exploring our hobby. You can even contribute to this often chaotic, occasionally illuminating community. Section 15.8.12 at the end of this chapter points you to free, online tools for creating your own tutorial videos and screencasts.

15.2 Selecting the Right Computer

Hoo boy…this topic could really open a can of worms.

It could open a can of worms because computer partisans are among the most loyal and blinkered individuals in the world. These happily obsessed folks can expound enthusiastically for hours on such eclecticisms as front-side buses, DDR3 memory, and caching strategies.

Luckily, you can just let them expound, since for your faceting needs, just about any computer will do. In fact, for the purposes of connecting online, that ten-year-old PC at the local library is more than enough. If you want to install your own software, such as GemCAD, you will probably need your own machine, but again, very modest hardware will suffice.

Photo-realistic, three-dimensional rendering, described later in this chapter, is a completely different kettle of fish. If you decide to explore the art of virtual gemstones, you will require some serious computing horsepower. More precisely, you won't *need* a powerful computer to get started with rendering, but you will soon *want* one. I currently use an eight-core hyper-threaded workstation for this purpose, with at least one additional machine slaved over the net (expound, expound, expound...). Guess what? I usually have to wait a while for a detailed rendering.

The good news is that for 99% of the faceting you will want to do on a computer, that slightly out of date box in the basement will be fine. And, as explained below, you don't even have to worry too much about exactly what kind of box it is.

Windows? Macintosh? Linux? Help!

Coke or Pepsi? Boxers or Briefs? Wax or Epoxy? These are some of the eternal questions with which the modern gem cutter must contend. Here's another: Windows, Macintosh or linux ?

Computers come in a wide variety of shapes, sizes, and cost categories, but it is an interesting insight into how computers integrate with society that there are only a handful of options in terms of *operating systems*.

The operating system, or OS, is the software which controls the computer and provides compatibility with externally produced programs and files. As such, it is the common language, the *lingua franca*, of computers: if your software can speak my OS, your software will work on my box. After an initial flurry of possibilities, the computer industry has settled on essentially three options in terms of operating systems for consumer class computers: Windows, Mac OS, and Linux.

Figure 15-1 Almost all consumer grade computers run Microsoft Windows, Apple Mac OS, or Linux.

The Windows operating system, first offered by Microsoft in 1985, is far and away the most popular OS in the world, with approximately 90% of the personal computer market share. The various flavours of Windows work on everything from mobile phones to netbooks to large server farms. Mac OS X, a UNIX-based operating system that appeared on Macintosh computers in 2001, enjoys increasing popularity in the scientific community, and it has always been the standard for publishing and the visual arts. Linux is also a variant of UNIX, and its open architecture and community-supported software base have appealed to the geeks among us for decades.

So. Three different operating systems. As an amateur gemstone cutter, which one is for you?

The short answer is Windows.

The reason for this is simple: the essential software tools of our craft are all based on the Windows operating system. Whether you use GemCAD, GemRay, BOG, or any of the half dozen or so other gemstone design and optimization programs out there, you will almost certainly be using it on a Windows machine. Period.

The somewhat longer answer is also Windows.

This answer is somewhat longer for the following reason: although you will have to run these programs under Windows, the operating system itself can run under a *different* OS (you may want to re-read this sentence). For example, you can have Windows in a window on your Mac OS or linux desktop. Or, within the Microsoft environment, you can have one version, say XP, working in a window while the main machine runs Win7. This is all made possible by the magic of something called *virtualization*.

Virtualization means that we are no longer bound to a single way of thinking and working. In terms of operating systems, you really can have it all. I am a living, breathing example of this. A piece of computer history, an original 128K Macintosh "toaster," now thirty years old, has pride of place in my office, and I have been an Apple fanboy since I realized that 1984 truly wouldn't be at all like 1984 (yes, my linux friends, that is when I drank the Kool-Aid). And, although my initial BOG development took place on a PC (see Section 15.3.2 below), I haven't used a Windows computer for the better part of a decade.

I use a free utility called VirtualBox to run Windows on my Mac (Figure 15-2). All of the gem designs in this book and all of the GemCAD, GemRay, and BOG output were produced using these tools. You can learn more about VirtualBox at www.virtualbox.org. Also, the BOG website (www.boghome.com) contains complete instructions for installing and running these programs.

There are multiple alternatives for running Windows under other operating systems, including offerings from Microsoft, Oracle, Parallels Inc., and VMware. Consult the list of "Virtualization / Emulation Tools" in Section 15.8.12.

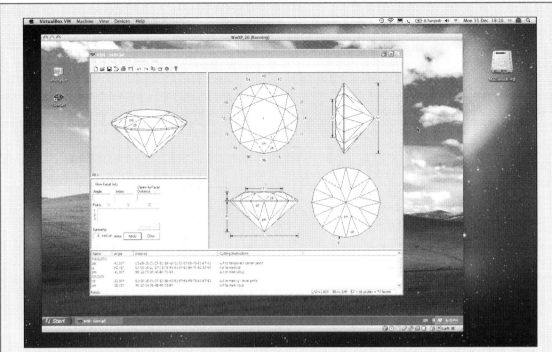

Figure 15-2 Virtualization tools such as VirtualBox let you run Windows programs, including GemCAD, under other operating systems. Look carefully at the screenshot – yes, that is indeed GemCAD running on a Windows XP virtual computer which is, in turn, running "inside" a Mac.

15.3 Gem Design and Optimization Software

If access to information and contact with fellow hobbyists on the Web have not convinced you to join the computer revolution, then the various gem design and optimization programs should. In a word, such software has revolutionized the world of gem creation, allowing even rank amateurs to try their hand at design, or at least to optimize their cutting angles for top performance. The following paragraphs provide an overview of the software available to help you create and optimize gemstone cuts. Chapters 16-18 contain more ideas on how to get started with gem design, and you can satisfy your interest in the history of gem design and optimization software by reading Chapter 9 of Broadfoot and Collins *Cutting Gemstones*. Chapter 9.1 of this book will help you track it down.

15.3.1 GemCAD Family

GemCAD is the flagship of a suite of programs produced by Robert Strickland. These include the GemRay ray tracing program, as well as smaller utilities for making animations of a moving gemstone.

You can think of GemCAD as a virtual faceting machine on your computer. As in the real world, you execute a sequence of facets by specifying cutting angles, index wheel settings, and target meet points. Unlike in the real world, however, the virtual faceter within GemCAD cuts angles with essentially infinite accuracy and precision, and most importantly, allows multiple levels of Undo. Wouldn't that be nice to have on your Ultra Tec?

Although primarily a design aid for creating new gemstone cuts, GemCAD is also an excellent proofing tool. Particularly with older published designs, there is no guarantee that a certain gem can actually be cut as described. GemCAD to the rescue! If you can cut something in GemCAD, you should be able to produce it on your faceting machine. The program is also an excellent means to test and verify alternate cutting sequences.

DOS GemRay and the other pre-Windows programs are getting somewhat long in the tooth[1], and their wider use is hampered by the fact that, with Vista and Windows 7, Microsoft dropped all support for DOS software. Virtualization tools can help: for example, using VirtualBox, you can run Windows XP and hence GemRay in a Vista or Win7 window. See "Windows? Mac OS? Linux? Help!" on page 192 and the online resources in Section 15.8.12 for more information.

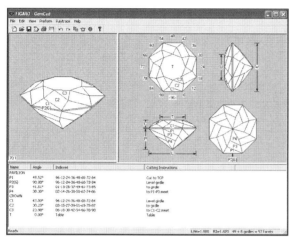

Figure 15-3 The Windows GemCAD program lets you design and adjust gemstones using an intuitive, user-friendly interface.

GemCAD costs $95 and is available at www.gemcad.com. You can download a 30-day trial version and immediately start working. GemRay and the other DOS-based programs are a free download at gemcad.com. You will also find an earlier, DOS version of GemCAD, which is also free. However, I recommend that you use the full Windows version for at least a couple of reasons. First, the DOS version has limited resolution, no support for 3D visualization, and only a single level of undo. Second, and most importantly, GemCAD represents a significant investment of time and effort on the part of Robert Strickland, a fellow amateur gemstone cutter. Supporting him supports us.

Want to learn more? Robert Strickland has produced excellent online manuals for both GemCAD and GemRay at www.gemcad.com. Also, these programs are my tools of choice for gemstone design and optimization, so you will find references to GemCAD and GemRay scattered throughout this book. For example, Chapter 18 presents a case study using these programs to design a gem.

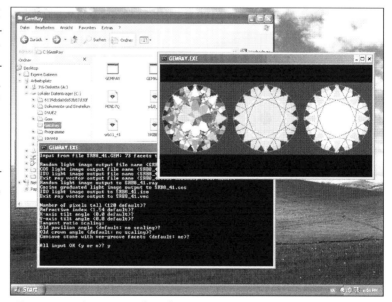

Figure 15-4 GemRay and its close cousin, GemRayX, are DOS programs which produce reasonably realistic grayscale renderings of gemstones.

---

[1] This situation appears to be changing, at least for GemRay. See the note on page 322.

Kiss the Sky with GemRay

For those of us old enough to associate purple haze with something other than inclusions in amethyst, the phrase "kiss the sky" has had a special resonance, evoking a particular time in our planet's cultural history. Gemstones can have a similar, profound effect on our emotions, and to close this admittedly strained metaphorical circle, well-designed gemstones should literally kiss the sky.

Yes, yes. I know. A generation of kids and especially their parents have wondered and debated what Jimi Hendrix actually meant with those lyrics, but in the case of gemstones, the relationship to the surrounding lighting environment – the sky – is of critical importance. A properly performing gemstone returns a significant fraction of the light from the environment to the viewer's eyes, and thus the makeup of that environment, the intensity, colour, and spatial distribution of light sources, has a profound influence on the visual impact of the stone.

You have almost certainly figured this out by now. Five minutes in a shopping mall jewelry store, with its array of high intensity point lighting, carefully composed glass cabinets, and selection of decor, is enough to tell you that only half the magic of a gem lies within the stone itself.

Need further proof? Download and fire up the DOS GemRay program with your favourite gemstone design. When you initiate the ray trace, GemRay produces three separate renderings of the stone (Figure 15-5). Unless you have selected a pathologically weird design, the three images should be dramatically different.

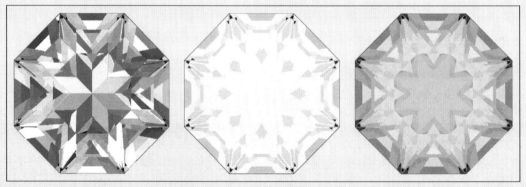

Figure 15-5 GemRay ray traces the stone using three different models for the lighting environment. From left to right, these are the Random, Cosine, and Isometric traces of the Parapet gem design, which appears in Chapter 19.1.6.

How does one gemstone produce such differing visual appearance?

To shamefully misquote the Bard, the answer, dear Brutus lies in the sky…

GemRay, like all ray tracing programs, needs to consider the gemstone in context, in its environment. Reduced to its simplest form, this environment consists of the "ground" beneath the gem and the "sky" above (Figure 15-6). In order to provide both a subjective and objective impression of gemstone performance, GemRay adopts three different models for the sky: Random, COS, and ISO.

Figure 15-6 The optical environment of a gemstone includes both the ground and sky.

Here's a short explanation of how it works, adapted directly from Robert Strickland's excellent documentation at www.gemcad.com/gemray.htm. Imagine the gemstone sitting face-up below the dome of a planetarium. The floor, or "ground" is completely black, in the sense that no light can enter the rear of the stone, and any rays that either miss the gem or exit the pavilion are lost. The three lighting models correspond to three types of illumination projected onto the dome above the gem, in other words, three different "skies" (see Figure 15-7).

The Random model contains a mottled blend of bright and dark areas and corresponds to the mixed lighting environment that you are most likely to encounter when viewing a gem. As a result, the Random ray trace (Figure 15-5) is the most "realistic," allowing you to see subtle reflectance patterns as adjacent facets pick out different points on the sky. The COS or cosine sky model is bright at the zenith, darkening steadily to black at the horizon. Finally, the ISO or isotropic sky model has uniform illumination, like a very cloudy day.

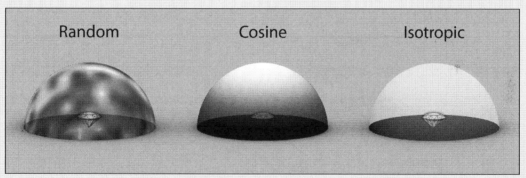

Figure 15-7 The Random, Cosine, and Isotropic lighting models.

The Random ray trace is obviously helpful in comparing and optimizing gemstone designs, but what is the use of the COS and ISO models?

Great question. Two great answers.

The first answer is straightforward. The ISO ray trace lets you make an objective measure of how much light the gem sends toward the viewer from the environment. Yes, this is the famous "ISO Brightness" quoted in many gemstone cutting diagrams (see Chapter 5.1.1). Uniform illumination is essential to this calculation, since, for example, a gemstone could get unlucky with the Random lighting model and show the viewer a lot of dark patches on the sky. Tipping the gem or moving the sky around slightly would produce a significantly different light return.

The second great answer is subtle. Take another look at the COS and ISO ray traces in your GemRay output (Figure 15-5). If they look pretty much the same, then it is clear that darkening the horizon has little effect on the appearance of the gem. This means that the stone is preferentially returning light to the viewer from the zenith. Read the previous sentences again – you have to understand what's going on, or the rest of this discussion will make no sense.

Now imagine the opposite situation: the COS and ISO ray traces have qualitatively different patterns. This clearly indicates that "turning on the lights" at the horizon has a profound effect, and hence the gemstone is sending you a lot of light from low down in the sky.

The bells of conventional wisdom should now be ringing in the hallways of your mind. Like me, you probably learned on the knee of your faceting teacher that rays striking the crown at low angles tend to increase dispersion. It is also clear that a gem which captures light from its horizon will be less susceptible to the "head shadow" effect (Figure 15-8 and Figure 15-9).

Figure 15-8 The head shadow phenomenon refers to the fact that when we stare at a stone, we tend to block out beneficial light sources in the environment. The scene: late afternoon light streams in through the large windows, while ceiling spotlights and large torchière lamps provide an interesting, luminous environment. Figure 15-9 shows what you see and what the stone sees.

Both the GemRay and BOG programs take advantage of this COS-ISO difference. The "X" version of GemRay, called GemRayX, uses the COS-ISO difference to provide a measure of the dispersion of the stone. It also includes a specific option for including head

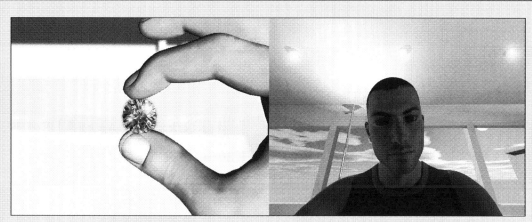

Figure 15-9 The head shadow effect. You are admiring a gemstone as shown in Figure 15-8. What you see (left). What the stone sees (right).

shadow. BOG, on the other hand, contains an "Illumination" optimization target which simply measures the difference between the COS and ISO images. Separate ray traces at different wavelengths provide an estimate of the dispersion. You can also run the newest version of BOG with either GemRay or GemRayX. Turn to Section 15.3.2 and Chapter 18.5 to learn more.

Hopefully, through the vaguely purple haze of this long explanation, you should have a greater appreciation of the importance of the sky to gemstone appearance. You should also be able to learn more from GemRay output and convert this knowledge to better real-world performance. Rock on. Literally.

15.3.2 BOG

BOG is the Better Optimizer for GemRay, a free program which uses DOS GemRay to optimize the crown and pavilion cutting angles of a gem. Full disclosure: I am the developer of the BOG program, so mention of it in this book may be prompted by more than its total awesomeness.

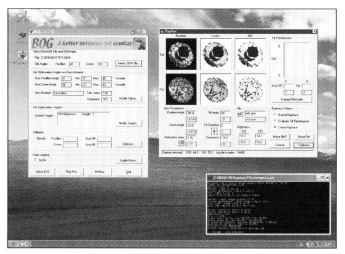

Figure 15-10 BOG uses DOS GemRay to optimize cutting angles.

The underlying principle of BOG is straightforward: GemRay produces a simulated image of the real-world stone, based on the user-supplied gem design, cutting angles, viewing geometry, and gemstone material. It also calculates familiar values related to optical performance, such as ISO brightness. All BOG does is repeatedly call GemRay, continuously changing the cutting angles of the pavilion and crown in order to maximize the user-specified measure of "goodness" – the so-called Merit Function.

Inputs to the merit function include overall (ISO) brightness, illumination effects, tilt performance, sparkle, and fire. The user can mix and match these parameters to achieve the desired optimization (see Chapter 18.5.2). The resulting angles serve as input to GemCAD or other tools for performing tangent ratio scaling (see Chapter 10.6.1).

BOG is a free download at www.boghome.com. You can learn more about BOG from the online documentation, and Chapter 18.5 shows a case study of optimization. Also, Chapter 16.7 uses BOG's sparkle and fire calculations to evaluate whether gem designs with an odd number of main facets truly outperform their even-numbered brethren.

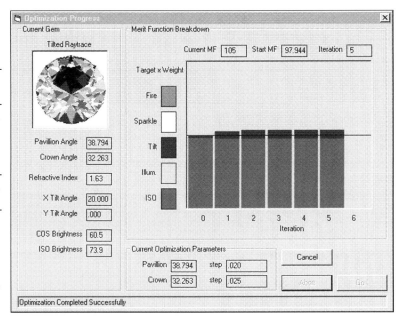

Figure 15-11 BOG optimization of a gem for ISO brightness and Tilt Performance.

15.3.3 Other Gem Design and Evaluation Tools

A number of additional software tools exist to help with gemstone design. These range from basic ray-tracing and visualization programs to gem cut databases to professional diamond design software. Google "gem design software" to begin your exploration.

15.4 Photo-Realistic Rendering Software

I keep going on about how computers have changed everything. Sorry, but it's really true, and I am about to go on about it some more. Section 15.3 describes the GemCAD and BOG programs, which let you cut an optimized gemstone entirely within your computer. This section focuses on additional software tools which enable you to visualize your masterpiece, long before lowering stone to the lap. These 3D rendering programs include realistic lighting effects and even allow you to mount your gem in jewelry and hang it around someone's (virtual) neck.

If you've seen the film Avatar, then you know what I am talking about: creating a realistic-looking world within your computer. Of course, the goal here is not to sell a billion dollars worth of movie tickets and popcorn, but rather to give you a preview of the ultimate appearance of your gemstone. This is not only fun, but also it allows you to make design modifications and material choices before cutting into that expensive piece of gem rough. It might even teach you a thing or two about how light and gemstones work together.

Here's the best part. The programs you need to do this are *free*. They're not necessarily easy to learn or use, but they're free. Three cheers for community-based software development!

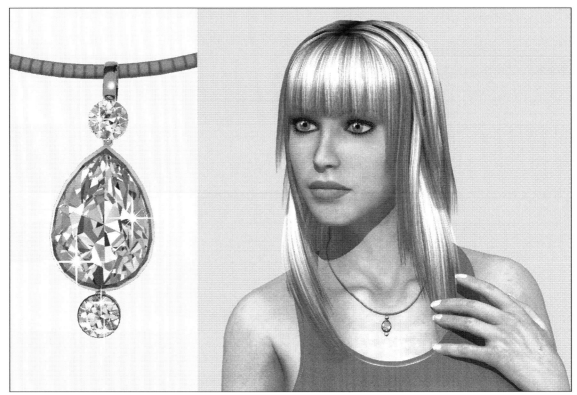

Figure 15-12 Modern 3D rendering software can produce realistic visualizations of jewelry. Neither this person nor her necklace exists in any form in the real world. The pendant is an aquamarine Superpear96 from Long and Steele (see Chapter 9.1), accented by a pair of diamond SRBs. The difference in refractive index is clear, and the full colour rendering includes dispersion effects.

Note 1: Needless to say, there are 3D rendering software packages which are not free. In fact, there are several out there which are *emphatically not* free. One that I particularly would like to try costs more than my car. Nevertheless, despite the apparently lucrative market for such software, at least a couple of very usable, public domain photo-realistic renderers exist. Give them a try!

Note 2: Strictly speaking, DOS GemRay belongs in this category, and not just because it, too, is free. GemRay uses the same optical ray-tracing principles as do the more sophisticated programs described below. However, as a quick-look tool, GemRay doesn't offer many options in terms of gemstone properties – it doesn't do dispersion, for example – and you certainly can't trace multiple gems, jewelry, or people in your scene. Nevertheless, nothing beats GemRay in terms of getting a quick idea of the real-world appearance of a gemstone design. And, unlike the high-horsepower renderers, GemRay performs additional calculations, such as the ISO brightness, which can be very useful in gem design and optimization.

The following sections describe one public domain rendering solution based on the Blender and LuxRender software packages. The text also takes you by the hand, leading you through the creation of your first 3D scene and the generation of a photo-realistic image of a gemstone. I have tried several freeware and commercial programs, and this combination appears to be the best overall for hobby faceters. My opinion is by no means authoritative, and – guess what? – the world of software and computing can change with time. Consult the resources listed at the end of this chapter and follow the online discussion groups to stay up to date.

15.4.1 Blender / LuxRender

Blender is free, open-source 3D rendering software that runs on all major computer platforms, including Windows, Mac OS, and linux. Although not as easy to learn as some commercial packages, Blender is a very capable program which can produce photo-realistic imagery of your gemstones. Did I mention that it was free? Yippee!

Actually, like most photo-realistic renderers, Blender is a *biased* ray tracer. This means that the calculations within Blender give up some realism for speed. Based on my experimentation, this unfortunately means sacrificing a lot of the real-world look of gemstones. For example, biased rendering software rarely handles absorption, total internal reflection and dispersion correctly. Yes, that is a big problem – maybe not for creating a friendly, ten-foot-tall blue alien, but for gemstones, it's a big problem.

Fortunately, there are a few *unbiased* or physically-based rendering packages out there, and at least one of them, LuxRender, integrates beautifully with Blender. Physically-based renderers take the opposite approach to the biased ray-tracer, sacrificing speed for realism. For example, LuxRender can use the full spectrum of light in producing its imagery – think realistic dispersion and fire. Like Blender, LuxRender can be a bit of a challenge to learn and use, but like Blender, it is free!

This difference in ray tracing approach is the reason why you need two separate programs. Blender serves as a general-purpose, flexible scene creation and rendering tool. In other words, it lets you easily manipulate objects, lights, and cameras within a virtual 3D world. However, as a biased renderer, Blender cannot do such a great job of rendering the interaction of light with gemstones. For that, you need the LuxRender package, which works as a plug-in to Blender.

Explaining in detail how to use Blender and LuxRender is far (really, really far) beyond the scope of this book, but the next section contains a tutorial which should give you a flavour of the process. There are plenty of additional online resources to help you on your way. Also, Section 15.6 describes how gemstone rendering works.

15.5 Your First 3D Rendering

Blender and LuxRender are great programs, but the learning curve can be a bit daunting, especially if you are unfamiliar with 3D rendering concepts. This section will hopefully provide you with something I sorely missed when I first fired up the software: a helping, sympathetic hand.

To give you a sense of the investment required to get going, it took me about the same amount of time, starting from zero, to cut a virtual gem within Blender/LuxRender as it would to complete a real stone on my faceting machine. Of course, most of this time involved learning the interface and idiosyncrasies of the software. Now, my virtual faceting machine is a relative speed demon.

The overall goal is to produce a reasonably realistic image of an existing gemstone design. In computing terms, this means taking an input GemCAD file and generating an output image in PNG or JPEG format, based on your choice of gem material, lighting, and so forth.

Here are the steps you will be following in the remainder of this tutorial: First, you will need to download, install, and fire up the Blender software. You will then generate a scene by importing the gem and creating a ground plane. After that, you will set up a suitable "sky" to ensure a varied and interesting lighting environment. LuxRender comes next. After downloading and installing the Blender-specific version, you will set appropriate parameters for the rendering before finally executing the ray trace. With any luck, you will end up with something that looks something like a gemstone.

Note: The following tutorial assumes Blender version 2.63 and LuxBlend exporter version 2.5. The location and appearance of windows, buttons, and menus may be somewhat different in your distribution. Also, by necessity, the explanations below are relatively bare-bones. For example, the text does not include instructions for moving objects within the scene, adjusting the location and characteristics of the rendering camera, and so forth. Complete documentation and tutorials for Blender exist all over the Web. Google and ye shall find...

15.5.1 Download, Installation, and Start Up

You can download Blender at www.blender.org. Installers exist for all popular versions of Windows, Mac OS X and Linux. Just follow the instructions and you should end up with a double-clickable icon in the appropriate directory. Note that it is probably worth firing up Blender and learning the interface before you start working with LuxRender.

By default, Blender unhelpfully places a gray cube in the middle of your scene at startup (Figure 15-13). I probably burned about twenty minutes figuring out what was going on and deleting the darn thing. You can do better by simply making sure that the cube is selected (**right click** on it – the cube should have an orange outline) and then hit the "**x**" key and confirm that you want to erase the selected object. Voilà! A clean three-dimensional canvas in which to set your scene.

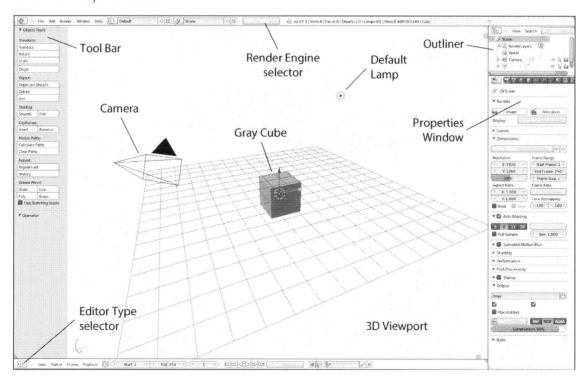

Figure 15-13 The Blender program starts up with a gray cube in an otherwise empty scene. Note that I have modified some user interface components for clarity (background colours, hiding the timeline, etc.).

15.5.2 Setting the Scene

A major challenge in assembling your scene will be importing the gemstone itself. GemCAD can export a design in a relatively old 3D format called DXF. Load up the gem you want within GemCAD, and then select the **File:Export** menu item. The program will prompt you for a name, location, and most importantly, the file format for the export. GemCAD defaults to the VRML, or Virtual Reality Machine Language format. Instead, you should select the **Autodesk DXF** format (Figure 15-14).

Back in Blender, you should create a new scene (**File:New** and acknowledge that you want to erase everything). Once again, you will have to delete our friend, the gray cube, before proceeding.

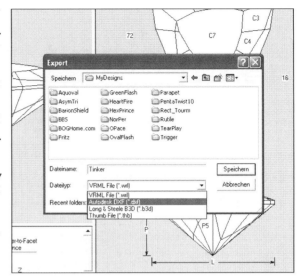

Figure 15-14 Exporting a gem design from GemCAD as a 3D DXF file.

To import the gemstone, select **File:Import:Autocad (.dxf)…** A dialog box will pop up, prompting you to navigate to and select your file. When you have done so, the gem should appear more or less in the middle of your scene. By properly setting the viewports, you should also see the camera and a default light (Figure 15-15).

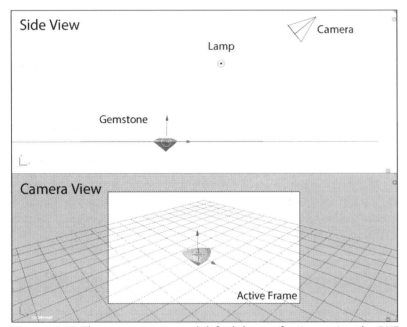

Figure 15-15 The gem, camera, and default lamp after importing the DXF file from GemCAD. Consult the Blender documentation to learn how to split the screen and adjust your view location, zoom factor, etc.

Note: Some distributions of Blender do not come with the DXF importer automatically enabled. If this is the case, select the **File:User Preferences** menu item, and then enable the **Import-Export: Import Autocad DXF Format** option in the **Addons** tab. Don't forget to issue the **File: Save User Settings** command before continuing.

Select **Render Image** from the **Render** menu. You should be rewarded with a very quick, but very ungemlike picture of your design (Figure 15-16).

Alternatively, you can press the **Image** button in the **Render** tab in the **Properties Window** on the right side of the screen (just under the Properties Window arrow in Figure 15-13).

Why does it look so bad? The answer is material and texture. Every object in the real world has physical properties describing how it interacts with light. So far, your gemstone has only

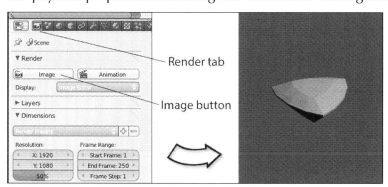

default properties selected by the program. Based on Blender's taste in cubes, the drab appearance of your gem should come as no surprise.

Figure 15-16 A quick rendering of the gemstone using the default material properties. Encouraging, but far from the real thing.

Note that Blender may have replaced your **3D Viewport** with the rendered image. To get back to work, select **3D View** from the **Editor Type** selector at the bottom left of the window (see Figure 15-13 for the location of this selector).

You will fix the material/texture problem later with LuxRender settings, but first, you need some ground. Use the **Add:Mesh:Plane** menu command to add a two-dimensional plane to the scene. Adjust the plane and gemstone until you have a satisfying arrangement in the camera view (see Figure 15-17) Yes, this is where you *really* have to become comfortable with the Blender interface.

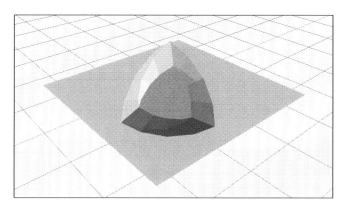

At this point, Blender's job is essentially complete. Use the **File:Save As** menu command to write a copy of your work to disk. If you haven't yet installed LuxRender, you should quit Blender at this point (**File:Quit**).

Figure 15-17 The completed Blender scene.

15.5.3 Materializing and Texturizing

Material and texture properties are intimately connected with the rendering process. As a consequence, you will have to set the gem and ground properties with the rendering package (LuxRender) installed. Fans of these programs will point out that Blender and LuxRender make a good-faith effort to communicate, and most object properties set in Blender will come over to LuxRender more or less unscathed. It turns out, however, that the material parameters needed for accurate gemstone rendering are not among these properties.

Let's get started. You will need to download and install the LuxRender package from www.luxrender.net. Pay particular attention to the installation instructions. Depending on the type of operating system, you may have to select certain options to ensure that LuxRender works with Blender.

As with the Blender installer, you should end up with a stand-alone LuxRender application that can be started with a double click (Figure 15-18). This is a good way to check that the program installed correctly, but you won't be using LuxRender this way. Instead, you will use the LuxBlend exporter that should now be a part of Blender.

Start up Blender again and load your scene (**File:Open**). Clicking on the **Render Engine** selector at the top of the user interface (see Figure 15-13) should reveal a new option: **LuxRender**.

With LuxRender selected as your engine of choice, you are ready to begin assigning material properties. Right-click on the gem to select it. Check for the familiar

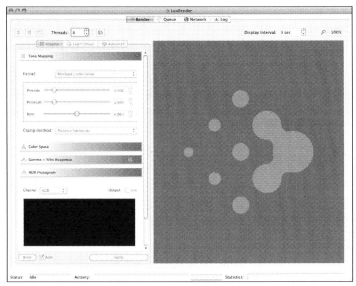

Figure 15-18 The stand-alone LuxRender application. You will see this window again when Blender launches the rendering.

orange outline before mousing over to the **Properties** window. You are likely still in the Render panel, the one with the small camera icon at the top. About a half-dozen icons to the right, you will find the friendly checkerboard sphere indicating the **Material** panel. Click on the symbol (Figure 15-19) to activate it.

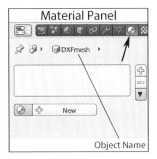

Somewhat confusingly, Blender presents you with an almost empty panel with the word "DXFmesh" at the top. This is, in fact, the name of your gemstone object – recall that it started its Blender life as an Autocad DXF file. You can change the name of this and other objects by double-clicking the appropriate entry in the **Outliner** (Figure 15-13 locates the Outliner).

Figure 15-19 Click on the small checkerboard sphere icon (arrow) to bring up the Material panel. Note the obscure Object Name for the gem.

Back to the **Material** panel. You must assign a material to your newly renamed gem before proceeding. Click on the **New** button at the bottom of the panel to create a new material. Suddenly, your empty window is full of options! Following along in Figure 15-20, you can immediately name the new material by double clicking on the ID Name field. You should then set the **Material type** to **Glass**. Almost instantly, Blender presents you with LuxRender options for this material. Move your mouse down to the **Choose preset** drop-down menu and click.

Look at that! A **Gemstones** option! Mousing over it reveals a plethora of choice (Figure 15-21). Select your favourite (I chose **Diamond**) and notice how Blender updates the **IOR** (index of refraction) field at the bottom of the panel.

Your ground plane deserves a new material as well. Right-click on it in the **3D Viewport**, and then click the **New** button in the **Material** panel of the **Properties** window. Name it, and for the **Material type**, select **Glossy**, since nothing in the real world is truly **Matte**. Let's try a checkerboard texture. For this, you will need to find or create an image of a checkerboard, in other words, alternating black and white squares. The file can be JPEG, PNG, BMP, or any of a half-dozen additional common formats. Google, grab, or grow your own...

To create the checkerboard texture for your new material, click on the **Textures** icon at the top of the **Properties** window (the one with the red and white checkerboard). You are again confronted with a mostly empty panel. Click the **New** button at the bottom. As before, many new fields should appear. The topmost of these lets you enter a name by double clicking. Set the **Type:** to **Image or Movie** and make sure that the **LuxRender type** is **Use Blender Texture**. Next, use the **Open** button at the bottom to navigate to and select the image file of the checkerboard. Finally, make sure that the **Mapping Type:** is set to **Planar**. You can find this setting by clicking open the sub-panel called **LuxRender2D Texture Mapping**. Figure 15-22 shows you where you should end up.

In order for it to take effect, you must assign your new texture to your ground plane material. Click back to the **Material** panel and look for the **LuxRender Glossy Material** sub-panel (note: it may be closed, requiring you to click on the small triangle). You need to set the **Diffuse color** to your new texture. Click on the **T** button to the right of the **Diffuse color** field and then click on the **red checkerboard texture** button that appears below. Select your checkerboard texture to complete your ground plane material.

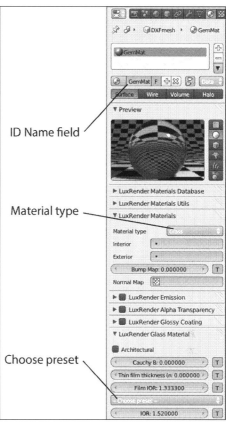

ID Name field

Material type

Choose preset

Figure 15-20 Setting the Material options for your gemstone.

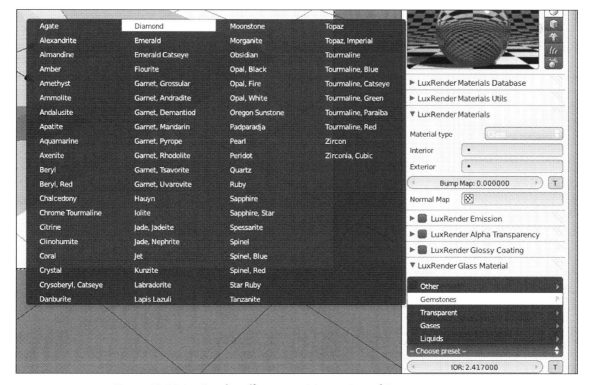

Figure 15-21 LuxRender offers an enticing variety of Gemstones presets.

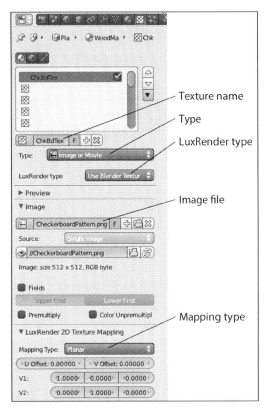

Texture name

Type

LuxRender type

Image file

Mapping type

Figure 15-22 The Textures panel of the Properties window after setting up the checkerboard.

There is one more major step required before you can execute the rendering. So far, you have a gemstone, a ground plane and the default lamp. That's it. The three objects might as well be floating in the blackness of space. To ensure a pleasing reflectance pattern from your gem, you need an interesting *sky*. If this doesn't strike you as incredibly important, then you remain in a purple haze (see "Kiss the Sky with GemRay" on page 196).

The easiest way to add a lively lighting environment to the scene is with a *hemispherical lamp*. Equipped with an appropriate screen or texture map, the hemispherical lamp becomes the equivalent of the GemRay sky depicted in Figure 15-7, illuminating the scene from all directions.

Adding a hemispherical lamp to your scene is simplicity itself. Select **Add:Lamp:Hemi** from the menu bar at the top of the screen. It may not look like much has happened, but if you poke around in the **3D Viewport**, you should be able to spot the new lamp – look for a pair of orange arcs defining the hemisphere. If you can't find it, make sure that **Hemi** is selected in the **Outliner**.

You may also notice a new icon in the **Properties** window, to the left of the **Textures** icon. It looks like what it is, a hemispherical lamp. Click on it to reveal the **Object Data** for the Hemi lamp. There are two important settings here, both in the **LuxRender Hemi Lamp** sub-panel. First, make sure that **Infinite** (not Distant) is selected. This places the source of light infinitely far away, like a true sky. More importantly, however, it allows you to specify an image as the *environmental map*. Here is where the interesting lighting comes in.

Click on the **browse** button (the small folder icon) at the right of the **HDRI Map:** field. This will open a file browser which will let you navigate to and select a suitable sky image. I typically use a high contrast image very similar to GemRay's Random sky as the lighting environment. In fact, as the field name suggests, you can use a High Dynamic Range Image (HDRI) here for extra "pop." These files are usually of type ".hdr" or ".exr". If you don't have an obviously suitable image, pick anything with a lot of varying brightness across the frame. Even that vacation snapshot will do…

15.5.4 Rendering

The end is in sight. There are just three easy steps to go. Honestly.

The first is to select an output file location under the **Render** panel of the **Properties** window. Look for the **Output** sub-panel and click on the folder icon to bring up a file browser. Navigate to a suitable directory for your rendering and **Accept** the selection.

The penultimate step is to check the type of rendering using the **LuxRender Render Settings** sub-panel of the **Render** panel. It is probably already correct, but verify that you will be doing **Bidirectional** rendering with the **Metropolis** sampler (Figure 15-23)

That's it. You're ready to roll.

The very final (I promise) step is to execute the rendering. As a precaution, save your work (**File** menu) and then select **Render Image** from the **Render** menuf, as you did way back on page 204.

Blender should launch the LuxRender stand-alone application in a new window. Slowly but surely, the image of your gemstone should appear. Depending on the hardware configuration of your computer, getting a decent rendering could take several to many minutes. Note that LuxRender will continue to improve your image until you tell it to stop using the **Pause** button. You also needn't worry about a computer crash: LuxRender regularly saves the newest version of the rendering in your specified Output folder. Why not go polish a couple of facets in the real world while you wait? Figure 15-24 shows what you can expect when you get back.

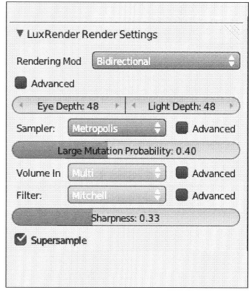

Figure 15-23 LuxRender set up for Bidirectional rendering with the Metropolis sampler.

Figure 15-24 Your first photo-realistic rendering of a gemstone. Congratulations! You should notice considerably more detail in the reflectance pattern compared to GemRay output. Note also that LuxRender's "environment" setting is somewhat different from GemRay's "sky" – the high contrast image on the Hemi lamp appears both above and below the "ground."

Actually, I lied.

Pushing the **Render** button wasn't the final step. In fact, it was really only the beginning. The true final step is up to you. This tutorial has only scratched the surface of Blender and LuxRender, but you should now be ready to begin exploring on your own. Here's a good place to start: try a nonzero **Cauchy B:** value on the gemstone's **Material** panel. Cauchy B is another way of saying dispersion or fire. How cool is that? For reference and further play, Table 12-7 contains IOR and Cauchy B values for some common gem materials.

Incidentally, with dispersion turned on, your renderings will take a long while to complete. This closes the circle opened in Section 15.2: while you are waiting, you will have plenty of time to check out the high-end machines at your local computer shop…

You can also modify and improve the scene around your gemstone. Why not try a wood grain texture for the ground plane? How about a spot lamp or two? You can even explore some of the modeling tools in Blender to create jewelry to show off your gem. The entirely virtual sapphire ring on the cover of this book (and in Figure 16-30) shows what is possible.

Blender and LuxRender are very popular, user-supported programs, and there are literally hundreds of examples and tutorials available on the Web. Follow your mouse. Is there some feature that simply does not exist? Do you really need an automatic needle inclusion generator? Roll your own! (and see Figure 6-12). As open-source software projects, both Blender and LuxRender grow and prosper based on the input of users.

15.6 Computing Gemstones in 3D

Note: This section provides additional information about the methods used in three-dimensional ray tracing of gemstones. It is not necessary to read and understand this material in order to produce realistic looking gemstone renderings, to say nothing of cutting a beautiful gem on your faceting machine. Nevertheless, the techniques involved relate directly to the interaction of light with matter, and hence should increase your understanding of how gemstones perform their magic.

How do programs like GemRay and Blender work? How can they make an accurate two-dimensional representation of a three-dimensional scene?

The answer lies in the realms of *three-dimensional ray tracing* and *planar geometric projections*.

15.6.1 Three-Dimensional Ray Tracing

Three dimensional ray-tracing is exactly what the name implies – the tracing of rays of light along the x, y, and z spatial axes, modifying the direction, colour, and brightness of the light as demanded by the materials with which it interacts. Chapters 10, 11, and 12 provide a great deal more detail on the subject, but it is worth briefly revisiting that material here, using an example tailored to the problem of ray tracing.

Figure 15-25 shows a situation you have seen before. A light ray travels through the air (1) until it strikes the surface of a gemstone. Due to Fresnel effects (see Chapter 11.8), a small portion of the ray reflects off the surface of the stone (2) and heads off into the sky. The remainder enters the gem, bent somewhat on entry by refraction (R). The ray continues into the stone (3), where absorption takes place. By selective removal of certain wavelengths of light, this absorption produces the colour in gemstones (Chapter 12.3.1), as well as an overall darkening due to non-specific absorption and scattering.

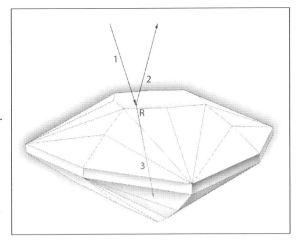

Figure 15-25 The path of a light ray entering a gemstone. See text for details. Note also that Chapters 10.3 and 10.4 provide more information and the gory mathematical details of what is happening here.

When the ray reaches the bottom of the gem, a number of things can occur. If the incidence angle is greater than the critical angle for the material, total internal reflection will redirect the ray back into the stone, producing further absorption. If the angle is below critical, good old Augustin-Jean Fresnel takes over once again, producing fractional reflection back into the gem and fractional transmission in the form of leakage out of the pavilion.

The result of all this is not one light ray, but rather a hierarchical "tree" of rays. Figure 15-25 shows three such rays: a "mother" (ray 1) and two "daughters" (rays 2 and 3). The goal of 3D gemstone rendering is to inject mother light rays into the scene and follow all the daughters – and daughters of daughters – until they strike some part of the "ground" or "sky," or until they have traveled so far through absorbing gem material that all light is extinguished.

Caveat 1. In reality, of course, the amount of bending at R depends on the wavelength of the light: the angle varies for different colours, producing the phenomenon of dispersion or fire. Reproducing this effect requires that the software split not only the intensity of the light at the surface, but also the angle as a function of wavelength. Yes, this adds lots of daughter rays to the tree, and although computationally intensive, such calculations are straightforward. See the comments on computing horsepower at the end of the previous section.

Caveat 2. If you really want to get down into the nitty-gritty physics of the situation, all kinds of things depend on other things. For example, the amount and polarization state of the light reflected at the interior and exterior surfaces of the gem depend on both wavelength and the incident angle. For pleochroic materials (Chapter 12.4), the refractive index and absorption depend on gem orientation, polarization, and wavelength. Daughters upon daughters upon daughters – this could get complicated. Luckily, most of these effects are relatively small in the real world, and ray-tracing software usually ignores them.

15.6.2 Planar Geometric Projections

A fancy term for a simple thing. Planar geometric projections are the mathematical operations which map the three-dimensional distribution of light in the scene onto the two-dimensional *viewport* of your computer display. Figure 15-26 shows the concept. The viewport is a plane located between the viewer and the three-dimensional scene. This plane intercepts the

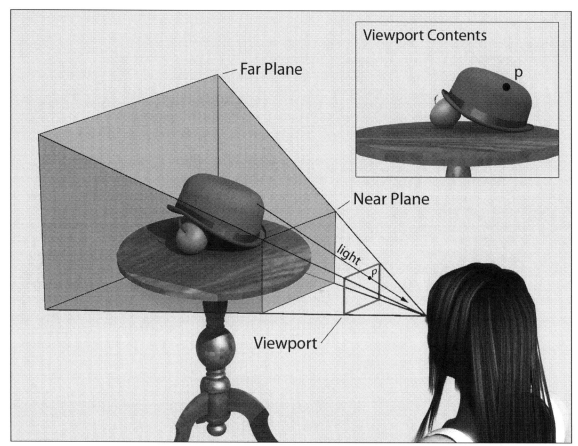

Figure 15-26 Planar geometric projection. Objects in the observer's field of view, typically restricted to the volume between a near plane and a far plane, send light through the viewport into the observer's eyes. All rays traveling in the correct direction and passing through a certain point, labeled p above, will contribute to the cumulative brightness and colour at that location in the scene.

light rays traveling to the viewer's eye. By assigning the appropriate colour and intensity to the intersection point on this projection plane, the computer can build up a two-dimensional representation of what the viewer sees.

More specifically, the computer needs to know exactly what colour and brightness to assign to a certain point on the viewport. Figure 15-26 demonstrates that this is equivalent to knowing the colour and brightness of all possible light rays passing through the point *p* and heading directly toward the observer's eye. The total colour and brightness will then be the sum over all of these possible rays. Simple.

There is a serious problem here, however. Have you spotted it? Only those rays which pass through the projection plane in the correct direction can enter the viewer's eye. For a given ray bouncing around the scene, what is the likelihood of that? Here's a hint: vanishingly small (see also Section 11.9.1). In fact, it would take an almost unbelievable stroke of luck to fire a random light ray into the scene, have it rattle around a bit, and then exit through the viewport at exactly the right angle. Since the chances are almost infinitely small, you need to fire an almost infinitely large number of rays to make sure that you can form the image. Also, since you know that light rays can split into multiple daughters when entering or leaving a transparent material such as a gem, you have to fire even more rays into the scene to account for this multitude of possibilities.

Don't go scouting around for surplus Cray supercomputers on eBay quite yet. There is a very clever solution to this conundrum, and it lurks in Chapter 11.6: light is reversible. That wonderful little fact makes ray tracing possible.

Here's the idea. You want to know the brightness and colour at a point in the viewport projection plane. This means following light rays from the scene to the viewer's eye, while properly accounting for reflection, refraction, and absorption. But you are really only interested in rays that end up traveling through this plane in the correct direction. Why not turn the situation around and fire light from the viewer's eye into the scene?

Imagine Superman sitting at the computer with laser beams coming out of his eyes (Figure 15-27 – this is finally getting interesting, right?). The laser rays will pass through the viewport with the correct direction, since you have set it up that way. The processes of reflection and refraction at surfaces are reversible, and hence, when the rays encounter a surface, the computer can split them appropriately, calculating the angles of reflection and refraction for the daughters and the amount of light to assign to each. These daughter rays propagate further into the scene, encountering additional surfaces and splitting as they go. In fact, you have created another "tree" of light rays, but this one is subtly different from that in Figure 15-25. Rather than starting with a single light ray injected into the scene, the "trunk" of this tree corresponds to the bundle of rays that end up exiting the scene with the correct position and direction to light up one pixel.

Figure 15-27 Computerized rendering follows light rays directed into the scene from the viewer's eyes, rather than the other way around. When the light encounters an object, the computer splits the rays according to the laws of reflection and refraction and then follows the "daughter" rays further into the scene.

The colour of this pixel will be the cumulative colour of all of the branches. For example, if the ray from Superman's eye enters the scene and misses the gem and the nice wooden table, the colour of the pixel will be the same as that of the "ground." If the ray strikes the gem, a portion, say 5% of the total, will be reflected toward the "sky "as at point R in Figure 15-25, while 95% will continue into the stone. The final image pixel will then contain the sky colour at a 5% level, with the remainder appropriately shaded by whatever the refracted ray and its daughters encounter. For the simple rendering of a gemstone shown in Figure 15-27, such colourants will be the absorption within the gem itself, the table, the ground, or the sky. Since the branching and sub-division of light could, in principle, go on forever, most ray tracing programs limit the number of times that a single ray can split. Figure 15-28 shows the effect of varying this quantity.

Armed with your knowledge of the inner workings of rendering software, you should be able to understand the differences in Figure 15-28. With a single "bounce," the program can generate only the reflection of the sky colour on the surface of the gemstone and cube, as

Figure 15-28 Rendering of a gemstone with one, two, four, and sixteen levels of ray splitting.

well as the shadowing by the stone on the top of the cube. Further splitting of daughter rays is suppressed. With two bounces, the sky colour reflected off the surface of the gemstone becomes visible in reflection on the cube, but internal reflections within the gem show no detail. Consult Figure 15-25 to convince yourself that this makes sense: two bounces do not suffice to provide information on the eventual sky or ground colour encountered by the daughters of ray 3. The four-bounce image gets much closer to reality, although a comparison to the sixteen-bounce frame shows important differences in detail and realism (book printing technology makes the difference less obvious here, but look, for example, at the reflection of the girdle in the cube).

For a rendering containing refractive elements such as gemstones, each additional bounce can approximately double the number of rays in the scene, and hence rapidly increases the computing time. As a result, professional 3D artists are very parsimonious with scene depth – that is, the number of permitted generations of daughter rays. A large, photo-realistic rendering of a gemstone, including dispersion, can literally take days on a home digital computer. Those of us who love the real thing even more than our virtual gemstones are quick to point out that these tiny, real-world, "analog computers" manage the same trick in about a ten-billionth of a second (see page 54). Take that, Microsoft.

Interested in learning more? Want to write your own ray-tracer? Chapter 9.4 contains a number of references on 3D geometry and ray tracing.

15.7 Other Software

Web access, gem design and optimization, 3D rendering…there is a whole world of computerized faceting out there to explore and learn. Important and enabling as these programs are, they will likely form only a part of your computerized faceting toolbox.

What are these other tools and where do you find them?

To answer the second question first: on your disk drive. If you are already a computer user, then you no doubt employ a variety of programs and utilities in your day-to-day life. Word processing software, image manipulation programs, spreadsheets and many other types of software can all help you get more out of gem cutting. Have you taken maximum advantage of them in your hobby?

To help answer the first question, this section presents a list of useful programs and how you might use them. Note that the following entries may refer to commercial packages (Microsoft Word, Adobe Photoshop…) to represent the overall category. While the commercial software is unquestionably of high quality, in almost all instances, very capable free or shareware versions exist.

Word Processors

Examples: Microsoft Word, Pages, OpenOffice Writer etc.

In addition to their basic purpose, creating formatted text files, word processors often have additional functionality that can enhance your faceting experience. Some examples:

- mixing of graphics and text to make catalogs, instruction manuals, etc.
- table manipulation tools, including simple calculations
- automatic export to HTML format for making websites

- creation and automation of form letters
- maintaining cutting logs, notes, etc.

Graphics Software

Examples: Photoshop, Illustrator, CorelDraw, Bridge, iPhoto, OpenOffice Draw etc.
- colour correction and manipulation of gem images
- photo catalog organization, management, searching, etc.
- creation and modification of diagrams, charts, etc.

Page Layout and Presentation Software

Examples: Quark XPress, InDesign, PowerPoint, Keynote, OpenOffice Impress, etc.
- creating newsletters, sales brochures, posters
- giving presentations, lectures, etc.

Spreadsheet Software

Examples: Excel, Numbers, OpenOffice Calc
- tangent ratio scaling (see Chapter 10.6.1)
- gem weight and rough cost calculations
- monitoring rough prices
- business management

Website Creation Software

Examples: Adobe Dreamweaver and Muse, Microsoft Expression Web, SeaMonkey etc.
- creating and maintaining websites
- e-commerce

15.8 List of Network Resources

Listing network resources in a printed book is a risky business, since the Internet is an extremely dynamic place. Web sites change their addresses, and individuals and business regularly disappear, transform themselves, and reappear.

Nevertheless, there are a number of network resources that are stable, in the sense that, as of the end of the first decade of the 21st century, they have been around for ten years or more. In case you didn't know, this is *forever* on the Web. The following pages provide the addresses of these and other network resources, as well as a short description and comment on each. Needless to say, given the nature of the Web, this list is far from comprehensive.

In order to track future changes, I have established (guess?) a web site! The first item listed below is the "official" web site of *Amateur Gemstone Faceting*, and you can point your browser there anytime to get the latest information on faceting on the Web. You can also help keep this resource up to date. Send additions and corrections to tom@facetingbook.com

15.8.1 General Information and User Groups

`facetingbook.com`
The "official" website of this book, where you can find updates (including the following links), corrections, and other information.

`gemologyonline.com`
A great web resource containing information on gems, gem materials, and all types of lapidary arts. It also hosts a very dynamic forum with expert contributors.

`usfacetersguild.org`
Home of the United States Faceter's Guild, hosting faceting diagrams, helpful tips, and web links. You can also join the lively online discussion group on Yahoo.

`gemsociety.org`
The International Gem Society website. Plenty of information on gem materials, gemology instruments, book reviews, and even a fun activity area for kids.

`gemaddicts.com`
A very useful site that maintains up to date information on gem treatments, new finds, and business ethics. The site hosts a list of "Safe Vendors" of gems and lapidary equipment.

`texasfacetersguild.org`
Web home of the Texas Faceter's Guild. They also have an online discussion group. Join by e-mailing TxFacetorsGuild-subscribe@yahoogroups.com

`ganoksin.com/orchid/orchid.htm`
Orchid is a moderated forum for gems and jewelry. They also host a collection of helpful articles on specific topics.

`gemcutters.org`
Home of the International Lapidary Association. Lots of great stuff here, but it seems to have been inactive since 2006.

15.8.2 Clubs, Guilds, and Schools

`usfacetersguild.org/guilds.shtml`
The USFG maintains a list of faceting guilds worldwide. Use this link as a starting point.

`lapidaryclub.org`
The Old Pueblo Lapidary Club in Tucson, Arizona. This is where I learned to cut, and it hosts an annual "hobnob" during the massive Tucson Gem Show (see Chapter 6.2.2).

`facetorsguild.com.au`
The Australian Facetor's Guild sponsors the renowned International Faceting Challenge, arguably the grandaddy of all faceting competitions.

`ukfcg.org`
The UK Facet Cutter's Guild.

`lapidaryworld.com`
Comprehensive lists of gem and mineral clubs worldwide, as well as other information.

`rockhounds.com/rockshop/clublist.shtml`
List of over 900 mineralogical, lapidary, and fossil clubs in the United States.

`lapidaryschool.org`
>   This is the web home of the Willliam P. Holland School of Lapidary Arts in northern Georgia, USA. They offer week-long beginner and intermediate faceting classes.

`northcoastlapidary.com`
>   Jim Perkins trains students on a one-on-one basis during his 5-day faceting course.

`facetingacademy.com`
>   Gemstone artist John Bailey offers a 4-day basic and a 5-day advanced class.

`riodoce.com/lapidary-instruction`
>   The Rio Doce gem mine in North Carolina provides individual training broken down into six, one-week segments.

`diamondschool.com`
>   The American Institute of Diamond Cutting in southeast Florida runs 3-month courses at the beginner, intermediate, and advanced levels.

`free-form.ch/fac.html`
>   Free Form Artists of Montreux, Switzerland hold single-day classes in faceting. Also offered in Dar es Salaam, Tanzania.

15.8.3 Gem Ethics –Jewelry Organizations and Government Agencies

`cibjo.org`
>   The World Jewellery Confederation (CIBJO). Download their Official CIBJO Gemstone Book at `download.cibjo.org`

`agta.org`
>   The American Gem Trade Association (AGTA). Click the DISCLOSURE link to view their Code of Ethics and Gemstone Enhancement Codes.

`ftc.gov/bcp/guides/jewel-gd.shtm`
>   The USA Federal Trade Commission (FTC) maintains an ethics guide for the jewelry industry (see Chapter 13.5).

Wayback the 404

Don't you hate getting 404'd?

Getting 404'd refers to the experience of receiving an HTTP 404 error code, indicating that you have tried to access a non-existing or dead link on the World Wide Web. This experience has now grown to be part of the online culture, spurring a flood of imaginative 404 message pages. Google "funny 404 page" and prepare to waste an hour.

What to do when you get 404'd?

The obvious first step is to verify the web address that you entered. If you are sure that a link should work, the site may be down either temporarily or permanently. In the latter instance, try using the Wayback Machine at `www.archive.org`. This fabulous resource was developed during the late 1990's by the Internet Archive, a non-profit organization, based in San Francisco. Just surf to archive.org, paste in your link, and then select a previously taken snapshot of the site from the chronological list. The Wayback Machine has saved my bacon on a number of occasions. As I said, a fabulous resource.

15.8.4 Online Gemstone Designs

`facetdiagrams.org`
> A massive database of online diagrams based on Long and Steele's Datavue program. Set up by Robert Strickland of GemCAD fame, facetdiagrams.org is growing daily with designs contributed by the community.

`rockhounds.com/rockshop/gem_designs/design_index.shtml`
> Bob Keller's online collection of over 150 gemstone designs, including Sun Twist from Chapter 16.2.2.

`rockhounds.com/oplc/cd_online/`
> Online version of the Old Pueblo Lapidary Club's CD, including 60 unique designs and links to plenty of additional faceting information.

`faceters.com`
> In addition to selling collections of his gem designs, Jeff Graham offered almost 40 cutting diagrams free of charge on his website. Although no longer directly online, Jeff's website is accessible on the Wayback Machine (see opposite page).

`boghome.com/TomsPages/MyDesigns/index.html`
> The web home of the BOG gem optimization program also hosts 15 gem designs, many of which are mentioned in this book.

15.8.5 Faceting Books and Reference Materials

`worldcat.org`
> Worldwide library search – 1.5 billion items. See page 354 of Volume 1.

`diamondcuttingbook.com`
> Website of Basil Watermeyer, originator of the barion design (page 246).

Commercial sites selling faceting related books:

`gemologyonline.com/books.html`

`cuttingrocks.com/catalog_books_faceting.shtml`

`gemcutter.com`

`theimage.com/books/books.html`

15.8.6 Information on Gems and Minerals

These websites provide encyclopedic information on gem species, minerals, and localities:

`webmineral.com`

`mindat.org`

`minerals.net`

15.8.7 Online Gemology Courses and Learning Material

`bwsmigel.info`
> Course material from an introductory class on gemology.

`nature.berkeley.edu/classes/cps2/`
> Material from a Gems and Gem Material Class at Berkeley.

ruby-sapphire.com
>   Home to a large collection of articles, opinion, book reviews, etc.

attawaygems.com/NMFG/Lets_talk_gemstones_index.html
>   A collection of articles by gemologist, Edna B. Anthony.

15.8.8 Faceting Machine Manufacturers

This section contains links to the manufacturers of the most popular current faceting machines. To track down other hardware, consult Chapter 2.8.

gravescompany.com
>   The Graves Company (Mark I, Mark IV, Mark 5XL machines)

facetron.com
>   Jarvi Tool Co. (Facetron machine)

jerseyinstruments.com
>   Jersey Instruments (Patriot, Tom Thumb machines)

polymetricinc.com
>   Poly-Metric Instruments Inc. (Xristal-Tek 99, Scintillator 88, O.M.F, Xristal-Tek 87)

ultratec-facet.com
>   Ultra Tec (V5, V2, Concave, and Fantasy machines)

15.8.9 Lap Manufacturers

gearloose.com
>   Website of the gearloose family of faceting products (see page 76 of Volume 1).

raytechgemprocessing.com/lapidary/diamond-products/facets-tomb-stone.php
>   Home of the NuBond and Fast Lap, as well as bonded steel, copper and tin laps.

gemartservices.com/pol.htm
>   The Pol-A-Gem cerium oxide permanently charged polishing lap.

lightninglap.com
>   Web home of the Lightning Lap, as well as the MagDop, Beast polish, and more.

abrasive-tech.com
>   Website for Crystalite cutting laps.

15.8.10 Synthetic and Simulant Gemstone Material

morioncompany.com
>   Morion manufactures an array of synthetic gemstone materials and sells it by the carat.

roughmanmadegems.com
>   This company offers synthetic garnets and CZ, as well as recrystallized corundum.

creativegems.com
>   Grady and Phyllis Harris offer a variety of synthetics and simulants.

gemcutter.com/syn-ruf.htm
>   The Facet Shoppe carries all manner of faceting supplies, from machines to natural and synthetic rough.

15.8.11 Other Manufacturers

This section lists manufacturers of specific products mentioned in this book.

Findings and Mountings:

`tripps.com`

`riogrande.com`

`stuller.com`

`firemountaingems.com`

Immersion Fluids for both refractive index (Chapter 4.5) and density (page 121):

`cargille.com`

`geoliquids.com`

Miscellaneous Manufacturers and Dealers:

`edmundoptics.com`
> Edmund sells a huge variety of optical components, including the first-surface mirrors discussed in Chapter 7.6.4.

`usdigital.com/products/encoders`
> This company manufactures incremental optical encoders, such as those needed to upgrade your faceting machine with a precision digital protractor (Chapter 20.8).

`en.nanotec.com`
> European manufacturer of optical encoders suitable for the faceting machine upgrade described in Chapter 20.8.

`arduino.cc`
> The home of all things Arduino. See Chapter 20.8.

`sparkfun.com`
> An electronics tinkerer's paradise. You can find almost anything here, including Arduinos and the liquid crystal displays discussed in Chapter 20.8.

`adafruit.com`
> Another hobbyist electronics superstore for Arduino projects and related hardware.

15.8.12 Software

Gem Design and Optimization Software:

`gemcad.com`
> The home of Robert Strickland's excellent GemCAD and GemRay programs.

`boghome.com`
> Website of the BOG optimization program (see Section 15.3.2).

`octonus.com`
> The DiamCalc and GemAdviser programs help you visualize and adjust gem properties to maximize impact. Geared toward diamonds.

`www.northcoastlapidary.com/?p=434`
> Jim Perkins hosts a downloadable version of Anton Vasiliev's Facet Designer software.

Software for Three-Dimensional Rendering (Section 15.4):

`blender.org`
> Home of the freeware Blender program.

`luxrender.net`
>   Physically-based renderer plugin for blender.

`povray.org`
>   Alternate freeware rendering program.

`3dlapidary.com`
>   Website hosting 3D models of various gemstone designs in common formats.

Virtualization / Emulation Tools - These programs let you run Microsoft Windows within another operating system (see page 192):

`virtualbox.org`

`microsoft.com/windows/virtualpc/`

`oracle.com/us/technologies/virtualization/index.html`

`parallels.com`

`vmware.com`

Free online tools for creating your own video tutorials (see page 191):

`screencast-o-matic.com`

`screenr.com`

15.8.13 Miscellaneous

`archive.org/details/plinysnaturalhis00plinrich`
>   Pliny the Elder's 37-Volume *Historia Naturalis*, all readable online!

`folds.net/diamond_design`
>   Marcel Tolkowsky's monograph on diamond design.

`gemval.com`
>   Online gemstone appraisal service. Access to valuation of most coloured gems is free, although some will require a subscription.

`rocktumbler.com/blog/fee-mining-and-digging-sites`
>   Extensive list (with links) of fee dig sites in the USA and Canada.

`timantit.com/laser/laser.asp`
>   Another take on the laser transfer cheat technique described in Chapter 7.6.4.

`gemologyproject.com/wiki/index.php?title=Dichroscope`
>   Detailed description, including video, of the principle and operation of the dichroscope.

Various Depth of Cut Indicator Implementations (see Chapter 20.7):

`usfacetersguild.org/articles/dave_wooley/beale_wooley_indicator`

`jewelcutter.com/sapphire`

`rockhounds.com/rockshop/gem_designs/kavan_bw_installation`

`gearloose.com/j2.html`

`boghome.com/TomsPages/Micrometer.html`

Faceting Machine Alignment:

`lapidaryworld.com/pdf/faceting_machine_alignment.pdf`

`usfacetersguild.org/articles/paul_head/machine_alignment`

Build Your Own Faceting Machine:

`books.google.com`
> Enter "Make Your Own Gemstone Faceting Machine" in the search box to link to the article shown in Figure 2-22.

`gearloose.com/why.html`
> Instructions and drawings for the Revision H faceting head by Gearloose.

True Miscellany:

`azotic.us`
> Manufacturers of Mystic Topaz (see page 152).

`urbandictionary.com`
> An invaluable resource with which you can catch up on all the latest lingo and memes, including the definition of facetable. Warning: occasionally (often) not safe for work.

`bls.gov/cpi`
> The USA Bureau of Labor Statistics is the home of the consumer price index (referenced in Chapter 6.5).

16

Designing Your Own Gemstone

I am not going to teach you how to design gemstones.

I know what the chapter title says, but I am not. I would if I could, but I can't so I won't.

Ultimately, gemstone design is an artistic, creative, act that comes from within. Yes, there are general guidelines, which I will try to explain. And yes, there are useful tools out there that can simplify and amplify the creative process, and I will also try to explain those. Nevertheless, the act of gemstone design will have to come from you.

This chapter will do its best to get you on the road to creating unique gemstone designs. It starts with some discussion of general principles of how inspiration can be translated to stone, and then explains some of the tools and techniques for turning that inspiration into an actual design. The next section contains a compendium of hints and observations on maximizing the visual impact of your creative efforts. The final part of the chapter gives two examples of how you can use gem software to gain insight into the design process.

Note that this is the first of three chapters on gem design. Chapter 17 focuses on various techniques for achieving your desired gem outline, while Chapter 18 brings everything together with a case study illustrating in detail how one gem design, called Briar Rose, came into being.

16.1 The Perspiration of Inspiration

As emphasized on the previous page, no individual teacher or textbook can explain how to be creative, and each person's approach to the process of coming up with a gem design concept will be different.

There are, however, a few obvious sources of inspiration, and I have used all of them:

1. Modification or adaptation of an existing design

2. Cuts inspired by objects or phenomena, such as flowers, sunsets, etc.

3. A specific design goal, for example maximizing sparkle, fire, or colour separation

4. Inspiration from the shape of (expensive) gem rough

5. Random play

Of these, the first is the most straightforward, at least in terms of getting started with putting your ideas down on paper or screen. There are a multitude of published designs out there that you can use as a starting point for your personal creative exploration. Section 16.2 below gives some ideas and examples of how to take inspiration from existing designs.

The entrancing geometries of gemstones often reflect or evoke phenomena in the real world. This should not come as a surprise, since many of the most visually pleasing aspects of gems, for example their symmetry (see Chapter 10.7), are also central to the appeal of natural objects, such as snowflakes or starfish. Finding inspiration in such objects is therefore a natural source of creative expression.

Occasionally, a particular type of gem rough may prompt a design idea. For example, pleochroic gem materials (Chapter 12.4) can produce striking visual effects when the light rays traveling along one optical axis of the gem are kept separate from those traveling along a different axis. The colour play that distinguishes an andalusite gemstone depends on proper design to achieve this.

It may sound bizarre or, more likely, vaguely ridiculous, but gem rough can talk to you. No, I don't mean actually speaking, and I have, to my knowledge, never been observed in conversation with a chunk of rock – a recalcitrant, half-completed gem on the faceting machine… that's a different matter. The stone shape and play of light in raw gem material can suggest a design, and I commonly carry around a particularly interesting or valuable piece of rough for days, taking it out when opportunity or inspiration strikes (see page 211 of Volume 1). Of course, financial considerations may also come into play: the goal of maximizing yield can certainly focus the design exercise into particular avenues.

Finally, the computer age has ushered in a new way of designing gemstones: random play. Once you gain experience with GemCAD and other design tools (Chapter 15.3), you are free to experiment, trying new shapes, facet combinations, and symmetries. Working through a design theme and investigating different variations has never been easier, and the computer allows you to save each branch of your exploration as a separate file for later refinement. Yes, traditional gem cutters often "design at the machine" (see page 309 of Volume 1), but there are clear limits and shortcomings to this type of experimentation. For example, designing directly on the lap has exactly zero levels of "Undo."

These (and other) sources of inspiration can, of course, be combined. For example, the starting point for a design may be the outline of an existing piece of gem rough (inspiration number 4 above). After establishing the appropriate girdle outline based on the stone, you may then begin experimenting with, for example, snowflake-like facets (number 2).

Am I Ready?

You may find gemstone design a daunting prospect. On the one hand, the traditional designs, such as the standard round brilliant or emerald, represent the accumulated wisdom of thousands of master cutters over hundreds of years. On the other hand, modern computer-based design tools, while quite affordable, can appear bewilderingly complex at first glance.

The simple answer is that, if you feel the inspiration to create new gem cuts and are willing to invest a little time and money, then you are undoubtedly ready to give it a try. I created my first gemstone design less than two years after starting the hobby, and after cutting only a handful of stones.

A basic knowledge of how a gemstone works (see Chapter 11), coupled with some inexpensive software tools (Chapter 15.3), are the only prerequisites. The rewards can be immense: nothing is more satisfying than presenting a friend or family member with a beautiful gemstone of your own creation, from beginning to end.

16.2 Modifying an Existing Design

Let me guess.

My guess is that the very first stone that you cut was not one that you designed yourself.

Let me guess again.

My second guess is that you haven't always strictly followed the cutting prescription laid out in the gem design. Maybe you adhered exactly to the instructions for that first stone, but sooner or later, a nasty inclusion or a cutting error forced you off the straight and narrow into some freestyle invention at the faceting machine.

Welcome to the world of gem design!

In fact, most faceters will improvise or change things on the fly when the need arises. While I would not categorize such activity as gem design *per se*, modifying an existing prescription to suit a particular situation is definitely a step down that path.

Such modification can be as simple as adding a few accent facets when cutting a particular design from a larger piece of gem rough, or omitting a few facets for a smaller stone. You can try splitting existing facets in two (or three…or four…). The seemingly infinite variations of the SRB are an expression of this desire to give an old standard a fresh new look (see Figure 16-1 and "Reinventing the Split" on page 229). You can even literally put a new twist on an established design. The crown of the Figaro cut (Figure 16-33) is a cork-screwed SRB.

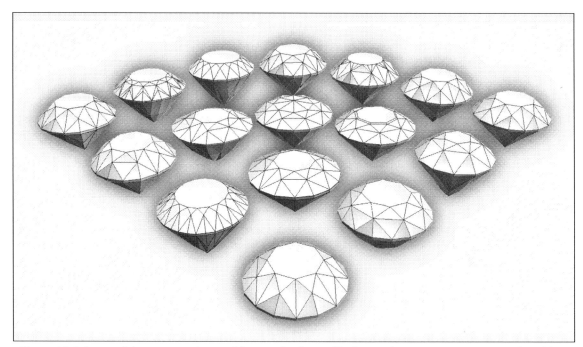

Figure 16-1 Some of the many variants of the standard round brilliant. These permutations arise by adding additional connecting and accent facets.

16.2.1 Mix and Match

Pushing the envelope a little further, you may wish to try a different crown on top of the prescribed pavilion. Although there may seem to be an infinite number of possible gem designs out there, the range of girdle outlines – at least those that are practical to cut – is considerably more limited. This is partially due to the fact that symmetry produces visual interest. It also has a lot to do with the requirement that faceted gemstones be convex solids (see Chapter 1.2) and the practicalities of gemstone setting – no jeweler will stock or manufacture an infinite variety of findings.

Figure 16-3 and Figure 16-4 show the standard girdle outlines as categorized by the great gemstone designers and teachers, Robert H. Long and Norman W. Steele. Their series of books is essential reading for any faceter (see Chapter 9). While this gemstone "zoo" may appear quite diverse, perhaps 90% of all designs fall into the half dozen or so most popular categories.

The bottom line? Many girdle outlines are identical, particularly for round and symmetrical stones, offering the possibility to mix and match.

In addition to providing a reasonably gentle introduction to gem design, mixing and matching pavilions and crowns with the same outline can lead to striking results. Figure 16-5 shows the same pavilion mated to three different crowns. Differences in symmetry and overall design approach between the two halves of the stone can multiply the interest of your gems.

Mixing and matching is fun and easy. How easy? "Am I Ready?" on the previous page notes that I designed my first gemstone after two years in the hobby. I lied. If mixing and matching counts as design – and I think that it does – then my third gemstone was an original (see Table 5-1).

A couple of words of caution: First, while this type of experimentation is often very successful, it can also lead to disappointing results. As always, I recommend trying new ideas in the computer before committing them to valuable gem rough. Second, things can go disastrously wrong if your pavilion and crown don't actually line up. Don't automatically assume that the outlines are identical. Check the facet layout of the girdle very carefully, or better still, test cut your creation in the computer.

Reinventing the Split

Look again carefully at Figure 16-1. In their attempts to put a new spin on an old standard, gem designers have tried a number of tricks, but the majority of the SRB variations they've come up with involve splitting the main facets. Some have vertical splitting, like the gem sitting front and center, while others, such as the stone to its immediate right, exploit horizontal splitting. Careful examination of the figure will show other gems which use both.

Why all this rectilinear thinking? Why not try something a bit different, like splitting the mains diagonally?

That's the idea behind the lovely Viviant design (Figure 16-2), created by my friend and colleague Dave Thompson. Both the pavilion and crown mains are split diagonally. A slight offset in index setting is the key to this bit of genius.

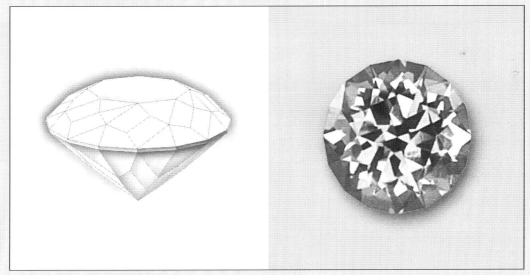

Figure 16-2 The Viviant gemstone design (left) uses diagonal splitting of the pavilion and crown mains to achieve a unique variation on the SRB. A 4.5-carat Viviant cut in flawless citrine (right).

It's a lovely design and it produces a knock-out stone, but Viviant carries a deeper message. Even the oldest of old standards still offers the opportunity for trying a new twist. All it takes is a little "out of the box" or dare I say, "diagonal," thinking. The Heidelberg Brilliant in Chapter 19.3.2 is another Dave Thompson take on this idea.

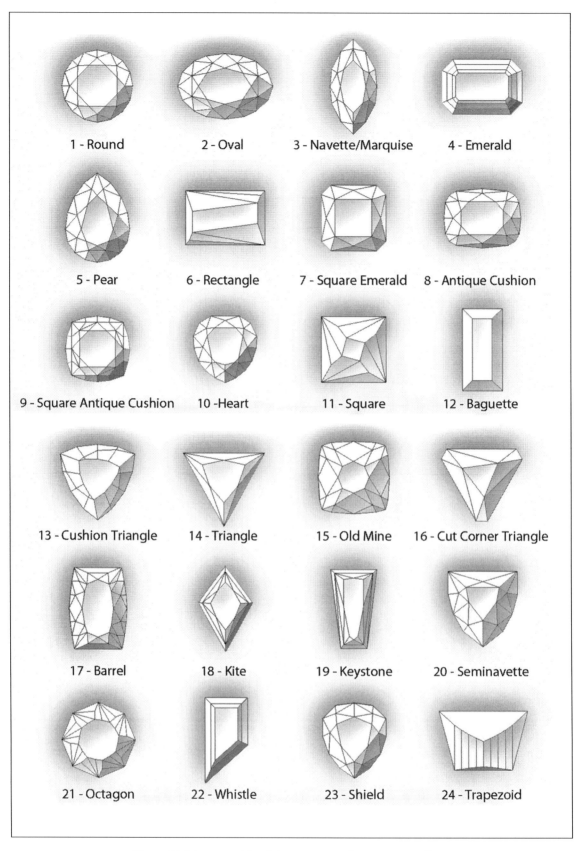

1 - Round 2 - Oval 3 - Navette/Marquise 4 - Emerald

5 - Pear 6 - Rectangle 7 - Square Emerald 8 - Antique Cushion

9 - Square Antique Cushion 10 - Heart 11 - Square 12 - Baguette

13 - Cushion Triangle 14 - Triangle 15 - Old Mine 16 - Cut Corner Triangle

17 - Barrel 18 - Kite 19 - Keystone 20 - Seminavette

21 - Octagon 22 - Whistle 23 - Shield 24 - Trapezoid

Figure 16-3 Long and Steele's taxonomy of gemstone outlines.

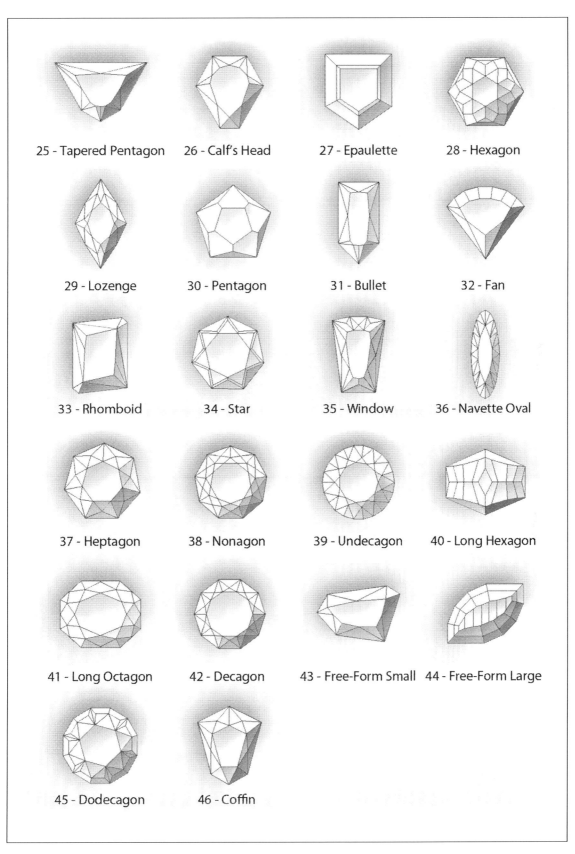

Figure 16-4 Long and Steele's gem outlines (continued).

Figure 16-5 The same pavilion matched to three different crowns produces strikingly different optical appearance. All three gems have a simple 16-facet "reflector" pavilion. From left to right the crowns are: SRB, Step Cut, and Checker. Note that these gems do not exist in the real world. This is a 3D virtual rendering as described in Chapter 15.5.

16.2.2 Spinning with Symmetry

How about more radical variations on an existing design that you like? One obvious approach is to try the cut in a different symmetry. Back in the day, when I first started faceting gemstones, I stumbled upon Sun Twist by Keith Sanker (see Figure 16-6). It's a great design, and it was the first "non-standard" gem that I cut. That was gemstone number five for me, and I liked it so much, it turned out to be gemstone number six as well (see Table 5-1).

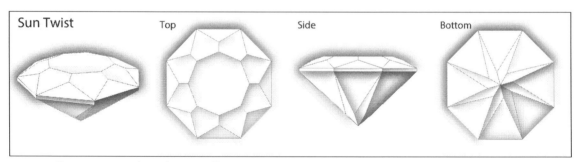

Figure 16-6 Keith Sanker's excellent Sun Twist design is available online – see Chapter 15.8.4.

Sun Twist is deceptively simple. The combination of a radially-symmetric pavilion with a simple, non-meet point, mirror-symmetric crown produces a surprisingly complex and lively gem (see Chapter 10.7 if you don't understand the difference between radial and mirror-image symmetry).

I wanted to try Sun Twist in a radically different form – pentagonal. I had just received a new 80-tooth index wheel, which opened the door to five-fold symmetric stones. The result was Twist5 (see Figure 16-7 and Chapter 19.1.2). The Sun Twist pedigree is obvious – note the "twisted" secondary pavilion facets and the floating, 60%, non-meet point table.

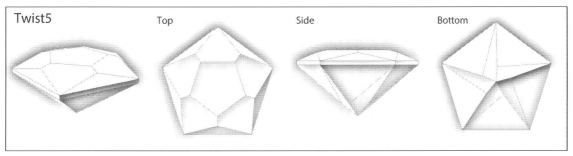

Figure 16-7 Twist5 is a five-fold symmetric variant of Sun Twist (Figure 16-6).

Despite its obvious heritage, Twist5 has a completely different look to that of Sun Twist, and a casual examination of the gemstones cut from the two prescriptions would not reveal a clear connection. Is Twist5 a unique, new design? I would argue not, since it is a simple transformation of an existing cut to a new symmetry. Nevertheless, exploring your favourite gemstone design in alternate forms can be very rewarding and occasionally surprising.

Incidentally, both Sun Twist and Twist5 should look vaguely familiar to you. The GeM101 cut presented in Chapter 5 is a hexagonally-symmetric variant of the same design, with a second slight twist applied to the crown. True originality can be an elusive goal, since there are very few new ideas, or new twists on old ideas, under the sun.

Inspiration versus Derivation

Is it theft to appropriate significant design elements from someone else's work?

Great question, and it's an issue that raises all kinds of ruckus in the online discussion groups. I am not a lawyer, and copyright law varies throughout the world, but you are fairly safe if you draw inspiration from published designs, as long as it is for your own private enjoyment.

In other words, it should not be a problem if your design is derivative of an existing work. Go ahead and cut the darn thing and sell the stone if you want. The situation gets a little murky if your gem cut is strikingly similar to a copyrighted design, or if you advertise your creative efforts as uniquely yours. Needless to say, you can expect legal trouble if you try to market a book of original designs that are not.

Short version: Use common sense.

16.2.3 Playing with Proportions

In addition to playing with symmetry, there is another, even more radical way of modifying an existing gemstone design to your particular taste – stretching. A standard oval brilliant is simply a stretched SRB, and the same strategy can be applied to many designs. For example, I created a very simple square reflector called Fritz (the design is available online at www. boghome.com). Figure 16-8 shows a 2-carat Fritz cut in Brazilian seafoam tourmaline. What the picture does not show is how the jagged angular reflections flash and shift as the stone is rocked. Incidentally, the name comes from the similarity of this to the behaviour of an old television "on the fritz," back when televisions were (a) analog, and (b) contained picture tubes instead of flat-panel displays.

I really liked how Fritz balanced an interesting play of light with showing off the intrinsic colour of the tourmaline. Having laid hands on a beautiful piece of Tajik golden beryl, I wanted to give Fritz another try. There was a problem, however. The rough was a long, flawless crystal in the classic hexagonal habit that beryl exhibits (see Figure 12-33). The usable volume of rough would produce a stone with a much greater length to width ratio (L/W~1.5) than that of Fritz (L/W=1.0). See Chapter 10.8.1 if you don't understand what length to width ratio means and where to find it.

Figure 16-8 The Fritz reflector design cut in seafoam tourmaline.

The solution was to stretch the design! "Putting on the Fritz..." below explains exactly how I did it using GemCAD, and Figure 16-9 shows the result. Want to put on your own Fritz15? Chapter 19.2.1 contains complete cutting instructions.

It turns out that GemCAD can do a whole lot more than just stretching, including such tricks as rotating and reflecting the gem. Combining these commands offers almost limitless opportunities for play. For example, Figure 16-13 shows how a combination of stretching, rotation, and reflection can produce an elongated rectangular cushion starting from a standard round brilliant. There are other ideas for design modification in the GemCAD manual. Get it and play!

Figure 16-9 The Fritz15 design is a stretched version of Fritz (and rotated 90° compared to Figure 16-8), here cut in flawless Tajik golden beryl.

Putting on the Fritz...

Here's how I turned the square Fritz design into a longer (L/W=1.5) cut, cleverly called Fritz15.

GemCAD offers the option of changing the proportions of a gemstone with a couple of clicks of the mouse. Figure 16-10 shows the Fritz design loaded into the program. Executing the **Scale...** command under the **Edit** menu brings up a dialog box called **Stretch or Shrink** (Figure 16-11). Selecting the **X** direction and the appropriate **Multiply By** value produces the result shown in Figure 16-12 and Chapter 19.2.1.

Done. That was easy, wasn't it?

Not so fast. There are at least a couple of problems with blithely stretching a gem design and going at it on the faceting machine.

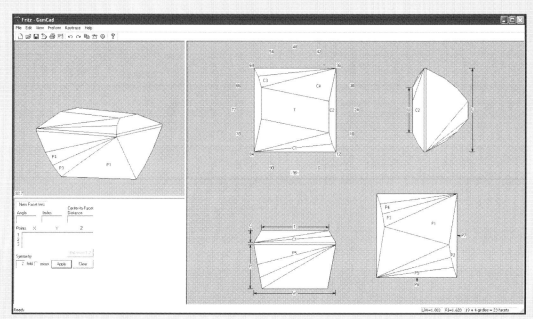

Figure 16-10 The original Fritz design loaded into GemCAD.

The first and most critical problem arises from the fact that stretching a particular arrangement of facets does a whole lot more than just change the gem outline. If the meet points are preserved, this process will inevitably change both the cutting angles *and* the indices of the facets (see also page 33). The angles will, in general, work out, but Murphy's Law dictates that in all but the luckiest instances, you won't end up with whole-number index gear settings. Instead, you'll get fractional indices, like 8.3 or 56.5. Yick.

Is it time to give your cheater a serious workout and attempt to cut a design with fractional indices? The cheater is, after all, formally known as the "index splitter" (see "Cheat to Win…" on page 25 of Volume 1). Luckily, the answer is no. As part of the stretching process, GemCAD will try to round the resulting index wheel settings to whole number values. In doing so, it will present you with the option of using an alternate index gear and will even evaluate the relative error in such rounding for various wheels, including those with 64, 72, 80, 84, 88, 96, and 120 teeth. Although few of us actually have such a large selection of index gears, this rounding function can really save your bacon.

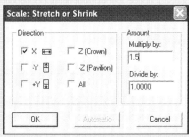

Figure 16-11 The Scale: Stretch or Shrink dialog box.

Occasionally, however, GemCAD will fail to find a suitable set of rounded-off facet indices. In this instance, it will alter the design as you specified, leaving fractional values in the prescription. At this point, you have several options, including trying a different stretch factor, altering the input design somewhat, or in the most desperate of circumstances, giving your cheater that serious workout.

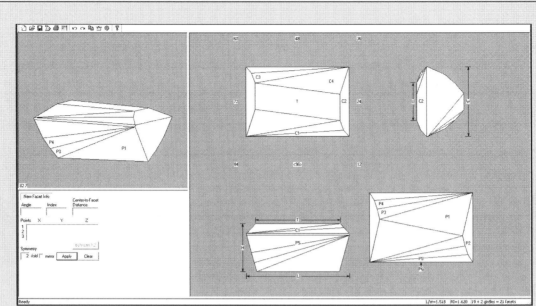

Figure 16-12 Fritz15, a L/W=1.5 version of the original Fritz design.

It turns out that I did not have to confront such options in converting the Fritz design to Fritz15: GemCAD returned whole number indices without difficulty. The reason for this is subtle, but it has to do with the arrangement of meet points along the (now) long dimension of the stone. GemCAD was able to jiggle the cutting angles around enough to preserve the meet points without splitting an index. Although not originally intended, this "stretchability" is an advantage of Fritz-type designs.

The second problem associated with stretching a design relates to the cutting angles. GemCAD will not add or subtract facets, so stretching a certain gem layout will inevitably change the angles. For example, the P1 pavilion facets in the Fritz design become longer in the x direction, yet the depth of the stone does not change. This means that the P1 cutting angle goes down, and we all know about the potential consequences of that (see also the comments on elongated designs on page 256). At the very least, you should check the modified cut for optical performance using your favourite software tool (see Chapter 15.3). As a matter of routine practice, I always re-optimize a design after changing its proportions. In the case of Fritz15, this optimization not only improved the light return, but also it restored the dynamic, "Fritzy" reflection pattern in the spirit of the original gem.

16.2.4 Acting on Inspiration

The final and most sophisticated way of modifying an existing gemstone cut is to incorporate your own interesting design elements or facet sequences into the prescription. Have you cut a gem with a particularly pleasing reflection pattern near the culet? You can try grafting the culet area of this gem onto the design. Has a certain sequences of facets – say a spray of triangular facets near the girdle – produced an interesting effect? Give it a try.

My own design, Keystar, is a good example of such "indirect" inspiration. Fairly early on in my faceting adventures, I cut a citrine in the excellent Pat's Points design by Jeff Graham (available in his fourth volume "Money Cuts" – see Chapter 9.2). The resulting gem was a

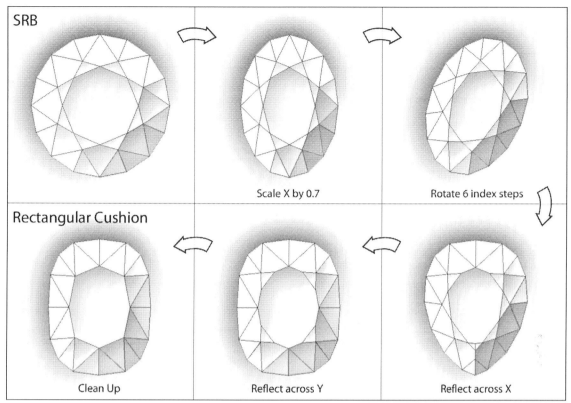

Figure 16-13 Combining GemCAD commands to create an entirely new gemstone design. The final "clean up" step involved deleting the small star facets and re-cutting a couple of crown breaks to the existing meet points.

beauty, with striking optical performance and interesting proportions. Best of all, Pat's Points was ideally suited to the odd shape of my piece of citrine rough. When I later acquired a promising hunk of Nigerian Rubellite with approximately the same shape, I knew what I wanted to try: a brilliant keystone of my own design.

Figure 16-14 shows the Pat's Point's design next to my own effort, the "Keystar" (you can find the cutting prescription for Keystar in Chapter 19.2.5). Despite the fact that they are two very different designs – reflector versus brilliant pavilion, different girdle outline, etc. – the inspiration is obvious. A careful examination of the two cutting prescriptions shows similarities in the method for establishing the girdle outline as well, although this "OMNI" approach is common to all barion-type designs (see page 246 and Chapter 17.4).

Modifying an existing gem cut offers a gentle introduction to the process of gemstone design. Whether you simply add a few accent facets, mix and match various pavilions and crowns, experiment with symmetry and stretching, or use individual aspects of an existing design as a springboard for your own creativity, you will find yourself asking the all-important "what if" question. What if I did this? What if I tried that? Asking those questions means that you are on your way.

16.3 Gemstone Design – Tools and Techniques

To shamelessly misquote Dickens, it is the best of times for the beginning gemstone designer. In the past, the lack of suitable tools made gem design a hit-or-miss proposition. In other words, it was the worst of times. Given the cost of rough and the necessary investment in

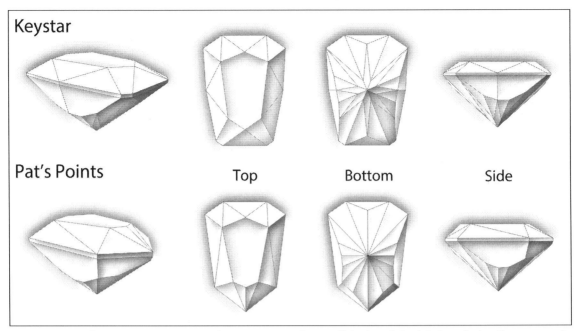

Keystar

Pat's Points   Top   Bottom   Side

Figure 16-14 The Keystar cut (top row) drew inspiration from Jeff Graham's Pat's Points design (bottom row).

time, "designing at the machine" was not for the faint of heart (see page 309 of Volume 1). Although experience and pre-planning on paper certainly helped, the advent of inexpensive calculators and computers has ushered in a golden age for beginning gemstone designers.

This section brings together some of the material presented elsewhere in this book – information about cutting techniques and design tools – to show you how real-world gem design works. It is followed by a more-or-less random compendium of guidelines for gem design gleaned from my own experience and from textbooks and online discussions of the topic.

16.3.1 Outlining Your Design

Inspiration has struck. You know what you want to do. "What if…?" seems to be just about the most important question in the world…

What next? Or more specifically, What first?

Before you head off into the wilderness of GemCAD, take a moment to consider strategy. Although others may disagree, I believe that as a beginner, you should design your gemstone just like you would cut it. And with a few gems under your belt, you should recognize that a good design is built on the foundation of the girdle outline, and that the pavilion should be cut before the crown.

So…to begin at the beginning, you need to transfer your creative inspiration into a girdle outline. How do you do that?

Establishing an accurate gem outline is a broad and interesting topic – broad enough to merit its own chapter, in fact. The chapter after this one explains the various techniques for transferring your ideas from brain to paper to stone. These methods may have obscure names – ECED, CAM, OMNI, CLAM – but they are firmly grounded in the design principles laid out here and in the mathematics from Chapter 10.

The next chapter also gives real-world, worked-through examples of establishing the girdle outline based on some of the designs from Chapter 19. To generate the girdle outline for your own creative enterprise, you need to decide which of these techniques is most suitable.

Here's a foretaste of what's to come with a bonus question at the end...

If your design is a round or other highly symmetric shape, you can almost certainly start with the appropriate number of facets cut at the same angle to a temporary (or final) center point. Then place the girdle facets to establish the outline (see Figure 16-15).

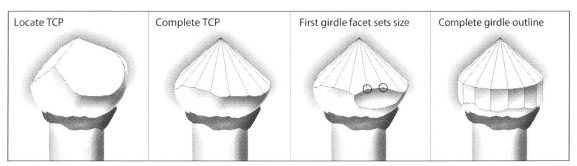

Figure 16-15 To generate the outline for a round gem, use the appropriate number of facets cut to a temporary center point (TCP). Three facets distributed around the gem locate the TCP (left panel – see also page 158 of Volume 1). When you are satisfied, cut the remainder of the tier to this reference point (second panel). The first girdle facet, cut at the same index as one of the angled facets, establishes the overall gem size (third panel). Completing the girdle facets based on the existing meet points (circled) generates the desired gem outline (right panel).

More complicated outlines require more complicated approaches – all those CAMS and CLAMS. Chapter 17 provides some hints on selecting the appropriate technique. Using a sketch, measurements, and GemCAD (or other program), you should be able to find your way. Working through the examples in the text will be excellent practice.

Bonus question: The method illustrated in Figure 16-15 is the simplest instance of one of the big three outlining techniques: CAM, OMNI, CLAM. Which one (or two?) is it?

16.3.2 Building on the Girdle

With the solid foundation of the girdle in place, you are ready to build your gemstone. I typically begin with the pavilion, just as in the cutting process. The reasons for the pavilion-first cutting order have a lot to do with running out of gem rough and other real-world considerations (see "The Great Debate" on page 304 of Volume 1). Obviously, such concerns don't apply at the design stage on the computer. Nevertheless, I prefer and recommend starting with the pavilion design for one very good reason: it can be difficult to get the pavilion to work out.

What do I mean by "work out"?

A lot of things have to come together in the pavilion. Not only must the facets produce a pleasing reflection pattern, but also the cutting angles have to work together to prevent windowing on the first or second bounce (see Chapter 10.4). The facets should also build upon one another, creating clear meet points to simplify the cutting process. Finally and most importantly, the pavilion carries the lion's share of the responsibility for producing a visually interesting and appealing gem. It ain't easy being a pavilion.

Cutting Evolution, a Two-Page History of Diamond Design

It is clear that humans have recognized the magic of gemstones, and of diamonds in particular, for over two thousand years. Although our friend, Pliny the Elder, mentioned diamonds, or adamas, in his masterwork *Natural History* at the end of the first century, analysis of Sanskrit texts shows that diamond trading was active in India some five hundred years earlier. See the Index entries for more on Pliny's contribution to faceting.

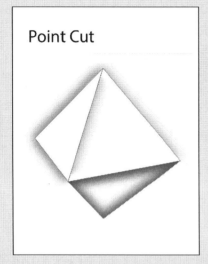

Point Cut

Craftsmen of these early times did not have the tools or understanding to work this hardest of all substances, and thus diamonds were appreciated in their natural crystal form, usually octahedral. At the beginning of the Middle Ages, the realization that only a diamond could cut a diamond led to the development of machinery for modifying this shape. However, early gem polishers merely sought to improve the visual appearance of diamond crystals, smoothing the faces and removing flaws to achieve the desired octahedral form. The result was the first of all diamond gem designs, the **Point Cut**.

Figure 16-16 The Point Cut mimics the natural octahedral shape of diamond crystals.

By the middle of the 15th century, European gem cutters had begun sawing off a portion of the octahedron, creating the **Table Cut**. With a recognizable pavilion, girdle, crown, and table, this design was the precursor of all modern gemstones. Nevertheless, the proportions and hence the optical performance of these early faceted gemstones were very poor: much of the light return was due to the surface luster of the diamond (Chapter 12.7.2) and not as a result of total internal reflection.

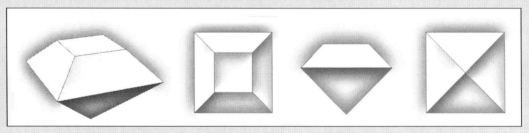

Figure 16-17 The Table Cut is a simple modification of the native diamond crystal.

The mid 15th to 16th century saw a couple of major innovations in gemstone design. First, a Flemish diamond cutter named Lodewyk van Berquem recognized the importance of symmetry to gemstone performance. The pear-like **Pendeloque** and elongated **Briolette** designs were the result. Toward the end of this period, the **Rose** or **Rosette Cut** appeared in Europe, perhaps influenced by earlier rose-type diamonds from India. This design couples a symmetric crown consisting of triangular facets to a flat back. With the eye of a modern gem designer, it is tempting to look at the rose cut with scorn, but it represented a major improvement in optical performance over the table cut, and the rose dominated the European diamond cutting industry until the late 1800's.

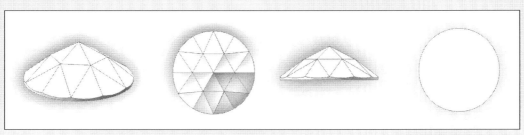

Figure 16-18 The Rose Cut has a faceted crown and a flat back.

In the meantime, jewelry makers developed techniques to apply metal to the back of glass gemstones in the early 1700's. This approach is reminiscent of modern-day mystic topaz (see "Foiled Again" on page 152), and it improved light return significantly, producing the showy glitter that was central to the fashion of the day.

The first examples of what we would call brilliant cut diamonds began to appear in the mid-1600's. Early versions had a simple crown with seventeen facets. Known as **Double-Cut Brilliants** or **Mazarins** after Giulio Raimondo Mazzarino, the prime minister of France during the reign of Louis XIV, these early brilliants improved markedly the light return of cut diamonds. In the late 17th century, a Venetian gem cutter named Vincenzo Peruzzi increased the number of crown facets to 33, producing the **Triple-Cut Brilliant** or **Peruzzi** design. Although it has somewhat sharper corners, following the octahedral shape of the diamond crystal, the Peruzzi design is a close cousin of what is now known as the **Old Mine Cut**.

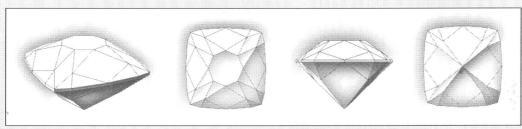

Figure 16-19 The Old Mine Cut is very similar to the ground-breaking Peruzzi or Triple-Cut Brilliant design of the late 17th century.

The development of bruting, that is, the rounding of one diamond with another, led to the **Old European Cut** in the 1800's. This design, with its rounded shape, shallower pavilion, and symmetric facet layout, is the direct precursor of the **Standard Round Brilliant**, which was pioneered in the early twentieth century by Marcel Tolkowsky and

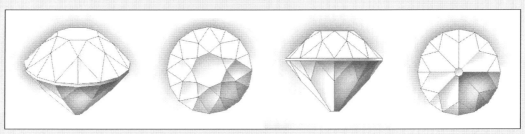

Figure 16-20 The Old European Cut, developed in the 19th century, paved the way for the modern standard round brilliant. Note the culet facet parallel to the table. This was a common feature of early diamond designs.

others (see below for more on Tolkowsky and page 263 of Volume 1 for a modern take on the Old European Cut). Since Tolkowsky's time, the number and variety of diamond cuts has grown enormously.

Well, so much for history. Let's get back to gem design (besides, I have exceeded my two-page allotment). Interested in learning more about the history of gemstone cuts? There are a number of excellent reference books available – see Chapter 9.

Crowns, on the other hand, are relatively straightforward and forgiving. You can explore a wide range of angles and pairings without unduly damaging the optical performance of the gemstone.

It therefore makes sense to make sure that you have the hard part, the pavilion, under control before expending effort on the remainder of the gem. The most beautifully designed crown in the world will be of no use if it cannot be mated to a suitable, high-performance pavilion.

How do you actually go about designing either the pavilion or the crown? That is the 64,000-dollar question, and as promised on the first page of this chapter, I cannot explain it to you. There are, however, general principles which apply to the majority of gemstone designs.

For example, I prefer meet point designs, since they allow accurate cutting and a clear sequencing of facets, (see Chapter 8.7 for an explanation of the meet point faceting technique). Since the process of establishing the gem outline usually creates meet points at the girdle, I tend to design from the outside-in, that is, I place additional facets at the girdle meets and work my way inward to the culet. The obvious exception to this practice is when the initial, girdle-establishing center point is not temporary. This happens in simple, reflector-type designs or when cutting from the inside out to save gem rough (see page 282).

Of course, the number, placement, and size of these subsequent facets depend on the desired effect – in other words, on your personal artistic vision. Section 16.5 below contains a compendium of tips and techniques that usually lead to aesthetically pleasing results. Nevertheless, there are no cut and dried rules in this game, and there is simply no substitute for experience and just trying a whole lot of alternative approaches. Luckily, computer tools such as GemCAD allow you to experiment rapidly and risk free. In fact, a quick survey of my GemCAD design folders shows 5-10 intermediate "explorations" saved as separate files for each ultimate design.

16.4 Design Tools

The first gem designers had very limited design tools: their eyes and the actual gem rough. Perhaps some enterprising cutters worked things out in advance with paper and quill (the kind used with ink), but the relative crudeness of contemporary cutting tools, coupled with the high cost of precious stones and a lack of understanding of the interaction of light with matter, meant that most early gem designs were simple and close to the native crystal form. This was particularly true for diamonds (see "Cutting Evolution, a Two-Page History of Diamond Design" on page 240).

In fact, it was not until the advent of diamond saws and other high quality jewelry tools in the early twentieth century that the modern standard round brilliant appeared. Marcel Tolkowsky, a Belgian diamond cutter, is credited with this design breakthrough. Perhaps more importantly, Tolkowsky placed the process of gemstone design on a firm physical and mathematical footing, and his tables of optimal pavilion and crown angles for diamonds became the industry standard for decades. Incidentally, Tolkowsky's original 1919 monograph on diamond design is available electronically on the web (see "Surf Hunting" on page 190). It makes very interesting reading.

More recent mathematical models have improved upon Tolkowsky's pioneering effort by including more than two internal reflections in the optimization process, for example. The "classic" faceting textbooks of the late twentieth century include tables and diagrams of ideal angles based on these calculations. Chapter 9.1 can help you track down these references.

The information age has, in my opinion, blown all of this history out of the water. While it is difficult to compete with decades of experience, craftsmanship, and trade lore, the arrival of inexpensive calculators and especially computers has made high quality gem design accessible to the casual hobbyist. Chapter 15 has a great deal more to say about this revolution. Given a little practice, you too can gain Tolkowsky-like insight into how gems work, without all that mucking about with cosines and graph paper. Sections 16.7 and 16.8 below provide a couple of examples.

Believe the Software

Computers are your friend. They really are.

They can save you huge amounts of time. They can save you huge amounts of rough. You should believe what they tell you about your gem design. Faceters tend to be a skeptical, curmudgeonly lot, but we have to get over it.

For example, GemRay can help predict the visual appearance of a gem long before stone meets lap. Playing around with optimization tools like BOG can lead to insights into general design principles, as well as help in the selection of specific design elements and angles. Photorealistic rendering software, such as Blender and LuxRender, can even provide you with a near-perfect impression of your gem's ultimate appearance. See Chapter 15 for more information on these programs.

These tools confirm well-understood design guidelines and lore, such as the correlation of higher crown angles with better tilt performance and dispersion. They can also help settle long standing arguments about gem design, such as the value of odd-numbered symmetry (see Section 16.7 below), or the actual best cutting angles for a particular design and gem material (see "A Critical Look at Culets" on page 64).

What tools do you need? I own and recommend GemCAD. Not only is this program inexpensive and easy to use, but also its author, Robert Strickland, is a dedicated amateur gem cutter and all-round good guy. For the price of a single decent piece of tourmaline rough, you can have some pretty hefty design horsepower at the click of a mouse. I also use some free angle optimization software called BOG, written by another amateur gem cutter who at least tries to be an all-round good guy. Chapter 15.3 contains further information on GemCAD and BOG, and Chapter 18 uses these tools in a real-world case study of gemstone design.

Don't Believe the Software

Don't trust your computer. Who are you going to believe? A pile of silicon and wire or your own hard-won experience?

If you get the sense that this chapter is sending mixed messages on the value of computers to gem design, then you are exactly right. The earlier comments about the savings in time and gem rough are 100% valid, but you should not take your computer output too seriously.

Here are a couple of reasons why. First, objective measures of gemstone performance, such as the ray traces and ISO brightness returned by GemRay, can be a useful guideline, but they can also deceive. For example, dark areas on the ray trace may not end up dark in the final gemstone. Because of the way that GemRay traces the light paths within the stone, the dark areas may actually be "trapped rays," not light leakage. Trapped rays occur when more than a specified number of total internal reflections take place within the gem (see also Chapter 15.6). Such behaviour can lead to longer light paths and hence better colour saturation and an improved, not degraded, appearance. Manually checking darker areas using the GemCAD ray trace tools can help, as can your hard-won experience, darn it!

The second reason that you shouldn't take your computer too seriously is the fact that it is a computer, not a human being. There is nothing magical about high brightness values, for example. Check the ISO reflectance returned by GemRay for your favourite design. I bet that you will not be overwhelmed. To quote the great gem designer Fred van Sant: "I personally do not consider brightness important in itself – if I want to look at a lot of white light I can shine a flashlight into my eyes…" The same applies to choices of facet layout and cutting angles for visual impact. As emphasized in Chapter 18.5.4, I will always select an aesthetically appealing reflection pattern over a less attractive one with objectively better performance. Remember that gemstone design is an art that can be helped by science – just don't let the science get in the way. To quote another great gemstone designer, Jeff Graham, "Programs and modern gemstone designing tools, while they are powerful and beyond a doubt very beneficial, they have no art and soul."

I will leave the last word to Frank Gehry, the brilliant architect who has brought us such wonders as the Guggenheim in Bilbao, Dancing House in Prague, and the Disney Theater in Los Angeles. He has also been a driving force in innovative software for architectural design. If any artist were a computer nut, it would be Frank Gehry. To quote a line from *Gehry Talks: Architecture and Process*, "the computer is a tool, not a partner, an instrument for catching the curve, not for inventing it…"

16.4.1 Other Design Tools

GemCAD and an optimization program like BOG can form the core of your design arsenal, but as you experiment and learn, you will realize that a number of other tools can simplify, speed up, and generally enable the design process.

For example, a drawing program like Illustrator or Photoshop allows you to sketch with straight lines and almost infinite "Undos," an essential feature which is absent or awkward with more traditional pen and paper. Even if you are a "back of the envelope" doodler when it comes to ideas, a scanner, coupled with drawing software, lets you capture and measure your creative efforts, converting them into more usable units, such as facet angles and indices (see Chapter 17). Finally, drawing programs allow you to create additional design tools, such as the CAM protractor and OMNI overlay described in the next chapter. Turn to Chapter 15.7 for more software ideas.

Design tools exist beyond the virtual world of computer programs and onscreen menus. In addition to the pen, paper, scanner, and protractors mentioned in the previous paragraph, you will likely find yourself using a camera, ruler, and calculator. Oh. And another handy little tool known as your brain. The indirect message here is that all of these tools can assist the design process, but they are not a substitute for the good old inspiration and perspiration mentioned at the beginning of this chapter. See "Don't Believe the Software" opposite for more wisdom on bringing your brain to the faceting process.

A Word from the Master...

"To compute or not to compute. That is the Question. Whether 'tis better to suffer the wrong angles and other errors of outdated or outrageous designs, or to take up a computer against them – to correct and improve – to achieve a more perfect design – 'Tis a goal much to be desired..."

- Fred van Sant, Master Gemstone Designer

16.5 Design Guidelines – Colour and Sparkle

This chapter began by stating that I am not going to teach you how to design gemstones. The following two sections of this chapter are exactly where I am not going to do so.

(Pause for dramatic effect)*

More specifically, the following paragraphs and Section 16.6 present a number of guidelines and tips for gemstone design. What they don't do is provide a prescription for the design process itself. As a profoundly individual expression of your creative impulses, you are going to have to work that one out for yourself. My recommendation? Scan through the following items, download GemCAD, and have at it. The case study in Chapter 18 can also provide some insight.

---

* and to acknowledge the brilliance of Joseph Heller

16.5.1 Designing for Colour and Sparkle

Depending on the saturation of the gem material, the first thing that a person will notice is either the colour or the reflection pattern of your faceted gemstone. There are a number of ways to enhance these properties to achieve the effect that you desire. For example, a profusion of small facets tends to gives more "action" or sparkle. Larger facets emphasize colour. The following paragraphs give additional guidelines on punching up (or down) the colour and sparkle of your gem design.

16.5.2 Colour

Chapter 12.3.4 explains that longer light-paths through a gem lead to deeper colour. To enhance the colour of paler materials you could deepen the design. For example, conventional wisdom holds that the Barion cut, with its pronounced belly-like pavilion, will intensify colour (but see "The Brilliant Barion" below). Note that you should not deepen a gem design simply by applying tangent ratio scaling, since this can radically alter the optical performance. (Chapter 10.5.2 rants a great deal on this issue). Finally and most effectively, you can deepen colour by cutting a particular design only in larger sizes for paler rough. This is not strictly a design decision *per se*, but it gets the job done

The converse is of course also true. I'm betting that you have at least one piece of garnet in your rough collection that is a beautiful wine-red when held up to the light, but a useless coal black when set down on a white piece of paper – and we all know that the white-paper test provides a reasonable prediction of the final colour of a gemstone (see "When is Too Much Too Much?" on page 90). You can reduce the colour saturation of a gem by taking strategies exactly opposite to those of the previous paragraph: try to make the design shallower, and under no circumstances cut a large gem from such material.

In the instance of very deep colour saturation, you can produce a design which "fails" as a gemstone, in the sense that the pavilion allows light to leak through. Tangent ratio scaling can help here. You can even create a gem with two tables – one on the front and one on the back (Figure 16-22). Such tablet-type designs act more like windows than gemstones and are used for intensely coloured gems in pendants, earrings, etc. For obvious reasons, these strategies will not work for settings such as rings, which do not allow proper illumination from the rear.

The Brilliant Barion

Earlier in this chapter, I encouraged you to begin your personal gem design journey by trying to mix and match pavilions and crowns, all driven by the spirit of the question "What if...?"

Here's an interesting and important What if: What if you combined the sparkle of a brilliant pavilion with a non-round crown, such as that of an emerald or step cut?

The much renowned and much loved Barion design answers exactly this question. Originally created in October 1970 by South African diamond cutter Basil Watermeyer, the Barion has spread far beyond the diamond world, and has become an essential element in many gem designs. This is because the process of generating a Barion pavilion allows the mating of a brilliant culet with just about any overall gem outline (Figure 16-21).

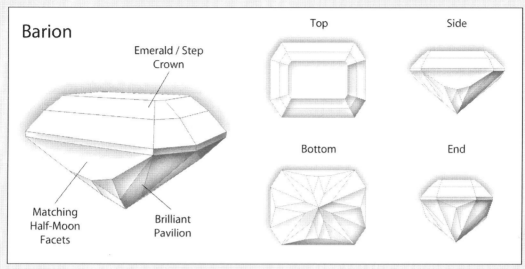

Figure 16-21 A Barion emerald. The Barion design concept allows the fusion of a brilliant pavilion with a non-round gem outline. The large half-moon facets do the lion's share of the work in achieving this minor geometrical miracle. Such large, steep facets are a classic feature of the Barion cut. See also Chapter 17.4.

Interestingly, the design wasn't intended to do anything of the sort. Watermeyer modestly admits that the discovery of the Barion was a bit of a lucky accident as he was trying to introduce some scintillation into the emerald cut. He recognized the value of the concept in bringing sparkle to non-round gems, thus allowing greater yield without impacting brilliance. Nevertheless, the relatively conservative diamond community of the time was slow to recognize the importance of the Barion.

The current coloured gem community displays no such reticence, and you will encounter the Barion concept everywhere you look among published gemstone designs. Sooner rather than later, you will be doing something very much like what Watermeyer did with your own creative efforts. Chapter 17.4 explains how to get started.

One final word on the Barion – at least until you get to the real-world design example in Chapter 17.4 . You will almost certainly hear that Barions are a good choice for relatively pale gem rough, since the resulting stones are deeper and hence provide greater saturation. In fact, you may even be told that the whole Barion concept exists to deepen both the geometry and colour of gemstones. Be skeptical. Be very skeptical. Chapter 10.5.2 contains a poorly restrained rant about the physical depth of gemstones, path lengths, and the corresponding increase in optical performance. Barions are no different. While they are somewhat deeper than traditional designs, the real purpose of the Barion is to bring the sparkle of a brilliant pavilion to a non-round gem.

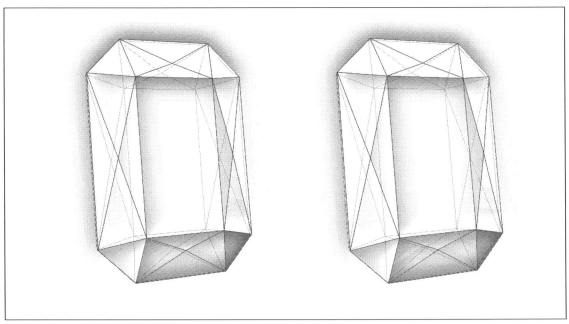

Figure 16-22 A tablet-type design can highlight the colour of saturated gem material. Yes, this is another one of those annoying 3D drawings. See page 74 for instructions on viewing the image, and Chapter 19.2.3 for a real-world design.

16.5.3 Sparkle

Sparkle is the property of a gemstone which causes it to scintillate as though it is literally throwing off sparks. Unlike colour, the sparkle of a gem is a fundamentally dynamic quality that can only be experienced in person, with the stone and the viewer moving through a rich lighting environment. Some people refer to this property as "brilliance," "action," or "scintillation." However you describe it, and whatever you call it, you know sparkle when you see it. And if you are still reading at this stage in this book, I am certain that you know exactly what I am talking about.

Also unlike colour, which has a very physical origin in the chemistry and structure of matter (see Chapter 12.3), sparkle is hard to describe and is perhaps impossible to quantify. Nevertheless, the BOG program attempts to do so (see Section 16.7). Despite its fleeting quality, there are a number of design strategies for improving the sparkle of your gemstones. The following paragraphs present some tips and ideas, in no particular order.

I find symmetric reflection patterns, such as those produced by an SRB, to be very pleasing. As the gem or the viewer moves, the sunburst pattern in the base of the stone scintillates as individual facets light up, but the overall design aesthetic remains. Brilliant-type pavilions produce this effect, even in non-round gem designs and even when combined with non SRB-type crowns (Figure 16-23). This ability is the beating aesthetic heart of many Barion-type designs (see page 246).

Figure 16-23 A brilliant-type pavilion produces centrally-symmetric sparkle, even when combined with a checkerboard crown. This is the Topo design, available online at www.bog-home.com, here cut in blue topaz.

Somewhat paradoxically to the above, I also really like random reflection patterns, with no clear symmetry or center. Figure 16-24 shows an example of a very simple, apparently symmetric gem design producing a wildly random and interesting reflection pattern. Although both this image and Figure 16-23 are static, trust me: the dynamic reflection patterns, though both pleasing, could never be mistaken for one another.

How do you achieve an exciting and aesthetically pleasing random reflection pattern? Great question, and the answer isn't as simple as it is in the case of the centrally-symmetric brilliant. I have found that pavilions with radial symmetry are effective at randomizing reflection patterns (see Chapter 10.7 for a complete explanation of radial symmetry). Specifically, a gem with a "twisted" pavilion, such as Sun Twist, Twist5, or Tris de Garnet (see Section 16.2.2 and Figure 16-24), can throw a wonderfully random wrench into the gears of an otherwise symmetric design. There are no hard and fast rules for optimizing this effect, however, and the best strategy is to experiment within your design software of choice.

Incidentally, it is one of the many wonders of our hobby that a seemingly simple gem cut, or a seemingly trivial modification to an existing design, can produce entrancingly unique, complex, and dynamic reflection patterns. Ray tracing is difficult enough to do on a computer and practically impossible in your head. The lesson here? Don't judge a design by the cutting diagram – you will almost certainly be surprised, and with a little attention to your own designs, you will be amazed.

Figure 16-24 Even a simple gem cut can produce dynamically random reflection patterns. This design, called Tris de Garnet, has only 9 pavilion and 9 crown facets. Chapter 19.1.4 contains the cutting prescription, and Chapter 15.5 explains how to execute a 3D rendering like this.

Mixed Cuts

"The Brilliant Barion" on page 246 asks what would happen if you combine the sparkle of a brilliant pavilion with the flexible shape of a step cut crown. Let's turn that question on its head and do the exact opposite:

What if you combined the high weight retention of a step cut pavilion with the visual sparkle of a brilliant crown?

The answer here is the Mixed Cut, a design approach that has been around for about half a century. Although the original Mixed Cuts were indeed brilliant crowns set atop emerald-type pavilions, the term has evolved somewhat to include such designs as the Princess Cut (see Figure 18-2), as well as other combinations of cutting style. In fact, some authorities consider the Barion, which started as the exact opposite, as a legitimate class of Mixed Cut.

16.5.4 Size and Distribution of Sparkle

Whether symmetric or random, the reflection pattern will be more pleasing when there is an even distribution of sparkle action across the stone. For example, many square designs suffer from a mix of large flashes at the center of the gem and tiny flashes in the corners. Teardrop and pear cuts are also notorious for gathering busy, tiny, flashes in the narrow part of the stone (Figure 16-25). The great gem designer Fred van Sant warned us all about such corners: they can act as a light funnel, either concentrating visual impact and pinfire (see page 252) or sucking the life out of your gem.

Note that in practical design terms, a uniform distribution of facet sizes does not necessarily yield a uniform distribution of reflection! Combining and/or splitting pavilion facets may help (see Figure 16-1), but the effect can be unpredictable. Some designers recommend reducing the number of facets in the corners, but there is no guarantee that this will improve the situation. As always, check your work in your favourite gem-rendering program (Chapter 15) before putting stone to lap.

An exception to the rule of uniform reflection pattern is the observation that a variety of flash sizes can produce a pleasing effect, provided of course that the different sizes are well mixed. This variety ensures that the body colour of the gem comes through in the larger flashes, while the smaller ones provide visual interest, scintillation, and in the case of dispersive materials, pinfire (see next section). Again, there is no prescription for producing this effect. Experience and testing on the computer are the way to go.

Figure 16-25 An uneven distribution of sparkle produces a less appealing gem. The reflection pattern is tiny and busy at the top of this Gem-Ray image, contrasting sharply with the larger flashes from the center of the stone. The cut gem (inset) shows the same problem.

Deliberately Bad Design – The Deck Prism

I love maritime museums, and one of the best of them is lurking in Pennsylvania on the south shore of Lake Erie, about halfway between Buffalo, New York and Cleveland, Ohio (the fact that three major states share this 200 mile (300 km) stretch of shoreline is a measure of the importance of waterways to early North America). The Erie Maritime Museum offers its visitors a unique perspective on early 19th century shipbuilding and the role of wooden sailing vessels in the War of 1812..

It also offers a unique perspective on bad gemstone design.

Let me explain. Before the advent of iron ships and electricity, life could be pretty dark below decks. Oil lamps were an expensive and potentially flammable option, but many vessels opted for a more elegant approach: the deck prism. A deck prism is essentially a glass gemstone with a very deep pavilion and no crown (Figure 16-26). By now, you should recognize immediately that this configuration will never work well as a gem:

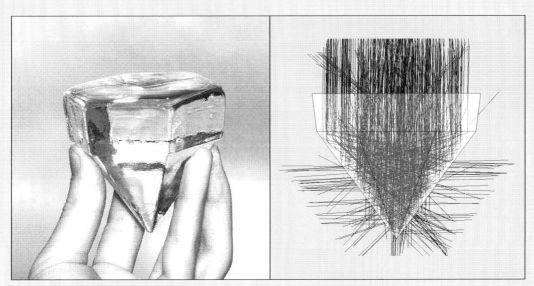

Figure 16-26 A deck prism combines a deep reflector pavilion with a table facet. A glass reproduction of a 19th century deck prism (left) and the resulting ray paths in GemCAD (right).

light entering the "table" will experience one internal reflection on a steep facet, but the depth of the pavilion will guarantee that no second reflection occurs (see also Chapter 10.4). Light will leak out the side.

Although it may be awful as a gemstone design, the deck prism is a great way of getting light below decks, and you can see them in action in Erie, Pennsylvania. The pride of the maritime museum is the reconstructed brig U. S. Niagara, which played a pivotal role in the Battle of Lake Erie. The Niagara is one of only two surviving ships which served in the War of 1812 (the other is the USS Constitution, which remains an active Navy vessel).

If you get the opportunity to visit, take it. While walking topside, you will see several hexagons of glass set flush into the deck. These are the "tables" of the prisms. Down below, you can experience the positive side of bad gemstone design (Figure 16-27).

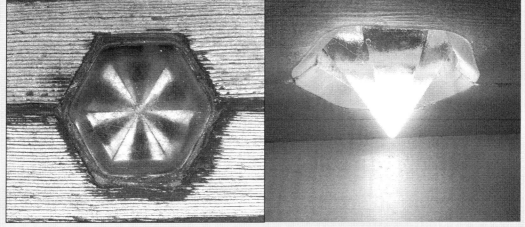

Figure 16-27 A topsides view of a deck prism installed in the U. S. Brig Niagara (left). Leakage out of the "pavilion" illuminates the lower deck (right).

16.5.5 Trading Colour against Sparkle

All this talk of colour and sparkle raises the obvious question: "Can't I get both?"

The short answer is no, not usually. The design considerations that tend to emphasize colour often reduce the impact of sparkle. The converse is also true, and most pieces of gem rough will not allow a completely free choice (also see page 91).

The somewhat longer answer is that you probably don't want it all, at least not in every circumstance. Some gem materials, such as pale aquamarine, simply won't produce intense colour, and for such stones, it is more productive to create a design which enhances sparkle. Most emerald falls in the opposite category. Although its body colour is a lovely, intense green, the internal flaws of natural emerald will often foil any attempt at achieving a dynamic, sparkling effect, not that such scintillation is a good idea in the first place – see below. Intense colour saturation presents a similar problem: complex and interesting scintillation patterns arise due to the interaction between the facets of the crown and pavilion. If light absorption dims the effect, this interaction will no longer be so striking. Also, dynamic sparkle relying on multiple reflections will be lost.

Facet size can be an important factor in the tradeoff between colour and sparkle. Larger facets make the gem behave like a coloured filter: light enters the stone, bounces a couple of times, and then exits through the crown toward the viewer. All along this path, the electrons in the crystal lattice are doing their work, subtracting the appropriate wavelengths of light to produce the lovely, rich colour of the gem (see Chapter 12.3). The large facets ensure that the visual impact of this filtering process is not diluted by the presence of multiple, small, ever-changing flashes.

Of course, at the microphysical level, the same filtering process takes place in a gemstone with smaller facets. Given the same lighting conditions, gem material, and path-length, the colour emerging from such a stone would be identical to that from its larger-faceted cousin. The difference is one of perception. Under typical viewing circumstances, tiny facets tend to produce a profusion of tiny points of light, but our eyes are not very good at judging the colour of such points. Have you ever noticed that the stars in the night sky have different colours? I bet not, but trust me, they do. Our eyes and brains are just not well engineered to appreciate the colour of points of light, and our gem designs should reflect this fact. Remember: colour and sparkle are literally in the eye of the beholder.

There is one exception to this size versus colour rule: pinfire. Pinfire refers to the tiny flashes of coloured light brought about by the combination of dispersion in a gem and splitting of colour by facet junctions (see Chapter 12.6). Pinfire is what makes a diamond a diamond, and smaller facets can help enhance the effect (Figure 16-28). Note that this does not contradict the statements in the previous paragraphs. Smaller facets tend to overwhelm the effect of the intrinsic body colour of a gem, but they can be useful in creating colour by splitting already dispersed light into pinfire.

One other aspect of this tradeoff between colour and sparkle deserves mention: gem size. Section 16.5.2 notes that larger gems lead to longer light paths and hence more intense colour. Smaller gems produce the opposite effect. It should be obvious to you by now that gem size also affects the relative prominence of colour and sparkle. The same gem design cut in a smaller piece of rough will produce proportionately smaller flashes and hence alter the balance away from colour and toward scintillation.

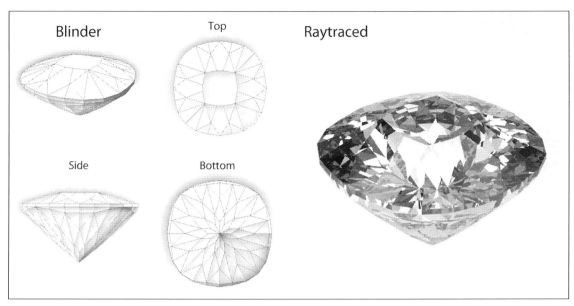

Figure 16-28 The Blinder design from Chapter 19.3.6 was an exercise in enhancing pinfire. A combination of many small facets with a highly dispersive gem material produces multiple tiny flashes of colour. Gem design (left) and 3D computer rendering in rutile (right). The extreme optical properties of this material produce sparkle and pinfire, even when viewed at an oblique angle.

16.5.6 Perfect Balance

All this balancing prompts an obvious follow-on to the question at the beginning of the previous section: Larger facets tend to emphasize colour, while smaller ones lead to sparkle. Won't middle-sized ones give me both?

Again, sadly, the answer is no, not usually. Achieving the delicate balance between colour and scintillation is difficult. The internal saturation of gem material can be difficult to judge beforehand, and the exact visual impact of scintillation is not readily quantifiable. And, as the previous paragraphs emphasize, the two effects interact with each other: internal colour modifies the sparkle, while scintillation can influence colour perception.

Put another way, each sample of rough will demand a slightly different balance in the gem design to achieve perfect colour and sparkle. Designing for colour or designing for sparkle is relatively straightforward. Trying to get both – hitting the sweet spot between the two – is possible, however. You know the gemstones that work. They are the magic ones that you will not sell for any price. I would say that I get it right or close to right about a third of the time. Experience in gem design and rough selection can help, but you are very likely to be surprised – and sometimes disappointed – when you pop the stone off the dop.

16.6 Miscellaneous Design Tips

This section contains random hints for improving your gemstone designs.

- This tip may be an obvious one, but in the heat of design passion, it can be easy to neglect. You can use *both* facet angles *and* facet indices to make your meet points and achieve the desired effect. I don't know how many times I have tried to finish up the last details of a design, but have found that a certain facet tier simply won't "click" for any input angle. Try a different index, Einstein.

• A critical review of my gem designs would reveal a predilection for multiple facets meeting at the girdle (Figure 16-29). There are two reasons for this, one aesthetic and one practical. Although I have no way of proving it, my impression is that such "girdle fans" produce lots of interesting and appealing sparkle. On the practical side, I frequently design (and cut) inward from the foundation of the girdle (see Section 16.3.2), and it is quite straightforward to build an effective design from such fans.

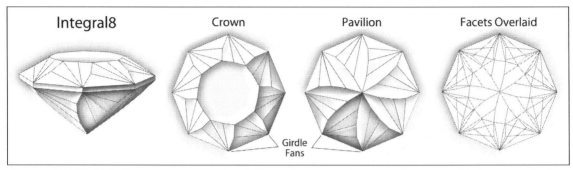

Figure 16-29 Multiple facets meeting at the girdle produce appealing scintillation. In this instance, the fans have radial symmetry (Chapter 10.7) and are stacked in opposite directions (rightmost drawing), producing even more action. This is the Integral8 gem design, available online at www.boghome.com. Figure 16-30 and the cover of this book show a computer ray trace of Integral8 as it performs in sapphire.

• Use your crown and pavilion as a team to multiply facets and increase the amount and quality of sparkle. Gemstones are often viewed straight on, with the eye more or less aligned with the center of the table and the culet. Crown and pavilion facets which directly overlap will line up in this configuration, killing a lot of the potential "action" in the stone. The classic emerald cut is perhaps the worst transgressor in this regard, although to be fair, emerald cuts are not intended to produce sparkle (see Figure 16-31 and Section 16.5 above). Some designs, on the other hand, make an explicit effort to split the light in different directions with the crown and the pavilion. The classic princess cut, bar rounds, opposed, bars, etc., come to mind. This "cross-splitting" produces interesting and complex reflection patterns with relatively few facets. The Slice cut is a direct exercise in this type of design (Figure 16-31 and Chapter 19.3.3). Briar Rose, the case study in Chapter 18, is another example.

• You can get a quick and dirty impression of how your pavilion will work by adding a simple step cut crown in GemCAD. The process takes only a moment or two, and allows you to gauge the visual impact of your pavilion facets without too much additional distraction. I just place two tiers of step facets at 35° and 25° at the same index wheel settings as the girdle. A final table facet approximately 50% of the width of the gem completes the design and lets you ray trace, optimize, and so forth. Figure 18-23 shows how I used this technique to do a sanity check on the pavilion of Briar Rose.

Figure 16-30 Computer generated image of the Integral8 design in sapphire. Yes, this is the top-down view of the rendering on the cover of this book.

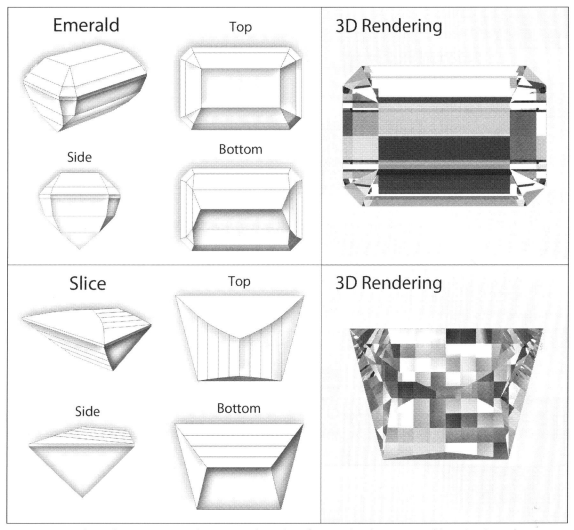

Figure 16-31 Aligned versus opposed crown and pavilion facets. The classic emerald cut (top) produces overlapping crown and pavilion reflections, minimizing sparkle while enhancing the perception of colour. The aptly named Slice design (bottom), deliberately cuts up the incoming light in perpendicular directions using the crown and pavilion. The cutting prescription for Slice appears in Chapter 19.3.3. See also Figure 6-28.

•You can expand your creative universe in conventional as well as unconventional ways. Splitting facets is a common approach (see page 227). Leaving some facets unpolished is less often seen. Doing so can have a dramatic effect, but of course, such a strategy is more suited to gem cuts which emphasize colour over sparkle. You can even try adding new, unpolished facets to an existing design to produce an image or to convey a particular message. Figure 12-27 shows an example of this.

•Here's one that is personal, and perhaps a bit odd. I like triangular facets. They produce an aesthetically pleasing layout and reflection pattern. I don't fancy quadrilaterals, or four-sided facets. On the cutting diagram, they just don't look right, somehow – almost as though the creator couldn't tie up a "tight" design. Kite-shaped facets, that is, long and thin quadrilaterals, are Ok, however. In general, consistent facet shapes (in terms of their length-to-width ratio) look better than a mixture of broad and narrow ones. Don't ask me why. And yes, the sparkle of a well-designed gemstone completely overwhelms all such considerations (Figure 16-32).

•You should always keep in mind exactly how much information you need to define a facet. This will help you understand whether a certain circumstance demands a meet point, for example. Geometry buffs know the answer: you need three bits of information to define a plane, and hence a program like GemCAD needs three numbers to lock down a facet. Table 16-1 shows the most common combinations. Note that, given sufficient information, GemCAD will happily generate a cutting angle and index. However, you might have to adjust things somewhat. For example, clicking on three points in the cutting diagram will produce an angle and an index wheel setting, but the latter might not be a whole number. See the GemCAD manual for more information.

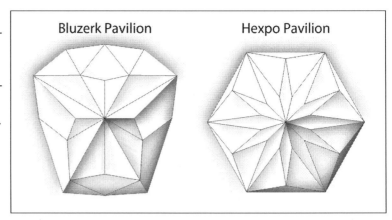

Figure 16-32 In my eyes, the design on the left is awful, while the one on the right is quite pleasing. This is not just a question of symmetry. Triangles and kite-shaped facets look nice. Quadrilaterals do not, unless they are long, thin, and hence kite shaped. Those quadrilaterals on the sides of Bluzerk look sloppy to me. I feel that mixing broad and narrow facets is a no-no as well. Ok, I am a bit weird, and for what it's worth, I am responsible for both designs. You can find them online at www.boghome.com.

Table 16-1 The most common ways of supplying three pieces of information to define a facet and what you should watch out for.

Information	Things to Check
1 angle + 1 index + 1 point	Presumably input values are fine
2 points + 1 index	Verify that the resulting cutting angle is Ok
2 points + 1 angle	Verify that the resulting index is Ok (whole number)
3 points	Check both the cutting angle and index

•Longer gemstone designs – those with a larger L/W ratio – will require a greater range of cutting angles. This may not be obvious at first glance, but a little playing around with GemCAD should make it clear. Since all sides of a gemstone have to converge at the culet or keel starting from the same girdle, the sides closer to the culet / keel must do so in less physical space and are hence steeper. This phenomenon connects directly to the next tip.

•Higher index materials can tolerate a greater range of cutting angles, a fact discussed in detail in Chapters 12.5.1 and 10.4. Coupled with the previous tip, this means that it can be a challenge to make a long design work in low index materials. Splitting facets can help somewhat. Note that many elongated gem cuts seek to emphasize colour, not sparkle, and hence reduced scintillation performance may be acceptable.

•Adjacent facets with closely spaced angles and index wheel settings make cutting and polishing more difficult. For example, small cutting angle errors can blow up (Figure 16-33) and agglomeration can cause scratching (Figure 8-31). Also, tweaking the polish on adjacent facets with similar angle and index settings can lead to rounding and even curving of the facet edges (see "Throwing a Curveball" on page 333 of Volume 1). Closely-spaced facets can be very useful in tying together a gem design, however, so such effects may be hard to avoid.

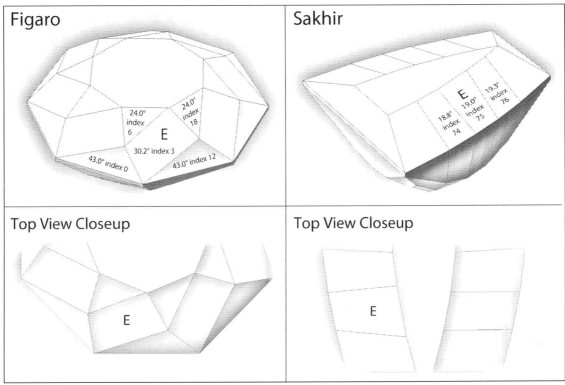

Figure 16-33 Adjacent facets with similar angle and index settings can lead to visible cutting errors. In both instances above, the facet marked E was cut 0.1° off the correct angle. In normal circumstances (left), this produces a minor error that can easily be corrected or even ignored. With closely spaced facets (right), the same error is unacceptable. As a consequence, the Figaro design is relatively easy to cut, while Sakhir is not. You can find the Figaro design online at www.boghome.com.

• This one may be blindingly obvious, but you need to place the crown and pavilion break facets at the same indices as the girdle facets. Failure to do so will lead to an uneven girdle and dirty looks from whoever has to set the gem (see also Section 16.2.1). Note that this does not necessarily place strong constraints on your creativity. For example, in its most general form, the Barion design uses girdle-matching "half-moon" facets to connect the pavilion to a girdle of a different shape (see "The Brilliant Barion" on page 246).

• Here's some controversial conventional wisdom – designs with an odd number of mains produce more complex, interesting reflection patterns. This is because light entering the crown through large facets will be more likely to encounter a pavilion facet edge before re-emerging toward the viewer. The idea is simpler than it sounds – look carefully at Figure 16-37 on page 260. Note that this is a specific instance of an earlier tip, which suggested that you use the crown and pavilion as a team to produce scintillation.

Not everyone believes this bit of wisdom, and you are sure to provoke a "lively" discussion at the lapidary club with this one – it

Figure 16-34 Gem designs with an odd number of mains enhance the splitting of reflections. The stone on the left is a nine-fold symmetric SRB, while the one on the right has the "standard" eight-fold symmetry. Both are computer rendered in sapphire.

is right up there with politics, religion, and wax versus glue. The next section tries to bring some light to the heat.

•Again, this may be blindingly obvious, but if you are having trouble bringing together an elongated design with a culet, consider using a keel. Try splitting the keel into two (or four, or more) segments to tighten the design and improve performance.

•Before finalizing your design, set the symmetry to 1-fold, non-mirror in GemCAD and cut the gem as you would in the real world – one facet at a time, not tier by tier. Although the symmetry option saves you time at the computer, it can do things that are not realistic, for example accurately cutting an entire tier of identical facets to the correct depth without the help of meet points. The girdle outline shown in Figure 17-22 is an example of this. A single GemCad command could chop out the gem like a cookie cutter. Doing so at the faceting machine with the necessary accuracy is significantly more challenging.

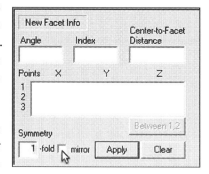

Figure 16-35 As a final check of your design, set the symmetry option in GemCAD to 1-fold non mirror and cut all of the facets one by one, just as you would on the faceting machine.

16.7 Against the Odds...

I like to be against the odds...
With me, it's just the satisfaction of the game. Just performance.
- Barry Bonds

Ok. I have to admit that the great ball player, Barry Bonds, was not referring to gemstone design when he made the foregoing remark about "the odds" and "performance." Nevertheless, the question of the true performance benefits of odd-main designs raises almost as much controversy among faceters as the discussion of Bonds' true place in the pantheon of baseball greats does among sports fans.

So, what is the truth? Do odd-main gemstones out-perform their even-symmetry brethren? Or is the promise of improved performance a myth, perhaps promulgated by less than scrupulous index wheel salesmen? Let's try to find out. Incidentally, both this section and the next one provide examples of how you can use your brain and a computer to discover your own design principles and gain insight into how gemstones work.

16.7.1 Do Odd-Main Gemstones Give Better Performance?

Some Ground Rules

As with all controversies, the first step in getting to the answer is agreeing on the question. In this instance, there are two ground rules to settle.

1. What is an odd-main gemstone?

Exactly what it says: An odd-main gem is a (symmetrical) stone with an odd number of main facets. For example, a standard round brilliant cut with nine-fold symmetry on a 72-tooth index wheel is an odd-main gemstone (Figure 16-36).

2. What is meant by performance?

Traditionally, faceters look at the overall fraction of light returned to the viewer as a measure of the optical performance of a gem. In GemCAD-speak, this corresponds to the ISO brightness given by a ray trace within GemRay. Refer to Chapter 15.3 and the GemRay documentation if you don't understand this.

At this point in this book, you should realize that light return is by no means the only or perhaps even the best way of judging the performance of a gem. For example, scanning through the previous sections should convince you that other factors, such as colour, visual interest, sparkle, and fire, all contribute to the impact of a stone. A fair evaluation of odd-main designs must consider several of these factors.

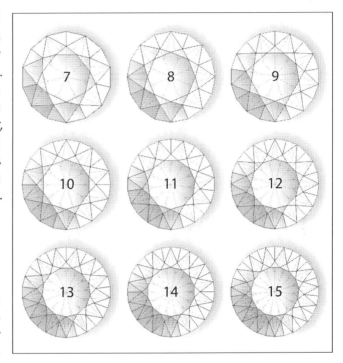

Figure 16-36 SRB gemstones cut with seven through fifteen-fold symmetry. Such gemstones are termed odd-main if the symmetry is odd.

Pre-Game Theorizing

Why should an odd-main design have better ISO brightness? Beats me. ISO brightness is a measure of how much light entering the crown from the environment gets re-directed back upward into the viewer's eyes. This is largely a function of facet angles, and a nine-fold symmetric gem will have pretty much the same cutting angles as a ten-fold gem of the same basic design. I therefore feel comfortable in hypothesizing that there should be little difference between even and odd-main designs in terms of ISO brightness. Adding to my comfort is the fact that I have already performed the experiment and hence know the answer...

On the other hand, there are very good reasons to anticipate improved sparkle and fire from odd-main designs. It all has to do with the point raised earlier in this chapter about the pavilion and crown working together to produce interesting reflection patterns.

Let's try a thought experiment involving the simplest possible case: light enters the table of a standard round brilliant gemstone, bounces a couple of times off the pavilion facets, and re-emerges toward the viewer (Figure 16-37). Note that Chapter 10.4 uses exactly this situation to draw conclusions about cutting angles and gem performance.

Light entering the gem from directly above will always be reflected across the symmetry axis of the stone – that is, it will pass through or near the line joining the culet with the center of the table. This means that the rays will, in general, bounce upward and emerge from the

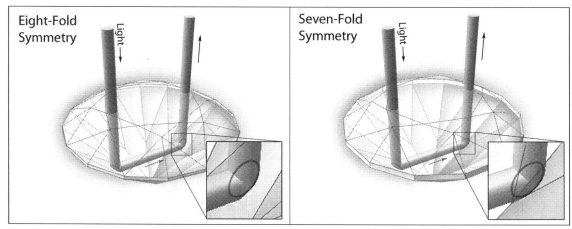

Figure 16-37 A bundle of light rays traversing a gemstone with an even (left) and odd (right) number of pavilion mains. In the even case, the emerging light encounters a similar arrangement of facets (see circular footprints), while in the odd case, a pavilion main facet center is always paired with an edge on the opposite side. See text for details.

crown area more or less directly opposite from where they entered. For an even-symmetry gem the arrangement of facets at the point of entry and emergence will be similar – effectively, the facets will "stack up" or overlap in much the same way as do the pavilion and crown facets in the emerald cut (see Figure 16-31 and adjacent text).

With the odd-main gem, however, the facet arrangement will be completely different. For example, if the entering rays strike the center of a pavilion main, the second pavilion bounce will take place in the neighbourhood of a facet junction, (Figure 16-37). This will split the incoming beam into two parts that will head through the crown in different directions. The reverse situation will occur for light that strikes the edge between main facets on the first bounce. Light is, after all, reversible (see Chapter 11.6), so you can just reverse the arrows in Figure 16-37. Yes, this is very much like crossing pavilion and crown facets in a design like Slice (Figure 16-31).

The effect of all this splitting in the odd-main case should be increased scintillation and fire. In the case of scintillation, the extra "action" arises out of what is effectively a larger number of facets on the pavilion – the equivalent of facet splitting to increase visual impact (*i.e.* Figure 16-1). For dispersion-induced colour or fire, the split-facet effect is more likely to cause separation of colours, as explained in Chapter 12.6 and Figure 12-22.

At this stage, the skeptical reader will point out that very few rays enter and exit a real-world gemstone in the manner depicted in Figure 16-37. For example, such geometry would require that the source of photons be in or near the viewer's eyeball. Superheroes (see Figure 15-27) and those suffering demonic possession aside, this situation is unlikely. Nevertheless, the effect of facet splitting in odd-main gemstones is very real, even in the instance of more realistic, slanted rays. Try the Waytrace command in GemCAD if you don't believe me.

Still not convinced? Figure 16-38 shows side-by-side GemRay ray traces of tourmaline SRB's with eight through eleven-fold symmetry over a range of viewing angles. Despite their comparable number of facets, the odd-main gems clearly show a richer, more finely structured reflection pattern (although the difference is admittedly less striking when the stone is tilted).

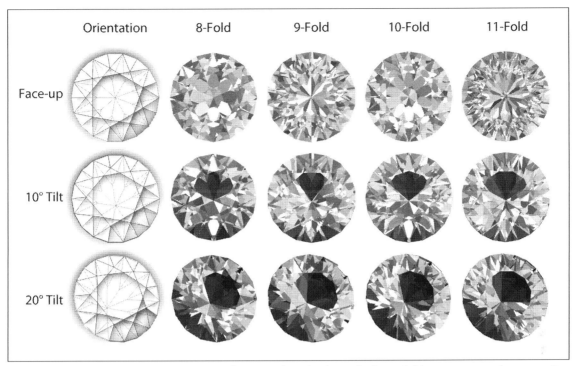

Figure 16-38 GemRay random ray traces of SRB's with eight through eleven-fold symmetry cut in tourmaline for several viewing angles. The odd-main designs produce a more visually interesting reflection pattern.

The Main Event

So much for theories. What about reality? Do odd-main gems perform better or is it a hoax?

Settling arguments like this requires objective measurements. After all, as the great U.S. senator Daniel Patrick Moynihan is credited with observing, everyone is entitled to his or her own opinions, but they are not entitled to their own facts.

There is a problem, however. Yes, it is possible to quantify the ISO brightness of a gemstone design in an objective way – just run it through GemRay – but how can you measure the sparkle and fire?

For this experiment, I have adopted the sparkle and fire metrics used in the BOG gemstone optimization program. A full explanation of the calculation is beyond the scope of this book, but the idea is straightforward: if a gemstone's appearance changes markedly for a small tilt in viewing angle, then that gemstone has lots of sparkle. Yet another information rich sentence. Read it again and refer to the BOG online documentation for further details.

Of course, poor tilt performance – that is, windowing through the pavilion as you change the viewing angle – shouldn't count as good sparkle.

Fire can be evaluated essentially the same way: if the reflection pattern changes dramatically for different wavelengths of light – say, for violet versus red – then that gemstone will exhibit plenty of fire. Again, no leaking out of the pavilion allowed.

Figure 16-39 shows an example of how it works. The difference between GemRay's random ray trace for the two angles (or the two wavelengths) gives the amount of sparkle (or fire).

Comparing those numbers to a "standard" SRB, one with eight-fold symmetry, should then give an indication of how odd-main gems really perform.

Ideally, this test should employ proper measuring equipment on real gems cut in identical material in the real world. However, even if this were possible or practical, there would still be challenges associated with quantifying the subjective effects of sparkle and fire. In my experience, the random ray trace in GemRay accurately reflects the appearance of cut gemstones, and hence it is a reasonable option to perform the experiment entirely within the computer.

Figure 16-39 GemRay ray traces for an 11-main SRB with viewing angle tipped by 2° (top) and for refractive indices corresponding to red and violet light in quartz (bottom). The difference image (rightmost column) shows where sparkle and fire occur (darker means a greater difference). The total amount of non-zero values in the difference gives a measure of sparkle and fire.

So, what is the answer?

Figure 16-40 shows the ISO brightness for the nine gemstones depicted in Figure 16-36. The fractional light return increases steadily with increasing number of sides up to about nine or ten-fold symmetry. The reason for this is somewhat subtle: as the number of main facets increases, the gem becomes more and more perfectly circular, which means that the main and break angles become more and more "ideal" for light rays entering at skew angles. At a certain point, the marginal increase in performance levels off, and there is no brightness benefit in increasing the symmetry of the gem.

Back to the main point, however. As expected (particularly if you were comfortable in knowing the answer in advance), there are no significant differences between odd and even symmetry. In other words, in terms of light return, odd-main designs do not outperform even-main designs. This observation may be the basis of the widely held skepticism about the advantages of odd symmetry.

How about the other two factors, sparkle and fire? Figure 16-41 shows the amount of sparkle and fire for the same series of gemstones with increasing number of pavilion mains. Note that, unlike ISO brightness,

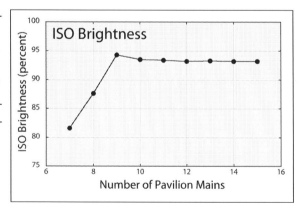

Figure 16-40 The ISO brightness or light return for standard round brilliant gemstones as a function of the number of pavilion mains. The ISO value increases with the number of sides, but there is no evidence for better performance for odd-main designs.

there is no absolute measure for these quantities. In other words, the amount of black and gray sprinkles in the "Sparkle" and "Fire" images in Figure 16-39 has no direct meaning in the real world. To allow comparison, Figure 16-41 plots the sparkle and fire values relative to that of an eight-sided SRB (hence the value 1.0 for sparkle and fire for eight pavilion mains).

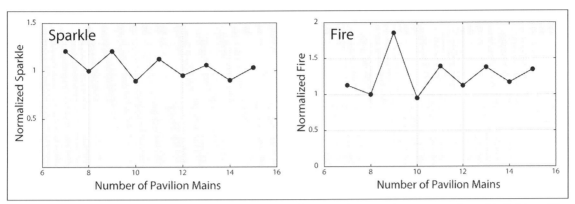

Figure 16-41 *The same type of plot as the previous one, this time showing the amount of sparkle (left) and fire (right). Note that the values have been scaled to 1 for the eight-fold symmetric standard round brilliant.*

Here, the situation is completely different from the ISO brightness trend. The sawtooth appearance of the curves clearly shows that both sparkle and fire are improved in the case of odd-main designs! For example, an SRB with eleven-fold symmetry has more sparkle and fire than either the ten-fold or twelve-fold version. As measured this way, odd-main designs are clearly better.

Take that, skeptics.

There are a couple of other things to notice in Figure 16-41. First, for both sparkle and fire, the difference between odd and even decreases as the number of sides goes up. In other words, the teeth of the sawtooth get smaller for higher symmetry. This makes all kinds of sense, since sparkle and fire depend on the "facet doubling" and "spectrum slicing" effects mentioned earlier. From an overall geometric point of view, the difference between odd and even symmetry becomes smaller and smaller for these effects as the number of pavilion mains increases. The lesson here? Don't bother buying that custom 68-tooth index wheel for 17-fold symmetry, since 16-fold symmetry on a good old 64-tooth wheel will do just about as well.

The other trend in Figure 16-41 is the apparent decrease in sparkle with increasing number of sides, independent of oddness or evenness. This is probably related to the fact that gems with lower number of sides will have larger facets. When tilting the gem causes such larger facets to "light up," the relative impact is greater than for the higher-symmetry designs.

The Final Score

What's the bottom line? It appears from these admittedly limited tests that the old saw about odd-main gemstones is at least partially true. While there is no clear improvement in overall light return, the overlapping of facet centers with facet edges in odd-symmetry designs enhances the splitting effect that improves both sparkle and fire. This improvement is more dramatic for gems with fewer sides, so it may be time to start saving pennies for that 84-tooth (seven-fold) or 72-tooth (nine-fold) index wheel.

A couple of words of caution before you bravely face the odds: first, there are relatively few odd-main designs out there, particularly in the higher symmetries. Of course, you are on your way to becoming an accomplished gemstone designer, so this is no real impediment. Second, you may encounter some resistance, or at least dirty looks, from your jeweler when it comes time to set your masterwork, since standard findings assume standard symmetry, and this usually means an even number of sides.

16.8 The Science of Art

Can you scientifically analyze art?

Most thinking people would say no. Science involves the measurement, classification, and explanation of phenomena in the world around us. Art, on the other hand, flows from a place that is not well characterized by measurements, and it inspires feelings that are hardly subject to classification and scientific explanation.

Our art form – the design and faceting of gemstones – is a little bit different.

The Foreword to this book tried to address this issue, noting that faceting represents a unique blend of art, science, and mathematics. It makes sense, then, that at least part of our craft may be susceptible to objective analysis. I say only part of our craft, because nothing in any of my physics books can explain the creative process of gem design, nor quantify the feeling of looking into a unique stone of your own creation.

In any case, to paraphrase Admiral Farragut, "Damn the considerations of aesthetics and intangible artistic impulses, full speed ahead..."

Here's my experiment: I laid my hands on approximately 100 modern gem designs optimized for a variety of materials and extracted the numerical information from each. This information included the geometric properties of the gems (essentially length, width, height, volume factor, and all the cutting angles), as well as the target refractive index. I tried to select a wide range of designs in terms of overall shape, symmetry, and gem material, and the list of creative talent responsible for this collection includes some of the greatest names in modern gem design. To provide additional variety, it also included me and the designs in Chapter 19.

The result was a reasonably impressive table of numbers, suitable for any second-rate Excel jockey. Suddenly, art had become science.

What can this mass of information reveal? Well for starters, a few clicks of the mouse reveal that the 100 gem designs have an average length to width to height ratio of 17 x 15 x 10, although no single design has this ratio.

The median value may represent a better measure of the range of gemstone designs. Recall from high school that the median value is the exact middle value: half of the other values are larger and the other half are smaller. Thus, if Bill Gates wanders into a crowded bar, the average income of the patrons goes up a lot, while the median income barely changes. Interestingly, the gem design with median length to width ratio has proportions 15.5 x 15 x 10, indicating that roughly half the gem designs have L/W~1. This essentially means rounds or squares. Both the average and median values demonstrate that the total depth of most gems is 2/3 of their width, a very useful fact when evaluating rough (see page 228 of Volume 1).

Figure 16-42 plots the L/W and H/W ratios for the 100 gems. As expected, a substantial fraction, roughly 60%, have L/W~1, and there is a clear trend to design to "natural" ratios, such as 1.2, 1.5, 2.0 and so on. A symmetric hexagon has L/W=1.155 (page 41), and this value appears frequently as well. The range of H/W is considerably more limited, never dropping as low as 0.5 and exceeding 0.8 in only a few cases. This, of course, is more a reflection of how light works – a reflection of (total internal) reflection – rather than the limited vision of the designers. Gems outside this range of H/W will simply not perform well.

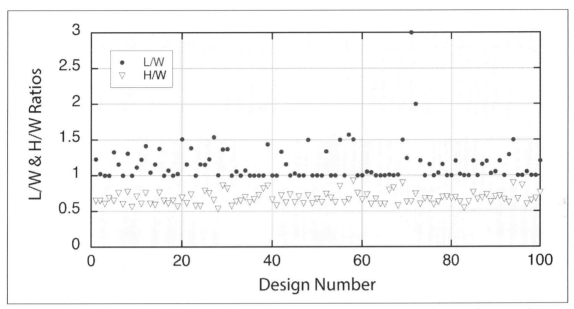

Figure 16-42 The Length to Width (circles) and Height to Width (triangles) ratios of 100 random gem designs.

I could go on and on…For example, Figure 16-43 shows the distribution of design refractive indices. Taller bars mean more gems target that type of gem material. With the exception of a couple of designs for fluorite and opal (n~1.45), along with one for rutile (n=2.62), the lion's share of gem cuts are intended for quartz, tourmaline, and a mix of garnet and corundum.

More than 85% of the gem designs have mirror versus radial symmetry. While this certainly reflects the popularity of the two design aesthetics, at least some of the difference relates to the fact that a gem with both mirror and radial symmetry, for example the SRB, gets labeled as mirror (see Chapter 10.7).

Figure 16-44 shows the relative popularity of the order of symmetry, that is two-fold versus four-fold versus eight-fold and so on. Unsurprisingly, one, two, three, four, and eight-fold symmetry dominate the field.

I hope that you agree that this is all great fun, but is there a deeper message here, beyond subjugating art to science?

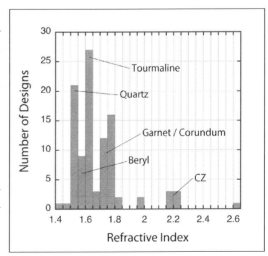

Figure 16-43 The distribution of design refractive index, showing peaks associated with popular gemstone materials.

I think that there is. In an era in which mass-production gemstones, both human and robot cut, proliferate and improve in quality year after year, it will become increasingly difficult for amateur faceters to distinguish themselves. Targeting unique portions of the gemstone "design space" is one effective strategy.

In fact, I now recognize that I have been doing this subconsciously all along: Only about 40% of my own designs have L/W~1, the reverse of the overall trend. I like to try a variety of different materials, including the two most extreme refractive indices in the group. Although they represent only about a quarter of the total, my designs account for roughly two thirds of those with radial symmetry. Finally, I tend to avoid four-fold symmetric designs: my personal version of Figure 16-44 has a bar for 4-fold symmetry that is half the height of that for 3-fold, again the opposite of the overall trend.

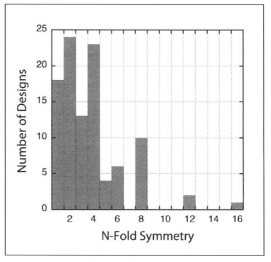

Figure 16-44 The distribution of gem symmetry, for example four-fold vs eight-fold.

I hope that the last two sections, and indeed this entire chapter, have convinced you that, among the seemingly chaotic profusion of gem cuts out there, some underlying design rules exist. More importantly, I hope that this chapter has inspired you to discover your own design principles and to put them into action with your own creations. The next two chapters should help you on your way.

17

Establishing the Gem Outline

Every gem design is built on a foundation, and that foundation is the girdle outline. Getting the outline right means getting a symmetric, pleasing stone with easy to follow meet points. In other words, pure faceting pleasure.

Because of its central importance to a successful outcome, gem designers and faceters have developed a number of techniques which can help you turn your ideas and sketches into the outline of a beautiful, cuttable stone.

The methods described in this chapter, known as CAM, OMNI, and CLAM, lie at the interface between cutting and design. In fact, you may have executed dozens or even hundreds of existing gem designs without realizing that you were following established procedures for getting the girdle outline right. Understanding these techniques is a great help if you enjoy creating free-form gems at the faceting machine, but it is an absolute prerequisite if you plan to come up with your own, unique designs.

The following pages introduce each of the techniques, provide you with insight into how they work, and most importantly, supply a real-world example of their execution.

17.1 Introduction

Here's an idea. Why not spend a relaxing afternoon picking through the gravel on your driveway, looking for stones that are naturally rounds, ovals, emerald-shaped, marquise, or briolette?

I know that this sounds like enormous fun, but you can also take my word for it that natural stones rarely come pre-shaped to an obvious gem outline, and the chances of finding a sample that is simultaneously properly shaped and inclusion-free are vanishingly small.

Most early gem cuts followed a very regular geometric design, such as a square or an octagon (see "Cutting Evolution, a Two-Page History of Diamond Design" on page 240). While initially inspired by the form of natural crystals, particularly diamond, such shapes are easy to produce on the faceting machine, for example by placing a number of facets at the same angle and mast height, and then cutting the girdle – more on this technique later (and also see Figure 16-15).

Over the decades, changing fashion and improved equipment have led to the development of more complex and adventurous gemstone shapes. Establishing these gem outlines with the accuracy needed for meet point faceting can be quite a challenge. Luckily, clever designers have developed a number of strategies for creating these shapes. Which one you choose for your own personal creation depends on your design goals and whether the facets you cut to establish the outline will form part of the final gem. Experience is a big help here, and as often happens, you can reach your target by more than one road.

A (nearly) final gentle warning before getting into the nitty-gritty of CAMs and CLAMs: Although it is often the first step in the gem cut, you should not confuse establishing the girdle outline with pre-forming. Pre-forming is a generally crude grinding or cutting step, which produces the approximate gem shape in order to save time and lap wear on the faceting machine. Chapter 8.3 provides further information.

Establishing the gem outline, on the other hand, refers to a variety of techniques to generate the precise arrangement of *final* girdle facets. As a side benefit, the procedures described in this chapter usually lead to reference meet points on which the pavilion and crown are built.

Here's the final gentle warning: Somewhat confusingly, the GemCAD program refers to facets used to establish the gem outline, but later cut away, as pre-form facets. I occasionally do the same, although I usually preface the term with the appropriate method to make things clear (*i.e.* "CAM pre-form facets"). Don't worry if this sounds complicated. It really isn't, and by the end of the chapter, all should be clear as quartz…

17.2 Why Not Cut the Girdle Directly to the Desired Outline?

Plenty of designs, including the classic standard round brilliant, have girdle facets that are equidistant from the gem centerline. In principle, then, you can set the quill angle to 90° and just dial in the appropriate sequence of settings on the index wheel, cutting all the girdle facets to the same depth. Some faceters refer to this method of establishing the girdle outline as **ECED** – Equal Center to Edge Distance.

The ECED technique is a very traditional way of establishing the gem outline. Unfortunately, it doesn't work that well. (This remark will inevitably trigger howls of protest from some very skilled faceters, who may also argue that sensible cutting procedure begins with the crown – see "The Great Debate: Pavilion-First or Crown-First?" on page 304 of Volume 1).

Outline? Which Outline?

Can you draw an angelfish?

Most people would come up with something like the image to the right. Actually, people with artistic abilities like mine would never come up with something like this in a million years, but let's move on…

These beautiful freshwater fish are loved by aquarists (a bit crazy like us, but with aquariums instead of faceting machines) for their dramatic vertical striping and lacy fins. The stripes help them hide among the roots and grasses in their native rivers of Columbia, Venezuela, and Brazil.

If you were a smaller fish or insect living in one of those rivers, however, you might draw something more like the drawing to the left. This is your last view of an angelfish before becoming lunch.

The point here is that gemstones (like angelfish) can have a dramatically different outline, depending on your point of view (or your position in the food chain). When faceters refer to the gem outline, they always mean the outer boundary of the stone when viewed from above, looking directly down onto the table (Figure 17-1)

This definition may seem somewhat arbitrary, but it is firmly rooted in the history and technique of gemstone faceting. Turn to Chapter 2.1 to learn more about the connection between gemstone anatomy and the geometry of faceting machines.

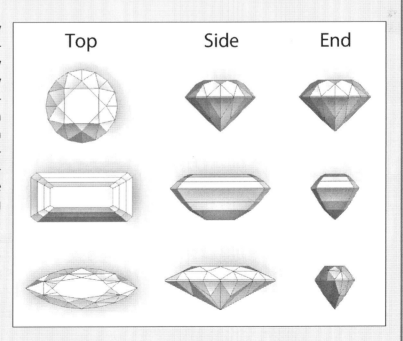

Figure 17-1 Top, side and end views of a standard round brilliant, emerald cut, and marquise. The gem outline refers to the top view.

There are complicated reasons, both human and mechanical, why directly cutting the girdle to depth doesn't work. Variations in hand pressure, coupled with machine flexure and other factors, will almost always lead to asymmetries, or a de-centered stone, or both. Simply stated, it is difficult to cut a series of facets to the exact same depth, particularly when the quill is horizontal. Building the remainder of the gem on an asymmetric or de-centered foundation will lead to frustration, and as a result, I do not generally recommend the direct girdle cutting, ECED technique.

Cutting to meet points is considerably more accurate. The three methods explained in this chapter – **CAM**, **OMNI**, and **CLAM** – are built on this fundamental principle. They offer alternatives for placing the girdle facets accurately, and most importantly, they rely on meet points and easier-to-establish facets.

Nevertheless, there will be instances when you have to cut the girdle directly. For example, when executing a particular design, there may be insufficient material to allow a proper CAM outline. In these instances, you should take extra care and time to ensure an accurate girdle. Try to keep constant, light pressure on the stone to avoid mast and quill flexure, and use whatever means you have to check for equal depth of cut (see Chapter 20.7). A girdle rest may also help (Chapter 4.11.4).

Outline by Design...

If you are cutting an existing, well-executed gem design, the easiest way to establish the girdle outline is to do nothing – nothing, that is, beyond following the instructions. Well-behaved designs with proper cutting diagrams will take care of their girdle outlines as a matter of course. Executing the facet tiers in the proper order and hitting the prescribed meet points will ensure a correct outline and a successful gemstone.

Incidentally, while you are doing this nothing (i.e. just following instructions), why not try to determine how the designer managed to create the gem outline? The actual method will almost certainly be one of those described below, or a combination of techniques. Understanding how the gem outline happens will give you a deeper understanding of the design and will help you with your own creative efforts.

17.3 Center-point Angle Method (CAM)

The Center-point Angle Method (CAM) is the most widely used technique for establishing a desired gem outline. CAM involves cutting a series of angled facets which meet at a common center point. This is followed by a series of 90° facets at the same index wheel settings. These vertical facets form a level girdle and chop out the correct outline like a cookie cutter (it is a geometric fact of faceting life that an angled facet cut at the same index as a girdle facet will always intersect that girdle facet along a line parallel to the girdle). Often, the angled facets, like the center point, serve only to establish the girdle outline and will be cut away at a later stage.

Be There or Be Square

Rectangular designs often call for a direct cut or ECED outline. In this instance, the facets come as two pairs, each with its own center distance. Typically, the cutting diagram will then specify a length to width (L/W) ratio. To cut such a design, you have to simultaneously ensure that each facet in a pair is the same distance from the center, and that the ratio of distances between the pairs has the prescribed L/W ratio.

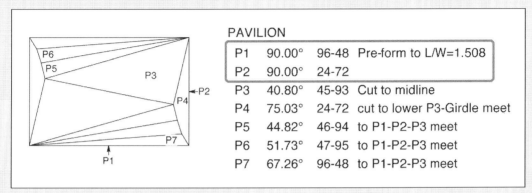

PAVILION			
P1	90.00°	96-48	Pre-form to L/W=1.508
P2	90.00°	24-72	
P3	40.80°	45-93	Cut to midline
P4	75.03°	24-72	cut to lower P3-Girdle meet
P5	44.82°	46-94	to P1-P2-P3 meet
P6	51.73°	47-95	to P1-P2-P3 meet
P7	67.26°	96-48	to P1-P2-P3 meet

Figure 17-2 A rectangular design will often establish the gem outline via two pairs of equidistant girdle facets and a length to width ratio. This is an extract of the Fritz15 design from Chapter 19.2.1.

This approach suffers from the same challenges as traditional ECED, with the additional complication of getting the L/W ratio right. If the amount of gem rough permits it, I always use the CAM technique for such designs. Section 17.3 explains how.

17.3.1 How Does CAM Work?

Note: Understanding how CAM works will give you a deeper insight into gemstone design, but understanding CAM is not strictly necessary to exploiting it. This section explains the reasoning behind the Center-point Angle Method. Turn over a few pages to Section 17.3.2 to get straight down to business.

Let's begin with a seemingly simple question: What exactly defines the gem outline? Yes, yes, the gem outline is the envelope of girdle facets when viewed from above (see page 269), but how does one actually define this envelope?

In order to understand the geometry and mechanics of CAM, the definition of the gem outline needs to be a little more precise. Here's a good working description: the gem outline is defined by a series of 90° facets cut at specific distances from the gem centerline and at specific settings of the index wheel.

The original problem can then be re-formulated: How does one determine the appropriate set of distances and index wheel settings to establish the desired gem outline?

This may sound like a trivial restatement of the original question, but from a gem designer's viewpoint, it does break down the general problem – establishing the gem outline – into two separate, specific goals: getting the index wheel settings right and getting the distances right.

Because the gem outline consists of connected straight lines, you can measure the individual index wheel settings directly from a sketch using a protractor, or calculate them based on the symmetry of the stone. See Section 17.3.2 below. Getting the distances right is a little more complicated.

Warning! Trigonometry ahead!

Don't panic…it's actually pretty simple trigonometry, and if you know anything about tangent ratio scaling of a gem (see Chapter 10.6), you already have all the trigonometric tools you need.

Figure 17-3 illustrates the problem: girdle facet G must be placed a controlled distance d away from the gem's centerline. Also shown is a special point on this centerline. Labeled TCP in the figure, this point is the famous (future) Temporary Center Point, which will be formed by the intersection of a number of angled facets. Confused? Be patient. All will become clear soon enough.

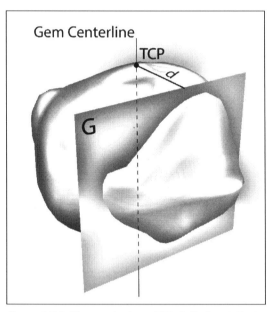

Now take a look at Figure 17-4. Translating d into a cutting angle θ involves the simple realization that all inclined facets F cut through the TCP and meeting a level girdle line will have the same distance h shown in the figure. If they didn't, the girdle would not be level. Note that different facets can have different θ and d, but for a level girdle, h will be fixed. This is another one of those information-rich paragraphs. Make sure that you understand it.

Figure 17-3 The goal: place 90° girdle facet G at a distance d from the gem centerline. TCP is the future Temporary Center Point.

The ratio h/d is simply the tangent of the cutting angle θ (refer to Section 10.2 if this is not absolutely clear). Therefore, for a given h, you can readily calculate the correct θ to give the desired d. There. Well done. You barely noticed the trigonometry, right?.

A quick note in passing: barring serious mechanical problems, you can set θ very accurately on your faceting machine, more accurately, in fact, than you can set or measure a depth of cut, such as d. This is why the CAM technique is superior to cutting the girdle directly (see Section 17.2).

Bundling all this into a method is now easy. Imagine that you need to cut two facets, F1 and F2, at distances d1 and d2 from the TCP, respectively (Figure 17-5). A little doodling leads to the relationship:

$$\frac{d_2}{d_1} = \frac{\tan \theta_1}{\tan \theta_2}$$

This manipulation cleverly eliminates *h* from the scene – a good thing, since in most circumstances, you want only the cutting angles and do not particularly care about the value of *h*.

Generalized to the entire gem outline, CAM then works as follows: cut a series of inclined facets to the TCP at the appropriate index wheel settings given by the drawing or gem symmetry. The exact angle for each inclined facet comes from the desired distances d1, d2, etc. via the simple formula above. You then cut the girdle facets one after the other, using the meet point created at the previous step (circled in panel c of Figure 17-5).

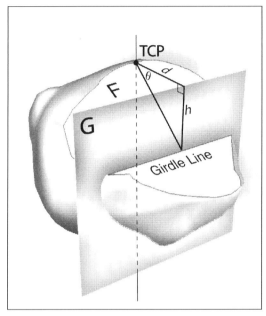

Figure 17-4 The tangent of the cutting angle θ is given by the ratio h/d.

Advanced trigonometrists and readers with good horse sense will have already noticed a problem here. For a given pair of distances, the equation gives a ratio of angles, but not the angles themselves. What to do? The short answer is that you fix one of the angles and work out all the others from there. More about this in the next section.

A final comment on the relationship between the cutting angle and the distance of a girdle facet to the centerline of the gem: Your hard-won trigonometric understanding from Chapter 10 (particularly the optional fun on page 6) leads you to the realization that steeper angles, that is, larger *θ*, with the quill closer to horizontal, will yield shorter distances *d*, in other words, girdle facets closer to the centerline of the gem. You might even have figured this out using your good old horse sense. In any case, this realization will be very useful later on.

17.3.2 Using CAM

The previous section explains how the Center-point Angle Method breaks down the problem of establishing the gem outline into two more practical exercises: (1) finding the correct index wheel settings for the girdle facets; and (2) figuring out how to cut them at the right distance from the centerline of the stone.

This section throws theory to the winds and gets down to brass tacks (another one for the Mixed Metaphor Hall of Fame). More specifically, it will explain exactly how to derive the correct index wheel and angle settings to execute CAM. Don't worry if it seems a bit complicated. It's not, and Section 17.3.3 will lead you step by step through a real-world example.

Determining the Index Wheel Settings

For a symmetric gemstone, finding the correct index wheel values is really easy: just look at the design and calculate the correct settings by dividing the number of teeth on the index wheel by the number of sides on the gem. For example, if you want to cut a rectangle, index settings of 0-24-48-72 will do the job, since 96/4=24 (assuming of course that you are working with a 96-tooth wheel). A symmetric twelve-sided stone uses indices 0-8-16-24-32-40-48-56-64-72-80-88. Of course, these values can be offset by a fixed amount. For example, 3-11-19-27-35-43-51-59-67-75-83-91 will also produce a symmetric, 12-sided outline.

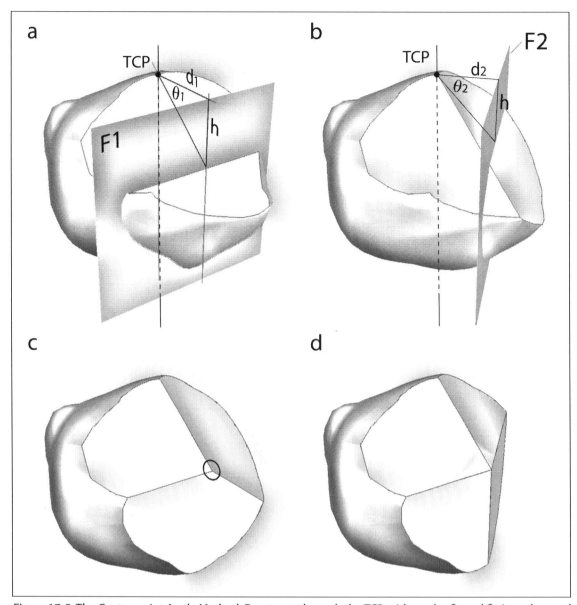

Figure 17-5 The Center-point Angle Method. Facets cut through the TCP with angles θ_1 and θ_2 (panels a and b) will let you create a level girdle with 90° facets at distances d_1 and d_2, respectively (panels c and d). The first girdle facet (panel c) sets the overall size of the gem and creates the meet point (circled) for the second facet. Cutting that facet (panel d) creates a meet point for the third. And so on…Question added in press: why are you faceting a lemon?

Gems with irregular or no symmetry can be a little harder to figure out. In these instances, the easiest solution is to estimate the girdle indices based on a drawing. Viewed from above, the outline is a series of connected straight lines at different angles. You can measure the angles from the drawing and translate them directly to index settings. For example, each tooth of a 96-index wheel is 3¾ degrees (360°/96=3.75°). A portion of the girdle on the drawing at 29° from the horizontal would then be close to index 8, since 8 x 3.75 = 30. You can measure all of the girdle segments this way and come up with a decent approximation of the desired outline by rounding to the nearest index. A simple overlay printed on transparent plastic can be a real help (see "A CAM Protractor" opposite). The next section shows a real-world example of this process.

A CAM Protractor

Tired of tapping away on that calculator? Can't remember if one index step is 3.25° or 3.75°? Why not make a simple plastic overlay that does the math for you?

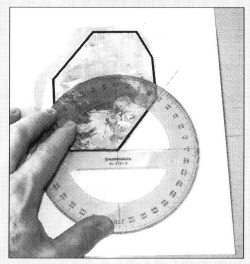

Figure 17-6 A transparent plastic protractor for measuring angles in degrees.

A protractor is a transparent plastic device for measuring angles in degrees (Figure 17-6). Hard core nerds may even have one that does radians (or even grads and gons!). For better or worse, faceters use a different unit of angle measure: one tooth of their index wheel.

An appropriate protractor can simplify your life, particularly when translating a gem sketch into a real world design. Figure 17-7 shows just such a device, in this case matched to a 96-tooth index gear. You can copy or print this design onto transparent plastic and use it as an overlay to read off index settings directly from the drawing. Printable versions for a variety of common index wheels are available at this book's website: www.facetingbook.com.

Alternatively, you can scan or import the CAM protractor into your computer or create your own with a program such as Adobe Illustrator. If the gem sketch is also somehow digitized, the entire process of matching index settings to the gem outline can take place in the virtual world behind your computer screen.

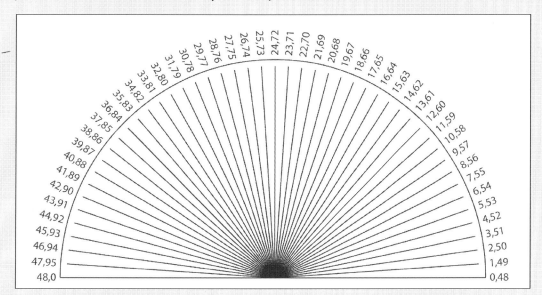

Figure 17-7 A simple overlay printed on transparent plastic lets you read off index wheel settings directly from a sketch. This CAM protractor has markings every 3.75°, corresponding to a 96-tooth wheel. Each line shows two possible indices, one for each side of the gem. For example, a vertical line can be either index 24 or 72.

Getting the Distances Right

So much for the index wheel settings. As explained in Section 17.3.1, getting the distances right is a little more complicated. Specifically, you need a way to place the girdle facets at exact, known distances from the centerline of the stone. This is done by adjusting the cutting angles of a series of facets cut through a temporary center point, and then placing 90° facets at the same index wheel settings. See the previous section if this is not clear.

Since the goal here is to establish the outline, not cut the gem itself, you don't want to remove any material that will be needed later. This means ensuring that the steepest of the angled facets through the TCP – that is, the one which will produce the girdle facet closest to the centerline – is shallower than all of the pavilion angles in the design itself (yet another sentence that contains too much information – it's worth a re-read).

The piece of gem rough may have a say in your decision about the appropriate range of angles for the CAM method. Here's why: The previous paragraph argued for shallow angles, in order to not remove any part of the future gem. On the other hand, the angled facets must be steep enough to reach from the TCP to the eventual girdle outline. Figure 17-8 should make the situation clear.

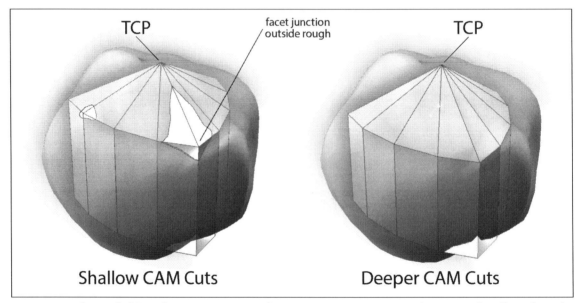

Shallow CAM Cuts   **Deeper CAM Cuts**

Figure 17-8 The angled CAM facets must connect the temporary center point to the eventual girdle outline. The shallower CAM cuts (left) will not produce all of the meet points needed to generate the entire girdle – critical intersections will be outside of the stone. Somewhat steeper angles (right) do the job, but of course, you should ensure that the CAM angles are shallower than the eventual pavilion angles.

Putting It All Together

The overall procedure follows naturally: Determine the index wheel settings based on a drawing of the gem or its symmetry. Cut the steepest angled CAM facet through the TCP a few degrees below the shallowest pavilion angle. Calculate the remaining target angles based on their corresponding distance and the trigonometry from the previous section:

$$\text{target angle} = \tan^{-1}\left(\tan(\text{steepest angle}) \cdot \frac{\text{shortest } d}{\text{target } d}\right)$$

A final remark on the inclined CAM facets through the TCP: depending on the gemstone geometry (and despite all the dire warnings above), these facets don't necessarily have to be cut away at a later stage. The inclined facets, or at least parts of them, can, in fact, end up in the final gem (see "Inadvertent CAM" on page 280). This may influence your selection of angles to execute CAM, so think before you cut.

17.3.3 Real World CAM

All the trigonometry and mixed metaphors in the world aren't worth a hill of beans without a real world example.[1] This section shows by example the detailed steps needed to generate an arbitrary gem outline using CAM. In this case, the outline was inspired by the desire to get the most out of a very pretty piece of tourmaline rough that had a somewhat skewed cross section (Figure 17-9), but the inspiration can come from a variety of sources (Chapter 16.1).

As explained in previous sections, you need to know the index settings and centerline distances of the desired gem outline in order to proceed. You can work from a sketch of the rough, but these days, it is much easier to take advantage of some of our electronic toys to get the job done.

One option is to take a digital photograph of the stone from the right point of view and print out an enlarged version to measure. Alternatively, you can place the rough on a flatbed scanner to capture the outline (Figure 17-10). Your favourite tweezers or calipers can help hold the stone in place against the glass in the scanner. Note that some scanners (like mine) produce a slightly skewed viewpoint for three-dimensional objects, and you may have to examine the image carefully to see exactly the region you want.

Figure 17-9 A beautiful but slightly odd-shaped piece of tourmaline rough provided the impetus for creating an arbitrary gem outline.

You will need a few simple tools, in addition to the printout or sketch of the stone. A standard ruler will give the distances of the outline segments from the centerline, while a student's protractor will help with the angles. A CAM Protractor (see page 275) will help even more. Finally, a good sharp pencil rounds out your toolbox.

Advanced computer mavens may eschew these primitive analogue devices, making all of their measurements directly onscreen with a digital drafting program such as Adobe Illustrator. Explaining how to do this is well beyond the scope of this book, and besides, advanced computer mavens never read instructions anyway.

Figure 17-10 A flatbed scanner can produce surprisingly helpful images of the outline of gemstone rough. Note the slightly tipped viewpoint, which can make identifying the edges a bit of a challenge.

---

[1] And "hill of beans" is one heck of a metaphor. Any phrase used by both P. G. Wodehouse and Humphrey Bogart deserves our utmost respect.

The Outline of an Outline

Let's begin by simplifying things. Specifically, you should examine the image or sketch and break it down into a few line segments. Yes, a 47-sided outline may trace the periphery of the stone very accurately, but it will be an arrestingly unrewarding exercise to cut it. Also, recall that the pavilion and crown facets of essentially all gemstones provide refinements to the overall outline. This usually means placing facets at different index wheel settings than the girdle. You don't want to use up all the notches on your index wheel, at least not immediately.

Figure 17-11 shows a good compromise for the tourmaline rough. This eight-sided outline follows the skewed crystal structure pretty well. Note that the pattern has through-center or radial symmetry (see Chapter 10.7), and that there are four pairs of equidistant segments. This can reduce the number of mast height and cutting angle changes, and such symmetry almost always produces interesting reflection patterns.

You know by now that measuring the angles of the outline segments (and hence the index wheel settings corresponding to the girdle facets) is a breeze, but how do you get the other piece of the puzzle, the centerline distances? You should start with finding the centerline itself.

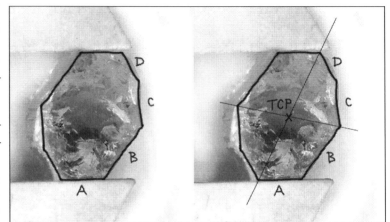

Figure 17-11 Reducing the gem outline to a series of line segments (left). Ideally, the rough will allow a relatively simple solution with interesting symmetry. If not, try to find the best compromise between accuracy and complexity. Label the individual segments to keep track. Connect opposite vertices to locate the center point (right).

Identify the centerline (or temporary center point) of the gem as best you can. If the outline has reasonable symmetry, try the intersection of a pair of lines connecting opposite vertices. Mark the TCP on the drawing (Figure 17-11).

The centerline distance to each girdle segment is the perpendicular distance between the TCP and that segment. In other words, it is the distance between the center point and the girdle measured along a line at 90° to the segment. To measure the distance, you first have to draw these perpendicular lines. Time to wield your trusty pencil, protractor, and ruler.

Figure 17-12 shows how this is done. The procedure should be familiar to any home carpenter. Note that the perpendicular line through the TCP does not necessarily pass through the midpoint of the girdle segment! In fact, in some cases, such as segment D in the figure, the perpendicular line may lie beyond one of the ends.

That's it for geometric constructions – you can put the pencil away. The next step is to measure the individual (perpendicular) distances and segment angles.

The distances are easy. Simply lay the ruler down on the perpendicular line and measure. Note the distance, in centimeters for example, next to the segment label. Ok…so you weren't 100% done with the pencil.

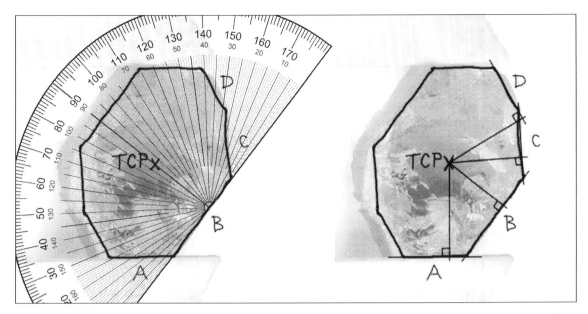

Figure 17-12 Using the protractor and ruler, draw a line through the TCP perpendicular to each segment of the outline. You can do this by placing the protractor on the sketch with the TCP on the 90° line and the base of the protractor square with the edge of the stone. The left panel shows this for edge B. Then make a mark at the bottom of the 90° line (near the letter B above). Joining this mark with the TCP using a ruler establishes the needed perpendicular line. Do the same for the remaining three labeled segments (right panel). Note that by this choice of symmetry, you do not have to measure the four remaining unlabeled segments – they will have the same distance and the opposite index wheel setting (i.e. 12-84 for a 96-index wheel).

The next step is to derive the index wheel settings by measuring the angle of each outline segment using the protractor. The only subtlety here is keeping track of where zero degrees is. Remember that in modern cutting diagrams, facets directly below the TCP (i.e. the 6 o'clock position) are at index zero. It makes sense, then, to define this direction as zero degrees and work outward from there. Figure 17-13 shows the result.

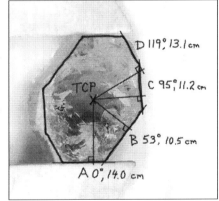

Figure 17-13 The distances and angles of each of the four unique outline facets.

From Measurement to Design

The pieces are now in place: you have all the required information to convert the distances and directions to a prescription for cutting this custom gem outline.

As noted several times above, transposing the segment directions into index wheel settings is dead easy: for a 96-tooth index wheel, simply divide the angle in degrees by 3.75 and round the result to the nearest integer. Don't worry about the rounding: you will always be within half an index of the best setting, which is plenty good enough for a reasonable gem outline. The final column of Table 17-1 shows the resulting index wheel settings.

Inadvertent CAM

By now, you should have a deep enough understanding of the Center-point Angle Method to realize that you have been using it all along.

Specifically, gem designs with simple symmetry, such as the standard round brilliant, use the CAM technique to establish the stone outline. This awful truth has been concealed for two reasons.

First, symmetric gems have a single centerline-girdle distance *d*, and hence need only a single cutting angle *θ* to get things right (see Figure 17-4). No fancy trigonometry here. Second, the nature of these designs allows you to use the angled facets as part of the final gem (the pavilion breaks in the case of the SRB). No temporary facets here. Pretty sneaky, eh?

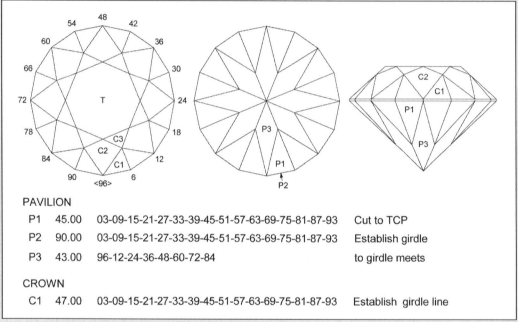

PAVILION

P1	45.00	03-09-15-21-27-33-39-45-51-57-63-69-75-81-87-93	Cut to TCP
P2	90.00	03-09-15-21-27-33-39-45-51-57-63-69-75-81-87-93	Establish girdle
P3	43.00	96-12-24-36-48-60-72-84	to girdle meets

CROWN

C1	47.00	03-09-15-21-27-33-39-45-51-57-63-69-75-81-87-93	Establish girdle line

Figure 17-14 The standard round brilliant cutting prescription uses the CAM technique to establish the gem outline. The P1 facets are the CAM angled facets, and the P2 girdle facets establish the gem outline. See also Figure 16-15.

Converting the distances to cutting angles is a bit more of a chore. The previous section explains that you should begin with the line segment closest to the TCP – that is, the one with the smallest measured distance. For the tourmaline shown here, this is segment B. Segment B will have the steepest CAM facet, and you need to stay shallower than any of the pavilion facets while ensuring that the angle is steep enough to place all of the future girdle meets within the rough (Figure 17-8). This usually means picking an angle that would clearly window in any gemstone material. For mathematical simplicity (a nice way of saying laziness), I selected 35°, well below any reasonable pavilion angle for tourmaline, but perhaps not for diamond. This value appears in the Cutting Angle column for segment B in Table 17-1.

Time to use the formula from page 276 to calculate the remaining cutting angles. Column 4 of Table 17-1 shows the results.

Table 17-1 The index wheel settings and cutting angles corresponding to the arbitrary gem outline. The boldfaced values are fixed and the others calculated relative to them.

Segment	Distance (cm)	Direction	Cutting Angle	Index
A	14.0	0°	27.71°	**0 – 48**
B	10.5	53°	**35.00°**	14 – 62
C	11.2	95°	33.28	25 – 73
D	13.1	119°	29.30	32 – 80

A Prescription for Success

The final step is to assemble the cutting prescription and test it, either using a computer program such as GemCAD (see Chapter 15.3.1) or for the supremely confident, directly on that expensive piece of rough. I am never supremely confident, an attitude well-justified by long and bitter experience.

Here's what to do in GemCAD: Begin by placing the angled facets using the cutting angles and index wheel settings in Table 17-1. Next place 90° facets to create the girdle outline as shown in Figure 17-15. Note from the figure that the GemCAD entries reflect the fact that this design has two-fold radial symmetry. See Chapter 10.7 for clarification.

And you're done! An overlay of the GemCAD drawing on the original image shows that this technique has done a pretty good job (Figure 17-16).

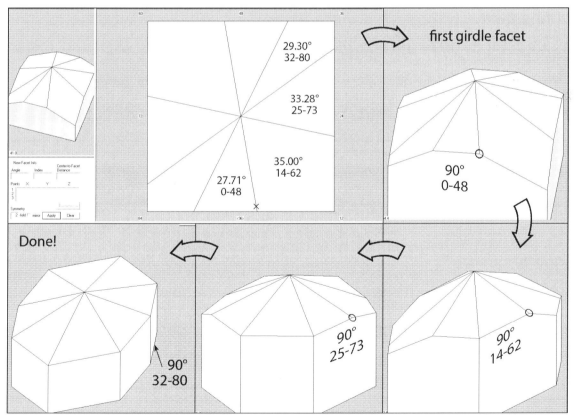

Figure 17-15 Producing the desired gem outline with four pairs of angled facets and their corresponding 90° girdle cuts placed at the circled meet points.

The End is Just the Beginning

This section has explained how to use the Center-point Angle Method to create a set of cutting instructions that will produce an accurate gem outline, thereby maximizing yield. The CAM technique can be applied to almost any circumstance, from the humble rectangular cut to the most spectacular of free-form designs.

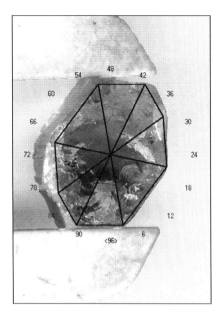

Of course, the design process for this lovely piece of tourmaline has just begun. Carrying these ideas forward to a complete concept is well beyond the scope of this chapter. Chapter 16 provides further tips and insight into the art of gemstone creation. If you just can't stand the suspense, the final gem design, called Scrambler, appears in Chapter 19.2.7.

How well did CAM optimize the design for this odd-shaped piece of tourmaline? Here's the punch line: using the Center-point Angle Method to match the design to the rough gave a carat yield of almost 40%, and most of the loss was due to the height, not the outline, of the final gem. Short version: CAM rules.

Figure 17-16 The prescription derived using the CAM outline technique matches the original gem rough.

Saving Stone with Clever CAM

Establishing the gem outline with a technique like CAM is great – you can produce an arbitrary shape using only a sharp pencil and some sharp wits (and a Sharp calculator, for those who desire a certain consistency of style).

Yes, CAM is great for shaping gems, but did you know that it can also save rough? I don't mean by ensuring that the design matches the shape of the raw stone. That's fairly obvious. It turns out that, independent of the shape of the rough, executing a clever CAM outline can lead to significant savings in stone for some types of gem designs. This allows you to produce a larger, more valuable gem.

To see how, let's take a concrete example, or more accurately, a garnet example. Figure 17-17 shows the facet layout for "Tris de Garnet," a relatively simple but visually interesting triangle cut designed for garnet. More details on Tris de Garnet, including cutting instructions, appear in Chapter 19.1.4.

The "normal" way of producing such a gem outline is to cut the pavilion break facets to a Temporary Center Point, and then to place the girdle facets at the same index wheel settings. In other words, cut B1 and B2 to a TCP, and then cut G1 and G2 at the same indices (Figure 17-18). Cutting the M1 facets to the girdle meet points completes the pavilion. This was how I initially designed the gem. And yes, this is an instance where the CAM facets are the final facets (see "Inadvertent CAM" on page 280).

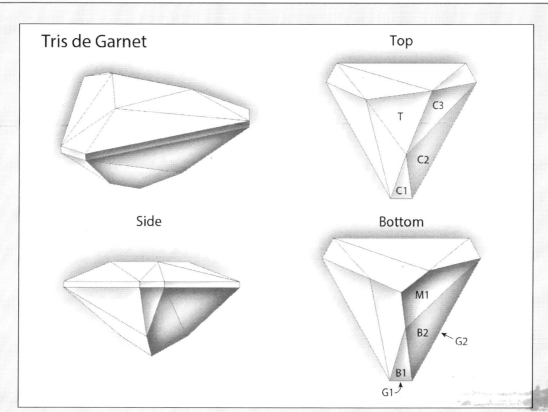

Figure 17-17 The Tris de Garnet gem design.

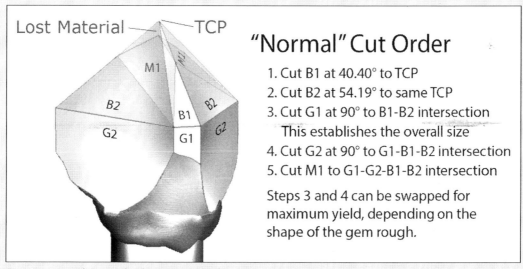

"Normal" Cut Order

1. Cut B1 at 40.40° to TCP
2. Cut B2 at 54.19° to same TCP
3. Cut G1 at 90° to B1-B2 intersection
   This establishes the overall size
4. Cut G2 at 90° to G1-B1-B2 intersection
5. Cut M1 to G1-G2-B1-B2 intersection

Steps 3 and 4 can be swapped for maximum yield, depending on the shape of the gem rough.

Figure 17-18 The standard cutting order for producing the Tris de Garnet pavilion uses B1-B2 and G1-G2 as CAM outline facets. Placing the M1 facets cuts away the Temporary Center Point and results in lost material at the tip of the stone.

Figure 17-18 illustrates an obvious problem with the "normal" cutting order. The tippy-top part of the stone, where the Temporary Center Point was, has been cut away by the subsequent placement of M1. All of the lovely gem rough above the final culet point and the main facets has been lost. Wouldn't it be nice if this didn't have to happen?

Clever CAM to the rescue! Watch…

Instead of cutting B1 and B2 to their final angles, let's tangent-ratio these facets to produce shallower CAM cuts (see Chapters 10.5 and 10.6 if you don't understand the tangent ratio). The exact angles will depend on the shape of the gem rough, but make sure that they are a few degrees shallower than the M1 facets. Sections 17.3.2 and 17.3.3 contain further tips on selecting appropriate CAM angles.

The original gem rough for Tris de Garnet allowed cutting angles of 22.5° and 34° for the CAM angled facets. Cutting 90° facets at the same indices gives the correct gem outline (Figure 17-19).

Now here comes the clever part…Instead of working from the outside in – that is, using the girdle meet points to place the break facets – you can now work from the inside out. In other words, now that the girdle outline is under control, you can cut the M1 facets directly to the center point created by the shallow CAM facets and make it the culet of the final gem.

The first panel of Figure 17-20 shows the result. The intersection of the M1 facets with the girdle creates meet points to place the breaks (center panel). Cutting B1 and B2 at the design angles completes the pavilion (right panel).

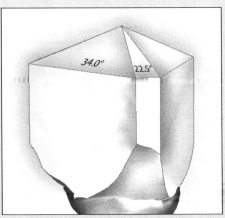

Figure 17-19 Shallow CAM facets give the correct gem outline.

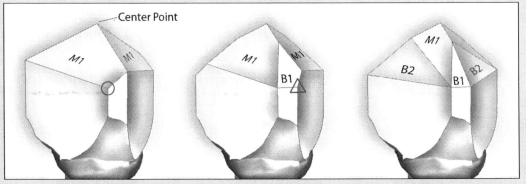

Figure 17-20 Cut the M1 facets to the center point created by the CAM facets (left). This produces target meet points for the B1 facets (circled). Cutting this first tier of breaks (center) creates meet points (triangle symbol) for the final B2 facets (right).

What have you gained? Well, you didn't cut away that tippy-top bit of the gem rough. In fact, this "Clever CAM" has effectively placed the shape higher up in the raw stone, thereby saving valuable gem material. Figure 17-21 makes the situation clear.

In the case of the original Tris de Garnet, there was insufficient rough to produce the final gem size using the "classical" cutting technique – the one in the prescription. At something well north of $40 per carat for top Merelani mint garnet, I faced a difficult choice: cut a smaller stone or abandon the design. In the end – and after lots of playing around in GemCAD – I realized that an inside-out cutting order would allow a larger, more valuable gem. Of course, I had to cut an "extra" CAM outline when it wasn't strictly necessary, but the savings in rough more than made up for the effort.

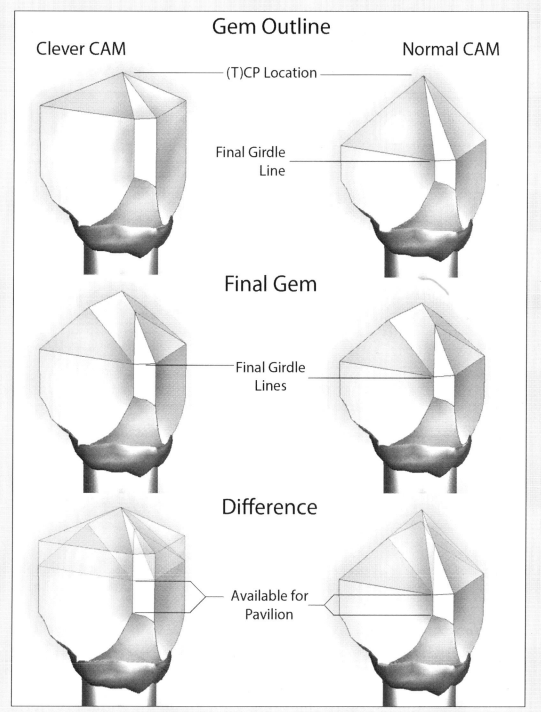

Figure 17-21 A Clever CAM outline (left column) can result in significant savings in gem rough. This may make the difference between having sufficient material for the crown or not. It also can lead to a larger, more valuable stone.

Note that Tris de Garnet has 54° pavilion break facets (B2), quite a large value as these things go. The Clever CAM technique works best for stones that have steeper angled facets meeting the girdle, since the amount of tippy-top that you don't cut away increases for steeper breaks. These savings will be correspondingly lower for designs with moderate angles. Steeper pavilion break angles are a feature of elongated gem designs, as well as those, like Tris de Garnet, which have a combination of narrow (i.e. G1) and wide (G2) girdle facets.

An important cautionary note: not all gem designs feature sets of angled facets, such as B1 and B2, that should be cut to the same TCP to create the gem outline. You should always check the cutting instructions, or do a quick test in a program such as GemCAD.

The Briar Rose case study in Chapter 18 is another example of a gem cut that can benefit from Clever CAM. As you follow the process of conceptual development laid out in that chapter, try to figure out a better sequence for producing the outline. If you get stuck, Chapter 19.2.8 contains both the "classic" and "clever CAM" cutting prescriptions.

Incidentally, there are very few new ideas under the sun (see page 233). Although references to it are hard to find, this Clever CAM technique sounds very much like the Zero Vertical Loss Method advocated by the great gem designer, Fred van Sant.

A final word to appease language lovers who demand precise terminology: You are correct…the Temporary Center Point generated with Clever CAM is not, in fact, temporary.

17.4 The OMNI Method

The OMNI method of achieving an accurate gem outline is second only to the CAM technique in popularity among faceters. The two approaches are quite similar. In both cases, a series of angled facets define a center point, followed by 90° girdle facets which establish the actual outline. Unlike with CAM, however, the inclined facets in the OMNI method are always cut at the same angle and at regularly spaced index wheel settings. This produces a pleasing, symmetric, "brilliant" pattern, and as a result, OMNI facets almost always end up as part of the final design. Of course, since the gem outline will not typically be circularly symmetric, the inclined and girdle facets will not be at the same index wheel settings. This produces an initially uneven girdle line, which must be addressed by subsequent cutting steps. Don't worry if this explanation is a bit overwhelming. All will be made clear below.

Incidentally, if you have absorbed the material in Chapter 16, you are probably experiencing a sense of déjà vu (or for the francophones out there, déjà lu). Barion gemstones match a brilliant pavilion with a non-round gem outline, and in fact, the OMNI method is at the heart of successful barion design (see "The Brilliant Barion" on page 246).

17.4.1 How Does OMNI Work?

The previous paragraphs explain that the OMNI method lets you assemble a gem with a brilliant-type pavilion and a non-round outline. This section examines the motivation and mechanics of OMNI from a slightly different viewpoint: given a desired gem outline (from a sketch, for example), how can you connect the desired girdle facets in a controlled way? As with Section 17.3.1, understanding this material is not a prerequisite to using the OMNI method. Skip ahead to Section 17.4.3 to get started immediately with real-world OMNI.

The first part of this chapter defines the gem outline as a series of line segments at specified index wheel settings and distances from the stone centerline. That is certainly one way to look at the situation, but it is by no means the only way.

Actually, it is simpler to think of the gem outline as simply that: the outline. If asked to sketch your desired gem, you would probably begin by tracing around the perimeter of the cross section of the stone, connecting one segment to the next without thinking about how far each one is from the center.

There is a fundamental problem with this approach, however, and it involves figuring out exactly where to place the 90° girdle facets. Let's take the simple case of the six-sided outline shown in Figure 17-22. Measuring this sketch as described in Section 17.3.3 yields index wheel settings of 12-20-44-52-76-84. Note that these settings are not uniformly spaced.

Right. Time to dive right in and cut the first girdle facet at index 12. The shape and internal qualities of the gem rough will determine its exact distance from the centerline, and in most instances, this choice will establish the final size of the gem. Figure 5-30 shows the general idea.

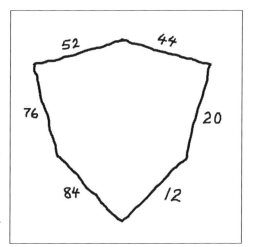

Well that was easy. Time to move on to the second girdle facet. You dial in index 20 and start cutting. Almost immediately, a worrying question floats up from the back of your mind. You knew how to start cutting this second girdle facet, but how – and more importantly, when – do you stop? The rightmost panel of Figure 17-23 illustrates the conundrum.

Figure 17-22 Sketching the outline of a six-sided triangular shield design. Measuring the angles of the perimeter segments gives the appropriate index wheel settings, here for a 96-tooth gear. Section 17.3.3 explains how to do this.

Like a ship in fog, you have no reference points to guide you to the correct depth of cut. You could, in principle, stop almost immediately or grind the entire stone away. In any case, you will almost certainly not guess the correct depth.

Yes, it is possible to measure the depth of cut from the sketch (as in Figure 17-13), but most faceting machines do not have accurate mast height adjustment. Nor do they make it easy to set the distance of a facet from the gem centerline. Also, machine flexure and other effects complicate the process, particularly when the quill is horizontal (see Section 17.2). Achiev-

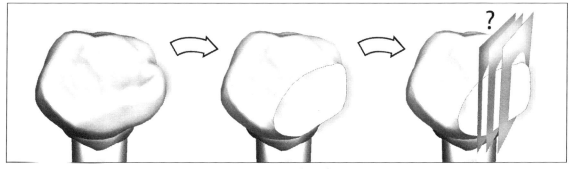

Figure 17-23 Cutting an initial 90° facet at index 12 based on the shape and internal flaws of the rough gem is straightforward, but where do you place the second cut?

ing an accurate outline can be very difficult, even for symmetric stones, which require no mast height changes at all. This is why the cutting prescription for that most symmetric of gems, the standard round brilliant, starts with a temporary center point and ends with the girdle. Turn back to page 270 for more opinion on this issue.

You clearly need some sort of reference to help place the second and subsequent girdle facets. OMNI provides that reference.

The heart and soul of the OMNI technique is the use of *equally spaced, angled facets* to clear away the metaphorical fog and establish reference meet points for cutting the girdle. These facets are cut at the same angle and at uniformly spaced index wheel settings, (for example, six facets cut at 43° at index 8-24-40-56-72-88 on a 96-tooth wheel – see top center panel of Figure 17-24). They form a center point and a series of radial edges, which intersect the future girdle and provide meet point targets. This sounds a lot more complicated than it is. Read on…

OMNI takes advantage of the fact that the intersection of two planes defines a line, while the intersection of three planes defines a point (Persnickety geometers would insist on use of the term "non-parallel planes." You can always spot the persnickety geometers: they are the ones sitting with the nerdy physicists at parties – see page 122.)

For OMNI, the three planes consist of two of the angled facets and one girdle facet. As with CAM, a pair of angled facets and the first 90° cut define the meet point target for the second 90° facet. This second girdle cut, coupled with the next pair of angled facets, forms the meet point reference for the third girdle cut, and so on around the stone. Let's take the outline and index settings shown in Figure 17-22. Putting the previous sentences into practice results in the OMNI outline sequence shown in Figure 17-24. Note that the angled and girdle facets do not have the same index, producing an uneven girdle line.

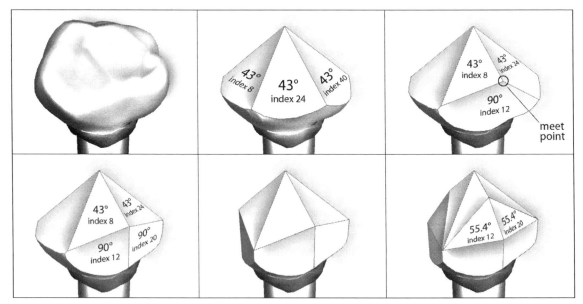

Figure 17-24 Two angled facets and one girdle facet form the meet point reference for subsequent girdle cuts. Original gem rough (top left panel). Six equally spaced, angled facets cut to a center point (top middle). The first girdle facet at index 12 (top right). Note that it does not have the same index wheel setting as either angled facet that it intersects. The second 90° facet cut at index 20 to the meet point created by the first (bottom left). The completed gem outline (bottom middle). Note the uneven girdle line. This can be corrected by a set of intermediate angle facets at the same index wheel settings as the girdle (bottom right).

17.4.2 Symmetry: The Key to OMNIpotence

It all sounds beautiful and easy…just cut a series of angled facets at regular index wheel settings to a center point, and then chop out your gem according to the indices corresponding to the actual outline you want. Yes, yes. This gives an uneven girdle line, but that's what later facets are for, anyway.

OMNI is particularly nice in that you can cut the angled facets with a single mast height setting, and the regular symmetry means that, in the final gem, these facets will look great as-is. All is well with the world. Right?

Well, partially right. The fly in the ointment is that the regularly spaced index settings for the angled facets restrict the girdle meet points to a series of radial lines (Figure 17-25). This was not a problem for the outline in Figure 17-22, due to the simple symmetry of the design. However, if a set of symmetric radial lines misses a bunch of your girdle intersections, you are out of luck.

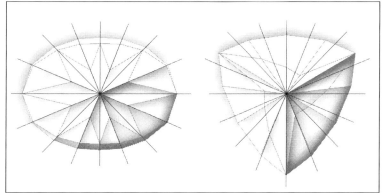

Figure 17-25 The OMNI technique restricts the vertices of the gem outline to a series of evenly spaced radial lines. The left-hand outline is fine for this sixteen-fold symmetry. The right-hand one is not.

There are a couple of ways around this restriction. First, you can start with more angled facets cut through the center point. More radial lines mean more meet point possibilities for defining the gem outline. Of course, this solution can cause additional problems. For example, cutting 96 angled facets would be a time consuming nightmare, and it would use up all of the index wheel settings needed to add visual interest with later facets.

The other option is to break the symmetry of the angled facets, for example, by not cutting them at regularly spaced index wheel settings or constant angles. Bonus points if you recognize the CAM technique as just such a generalization of OMNI. Many oval gem designs do precisely this to accommodate the more distant girdle facets. Nevertheless, it can be a bit of a chore to determine which set of index settings and angles will produce the direction you want. More on this in Section 17.5…

Given all these considerations, the key to the OMNI technique is to find the correct symmetry for the angled facets. For some designs, such as the triangle shield shown in Figure 17-22, the choice is obvious and straightforward.

For more complex or free form designs, however, I recommend using a simple mechanical aid, such as an OMNI protractor (see next page). The next section uses this device to help execute a real-world OMNI outline.

An OMNI Protractor

The OMNI technique lets you "connect the dots" to create a gem outline, as long as those dots lie along a set of radial lines created by equally spaced, angled facets intersecting at a center point. But how can you pick the best set of radial lines? In other words, which index settings should you use for these angled facets?

Assuming that you are working from a sketch of the desired gem, the best way may be to generate an overlay printed on transparent plastic (Figure 17-26). As with the CAM protractor described on page 275, you can use several methods to produce the overlay, ranging from an indelible thin-line marker on an overhead projector transparency to fancy drawing programs and laser printers. And yes, computer virtuosi can execute the entire process, from sketch to final design, using electrons alone.

The overlay should include all simple symmetries for each index wheel. This is 6, 8, 12, 16, and 24-fold symmetry for a 96-tooth wheel. Lower symmetries are possible (see Table 10-2) but they are effectively covered by this group of five. Placing the overlay on the sketch allows you to try various symmetries for the best match before committing to your OMNI facets. Section 17.4.3 uses just such a tool to generate a Barion-type keystone pavilion.

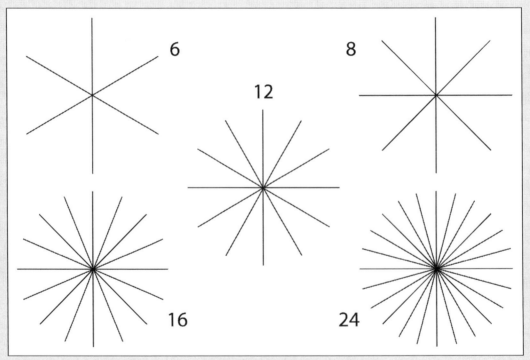

Figure 17-26 A series of radial lines with various symmetries printed on plastic helps with the selection of correct index wheel settings for the OMNI method. As with the CAM protractor in the previous section, you can download printable versions of the OMNI overlay at this book's website: www.facet-ingbook.com.

17.4.3 Real World OMNI

For those of us who hate learning from textbooks, the OMNI method offers two profound benefits. First, it is blessedly free of trigonometry, and second, the best way to understand

OMNI it is to actually do it. This section will use the OMNI technique to generate the gem outline for a keystone cut, called Keystar.

As often happens, the original inspiration for the gem design came from a beautiful piece of rough – in this case, a flawless portion of a larger crystal of Nigerian rubellite – as well as an existing gem cut (see Chapter 16.2.4). Figure 17-27 captures the outline of Keystar in the form of a sketch.

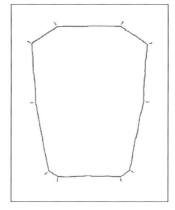

Figure 17-27 The desired keystone gem outline. Note that the long sides are broken into two segments.

We interrupt this explanation of the OMNI technique for a brief intermission on the practicalities of gem design, (an intermission which arguably belongs in Chapter 16). Note the split in the middle of the long sides in Figure 17-27. Although single segments would have been a better match to the original rough, splitting the long sides creates a pair of targets for subsequent pavilion facets, which in turn produce greater visual interest.

End of intermission…time to wield the mighty OMNI protractor.

Take up your OMNI protractor, whether it be a piece of transparent plastic, a sheet of tracing paper, or a digital image file, and overlay it on the sketch of the gem outline. Try different degrees of symmetry in order to achieve a decent match to as many vertices of the keystone as possible. A few moments of concentrated play should lead you to the conclusion that sixteen-fold symmetry does a reasonable job of hitting the target vertices (Figure 17-28). The necessary angled facets will then fall at index settings 3-9-15-21-27-33-39-45-51-57-63-69-75-81-87-93. The two outer corners on the bottom are problematic, but you can use a trick to nail those ones as well. More on this presently…

The next step is to use the same method as with CAM to estimate the correct index wheel settings for the 90° girdle facets. If necessary, turn to Section 17.3.3 for a refresher.

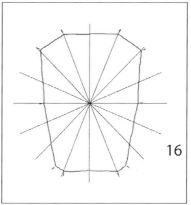

Figure 17-28 Sixteen-fold symmetry matches the keystone shape reasonably well. Eight of the ten vertices lie close to the radial lines.

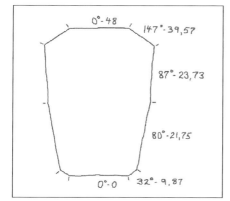

Figure 17-29 The measured angles and index wheel settings for the keystone gem outline.

As before, you can use the CAM protractor overlay or a regular protractor and some simple math. This yields the index settings shown in Figure 17-29.

With the correct index wheel settings in hand for both the angled and 90° facets, you are ready to start cutting the OMNI outline, at least in the low-risk world of GemCAD.

Begin with the sixteen angled facets cut to a center point. The exercise with the overlay (Figure 17-28) told you that these should be placed at index settings 3 9 15-…-81-87-93 to produce a left-right symmetric pattern. As with the CAM technique, it is generally best to select a cutting angle well above the shallowest pavilion facet, although as noted above, OMNI angled facets often form part of the final design. Here, you should use 35° – like the kiddie pool, shallow enough to keep almost anyone out of trouble. Figure 17-30 shows the outcome of the first cut.

Before embarking on the 90° facets, let's pause for a bit of strategic thinking. You know that each girdle cut forms the meet point for the next one (Figure 17-24). You also know that the girdle intersections at the bottom outer corners will cause trouble, since they don't really fall along the sixteen-fold radial lines (Figure 17-28). It makes sense, then, to do as much as you can with standard OMNI before resorting to more complicated measures. This means starting at the "top" of the gem – i.e. index 48 – and working your way as much as possible around the stone. Of course, with real material, other factors, such as the shape of the gem rough or inclusions, might alter this approach.

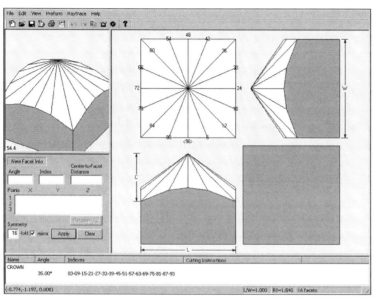

Figure 17-30 The sixteen angled facets cut to a temporary center point.

Enough strategizing. Begin with the first 90° girdle facet at index 48. This cut will establish the overall size of the gem and create two meet points for subsequent girdle facets (Figure 17-31).

With a couple of clear targets in view, you can dial in index settings 39 and 57 and cut the second pair of 90° facets. This, in turn, will generate meet points for the third pair of girdle facets at 23-73. And, like any civic-minded OMNI facet, this pair of cuts will pass on the goodness, establishing the meets for 21-75. It all runs smooth as clockwork (Figure 17-32).

Smooth as clockwork, that is, until you need an extra hour-marker between 4 and 5. You have completed all of the possible 90° cuts, given the sixteen-fold symmetry of the angled facets. To proceed, you will need some sort of reference point for the girdle cuts at 9-87.

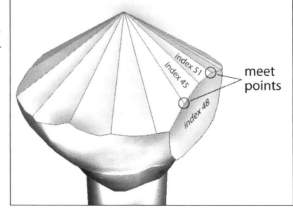

Figure 17-31 The first 90° facet at index 48 establishes two meet points for the subsequent cuts.

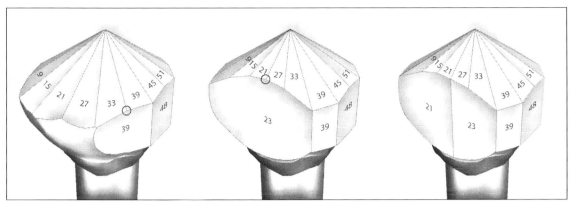

Figure 17-32 Daisy-chaining of girdle meet points in the OMNI technique. The girdle is level at index 39-57 and 21-75, since both the angled and 90° facets share these settings.

Finessing Additional Meet Points with OMNI

Here's a cool trick. Recall that the major difference between the CAM and OMNI methods is that for OMNI, the angled and 90° facets are not, in general, cut at the same index wheel settings. This results in an uneven girdle line, which is particularly apparent in Figure 17-32. Additional angled facets, cut at the same index settings as the girdle, can correct the situation (see the lower right panel of Figure 17-24 and Figure 16-21).

So. You have to level the girdle anyway. Why not kill two birds with one stone and establish the meet points for the rest of the gem outline at the same time?

Here's how. Note that there are both angled and 90° facets at index settings 39-57. Hence, this location represents the level girdle line (yes, index settings 21-75 also match, but 39-57 is the deepest point on the girdle line). You will need to place additional inclined facets at index settings 23-73 and 21-75 to continue the level girdle. Eagle-eyed readers will also note the necessity of such a cut at index 48. And yes, these facets are, in fact, the equivalent of the famous "half-moons" in the Barion gem design, (see "The Brilliant Barion" on page 246).

These girdle-leveling facets are generally steep, in order to avoid cutting away too much of the existing facets. This is particularly true if, as usually occurs, the OMNI angled facets form part of the final design. Note, however, that you should limit the cutting angle to about 70° or less to avoid dirty looks from whomever has to eventually mount the gem in jewelry.

In general, these steep half-moon facets do not hurt the overall optical performance of the gem. In fact, they are often used to deepen the pavilion of a design and, according to many, produce better colour from less-saturated gem rough. Turn to Section 10.5.2 for my admittedly controversial opinion on this issue.

Based on experience and a little fooling around with GemCAD, you should cut the first set of steep facets at 70° and index 23-73 through the meet points on the deepest girdle line. This produces a pair of new meet points on each side of the gem (square symbols in Figure 17-33).

With two meet points, you just need an index to define the next angled facet (see Table 16-1), but you already know that this facet must be at 21-75 to produce a level girdle. After you have entered the two meet points and the required index, GemCAD informs you that the

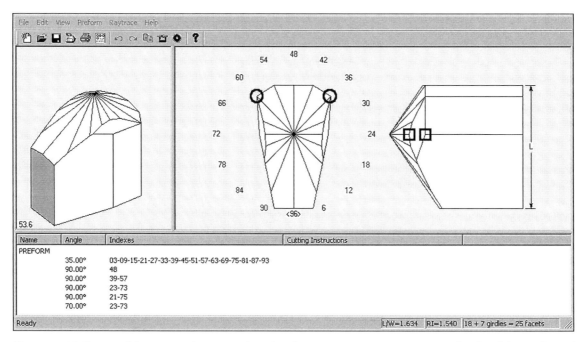

Figure 17-33 Steep 70° facets at index 23-73 placed at the pre-existing meet points (circles) level the girdle and create two pairs of new meet points for the next steep facets (squares).

appropriate cutting angle is 70.32°, which seems like a fine angle – relatively close to that of the previous half-moon facets and nowhere near a value that will get you in trouble with either windowing or your jeweller (Figure 17-34).

These facets have (surprise!) produced a new pair of lovely meet points on the girdle, close to the locations you need, the two vertices on the original sketch that did not correspond to sixteen-fold symmetry (Figure 17-34). These meet points will allow you to complete the girdle.

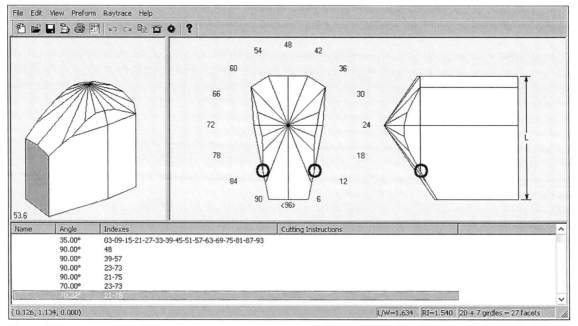

Figure 17-34 A second pair of steep facets at 21-75 continues the process of leveling the girdle, and also produces the sought-after reference points (circles) for completing the gem outline.

You are almost done. Using the newly created meet points, you can continue with the girdle facets and complete the gem outline. A pair of 90° cuts at index 9-87 produces the targets for the final girdle facet at index setting 0. The result is a completed gem outline very close to the original goal (Figure 17-35).

Congratulations! Your OMNI outline is complete!

A final note: This exercise is based on the Keystar gem design from Chapter 19.2.5. Take a careful look at the cutting prescription. As so often happens, the OMNI facets themselves ended up in the final design.

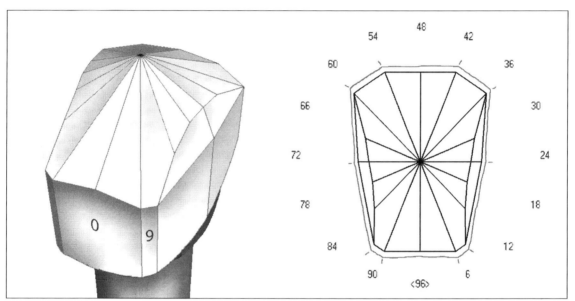

Figure 17-35 Placing the final girdle cuts at index 9-87 and 0 completes the gem outline. A comparison with the original sketch (right) shows how well you have done.

CAM versus OMNI

So far, this chapter has highlighted the two most important strategies for establishing the gem outline, the Centerline Angle Method (CAM) and the OMNI technique.

Which one should you use?

The answer sounds facetious: Just use the one that works best under the circumstances. Figuring out which one this actually is takes experience, and unsurprisingly, it depends a great deal on the gem design you are aiming for.

CAM allows exquisite control over the outline, and it is not dependent on your having girdle vertices that line up with nice, evenly-spaced, symmetric locations. CAM outlines also naturally produce a level girdle line without additional steep, Barion-type facets.

On the other hand, the OMNI technique unquestionably involves fewer changes of cutting angle and mast height, and the OMNI facets usually appear in the final design, thereby saving effort. Some faceters also claim that the OMNI method requires less extra gem rough. In any case, it is very clear that CAM does not do well on elongated designs, since this requires a large range of cutting angles, meaning you either run out of stone or are forced to cut uncomfortably steep angled facets. "Clever CAM" can help in these circumstances (see page 282).

The short answer is that, if the design is naturally simple and symmetric, or if you are aiming for a more deep-bellied, brilliant pavilion, try the OMNI method. Otherwise, go with CAM. In either case, it is safest and best – and in my view, mandatory – to test cut the gem outline in a program such as GemCAD.

17.5 Corner Locator Angle Method (CLAM)

The CAM and OMNI approaches are by far the most popular methods for establishing the gem outline, but there are times when neither will do. This has spawned the development of a third technique, called the Corner Locator Angle Method, or CLAM.

In many ways, CLAM is a variant of OMNI, in that the goal is to establish radial lines outward from a center point to generate meet points for the 90° girdle cuts (see Section 17.4). As with the OMNI method, CLAM facets also frequently end up as part of the gem design. Unlike OMNI, however, the cutting angles are not equal, and the index wheel settings are not symmetric and evenly spaced.

The basic goal of CLAM is to use a pair of angled facets to establish a direction out to a future girdle vertex – hence the name "corner locator." Figuring out the correct combination of angled facets to produce the desired direction is a matter of calculation (see below) or experimentation (hopefully in GemCAD and not in expensive stone).

Note that this section, unlike those which previously dealt with CAM and OMNI, will combine theory, practice, and a real-world example into one happy bundle.

Figure 17-36 shows the desired gem outline, including the girdle facet index wheel settings measured exactly as with CAM and OMNI (turn back to previous sections, if you don't understand how to do this).

Time to sit down at the virtual faceting machine known as GemCAD. You will begin by generating four angled facets to create the temporary center point. Since you know that the design will be elongated left-right, it makes sense to place these facets with index wheel settings somewhere near the top and bottom, that is, near index 0 and 48 on a 96-tooth wheel (think about it…this actually does make sense).

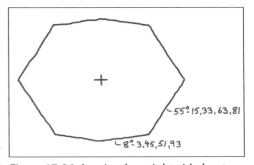

Figure 17-36 A simple eight-sided stone whose shape will be established using the CLAM technique. Due to the two-fold, mirror symmetry, two segments define the entire outline.

Again, absent other considerations, it seems sensible to start with a level girdle line by selecting the same index wheel settings for the angled facets as for the girdle cuts measured in Figure 17-36 (see the first paragraph of Section 17.3 for more on this). The plan is to use these angled facets in the final design, so a cutting angle of 41° seems reasonable. Figure 17-36 dictates index settings of 3-45-51-93 for this initial cut. Figure 17-37 shows the result.

Incidentally, don't worry at this stage if these choices seem arbitrary or difficult to figure out for yourself. They will make more sense as you gain experience in gem design, and besides, the real goal here is to illustrate the motivation and mechanics of CLAM. Onward…

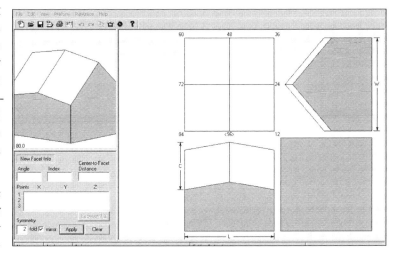

Figure 17-37 Four angled facets at 41° placed at the same index wheel settings as the corresponding segments of the future girdle.

You can now go ahead and cut the first 90° girdle facets at index 3 and 93. This sets the ultimate size of the gem (Figure 17-38). In principle, you could also cut the other two facets of this tier at 45-51, but if you were working with real stone and not electrons, these facets would require accurate 90° cuts to the exact same depth, since there are not (yet) any meet points to guide you (see the tip on page 258 about test cutting in GemCAD for more about this). As a result, you should forego the 45-51 girdle facets for the moment.

What next? Great question…no easy answer.

It turns out that you are in a very similar situation to that portrayed in Figure 17-23 in the previous section. The next 90° facets are at index 15-81, but there is no way to tell how deep to cut them: there is no meet point defining the intersection of the girdle facets at index 3 and 15 (or 93 and 81). To proceed, you will need a method to locate the corner. Guess which one you'll use…

The heart and soul of the Corner Locator Angle Method is to cut two sets of facets to the same center point, but at different angles and index wheel settings. These facets intersect, producing radial lines outward from the center point in (hopefully) controlled directions. As with the OMNI method, these radial lines will produce meet point targets for the girdle cuts which will define the gem outline.

A quick bit of protractor work on the sketch (Figure 17-36) indicates that you need such radial lines at about 42° from the six o'clock (or index zero) position (Figure 17-39).

Time to locate some corners…The initial angled facets at 41° and index 3-45-51-93 established the center point. Now cut four more facets to this center point at 38.5° with index wheel settings 6-42-54-90 (Figure 17-40).

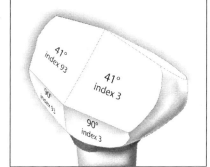

Figure 17-38 The first two 90° facets begin the girdle and establish the overall size of the gem.

Look! Four wonderful radial lines at approximately 42°! Exactly what you need to go forward. Ain't CLAM great?

Well, mostly yes. While the applause slowly dies down, that smart kid in the front row asks how you magically knew the cutting angle and index settings for the second set of angled facets. Hmmph – that kid will probably become a persnickety geometer one day...

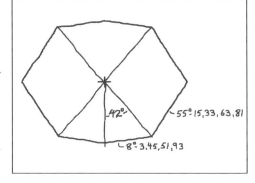

Figure 17-39 Radial lines at 42° from the center point locate the required corners of the gem outline.

It's actually a great question, and the answer can be as simple or as complicated as anything in this book. At one level, experience allows a very good guess of facet combinations to produce the desired outcome. Alternatively, a few minutes of play in a program such as GemCAD leads directly to a workable set of angled facets. Just make sure to use the Windows version, with plenty of levels of Undo. For the hard-core folk out there, the ones who are geometrically inclined, there is even a mathematical solution. Read on...

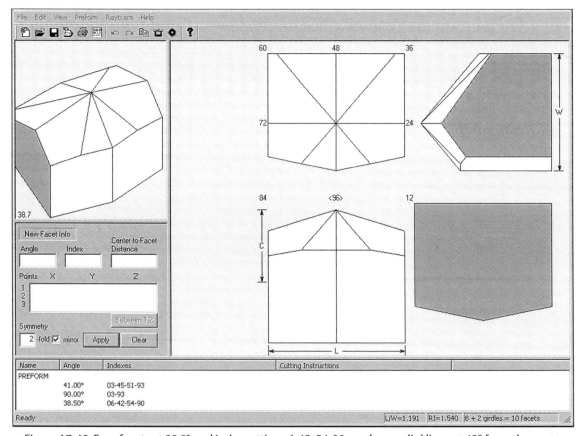

Figure 17-40 Four facets at 38.5° and index settings 6-42-54-90 produce radial lines at 42° from the center point, in exactly the correct direction to locate the future corners of the gem.

17.5.1 CLAM Math

Note: This section describes the mathematics of the Corner Locator Angle Method. Understanding this material is not a prerequisite to successfully using CLAM, particularly if you can work with GemCAD to find suitable angles and index settings.

The Corner Locator Angle Method uses two sets of angled facets cut through the same center point to define radial directions to the vertices of the gem outline. This procedure is readily expressible in terms of geometric entities such as points, lines, and planes. Figuring out how to cut a pair of angled facets to produce a controlled radial direction is then just a matter of solving a few trigonometric equations. Nothing could be simpler.

(...nervous chuckle and adjustment of necktie...)

Actually, many things are simpler, and the equations required for CLAM are somewhat ugly, even if the idea is straightforward. No matter...Let's forge ahead.

CLAM locates the corner by intersecting two planes – in other words, two facets. Chapter 2.1.1 explains that the location of such facets can be defined by two angles and a distance, the equivalent of cutting angle, index wheel setting, and mast height.

It turns out that there is another, geometrically identical way of defining a plane using a reference point on the plane and a direction perpendicular to it. Figure 17-41 compares these two definitions.

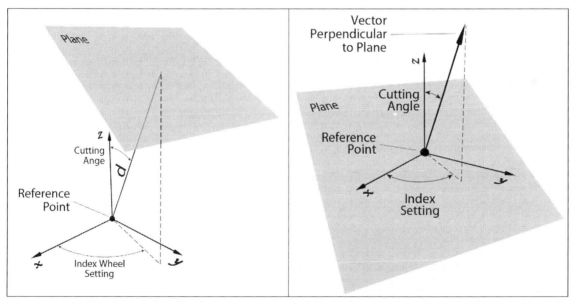

Figure 17-41 A flat plane defined by the cutting angle, index wheel setting, and distance d from a point (left). A flat plane defined by a reference point on the plane and a direction vector (right). This direction vector is a combination of the cutting angle and index wheel setting.

The CLAM technique uses two angled facets through the same center point. Look again at the right panel of Figure 17-41. If this center point is the reference, the description of a facet can be simplified to just the direction vector. With CLAM, the intersecting facets share the same reference point, and hence the geometry simplifies to two vectors (Figure 17-42).

Look carefully at Figure 17-42. The goal is to know and control the direction of the intersection line between the two planes. More specifically, you want to be able to dial in facets – or equivalently find the direction vectors – which produce the desired line in the X-Y plane (i.e. as viewed from above). Even more specifically, you want to pick cutting angles and indices which produce the target angle θ.

The key to solving this conundrum is the realization that the line of intersection of the two planes is perpendicular to both of the direction vectors. Yup...another information rich sentence. Read it again and use Figure 17-42 to convince yourself that it's true.

Once you recognize the essential perpendicularity of the situation, you can bring some fairly standard mathematical tools to bear. For example, the so-called cross-product of two vectors is a third vector perpendicular to both of them. Sounds pretty useful, given the geometry of this intersection problem.

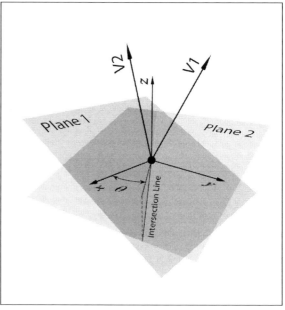

Figure 17-42 Two angled facets cut through the same center point intersect to form a radial line at angle θ in the x-y plane. The two vectors, labeled V1 and V2, are perpendicular to their respective planes.

From this point on, it's just math. Pretty gory math, but math nonetheless. The result is a fairly simple prescription for calculating the direction of the intersection line of two facets.

Mathematical Prescription for CLAM

For each angled facet, define two quantities related to the index wheel setting and cutting angle:

$$R = \tan i \quad \text{and} \quad Q = \frac{1}{\tan c \cdot \cos i} \, ,$$

where c is the cutting angle and i is the index wheel angle. Note that both of these angles are measured in degrees, and hence:

$$i = \text{index} \cdot D \, ,$$

where D is the number of angular degrees per index wheel step (3.75 for a 96 tooth gear).

The intersection line between the facets lies at angle θ given by:

$$\theta = \tan^{-1} \left(\frac{Q_1 - Q_2}{R_1 \cdot Q_2 - R_2 \cdot Q_1} \right) \, ,$$

where the 1 and 2 subscripts refer to the individual intersecting facets. This equation gives the direction of the CLAM locator line for any combination of facets. Pretty neat, and a fun mathematical adventure if you want to derive it yourself, but you need cutting instructions, not the direction of a line. Is this equation of any use?

Yes, partially. The problem is that mathematics is not magic, and you can't get more information out than you put in. Specifically, this equation supplies the direction θ for four input variables (two cutting angles and two index settings). Different combinations of cutting angles and indices can, in fact, produce the same θ (you may recognize that tangent ratio scaling is a special case of this fact – one which seeks to change c without altering i or θ).

As a result, it is not possible to derive a unique pair of facets for a given θ. In mathematical terms, this is a many-to-one problem. The formula can help if you supply some of the inputs, however. For example, if you know the cutting angle and index for facet 1, and the index wheel setting for facet 2, you can uniquely determine the cutting angle for facet 2 to produce the desired direction. Here's the answer (and it's another amusing derivation for the mathematically brave):

$$c_2 = \tan^{-1}\left(\frac{\sqrt{1+R_2^2}}{Q_1} \cdot \frac{1+R_1 \cdot \tan\theta}{1+R_2 \cdot \tan\theta}\right).$$

For the gem outline you are working on here, facet 1 has cutting angle 41° and index angle 11.25° (index 3 and 3.75° per tooth – see Figures 17-36 and 17-37). The second facet has index angle 22.5° for the assumed index (6). This gives:

$$R_1 = 0.199 \; ; \; R_2 = 0.414 \; ; \; Q_1 = 1.173,$$

which, when plugged into the previous equation, yields:

$$c_2 = 38.40°$$

This is within a tenth of a degree of the value I came up with by playing in GemCAD (see Figure 17-40), and in fact, it yields an intersection line exactly, not approximately, 42° from the 96-index position. CLAM really can locate corners!

The foregoing assumed an index for facet 2 and calculated the cutting angle c. In principle, similar manipulations would yield the index wheel setting for a given cutting angle, but the mathematics is far more gory. I would also argue that working CLAM this way doesn't make much sense. You would almost certainly end up with a fractional index setting, such as 12.347, which would require you to round off and calculate the cutting angle anyway. In my view, it is far better to pick a reasonable index and derive the angle from the equation above. And here's a final, somewhat sheepish admission: I never use these equations…for me, playing in GemCAD is a quicker way to CLAM.

17.5.2 CLAMming Up

Phew! Enough math. Time to finish the gem outline…

With the corner accurately located, you can now place the next 90° girdle cut with index 15 at the intersection of the first girdle facet and the CLAM intersection line (top left panel of Figure 17-43). This, in turn, generates the meet point for the next girdle facet at index 33 (top right panel). In fact, this process generates a cascade of meet points around the stone, allowing you to complete the desired girdle outline accurately and effortlessly. Figure 17-44 shows how well the CLAM technique reproduces the desired shape.

As with the examples for CAM and OMNI, the CLAM gem outline establishes a firm foundation, but the process of gem design has just begun. This exercise ultimately resulted in

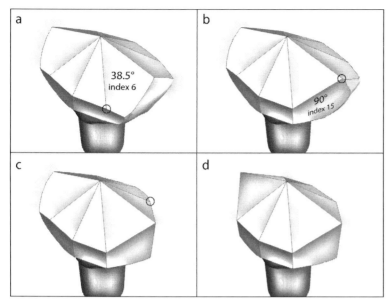

Figure 17-43 The Corner Locator Angle Method produces reference meet points to establish the gem outline. The first 38.5° facet locates the corner, producing a girdle meet (circled in a); A 90° cut through this meet point at index 15 generates the next meet point for the girdle facet at index 33 (panel b); Placing the next girdle facet generates the meet point for the 90° cuts at 45 and 51 (panel c); Cascading meet points around the stone lets you complete the gem outline (panel d).

CLAMour, a bright yet simple gemstone design for garnet. You can find the cutting prescription for CLAMour in Chapter 19.1.5.

Bonus questions: the gem outline for CLAMour is slightly modified from the one shown here. Can you spot the difference? Can you explain it?

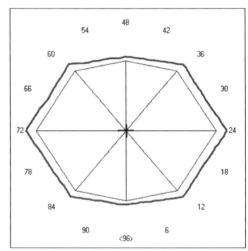

Figure 17-44 A comparison of the CLAM gem outline with the original sketch shows how well you have done.

17.6 A Final Word on Gem Outlines

I know. This chapter contains a lot of information and a lot of math.

Nevertheless, I hope that you now appreciate that the CAM, OMNI, and CLAM methods (and even ECED) are at the very heart of both gem cutting and design. Mastering these techniques will enable you to produce almost any gem outline imaginable, and they should open the door to your own novel designs.

18

Case Study: Designing the Briar Rose

In emphasizing the diversity of approaches to solving a problem, my high school geometry teacher used to say that "there are many ways to skin a cat." This is doubly true of the process of gemstone design, which, after all, combines geometry with artistic creativity. Ultimately, you will have to explore your own path, but there are certain strategies and techniques which can improve the likelihood of a successful outcome.

Chapter 16 addresses the general issue of gemstone design, including working with sources of inspiration and identifying helpful tools. It also provides a semi-random collection of tips and tricks for getting the job done. Chapter 17 covers the critical issue of establishing an exact outline as the foundation of the gem. With all the necessary background information in place, it is now time to bring your knowledge together in a real-world example of gem design.

This chapter follows the full cycle of development of a new gemstone cut, called Briar Rose, from inspiration and conception to design and optimization. This is not intended to be an exhaustive explanation of how to create new and interesting gemstone designs – no textbook could explain that. Rather, this chapter is a case study of a single design. Hopefully, you will find the approaches illuminating and useful. Note also that this chapter uses GemCAD and BOG for design and optimization, respectively. Following the process on your computer will also give insight into how these programs work.

18.1 Royal Inspiration

Chapter 16.1 explores a number of sources of creative inspiration. These include building on an existing gem cut, mimicking objects or phenomena such as flowers and stars, pursuing a specific design goal such as maximizing scintillation, drawing inspiration from the natural shape of the gem rough, and indulging in random play at the computer or faceting machine.

As explained on page 227, these (and other) sources of inspiration can be combined. In the case of the Briar Rose, the creative impetus came from two directions. First, I managed to acquire a very beautiful piece of blue-green tourmaline (Figure 18-1). Material of this colour and quality has sadly become more and more rare in recent years. It has also become increasingly expensive. Therefore, any design would have to maximize the yield from this natural crystal shape.

Figure 18-1 The tourmaline rough that inspired Briar Rose. Note that this image is from a flatbed scanner. It is an extract of my rough log for a gem show. See page 206 of Volume 1 for an explanation.

The second inspiration was a desire to attempt a conventional design – the Princess cut – in a non-conventional shape: the distorted hexagonal outline of a natural tourmaline crystal.

Figure 18-2 shows a typical, square Princess cut. Note how the pavilion facets radiate away from the corners. The overlying crown facets echo this layout, resulting in multiple, large flashes. Given good body colour in the gem rough, the Princess design produces spectacular results.

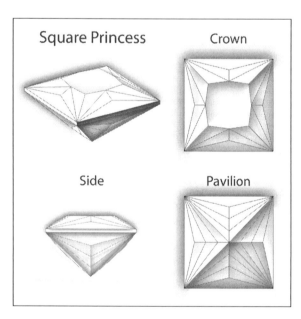

But how can you cut a rectangular design in a (distorted) hexagon? It's sort of like hammering a square peg into a round hole.

Doodling. That's how. A combination of playing around with pencil, paper, and computer led to the concept in Figure 18-3. As with the original Princess, the "Hexed Princess" has pavilion fan facets radiating away from its corners. To maximize sparkle, it features non-overlapping crown facets offset from the pavilion facet fans. See page 254 for more on getting the pavilion and crown facets to work together.

Figure 18-2 A square Princess-type cut showing the fan-type facets radiating from the corners.

While this sketch is admittedly relatively crude, all of the elements are in place to begin working with GemCAD. Developing an initial inspiration into a workable concept such as that in Figure 18-3 is not a straightforward, linear process. Nor is there a simple way to explain how to do it. In the case of Briar Rose, it took me about a week, broken up into scattered sessions of thinking and sketching, interspersed with longer periods of inactivity and passive mental "brewing." Your particular experience will almost certainly differ, but you should expect that your brainstorming will be governed by both external and internal factors, such as other distractions, perceived progress, and so on. You should not rush this critical, creative phase of the process, however. Let your design grow along with your relationship to it.

18.1.1 The Briar Rose Design Concept

Figure 18-3 shows that Briar Rose is a relatively conventional design, in the sense that it is symmetric, has a centered culet, and generally doesn't "break the rules" of a traditional gemstone. There are challenges, however. For example, multiple facets radiating from a single girdle vertex inevitably lead to a series of tiers with similar angles, similar indices, or both. Such a design can be difficult to cut if your faceting machine is out of alignment or does not allow accurate angle settings at the 0.1 degree level (see also page 256).

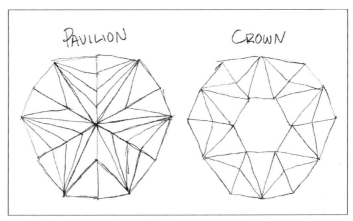

Figure 18-3 Pencil sketch of Briar Rose. Note how the pavilion and crown fan facets are at alternating points on the gem outline. This should maximize scintillation, although it is admittedly a slight twist on the classic Princess approach.

In order to maximize yield, the Briar Rose design adopts a girdle outline close to the shape of the original, tourmaline crystal. This choice also naturally places the symmetry (i.e. dop) axis of the stone along the c-axis of the crystal, hopefully maximizing the impact of the stone's fine colour (see page 232 of Volume 1). Tourmaline is pleochroic. Choosing a skewed symmetry axis will mix the colours from the various axes. While sometimes desirable, the results can be disappointing and are almost always a little surprising.

A Rose by Any Other Name

Naming your gemstone design is part of the creative process, and settling on an appropriate moniker can be both fun and frustrating. And, just as different designers approach a new project differently, you will encounter a variety of philosophies regarding the naming of gem cuts.

For example, some designers choose a very literal name, or one that indicates a logical placement in a sequence of designs. "Garnet Oval Barion" or "Marquise #7" are obvious (if fictional) examples of this type. Others personalize the design, naming it either eponymously or in honour of a friend or public figure. "George's Brilliant" or "A Heart for Suzie" fall into this category. A third approach, to which I subscribe, is to name the design for a particular unique aspect or association. The "Green Flash" and "Slice" designs in Chapter 19 are good examples.

Whichever philosophy you adopt, you should not feel rushed into naming a new and unique gemstone design. Cut the stone first, and use the time at the machine to explore your relationship with the design. You will often find that your original name is completely inappropriate, or you will be suddenly struck with an inspiration.

So why "Briar Rose?" As mentioned in Section 18.1, this design was inspired by the shape of a beautiful piece of blue-green tourmaline and the desire to attempt a princess-type cut in a hexagonal form. In other words, this cut is a hexed princess – like Sleeping Beauty. Now "sleeping" is a bad adjective to connect with a supposedly brilliant gem. In fact, aficionados often use the word "sleepy" to describe a stone that simply doesn't perform, whether due to poor design, internal flaws, or bad polish.

Sleeping Beauty is therefore out as a name. The story of the hexed princess, as with so many Disney recreations, dates back to the famous brothers Grimm (and even earlier). In the Grimm version, the girl is named "Dornröschen," or Briar Rose. Given the symmetric "petalled" nature of the design, the association with a flower makes the name Briar Rose doubly meaningful.

Independent of what you call your design, the cutting prescription should contain your name, the date of creation, the gem species for which it is intended, and other useful information, such as the ISO brightness. The printed output of the GemCAD program has both header and footer areas for this purpose. See Chapter 19 for examples.

Let me end with a bit of mildly curmedgeonly philosophizing. Thanks in advance for your forbearance…At the end of the day, the name of a gemstone design is like the wrapping on a gift – it can enhance the impact of your efforts, but it is ultimately less important than the quality of the content. In a similar way, new parents agonize, sometimes for months, over possible names for their child. All their worries about possible negative associations are wiped away by the appearance of their offspring, and thereafter, the chosen name has only one real association. The same is true for other acts of creation, including gemstone design.

18.2 The Pavilion: From Inspiration to Design

Translating your creative inspiration into a successful gem design is the next challenge. Happily, there are a number of straightforward techniques and tools to simplify this process, (see Chapters 15.3 and 16). Given a well thought-out concept, transforming your ideas into a cuttable gem design can be easy and fun.

18.2.1 Into the Breach – Briar Rose meets GemCAD

Note: It will improve your insight and understanding of this case study to follow along on your computer. This chapter presumes that you have both GemCAD (Windows version) and the BOG optimization program installed and running. See Chapter 15.3 to learn more about these programs. The following sections also adopt the pavilion-first design philosophy. Other tools and techniques are possible, and I am sure that choosing the best option would make for a fine and lively debate. Some other time…

Note also that, as with all software explanations in this book, **bold-faced** *text corresponds to user input and onscreen items, while wording such as* **"Raytrace: Properties…"** *refers to the* **Properties…** *command under the* **Raytrace** *menu.*

Start GemCAD by **double clicking** on its icon. You should see a blank screen with multiple sub-panels (Figure 18-4).

Let's orient ourselves…(and note that much of the material in this chapter is covered in the excellent GemCAD manual available online at www.gemcad.com). Once you start designing, the panel to the upper left will contain a 3-dimensional rendering of your stone. This rendering can be manipulated by dragging with the mouse to view all sides of the design. Below the 3D window is a gray sub-panel for manually entering values for the individual facet angles, indices, and symmetry characteristics of the gem (more on this later).

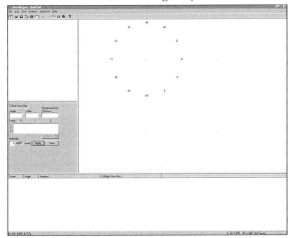

To the right of these panels lies the large, plan-view window, which will show projections of the gemstone along various lines of sight. Note the circle of guide numbers to the upper left; these correspond to the index wheel (if you don't see the numbers, select **View:Zoom:Zoom Out**). Briar Rose uses the most common, 96-tooth wheel. If you don't see the value **<96>** at the bottom of the cutting circle, select the correct wheel from the **Edit: Index Gear…** menu.

Figure 18-4 If you don't see all the GemCAD sub-panels, move your mouse to the relevant edge. When the icon changes to a double-headed arrow, **click and drag** *the edge inward to reveal the sub-panel. You can also use this method to adjust the sizes of the individual areas to your liking.*

Finally, at the bottom of the screen lies the white, cutting recipe area. Information describing the individual facet tiers will appear here as you progress.

18.2.2 Establishing the Correct Gem Outline

Note: Chapter 17 emphasizes the importance of an accurate gem outline to your faceting success. It also explains several techniques for translating a sketch into a cutting prescription. You may want to review that material before proceeding.

Briar Rose is a fairly symmetric design, yet it does not have a brilliant type pavilion. The guidelines laid out in Chapter 17, particularly in "CAM versus OMNI" on page 295, argue strongly for a CAM outline approach. As it turns out, that is exactly what I did in designing the gem. In fact, the method I used to translate the sketch of Figure 18-3 into a CAM outline follows Chapter 17.3.3 so closely that it doesn't bear repeating. Here are the angle and index combinations that worked for the inclined CAM facets:

39° at indices 14-18-46-50-78-82
37° at indices 2-30-34-62-66-94

If you don't understand what these numbers mean, review the material in Chapter 5.1.1. Note that the two cutting angles, 39° and 37°, are close to "final" angles for a tourmaline gem, in the sense that they are considerably steeper than typical CAM "pre-form" angles. Don't worry about this for now. The goal here is to establish the outline. There will be plenty of time, as well as the tangent ratio method, to deal with the exact angles later.

Before starting to create these facet tiers, you should understand and **enter** the appropriate gem symmetry values in the gray, numerical entry sub-panel in GemCAD (Figure 18-5). Note that these values are not fundamental to the gemstone design process. Rather, they simply serve as an aid in creating multiple facets for a single tier in one step. As such, you can freely change the symmetry values during the design process. For example, some tiers may have mirror symmetry, while others do not. Note also that having incorrect entries in these fields can lead to unexpected and undesirable results. If GemCAD is not generating facets as you think it should, check the gem symmetry settings.

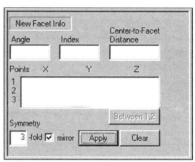

The outline of Briar Rose has three-fold, mirror-image symmetry. This is because each girdle facet has corresponding facets distributed at 120° (i.e. three-fold) around the midline of the gem, and the design is left-right (i.e. mirror) symmetric. If you don't understand this, review the material in Chapter 10.7.

Since the CAM technique uses a common center point to establish the girdle outline, you can begin with either of the two tiers, 39° or 37°. Given a choice, I usually start with the steepest set, although this is purely a matter of taste.

Figure 18-5 Briar Rose has three-fold, mirror symmetry.

But where to begin? There are no points of reference to help place the initial facets: you are facing a blank screen. It turns out that GemCAD knows that the initial set of facets will often be cut to a common center point. You therefore need to provide only an angle and an index.

Enter the values **39°** and **14** in the angle and index fields respectively of the **New Facet Info** panel on the left. You can also use the shortcut **Ctrl-A** to pop up an angle entry dialog and **Ctrl-I** for the index. With correct values in the angle and index text fields, click the **Apply** button or hit the **Enter** key.

Shazzam! GemCAD cuts a total of six facets at the appropriate settings – see the recipe window at the bottom of the screen (Figure 18-6). This would not have happened without correct values in the symmetry fields. You can type **Ctrl-Z** to undo and try different symmetries to see the effect. Note also that there are white and gray coloured facets in the various views. These correspond to defined and undefined areas of the gem, respectively.

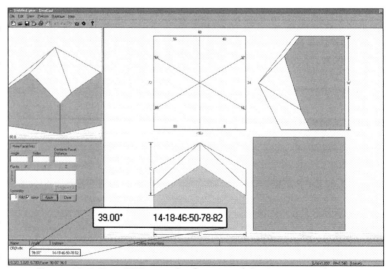

Figure 18-6 GemCAD cuts the first tier of the Briar Rose design.

When you are done, the views should show white facets only. At some point, you may see some gray facets where you don't think that they should occur. Over-scaling of the gem may be responsible. Try adjusting things in the **Edit: Scale** dialog box.

Congratulations! You have just created the starting facets for the Briar Rose design. The second set, at **37°**, is next. Enter this angle and index **2** into the appropriate boxes. Note, however, that unlike with the first tier, GemCAD does not automatically assume a center point for subsequent facets. You need to specify the angle, index, *and* location.

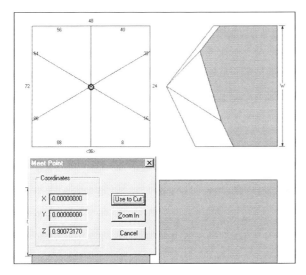

In order to tell GemCAD where to cut these facets, place your mouse over the existing center point in any of the plan views (large window to the upper right). The cursor should change to a small circle. **Click** on the center point and choose **Use to Cut** to tell GemCAD the location (Figure 18-7). If you don't see the expected dialog, your mouse was not close enough to the existing meet point. **Cancel** the operation and try again.

*Figure 18-7 **Select** the center point for the second tier. Note the circle at the location of the cursor.*

Note how the **Apply** button in the **New Facet Info** panel has changed to the **Cut Facet** button: GemCAD now has sufficient information to know how and where to cut the second tier of facets. Go ahead and click **Cut Facet**. You should be rewarded with a second tier as shown in Figure 18-8.

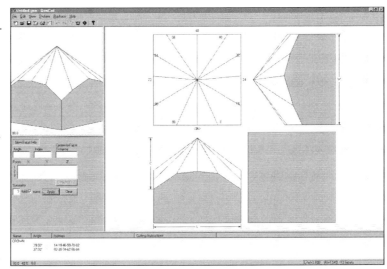

Figure 18-8 GemCAD cuts the second tier of facets to the original center point

This is a classic CAM approach, and these two angled facet tiers define the outline of the gemstone. As an experienced CAMmer, you know that 90° facets cut at the same index wheel settings will produce a level girdle line. You therefore need to cut two tiers as follows:

90° at indices 14-18-46-50-78-82
90° at indices 2-30-34-62-66-94

You don't currently have a meet point at which to begin placing these facets. **Click** on the top view of the gemstone as shown in Figure 18-9. Make sure that you are on the vertical facet

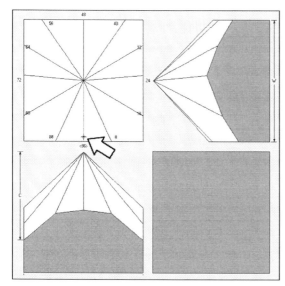

*Figure 18-9 **Click** on the edge to set a new point (arrow). Note the cross-shaped cursor.*

edge but not close to one of the existing facet intersections – the cursor should NOT change to a small red circle as it did before.

The **Point on Edge** dialog should pop up (Figure 18-10). You can examine some of the options if you want, but if you are happy with the location, accept the point by clicking **Use to Cut**.

Presumably, you placed the point close to the (gray) edge of the gem. On an actual piece of rough, you would begin cutting the girdle at the index which defines the size of the final gem – in other words the facet that produces the maximum possible yield while removing all of the rough edges, inclusions etc. Figure 5-30 illustrates the idea.

Now enter the appropriate angle (**90°**) and index (**2**). Again, GemCAD tells you that it has sufficient information by presenting the **Cut Facet** button. **Clicking** it should result in the first set of six girdle facets distributed around the gem (Figure 18-11).

Placing the second set of girdle facets is easy, since you now have a meet point created by the previous cut (circled in Figure 18-11). Move your mouse to the meet point, check that the cursor is a red circle, and **click** to identify this location for the next set of facets (Figure 18-12). As before, enter the ap-

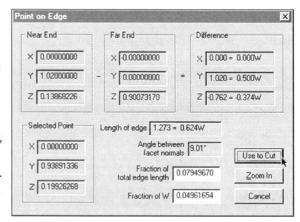

*Figure 18-10 The Point on Edge Dialog. Accept the suggested values and click **Use to Cut**.*

propriate angle (**90°**) and index (**14**) before clicking the **Cut Facet** button to place the second girdle tier (Figure 18-12). This completes the gem outline. Nice going!

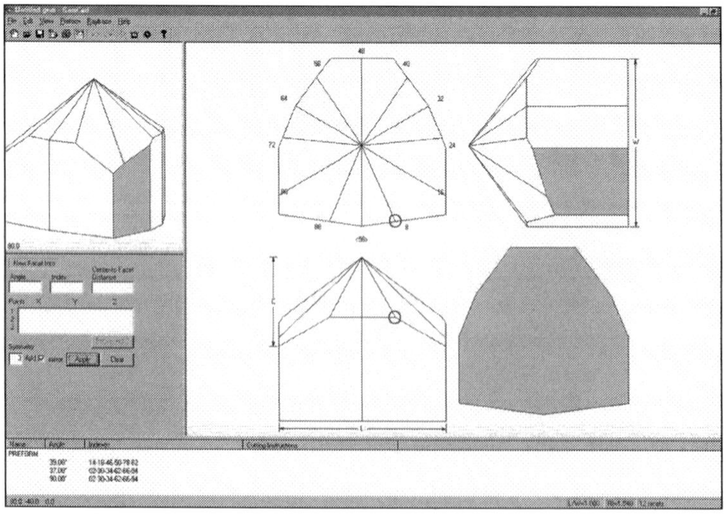

Figure 18-11 The first set of girdle facets, cut at index 2, produces a meet point (circled) for the next girdle tier.

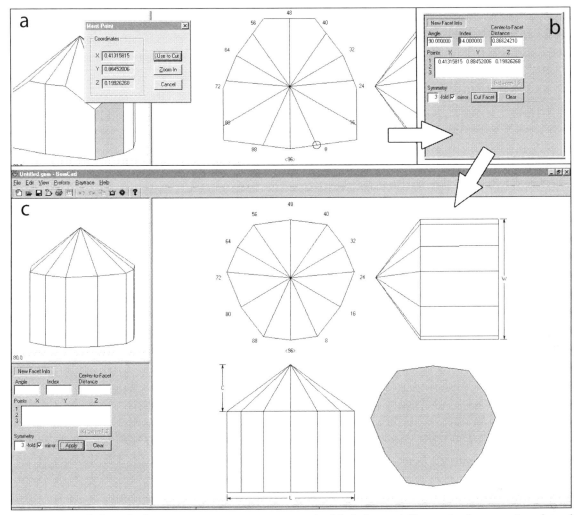

Figure 18-12 **Click** *on the facet intersection to set a meet point (circled at top). Then* **enter** *the correct angle and index for the second set of girdle facets (upper right). Clicking on* **Cut Facet** *finishes the girdle outline (bottom).*

18.2.3 Turning the Outline into a Princess

You now have the correct outline of the gemstone and can begin the process of laying down the characteristic fan-like Princess facets. Referring back to the sketch in Figure 18-3, it is clear that you will need to place these facets at the appropriate girdle meet points. What is less obvious is that the fan facets must get shallower as you go from the girdle to the culet of the gem. In other words, the facets that adjoin the girdle have a larger cutting angle (that is, the quill must be more horizontal) than do the facets that meet at the culet.

You will also soon realize that the current center point will be cut away by this process. Given the desire to make this a meet point design (see Chapter 8.7), you probably want to start at the girdle and then cut the fan facets successively inward toward the culet (see Figure 18-13). You can, in fact, do the exact opposite, executing a "Clever CAM" (see page 282), and perhaps save some valuable gem rough in the bargain. The cutting prescription for Briar Rose in Chapter 19.2.8 shows both possible sequences. The following paragraphs presume the classic "outside-in" order.

The first set of fan facets, labelled "1" in Figure 18-13, meets the girdle and extends approximately ¼ of the way to the culet. You already know how to tell GemCAD about the meet point: place your mouse over the correct girdle facet intersection, look for the red circle, and then **click**. Accept the point by clicking **Use to Cut** (Figure 18-14).

The next step is less obvious. GemCAD needs more information in order to proceed (see Table 16-1), yet there are no further meet points or other guides to help. The one piece of information that you have not yet used, however, is the fact that the fan facet should end up about a quarter of the way from the girdle to the culet.

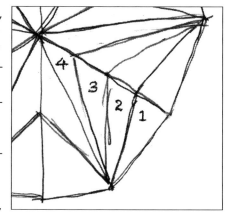

Figure 18-13 The classic cutting order for the pavilion fan facets.

You have already used the Point on Edge dialog in placing the first girdle facets, and you can use it again to specify the location of the first fan tier. Place your mouse on the edge between the 14-index and 18-index facets as shown in Figure 18-15. The location should be approxi-

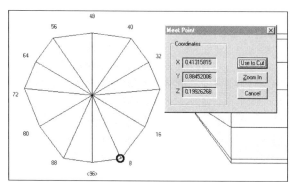

mately ¼ of the way in from the edge. **Click** to pop up the **Point on Edge** dialog. Note the field labeled **Fraction of total edge length**. I actually managed to get pretty close to the desired location. You can either accept the point as is, or type **0.25** into the field to ensure absolutely accurate placement.

*Figure 18-14 **Select** the correct meet point for the first fan facets.*

With two points defined, you now need to figure out which index the first fan facet will have. Clearly, both 2 and 14 are excluded, since they would simply recut the existing facets on each side of the girdle meet. Experience and some playing with GemCAD also dictates that the remaining fan facets, labeled 2-3-4 in Figure 18-13, must be cut at successively smaller indices to produce the desired effect. If you don't yet have this experience or you don't believe me, now is a great time to save your work and play around a little bit. It's also yet another occasion to be thankful for the multiple Undo's in Windows GemCAD.

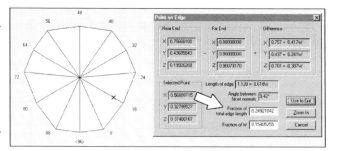

*Figure 18-15 Set "Fraction of total edge length" to **0.25**.*

A little experimentation leads to the conclusion that index 13 is the correct choice. Enter **13** in the **Index** field of the **New Facet Info** panel, and then click **Cut Facet** to see the result (Figure 18-16).

You can place the remaining fan facets in a similar manner. For example, the next tier will require the same girdle meet point and a **Point on Edge** value of 0.333, since it will occupy one third of the remaining distance to the culet. The aforementioned experience and experimentation lead to an index of 12 in the Index field. **Enter** this value and click **Cut Facet** to see the result (Figure 18-17).

The way forward should now be clear. Use 50% of the remaining edge and an index of 11 to create the third tier of fan facets (Figure 18-18). Note that this will also define the final center point, and hence pavilion depth, of the gem.

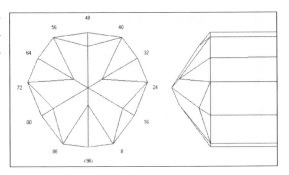

Figure 18-16 The third pavilion tier creates the first set of fan facets.

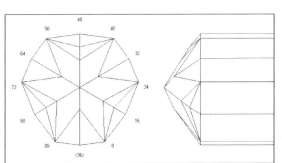

Figure 18-17 The next cut produces the second set of fan facets, which occupy a third of the distance from the first fans to the culet.

The final step in designing the pavilion is to refine the "Princess" appearance by closing the last fan facets. They appear as quadrilaterals, not triangles, and as page 255 makes clear, I don't like quadrilaterals. You can achieve this refinement by joining the final culet meet point with the original girdle meet (near the "8" index in the figures). **Select** the two meet points as shown in Figure 18-19.

Logic and experimentation once again dictate the index for this final set of pavilion facets. Enter the value **10** in the **Index** field of the **New Facet Info** panel, and then click **Cut Facet**. The pavilion is complete! (Figure 18-20) Congratulations!

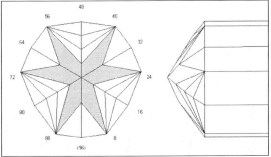

Figure 18-18 (above) The third set of fan facets defines the final culet. Note that the remaining facets (shown in gray here) still need to be converted to triangles.

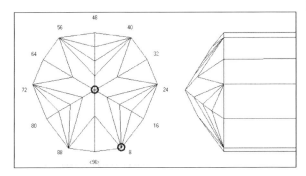

Figure 18-19 (left) The two meet points for the final pavilion tier.

18.2.4 Whoaa! Wait a Minute Here…

Have you been paying attention to the Cutting Instructions panel at the bottom of the screen? Figure 18-21 shows the current prescription for cutting Briar Rose (Note: your values might be slightly different). You have been blithely designing away using meet points, and not really paying attention to the angles. Except for the initial pair of facet tiers, and of course the girdle, all of the angles are below the critical value for most common gem materials! For example, a piece of tourmaline inspired the Briar Rose design, but tourmaline windows at 38°. Only one of the facet tiers is safe!

Not to worry. This is a fairly normal state of affairs in gem design. You have been concentrating on getting a pleasing facet layout in an easy-to-execute meet point design. Now, you can work on the angles.

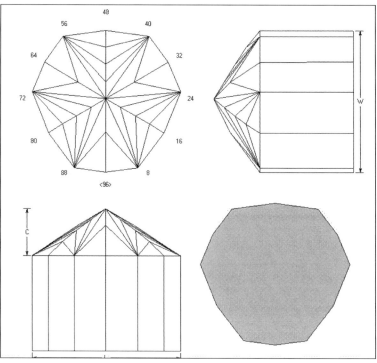

Figure 18-20 The pavilion of Briar Rose is complete…or is it?

18.2.5 Closing the Window

GemCAD has a built-in facility for stretching or compressing a design while retaining the overall appearance of the gem, its so-called *plan view* (this is the **Top View** in GemCAD). Normally, such stretching or compressing is used to adapt a design for gem material with a significantly different refractive index, or to flatten the crown when running out of rough (but see Chapter 10.5 for my opinion of these practices). The key to the technique is the tangent ratio. Here, you can use GemCAD's built-in tangent ratio scaling function to ensure that all of the pavilion facet tiers are above the critical angle.

Name	Angle	Indexes
	39.00°	14-18-46-50-78-82
	37.00°	02-30-34-62-66-94
	90.00°	02-30-34-62-66-94
	90.00°	14-18-46-50-78-82
	34.96°	13-19-45-51-77-83
	33.26°	12-20-44-52-76-84
	32.39°	11-21-43-53-75-85
	31.96°	10-22-42-54-74-86

Figure 18-21 These pavilion angles will cause problems.

Tangent ratio scaling with GemCAD is straightforward. You just **click** on any facet, review its current angle, and then enter the new desired value. The entire half of the gem – pavilion or crown – will be scaled accordingly. Chapter 10.6.1 explains the process in detail.

Here, you want to ensure that there will be no windowing for tourmaline. In other words, the shallowest angle should be 38° or greater. The final facet tier has the lowest angle, so **select** one of these facets as shown in Figure 18-22. Note that you can also **click** on the appropriate line in the **Cutting Instructions** panel at the bottom of the screen.

The current angle is 31.96°. **Double-click** this value and enter **38**. Clicking on **Apply** will stretch the pavilion as desired.

*Figure 18-22 **Click** on one of the facets of the shallowest tier to display the current angle. Enter the new angle (**38°**) in the appropriate box and then click **Apply** to perform the tangent ratio.*

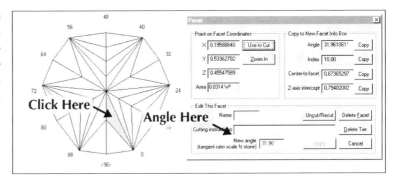

Take a quick look at the prescription down in the **Cutting Instructions** panel. Now, the pavilion angles range from 38° to 45.4°. Don't worry at this stage that 38° is very close to the critical angle for tourmaline – you will be optimizing the design for brightness and tilt performance later on.

18.2.6 A Pavilion Sanity Check

At this point in the design process, I usually do a sanity check on pavilion performance by placing a step-cut crown on the gem and ray tracing the result (see also page 254). This only takes a couple of minutes in GemCAD. Simply execute the dop transfer (see next section) and then place a couple of rows of facets, at 35° and 25° for example, at the same index wheel settings as the girdle. Make each tier about one quarter the distance to the center and complete the temporary crown with a 50% table (Figure 18-23). You can skip ahead to Section 18.4 if you have trouble entering the cutting values for the table.

Step cuts produce a minimum of sparkle (Chapter 16.5), and hence this configuration gives you a relatively clear view of how well the pavilion handles light. You can use GemRay for this purpose, or even try a quick optimization in BOG (see Section 18.5). For a real whiz-bang view, try a photorealistic ray tracer such as Blender (Chapters 15.4 and 15.5).

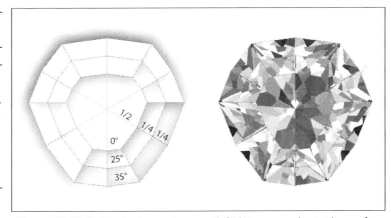

Figure 18-23 A simple step-cut crown (left) lets you evaluate the performance of the pavilion. GemRay ray shows that all is well (right).

18.3 Crowning the Princess...

With the pavilion complete, you are now ready to focus on the crown. Just as in the real world, however, you have to transfer the stone in order to work on the other side. GemCAD insists on this, since angles are always specified between 0° and 90°, as on a faceting machine. Without the option to transfer the gem, you would have to specify angles greater than 90° or less than 0°. You would also get confused.

Transferring a gemstone is almost infinitely easier in GemCAD than in reality (see Chapter 7). Simply **click** the small transfer jig icon in the toolbar and voilà! Instant and perfectly aligned transfer! (Figure 18-24).

Figure 18-24   Click the transfer jig icon to begin working on the crown.

18.3.1 Designing the Crown

In my experience, the design process for the crown of a gemstone is usually considerably easier than for the pavilion. There are a number of reasons for this (see also Chapter 16.3.2):

1. Most obviously, there are fewer constraints on angles, since total internal reflection is (hopefully!) irrelevant for the upper part of the gem.

2. In addition, the crown generally has less influence on the overall performance of the design, and hence a sub-optimal crown is considerably less disastrous than a problematic pavilion. This is because the crown influences the light rays by *refraction*, whereas total internal *reflection* drives the performance of the pavilion – see Chapter 11 for a detailed explanation of these phenomena. Still skeptical? Consider this: changing the angle of a crown facet by 1° will change the direction of a light ray refracted into the gem by less than 1°, often substantially less (think about it…this makes sense). Changing a pavilion facet by 1°, however, will alter the ray's direction by 2°, or perhaps far more if the change causes windowing.

3. Finally, the layout of the pavilion pre-determines a number of choices in designing the crown. For example, aesthetics and mounting requirements argue for a constant-thickness girdle. This can only be achieved if the crown break facets have the same index wheel settings as the pavilion break facets. As a result, many of the decisions for the first two tiers of crown facets for Briar Rose have already been made (see below).

18.3.2 The First Crown Tiers

In the case of Briar Rose, a uniform girdle thickness (point 3 above) will require crown break facets at indices:

14-18-46-50-78-82

2-30-34-62-66-94

This establishes the index wheel settings for the first facets of the crown. The location of these facets is also pre-determined: you should cut them to a depth that produces an appropriate girdle thickness. See? Designing the crown is easy!

Unfortunately, index and location alone do not a facet make (see Table 16-1). You need at least three pieces of information. In this instance, you need to specify the cutting angles for the 12 crown facets that define the girdle.

But which angles?

Once again, aesthetics come to the rescue. Briar Rose aims to reproduce aspects of a Princess cut in a hexagonal gem. This means that there is a definite spatial relationship between the crown and pavilion facets (see Figure 18-3). Basically, the edges defining the intersections of the crown break facets should overlay those in the pavilion.

It turns out that you must cut the first two crown tiers at angles that bear a specific relation to the pavilion break facets below them. If you don't, they simply won't line up. How can you guarantee alignment between the pavilion and crown breaks? Think tangent ratio. Our old friend from Chapter 10 will help line up the edges.

In fact, all will be copacetic if the ratio of the tangent of the cutting angle of the first tier of break facets to that of the second tier of break facets is the same for both the pavilion and crown. Sorry again for an information-rich sentence. Yes, it merits a second read-through...

Indeed, since you know that you can freely stretch either half of the gem, picking the appropriate angles is actually a lot easier than explaining all of this. Short version: you can start cutting the crown exactly as you started the pavilion:

39° at indices 14-18-46-50-78-82
37° at indices   2-30-34-62-66-94

Try it, you'll see – you can skip ahead for the details, but Figure 18-25 shows the effect. Again, I encourage you to experiment in GemCAD to convince yourself of the truth of this. Again, I encourage you to give thanks for **Undo**. Another great feature of Win GemCAD, **Hidden Lines** under the **View** menu, is a great help for this kind of thing.

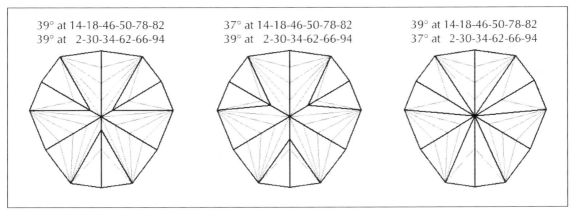

Figure 18-25 Lining up the crown and pavilion facets. The panels show three different choices for the cutting angles of the first two crown tiers. The dark lines indicate the crown facets, while the Hidden Lines option in GemCAD portrays the pavilion in light gray. Only when the crown angles match the pavilion angles do the facet edges line up (right panel).

Armed with the location, indices, and angles, you can readily cut these first two crown tiers in GemCAD. Begin by **selecting** a point which defines a pleasing girdle thickness. Refer to page 44 for opinion on the seemingly endless debate about how thick the girdle should be. For now, **pick** a point as shown in Figure 18-26.

Click the **Use to Cut** button to dismiss the dialog, and then enter **39°** and **14** in the **Angle** and **Index** fields, respectively, of the **New Facet Info** panel. Clicking **Cut Facet** completes the first crown tier (Figure 18-27).

In what by now must seem a routine, yet still moderately miraculous way, the first crown cut has produced a level girdle and a meet point target for the second tier. **Select** the meet point (Figure 18-27), enter **37°** and **2** into the appropriate fields, and then **cut** the facets as shown in Figure 18-28.

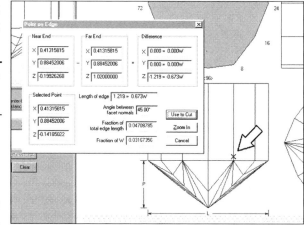

Figure 18-26 *Select a **Point on Edge** to define the first crown facet tier and girdle thickness.*

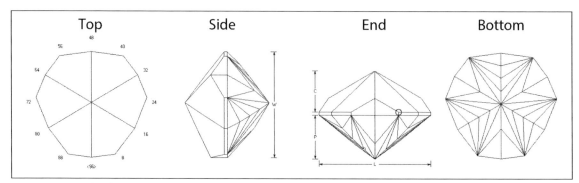

Figure 18-27 *The first tier of crown facets in place. The circle in the end view (third image) indicates the meet point for placing the second tier.*

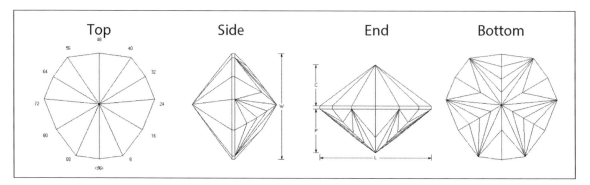

Figure 18-28 *The second tier of crown facets completes the girdle.*

Seeing is Believing

If you haven't done so already, now would be a good time to turn on the **Hidden Lines** option in GemCAD (under the **View** menu). Particularly in the case of Briar Rose, you want to ensure that the crown and pavilion facets line up properly. Note that this may be a bit anticlimactic. If your alignment is good, the relevant pavilion facet edges will hide exactly underneath the intersections of the first two crown tiers (rightmost panel of Figure 18-25).

18.3.3 Fanning the Crown

With the first two crown tiers under your belt (or perhaps more appropriately, over your girdle), you can now move on to establishing the "Princess" and added-sparkle characteristics of the design. Refer back to Figure 18-3. Specifically, you need fan-like facets on the crown spreading from those girdle vertices which do not have fans in the pavilion, in other words, from the meet points at indices 96-16-32-48-64-80.

The approach here is essentially the same as for the fan facets on the pavilion. There is an obvious set of girdle meet points from which the fans should spread, and a glance at the pencil sketch shows that the first set should start at about a third of the distance to the center of the stone.

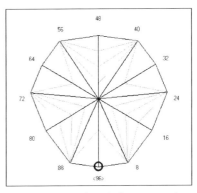

Begin by **selecting** one of the target girdle meet points – at index 96, for example (Figure 18-29). Then **select** a point about a third of the way in on the facet edge to the right (Figure 18-30). As before, you can either accept the point you created, or enter an exact value in the **Point on Edge** dialog.

Figure 18-29 The girdle meet point for the first crown fan facets.

Two points and an index are sufficient to define a facet tier. You have the two points, so you just need to find the appropriate index. As with the pavilion, experimentation and the lifesaving Undo feature of GemCAD are generally the best way to proceed. Unlike with the

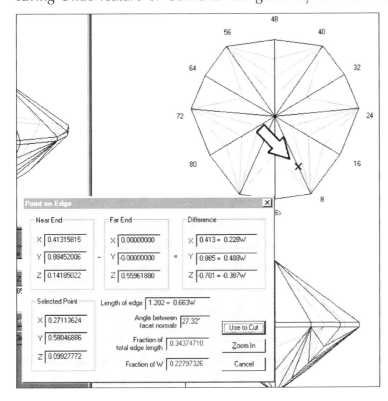

pavilion, however, you have very little choice. Note that there are crown break facets at index 94 and 2. You need to place one fan facet on either side of the crown break intersection along index 96 (or zero). A facet at index 2 (or 94) would simply overlap the current breaks (try it). This means that the choice is limited to any facet index between 0 and 2 (or between 94 and 96). Some choice.

*Figure 18-30 **Select** a point approximately 1/3 of the way in from the girdle to the center on the facet intersection along index 8. Note that **View: Hidden Lines** has been toggled on within GemCAD. This helps you visualize the alignment between pavilion and crown.*

Enter the value **1** in the **Index** field of the **New Facet Info** panel and click **Cut Facet** to place the first crown fans (Figure 18-31).

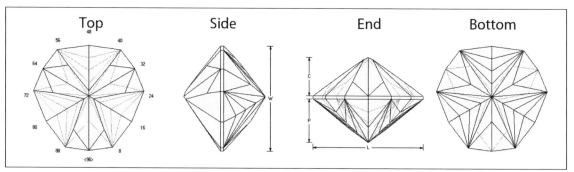

Figure 18-31 The first crown fan facets.

Placing the complementary set of crown fan tiers is now straightforward, since there are a couple of sets of obvious meet points: the remaining girdle meets and the newly created meet points 1/3 of the way up the crown. **Click** on the appropriate spots as shown in Figure 18-32 and **Use to Cut**.

Again, you have two points and you need an index. And, as with the previous tier, this index must occur somewhere between the existing breaks, here at 14-18, and the symmetry line for this set of facets, which is at index 16 (refer to the pencil sketch and Figure 18-31 if this is not clear). As before, you have no choice…for the facet joining the meet points shown in Figure 18-32, index 15 is the only option. **Enter** this value and click **Cut Facet** to place the second set of fans (Figure 18-33).

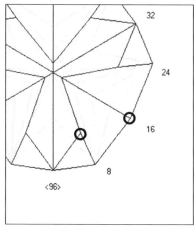

Figure 18-32 The meet points for the second crown fan tier.

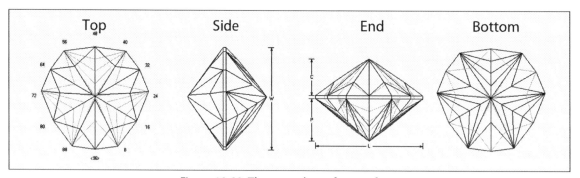

Figure 18-33 The second set of crown fans.

It is now time to place the final two sets of crown fan facets. These are along the symmetry lines mentioned in the previous paragraphs: index 96-32-64 for the first set and 16-48-80 for the second. Begin by **clicking** on the girdle meet point at index 96. Accept the meet point and then enter the (known) index: **96**. Two out of three pieces of information are in place.

Again, there is no clear facet intersection to define a second point. The pencil sketch indicates that this tier extends about 30-40% of the distance between the existing crown fan facets and the center of the gem. **Click** on the approximate location and either accept the **Point on Edge** value or enter it manually. Click **Cut Facet**. Figure 18-34 shows the result. As always, if you are unsatisfied, you can type **Ctrl-Z** and try again.

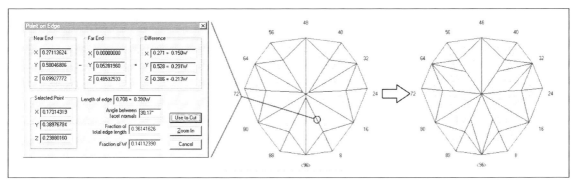

Figure 18-34 **Click** *on the circled point to place the third crown tier.*

Placing the final tier of crown facets is trivial: you have the symmetry meet points (16-48-80) at the girdle, the required indices of the facets (also 16-48-80), and the meet points created by the previous tier of facets. **Clicking** on the appropriate locations and **entering** the correct values completes the crown (Figure 18-35). The end is in sight!

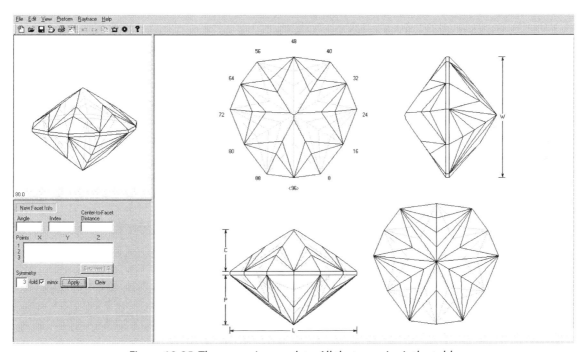

Figure 18-35 The crown is complete. All that remains is the table.

18.4 Tabling the Issue

Chapter 16.3 recommends that you create your gems on the computer in the same order as you would on the faceting machine – pavilion first, then crown, and finally table. With the pavilion and crown of Briar Rose now complete, you just have to place the table to finish the design.

The table is presumably a facet like any other, and it needs three inputs, for example, a meet point, the cutting angle, and an index. A cursory examination of Figure 18-35 shows that suitable meet points are in place, and any self-respecting table is happy with a cutting angle of 0°, but which index should you use?

The answer is that it doesn't matter. If you think about it, facets at 0° are at any index (or all indices). In fact, if you enter **0°** into the **Angle** field of the **New Facet Info** panel, you don't even have to enter an index at all. Tables, like the first cut of a new design (page 308) are an exception to the rules defining the minimum information needed to define a facet (see Table 16-1 on page 256). All you need is one point, and of course the angle, which is zero degrees.

Click on one of the meet points defined by the last tier of crown facets and enter **0** for the angle. The **Cut Facet** button becomes activated, since GemCAD already has enough information. **Click** it to finish the Briar Rose design (Figure 18-36).

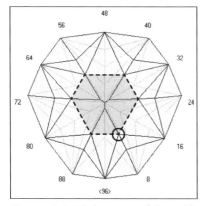

Figure 18-36 **Select** one of the table meets (circled) and then enter a cutting angle of **0°** to produce the table.

PAVILION		CROWN	
45.40°	14-18-46-50-78-82	39.00°	14-18-46-50-78-82
43.34°	02-30-34-62-66-94	37.00°	02-30-34-62-66-94
90.00°	02-30-34-62-66-94	35.35°	01-31-33-63-65-95
90.00°	14-18-46-50-78-82	36.66°	15-17-47-49-79-81
41.20°	13-19-45-51-77-83	34.73°	96-32-64
39.40°	12-20-44-52-76-84	35.74°	16-48-80
38.47°	11-21-43-53-75-85	0.00°	Table
38.00°	10-22-42-54-74-86		

Figure 18-37 The final, non-optimized, GemCAD cutting prescription for Briar Rose.

18.4.1 Whoaa! Redux

The gem is complete and you can lean back and appreciate the fruits of your efforts, but a vague worry is stirring in the back of your brain. As before, you have been beavering away happily with crown meet points and facet layout without thinking about angles. The design looks great, but will it work?

A glance at the actual cutting prescription at the bottom of the screen (Figure 18-37) should set your mind at ease. As an inadvertent side effect of mimicking the first two pavilion cuts, the range of crown angles is pretty reasonable. Phew!

Now is no time to rest on your laurels, however. And given their propensity for prickliness, no time to rest on your briars, either. The next step is to optimize the design for best performance.

18.5 Optimizing Briar Rose with BOG

Note: As this volume went into final production, rumours began appearing about an imminent new version of GemRay capable of optimizing gemstones. Based on initial impressions of the pre-alpha software previewed on YouTube, this program will have significant impact.

I toyed with the idea of removing the material in this section, since it may soon be obsolete. However, I decided against this course of action in the end, since those same initial impressions indicate that the new program is very similar in form, philosophy, and function to BOG. In other words, the approach to optimizing gemstone cutting angles, as explained below, should remain the same.

The process of gem optimization involves scaling the pavilion and crown in a controlled way using the tangent ratio technique, with the goal of maximizing visual impact. This section will presume the use of the Better Optimizer for GemRay, also known as BOG. This is a freeware program intended for use in tandem with the (also free) DOS GemRay software for tracing light through gemstones. Chapter 15.3 contains further information about both programs, and you can learn a great deal more from their respective websites listed in Chapter 15.8.12.

Note that you should not consider the following sections as a beginner's BOG tutorial. I presume that you have the program up and running. The explanations are also correspondingly brief. Point your browser to the BOG website for detailed instructions on installing the software and several tutorials to help you explore various features of the program.

18.5.1 How BOG Works

BOG uses the tangent ratio technique to scale the pavilion or crown, and then calls GemRay to perform a ray trace. Based on the results, BOG decides whether the gem has improved or not and then adjusts the angles accordingly. Pretty simple.

Actually, like just about everything else in our hobby, it's a little more complicated. For example, here's an excellent question: What exactly does "improved" mean in the previous paragraph? Here's another: How does BOG know when to stop?

The process of gem design optimization can be likened to mountain climbing (see Figure 18-38). Imagine a world in which one grid direction, for example east-west, corresponds to the current pavilion reference angle, and the other, north-south, corresponds to the current crown reference angle (recall from Chapter 10.6 that the tangent ratio method relies on reference angles for scaling). The altitude at any point is a measure of how good the gem is with that particular combination of pavilion and crown angles. BOG calculates a merit function to determine this altitude or gem quality. Finding the best gem then becomes a problem of finding the highest peak within the area defined by an acceptable range of pavilion and crown angles, essentially within the edges of the world in Figure 18-38.

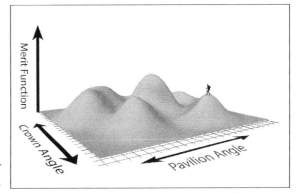

Figure 18-38 The gem optimization world. The intrepid mountain climber is searching for the highest peak.

How do you go about finding the highest peak? Finding the maxima (and minima) of surfaces is a very important problem in all areas of science and engineering, and there are a large number of peak-finding algorithms in use. BOG implements the simplest and most robust of these, a so-called grid search. Imagine that you are a mountaineer dropped down somewhere on that world with the task of finding the highest peak. To do a grid search, you would begin by taking a step in one direction, say east. If the terrain goes up, you take another step.

If, on the other hand, the terrain goes down, you reverse direction and start looking west. Having selected a search direction, you carry on taking steps until the ground stops getting higher.

At this point, things go downhill to both the east and west. The obvious strategy is to begin exploring north-south in the same way. When that is no longer productive, you switch back to searching east-west. And so on. The grid search algorithm within BOG has a few additional bells and whistles. For example, before switching to the perpendicular grid direction, it uses the altitude of the last three steps to make a more accurate estimate of the highest point before setting off at right angles. It also continuously adjusts the size of the steps, based on how long it took to exhaust a certain grid direction. Like all grid-search strategies, the algorithm in BOG stops searching once the step size is below a user-specified value. I usually pick something like 0.05°, which is about the limit of what I can reliably dial in with my faceting machine anyway (see page 396). There's the answer to question 2 from the beginning of this section.

Although you would look pretty silly doing this on a real mountaintop, it is clear that this simple strategy inevitably leads to the highest point in the vicinity. There is another problem, however. Look again at the terrain in Figure 18-38. The grid-search strategy will lead to a peak, but not necessarily the highest peak. In other words, this algorithm (like most) really finds the local, not absolute maximum. Depending on where you set out – in other words, depending on your choice of initial pavilion and crown angles – you may not find the best gem.

This problem is also well known, and there are a variety of solutions. BOG again adopts the simplest strategy, so-called Merit Function Mapping. This technique essentially boils down to calculating the altitude on a grid of pavilion and crown angles. This helps identify multiple peaks and good starting points for the optimization algorithm. Turn to Section 18.5.5 to see how Merit Function Mapping helps select the best angles for Briar Rose.

18.5.2 The Merit Function

Back to question 1, the one about what improvement really means. BOG optimizes a gem by maximizing a so-called Merit Function. The Merit Function (or MF) is a numerical value assigned to the quality of a gemstone design, based on a set of user-specified criteria. BOG supports five different measures, or Targets of gem merit, as described in Table 18-1. Considerably more information on these MF components appears on the BOG website.

The overall merit function value – the altitude in Figure 18-38 – is the mathematical sum of the merit functions of the individual Targets, each multiplied by a weighting factor:

$$MF = ISO \cdot W_{ISO} + Illum \cdot W_{Illum} + Tilt \cdot W_{Tilt} + Sparkle \cdot W_{Sparkle} + Fire \cdot W_{Fire}$$

where W_x is the weight associated with optimization Target X.

You can see where this is going. BOG varies the pavilion and crown angles and evaluates the corresponding MF. Using the peak-finding algorithm described in the previous section, the program zeroes in on the combination of angles which produces the highest Merit Function. There's the answer to question 1.

Table 18-1 The gemstone optimization Targets used by BOG.

Optimization Target	Comment
ISO Brightness	Calculated by GemRay. Overall brightness for uniform illumination.
Illumination Response	Maximizes impact of rays entering the gem at large angles; reduces head shadow effects and may improve dispersion (see also the discussion starting on page 196).
Tilt Performance	Minimizes brightness loss due to windowing when the gem is tilted.
Sparkle or Scintillation	Maximizes scintillation or "action." See page 261.
Dispersion or Fire	Maximizes dispersion. See page 261.

Optimizing in this way brings up the inevitable challenge of comparing apples to oranges. How does a 5% change in ISO brightness compare to a little more scintillation or a somewhat improved tilt response? In other words, how do you determine the weighting factors in the equation for MF?

Rats! Another great question, and unfortunately, this one has a less than satisfying answer: trial and error, combined with experience using the program and specific design goals, leads to a reasonable selection of weighting factors and a well-optimized gemstone. The BOG website offers further wisdom and advice.

18.5.3 Real World BOG

Begin by **double-clicking** on the BOG icon. You should be presented with a DOS window for running GemRay and the BOG main control window (Figure 18-39).

The optimization workflow runs from top to bottom in this window. The first step is to load the Briar Rose design. Click the **Select GEM File...** button. BOG presents you with the file and reference angle selection dialog box (Figure 18-40).

Figure 18-39 The main window for running BOG. Note that BOG always re-loads the parameters from when you last used the program. Don't be surprised if some of the fields already have entries.

Navigate to the Briar Rose GemCAD file using the top part of the panel. With the correct file highlighted, click the **Extract Angles** button. This scans the prescription and presents you with the pavilion and crown angles. You need to **select** one of each as a reference for the optimization process (see Chapter 10.6 if this is not clear). It doesn't really matter which angles you choose. I tend to work with either the main or break facets. Note, however, that the remainder of this optimization tutorial assumes the angles shown in Figure 18-40. Click **Ok** to continue.

The next step is to inform BOG about the gem material and the range of angles you wish to explore. Click the **Modify Values...** button in the main window (second from the top on the right hand side) to open the appropriate dialog box (Figure 18-41).

The meaning of the angles should be clear. BOG begins with the starting values and varies them within the range set by the minimum and maximum. If the optimization process drives things outside of this window, the program stops and warns you that one or both angles are out of range. **Enter** the minimum and maximum values as shown. You will modify these later in the optimization process. You should also inform BOG that Briar Rose is intended for tourmaline. **Select** the appropriate entry from the list as shown and then click the **Ok** button to proceed.

At this point, it is worthwhile to check that all is well by having BOG ray trace the gem. Click on **PlayPen** at the bottom of the main control window and when the dialog box appears, click **Raytrace** at the lower right. You should be rewarded with three views of

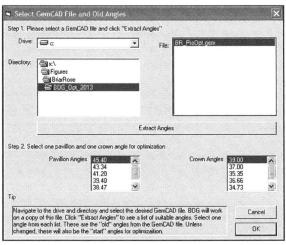

Figure 18-40 The file selection and reference angle entry dialog box.

the original Briar Rose, based on the Random, COS, and ISO lighting models (Figure 18-42; refer to page 196 for an explanation of these lighting models). BOG also informs you, among other things, that the ISO brightness of the gem is about 78%. Not bad for a (semi-random) start, but you can do better. While you are here, feel free to explore the other features of this window – it is the PlayPen after all. When you are done, click **Cancel** to return to the main window.

The next step is to identify and balance Merit Function targets. In the main BOG window, click **Modify Targets…**, the third button in the workflow. A small window with six tabs should appear, one for entering weighting factors and one for each of the five BOG Op-

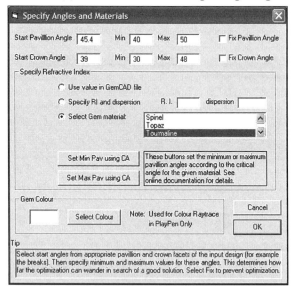

*Figure 18-41 The **Specify Angles and Materials** dialog box. BOG automatically enters the reference angles from the GemCAD file as starting values.*

timization Targets (Figure 18-43). I usually optimize designs for ISO brightness and Tilt. Sorry once again, but this is a case of experience dictating action. There will be plenty of time to explore other options later on. Let's forge ahead…

Enter the ISO and Tilt weights as shown in Figure 18-43. Make sure that the **Use** boxes for both ISO Brightness and Tilt are checked and then **click** on the **ISO Brightness** tab. BOG helpfully reminds you that there are no further parameters needed to evaluate this Target, so move on to the **Tilt** tab (Figure 18-44). Here, you must specify the direction and amount of tilt used to assess the gem's performance. **Enter** the values shown and then click **Ok** to complete the optimization target specification process.

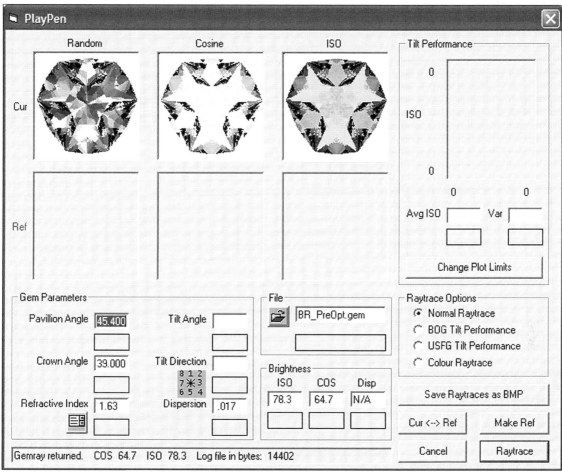

*Figure 18-42 Briar Rose ray traced in the **PlayPen**.*

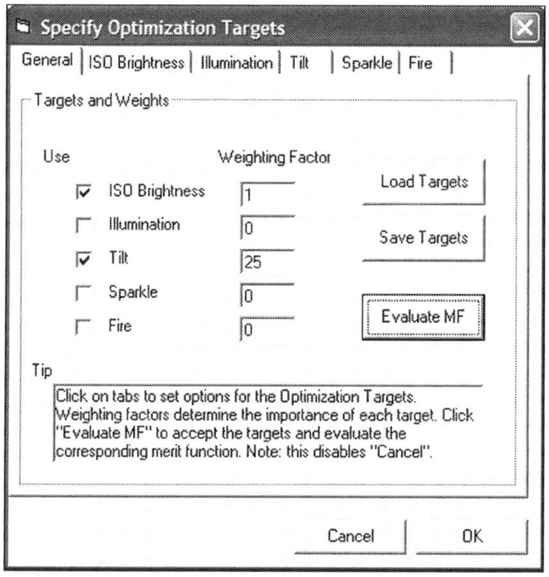

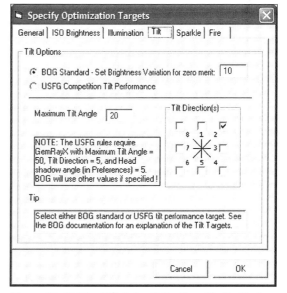

*Figure 18-43 The **Specify Optimization Targets** dialog box.*

*Figure 18-44 The **Tilt** tab of the **Specify Optimization Targets** dialog box.*

18.5.4 Optimizing Briar Rose

You are finally ready to optimize! In the main BOG window, Click **Optimize…** BOG pops up the Optimization Progress window (Figure 18-45). This window will present a great deal of information in a moment or two, so you might want to examine it carefully before clicking **Go!** at the bottom right.

BOG should start its work, varying first the pavilion and then the crown angles, tipping the gemstone as it goes. You can follow the action in the **Current Gem** window on the left and watch the angle, brightness and Merit Function values evolve. BOG also illustrates its progress graphically, showing the improvement as a serious of stacked bars in the plot on the right. Just when you start to get the hang of what's going on, BOG will stop, informing you in text superimposed on a friendly green background that its optimization is complete (Figure 18-46).

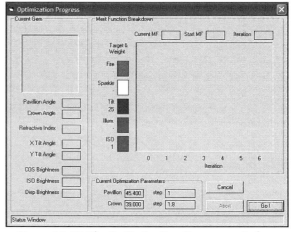

Click **Cancel** to return to the main window and note that BOG has recorded the optimized pavilion and crown angles, as well as the **Start** and **Final MF**, in the **Optimize** sub-panel. Note also that your angles may be somewhat different from those shown, due to minor differences in the input gem prescription and BOG-internal settings.

*Figure 18-45 The **Optimization Progress** window.*

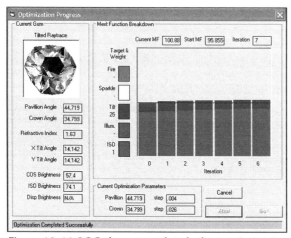

Figure 18-46 BOG has completed the optimization of Briar Rose, increasing the overall Merit Function by about 4% compared to the starting value.

In principle, the process is now complete, and you could use your favourite tool to tangent ratio the pavilion and crown to these better values (see Chapter 10.6.1). That would be blindly following the computer's suggestions, however, and this is rarely a good idea. The darn thing is supposed to help us catch the curve, after all, not invent it (see page 244).

I always check the optimization output for at least two good reasons. First, the computer can easily get confused (or stated more precisely, the computer can easily execute your confused instructions). The optimization process – that is, our intrepid mountain climber – may have wandered away and got lost, or it may have scaled a minor peak (see Section 18.5.1). Second and most importantly, the computer has no real aesthetic sense. It merely measures objective values associated with brightness, tilt, etc. As a result, it may very well select a set of angles that yields good numbers but which produces a disappointing gem. This is something that a real-world faceter would never do. For example, I will always select a gem with a pleasing reflection pattern over one with a few extra percent of ISO Brightness.

So. There are two problems: checking whether BOG has found the true maximum MF and verifying that the result is nice on the eyes. Two problems, one solution. Enter the Merit Function Mapper…

18.5.5 Exploring MF Mountain

BOG's Merit Function Mapper is a conceptually simple tool that maps out the MF landscape for you. It does this by varying the pavilion and crown reference angles between their minimum and maximum values (Figure 18-41), calculating the Merit Function at each location, and then presenting you with an interactive graphical representation of the results. There is also an option to produce a grid of over a hundred separate ray traces. How cool is that?

Click **MFMap** at the bottom of the main BOG window to launch the Merit Function Mapper. Again, you should see a relatively busy dialog box, with which you should familiarize yourself before proceeding. The left side of the window should remind you of the **Optimization Progress** window (Figure 18-45), and in fact, it operates in the exact same way, showing you the current conditions as the calculation proceeds. The right hand side will contain the actual **Merit Function Map**. Note how the large box spans the minimum to maximum range of the pavilion and crown reference angles.

Click **Go** to set things in motion. BOG steps progressively through the pavilion and crown angles, mapping the Merit Function as it goes. When it is done, you should see a map of the MF values scaled appropriately to the colour bar below it (Figure 18-47).

Try **clicking** on one of the coloured squares in the map. The information panel on the left immediately presents the relevant details and image for that combination of angles, and the stacked bar to its right shows the balance between ISO Brightness and Tilt. Explore the landscape and see if you can see trends in relative optimization target values as well as overall MF. Can you find local maxima? Where is the tallest peak?

Clearly the best gem lies somewhere toward the bottom center of the map. You can zoom in on this area by restricting the minimum and maximum reference angles in the **Specify Angles and Materials** dialog box. Click **Cancel** to return to the main window, and then click the **Modify Values…** button to enter the values shown in Figure 18-48. Click **Ok** to return to the main window.

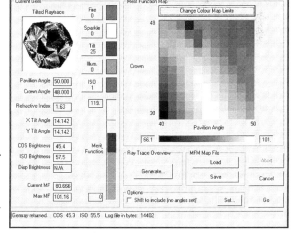

*Figure 18-47 The completed **Merit Function Map**.*

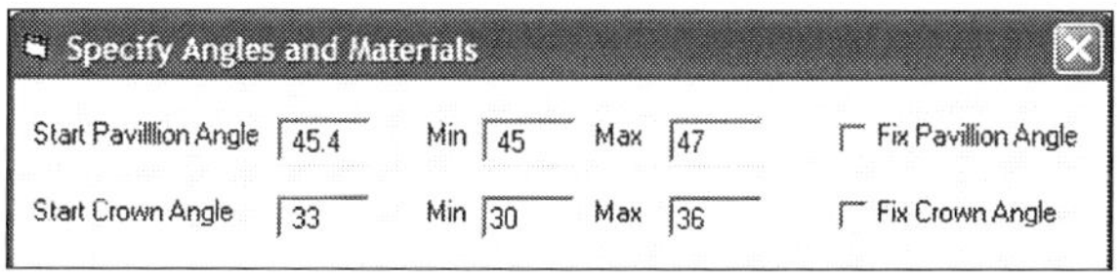

Run the **MF Map** once again. You will note that it now explores a considerably smaller region of the pavilion-crown landscape. **Click** various points on the map to see which reflection pattern is the most pleasing. You should notice that a fairly broad swath of MF Mountain has acceptable total per-

Figure 18-48 You can restrict the size of the Merit Function landscape using the Min and Max values of the reference angles.

formance but somewhat different reflection patterns. You can click the **Generate...** button in the **Ray Trace Overview** sub-panel to get a bird's eye perspective on the situation. Figure 18-49 shows the result.

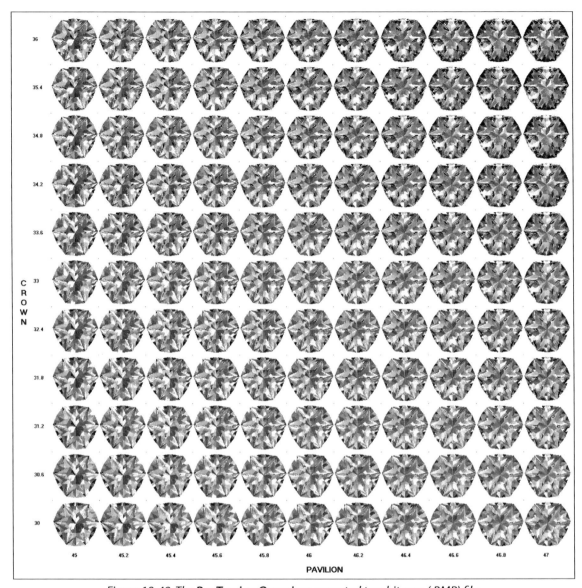

*Figure 18-49 The **RayTracing Overview**, exported to a bitmap (.BMP) file.*

I like the gem with pavilion 46° and crown 33° best. Again, this is an aesthetic choice, based on an overview of well-performing combinations. BOG has helped catch the curve.

As a final check, I usually compare the optimized gem with the original using the PlayPen. Return to the main window and then launch the **PlayPen** as before. You can play with two different gems at once in this window, using the current and reference buffers controlled by the buttons to the lower right. Figure 18-50 shows the optimized Briar Rose (**Cur**) above the original (**Ref**). Note that I also used the BOG Tilt Performance option in the right hand panel to generate the plots of ISO Brightness versus tilt angle.

BOG has done a fairly good job. The face-up ISO Brightness has increased from about 78% to almost 90%, and the optimized gem has improved Tilt Performance as well (upper line in the graph). Finally, and most importantly, the reflection pattern under Random lighting makes me smile...

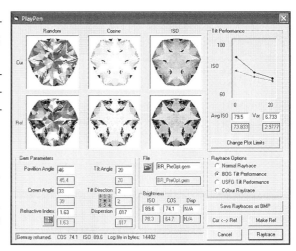

*Figure 18-50 A **PlayPen** comparison of the optimized Briar Rose (top row) with the original (bottom row) The plot on the right shows ISO Brightness versus tilt angle for the original (gray) and optimized (black) versions of the gem.*

18.6 Finishing Up

The foregoing pages have given a necessarily abbreviated view of gem optimization with BOG. You should repeat the process and explore the additional options at each step. To complete the case study, however, you have to incorporate the optimization results into the actual gem design.

Yes, this is a job for your favourite tangent ratio tool. Chapter 10.6.1 explains how to proceed using a variety of techniques, and Chapter 19.2.8 contains the final, optimized prescription. Note also that Briar Rose can benefit from the "Clever CAM" technique (see explanation starting on page 282). Given the relatively limited amount of extra gem rough (Figure 18-1), I actually executed the design using such an "inside-out" approach and managed to achieve more than 35% yield. Chapter 19.2.8 includes both versions of the cutting prescription: the classic "outside-in" approach detailed here and the "Clever CAM" strategy.

Of course, the proof of the pudding is in the eating, as Don Quixote so helpfully reminded us (and whom I badly misquoted on page 325 of Volume 1). Figure 18-51 shows the completed Briar Rose executed in that lovely piece of blue-green tourmaline. The front cover of this book tries to capture the gem in colour. I hope you agree that it's a knockout.

Figure 18-51 The completed tourmaline Briar Rose.

19

New Gemstone Designs

Although there is a huge and enticing range of gem designs available in books and online, many faceters take a surprisingly long time to expand their horizons beyond a few, well-established cuts. This is not necessarily a bad thing, since the visual impression of a particular design can be entrancingly different when executed in a different type or colour of gem rough. Nevertheless, the variety and beauty of modern gemstone cuts call out to the intrepid hobbyist, and this is one siren's song that you should heed.

This chapter contains diagrams and cutting instructions for twenty-one gemstone designs, ranging from simple cuts suitable for the beginner, up to complex gems that should challenge even the old hands at our craft. They are organized in three groups of increasing difficulty and, correspondingly, decreasing detail and explanation.

In addition to providing new (and I hope interesting) gemstone designs, this chapter will give you real-world experience in cutting techniques. Yes, you learned all about CAMs and CLAMs in Chapter 17, but here, you can put that knowledge to good use, producing some eye-catching gemstones.

19.1 Beginner Designs

At various locations in this book, I have complained about the pervasiveness of the standard round brilliant, not as a gemstone design *per se*, but rather as the traditional introduction to faceting for the beginning cutter. At the risk of being repetitive (again!), the SRB is *hard*. Hard enough, in fact, to discourage someone just setting out in our hobby.

It doesn't have to be so. My own introduction to faceting was gentle by comparison, with a much more forgiving design (see Chapter 5.2). But how can the beginner judge whether a particular gem cut is too ambitious? If you have read this far, you probably have some ideas: gem designs with multiple meet points per facet are a challenge, and cutting and polishing adjacent facets with very similar index and angle settings can lead to all kinds of pain. Nevertheless, wouldn't it be nice if there were a collection of gem designs suitable for the neophyte faceter?

This section gathers together half a dozen straightforward gem cuts with gently increasing difficulty. They include the **GeM101** design from Chapter 5, as well as a couple of variants, called **Twist5** and **Pyramid Twist**. **Tris de Garnet** is a deceptively simple cut which produces visually interesting random flashes from only nine pavilion and ten crown facets. The **CLAMour** design provides an introduction to the CLAM outlining technique from Chapter 17.5, while the final beginner's cut, called **Parapet**, approaches the SRB in terms of complexity and meet point requirements.

A couple of final notes before you set off to your faceting workshop. First, a 3D computer rendering of the gem accompanies each design in this and subsequent sections. Chapter 15.5 explains how you, too, can produce such images. Second, you may find that your gemstones appear reversed compared to the drawings shown here. Turn to page 303 of Volume 1 to learn how this happens and why you shouldn't worry about it.

19.1.1 GeM101

GeM101 is a simple, twisted reflector design that works well in both quartz and beryl. Chapter 5 explains in detail how to cut GeM101, starting with rough evaluation and selection and continuing through cutting, polishing, and finally showing off the fruits of your labour.

Due to its straightforward design, low facet count, and minimal meet points, GeM101 is the ideal beginner's stone. Nevertheless, the twisted pavilion produces surprisingly rich and interesting reflection patterns. Give it a try!

Figure 19-1 Three-dimensional computer image of the GeM101 design, here rendered in beryl.

Figure 19-2 shows the familiar top, side, bottom, and end views of the gem, while Figure 19-3 contains the cutting prescription (see also Chapter 5.1.1). The best way to learn to cut GeM101 is to follow the detailed instructions in Chapter 5. For your convenience, Figures 19-4 and 19-5 gather together images of the gem at each cutting stage.

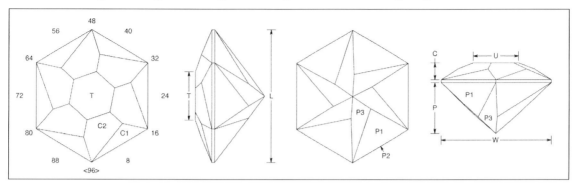

Figure 19-2 Top, side, bottom, and end views of the GeM101 design.

GeM101

Designed by Tom Herbst, January 2007
BOG optimized for ISO and Tilt
ISO 92% in Quartz
Angles for R.I. = 1.540
25 + 6 girdles = 31 facets
6-fold radial symmetry
96 index
L/W = 1.155 T/W = 0.423 U/W = 0.409
P/W = 0.444 C/W = 0.147
Vol./W³ = 0.222

PAVILION

P1	42.60°	08-24-40-56-72-88	Cut to TCP
P2	90.00°	08-24-40-56-72-88	Establish gem outline
P3	40.60°	07-23-39-55-71-87	Cut to girdle meets, new ctr pt

CROWN

C1	31.50°	08-24-40-56-72-88	Establish girdle thickness
C2	22.20°	05-21-37-53-69-85	Cut to girdle meets
T	0.00°	Table	Table - approximately 40% of width

Figure 19-3 The GeM101 cutting prescription.

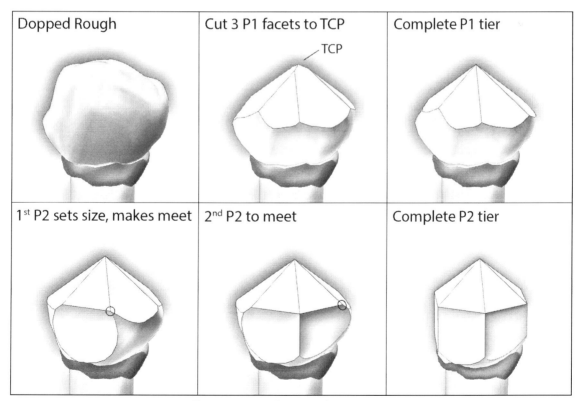

Dopped Rough	Cut 3 P1 facets to TCP	Complete P1 tier
1st P2 sets size, makes meet	2nd P2 to meet	Complete P2 tier

Figure 19-4 continues on the next page.

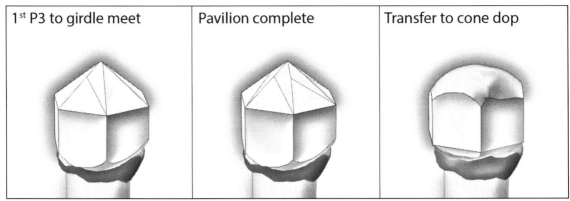

Figure 19-4 Cutting the pavilion of GeM101. Carefully dop the rough as explained in Chapter 5.4 (top left). Then, using the "cutting by ear" technique (Chapter 5.5.5), cut three P1 facets to a common temporary center point (TCP - top center). Complete the P1 tier to this same TCP (top right). The first P2 girdle facet sets the final gem size. Take care with this step, as shown in Figure 5-30. The intersection of this P2 facet with the P1 facets creates target meet points for the remaining girdle cuts (circled, middle left). Completing the P2 tier (middle center and right) establishes the gem outline. Carefully cut the first P3 facet to the girdle meet point (bottom left). Warning! The P3 facets come in very quickly. Complete the P3 tier (bottom center) and execute the dop transfer (bottom right and see Chapter 5.6).

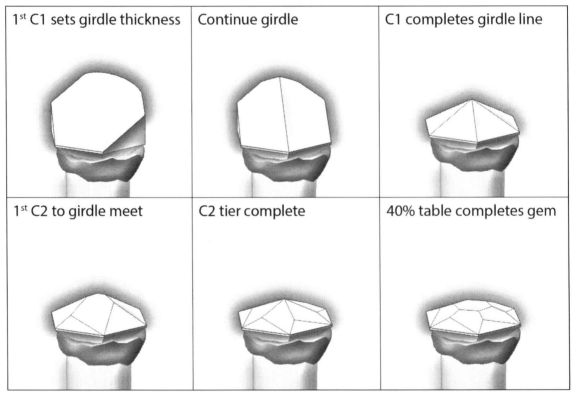

Figure 19-5 Cutting the crown of GeM101. Note: This sequence assumes that you have established the proper transfer cheat. See Chapter 5.7.1. The first C1 facet establishes the girdle thickness (top left). Continue and complete the C1 tier (top center and right), and double check that you have a level, continuous girdle. Cut the C2 facets to the girdle meet points (bottom left and center). These should come in more slowly than the P2 tier, since the angle and index difference to C1 is larger. Finally, float in a table facet approximately 40% of the width of the stone to complete GeM101 (bottom right and see Chapter 5.8).

19.1.2 Twist5

As explained in Chapter 16.2.2, Twist5 is a five-fold symmetric take on a pre-existing gem design, namely the excellent Sun Twist cut by Keith Sanker. You can find Sun Twist on the web (see Chapter 15.8.4).

In fact, both Twist5 and GeM101 take inspiration from Sun Twist, and all three gems perform well in low index material, despite the minimal facet count. Twist5 is arguably the easiest of the three to cut, but its five-fold symmetry means that you will need an 80 index wheel.

Figures 19-7 and 19-8 below show the standard gem views and prescription, respectively, while Figure 19-9 provides a step-by-step visual guide to cutting Twist5.

Figure 19-6 Twist5 rendered in quartz.

I really like the inverted pentagonal "mirage" in the reflection pattern. A comparison of Figures 19-1 and 19-6 demonstrates vividly how a small twist and a simple change of symmetry can produce a dramatically different visual effect.

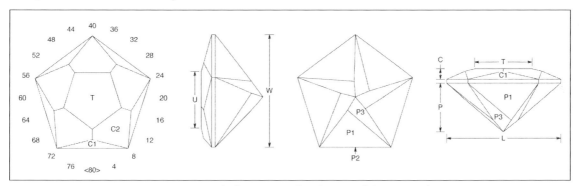

Figure 19-7 Top, side, bottom, and end views of the Twist5 design.

Twist5

by Tom Herbst, March 2002
BOG Optimized for ISO and Tilt
ISO 92% in Quartz
Angles for R.I. = 1.540
21 + 5 girdles = 26 facets
5-fold radial symmetry
80 index
L/W = 1.051 T/W = 0.490 U/W = 0.466
P/W = 0.418 C/W = 0.061
Vol./W³ = 0.168

PAVILION

P1	44.10°	80-16-32-48-64	Cut to ctr point
P2	90.00°	80-16-32-48-64	Level girdle
P3	41.59°	01-17-33-49-65	New ctr pt, girdle meet

CROWN

C1	25.00°	80-16-32-48-64	Establish girdle thickness
C2	10.00°	08-24-40-56-72	Cut to girdle meets
T	0.00°	Table	Center table, approx. 45% of W

Figure 19-8 The Twist5 GemCAD prescription.

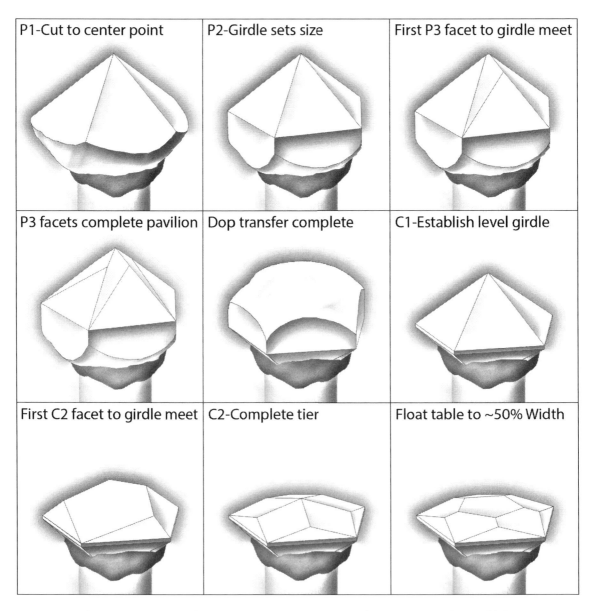

P1-Cut to center point	P2-Girdle sets size	First P3 facet to girdle meet
P3 facets complete pavilion	Dop transfer complete	C1-Establish level girdle
First C2 facet to girdle meet	C2-Complete tier	Float table to ~50% Width

Figure 19-9 The cutting sequence for Twist5 is very similar to that of GeM101. Begin by establishing a temporary center point (TCP) with three P1 facets. When you are satisfied, complete the P1 tier to this TCP (upper left). As before, the first P2 girdle facet sets the overall gem size, and the complete tier defines the outline of the stone (top center). Cut the first P3 facet to the P1-P2 girdle meet (top right). These facets are only a couple of degrees and one index step away from P1, so they will come in quickly. After completing P3 (middle left), transfer the stone and cut C1 to a level girdle line (middle center and right). The first C2 facet just touches the girdle meet (bottom left). Finish the C2 tier (bottom center) and complete the gem with a symmetric table cut to approximately 50% of the width of the stone (bottom right).

19.1.3 Pyramid Twist

Pyramid Twist is yet another take on the simple, twisted reflector motif of GeM101 and Twist 5. This time, the table is not free-floating, and the overall visual effect is more geometric and "clean." This design emphasizes colour over sparkle, so select your rough accordingly.

As the first design in this book with table meets, Pyramid Twist provides a gentle introduction to the challenge of cutting this most difficult of facets. The geometry buffs in the readership will point out at this stage that, with only three table meets, this should be no real challenge at all. Nevertheless, Pyramid Twist lets you hone your meet balancing skills, secure in the knowledge that everything, in principle, should work out.

Figure 19-10 Pyramid Twist rendered in quartz.

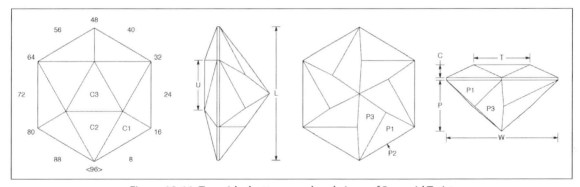

Figure 19-11 Top, side, bottom, and end views of Pyramid Twist.

Pyramid Twist

Designed by Tom Herbst, January 2007
BOG optimized for ISO and Tilt
ISO 94% in Quartz
Angles for R.I. = 1.540
22 + 6 girdles = 28 facets
3-fold radial symmetry
96 index
L/W = 1.155 T/W = 0.500 U/W = 0.433
P/W = 0.442 C/W = 0.111
Vol./W³ = 0.203

PAVILION

P1	43.50°	08-24-40-56-72-88	Cut to TCP
P2	90.00°	08-24-40-56-72-88	Establish gem outline
P3	40.50°	07-23-39-55-71-87	to girdle meets, new ctr pt

CROWN

C1	23.90°	08-24-40-56-72-88	Establish girdle thickness
C2	14.35°	96-32-64	to corner meets
C3	0.00°	Table	to 3 C1-C2 meets

Figure 19-12 The GemCAD prescription for Pyramid Twist.

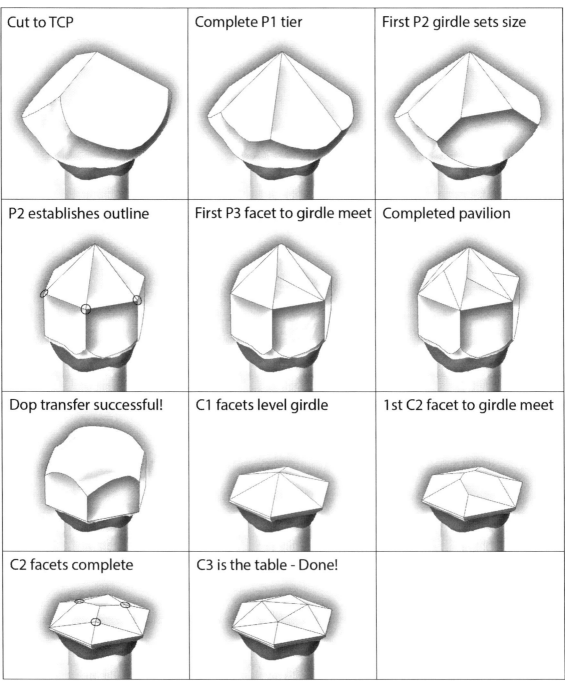

Cut to TCP	Complete P1 tier	First P2 girdle sets size
P2 establishes outline	First P3 facet to girdle meet	Completed pavilion
Dop transfer successful!	C1 facets level girdle	1st C2 facet to girdle meet
C2 facets complete	C3 is the table - Done!	

Figure 19-13 Cutting Pyramid Twist should by now be familiar territory. Begin with a TCP formed by three P1 facets (top left). Complete the P1 tier (top center) and use the first P2 girdle facet to establish the gem size (top right). Completing the gem outline provides meet points for the P3 facets (circled, second row left). The P3 tier completes the pavilion (second row center and right). After dop transfer (third row left), cut the C1 tier to a level girdle line and place the first C2 facet at the P2-C1 girdle meet (third row right). Finishing the C2 facets provides three meet points (circled, bottom left) for the table, which completes the gem (bottom center). Take care placing the table – over cutting at this stage means going back to C1, at least.

19.1.4 Tris de Garnet

As mentioned on page 334, Tris de Garnet is a simple design that produces lovely, random sparkles with only nine pavilion and ten crown facets. It also serves as a gentle introduction to the CAM technique of establishing the gem outline (see Chapter 17.3).

It turns out that Tris de Garnet was my very first gem design, and my initial cutting order used the standard "outside-in" CAM approach as shown below (Figure 19-17).

A very expensive chunk of Merelani mint garnet encouraged me to look for a better way. Figure 19-18 shows the "Clever CAM" inside-out cutting order, which really can save gem rough, particularly for shapes like Tris de Garnet.

Figure 19-14 Three-dimensional computer rendering of Tris de Garnet.

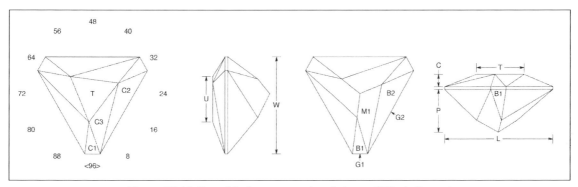

Figure 19-15 Top, side, bottom, and end views of Tris de Garnet.

Tris de Garnet

"Classic" cut order
by Tom Herbst, 2001
ISO 75% in garnet
Angles for R.I. = 1.730
19 + 6 girdles = 25 facets
3-fold radial symmetry
96 index
L/W = 1.155 T/W = 0.505 U/W = 0.470
P/W = 0.441 C/W = 0.127
Vol./W³ = 0.189

PAVILION			
B1	40.40°	96-32-64	Cut to TCP
B2	54.19°	16-48-80	to same TCP
G1	90.00°	96-32-64	Sets overall size
G2	90.00°	16-48-80	to G1-B1-B2 meet
M1	44.95°	14-46-78	to G1-G2-B1-B2 meet. Cuts away TCP
CROWN			
C1	21.21°	96-32-64	Sets girdle thickness
C2	32.30°	16-48-80	Level girdle
C3	23.36°	14-46-78	Cut to C1-C2 girdle meet
T	0.00°	Table	Table to C1-C2-C3 meet

Figure 19-16 The GemCAD prescription for the "classic" Tris de Garnet cutting order.

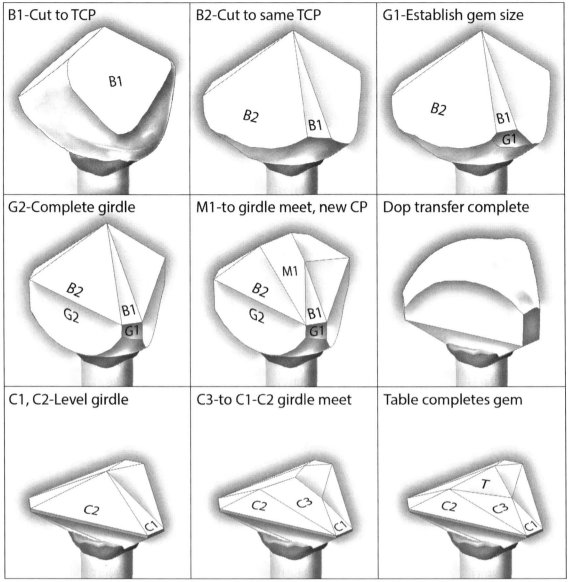

Figure 19-17 "Classic CAM" cutting sequence for Tris de Garnet. Compare this method for producing the pavilion with the "Clever CAM" approach in Figure 19-18.

You can read more about the Clever CAM approach and see a direct comparison of the two methods for cutting Tris de Garnet starting on page 282 of this volume.

Note: Eagle-eyed readers may notice a slight difference in the volume factor (Vol./W³) between the two prescriptions. How can this be, given that the two designs are supposedly identical? Here's a hint: GemCAD calculates the volume of the actual gem that you "cut." Although Tris de Garnet has fixed angles and meet points, there is one step for which you have complete freedom to place the facets where you want them. Still stumped? Here's another hint (and really a give-away): You can turn this freedom to your advantage, including increasing your yield as explained on page 44.

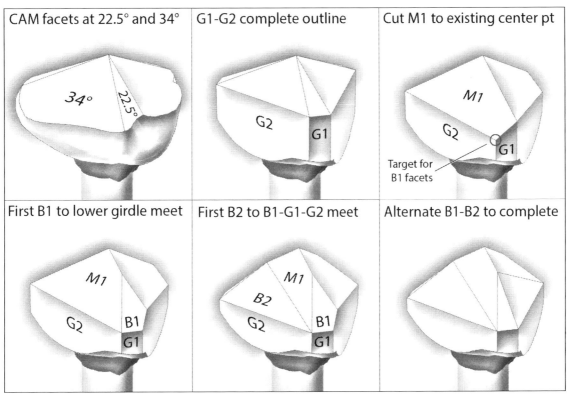

Figure 19-18 The "Clever CAM" approach to cutting the pavilion can save gem rough. The key is to use the center point of the CAM facets as the ultimate culet of the gem. Turn to page 282 to learn more.

Tris de Garnet

"Clever CAM" cutting order
by Tom Herbst, 2001
ISO 75% in garnet
Angles for R.I. = 1.730
19 + 6 girdles = 25 facets
3-fold radial symmetry
96 index
L/W = 1.155 T/W = 0.504 U/W = 0.470
P/W = 0.441 C/W = 0.127
Vol./W³ = 0.187

PAVILION

G1	90.00°	96-32-64	CAM outline 22.5 deg
G2	90.00°	16-48-80	CAM outline 34 deg
M1	44.95°	14-46-78	Cut to prev center - cuts away CAM
B1	40.40°	96-32-64	Cut to lower girdle meets
B2	54.19°	16-48-80	Same meet - levels girdle

CROWN

C1	21.21°	96-32-64	Sets girdle thickness
C2	32.30°	16-48-80	Level girdle
C3	23.36°	14-46-78	Cut to C1-C2 girdle meet
T	0.00°	Table	Table to C1-C2-C3 meet

Figure 19-19 The GemCAD prescription for the "Clever CAM" Tris de Garnet cutting order. Note that G1 and G2 result from CAM facets at 22.4° and 34°, respectively. The pavilion mains M1 subsequently cut these CAM facets away. See also Figure 17-19.

19.1.5 CLAMour

The CLAMour gem design, like Tris de Garnet, is deceptively simple, yet it holds a deeper, more mathematical secret. Hidden behind the apparently straightforward selection of index and angle for the first two facet tiers is the CLAM technique for establishing the gem outline. Chapter 17.5 supplies all of the mathematical (and practical) gore of the CLAM method.

Cutting CLAMour is, relatively speaking, simplicity itself, and the gem does a really nice job of balancing colour and sparkle. Figures 19-21 and 19-22 contain the usual 4-views of the design and its GemCAD prescription, respectively, while Figure 19-23 portrays, in abbreviated form, the cutting sequence.

CLAMour is a typical keel-type gem cut in the sense that it exploits what are effectively multiple "center points" along the base of the stone to keep the pavilion angles under control in an elongated design. While cutting the gem, try to understand

Figure 19-20 CLAMour, rendered in garnet.

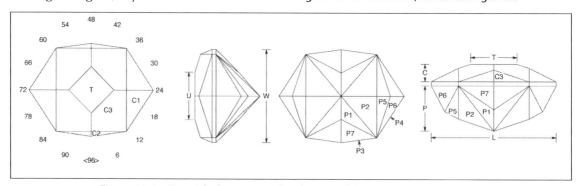

Figure 19-21 Top, side, bottom, and end views of the CLAMour gem design.

CLAMour

Designed by Tom Herbst, Mar 2007 - Jul 2013
BOG optimized for ISO and Tilt
ISO 80.2% in Garnet
Angles for R.I. = 1.760
33 + 8 girdles = 41 facets
2-fold, mirror-image symmetry
96 index
L/W = 1.382 T/W = 0.513 U/W = 0.513
P/W = 0.490 C/W = 0.189
Vol./W³ = 0.357

PAVILION			
P1	43.50°	03-45-51-93	Cut to TCP
P2	40.97°	06-42-54-90	to same TCP
P3	90.00°	02-46-50-94	Define size
P4	90.00°	15-33-63-81	Continue girdle
P5	43.98°	09-39-57-87	to P1-P2-P3-P4 meet
P6	65.93°	15-33-63-81	Same meet, level girdle
P7	46.06°	02-46-50-94	Same meet, complete girdle line
CROWN			
C1	30.20°	15-33-63-81	Define girdle thickness
C2	68.02°	02-46-50-94	Complete girdle
C3	24.57°	12-36-60-84	to girdle meet
T	0.00°	Table	Float in to 1/2 Width

Figure 19-22 GemCAD prescription for CLAMour. Note that P1-P2 locate the corner girdle meet using the CLAM technique. Turn to Chapter 17.5 for more.

how the keel comes together. If and when you embark on your own design adventures, your command of the keel will come in very useful.

I first cut CLAMour in some lovely synthetic GGG rough and was amazed. The design should work well in any medium to strongly saturated material. Try it yourself and see.

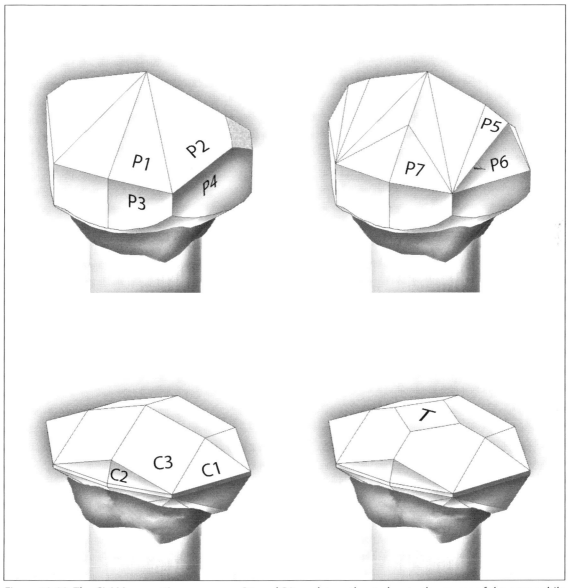

Figure 19-23 The CLAMour cutting sequence. P1 and P2 work together to locate the corner of the gem, while facets P3 and P4 establish the outline based on this reference (upper left). P5 through P7 level the girdle and add visual interest (upper right). The crown is relatively conventional, with C1 and C2 defining the girdle (lower left). The free floating table (lower right) has no meet points. While easier to execute in principle, you should monitor your progress carefully to ensure a pleasing, symmetric gem.

19.1.6 Parapet

What a difference a single facet can make. Parapet is essentially only a meet point and an angle setting different from the simplified SRB known as the eight-sided brilliant (this is the beginner's stone suggested by Vargas – see Chapter 9.1). Cutting C3 to half the length of the C1-C2 intersection rather than to the tip of C1 changes the look completely. You could, in fact, call Parapet an eight-sided brilliant suffering from star facets with delusions of grandeur.

Of course, there is more to Parapet than a simple tweak to a simple SRB. For example, the depth and cutting angle of C3 are carefully determined to ensure 90° angles, well balanced facet sizes, and a clean, geometric look. In fact, it was the resemblance of the crown to the top view of an old-fashioned castle tower that gave the gem its name.

Figure 19-24 A 3D rendering of Parapet in sapphire.

Parapet is the first gem design in this collection with more than three table meets. As an experienced (and perhaps persnickety) geometer, you no doubt realize that this presents a much greater challenge. Take care in centering the initial table cut as described in Chapter 5.8, and hopefully you will make most or all of the meets. If you have to over cut some of the meet points, you can go back and adjust things by lowering the angle of some of the C3 facets until the gem looks clean and balanced. This will, unfortunately, mess up the 90° top-down "parapet" look, but hopefully only a little. This post-table tweak is a variation on the technique described in "Shooting Stars" on page 345 of Volume 1. As I so often warn, however, check your strategy in GemCAD before committing your corrections to stone.

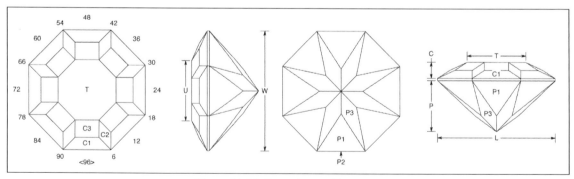

Figure 19-25 Four-views of Parapet.

Parapet

Designed by Tom Herbst, February 2007
BOG optimized for ISO and Tilt
ISO 94% in Corundum
Angles for R.I. = 1.760
41 + 8 girdles = 49 facets
8-fold, mirror-image symmetry
96 index
L/W = 1.000 T/W = 0.500 U/W = 0.500
P/W = 0.423 C/W = 0.134
Vol./W³ = 0.207

PAVILION

P1	42.60°	96-12-24-36-48-60-72-84	Cut to TCP
P2	90.00°	96-12-24-36-48-60-72-84	Establish outline
P3	38.03°	06-18-30-42-54-66-78-90	to girdle meets, new center pt

CROWN

C1	33.00°	96-12-24-36-48-60-72-84	Establish girdle
C2	26.43°	06-18-30-42-54-66-78-90	to Girdle meets
C3	24.66°	96-12-24-36-48-60-72-84	to half C1-C2 edge, C1 should be ~W/10
T	0.00°	Table	to C2-C3 meets

Figure 19-26 Parapet's GemCAD cutting prescription.

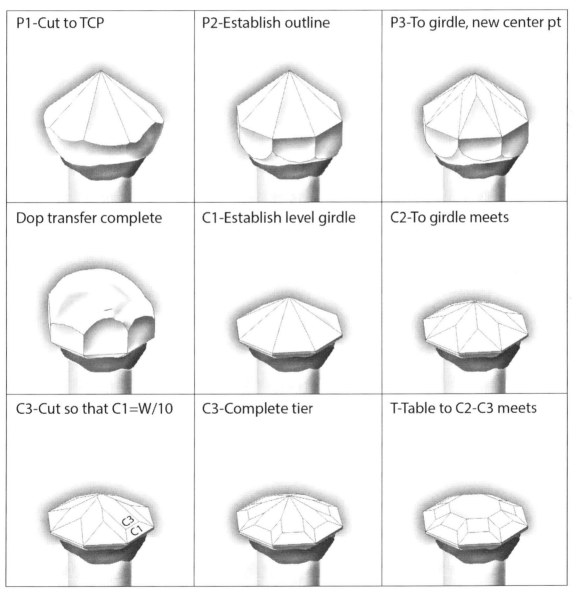

Figure 19-27 Cutting sequence for Parapet. The pavilion follows the conventional strategy of creating a temporary center point (TCP) to establish the girdle outline (top left and center). The C3 facets determine the girdle thickness (center), while the C2 and C3 tiers form the geometric "parapet" facet layout (next 3 panels). Note that the table has to hit eight meet points with this design (bottom right).

19.2 Intermediate Designs

Who's afraid of a few meet points? The table has to hit six of the darn things at once? No problem. Bring it on.

If you find yourself uttering statements similar to the above, you are probably ready to tackle some more difficult gem cuts. This section brings together nine intermediate designs to test your mettle. **Fritz15** is a rectangular reflector that produces dazzling geometric flashes. **Checkpoint** will teach you the secrets of checkerboard cuts, while **Tabula Rosa** illustrates how classic scissor facets can add interest to even the simplest of designs. Cushion triangles, such as **Tinkerbell**, always seem to surprise and satisfy with their rich and ever-changing reflection pattern. The **Keystar** design uses the OMNI technique to match a keystone outline to a brilliant pavilion. **Skew Tube** is another take on the geometric reflector, while **Scrambler** illustrates how a CAM pre-form can make the most out of odd-shaped rough. **Briar Rose** from Chapter 18 provides visual interest and a challenge to the cutter, due to its several fans of closely placed facets. The final intermediate design, **Green Flash**, requires off-center dopping and demonstrates how large angled facets can multiply the interest of an otherwise conventional brilliant pavilion.

19.2.1 Fritz15

Chapter 16.2.3 uses the example of Fritz15 to demonstrate how you can create an entirely new gem from a pre-existing design by playing with proportions. Fritz15 is a cleverly-named version of the Fritz design executed with a length-to-width ratio of 1.5. All those creative writing classes seem to have paid off...

The cutting prescription presumes that you have outlined the rough to L/W=1.508. You can do this by the traditional method of cutting opposed girdle facets to equal depth and measuring, or you can execute a suitable CAM outline. I tend to use CAM when the rough allows it, since misalignment and machine flexure can make cutting balanced girdle facets a challenge. See Chapter 17.2 for more on this issue.

Figure 19-28 Rendering of Fritz15 in tourmaline.

Take a close look at Figure 19-31. Like me, you may find that you have barely enough raw stone to complete the gem, or more likely, that the rough will not permit you to cut the P3 facets to the full length of the gem. This will certainly be the case if you use a CAM outline. The figure shows you how to alternate P3 and P4 cuts to go only as deep as you have to. As soon as the P3 and P4 facets meet, you can complete the pavilion.

Fritz15 produces lovely, irregular geometric flashes as you rock the gem. It's not a sparkler, and thus works best in beautifully coloured material. My first Fritz15 was in some amazing Tajik golden beryl, and it's a knock-out (see Figure 16-9).

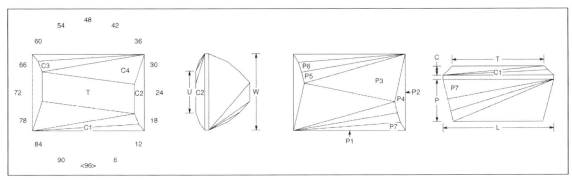

Figure 19-29 Top, side, bottom, and end views of Fritz15.

Fritz15Tourm

Designed by Tom Herbst 2002-2007
BOG Optimized for ISO (and Tilt)
ISO 70% in Tourmaline
Angles for R.I. = 1.620
19 + 4 girdles = 23 facets
2-fold radial symmetry
96 index
L/W = 1.508 T/W = 1.246 U/W = 0.547
P/W = 0.550 C/W = 0.119
Vol./W³ = 0.648

PAVILION

P1	90.00°	96-48	Pre-form to L/W=1.508
P2	90.00°	24-72	
P3	40.80°	45-93	Cut to midline
P4	75.03°	24-72	Cut to lower P3-Girdle meet
P5	44.82°	46-94	to P1-P2-P3 meet
P6	51.73°	47-95	to P1-P2-P3 meet
P7	67.26°	96-48	to P1-P2-P3 meet

CROWN

C1	38.00°	96-48	Establish girdle line
C2	42.32°	24-72	Finish girdle
C3	20.66°	47-95	to C1-C2 meet
C4	16.43°	46-94	to C1-C2 meet
T	0.00°	Table	Table

Figure 19-30 GemCAD prescription for Fritz15 in tourmaline.

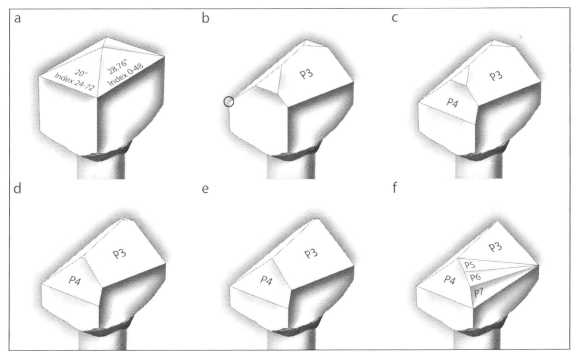

Figure 19-31 Generating the Fritz15 outline using shallow CAM facets. The combination in the upper left panel works well. Cut the P3 facets to the same depth (top center), creating a meet point (circled) for P4. Clearly, the P3 facets were not cut deep enough (upper right). Placing them deeper and then re-cutting P4 gets you close (bottom left). Iterate this way until P3 and P4 "close" the gem (bottom center). You can then cut the remainder of the pavilion (bottom right).

19.2.2 Checkpoint

Checkpoint mates a classic reflector pavilion to a checkerboard crown. There are two versions: a full checkerboard suitable for materials of "normal" refractive index (i.e. quartz and higher), and an apex crown variant that will work with extremely low index gems such as fluorite and opal. Yes, the apex crown version merely omits the table, which happens to be the central square of the checkerboard. Turn to page 21 for more on apex crowns.

I find it fascinating how inclined cuts can lead to rectilinear facets within a round outline (see Figure 19-38). It turns out that GemCAD makes this bit of magic relatively straightforward. Here's the secret: when placing intersection points for a facet, holding the shift key down restricts the target lo-

Figure 19-32 The apex crown version of Checkpoint rendered in fluorite.

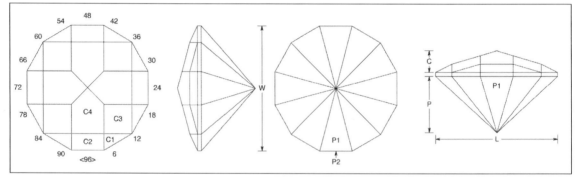

Figure 19-33 Top, side, bottom, and end views of the apex crown Checkpoint.

Checkpoint

Designed by Tom Herbst July 2007
BOG optimized for ISO and some tilt
ISO 94% in Fluorite of all things...
Angles for R.I. = 1.430
32 + 12 girdles = 44 facets
4-fold, mirror-image symmetry
96 index
L/W = 1.000
P/W = 0.450 C/W = 0.173
Vol./W³ = 0.204

PAVILION

P1	42.00°	96-08-16-24- 32-40-48-56- 64-72-80-88	Cut to TCP
P2	90.00°	96-08-16-24- 32-40-48-56- 64-72-80-88	Establish size

CROWN

C1	30.00°	08-16-32-40- 56-64-80-88	Establish girdle
C2	26.57°	96-24-48-72	Complete girdle
C3	22.21°	12-36-60-84	to corner meet
C4	16.10°	96-24-48-72	to C1-C2-C3 meet, new ctr

Figure 19-34 GemCAD prescription for the apex crown Checkpoint.

cation to exactly above/below or left/right of the last point entered. You can even select a reference point, clear it, and then hold Shift to force the desired facet vertex to be on a vertical or horizontal line from the reference. Very cool.

Examine the rendered images of Checkpoint carefully (Figures 19-32 and 19-35). While the traditional tabled version returns a pleasing mix of checkered and radial flashes, the low-index, apex crown gem produces a "mirage" at its heart – quite a different effect. You can try eliminating the table facet on other designs…just make sure to re-optimize the angles before cutting stone. Fisheyes make lousy mirages.

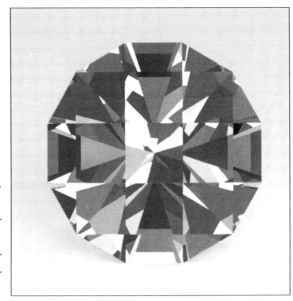

Figure 19-35 Three-dimensional rendering of the tabled version of Checkpoint in topaz.

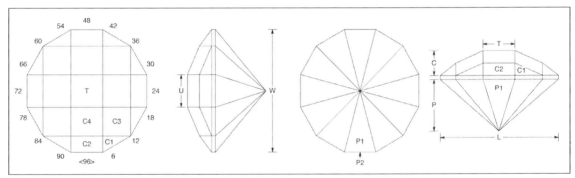

Figure 19-36 Top, side, bottom, and end views of the tabled Checkpoint.

Checkpoint (Tabled)

Designed by Tom Herbst, July 2007 / September 2013
BOG Optimized for ISO and Tilt
ISO 93% in Topaz
Angles for R.I. = 1.610
33 + 12 girdles = 45 facets
1-fold radial symmetry
96 index
L/W = 1.000 T/W = 0.268 U/W = 0.268
P/W = 0.423 C/W = 0.202
Vol./W³ = 0.224

PAVILION

P1	40.20°	96-08-16-24-32-40-48-56-64-72-80-88	Cut to TCP
P2	90.00°	96-08-16-24-32-40-48-56-64-72-80-88	Establish size

CROWN

C1	41.00°	08-16-32-40-56-64-80-88	Establish girdle
C2	36.98°	96-24-48-72	Complete girdle
C3	31.58°	12-36-60-84	to corner meet
C4	23.49°	96-24-48-72	to C1-C2-C3 meet
T	0.00°	Table	to C3-C4 meets

Figure 19-37 GemCAD prescription for the tabled Checkpoint.

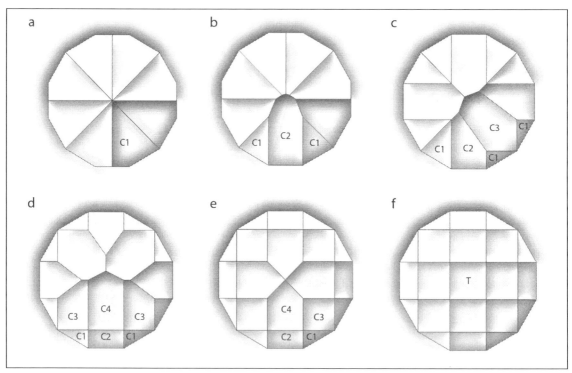

Figure 19-38 Fitting square pegs into a round hole. The C1 facets show conventional central symmetry (panel a). Placing the C2, C3 and C4 facets at the correct angles results in rectilinear "checkerboard" facets (next four panels). The final facet (panel f) distinguishes the tabled Checkpoint from the apex crown version (panel e).

19.2.3 Tabula Rosa

Tabula Rosa provides an appealing solution for all that dark garnet you have rolling around in your rough drawer. Don't try to deny that it is there...try Tabula Rosa instead. This design breaks the central rule of conventional gemstones with a "pavilion" as far below the critical angle as you can get: zero degrees. It thereby deliberately windows terribly, allowing light to pass directly through the gem like a...well, like a window. This leads to short light paths and correspondingly less internal absorption in saturated rough. Tabula Rosa also introduces you to scissor facets, which can add interest and sparkle to otherwise conventional shapes such as the rectangle.

Figure 19-39 A pair of Tabula Rosas (or should I say Tabulas Rosa?) rendered in garnet.

Needless to say, this gem requires a backless mounting. You should also take some care in dopping, since cutting Tabula Rosa requires a flat-to-flat dop transfer. Also, note the CLAM-like strategy for generating the gem outline (Figure 19-42). You can also just execute a conventional ECED type rectangular outline with L/W=1.411 (see Chapter 17.2).

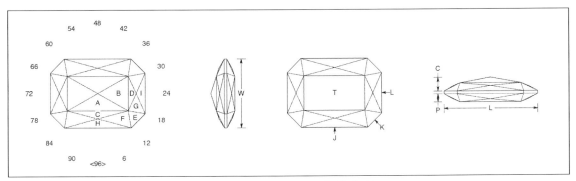

Figure 19-40 Four-views of Tabula Rosa.

Tabula Rosa

Designed by Tom Herbst, Apr. 2010-Oct. 2013
Inspired by Long & Steele's Super Emerald
Angles for R.I. = 1.540
42 + 8 girdles = 50 facets
2-fold, mirror-image symmetry
96 index
L/W = 1.411 T/W = 0.910 U/W = 0.499
P/W = 0.118 C/W = 0.118
Vol./W³ = 0.259

A	18.00°	96-48	A-B to temporary center point
B	10.10°	24-72	A-B cut away by table
C	19.08°	96-48	Cut to equal depth leaving 0.5 W clear
D	21.80°	24-72	to A-B corner meet (circled below)
E	29.55°	12-36-60-84	to same meet
F	24.94°	01-47-49-95	to same meet
G	24.94°	23-25-71-73	to same meet
H	30.00°	96-48	to C-F meet
I	27.99°	24-72	to D-G meet
J	90.00°	96-48	Girdle
K	90.00°	12-36-60-84	Continue girdle
L	90.00°	24-72	Finish girdle
T	0.00°	Table	Table cuts away A-B

Figure 19-41 The GemCAD prescription for Tabula Rosa. The crown is identical to the pavilion.

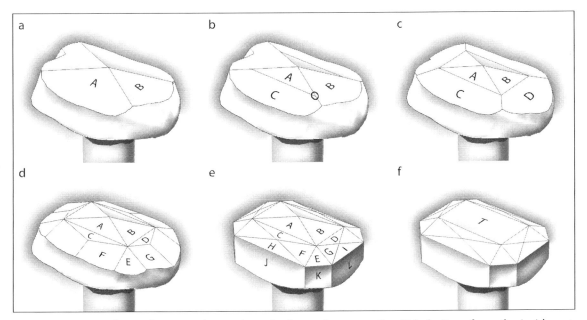

Figure 19-42 My admittedly somewhat awkward scheme for generating Tabula Rosa from the inside out, thereby not requiring an accurate L/W "pre-form." Tiers A and B act like CLAM facets, providing a guide for the placement of later cuts. Having discharged this duty, they are duly dispatched by the final, table facet. Of course, you do not need to repeat this exercise on the other side of the gem...the conventional "inside-out" order will work just fine.

19.2.4 Tinkerbell

Tinkerbell is a semi-classic triangular cushion, and it exhibits all of the entrancing scintillation that this type of design produces. The cutting procedure begins with a standard CAM outline to establish the girdle facets. Fans of gemstone symmetry will note that the pavilion is 3-fold mirror symmetric at this stage, but the highlight facets P5 to P8 break this symmetry down to 3-fold radial.

Breaking things can be good, and incidentally, it was these symmetry breaking highlight facets that inspired Tinkerbell's name. I was one of millions of Sunday-evening Disney watchers as a kid, and the outline of P5-P8 reminded me of Tinkerbell's wave of her magic wand at the beginning of each program.

Figure 19-43 Tinkerbell rendered in tourmaline.

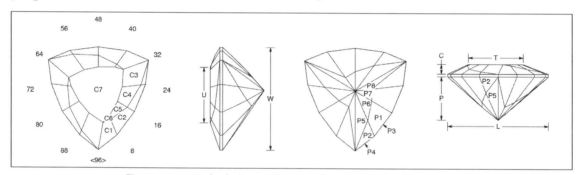

Figure 19-44 Tinkerbell, seen from the top, side, bottom, and end.

Tinkerbell

Designed by Tom Herbst, April 2005
BOG optimized for ISO and Tilt
ISO 88% in Tourmaline
Angles for R.I. = 1.620
49 + 12 girdles = 61 facets
3-fold radial symmetry
96 index
L/W = 1.007 T/W = 0.549 U/W = 0.539
P/W = 0.419 C/W = 0.094
Vol./W³ = 0.158

PAVILION

P1	46.92°	14-18-46-50-78-82	Cut to TCP
P2	43.92°	10-22-42-54-74-86	to TCP
P3	90.00°	14-18-46-50-78-82	Establish size
P4	90.00°	10-22-42-54-74-86	Complete outline
P5	40.91°	09-41-73	to corner meet
P6	43.34°	13-45-77	to P2-P5 meet
P7	42.85°	17-49-81	to P1-P6 meet
P8	37.97°	26-58-90	to P1-P7 meet

CROWN

C1	27.56°	10-22-42-54-74-86	Establish girdle line
C2	30.09°	14-18-46-50-78-82	Complete girdle
C3	21.01°	23-55-87	to corner meet
C4	22.70°	19-51-83	to C1-C3 meet
C5	22.30°	16-48-80	to C2-C4 meet
C6	19.49°	12-44-76	to C2-C5 meet
C7	0.00°	Table	Table

Figure 19-45 GemCAD prescription for Tinkerbell.

19.2.5 Keystar

Keystar is a keystone design inspired by Jeff Graham's excellent Pat's Points. In addition to producing a knock-out stone, Keystar provides a fine introduction to the OMNI technique of generating a target gem outline (see Chapter 17.4).

As explained on page 293, you have to use a sneaky trick to generate the meet points for the P8 and P9 girdle facets. Eagle-eyed readers will spot that Sepang in the next section plays the same game. Note also that, for Keystar, facet tiers P11 to P15 can be eliminated for smaller gemstones, or for a somewhat different look.

Like many barion designs, Keystar produces a lovely brilliant-type reflection pattern centered in a distinctly non-circular outline. The

Figure 19-46 3D rendering of Keystar in tourmaline.

key to this bit of geometric magic is girdle matching "moon" facets, in this case, P6, P7 and P10. Keystar produces plenty of sparkle, and hence will work well in less saturated rough.

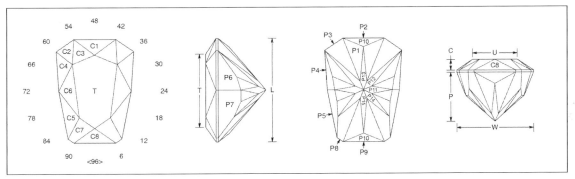

Figure 19-47 GemCAD four-views of Keystar.

KeyStar

by Tom Herbst (Feb 2002)
Angles for RI=1.62
ISO 86%
Angles for R.I. = 1.620
45 + 10 girdles = 55 facets
1-fold, mirror-image symmetry
96 index
L/W = 1.307 T/W = 0.924 U/W = 0.579
P/W = 0.616 C/W = 0.134
(P2 P9)/W = 1.307
Vol./W³ = 0.405

PAVILION

P1	42.10°	03-09-15-21- 27-33-39-45- 51-57-63-69- 75-81-87-93	Cut to ctr pt
P2	90.00°	48	Establish size
P3	90.00°	39-57	Level girdle
P4	90.00°	23-73	to P1-P3 meet
P5	90.00°	21-75	to P1-P4 meet
P6	72.64°	23-73	Level girdle
P7	72.93°	21-75	level girdle, P6-P1 mt
P8	90.00°	09-87	level girdle
P9	90.00°	96	Complete outline
P10	53.07°	96-48	level girdle

Figure 19-48 GemCAD prescription for Keystar (continued on next page).

P11	40.59°	24-72	to moon meet
P12	41.12°	36-60	to girdle meet
P13	40.97°	48	to P10 meet
P14	40.85°	12-84	to moon meet
P15	40.98°	96	to P10 meet
CROWN			
C1	34.36°	48	Establish girdle line
C2	28.00°	39-57	Level girdle
C3	25.22°	42-54	to girdle meet
C4	33.96°	23-73	level girdle
C5	34.42°	21-75	level girdle
C6	31.37°	22-74	to girdle meet
C7	23.70°	09-87	level girdle
C8	35.69°	96	level girdle
T	0.00°	Table	

Figure 19-48 (continued) The remainder of the Keystar GemCAD prescription.

19.2.6 Skew Tube

I just love surprising contrasts, and it has led to a number of gem designs which attempt to produce semi-random, chaotic flashes from a seemingly geometrically ordered gem layout. Skew Tube, along with Fritz and Fritz15, work well in intensely coloured rough, producing large flashes like a classic reflector design, but with a definitely skewed geometry compared to the gem outline.

Note that the default "outside-in" cutting order shown here can be somewhat wasteful of gem material. Beginning with the rough pre-formed to L/W=1.375 and working from the inside out can improve yield. See page 282 for more on these rough-saving strategies.

Figure 19-49 Skew Tube rendered in tourmaline.

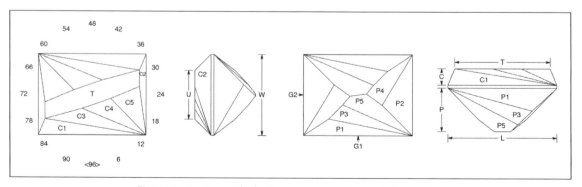

Figure 19-50 Top, side, bottom, and end views of Skew Tube.

SkewTube

Designed by Tom Herbst - Fall 2008
ISO 80% in Tourmaline
Angles for R.I. = 1.620
21 + 4 girdles = 25 facets
2-fold radial symmetry
96 index
L/W = 1.375 T/W = 1.202 U/W = 0.606
P/W = 0.536 C/W = 0.205
Vol./W³ = 0.522

PAVILION

P1	54.08°	96-48	Cut P1-P2 to TCP or better yet, start
P2	45.12°	24-72	with a L/W = 1.375 pre-form
G1	90.00°	96-48	Establish size
G2	90.00°	24-72	Complete girdle
P3	45.88°	01-49	to corner meet
P4	39.83°	26-74	to corner meet
P5	42.48°	02-50	to corner meet

CROWN

C1	46.10°	96-48	Level girdle
C2	67.16°	24-72	Complete level girdle
C3	21.35°	04-52	to corner meet
C4	19.80°	05-53	to corner meet
C5	19.26°	06-54	to corner meet
T	0.00°	Table	to C1-C2-C3 meet

Figure 19-51 GemCAD cutting prescription for Skew Tube.

19.2.7 Scrambler

Scrambler owes its unusual, distorted outline to my desire to get the highest yield possible from a beautiful yet oddly shaped piece of tourmaline rough. Clearly, symmetric designs were off the table, and I soon recognized that I would need to create something new. Scrambler was the result. By using the CAM outlining technique, a pencil, and my pocket calculator, I managed about 40% yield. Chapter 17.3 contains a complete description of the procedure.

There is more to Scrambler's pavilion than mere mathematics, however. Take a closer look…The overall outline comes from CAM, but the P1 facets, which are cut to the CAM center point, bear more relation to an OMNI design. They radiate outward at evenly spaced index wheel settings and a common

Figure 19-52 Three-dimensional rendering of the Scrambler gem design in tourmaline.

angle, thus ensuring a symmetric, starburst reflection pattern. As with OMNI, however, the facet edges must be matched to a non-symmetric outline. The solution is the classic "moon" facets of an OMNI-cut barion. Facet tiers P2-P5 perform this outline-matching task.

While very instructive and arguably interesting, I find the facet layout, particularly on the crown, to be less than aesthetically pleasing. Somehow, the mixture of narrow and wide triangular facets seems improvised and klunky. Nevertheless, Scrambler produces well-balanced, random flashes that conceal completely the somewhat unsatisfying facet layout. The gem works well with both pale and more saturated rough.

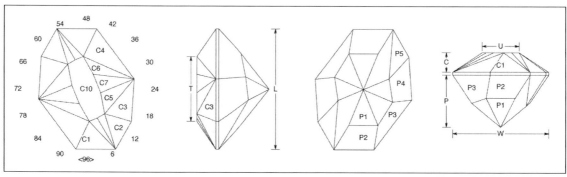

Figure 19-53 GemCAD top, side, bottom, and end views of Scrambler.

Scrambler

Designed by Tom Herbst July 2007
BOG optimized for ISO and Tilt
ISO 82% in Tourmaline
Angles for R.I. = 1.620
35 + 8 girdles = 43 facets
2-fold radial symmetry
96 index
L/W = 1.228 T/W = 0.660 U/W = 0.385
P/W = 0.531 C/W = 0.199
Vol./W³ = 0.327

PREFORM

	30.00°	96-48	CAM Outline
	37.62°	14-62	see Chapter 17.3.3
	35.76°	25-73	
	31.73°	32-80	
	90.00°	96-48	Cut CAM outline
	90.00°	14-62	
	90.00°	25-73	
	90.00°	32-80	Outline complete

PAVILION

P1	39.20°	96-12-24-36-48-60-72-84	To outline ctr pt
P2	43.17°	96-48	To lowest girdle meet
P3	63.13°	14-62	To girdle, P1-P2 meet
P4	55.05°	25-73	To girdle, P1-P3 meet
P5	47.52°	32-80	Finish girdle, to ctr pt

CROWN

C1	35.00°	96-48	Establish girdle thickness
C2	35.23°	16-64	Continue girdle line
C3	35.00°	23-71	Continue
C4	35.00°	34-82	Complete girdle
C5	28.19°	27-75	to C3-C4 girdle meet
C6	29.80°	32-80	to same meet
C7	27.79°	30-78	to same meet
C8	28.38°	06-54	to C1-C2 girdle meet
C9	28.11°	08-56	to same meet
C10	0.00°	Table	Table to four meets C1-C4 and C2-C3

Figure 19-54 Scrambler's GemCAD cutting prescription. Note that this CAM outline has slightly different angles than those shown in Table 17-1.

19.2.8 Briar Rose

There is not much more to say about Briar Rose. Chapter 18 explains the inspiration and design procedures that lead to the gem. It also includes a detailed look at how I optimized the pavilion and crown angles with the BOG program. Briar Rose is fun to cut, and it should work well with both pale and more saturated rough.

Figure 19-57 contains the GemCAD prescription for the standard "outside-in" cutting order. As mentioned in Section 19.2.6, this approach can be somewhat wasteful of rough. If, like me, you often find yourself working with the bare minimum of spare gem material, you might want to try the inside-out "Clever CAM" sequence shown in Figure 19-58.

Figure 19-55 Briar Rose rendered in tourmaline.

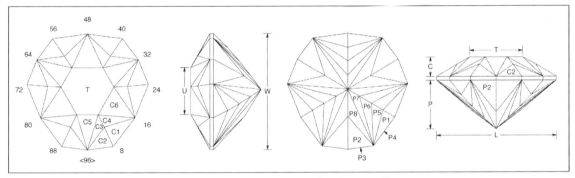

Figure 19-56 Top, side, bottom, and end views of Briar Rose.

Briar Rose

Designed by Tom Herbst, May-June 2006
BOG Optimized for ISO and Tilt
ISO 89% in Tourmaline
Angles for R.I. = 1.620
67 + 12 girdles = 79 facets
3-fold, mirror-image symmetry
96 index
L/W = 1.073 T/W = 0.468 U/W = 0.405
P/W = 0.420 C/W = 0.168
Vol./W³ = 0.219

PAVILION

P1	46.00°	14-18-46-50-78-82	Cut to TCP
P2	43.94°	02-30-34-62-66-94	Cut to same TCP
P3	90.00°	02-30-34-62-66-94	Define size
P4	90.00°	14-18-46-50-78-82	Complete girdle
P5	41.80°	13-19-45-51-77-83	to girdle meet
P6	39.99°	12-20-44-52-76-84	to same meet
P7	39.05°	11-21-43-53-75-85	to same meet
P8	38.58°	10-22-42-54-74-86	to girdle, center meets

Figure 19-57 Conventional cutting prescription for Briar Rose (continued on next page).

		CROWN		
C1	33.00°	14-18-46-50-78-82	Establish girdle
C2	31.15°	02-30-34-62-66-94	Complete girdle
C3	29.63°	01-31-33-63-65-95	Cut to girdle meet
C4	30.84°	15-17-47-49-79-81	Cut to girdle meet
C5	29.07°	96-32-64	to C3 girdle meet
C6	29.99°	16-48-80	to C4 girdle meet
T	0.00°	Table	Table

Figure 19-57 (continued) The remainder of the conventional Briar Rose prescription.

Briar Rose - Clever CAM

Designed by Tom Herbst, May-June 2006
"Outside-in" pavilion cutting order
Use same crown as conventional order

PREFORM

	25.00°	14-18-46-50-78-82	To center point
	23.46°	02-30-34-62-66-94	to same ctr pt
P3	90.00°	02-30-34-62-66-94	Establish outline, size
P4	90.00°	14-18-46-50-78-82	Complete outline

PAVILION

P8	38.58°	10-22-42-54-74-86	To outline center pt
P1	46.00°	14-18-46-50-78-82	to lower girdle meet
P2	43.94°	02-30-34-62-66-94	to same girdle meet
P5	41.80°	13-19-45-51-77-83	to same meet
P6	39.99°	12-20-44-52-76-84	to same meet
P7	39.05°	11-21-43-53-75-85	to girdle, center meets

Figure 19-58 Outside-in "Clever CAM" GemCAD prescription for Briar Rose's pavilion. The crown cutting instructions appear in Figure 19-57 above.

19.2.9 Green Flash

Green Flash is an interesting half-brilliant, half-reflector design that was inspired by a very pretty piece of Norwegian Peridot. The rough was reasonably well shaped for a circularly symmetric gem, but unfortunately, a significant fraction of the circle was included and/or missing. While staring at the stone one day, I realized that I could cut half of a brilliant pavilion on the good side, and use some large reflecting facets on the damaged side. The result was Green Flash.

Figuring out how to match half of a brilliant pavilion with half of a reflector was a challenge, and the cutting prescription shown here comes with a couple of important additional notes: First, you should cut P1 and P2 at index 15 and 81, as well as the other ten index wheel settings listed here. These

Figure 19-59 Green Flash rendered in Peridot using the freeware Blender / LuxRender programs.

additional "sacrificial" facets give you the girdle meet points needed for P3. Having discharged this duty, they dutifully disappear when you cut P4. The second warning relates to the initial dopping. The P1 facets define the symmetry center of the gem, and this will very likely be far from the center of your piece of rough. You should dop the stone centered on what will be the Temporary Center Point created by P1.

The name Green Flash comes from the atmospheric phenomenon seen at sunset (or sunrise), in which a distinct greenish glow accompanies the disappearance (or appearance) of the sun. Given its horizon-sunburst pattern and the fact that the design originally targeted peridot, the name is a natural.

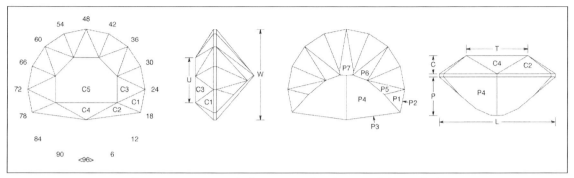

Figure 19-60 Top, side, bottom, and end views of Green Flash.

Green Flash

Designed by Tom Herbst, May-June 2003
BOG optimized for ISO and TIlt
ISO 85% in Peridot
Angles for R.I. = 1.650
36 + 12 girdles = 48 facets
1-fold, mirror-image symmetry
96 index
L/W = 1.330 T/W = 0.701 U/W = 0.496
P/W = 0.426 C/W = 0.201
Vol./W³ = 0.331

PAVILION

P1	41.36°	21-27-33-39-45-51-57-63-69-75	Cut to TCP (also at 15-81)
P2	90.00°	21-27-33-39-45-51-57-63-69-75	Define size (also at 15-81)
P3	90.00°	02-94	to bottom P1-P2 meets
P4	41.36°	02-94	to P1-P2-P3 meet
P5	39.48°	24-72	to girdle meet
P6	39.97°	35-61	to girdle meet
P7	39.81°	48	to girdle meet

CROWN

C1	35.73°	21-27-33-39-45-51-57-63-69-75	Establish level girdle
C2	54.68°	02-94	Complete girdle
C3	32.65°	24-36-48-60-72	to girdle meet
C4	46.66°	96	to girdle, C1-C2-C3
C5	0.00°	Table	Table

Figure 19-61 GemCAD cutting prescription for Green Flash.

19.3 Advanced Designs

The final section of this chapter offers six challenging cuts for the more advanced faceter. This challenge arises from several sources. For example, **Sepang** presents an unconventional cutting method, while the **Heidelberg Brilliant** features quite small accent facets. **Slice** is a non meet point design, requiring a good eye to achieve a balanced and symmetric reflection pattern. **Sakhir** is demanding in terms of both accuracy and precision, due to it multiple cuts at similar index and angle. The final two designs, **FanCZ** and **Blinder** are challenging due to their sheer number of facets, and in the case of Blinder, the danger of cumulative error building up over multiple tiers. Good luck and have fun…

19.3.1 Sepang

Sepang is an unusual fan-shaped design inspired by the Malaysian Formula 1 Grand Prix racing track on the outskirts of Kuala Lumpur. The most distinctive feature of the Sepang circuit is the Tower Grandstand, with its soaring roof inspired by the hibiscus, the national flower of Malaysia. The Sepang gem design tries to capture some of the same symmetry and beauty.

It is definitely worth cutting Sepang within the friendly confines of GemCAD before subjecting your valuable rough to the cutting lap. The facet order is somewhat unconventional and can involve a lot of changes of cutting angle and mast height. Nevertheless, seeing the fan-like outline take shape is both fun and instructive.

Figure 19-62 Sepang rendered in garnet.

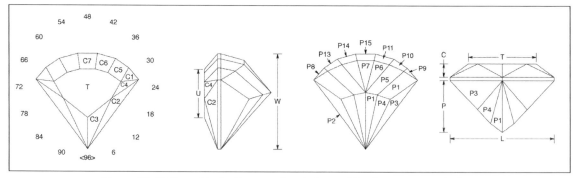

Figure 19-63 Top, side, bottom, and end views of the Sepang gem design.

Figure 19-64 The Tower Grandstand at Malaysia's fabulous Sepang Formula 1 circuit. Image by Eriang87, Wikimedia Commons.

Sepang

Designed by Tom Herbst, March 2004
BOG Optimized for ISO and Tilt
ISO 68% in Spessartite Garnet
Angles for R.I. = 1.810
34 + 9 girdles = 43 facets
1-fold, mirror-image symmetry
96 index
L/W = 1.116 T/W = 0.729 U/W = 0.510
P/W = 0.543 C/W = 0.140
Vol./W³ = 0.235

PAVILION

P1	46.40°	08-24-72-88	Cut to TCP
P2	90.00°	14-82	Establish size
P3	70.57°	14-82	to bottom P1-P2 meet
P4	50.29°	10-86	to same meet
P5	39.88°	30-66	to P1-P4 meet
P6	39.88°	44-52	to P1-P5 meet
P7	40.89°	48	to same meet
P8	90.00°	35-61	to P1-P2-P3 meet
P9	72.52°	35-61	to same meet
P10	73.14°	39-57	to P1-P5-P9 meet
P11	74.66°	44-52	to P5-P6-P10 meet
P12	75.03°	48	to P6-P7-P11 meet
P13	90.00°	39-57	Continue girdle
P14	90.00°	44-52	continue girdle
P15	90.00°	48	Finish girdle

CROWN

C1	41.16°	35-61	Establish girdle
C2	51.07°	14-82	to side meet (P2-C1)
C3	28.40°	10-86	to bottom meet
C4	41.88°	16-80	to side meet (P2-C1-C2)
C5	39.65°	39-57	Continue girdle
C6	40.52°	44-52	continue girdle
C7	40.58°	48	Finish girdle line
T	0.00°	Table	to 2 C2-C3-C4 meets

Figure 19-65 GemCAD cutting prescription for Sepang.

19.3.2 Heidelberg Brilliant

Say hello to a special guest. The Heidelberg brilliant was designed by my friend and colleague, Dave Thompson, who also produced the Viviant design described on page 229. In addition to producing excellent gem designs, Dave is an experienced, self-taught cutter, and he happens to be the person who first introduced me to faceting.

Dave designed the Heidelberg brilliant while living in – you guessed it – Heidelberg, Germany. Like the Viviant cut, this design is a novel variant of the Standard Round Brilliant. The tiny, radially-symmetric accent facets on the pavilion and crown really add a lot of visual interest and action. Nevertheless, these facets can come in very quickly, so cut them with care. On smaller stones,

Figure 19-66 The Heidelberg brilliant in sapphire.

consider switching off your lap motor entirely. Note also that the prescription shown here is an "inside-out" Clever CAM cutting order. Begin with shallow CAM facets to a final center point using the girdle indices, and then cut the outline.

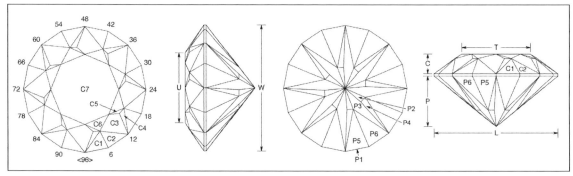

Figure 19-67 GemCAD top, side, bottom, and end views of the Heidelberg Brilliant.

Heidelberg Brilliant

Designed by Dave Thompson
BOG Optimized for ISO and Tilt
ISO 91% in Spinel
Angles for R.I. = 1.720
89 + 16 girdles = 105 facets
8-fold radial symmetry
96 index
L/W = 1.000 T/W = 0.555 U/W = 0.555
P/W = 0.400 C/W = 0.157
Vol./W³ = 0.196

PAVILION

P1	90.00°	03-09-15-21-27-33-39-45-51-57-63-69-75-81-87-93	Shallow CAM to ctr pt then cut girdle
P2	38.40°	01-13-25-37-49-61-73-85	to CAM ctr pt, makes uneven girdle
P3	38.71°	11-23-35-47-59-71-83-95	to same center point as P2
P4	38.87°	01-13-25-37-49-61-73-85	to girdle meet at index 96
P5	40.09°	03-15-27-39-51-63-75-87	to girdle and P2-P3-P4 meets
P6	39.99°	09-21-33-45-57-69-81-93	to girdle and same P2-P3-P4 meets

CROWN

C1	40.20°	03-15-27-39-51-63-75-87	Establish girdle thickness
C2	39.18°	09-21-33-45-57-69-81-93	Complete level girdle
C3	35.33°	11-23-35-47-59-71-83-95	to girdle meet
C4	36.76°	01-13-25-37-49-61-73-85	to same girdle meet and C1-C2-C3
C5	31.25°	01-13-25-37-49-61-73-85	to C1-C2-C3-C4 meet
C6	21.05°	06-18-30-42-54-66-78-90	to same C1-C2-C3-C4-C5 meet
C7	0.00°	Table	Table to tips of C5

Figure 19-68 GemCAD cutting prescription for the Heidelberg Brilliant.

19.3.3 Slice

I cut my first really costly piece of gem rough in Jeff Graham's classic Smith Bar design (available online – see Chapter 15.8.4). Smith Bar is a variant of the "opposed bar" concept, in which the pavilion has facets all running in one direction, while the crown has facets all running in the perpendicular, or opposed, direction. It may look a bit odd in the cutting diagram, but of course, we all know that well-designed gems make their pavilions and crowns work together. The result of all this opposition is, in fact, harmony in the form of entrancing, geometrically square flashes.

Slice is my take on the opposed bar. I wanted to try placing square flashes in an emphatically non-square outline. For optical

Figure 19-69 Slice rendered in quartz.

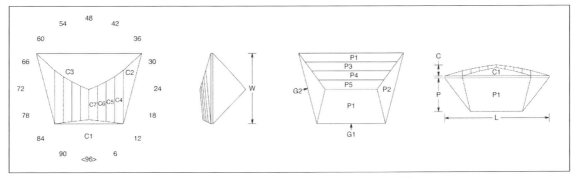

Figure 19-70 Top, side, bottom, and end views of Slice.

Slice

Designed by Tom Herbst, Feb-Mar 2006
BOG optimized for ISO and Tilt
ISO 86% in quartz
Angles for R.I. = 1.540
19 + 4 girdles = 23 facets
1-fold, mirror-image symmetry
96 index
L/W = 1.536
P/W = 0.478 C/W = 0.158
Vol./W³ = 0.385

PAVILION

G1	90.00°	96-48	To equal depth and final W
G2	90.00°	20-76	Equal depth until shorter G1 equals W
P1	44.50°	96-48	to equal depth, midline
P2	63.23°	20-76	Equal depth to level girdle
P3	43.50°	48	Cut until P1 = W / 8
P4	42.49°	48	Cut until P3 = W / 8
P5	41.48°	48	Cut until P4 = W / 8

CROWN

C1	63.35°	96	Establish girdle thickness
C2	20.50°	20-76	Continue girdle
C3	17.13°	48	Complete girdle
C4	16.75°	19-77	to corner meet
C5	14.19°	18-78	Cut until C4 = W / 8
C6	12.34°	17-79	Cut until C5 = W / 8
C7	10.95°	16-80	Cut until C6 = W / 8

Figure 19-71 GemCAD prescription for the Slice gem design.

and geometry reasons, such efforts always have trouble with acute gem corners (those with angles below 90°). Nevertheless, Slice does a reasonably good job of popping up surprising squares in a trapezoidal gem.

You can establish the outline as shown in the prescription, that is, by cutting the G1 girdle facets at 96-48 to equal depth and the final width, and then cutting the G2 girdle facets to equal depth until the shorter G1 facet equals the width (W) of the final stone. Alternatively (and if your gem rough allows it), you can do a CAM pre-form. Having studied Chapter 17.3, you should be able to work this out by yourself, but here's the answer anyway: cut CAM facets at 29.73° at 96-48 and 25.00° at 20-76 to the same common center, followed by 90° facets to chop out the proper shape.

Note also that placing the parallel facets on the pavilion and crown can be a bit of a challenge, since there are no meet points to guide you and the facets lie close together in cutting angle and (especially!) index. This can amplify the visibility of minor cutting errors (see Figure 16-33). Also, Slice's visual impact depends on the illusion of a perfect checkerboard, so take extra care.

19.3.4 Sakhir

Sakhir, like Sepang in Section 19.3.1, draws its inspiration from an architectural component of a Formula 1 race track, in this instance the inverted, truncated cone shape of the VIP Tower next to the circuit in Bahrain (see Figure 19-74). This gem design uses a classic OMNI approach to establish the girdle outline, and the symmetric P16 facets generate the typical symmetric starburst effect of a standard round brilliant. The geometrically parallel facets on the crown split this symmetry into horizontal bands and produce a unique reflection pattern.

Cutting the pavilion is for the most part straightforward; the challenge comes in placing C2-C6 on the crown. These facets are at low cutting angles and are almost par-

Figure 19-72 Sakhir rendered in beryl.

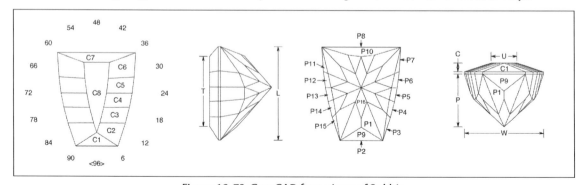

Figure 19-73 GemCAD four-views of Sakhir.

allel planes (same index and angle), amplifying any minor errors substantially (Figure 16-33). Nevertheless (and unlike with Slice), you will probably find that Sakhir's sparkle will conceal a variety of sins.

Note also that Sakhir has a deeper pavilion and shallower crown than most other gem designs. In fact, it has the second highest P/W – C/W value among the 100 or so diverse cuts discussed in Chapter 16.8. This may cause some difficulty in mounting.

Sakhir

Designed by Tom Herbst, March 2007
BOG optimized for ISO and Tilt
ISO 74% in Beryl
Angles for R.I. = 1.580
49 + 12 girdles = 61 facets
1-fold, mirror-image symmetry
96 index
L/W = 1.153 T/W = 0.864 U/W = 0.326
P/W = 0.652 C/W = 0.111
(P2 P8)/W = 1.153
Vol./W³ = 0.364

PAVILION

P1	44.30°	03-09-15-21-27-33-39-45-51-57-63-69-75-81-87-93	Cut to TCP
P2	90.00°	96	Establish size
P3	90.00°	19-77	to P1-P2 meet
P4	90.00°	20-76	to P1-P3 meet
P5	90.00°	21-75	to P1-P4 meet
P6	90.00°	22-74	to P1-P5 meet
P7	90.00°	23-73	to P1-P6 meet
P8	90.00°	48	to P1-P7 meet
P9	51.76°	96	Corner meet, level girdle
P10	69.36°	48	P1-P7 meet, complete girdle
P11	76.80°	23-73	Top corner meet
P12	77.24°	22-74	Continue barion facets
P13	77.37°	21-75	continue barion facets
P14	77.24°	20-76	continue barion facets
P15	76.80°	19-77	continue barion facets
P16	41.75°	96-12-24-36-48-60-72-84	Final ctr pt, 24-48-72 touch neighbours

CROWN

C1	33.37°	96	Establish girdle thickness
C2	19.62°	19-77	Continue girdle
C3	19.27°	20-76	continue girdle
C4	18.98°	21-75	continue girdle
C5	18.79°	22-74	continue girdle
C6	18.62°	23-73	continue girdle
C7	42.36°	48	to corner meet
C8	0.00°	Table	to C1 tip - one meet!

Figure 19-74 GemCAD cutting prescription for Sakhir, accompanied by an image of the VIP Tower at Bahrain's Sakhir Formula 1 circuit (inset - image by Navin Shetty Brahmavar, wikipedia).

19.3.5 FanCZ

I would like to say that FanCZ developed from a single design aesthetic, a single artistic vision. It emphatically did not. I had acquired a large chunk of lovely coloured cubic zirconia, and I wanted to try a fancier cut, hence the name FanCZ (get it?).

The pavilion came together via random play in GemCAD, a perfectly legitimate way to design gemstones, thank you very much (see Chapter 16.1). I did have an inkling of a plan, however…

With a larger stone in hand, I tried to avoid bringing all of the facets together at a single culet. FanCZ has three "sub-culets" distributed around the pavilion to collect long triangular facets, in addition to the conven-

Figure 19-75 FanCZ rendered in (naturally) CZ.

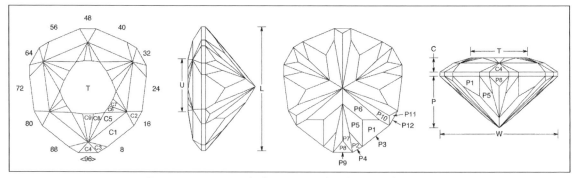

Figure 19-76 Top, side, bottom, and end views of FanCZ.

FanCZ

Designed by Tom Herbst, Oct. 2004
BOG optimized for ISO and Tilt
ISO 94% in CZ
Angles for R.I. = 2.160
85 + 18 girdles = 103 facets
3-fold, mirror-image symmetry
96 index
L/W = 1.024 T/W = 0.483 U/W = 0.439
P/W = 0.426 C/W = 0.117
Vol./W³ = 0.202

PAVILION

P1	42.97°	10-22-42-54-74-86	Cut to TCP
P2	41.97°	08-24-40-56-72-88	to same TCP
P3	90.00°	10-22-42-54-74-86	Set overall size
P4	90.00°	08-24-40-56-72-88	Complete girdle line
P5	41.63°	09-23-41-55-73-87	to P1-P2-P3-P4 meet
P6	40.70°	11-21-43-53-75-85	to P1-P3 girdle meet
P7	40.19°	01-31-33-63-65-95	to P5-P6 meet, breaks girdle
P8	41.68°	96-32-64	to P2-P4-P7 girdle meets
P9	90.00°	96-32-64	Same meet, repairs girdle
P10	40.57°	15-17-47-49-79-81	to center point, breaks girdle
P11	43.56°	16-48-80	to P1-P3-P10 girdle meets
P12	90.00°	16-48-80	Same meet, repairs girdle

Figure 19-77 GemCAD cutting instructions for FanCZ (continued on next page).

CROWN			
C1	29.93°	10-22-42-54-74-86	Establish girdle thickness
C2	33.64°	16-48-80	Continue girdle
C3	32.94°	08-24-40-56-72-88	continue girdle
C4	40.96°	96-32-64	Complete girdle line
C5	20.98°	10-22-42-54-74-86	to C4-C3, C2 tips
C6	16.20°	14-18-46-50-78-82	to C1-C2-C5 meets
C7	15.65°	16-48-80	to same meet
C8	10.71°	02-30-34-62-66-94	to C1-C3-C4-C5 meets
C9	10.37°	96-32-64	to same meet
T	0.00°	Table	to C5-C6-C8 meets

Figure 19-77 (continued) The remainder of the FanCZ cutting prescription.

tional central one. The crown shares this aspect. As mentioned on page 254, I really like facet fans meeting at a nexus on the girdle. On a larger stone such as this, my doodling in GemCAD led me to bring these nexus points inward and use "inverse" fans to the girdle. Figure 19-76 shows the result.

FanCZ is truly flashy in cubic zirconia. Given the facet count, you should probably stick to larger pieces of rough.

19.3.6 Blinder

When I set out to design a gem to maximize pinfire (see Chapter 16.5.5), rutile was the natural choice: this flame fusion synthetic material has a refractive index over 2.6, a birefringence value of 0.29, and a BG dispersion of 0.28. If those sound like dry, uninteresting numbers to you, go back and re-read Chapter 12. In fact, rutile has a considerably higher refractive index than diamond, and its dispersion is almost seven times as great. Talk about an extreme material…

Blinder takes maximum advantage of rutile's unusual properties. With 165 facets in a modified cushion Portuguese cut, Blinder really is a blinder. Under intense, spot lighting the gem produces a profusion of multicoloured points that are, frankly, breathtaking. In fact, the visual effect is arguably a bit over the top, and some people may think that the gem is somehow not "real."

Figure 19-78 Three-dimensional computer rendering of Blinder in rutile. The black and white image shown here doesn't do justice to the original picture, and certainly not to the gem itself.

As with any Portuguese-type cut, the challenge lies in both the sheer number of facets and the potential of cumulative error (see Chapter 8.9.4). Nevertheless, there is plenty of fun cutting in Blinder. As you proceed through the pavilion facet tiers, you may recognize how the P5-P7 "moon" facets match the circularly symmetric pavilion to the square cushion outline. In a very real way, Blinder is a Portuguese barion.

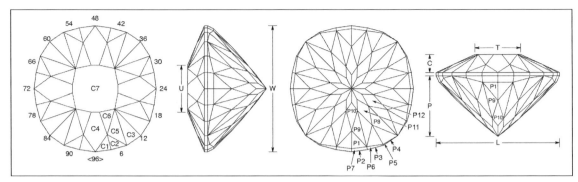

Figure 19-79 GemCAD top, side, bottom, and end views of Blinder.

Blinder

Designed by Tom Herbst, Nov04-Apr05
BOG optiimized for ISO and Tilt
ISO 92% in Rutile
Angles for R.I. = 2.620
141 + 24 girdles = 165 facets
4-fold, mirror-image symmetry
96 index
L/W = 1.000 T/W = 0.371 U/W = 0.371
P/W = 0.480 C/W = 0.144
Vol./W³ = 0.228

PAVILION

P1	45.37°	02-06-10-14- 18-22-26-30- 34-38-42-46- 50-54-58-62- 66-70-74-78- 82-86-90-94	Cut to TCP
P2	90.00°	02-22-26-46- 50-70-74-94	Establish size
P3	90.00°	04-20-28-44- 52-68-76-92	Continue outliine
P4	90.00°	09-15-33-39- 57-63-81-87	Complete outline
P5	64.04°	09-15-33-39- 57-63-81-87	Level girdle
P6	64.77°	04-20-28-44- 52-68-76-92	level girdle
P7	64.96°	02-22-26-46- 50-70-74-94	level girdle
P8	44.35°	11-13-35-37- 59-61-83-85	to girdle meet
P9	44.07°	03-05-19-21- 27-29-43-45- 51-53-67-69- 75-77-91-93	to P1-P6-P7 meet
P10	41.79°	96-08-16-24- 32-40-48-56- 64-72-80-88	to P8-P9-P1 meet
P11	38.66°	03-21-27-45- 51-69-75-93	to P9 tips
P12	38.66°	12-36-60-84	to P8 tips

CROWN

C1	26.97°	02-22-26-46- 50-70-74-94	Set girdle thickness
C2	26.77°	04-20-28-44- 52-68-76-92	Continue girdle
C3	26.03°	09-15-33-39- 57-63-81-87	continue girdle
C4	24.56°	96-24-48-72	to girdle meet
C5	25.27°	05-19-29-43- 53-67-77-91	to girdle meet
C6	23.49°	03-21-27-45- 51-69-75-93	to C1-C2 tips
C7	0.00°	Table	to C3-C5-C6 meet

Figure 19-80 GemCAD cutting prescription for Blinder.

20

Do-It-Yourself Projects
for the Frugal Faceter

Face it. Gemstone faceting is a hobby that requires a significant investment in terms of equipment, time, and money. Of course, those of us who are enthusiastic faceters reap fabulous returns on this investment, at least in terms of personal satisfaction. We also tend to reap a workshop full of tools, accessories, and assorted doodads, which enhance our enjoyment of the hobby.

This chapter collects together a number of do-it-yourself projects to expand and improve your faceting experience. The projects range from instruments for mineral identification to upgrades for your faceting machine. These projects can also require a substantial investment in time, but as the chapter title implies, doing it yourself can save a great deal of money over purchasing the commercial equivalents of these items.

A final warning and request: as with faceting itself, constructing these projects will require some mechanical aptitude and attention to appropriate safety measures. Please play safely.

20.1 Tools for Identifying and Characterizing Gem Rough

Identifying and characterizing gem rough is a discipline replete with devices. There are scales, refractometers, spectrometers, polariscopes, and on and on. While most of these can be acquired from your friendly neighbourhood gemology shop, the cost can be startlingly high. This section describes a couple of simple gizmos that you can whip together quickly to help you understand the properties of your gem rough.

20.2 A Density Measuring Device for Identifying Gem Rough

Many gem materials resemble each other, particularly in rough form. For example, it can be quite difficult to distinguish spinel from ruby, or to separate the various types and mixes of garnet. There are a number of non-visual characteristics that can help you identify gems, however. One very useful diagnostic is the *density* of the material, a topic covered extensively in Chapter 12.8.

Density is defined as the weight per unit volume, usually expressed as grams per cubic centimeter. (Actually, the formal definition of density is mass, not weight, per unit volume. There is a related quantity called *specific gravity*. Turn to page 121 for more on this). The density is a known and tabulated characteristic of the material, and most importantly for the field gemologist, it is independent of the size of the sample – all chunks of aquamarine, for example, have the same density.

20.2.1 Measuring Density

Although simple in concept and fundamental in importance, the density of matter proved surprisingly difficult to measure for early scientists. In fact, it took a genuine "Eureka!" insight on the part of an ancient Greek mathematician and physicist to come up with a workable technique.

Archimedes lived in Syracuse in modern Sicily during the third century BCE. As a member of the court of King Hiero, he contributed in many ways to the protection and improvement of Syracuse, including mechanisms for irrigation, advanced mathematics, and engines of war. But he is best known for his Law of Buoyancy, also called Archimedes' Principle:

The buoyant force of a body in a fluid is equal to the weight of liquid displaced.

In other words, an object placed into a liquid will weigh less. The reduction in weight is due to the buoyant force, and this force is equal to the weight of an amount of liquid with the same volume as the object.

Here's an example of how Archimedes' Principle works. Gold, which played a central role in Archimedes' discovery (see opposite page), has a density of 19.3 grams per cubic centimeter (commonly abbreviated to g/cc). Imagine an irregular nugget of gold that weighs exactly 19.3 grams. You know from the definition of density that the nugget must therefore have a volume of one cubic centimeter.

A Streak of Inspiration

Some of us do our best thinking while in the shower. According to legend, Archimedes recognized the law of buoyancy while taking a bath. King Hiero of Syracuse had asked Archimedes whether it was possible to determine the purity of a gold crown that the king had commissioned. While universally acclaimed as beautiful, the crown had raised suspicions that the goldsmith had mixed the precious metal with baser silver.

Writing a couple of centuries after Archimedes' death, the Roman architect Vitruvius relates how Archimedes, while lowering himself into a public bath, noticed that more and more water spilled over the sides. The bolt of insight struck, and Archimedes reportedly ran home through the streets of Syracuse, naked, shouting "Eureka! Eureka!" ("I have found it! I have found it!").

Now, drop the nugget into a glass of water, which has a density of 1.0 g/cc. The gold displaces its own volume – one cubic centimeter – of water. By Archimedes' Principle, the buoyant force is equal to the weight of this displaced water, i.e. one gram. Therefore, if you could weigh the gold in the water, you would come up with 19.3 – 1.0 = 18.3 grams. This is a reduction in weight of about 5%.

Bronze, another metal known in antiquity, has a density of about 8 grams per cubic centimeter (the exact value depends on the mix of copper, tin, and other metals). A nugget of bronze with the exact same shape and size as the gold would weigh 8 grams in air and 7 grams in water, a reduction of 12.5%. Aluminum has a density of 2.70 g/cc and was emphatically not known to Archimedes (look up the Google reference on page 224 of Volume 1). Dropping an identically shaped nugget of aluminum into water leads to a weight reduction of almost 40%.

How does this mental experiment help? Clearly, denser materials, such as gold, experience a smaller reduction in weight when immersed in water. More importantly, you can do a little mathematics and demonstrate the following relation:

$$\text{density} = \frac{\text{dry weight}}{\text{dry weight} - \text{wet weight}}$$

This will let you convert dry and wet measurements directly to the density of the unknown sample.

20.2.2 The "Suspension Gizmo" – A Simple Density Measuring Device

In this section, you will learn how to build a relatively simple mechanism based on Archimedes' moment of genius. This device, in combination with a good set of scales, will allow you to determine the density of small samples of gem rough with sufficient accuracy to identify the material. For those paying attention since Chapter 12, the suspension gizmo actually makes a measurement relative to water, and hence evaluates the specific gravity, not the density, of the sample.

Incidentally, density-measuring accessories are commercially available for several types of scales. Unfortunately, these products retail for $50-$100, far more than the ten-cent investment of the home-built device described here.

Basically, you need to measure accurately the weight of the sample in air and in water. The weight in air is straightforward – just place the piece of rough on the scales. Weighing something while it is immersed in water is a little trickier. For that, you will need to build a special gizmo.

Here is what you will need:

Item	Comment
High quality scales	0.01 g accuracy or better – see discussion of accuracy in Section 20.2.5 below.
Thin copper wire *ca.* 12 in (30 cm) long	1-2 mm thick. Should be easily bendable and fairly lightweight.
Braided copper wire *ca.* 1 in (3 cm) long	One strand needed for suspension wire.
Small cup or beaker approximately 2 oz (60 ml)	Large enough to accommodate larger pieces of gem rough.
Soldering iron and solder	To connect the components – alternative: epoxy.
Wire clippers, needle-nose pliers, etc.	To cut and shape the wire.

20.2.3 Constructing the Suspension Gizmo

1. Cut approximately 4 inches (10 cm) of the copper wire and, using needle nose pliers, bend the wire into a basket form suitable for holding the gem rough (see Figure 20-1).

2. Using the remainder of the copper wire, make a base ring, riser, and hook. You can make one continuous wire form, or connect smaller pieces using solder or epoxy cement. Figure 20-2 shows one possibility, but the exact configuration will depend on the shape and size of your scales. The base ring must be large enough to rest stably on the pan of the scales, while the riser must be tall enough to accommodate the small cup or beaker. Don't go overboard, however. A sturdy device that weighs 20 grams will not be very useful if the weight limit on your scales is only 10 grams.

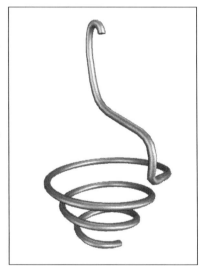

3. If necessary, strip the insulation from the braided copper wire and extract a single strand. This will serve as the suspension wire between the hook and basket. In order to maximize accuracy, this wire should be as thin as possible, but not so thin that it breaks easily.

Figure 20-1 Form a small basket out of copper wire.

4. Wrap one end of the suspension wire around the basket hook and solder in place. Adjusting the length of free wire, wrap the other end around the riser hook and solder. The basket should hang freely at a height suitable for lowering the basket into the water (see Figure 20-4).

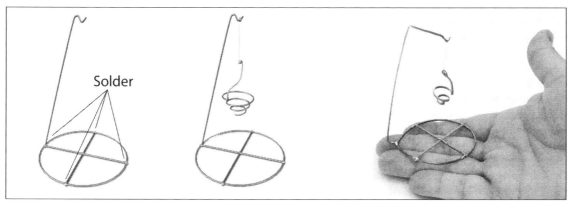

Figure 20-2 Solder together a base, which can rest on the pan of your scales, and a riser from which to hang the copper basket (left). Using a single strand of copper wire, solder the basket to the base and riser (middle). The completed suspension gizmo (right).

20.2.4 Example: Measuring the Density of an "Unknown" Garnet

Figure 20-3 shows a small piece of gem rough that needs identification. According to the dealer, the stone is rhodolite, one of the more valuable species of garnet. Let's check to make sure.

As with many of the red garnets, rhodolite is a mix of basic types – in this case, almandine and pyrope. The exact mix, and hence the density, can vary somewhat, but rhodolite typically lies in the range 3.7-4.0 g/cc.

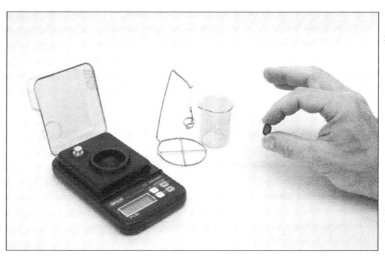

Figure 20-3 The putative rhodolite garnet whose identity needs confirmation. Measuring the wet and dry weight of the stone using accurate scales and the special gizmo will give the density of the material.

Measuring the density requires both the "dry" and "wet" weight of the sample, as well as the formula from the previous section.

Step 1: Place the gemstone sample directly in the pan of the balance. The rough in this example has a weight of 1.856 g.

As mentioned above, calculating the weight in water is a little more complicated. Just dropping the stone into the beaker and placing everything on the scale will not work. The reason for this is somewhat subtle, but it relates to the fact that, when the stone sinks, the water level rises, hence increasing the pressure at the bottom of the beaker – the water is deeper after all, and as any diver can tell you, deeper water means more pressure. This added pressure exerts a downward force on the beaker that exactly balances the buoyant force on the stone, and hence, the reading on the scales will not change. Besides, common sense dictates that you would get the exact same weight if you placed the stone next to, not in, the beaker of water. Hardly a measurement of "wet weight."

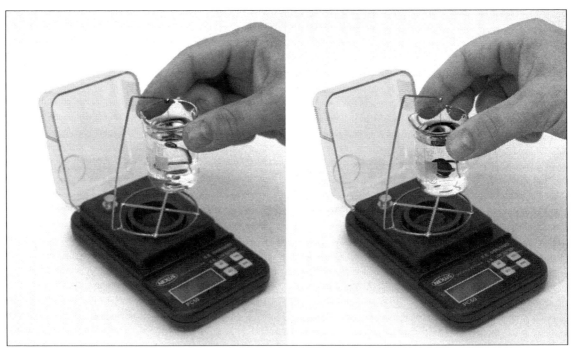

Figure 20-4 Weigh the suspension gizmo without (left) and with (right) the stone in the basket. The difference gives the wet weight of the stone.

Somehow, you have to weigh the wet gem without weighing the beaker or water. You can do this by hanging the stone from the suspension gizmo.

Actually, to get a proper net weight of the sample, you have to make two measurements. If you merely place the stone in the basket and submerge it in the beaker, you will be weighing both the stone and the suspension gizmo.

The solution? Two measurements: one with the stone in place and one without. The difference between these two values will be the weight of the alleged garnet in water. Confused? Don't worry. This step is far easier to demonstrate than it is to explain…

Step 2: Weigh the suspension gizmo (i.e. no stone) while submerging the basket in water. Make sure that no part of the basket touches the beaker. This measurement gives 6.040 grams with the basket immersed (left panel of Figure 20-4).

If you first placed the empty gizmo on the scales and then raised the beaker into place, you may have noticed that the reading went down. This happens because the buoyant force acts on the basket just as it will on the stone. You should aim to make all measurements at the same depth in the beaker, with the water line crossing the thin wire, not the basket or hook.

Step 3: Weigh the suspension gizmo containing the stone with the basket submerged to the same depth as in Step 2 (Figure 20-4, right panel). This sample rough plus gizmo weighs 7.414 grams wet.

In steps 2 and 3 above, make sure that no small bubbles adhere to the copper or stone during the measurement. Such bubbles will artificially increase the buoyancy and skew the results. See the next section for a discussion of accuracy.

Archimedes' Principle gives the density:

Step 4: Calculate the weight of the sample in water. Here, the weight is 7.414 – 6.040 or 1.374 grams. Surprise! The stone weighs less in water than in air!

Step 5: Calculate the density. For the presumed rhodolite, the formula gives a density of 3.85 grams per cubic centimeter.

Step 6: Celebrate the simplicity and effectiveness of a technique that was invented more than two millennia ago. However, please do not run naked through the streets.

The verdict? The sample has a density that is consistent with rhodolite garnet. A value of 3.85 g/cc excludes some gem materials with which rhodolite is occasionally confused. For example, you can be reasonably certain – and somewhat disappointed – that the stone is not ruby (density 3.97-4.05) nor red spinel (3.54-3.63).

20.2.5 A Word about Accuracy

As with any real-world measurement, this density determination is not exact. Not only are the scales imperfect, but also there may be inclusions and impurities in the sample that affect the results. And, as mentioned above, air bubbles will reduce the accuracy of the measurement.

Greater accuracy allows stronger statements about the identity of the gem material, and there are a few things that you can do to improve the reliability of the technique. Make several measurements at each step and use the average value. Ensure that the basket is completely immersed and not in contact with the beaker. Position the basket at the same height in the water each time, since the buoyant force affects the wet portion of the suspension wire as well (this is why the suspension wire should be thin). Finally, make sure that no water drops or other inadvertent contact with the scales can distort the measurements.

How accurately can you measure density with the suspension gizmo? The answer depends on a number of factors, including the accuracy of your scales and the weight of the stone. Obviously, higher quality scales improve the answer. Larger samples also produce greater accuracy, since the measurement error in the scales will be proportionately smaller. A less obvious effect arises from the greater wet-minus-dry weight for less dense stones (see Section 20.2.1). Again, the measurement error will be proportionately less if this difference is larger. Hence, the technique performs better on low-density materials.

There are formal ways of calculating the uncertainty in the density measurement. I will spare you the gory mathematical details, but Table 20-1 should provide a good guideline.

The importance of a decent set of scales is clear from the table: attempting a density measurement on a realistic-sized (i.e. affordable) piece of rough is pointless unless the measurement error of the scales is 0.01 gram or better.

The scales shown here have an uncertainty of 0.002 gram. Therefore, with a sample weight of slightly under 2 grams, the technique can determine the density of the rhodolite to an accuracy of about 1-2 %. In other words, the measured density is between 3.79 and 3.91 g/cc.

Table 20-1 Accuracy estimates for different scales, sample sizes, and densities. The upper table shows the percentage error for low-density gem materials as a function of sample size and accuracy of the scales. The lower table shows the same information for higher density rough.

Low Density Case* 2.7 g/cc	Simple Scales 0.1 g accuracy	Medium Scales 0.01 g accuracy	Fancy Scales 0.001 g accuracy
Small sample 0.5 g	unusable	20 %	2 %
Medium sample 2 g	unusable	5 %	0.5 %
Large sample 5 g	20 %	2 %	0.2 %

*appropriate for quartz, beryl, tourmaline etc.

High density case** 4.0 g/cc	Simple Scales 0.1 g accuracy	Medium Scales 0.01 g accuracy	Fancy Scales 0.001 g accuracy
Small sample 0.5 g	unusable	30 %	3 %
Medium sample 2 g	unusable	7 %	0.7 %
Large sample 5 g	30 %	3 %	0.3 %

**appropriate for garnet, corundum, zircon, etc.

20.3 An Inexpensive Dichroscope

A number of popular gemstone materials are pleochroic, that is, they display different colours along different crystal directions (see Chapter 12.4). Tourmaline is a great example. Many tourmalines show a distinctly different colour along the long axis of the crystal, the c-axis, compared to across the crystal. Sometimes the c-axis of a tourmaline will produce a highly desirable blue-green, while in other stones, the long axis may be completely dark, or "closed." The colour and beauty of the resulting faceted gemstone will vary dramatically depending on the orientation of the rough with respect to these crystallographic axes.

By now, you should be convinced that proper orientation can help ensure that your piece of rough tourmaline will turn into a beautiful and valuable gemstone. If not, turn to Chapter 6.7. But long before you consider orientation, you will confront a more fundamental problem: how can you be sure that that beautiful and valuable piece of gem rough is in fact tourmaline? With prices for rough indicolite running to hundreds of dollars per gram and questionable dealers proliferating, this problem is hardly a trivial one.

Ruby may be an even better example. Its strong pleochroism distinguishes it from much less valuable gem materials, such as garnet, with which it can be easily confused (see page 81 and page 377). Such confusion is not even necessarily the result of shady dealing, since ruby and garnet often come from the same geographic region and mines.

Luckily, you can exploit intrinsic pleochroism to help identify these valuable gem materials in the rough. Mineralogists use an instrument, known as a dichroscope, to reveal the various colours that pleochroic materials exhibit. Not only can such a device be used for the identification of gem species, but also a dichroscope identifies the location of the stone's crystallographic axes. Locating these axes will help you orient the rough for optimum colour and performance.

20.3.1 How does a dichroscope work?

Dichroscopes exploit the fact that the optical properties of a pleochroic mineral, including the colour, depend on the polarization state of the transmitted light (see Chapters 11.2.2 and 12.4). In one polarization direction, the gem has a particular set of transmission properties, while in the perpendicular (or orthogonal) polarization, it displays another set. If you can observe the light emerging from the stone in different polarizations, you should be able to discern differences in colour and brightness that are indicative of pleochroism.

Dichroscopes come in a variety of forms, but they all have the same basic function: take the light emerging from the stone, physically separate the two linear polarizations, and then present the operator with a side-by-side view for comparison.

But how can you physically separate the two polarizations? Rockhounds have an easy answer: calcite. This mineral, also known as Icelandic spar, is birefringent, meaning that the refractive index of the crystal is different for different polarizations. Thus, a light ray entering a birefringent material will split into two rays, one for each polarization, and these rays will continue into the crystal at different angles. This produces the familiar effect of doubling, in which objects viewed through calcite show two images (see Figure 12-12).

One simple form of dichroscope exploits this wonderful birefringent property. Simply mounting an appropriately sized and oriented piece of calcite in a tube with a magnifying lens does everything you need. Figure 12-14 shows how essentially all modestly priced commercial dichroscopes work.

But, in the spirit of do-it-yourself, the frugal faceter must ask what exactly is "modestly-priced?" You can expect to pay between $50 and $150 for a simple calcite-based dichroscope. Yikes! You call that modest?

This section explains how to put together a perfectly serviceable dichroscope for about two dollars, the cost of a small piece of calcite at a mineral show. Actually, I raided my existing rock collection and managed the job for less than a penny.

Here is what you will need:

Item	Comment
Calcite sample approximately 3/4" on a side (18x18x18 mm)	From a mineral show. An internally clean sample works best, but is not necessary.
Black electrical tape	Approximately 4-6 inches (10-15 cm) will do.

20.3.2 Building your Inexpensive Dichroscope

It doesn't get any easier than this. Constructing the dichroscope amounts to using the black electrical tape to block off all but a small, rectangular window on one side of the calcite. When done correctly, the crystal will split this input window into two side-by-side views of the two polarization directions. The only trick is to find the orientation and size of the window.

Step 1: Select a good piece of calcite for your dichroscope. In this context, "good" means one that does double images really well. Ideally, it should be undamaged and display the simple, distorted-cube, or rhombohedral, shape of a calcite crystal. This will ensure that you have clean "windows" on all sides through which to look. Of course, the crystal should be as free as possible from internal inclusions, cracks, and veils.

Step 2: Determine the orientation of the birefringence in your sample of calcite. A black dot on a white piece of paper is all you need. Try all 3 directions through the stone to find the cleanest and largest amount of image separation. Mark the best pair of faces and the direction of image split on the crystal with an indelible marker.

Step 3: Draw a small box on the paper and adjust both box size and the orientation of the crystal to produce two side-by-side boxes when viewed through the calcite (Figure 20-5). You will need to reproduce this box on the input face of the crystal using the black electrical tape, so you should note the appropriate orientation of the calcite for the next step.

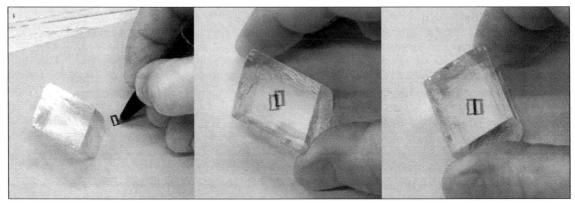

Figure 20-5 A small rectangle drawn on a piece of paper will help you determine the ideal size for the window (left). With the calcite in place, two rectangles appear (center). Proper window size and calcite orientation gives two, touching, adjacent views (right).

Step 4: Using small pieces of tape, block off three sides of a similarly sized window on one of the two faces corresponding to your selected direction through the crystal. The fourth side should be along the direction of image split (Figure 20-6).

Step 5: While looking through the calcite from the opposite side, carefully place a final piece of electrical tape on the crystal to complete the rectangular window (Figure 20-7). You will see that this immediately creates the two desired windows, side-by-side. The goal here is to position the last piece of tape such that the windows just touch without overlap. Take a moment or two to get this step right (Figure 20-8).

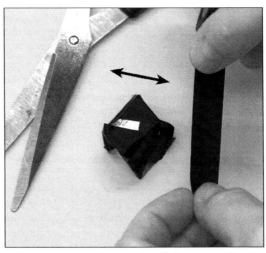

Figure 20-6 Tape three sides of the rectangle. The arrows show the direction of image split.

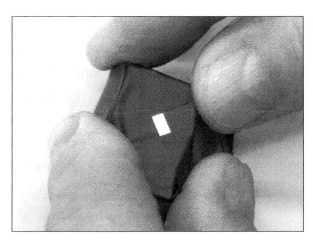

Step 6: Finally, use additional black tape to block off the other, unused, sides of the crystal. This will eliminate distracting stray light during use. Yes, this is the cheapo equivalent of the nice metallic tube in those $100 commercial dichroscopes.

Figure 20-7 Block off the fourth side of the rectangle so that the two output windows just touch each other (see Figure 20-8).

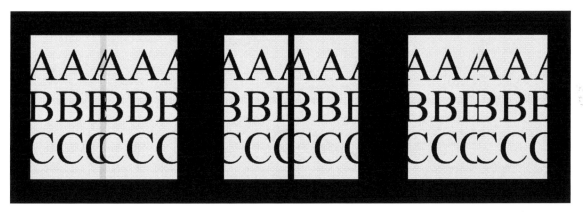

Figure 20-8 Getting the window right. The left hand image shows partial overlap, because the window is too large. The tape placement at center results in a too-small window and hence a black bar between the two views. The right-hand window is just right.

20.3.3 Using Your Inexpensive Dichroscope

You can immediately test your dichroscope on a known, pleochroic stone. For example, try a piece of tourmaline rough with distinct colours along different directions (Figure 20-9). When the two windows appear identical, you are looking down one of the optical axes of the crystal. Consult the web for further tips on using your dichroscope (Chapter 15.8.13 will help you get started).

You can also demonstrate the polarization splitting properties of this device using the blue sky on a clear day. Look through the dichroscope at approximately 90° to the sun (this works better close to sunrise or sunset). You should see a lighter and darker patch of blue, reflecting the fact that molecules and

Figure 20-9 Hold a piece of tourmaline against the input window face of the dichroscope and look through the other side of the device toward a bright background. You should see the two, distinct colours of this pleochroic material.

dust in the atmosphere selectively scatter polarized light. Rotating the calcite around the line of sight should cause the colour patches to alternate in brightness. This also works when it is cloudy, and some scholars believe that Viking navigators used Icelandic spar as a "sunstone" in exactly this way to determine the direction of the sun on overcast days.

There are many more interesting and surprising instances of polarization-dependent colour and brightness in our world. Use your new dichroscope to explore!

20.4 Add-Ons and Enhancements for Your Faceting Machine

All that remains of my very first car is a pair of fuzzy dice. And a ridiculous, racing-style, leather steering wheel. These cherished mementos of a much-loved automobile, long since crushed and melted – exploded cylinder head, rusty bumpers, and all – carry a powerful message: whether it is blowing your own horn with an outlandish bumper sticker or blowing your own hemi in a machine shop, our automotive culture has a strong tradition of customization and personalization of this most valued of machines.

It's the same way with faceters.

In your search for the perfect faceting machine, you have most likely come up a little short. Perhaps it is the way that the angle protractor works. Or the numbering on the cheater. Whatever the particulars, you almost certainly could name something you'd like to change. You manage to turn lifeless lumps of rock into beautiful gemstones, so you should certainly be able to spruce up and fine-tune your machine.

Enter the world of add-ons and enhancements. The following sections get you started with a description of a few modifications that will improve your cutting experience. But it is only a start. Yes, it provides some ideas and plans, but as you experiment, you will almost certainly come up with projects of your own.

20.5 A Better Drip Tank

Are you worried about what you are dribbling all over your valuable gemstones and laps? Have you read nightmarish stories about sediment build-up and even (horrors!) sand showing up in people's drip tanks? Do you want to do something about it?

This section explains how to build a Better Drip Tank using a commercially available water filter jug. Read on.

A Refreshing Glass of Inspiration

Drip tanks are arguably the simplest, and hence least engineered, parts of a faceting machine. Most commercial offerings are just plastic or metal buckets on a stick with a simple faucet to control water flow. Why they cost $30-50 or more is a mystery.

When I set out to put together my own hybrid commercial / homebuilt faceting machine (see page 53 of Volume 1), I recognized the need for a reliable drip tank, but in forthright acknowledgment of my cheapness, I refused to plonk down hard-earned cash for an overpriced bucket on a stick.

As time passed and more and more of the parts came together, the drip tank situation had not improved. Worries about water quality persisted, and I needed some sort of drip arrangement to cut stones. I began the slow transition to acceptance and resignation: I would have to buy something.

I was saved by a cold drink of water.

Sitting in our kitchen refrigerator was the perfect solution: a plastic Brita water jug. These clever containers have a built-in filtration system that can intercept nasty materials before they reach your stomach. Looking more carefully at the jug, I noticed that the handle was perfectly formed to sit atop a stick. Bucket and stick. With a filtration system to boot. Eureka!

20.5.1 Building a Better Drip Tank

This one is easier to show than to describe. Here is what you will need:

Item	Comment
Brita-type filter jug	Make sure that you can mount this readily on your faceting machine. For instance, many jugs have a hollow handle that will sit stably on the end of a rod.
Small plastic or metal faucet	To control water flow.
Plastic tubing and soft wire	To convey water to the lap at a controlled position. Make sure that the wire, when inserted in the tube, allows you to bend the plastic without restricting water flow.
Mounting rod	Holds the jug in place over the lap.
Glue	Epoxy or silicone sealant.

Determine the best location for the jug and install the mounting stick appropriately. On my machine, this involved bolting the stick to the aluminum top plate visible in Figure 20-10. A portion of the jug should overhang the lap but not obscure your vision nor limit your freedom of motion. Once again, the exact configuration depends on specific local factors, such as the layout of your faceting machine and work area, as well as the shape of the filter jug.

When you are satisfied, drill a small hole in the bottom of the jug at the appropriate spot and glue the faucet in place. This may involve epoxy or silicone bathtub sealant. In my case, it involved both, but I am not proud of the fact (turn to page 54 of Volume 1 to learn more about my relationship with bathtub sealant).

When the glue has set, attach the plastic tubing to the faucet and trim it to the correct length. Insert and trim a piece of soft wire to allow adjustment of the position of the tubing.

20.5.2 Using the Better Drip Tank

If everything went well, you should have no trouble operating your better drip tank. It is, after all, just a bucket on a stick (see previous page). The only complication arises from the filter. Consult the manufacturer's instructions, since some filters cannot be allowed to dry out, and they will require regular replacement.

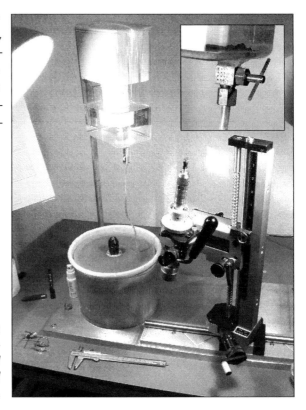

Figure 20-10 The Better Drip Tank mounted on a piece of square aluminum rod. Note the plastic tubing and soft wire to control the location. The original intravenous-drip-type valve has since been replaced with a more reliable brass fixture (inset).

20.6 A Transfer Cheat Thingy

Note that this section contains instructions that include the operation of mechanical tools that are potentially dangerous. Do not embark on this project without proper training and experience.

By now, it should be clear to you that I think that dopping is a big deal. Proper dopping procedure, and in particular, accurate dop transfer, is a prerequisite to a successful gemstone. Unfortunately, dopping technology has not improved much in the last several hundred years. Getting this critical step right is a source of endless frustration to the beginner, and yet for some reason, the classic texts devote a minimum of explanation to the topic.

Not so here.

In fact, Chapter 7 focuses exclusively on the subject of dopping and presents several alternative methods for executing the transfer accurately. One of those methods offered relief via a simple mechanical jig and promised instructions on how to build one. Those instructions follow. Hopefully, relief will follow as well.

20.6.1 Building the Transfer Cheat Thingy

Here is what you will need:

Item	Comment
Aluminum plate stock	Approximately 2.5 x 1 inches (6 x 2.5 cm) and 1/4 inch (6 mm) thick.
Access to machinist tools	End mill, drill press, tap set, etc. Please be careful.

Figure 20-11 shows the transfer cheat jig, and Figure 20-12 is a mechanical construction drawing that any machinist should understand. You can fabricate the device from practically any material ranging from plastic to metal. The one consideration is that the jig be softer than your dops to prevent damage and deformation. You will need access to a saw, drill press, thread tap, and potentially an end mill.

Figure 20-11 A simple device for aiding the transfer cheat. See Chapter 7.6.3 for more.

Fabricating a snug and repeatable clamping hole is a bit of a challenge. Doing so may be easier after finishing the remainder of the device. Just clamp the two halves firmly together and (carefully!) drill the hole. You should start with an undersized hole and then enlarge it with abrasive paper held against a drill bit. Keep working the hole until it clamps firmly to your dops.

If you don't have access to proper machine shop equipment, you should still be able to put together a decent facsimile using common tools. For example, you can drill and tap screw holes with a minimum of equipment. Alternatively, you can ask a machinist for assistance with the difficult steps. In my experience, shop people are uniformly friendly and accommodating. None of my "homebuilt" hardware, including the Transfer Cheat Thingy, would have been possible without their help.

Whatever construction path you choose, there are two primary considerations: First, and most obviously, the clamping mechanism must be reliable and easy to use. The whole point here is to preserve and transfer information about rotational orientation (see Chapter 7.3.2). A loose clamp will ruin your whole day.

The second consideration is that the base should be very flat and sit square on your master lap without gaps. Having a wider base as shown here is a help, since it will "average" over more area of the lap and hence minimize the effect of local bumps or surface contamination.

20.6.2 Using the Transfer Cheat Thingy

Step 1: Refer to Chapter 7.6.3

Step 2: Have fun.

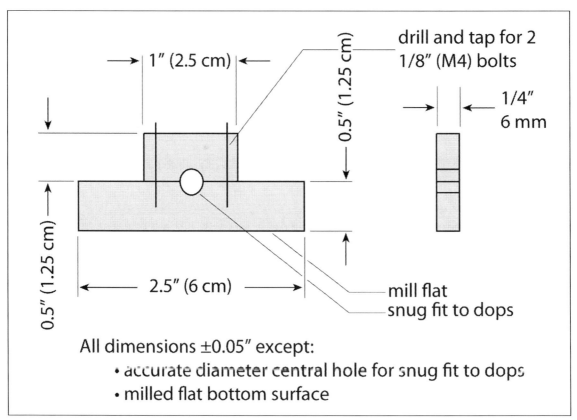

Figure 20-12 Construction drawing for the Transfer Cheat Thingy.

20.7 A Better Depth of Cut Indicator

Your initial faceting experience probably echoes mine. I didn't know how to start.

There were no lapidary clubs in my neighbourhood, I had no nearby faceting friends, and I just didn't know what to do. Eventually, circumstances permitted me to spend several months in Tucson, one of the epicenters of the gem-cutting world. I joined a club, found an instructor, and dove right in.

It soon became clear to me that the real problem was knowing how to stop.

Specifically, modern faceting machines and laps permit you to vaporize valuable gem rough in an alarmingly efficient way. Without careful control, balancing your facets is a process of cutting down to the deepest recent mistake. You should by now realize that this is not a good way of maximizing yield.

I learned on a Graves Mk IV, a fine beginner's machine which features a hard stop mechanism to prevent the type of over cutting mentioned in the previous paragraph (see Chapter 2.4 for more on hard and soft stops). It didn't work for me – I tend to have a heavy hand at the machine, and mast flexure plagued my early faceting experience.

20.7.1 The Depth of Cut Indicator

Discussion with friends and a bit of online research led to the discovery of the Depth of Cut Indicator (DoCI), a device which promised to give a clear signal when a prescribed amount of gem material had been removed. I vowed that when I put together my own dream machine (see page 53 of Volume 1), I would include such an indicator.

Most DoCI's rely on a now-ancient principle for measuring the position of an object. The idea is to place electrical contacts on two surfaces which approach each other as the measurement proceeds. These electrodes close a circuit when contact is made, and an appropriate indicator, such as a lamp or buzzer, announces the event. In the case of a faceting machine, one contact is typically on the quill, while the other is mounted to a fixed point on the cutting head. At the desired angle, the two electrodes touch each other and trigger the alarm (Figure 20-13).

The dynamic nature of a faceting machine permits an additional refinement. Minor machine wobble, coupled with hills and valleys on the lap, leads to intermittent contact as the final depth approaches. This means that the circuit will open and close repeatedly just as the electrodes come into contact. The resulting electrical signal is a square wave whose duty cycle – that is, the fraction of time that the signal is high versus low – increases as the two contacts come together (Figure 20-14).

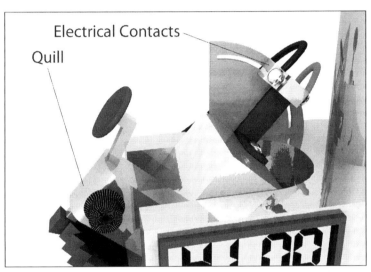

Figure 20-13 Electrical contacts mounted at a suitable location will signal when the desired cutting angle has been reached.

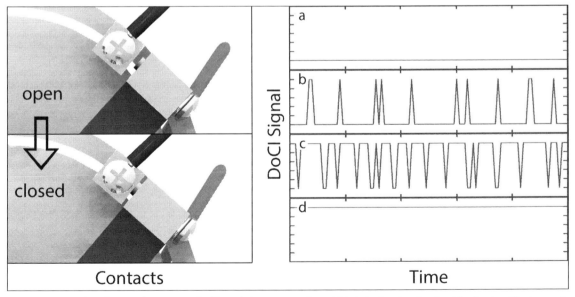

Figure 20-14 The electrical contacts (left) and the output signal (right) of a depth of cut indicator. During cutting, the electrical circuit is open and the signal is zero (a). As the two contacts approach each other, surface irregularities and vibration of the lap cause intermittent contact (b). The amount of time that the circuit is closed increases as the electrodes come together (c). Finally, with the two contacts firmly pressed against each other, the signal remains high (d).

In principle, then, you could make an even more accurate depth of cut by always stopping at the precise moment when the flickering signal has the same duty cycle. Unfortunately, however, human eyes and ears aren't very good at assessing the amount of flickering of a lamp or the intermittent squeal of a buzzer. You need a way of converting the rapidly alternating high and low signal into a continuously varying one.

At this point, readers with a mechanical engineering background are thinking springs and dashpots, while our electrical engineering colleagues have conjured visions of resistors and capacitors. In fact, most depth of cut indicators you will see on the Web adopt the mechanical approach, using the springs and dashpot of an analog meter to measure the duty cycle of the alternating signal.

Unfortunately, mechanical meters are an increasingly rare commodity in our modern digital world, and they were never cheap. They can also be finicky, and the exact arrangement of the device can spell the difference between a useful measurement of depth of cut and a fluttering, maddening mess. My particular mechanical meter was definitely in the fluttering mess category, and I thus set out to find another solution more in harmony with my electrical engineering friends.

Magicus Ex Machina

Incidentally, you may come across some extravagant claims on the Web regarding the functioning and capabilities of depth of cut indicators. I have read endless discussion group posts detailing sophisticated operating principles and ascribing to these humble devices almost magical powers for correcting everything from mast flexure to misaligned machines.

Don't believe it. Essentially all depth of cut indicators use simple mechanical or electrical mechanisms to convert a series of on-off pulses to a continuous signal, whose value corresponds to the amount of on versus off. They do so in a way which would be familiar to engineers of your grandparents' generation. No mysteries here.

Of course, knowing when the quill is at the same angle relative to the faceting head is of enormous value in producing consistent facet tiers – that is, after all, the whole idea. Nevertheless, the insight provided by the DoCI does not extend beyond this simple, valuable piece of information. It does not, for example, tell you anything about mast flexure or overall alignment, at least not directly.

Short version: Use a depth of cut indicator as one more tool in your arsenal, but don't rely on it for everything. Repeat your mantra: cut a little and look a lot.

20.7.2 Building the Better DoCI

The problem is simple: convert a rapidly varying on-off, or digital, signal into a continuously varying, or analog, one. The more time that the digital signal is high, the greater the analog signal should be.

It turns out that to do this, you need an electrical device which goes by the fancy name of integrator. Luckily, this fancy name accompanies one of the most simple of electrical layouts, known to many as the classic RC circuit. An RC integrator performs a time average of its input signal, and you can adjust the response, or time constant, by varying the resistance and or capacitance of its components. A shorter time constant means more responsiveness and flutter, while a longer time constant means a steadier signal, which will rarely reflect the instantaneous value of the input.

The circuit is almost unbelievably simple. Figure 20-15 shows the necessary components: a couple of resistors and a capacitor do the hard work, while a commercial voltmeter module measures the result. Easy peasy.

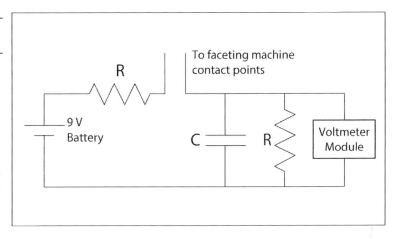

Figure 20-15 A simple RC integrator will convert the on-off signal input to a smoothly varying analog output.

Here is what you will need:

Item	Comment
Voltmeter module	For 0-10 V. Available at your local hobby electronics shack.
Resistors, capacitor	See text for details.
Machine contacts, wire	Configuration, type, and location will vary from machine to machine. See text.
Prototype board, 9V battery, enclosure	Available at hobby electronics shacks.

Assemble the components on a small hobbyist prototype board (Figure 20-16). In fact, the circuit is so simple that you could even put the RC parts together on a piece of cardboard and stuff it into the back of the meter module. Just don't start a fire with your soldering iron.

Two points deserve mention before you head off to Radio Shack:

Select the resistors and capacitor so that the RC product is approximately 1, giving a one second time constant. For example, I use 10 megaohm resistors and a 0.1 microfarad capacitor. Reducing either R or C will produce a more responsive, jumpy, output, while increasing them will smooth things further. Note also that the current draw of this circuit is very low. In fact, it is zero when the contacts are apart and about half a micro-Amp when the circuit is closed. The nine-volt battery will last a LONG time.

This better depth of cut indicator is a snap to build, but the real challenge lies in finding appropriate contacts and mounting points on your faceting machine. Given the diversity of machine configurations, I cannot hope to give coherent advice here. The best strategy will vary from manufacturer to manufacturer and from model to model. Figure 20-13 illustrates one common configuration, while Figure 20-17 shows how I installed the electrodes on a Poly-Metric Scintillator head. The online discussion groups (Chapter 15.1.3) are an excellent source of experience and wisdom in this area.

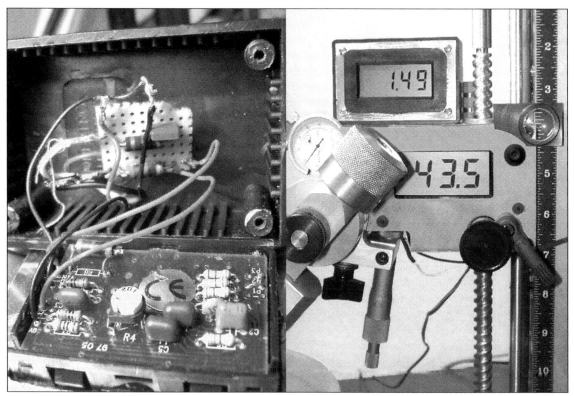

Figure 20-16 The simple RC circuit on a scrap piece of prototype circuit board mounted in a hobbyist's project box (left). Yes, I admit that it's not pretty. The commercial voltmeter module is face-down at the bottom of the image. The assembled depth of cut indicator atop a Poly-Metric Scintillator head (right).

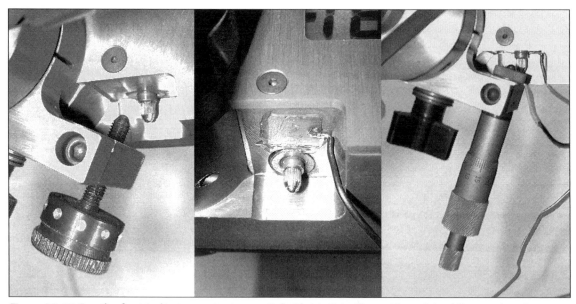

Figure 20-17 Depth of cut indicator contacts on a Poly-Metric Scintillator. The original fine angle adjustment knob provides a suitable location for the contacts (left). A small conducting plate glued to the underside of the faceting head serves as one contact (middle). The other contact is on the moving knob, here upgraded with a micrometer head for even finer control (right). See Chapter 15.8.13 for links to this and other DoCI conversions.

20.7.3 Using the Better DoCI

This electronic depth of cut indicator works exactly like its mechanical cousins. With the quill up and the circuit open, the meter should read zero volts. With the contacts touching firmly, you should see a steady signal whose value depends on component selection and the details of your meter module. Try tapping the circuit closed several times per second with the quill. This will produce an intermediate reading.

When cutting, you should stop before the meter reaches its maximum value. For subsequent facets of the same tier, try to stop cutting at the same reading. With a little experimentation and practice, you should soon be cutting exquisitely balanced tiers of constant facet depth.

It turns out that, despite its great virtues, my Better Depth of Cut Indicator did not last long in its original form. Turn to the next section to learn how you can incorporate its functionality into a sophisticated digital facet angle encoder. Easy peasy becomes fancy pantsy...

20.8 A Digital Facet Angle Encoder

This is a serious project.

Seriously.

On the one hand, it is a seriously cool project. It involves modifying your faceting machine to allow easy but extremely accurate and repeatable angle measurements. No more peering through a magnifying lens at vernier scales or wondering why your "digital" readout gives an answer that varies with time, temperature, or the Dow Jones Industrial Average.

On the other hand, this can also be a seriously complex project. Depending on the mechanical details of your faceting machine, it could involve manufacturing a new part or two. It certainly entails soldering together electrical components, and depending on your personal inclinations, it could involve writing some microcontroller code.

Like I said, seriously cool. Just remember that it may also be seriously serious.

20.8.1 Why Mess with My Fine Machine?

Great question. If you are completely happy with how well the angle indicator on your faceting machine works, read no further. If you are able to consistently dial in (and believe) your cutting angles to 0.1° or better, put the book down now. If you are ready, willing, and able to spend the better part of a thousand bucks on a commercial digital encoder system, go for it.

If, like me, you are none of these three things, however, you may be ready to invest the time and effort in a homebuilt digital encoder for your faceting machine. It should greatly improve both the accuracy and precision of your cutting, and if my experience is any guide, it will enormously increase your enjoyment of the hobby. And finally, if you really enjoy do-it-yourself projects – the tiny dropped components, the broken fingernails, the sharp sting of solder fumes up your nose – then this one will be a doozy.

20.8.2 Building the Digital Encoder

Still with us? Great! Here is what you will need:

Item	Comment
Optical encoder	2000 steps/revolution or better (see page 396).
Microcontroller	Arduino or equivalent (see Section 20.8.4).
LCD alphanumeric display	16 characters x 2 line or better…choose a standard module (page 403).
LEDs and beeper for feedback	Provides info on calibration and depth of cut (page 404).
Mechanical interface	Depends on faceting machine (see page 398).
Wire, solder, mounting hardware	To mount the encoder, microcontroller, and display on your faceting machine.

Accuracy versus Precision

Want to start a fight among engineers and scientists? Ask them about accuracy versus precision. Yes, they all had the exact meaning of these two words hammered into their skulls back in college, but a lifetime of careless usage almost always blurs the critical distinction between the two.

Accuracy refers to how close you come to the correct answer, whereas precision refers to how repeatable your answer is. One can be very accurate but imprecise, or conversely, very precise but inaccurate. Figure 20-18 shows the difference using a classic analogy. The archer on the left is very accurate – all of his arrows lie close to the bull's eye. On the other hand, none of them lie close to each other. While they were all fine shots, they were not repeatable, not *precise*. The archer on the right has the opposite problem. She can produce a tight, consistent cluster of hits. In other words, her shooting is very precise. Unfortunately, this nice, tight cluster is nowhere near where it should be – it is *inaccurate*.

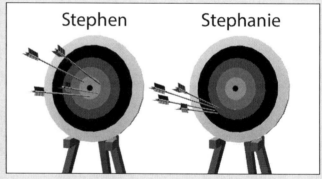

Figure 20-18 *Accuracy measures how close you come to your target, while precision measures how consistent you are. Stephen on the left has high accuracy but low precision, whereas Stephanie on the right has high precision but low accuracy. Faceters should try to hit the bull's eye every time…*

Needless to say, good cutting requires both accuracy and precision. It doesn't help much if you can nail a facet angle exactly, if you can only do it one in ten times. On the other hand, consistently dialing in exactly 43.5° brings no gemological joy when the desired angle was 43°.

The digital encoder described in this section should help with both accuracy and precision. Read on to see how and why.

There are three basic aspects to this project: the mechanics, the electronics, and the software. The mechanical part involves figuring out how to attach the encoder and display to your faceting machine. The details of this will depend on the configuration of your machine (see page 398). The example shown here is for a Poly-Metric Scintillator head, which requires a custom angle shaft extender and a simple project box available from your favourite hobby electronics store. The electronics aspect involves some simple hookups between the encoder, microcontroller, and display. Note that, for good measure, this project incorporates the depth of cut indicator (DoCI) described in Section 20.7. Finally, the software component is up to you. The simplest approach is to obtain an Arduino microcontroller and type in the program supplied below. If you are more adventurous – or more likely, filled with contempt at my coding practices – you can try your own hand at writing microcontroller programs on your platform of choice.

20.8.3 The Mechanics

This section begins with a few words on how faceting machines measure angles, and how an optical encoder can do a much better job. Then it's on to selecting an appropriate encoder and the more difficult chore of identifying a way to attach it to your particular faceting machine. This may require some help from your friendly neighbourhood machinist, so as usual, be prepared to buy beer.

Facet Angle Measurement

The original faceting machines – the so-called jamb-peg faceters – used the simplest of angle measuring devices: a board with various holes into which you would "jamb the peg," in other words, insert the fixed-length quill (see page 20 of Volume 1). Sadly, the beauty of this simplicity did not bring accuracy along with it, although an experienced cutter could certainly achieve precision (see opposite page). The most obvious shortcoming of using a pegboard and a fixed length quill is that the gem itself forms part of the triangle that determines the cutting angle (see Figure 20-19). This results in different angles for different-sized stones, or in the case of non-round cuts, an angle error that depends on the shape of the gem.

Modern faceting machines use a variety of mechanical and electrical means for determining the cutting angle. The purely mechanical devices typically employ a vernier scale, which in principle allows measurement to about a tenth of a degree, assuming, of course, that everything is properly aligned. Other machines, such as the Facetron, use gears and a mechanical counter to keep track of the angle (see Figure 20-20).

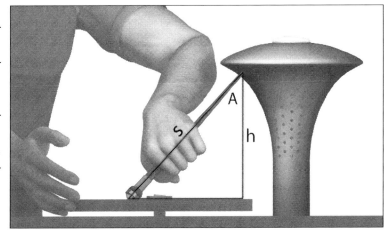

Figure 20-19 A Jamb-Peg faceter sets the cutting angle using multiple holes and the length of the quill plus gem. You know from Chapter 10.2 that the cutting angle A = cos⁻¹ (h/s), but s includes the size of the stone.

Figure 20-20 Mechanical angle measuring devices. A vernier scale on an Ultra Tec faceting machine (left). The hand crank and counter on a Facetron (right).

The newest generation of faceting machines sport what is called a "digital angle readout." In most cases, this is a mild misnomer, since they offer only a digital display of an analog measurement. Specifically, these machines contain an accurate potentiometer, a variable electrical resistor, attached to the facet angle shaft. Moving the quill rotates the potentiometer and a digital meter samples the resulting change of (analog) resistance. With high-class potentiometers, such an arrangement can achieve accuracy and precision in the neighbourhood of 0.1°, although many users report significantly larger drifts with time and temperature. For example, you set the angle to 42.5°, go have lunch, and on your return, you find that your waistline is not the only thing that underwent expansion in the intervening hour. Such drifts are extremely difficult to avoid in the analog world, and hence, the ultimate in accuracy and precision comes only with a truly digital device, such as an optical encoder.

Digital Optical Encoders

Note: This section explains the operating principle of optical encoders. While interesting, at least in my opinion, understanding this material is not absolutely essential to building a working facet angle encoder. Turn to page 397 if you want to skip this introduction.

Digital optical encoders overcome the uncertainty and drift inherent in analog circuits. They do this by exploiting a simple electro-optical concept known as the light gate, in which an opaque object interrupts a beam of light and signals to the control system that something must be done. The automatic door opener at your neighbourhood grocery store is a classic example (Figure 20-21), although ultrasonic sensors are steadily replacing light gates in this application. The right panel of Figure 20-21 illustrates the more relevant example of a toothed wheel with alternating black and transparent regions, which can be used to monitor the turning of a shaft.

A light gate is a simple, non-contact, on-off device. It produces either a positive signal or zero, depending on whether the sensor sees the light or not. As such, it is immune to the usual ills of the analog world, for example sensitivity to temperature. It also avoids all that error-prone squinting at tiny scratches on a vernier scale. Coupled with a computer to count the ones and zeros, a light gate can provide an accurate and precise way of measuring angles.

Of course, a simple wheel such as that shown in Figure 20-21 would be of little use on a faceting machine: the output signal indicates that the shaft is rotating, but it contains no information on where it is, which way it is turning, and how far it has gone. Most of us can

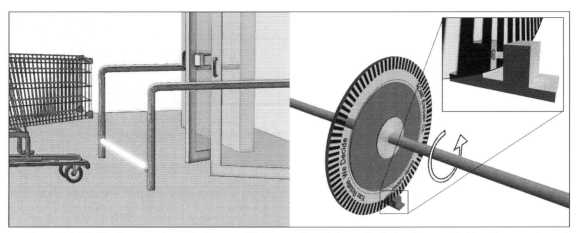

Figure 20-21 The interruption of a beam of light can signal the arrival of a shopper (left) or the rotation of a shaft (right).

already tell when the angle shaft on our faceting machine is moving. At least those of us who haven't been squinting too long…

How, then, can you measure the angle of a shaft? This is where the "encoding" part of the encoders comes in. Even a modest familiarity with computers and digital electronics should suggest one possible solution. Why not create multiple radial zones on the wheel and encode the angle as a binary number? Figure 20-22 shows how. Such a device is known as an *absolute* encoder, since it can measure the exact angle at any time without calibration.

That same modest familiarity with computers and digital electronics should also suggest why the absolute encoder is a particularly bad solution for a facet angle measurement. The answer is *resolution*. Let's say you want to measure the cutting angle to a tenth of a degree (see "The Resolution Resolution" on the next page). For a direct shaft connection (i.e. no gearing), you will want this resolution over 90°, a quarter of a rotation. This means that the encoder will have to distinguish 900 separate angles. Sparing you the math ($\log_2(900)$ in case you are interested) such an arrangement would require ten separate radial zones of the type shown in Figure 20-22. It would also require ten light detectors, as well as an uncomfortably small tolerance on assembly to prevent cross-talk between the channels. All in all, not a good (or inexpensive) choice.

Happily, there is a simple, inexpensive alternative to the absolute encoder. It is known as the *relative* encoder, and to no-one's surprise, the relative encoder measures things relative to a fixed reference point. Some manufacturers refer to these as *incremental* encoders. Rather than having a separate radial zone for each digit of the binary number representing

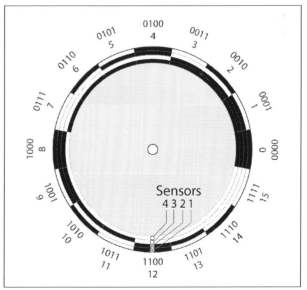

Figure 20-22 Radial coded zones allow multiple light sensors to measure the angle of the wheel, here shown as a binary number between zero (0000) and fifteen (1111). Yes, this four-zone absolute encoder will have poor angular resolution: the steps are 22.5° apart, far too large for high-quality faceting.

the angle, the relative encoder has only two such zones, which are created using a single set of dark bars and two light sensors offset from each other by half the width of the bars. Figure 20-23 illustrates the principle.

These two sensors give only the direction and distance of motion. Hence, they need a reference point to give an absolute angle measurement. This can be the closing of a mechanical switch or preferably, the use of a third radial zone with a single opaque bar (see Figure 20-23). Once per revolution, a transition on this third *index* channel indicates that the shaft is at the reference angle, and the control program can merely count steps from there.

In addition to their more modest assembly tolerances, relative encoders offer a very significant advantage over their absolute brethren: the achievable resolution does not depend on the number of radial zones on the wheel. In fact, the A and B sensors use the same bars, and you don't have to add another zone for each factor of two improvement. This means that relative encoders with the required resolution can be had for significantly less than $100, far less than what an absolute encoder would cost.

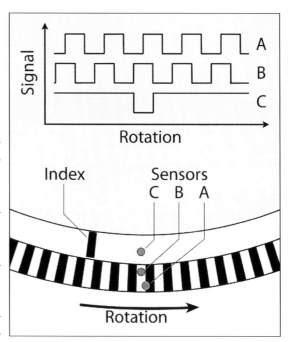

Figure 20-23 The Relative or Incremental Encoder can determine the direction of motion by determining which of the two channels ("A" or "B") went from dark to light, or vice-versa, before the other. You can convince yourself of this by following the signals in the plot from left to right and then from right to left. By counting the number of transitions, the device can keep track of how far the shaft has turned. A single opaque bar in the third "C" channel marks the absolute reference point and is sampled once per revolution by a third sensor.

The Resolution Resolution

How much angular resolution do you actually need?

Or, put another way, when are you just showing off? Most modern faceting diagrams show angles with at least 0.1° accuracy. In other words, the prescription calls for 42.3°, not 42°. The GemCAD software (see Chapter 15.3.1) expresses all angles with two decimal places, *i.e.* 42.34°. Most experienced faceters agree that this extra digit is somewhat superfluous, given the (often abysmal) state of alignment of many of our machines and our ability to set angles accurately (but see "Sufficient Accuracy" on page 111 of Volume 1 for more punditry on this issue).

You have no doubt learned, perhaps in a painful manner, that cutting angle errors translate directly into something visible, such as missed meets. The relationship between angle errors and visible flaws is a complex one, but based on the discussion in Section 4.11.6 and the overwhelming common wisdom of the faceting community, this project will assume that 0.1° resolution, particularly if it can be achieved with both accuracy and precision (see page 392), will be more than enough.

Thinking in the world of encoders, you will then need at least 3600 subdivisions per shaft rotation to reach this target resolution (360° / 0.1° = 3600). Figure 20-24 shows an example of a suitable device, the HEDS-6545 encoder with 2000 optical pulses per revolution.

Figure 20-24 This relative optical encoder, with 2000 optical pulses per revolution, provides enough angular resolution to give better than 0.1° resolution. The encoder wheel and light gate mechanism visible here are normally enclosed in a protective housing.

But wait! Didn't I just say that you needed 3600 steps per revolution? How can an encoder with only 2000 pulses possibly work?

The answer lies in Figure 20-25. Look at the signal patterns carefully. The passage of each black bar past the sensors, that is each optical pulse of the encoder, actually provides *four* separate signals. You can follow along in the figure. As the wheel rotates from one black bar to the next, channel A goes negative (1), then channel B goes negative (2), then channel A goes positive (3), then channel B goes positive (4). After this, the process repeats with the next black bar.

Voilà! Four steps for the price of one! As long as you keep careful track of the state of each channel, you can actually turn a 2000 step encoder into an 8000 step encoder! This corresponds to about 0.045° per step, or a little bit more than twice the resolution you need. All that is required is a little bit of clever software.

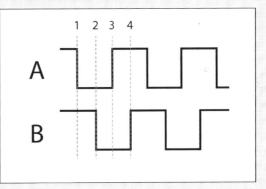

Figure 20-25 By monitoring the "on" and "off" states of channels A and B, you can effectively quadruple the resolution of the relative encoder. See text for details.

Incidentally, the last sentence of the previous paragraph is the second most popular phrase uttered by computer programmers. The first, of course, is "it must be a hardware problem…"

Your Real-World Encoder

Figure 20-26 shows how a real-world relative optical encoder goes together. These devices are available in a variety of formats from several manufacturers. You should expect to pay well under $100 for the entire package, including the encoder wheel, optical sensor block, and housing assembly. Chapter 15.8.11 provides links to several online retailers.

Whether you shop for your encoder online or through a paper catalog, you may be confronted with an intimidating array of options. The key things to watch for are the number of steps, the shaft diameter, single-ended versus differential outputs, the packaging and mounting details, and the presence of a third index channel to allow absolute calibration. Table 20-2 provides guidance.

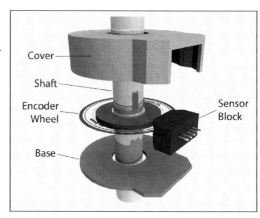

Figure 20-26 The components of an optical encoder. This one has a "through-shaft" configuration, so-called because the rotating shaft passes completely through the device. A suitable real-world encoder will fit in the palm of your hand and costs less than $100 (see also Figure 20-24).

For my faceting machine upgrade, I selected the HEDS-6545 encoder from Nanotec in Germany. This is very similar, both mechanically and electrically, to devices produced by U.S. Digital and Agilent. Choose the best encoder for you, depending on cost, availability, and most importantly, how easily you can mount it on your faceting machine.

Table 20-2 What to look for in a relative optical encoder.

Item	Value	Comment
Counts per Revolution	1000+	1000 counts gives 0.09° resolution. More is better, so look for devices with 2000 CPR or more.
Shaft Diameter	2-25 mm	Depends on the mechanical details of your mounting arrangement.
Single-ended or Differential Outputs	Single-ended	With differential, each signal line has its own ground. Single-ended is sufficient for short cable runs.
Packaging	various	Includes attachment details, holes for through-shaft mounting, etc. (see example below).
Index Channel	yes	A third channel with one pulse per revolution. Needed for absolute calibration (see page 396).

Mounting the Encoder

Here is where the rubber meets the road. Figuring out how, and indeed whether, your machine can accommodate an optical encoder is the single most challenging aspect of this entire project.

Note that modifying your machine may violate warranties and otherwise irritate the manufacturer. It may also ruin the calibration of the pre-existing angle measurement equipment. Ask your supplier or manufacturer before trying anything radical. My lawyer is now happy. Good luck to you.

Sorry, I can't be of much help in figuring out how to mount the encoder, unless of course you own the exact same faceting head as I do (a Poly-Metric Scintillator). If yours is different, the information in this section can serve as a general guideline only. No matter which machine you own, however, the basic idea is to figure out how to mount the encoder with minimum impact on the existing mechanics. In the case of my Scintillator, I wanted to preserve the potentiometer-based angle-measuring device as a backup. This meant somehow sharing the facet angle shaft. As you will see, it also meant fabricating a shaft extender.

Figure 20-27 shows the original hardware arrangement of the Scintillator. The potentiometer sits on the back of the faceting head and is connected to the angle shaft via a standard mechanical coupler.

I could see only one way to include the new digital encoder without losing the original mechanism: shifting the potentiometer backward and using a through-shaft encoder (see Figure 20-26 and Figure 20-28). Of course, the original potentiometer shaft was not long enough to extend through the encoder into its original coupler, so I was faced with the need to extend both the shaft and the housing of the faceting head. Employing my standard trick of turning beer into steel (see page 55 of Volume 1), I "encouraged" a machinist friend to fabricate a suitable shaft extender (see Figure 20-28 and Figure 20-29b). And, turning burden into opportunity, I chose to replace the back panel of the Scintillator head with a hobby electronics box that could accommodate the extended angle shaft plus encoder, as well as the microcontroller and display hardware described in the next section.

Figure 20-27 Removing the back cover reveals the original Scintillator angle measuring device, a precision potentiometer coupled directly to the angle shaft.

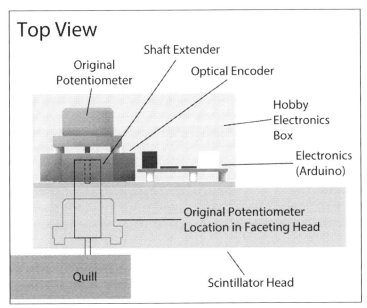

Figure 20-28 Shifting the original potentiometer backward and enclosing it and the new optical encoder in a hobbyist's electronic box.

Putting the whole thing together proved much simpler than I expected. The only hiccup came when I realized that I had arranged the various attachment and set screws in a way that the thing couldn't be bolted together, sort of like the classic case of putting the stitches on the inside of a soccer ball (how do they do that, anyway?) A modest re-jiggering with some spacers gave me the gaps I needed to tighten the final screws. Then of course, there was the slight rubbing of this on that, and the hole that was the wrong size, and...well, as you can see, an unqualified success as these things go.

Figure 20-29 chronicles the various steps in assembling the encoder mechanics. The final panel portrays the entire thing bolted together with the original potentiometer display still working (!) Panel i shows me bolting the microcontroller into the hobby project box. This tiny bit of electronic wizardry is the focus of the next part of the encoder project.

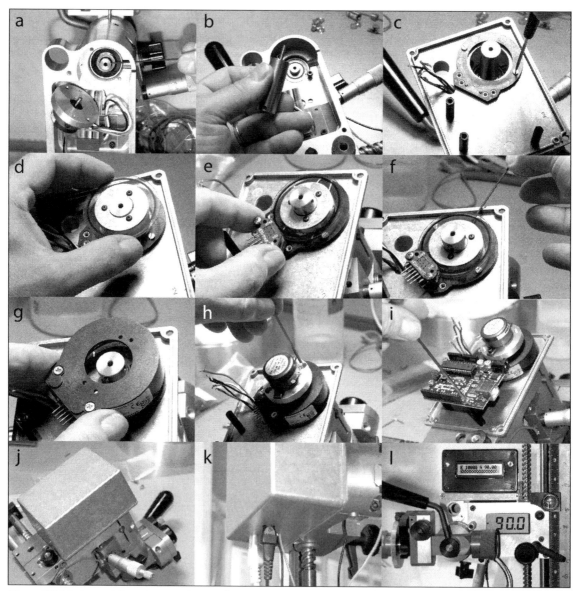

Figure 20-29 Assembling the encoder mechanics on a Poly-Metric Scintillator. a. Removing the original potentiometer. b. The shaft extender. c. The extender has been locked in place and protrudes through the top plate of the hobby electronics box, which is in turn bolted to the back of the Scintillator. The base plate of the encoder is next. d. Carefully mounting the encoder wheel. e. Bolting the sensor block in place. f. Locking the encoder wheel. NOTE: The orientation of the wheel sets the location of the index pulse. I chose to place the pulse so that it triggers each time the quill is raised above horizontal (at approximately 100° cutting angle). g. The cover encloses the optical encoder. h. Installing the original potentiometer at its new, more distant location on the top cover of the encoder (see Figure 20-28). i. Bolting the Arduino microcontroller in place. j. The hobby box protects all of the encoder hardware. k. Wiring emerging from the bottom of the encoder box. l. The 16 character x 2 line LCD display mounted atop the original, variable-resistor angle readout.

20.8.4 The Electronics

The mechanical parts are presumably under control, and they will produce a series of electrical pulses as the quill moves up and down. Unless you plan to follow these pulses with an oscilloscope or flashing LEDs, however, you are going to need some support electronics. Specifically, you must count and keep track of encoder steps, calculate the facet angle, and present the result in a usable form to the operator (this is you).

The Brains of the Operation

In the old days, for example when your faceting machine was (probably) designed, this sort of task was managed by discrete electronic components, such as logic gates, shift registers, and other Transistor-Transistor-Logic obscurities. Unless you have a fading orange copy of the Texas Instrument's TTL Data Book for Design Engineers gathering dust on your bookshelf, you will probably have no idea what I am talking about.

No matter. We are now in the era of the microcontroller, those seemingly miraculous tiny silicon dots which contain a complete computer, including memory, operating system, and interfaces to the outside world. Microcontrollers are everywhere from your wristwatch to the microwave oven. If your car was produced in the 21st century, it may contain dozens of individual microcontrollers. You may even be walking around with several in your pocket: many modern credit cards, and all mobile phone SIM cards, have a microcontroller lurking under those gold contacts.

The spectrum of microcontrollers suitable for hobby projects is thankfully more limited. And, while the entire encoder electronics do not have to fit within the thickness of a credit card, there are a few things that you should look out for, in order to make your life easier. Most importantly, the microcontroller should provide an easy environment for programming, downloading the code, and debugging. There is nothing worse – trust me, I've done it – than attempting to figure out what is wrong with a program written in binary or hexadecimal code, when your only hint of what's happening is a blinking error lamp.

Of course, the microcontroller should offer a wealth of input and output channels. You will need to detect pulses from the encoder and send control signals to the display. It would also be nice to have a few additional bells and whistles, such as signal lamps, an audio alarm, and a reset switch input. Finally, the microcontroller can also be made to sense continuously varying analog inputs, such as the signal produced by a depth of cut indicator (see Section 20.7).

Arduino Arguendo

I don't want to get into a fight. Particularly with computer and microcontroller people. They fight dirty. Yes, there are multiple platforms out there that can do the job, but I will make the argument that the Arduino microcontroller fits the bill perfectly (See Figure 20-30).

First of all, the Arduino is simple to use. There is a friendly graphical user interface (GUI) that is a free download and runs on most home computers, including those based on Windows, Mac OS, and linux. This GUI allows you to write code comfortably on a real screen, formatting and error-checking your efforts as you go (Figure 20-31). Incidentally, and somewhat mysteriously, Arduino programs are known as "sketches."

Downloading the sketch to the microcontroller is a mouse click and a USB cable away. The GUI and Arduino internals take care of all of the additional infrastructure, including managing the file transfer and re-starting. If you want to sound cool, or at least well informed, you can refer to the latter among friends as the "boot loader" process. No guarantee that they will remain your friends, however.

The Arduino is also electrically very simple, requiring only a DC power supply providing somewhere between 7 and 12 volts. The interface lines are compatible with standard electronic components, including the optical encoder and the liquid crystal display (LCD – see next section). There are also a pair of so-called "interrupt" lines, which greatly simplify working with an encoder – see below. The Arduino can even draw power from your home computer via the USB cable, although I would not recommend this as a long term solution: not only would the computer have to remain next to your faceting machine and switched on, but also some laptops may not provide enough USB power to supply the Arduino, encoder, and LCD at the same time.

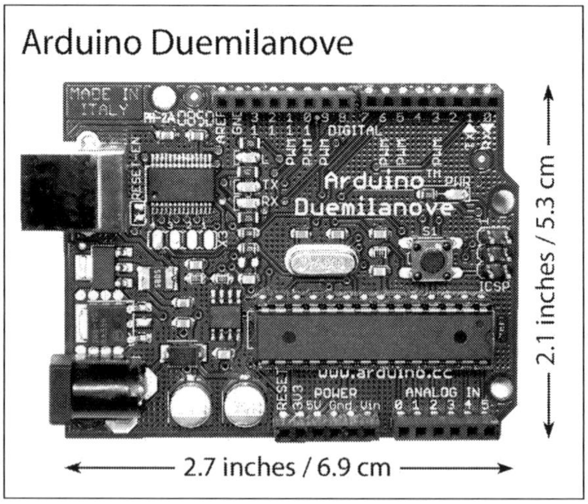

A number of manufacturers offer expansion boards, or "shields" for the Arduino. These add-ons open up an array of additional capability, including Ethernet, GPS, and Bluetooth interfaces. Want to read your current facet angle using your cell phone? It should be possible, although there are more than enough examples in our world that demonstrate that not everything that *can* be done *should* be done.

Figure 20-30 The Arduino microcontroller is an excellent open-source platform for operating the encoder. This is the Duemilanove model, first released in 2009 and since replaced by more capable yet completely compatible versions. Note the header plugs giving access to the fourteen digital and six analog ports. The large connectors on the left are for the USB computer interface and 9-volt power. See www.arduino.cc for complete information, including local vendors.

An even more important advantage of the Arduino is that there is a substantial user community out there on the Internet that has written and uploaded open-source (this means FREE!) modules to control a variety of devices, including some encoders and LCD's. These modules are available online, as is troubleshooting support via a number of forums. Finally, the Arduino is cheap. Depending on the model you select, you can expect to pay $20-$30 for the whole shebang.

Pardon Me, but What is an Interrupt?

Most computer code is *linear*, in the sense that one statement gets executed after another, exactly as written. While reliable and easy to understand, such an arrangement does not allow the software to react to important, time-critical events. In other words if the code currently being executed isn't looking for something to happen, that something might not get noticed.

Interrupts address this critical shortcoming of traditional software. The triggering of an interrupt causes the computer to jump to a pre-defined section of the code, execute the necessary statements to react to the event, and then return operation to the previous location. If written properly, interrupt driven software can combine the best of both linear programming and real-time reaction.

I selected the Arduino Duemilanove for the encoder project (Figure 20-30). The Duemilanove supports 14 digital pins for input or output (I/O), as well as 6 channels of analog input. Six of the fourteen digital I/O lines can also be used for analog output, although this feature is not necessary for the encoder project. Unlike some of the more compact Arduino implementations, the Duemilanove provides easy-to-plug header sockets for all of the input and output lines.

Figure 20-31 The Arduino graphical user interface simplifies the process of writing, transferring, and debugging microcontroller code. This short program or "sketch" flashes an LED connected to pin 13.

```
/* BlinkLED Sketch
 * This simply blinks an LED connected to pin 13 for one
 * second on and off - forever.
 */

int LED_Pin = 13;              // LED connected to pin 13

void setup()                   // This always runs at startup
{
  pinMode(LED_Pin, OUTPUT);    // Define pin as output
}

void loop()                    // This executes forever
{
  digitalWrite(LED_Pin, HIGH); // Turn LED on
  delay(1000);                 // Waits for 1000 milliseconds
  digitalWrite(LED_Pin, LOW);  // Turn LED off
  delay(1000);                 // Another second then loop back
}
```

Binary sketch size: 1,084 bytes (of a 14,336 byte maximum)

The Display

You will need an output device for the measurement – a display. Once again, I don't want to get into a spitting (or other body fluid) match with the true computer mavens out there, so please return quietly to your blogs and Cheetos. What you need is a simple and clear way to present the facet angle information to the user.

As with the microcontroller, selecting the optimal display seems initially to be a daunting task. There is a huge variety of suitable display types out there, and identifying the best can be a challenge. Luckily, the choice of the Arduino platform can narrow the field considerably.

A quick scan of the Playground area of the Arduino website (arduino.cc/playground) led me to the realization that the basic software package that I installed already included a module for driving liquid crystal displays! Specifically, the LiquidCrystal library contains all the commands needed to drive LCD's using Hitachi HD44780, Samsung KS0066, or compatible controllers. This may sound obscure, but it turns out that many liquid crystal displays fall into this category. I chose the Anag Vision AV1624 module, which has two lines of 16 characters, essentially because my local electronics hobby shop had it in stock and it cost less than $20 (see Figure 20-32). Chapter 15.8.11 can help you locate a suitable display.

One additional point deserves mention. These liquid crystal displays come with a variety of interfaces, including serial and 4/8-bit parallel. The LiquidCrystal library handles both the 4 and 8-bit parallel type, and most compatible LCD's can also do both. Nevertheless, the serial interface is also a fine, albeit slightly more expensive option. The Arduino Playground includes modules to drive these serial devices as well.

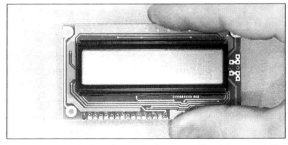

Figure 20-32 A simple 16x2 character liquid crystal display compatible with the Arduino software library.

Additional Feedback Doodads

In addition to the microcontroller and display, you will want some signaling devices to let you know that certain events have occurred, for example, successful power-up, calibration of the index channel of the encoder, and reaching the target depth of cut. The multiple output lines of the Arduino make adding LEDs a snap. I also procured a small, low voltage buzzer for audio feedback.

Wiring it All Together

I am not going to teach you how to solder. If you have made it this far, you probably already know how to solder, and if not, you certainly can figure out how to learn. The exact wiring configuration will of course depend on the details of the encoder, microcontroller, and display you have selected. Nevertheless, there are a few general guidelines:

1. If the microcontroller offers digital interrupt lines, make sure to connect these to the encoder A and B outputs. If your microcontroller offers more than two interrupts, consider connecting the encoder index output as well, although this will require a slight modification to the code in the next section.

2. Use ribbon cable and heat shrink tubing to prevent inadvertent contact between wires.

3. Wherever reasonable and practical, use detachable cables and connectors. This project involves a lot of inter-connects, and your hardware (and life) can get snarled quite quickly.

4. Test all solder joints for continuity and short circuits before proceeding.

5. Make a sketch of your soldering plan before you begin, and keep track of which wire is which. Commercial encoders, microcontrollers, and displays are reasonably foolproof, but they will not tolerate serious electronic stress, such as reversing the +9V and ground lines.

Figure 20-33 shows how I wired together the encoder, Arduino, and LCD display. Note the additional analog input for the depth of cut indicator, as well as the digital lines for a diagnostic LED, alarm buzzer, and reset switch. Because I was running out of digital lines on the Arduino, I chose the 4-bit parallel driver configuration for the LCD display.

20.8.5 The Software

At this point, you hopefully have the hardware and electronics – essentially the muscle and brains – of the encoder project in place. There is one final piece to the puzzle. The encoder needs some instructions on how to work: the control software.

Figure 20-31 shows what is perhaps an absurdly simple Arduino sketch, but it serves to highlight the basic code components you will need. All sketches have three elements: a declaration area followed by two routines called setup() and loop(). Guess what? The declaration

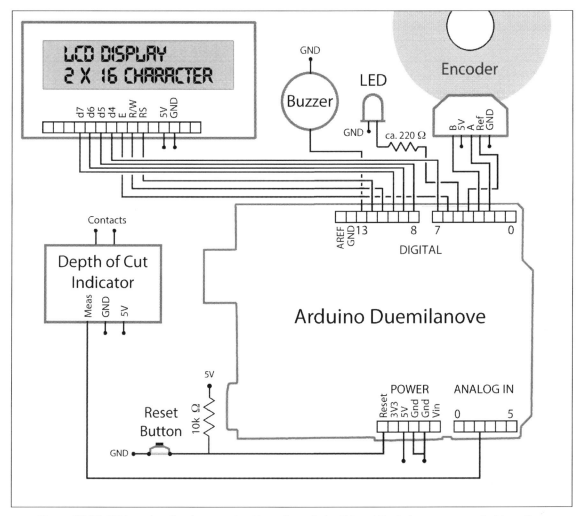

Figure 20-33 Wiring plan for the encoder. Note that all the 5V and Gnd pins are connected together.

area is used to make declarations, the setup() routine sets things up, and the loop() routine loops forever (or at least until a reset occurs, the device is turned off, or a new sketch is uploaded). As you will see, it is possible, and indeed highly recommended, to add additional routines. Due to its heritage in the popular C programming language, these Arduino code blocks, as well as multi-line statements, are enclosed in curly brackets. Each statement ends with a semi-colon for the same reason. Make sure that you understand everything in Figure 20-31…it's going to get a little more complicated from here on. If you have any questions, refer to the excellent online reference area at arduino.cc/en/Reference/HomePage

A listing of the encoder control software begins on the next page. As you can see, it is a considerably longer sketch than BlinkLED, so the following sections will examine it piece by piece. Note that I have manually added line numbers to simplify this discussion, and they should **not** be included when you type in the code. The GUI does keep track of line numbers, incidentally. For example, in Figure 20-31, the cursor sits in line 17 of the sketch, a fact duly reported at the bottom of the window. You can also download the sketch at this book's website: www.facetingbook.com

```
1    #include <LiquidCrystal.h>          // include the LiquidCrystal library
2    #include <WString.h>                 // include the String library
3
4    //=========================================
5    //
6    // We need to create the structures
7    // for interacting with:
8    //    1. The Rotary Encoder
9    //    2. The Liquid Crystal Display
10   //    3. The Depth of Cut Indicator
11   //
12   //=========================================
13   // Set up Rotary Encoder with:
14   // A on pin 2 (Interrupt)
15   // B on pin 3 (Interrupt)
16   // Index on pin 4
17   //
18   // NOTE: The value enc0 is the angle
19   //       for the index pulse location of the encoder.
20   //       This must be CALIBRATED!
21   //=========================================
22
23   #define pinA 2    // 2-3 are the interrupt-enabled inputs
24   #define pinB 3
25   #define pinI 4    // Index input
26   #define led 5     // LED indicator lamp
27
28   volatile unsigned int encPos;    // This is the current encoder count
29   unsigned int enc0 = 10411;       // Encoder counts at index pulse
30   unsigned int enc90 = 10000;      // Define 10000 counts at 90 degrees
31
32   boolean Aset;        // Whether we just had a positive going edge on A
33   boolean Bset;        //   and on B. These keep track of where we are
34   boolean newCal;      // This gets set at new calibration (index pulse)
35
36   float degPerStep = 0.045; // The number of degrees per encoder step
37
38   //=========================================
39   // Set up LiquidCrystal display with:
40   // rs on pin 12
41   // rw on pin 11
42   // enable on pin 6
43   // d4, d5, d6, d7 on pins 7,8,9,10
44   //
45   //=========================================
46
47   LiquidCrystal lcd(12, 11, 6, 7, 8, 9, 10);
48
49   unsigned int LCDchar = 16;   // No. of characters across (16 for LCD)
50   unsigned long cur = 0;       // Current time in milliseconds
51   unsigned long last = 0;      // Last sample time in milliseconds
52   unsigned long rate = 100;    // 100 ms update time for display
53
54   //=========================================
55   // Set up Depth of Cut Indicator with:
56   //   Analog Input on pin 2
57   //=========================================
58
59   unsigned int docPin = 2;     // Use pin 2 to measure depth of cut
60   unsigned int beep = 13;      // Pin connected to beeper
```

```
61   unsigned int docMax = 400;   // Voltage value for closed switch (measured)
62   unsigned int doci;           // Depth of cut indicator measurement (0-1023)
63   unsigned int doco;           // Output is doci scaled to the LCD display
64   unsigned int mthresh=8;      // Flash LED if exceeded - this is 1/2 display
65
66   unsigned int beepMax=10;     // How many cycles (of "rate") to keep beeping
67   unsigned int nBeep;          // How many so far
68
69   String Bar = String(17);     // To set up output display bar
70
71   //============================== SET UP ==============================
72
73   void setup()
74   {
75
76   // Encoder stuff
77
78     pinMode(pinA,INPUT);       // Define these as digital inputs
79     pinMode(pinB,INPUT);
80     pinMode(pinI,INPUT);
81
82     attachInterrupt(0,doA,CHANGE);  // Interrupt 0: RISING/FALLING on pinA
83     attachInterrupt(1,doB,CHANGE);  // Interrupt 1: RISING/FALLING on pinB
84
85     interrupts();              // Enabled by default, but just in case
86
87     pinMode(led, OUTPUT);      // sets the LED digital pin as output
88     digitalWrite(led,HIGH);    // Flash LED at start up
89
90   // LCD - Print a welcome message then set up display
91
92     lcd.print("Digital  Encoder");   // Static message
93     lcd.setCursor(0,1);              // Jump down to second row
94     lcd.print("facetingbook.com");
95
96     delay(2000);               // Wait a couple of seconds
97     digitalWrite(led,LOW);     // Turn off LED
98
99     lcd.clear();               // Erase, go to upper left
100
101  // Depth of Cut Indicator - Initialize output bar
102
103    Bar="                 "; // Initially blank
104
105  }
106
107  //============================== MAIN LOOP ==============================
108
109
110  // All encoder activity is interrupt driven. This routine measures the
111  // depth of cut indicator voltage and prints a bar on the second line
112  // of the LCD. It also updates the angle display based on the current
113  // value of encPos. This happens every "rate" milliseconds. It checks
114  // for a calibration more frequently - every time through the loop.
115  // Monitoring the A/B lines of the encoder happens with interrupts and
116  // updating of the steps occurs in routines doA() and doB(). This
117  // routine only calculates and shows the current facet angle.
118
119  void loop()
120  {
```

```
121
122    // Check for a new calibration and flash LED if it happened
123
124      if (newCal) {                    // Just did a cal - flash LED
125        newCal=false;                  // Reset value to false
126        digitalWrite(led,HIGH);        // Flash LED On
127        delay(100);                    // Wait 0.1 sec
128        digitalWrite(led,LOW);}        // Turn LED Off
129
130
131    // We only check the depth of cut every "rate" milliseconds
132
133      cur=millis();                // Grab number of milliseconds since startup
134      if (cur>last+rate) {         // We have waited long enough - update
135
136      last = cur;                  // Reset last to current for next check
137
138      doci = analogRead(docPin);     // Get current voltage (0-1023) from DOCI
139      doco = map(doci,0,docMax,0,LCDchar-1); // Scale 10-bits to LCD (0-15)
140
141    // If Depth of Cut Reached - provide audiovisual feedback
142
143      if (doco > mthresh){       // Reached desired depth of cut Need to flash
144
145            digitalWrite(led,HIGH);    // Turn LED on
146
147          nBeep=nBeep+1;                    // Increment beep counter
148          if (nBeep>beepMax){               // Long enough! Don't irritate!
149            digitalWrite(beep,LOW);}        // Switch off beep
150          else
151            digitalWrite(beep,HIGH);        // Switch on beep
152
153      }
154      else {
155          digitalWrite(led,LOW);        // Switch off LED
156          digitalWrite(beep,LOW);       // And switch off beeper
157          nBeep=0;                      // Reset beep counter
158      }
159
160    // Generate characters for Depth of Cut Bar display
161      for (int i=0;i<=doco;i++){         // Stuff full part of bar
162        Bar.setCharAt(i,'X');            // Use 'X' as the full character
163      }
164
165      for (int i=doco+1;i<=LCDchar-1;i++){   // Stuff empty part
166        Bar.setCharAt(i,' ');                // Use ' ' as empty character
167      }
168
169      lcd.setCursor(0,1);        // Go to beginning of display line 2
170      lcd.print(Bar);            // Print the bar chart result
171
172
173    // Now print out encoder and angle info
174      lcd.setCursor(0,0);                       // Go to line 1, char 1
175      lcd.print("                ");            // Clear line
176      lcd.setCursor(0,0);                       // Go to line 1, char 1
177      lcd.print("E ");                          // Shorthand for "Encoder"
178      lcd.print(encPos);                        // Print encoder value
179      lcd.setCursor(7,0);                       // Move across display
180      lcd.print (" A ");                        // Shorthand for "Angle"
```

```
181
182      lcd.print(90.0 + (1.0*encPos-enc90)*degPerStep);  // Angle in degrees
183
184    }
185    }
186
187    //==================== INTERRUPT SERVICE ====================
188
189    // These routines are called when a voltage transition, either upgoing or
190    // downgoing, on line A or B triggers an interrupt. First check whether
191    // the index pulse has also happened. If it has, Restore Aset and Bset to
192    // their initial values and set encPos to the measured reference value. If
193    // an index pulse did not occur, update the status by setting Aset in
194    // doA() or Bset in doB(). Then check the status of the other line - i.e.
195    // check Bset in doA() and Aset in doB().The direction of the transition,
196    // coupled with the last measured state of the other line, gives the
197    // direction of the move. Finally, increment or decrement encPos and
198    // return control to the loop() routine.
199    void doA(){        // Transition on pinA - either upgoing or downgoing
200
201      if (digitalRead(pinI) == HIGH){   // Check for index pulse
202        Aset=false;           // Reset these to have the same starting condition
203        Bset=false;
204        newCal=true;          // A new calibration has happened - Set flag
205        encPos=enc0;          // Reset encoder counts to reference value
206      }
207
208    else {                    // No Cal. Change on A - check which type and react
209
210      if (digitalRead(pinA) == HIGH){   // UP going transition on A
211        Aset=true;                       // We just had an upgoing transition
212        if (Bset)
213          {encPos=encPos+1;}             // Increment
214        else
215          {encPos=encPos-1;}             // Decrement
216      }
217
218      else {                            // DOWN going transition on A
219        Aset=false;                      // We just had a falling transition
220        if (Bset)
221          {encPos=encPos-1;}             // Increment
222        else
223          {encPos=encPos+1;}             // decrement
224
225      }
226    }
227    }
228
229    //======= B Interrupt ======
230    //
231    // See explanation in the doA() routine
232    //
233    void doB(){        // CHANGE transition on pinB
234
235      if (digitalRead(pinI) == HIGH){   // Check for index bit
236        Aset=false;           // Reset these to the same starting condition
237        Bset=false;
238        newCal=true;          // Set flag
239        encPos=enc0;          // Reset
240      }
```

```
241
242   else {                         // Change on B - check which type and react
243
244     if (digitalRead(pinB) == HIGH){   // UP going transition
245       Bset=true;                      // We just had an upgoing transition
246       if (Aset)
247         {encPos=encPos-1;}            // Increment
248       else
249         {encPos=encPos+1;}            // decrement
250     }
251
252     else {                           // DOWN going transition
253       Bset=false;                     // We just had a falling transition
254       if (Aset)
255         {encPos=encPos+1;}            // Increment
256       else
257         {encPos=encPos-1;}            // decrement
258
259     }
260   }
261 }
```

The Big Picture

Before delving into a line-by-line analysis, it is a good idea to have the Big Picture. In other words, what will the program do and how will it do it?

In the broadest sense, you want to improve your cutting accuracy and precision by keeping track of the position of a relative rotary encoder connected to the angle shaft of your faceting machine. A secondary goal is to measure the voltage from a depth of cut indicator. Both of these pieces of information – the facet angle and depth of cut condition – should be conveyed to the operator in a direct, effective manner.

Let's narrow this vision and focus on the job of monitoring the encoder. Given how they work (Section 20.8.3), this clearly involves sampling some signal lines and taking an action when they change. Two aspects of this are critical. First, you simply cannot afford to miss any A and B signal pulses from the encoder. If the microcontroller misses a transition from high-to-low or low-to-high, the whole scheme of determining direction and counts as shown in Figure 20-25 goes out the window. Missing steps means losing track of the current facet angle, and thereby tossing the goal of accuracy and precision out the window as well. You can avoid missing pulses by using interrupts, a topic dealt with in detail below.

The second critical aspect of measuring the facet angle with the encoder is calibration. For reasons of simplicity and cost, this project uses a relative or incremental encoder (see page 395). Translating the pulses from such a device into an absolute measurement requires that you monitor the state of the index line. Recall from panel (f) of Figure 20-29 that the encoder disk was oriented such that the index pulse occurs at about 100° facet angle, i.e. when the quill is lowered to or raised from its operating zone.

Ideally, you would monitor the index with an interrupt as well, but the basic Arduino Duemilanove has only two interrupt lines. Given this restriction, the best strategy is to measure the state of the index line every time an interrupt occurs on either of the other two lines. In principle, it is possible to move the quill so quickly that the program misses the index signal in the tiny interval of time between the A/B interrupt and the index measurement. If this happens, it means that the angle isn't recalibrated on that particular up or down-stroke of the quill, but re-calibration is not necessary every single time. In principle, only one calibration is needed at startup, and I have not been able to mess up the measurements on my machine, despite some rather rapid (and silly looking) quill waving.

Compared to the task of keeping track of the rotary encoder, the depth of cut measurement is a piece of cake (there is probably a clever birthday joke just waiting to jump out of that metaphor). The depth of cut indicator described in Section 20.7 produces a voltage which is zero when you raise the quill and which ramps up smoothly to several volts as the final depth of cut approaches. The software must simply monitor this voltage using one of the Arduino analog input lines. In order to provide clear visual feedback, the controller uses the top line of the display for the angle encoder information and draws a bar of "X" characters and blank spaces across the bottom line to indicate the depth of cut (Figure 20-34). In addition, when the specified threshold is reached, the program provides supplementary visual and auditory feedback – a fancy way of saying flashing a light and buzzing a buzzer.

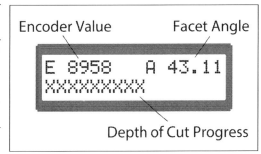

Figure 20-34 The two lines of the encoder display. The Encoder Value is the current encPos (see code listing)

The Declarations

Enough preliminaries. On to the code!

(And please recall that the line numbers in the code listing are only to help you follow along. Don't try to enter these into the sketch).

Lines 1 to 69 of the sketch contain all the necessary declarations. Most of these should be self-explanatory, either by the name of the item or the comments in the code.

Lines	Comment
1-2	Forces inclusion of the standard Arduino libraries for liquid crystal displays and handling character strings.
23-26	Defines the digital pins for channels A, B, and Index for the encoder, as well as the indicator LED output line. Note that on the Arduino Duemilanove, interrupts are enabled on pins 2 and 3 only.
28-30	Declaration of encPos, enc0, and enc90. The variable encPos is the current step count, while enc0 is the step count when the index pulse occurs. The value of enc0 determines enc90, the desired "zero-point" for the counter. I measured enc0=10,411 for a target enc90=10,000. See Section 20.8.6 below for more details. Note that the value of encPos will be modified outside of the loop() routine. Hence, it must be declared as volatile.
32-34	Declaration of critical Boolean (true/false) variables for keeping track of the last measured state of the three encoder channels.
36	Declaration of the number of degrees per step. For the HEDS-6545 encoder, degPerStep = 360° / (2000 x 4) or 0.045°. See "The Resolution Resolution" on page 396 to understand why.
47	Create a "LiquidCrystal" software entity with the listed pin assignments. For object-oriented programmers (the ones who sit alone at the end of the bar), this is equivalent to instantiating a member of the LiquidCrystal class. Drink up.

49-52	Declare variables associated with the geometry of the LCD and how frequently it should be updated.
59-64	Declare variables for the depth of cut indicator measurement. The variable doci contains the 10-bit (0-1023) measurement, which is scaled to doco, the number of X's to put in the display. Note that docMax, the value of doci when the depth of cut circuit is closed, must be measured in advance (see Section 20.8.6). The controller signals the appropriate depth of cut at half of the full range. Therefore, if doco exceeds mthresh – that is, half of the number of characters in the display – we have a winner.
66-67	Variables associated with controlling the beeper. You do not want a continuous beep when the stone is resting on the hard stop. Trust me, I tried it.
69	Declaration of a character string to contain the bar symbol for the depth of cut.

The Setup

Here, too, things should be pretty obvious…

Lines	Comment
73	Declaration of the setup() routine. Note the syntax, particularly the fact that all of the lines within a routine are enclosed by a master set of curly brackets.
78-80	Set all of the encoder digital lines to INPUT. The digital channels on an Arduino can act as either outputs (i.e. for an LED) or inputs (i.e. for measuring the signal level of an encoder channel).
82-85	Set up the interrupts. The Arduino Duemilanove has a pair of them, labelled 0 and 1, which are assigned to pinA and pinB, respectively. The second argument in the attachInterrupt command tells the microcontroller which routine to execute (doA or doB) when the corresponding interrupt occurs. The third argument instructs the Arduino to react to any change in the condition of the signal. Line 85 turns on the interrupt handler.
87-99	Some nice visual feedback at startup. First turn on the LED, and then present a suitable message on the liquid crystal display. After a couple of seconds, end the startup visuals by switching the LED off and clearing the LCD.
103	The variable "Bar" will contain a series of X's and blanks to simulate a bar display proportional to the voltage from the depth of cut indicator, (for example, "XXXXX "). Set the bar to all blanks to begin.

The Loop

And around and around we go…

Lines	Comment
119	Again, the routine must be declared properly and enclosed in curly brackets.
124-128	The newCal variable, if set true by one of the interrupt handling routines (doA or doB), indicates that the Arduino has detected the index pulse. At this point, the program just alerts the user that something has happened by flashing the LED for 0.1 second.
133-134	Humans operate at much lower data rates than computers. Therefore, the update rate for the display is every 100 milliseconds, set by the variable "rate." Also, the time constant of the DoCI is about a second (see page 389). Line 133 evaluates how many milliseconds have elapsed since the last power on or reset. If the time difference since the last update exceeds 100 milliseconds (the value rate – see line 52), it executes the large section of subsequent code (lines 136 to 182).
136	Reset the variable last for the next time interval check.
138-139	Read the analog voltage from the depth of cut indicator and scale the answer appropriately to fit in the 16-character display.
143-158	If the measured voltage exceeds the threshold, alert the operator by flashing the LED and beeping the beeper. Limit the beep to about a second or so to avoid undue aggravation. Otherwise, if the measured voltage is below the cutoff, make sure that things are dark and quiet.

161-170	Generate a character string, called "Bar," containing the appropriate number of filled ('X') and blank (' ') characters. Display this string on the second line of the LCD as visual feedback of the depth of cut.
174-182	Display the current encoder counts and facet angle on the first line of the LCD. This is arguably an "engineering" display, and you may wish to suppress the encoder counts in the final version of the software. At this stage, displaying the current value of encPos simplifies the absolute calibration, (see Section 20.8.6 below).

Interrupt Handling

The following explanation covers the contents of doA() only, since doB() is exactly the same in reverse, so to speak…

Lines	Comment
199	doA() is a self-contained routine, and hence requires proper declaration and curly brackets.
201-205	If the index pulse has occurred, restore Aset and Bset to their starting values, switch the newCal flag to true, and set encPos to the reference value enc0. This check occurs at the beginning of the routine to minimize the chance of missing the index pulse.
208-223	If there wasn't an index pulse, check the current state of channel A to see whether the interrupt was an up-going or down-going transition. Assign the appropriate value to Aset. Then, examine the last reported state of channel B, via Bset. The direction of the channel A transition, coupled with the value of Bset, determines the direction of motion (see Figure 20-25). Increment or decrement the current encoder counts (encPos) accordingly.

20.8.6 Calibrating and Using the Encoder

The hardware seems to be working, the code has been uploaded to the Arduino, and you are ready to attack your first gemstone.

Not so fast…There is one critical remaining step: absolute calibration.

Recall that this encoder is a relative or incremental encoder with a reference or "index" channel. When mounted properly, this arrangement can make accurate and repeatable measurements of the angle between the current position and the reference location. To make the system usable for faceting, however, you need to calibrate exactly where that reference location is.

The calibration method is a variant of the standard technique for verifying the cutting angle on any faceting machine. It involves installing an accurate metal rod in the quill and adjusting the machine so that a uniform gap exists between the rod and a reference lap (see Figure 20-35 and Figure 4-9). This defines precisely 90°.

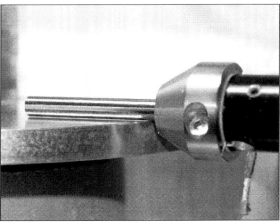

Figure 20-35 Use a precision steel rod held in the quill and a master lap to calibrate the 90° position very accurately.

Because the index on the encoder wheel triggers with the quill well above horizontal (see panel f of Figure 20-29 and page 410), the precise 90° orientation will be several hundred counts beyond. To calibrate the encoder, you need to determine exactly how many counts.

Actually, the code makes this easy: as written, it displays the current encoder counts (encPos) on the LCD display (line 178 of the code and Figure 20-34). Calibration is then a simple matter of noting down the number with the reference rod exactly horizontal. Add 10,000 to the value and insert it at the appropriate location in the sketch (see lines 29-30). Use the Verify button in the Arduino GUI to re-compile, upload the code, and you are good to go.

The depth of cut indicator requires a similar calibration to establish the value of docMax (see lines 61 and 139). For example, you could temporarily print the value of doci instead of encPos in line 178, and then enter into line 61 the doci measured with the contacts closed. Verify and upload the sketch to complete the calibration of the depth of cut indicator.

Using the encoder is a breeze. Just turn things on, wait for the friendly greeting (lines 92-94… feel free to customize this), and then move the quill past the reference point. The diagnostic LED should flash and the angle display will begin to track. Check that 90° is truly 90°. Move the quill down so that the depth of cut indicator electrodes make contact. You should see the corresponding signal in the lower half of the display and hear the buzzer. All is well, and you are ready to enjoy your new digital encoder.

20.8.7 Conclusion

Although the arrangement of my machine allowed me to preserve the original angle measuring hardware, I have found the digital encoder to be utterly reliable over several years of use. The Arduino controller is a tough little customer: despite multiple minor mishaps during construction, and several unintentional losses of power during use, it has unfailingly recovered, rebooted, and returned to operation within a second or two. Dialing in accurate and precise angles is now a pleasure. In short, I am not going back.

The Upgrade…

I got it bad…I can't leave things well enough alone.

It was only a few months after completing my digital angle encoder that I started having ideas…ideas for the next big improvement. How could I make the encoder even more useful and pleasant to use?

If you have compared the display hardware described here with the photo on the cover of this book, you know exactly where this is going. You see, my local electronics shop was offering a wonderful, backlit graphical liquid crystal display (GLCD)…and it didn't even cost that much…With 128x64 individually addressable pixels, a GLCD opens up all kinds of possibilities.

I began with the notion of having a larger angle readout. Beyond a certain age, and with various loupes and lenses stacked up in front of your eyes, it can be difficult to read a small character display, even a nice one such as that shown in Figure 20-32. A larger screen can also accommodate more information, such as the target angle you are shooting for and a more realistic "analog" display of the depth of cut.

After a few months of hard use, I had also realized that the Arduino is so robust that it does not need a reset button: if there is a problem (and there never is a problem), just unplug it and plug it back in. This realization freed up the push button shown in the last panel of Figure 20-29 and in Figure 20-33. What could a newly liberated button accomplish? Why not use it to bring up an entire separate screenful of information, for example the last ten target angles or even the entire faceting prescription?

Thus began the Encoder Mark II, whose primary screen graces the front cover of this book and whose secondary screen appears in Figure 20-36 below. Note the large friendly numbers for the angle display. I had to learn how to create and edit GLCD fonts to get just the right look (not that this was a burden or anything…as I said, I got it bad). Pressing the front panel button temporarily flips the display to screen 2. Pressing and holding the button stores the current angle in slot 1 of the Reference Angles and shifts all the others down. This first Reference Angle also appears as the Target directly above the angle display on the primary screen. Finally, the Depth of Cut progress bar boasts 128 glorious steps between no electrical contact and fully closed, as opposed to the sixteen steps of the original display.

Figure 20-36 The second screen of the Mark II Encoder upgrade lists the last ten reference angles.

Figure 20-37 shows the wiring diagram for the Mark II Encoder. Eagle-eyed readers will note that I have exploited the fact that you can, in fact, use the Arduino analog input pins as digital outputs. A careful inventory would also reveal that the circuit in Figure 20-37 uses absolutely every available port on the Duemilanove board. As it turns out, the software fills all but a tiny fraction of the limited memory within the microcontroller as well. Short version: the Mark II pushes the admittedly outdated Duemilanove to the limit. Unsurprisingly – and fortunately for the inevitable Mark III – the more modern Arduino boards have many more interface pins and a far larger program memory.

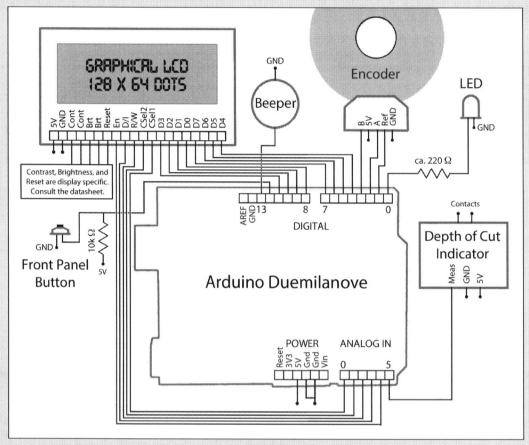

Figure 20-37 Wiring diagram for the Mark II upgrade. Please note that the GLCD pin assignment depends on both the display type and the model of Arduino. Consult facetingbook.com for more.

You can download the Mark II software at this book's website: www.facetingbook.com. On the site, you will also find a file containing the custom large angle display font, as well as additional tips and tricks to get your own Mark II up and running.

What next? Well, a few paragraphs back, I mentioned the notion of showing the actual faceting diagram on the display. The Mark II might have had this capability, but I ran into the difficulty of transferring files from a computer to the Arduino without a fixed cable connection. There was also the challenge of adding significant new capability with zero extra pins and almost zero extra program memory. The good news (in addition to the aforementioned more powerful boards)? There are both wifi and Bluetooth expansion cards in the Arduino line…and they really don't cost that much…

Acknowledgments

This book would not have been possible without the help, both direct and indirect, of many people. My first thanks go out to Dave Thompson and Rob Kulakofsky, who introduced me to the world of faceting. Dave also provided ongoing encouragement and inspiration, as well as several photographs and the design of the Heidelberg Brilliant in Chapter 19.3.2. I owe a debt of gratitude to Walt Heitland of the Vancouver Island Faceters Guild for the information in Chapter 2 about hand faceters in the Pacific Northwest. Armin Böhm and Lars Mohr provided expert assistance in the areas of precision machining and electronics, respectively, and Bernhard Grimm suggested the circuit in Figure 20-15. Brian in Oz posted online instructions for building a transfer aid similar to that described in Chapter 20.6. Several individuals and companies provided images. Their credits appear at the end of each volume.

I am also grateful to the many contributors to the online discussion groups, particularly the USFG Faceters List (groups.yahoo.com/neo/groups/usfgfaceterslist/info) and the Gemology Online Forum (gemologyonline.com/Forum/phpBB2/index.php). As mentioned in Chapter 15.1.3, there are many hundreds of miles between me and my nearest faceting acquaintance. The online community has been an incredibly helpful resource in preparing this book, providing information, wisdom, and vital online links.

I would also like to thank you, dear reader, for your interest in *Amateur Gemstone Faceting*. I very much welcome your feedback, and plan to incorporate suggestions in future revised editions. Send your comments to tom@facetingbook.com.

Finally, my deepest thanks go out to my amazing wife, Inge, and our two equally amazing sons, Matthew and Timothy, who have been tolerant and supportive over the several years that it took to complete this book.

I

Index

Note: This is a merged index from both volumes of Amateur Gemstone Faceting. Look for the volume number before each page entry. For example, I:69-73 refers to Volume 1, whereas II:148 is in Volume 2.

Image Credits

Unless stated otherwise below, all images in this book are the original work of the author.

CHAPTER 10

Figure 10-2 (right) Photograph of the pyramid of Khafre by Hamish2k at wikipedia.org This image is licensed under the Creative Commons Attribution-Share Alike 3.0 Unported license. For further details see: http://creativecommons.org/licenses/by-sa/3.0/ Modifications from the original: converted to grayscale, brightness and contrast adjustment.

Figure 10-4 Painting of the School of Athens by Raphael. The painting dates from 1509-1510 and is on display in the Apostolic Palace in the Vatican. This work is in the public domain.

Figure 10-30 Screen capture of Bob Keller's online tangent ratio calculator at:

   http://www.rockhounds.com/rockshop/gem_designs/tangent_ratio_form.html

CHAPTER 11

Figure 11-7 This portrait of Pierre de Fermat is a contemporary engraving and is hence in the public domain.

Figure 11-18 Caravaggio's Narcissus is on display at the Galleria Nazionale d'Arte Antica in Rome. This image is in the public domain.

Figure 11-20 (right) Image of the Fresnel lenses of a lighthouse courtesy Hannes Grobe. Licensed under the Creative Commons Attribution-Share Alike 2.5 Generic license. For further details, see: http://creativecommons.org/licenses/by-sa/2.5/deed.en. Modifications from the original: converted to grayscale, brightness and contrast adjustment.

Figures 11-26 and 11-27 by Tom Herbst. Adapted from René Magritte's 1964 painting The Son of Man.

CHAPTER 12

Figure 12-20 Photograph of refractometer courtesy of Krüss Optronic, www.kruess.de

Figure 12-30 Engraving of Pliny the Elder from the Wikimedia Commons. This image is a work of the National Institutes of Health, part of the United States Department of Health and Human Services. As a work of the U.S. federal government, the image is in the public domain.

Figure 12-44 This engraving of Gerolamo Cardano by an unknown artist is in the public domain.

CHAPTER 13

Figure 13-1 This photograph by PHGCOM of Pliny the Elder's Historia Naturalis is from the Wikimedia Commons. The photographer has released the image into the public domain. The book itself is a mid 12th-century manuscript from an abbey in Le Mans, France, and is now on display at the Musée de Cluny in Paris.

CHAPTER 16

Figures 16-3 and 16-4 by Tom Herbst. Adapted from the gemstone taxonomy from Robert H. Long and Norman W. Steele's Datavue database.

Figure 16-27 Photographs of deck prisms courtesy of Captain William Sabatini of the US Brig Niagara. You can visit the ship itself at the Erie Maritime Museum in Erie, Pennsylvania. Learn more about the Niagara at www.flagshipniagara.org.

CHAPTER 18

Figure 18-2 by Tom Herbst. The gem design portrayed is adapted from Jeff Graham's Gram Princess.

CHAPTER 19

Figure 19-64 Photograph of the Tower Grandstand at Sepang Circuit by Eriang87. This image has been released on wikipedia.org under the Creative Commons Attribution-ShareAlike 3.0 Unported license. Modifications from the original: converted to grayscale, brightness and contrast adjustment.

Section 19.3.2 Heidelberg Brilliant gemstone design by David Thompson.

Figure 19-74 Image of the VIP Tower at Bahrain's Sakhir circuit by Navin Shetty Brahmavar, released on wikipedia.org under the Creative Commons Attribution-ShareAlike 3.0 license. Modifications from the original: cropped, converted to grayscale, brightness and contrast adjustment.

CHAPTER 20

Figure 20-20 (left) Photo of a vernier angle scale on an Ultra Tec faceting machine courtesy of David Thompson.

Figure 20-20 (right) Photo of an angle counter on a Facetron faceting machine by Tom Herbst with the able assistance of Billy Bob Riley and the Old Pueblo Lapidary Club.

About the Author

Tom Herbst is an amateur faceter and all-round rock enthusiast. Born in eastern Ontario, Canada, he received his formal education in Montreal, Quebec, Waterloo, Ontario, and Ithaca, New York. A research astrophysicist in his "day" job, Tom specializes in the design, construction, and scientific exploitation of novel astronomical instrumentation.

Although he began collecting pretty rocks as a kid, it was not until his mid-thirties that Tom realized that creating gemstones is within everyone's grasp. A few faceting lessons and a homebuilt machine later, he was deep into the hobby and has never looked back.

Tom currently lives and works near Heidelberg Germany, along with his wife Inge, and their two teenage sons, Matthew and Timothy.

You can contact the author at tom@facetingbook.com

The author working on the proofs of Amateur Gemstone Faceting while on family vacation in 2013 (right).

Printed in Great Britain
by Amazon